"Compelling, candid, and highly revelatory. By examining in striking detail the remarkable life of Constance Baker Motley—a formidable lawyer turned politician turned judge—Tomiko Brown-Nagin makes a major contribution to several fields: race relations, women's studies, the study of the legal profession, and modern American history."

—*Randall Kennedy, Michael R. Klein
Professor of Law, Harvard Law School*

"In *Civil Rights Queen*, award-winning historian Tomiko Brown-Nagin recognizes an unsung American heroine. Through an intimate, behind-the-scenes journey into what Motley did, where she came from, and how she got there, we learn the keys to Black women's successes in the twentieth century. A dazzling life story that inspires readers to discover the Constance Baker Motley in ourselves."

—*Martha S. Jones, author of* Vanguard: How Black Women
Broke Barriers, Won the Vote, and Insisted on Equality for All

"Brown-Nagin brings a storyteller's art, meticulous research, and astute legal and psychological insights to the life and times of a central figure of the civil rights movement. Readers will never forget the woman whose outspoken, proud, and ferocious sense of justice changed her fortunes while she challenged America's racial apartheid, gender barriers, and day-to-day obstacles to human thriving."

—*Martha Minow, 300th Anniversary
University Professor, Harvard University*

"An immersive and eye-opening biography. Brilliantly balancing the details of Motley's professional and personal life with lucid legal analysis, this riveting account shines a well-deserved—and long overdue—spotlight on a remarkable trailblazer."

—Publishers Weekly (*starred review*)

Also by Tomiko Brown-Nagin

Courage to Dissent: Atlanta and the
Long History of the Civil Rights Movement

CIVIL
RIGHTS
QUEEN

CIVIL RIGHTS QUEEN

CONSTANCE BAKER MOTLEY

and the Struggle for Equality

Tomiko Brown-Nagin

Pantheon Books, New York

Library of Congress Cataloging-in-Publication Data
Name: Brown-Nagin, Tomiko, [date] author.
Title: Civil rights queen: Constance Baker Motley and
the struggle for equality / Tomiko Brown-Nagin.
Description: New York: Pantheon Books, 2022.
Includes bibliographical references and index.
Identifiers: LCCN 2021022495 (print). LCCN 2021022496 (ebook).
ISBN 9781524747183 (hardcover). ISBN 9781524747190 (ebook).
Subjects: LCSH: Motley, Constance Baker, 1921–2005. Judges—
New York (State)—Biography. African American judges—New York
(State)—Biography. Women judges—New York (State)—Biography.
Lawyers—New York (State)—Biography. Civil rights workers—
New York (State)—Biography. Civil rights—United States.
Equality before the law—United States.
Classification: LCC KF373.M64 B76 2022 (print) |
LCC KF373.M64 (ebook) | DDC 347.747/0234 [B]—dc23
LC record available at lccn.loc.gov/2021022495
LC ebook record available at lccn.loc.gov/2021022496

www.pantheonbooks.com

Jacket photograph: Constance Baker Motley, February 6, 1964.
World Telegram & Sun photo by Walter Albertin, Library of Congress,
Washington, D.C.
Jacket design by Emily Mahon

Printed in the United States of America
First Edition
2 4 6 8 9 7 5 3 1

IN LOVING MEMORY OF MY MOTHER,

Lillie Williams Brown

"Listen Lord - from the Slums"

Someone told me that a God made the world
 And everything from stone to wood ;
 And when He had finished it
 He said that it was good.

He worked on it six long days,
 On the seventh He rested content.
But I have often wondered
 If this is the place He meant.

Man made the slums where I live
 with its mountains of sin;
 They jammed the houses together
To keep beauty from entering in.

I often think that it is true
That real things have never been seen,
 ' Cause I've lived here all my life
And never saw grass that was green.

I don't think God made my world,
 'Cause it's misery not fun.
If HE made a beautiful place
This couldn't be the one.

yet someone said that there is a place
Where the sun shines bright all day;
 And that beautiful trees and flowers
 Have been planted along the way.

My days are dark and dreary,
yet I often wish I could
 See with my own eyes
The world that God called good.

When I see God I'll tell Him
That it's the sin which man has hurled
Upon His beautiful earth
which has devastated the world.

No longer am I sad , for someday
When my eyes close for good
I'll see in Glory
 The World the way I should.

                    Constance Juanita Baker - 15 yrs.
                      June 17, 1937

Contents

CIVIL
RIGHTS
QUEEN

Introduction

S am Terry was killed in cold blood. On February 27, 1949, a Sunday afternoon in rural Manchester, Georgia, about sixty-five miles south of Atlanta, white officers shot Terry—a veteran of World War II, a member of the "Greatest Generation," and a thirty-seven-year-old Black man—three times in the back, once in the side.

Terry had been arrested for a minor infraction that had nothing whatsoever to do with him. Two officers hauled him from his home and locked him in a jail cell. While he was detained, they unloaded their weapons on him, claiming he had resisted arrest and tried to break away from his cell. Terry died of his wounds two days later. In the aftermath, the local sheriff disclaimed all responsibility. His men had done nothing wrong, he said: "no evidence was found" that Terry had been "mistreated" by the arresting officers—the same men who shot and killed him.[1]

Terry's widow, Minnie Kate, flatly contradicted the sheriff. Sam had not resisted arrest, his wife asserted; suffering from the mumps, he had been in no condition to attack anyone, much less officers of the law. But Sam had protested—verbally—when the officers had "manhandled" Minnie Kate and briefly placed her under arrest on trumped-up charges. Angered by Sam's defense of his wife, the officers yelled, "Shut up, you black son-of-a-bitch or we'll kill you." Once they arrived at the jail, the officers "shoved" Sam into a cell, "followed him in," "slammed the door," and "immediately after" fired several shots at him. Minnie Kate, standing just outside the cell door, witnessed the events unfold; what she had seen and heard was an entirely unjustified shooting—a barbaric murder. What was more, Minnie Kate said, while Sam bled profusely from the gunshot wounds in his intestines, the officers had insisted that she had "better not holler," or she "would get the same thing."[2]

News accounts and an attending doctor confirmed critical elements of Minnie Kate Terry's version of events. The *Atlanta Constitution* established that the doors of the cell had been locked when officers repeatedly shot Sam Terry. And the doctor who treated the veteran after the incident said that he had been shot four times. But Minnie Kate had no recourse in the state of Georgia, which at that time was governed by Herman Talmadge, a vicious racist. So she reached out to the national NAACP and its lawyers. Along with her allies, Minnie Kate "urge[d]" the lawyers to take "action" to "see that this injustice is brought to the limelight" and the "guilty ones are punished." Murders of Black men "are spreading throughout the Southland." She was not wrong. A reign of terror that began around 1880 continued through the mid-twentieth century: during this time, white mobs across the South, aided and abetted by law enforcement, murdered hundreds of African Americans, and often targeted Black veterans.

Terry's death came to the attention of Thurgood Marshall, the chief counsel of the NAACP Legal Defense and Educational Fund (LDF, or Inc. Fund), and his legal assistant, Constance Baker Motley, then just three years out of law school. Springing into action, Motley wrote to Tom C. Clark, Attorney General of the United States, and requested a federal investigation. Marshall followed up with a letter to the Department of Justice, seeking the help of the Federal Bureau of Investigation. Nothing happened.

In 1950—more than a year after Minnie Kate Terry had buried her husband—Motley once again followed up with federal officials, to no avail. The Department of Justice closed the case, saying that the evidence was insufficient to support a prosecution. This failure to thoroughly investigate, much less prosecute, fit a pattern. Despite its wartime condemnation of the racism and violence of the Nazi regime, the U.S. government virtually ignored the wave of anti-Black terrorism—the all-too-frequent beatings, shootings, and lynchings of African Americans—that occurred in the postwar South. Veterans, who led a growing resistance to anti-Black oppression, were routinely victimized and in dire need of representation. Constance Baker Motley, then in her twenties, became one of the most prominent and tireless advocates for African Americans during this turbulent era.

By 1950, African Americans from not just the South but across the whole United States counted on Motley to stand up for racial justice and protect the rights of Black citizens. Handling dozens of cases at a time in a dizzying array of subject areas, she deployed her sharp legal skills to combat discrimination in the criminal legal system, in education, in housing, in the workplace, in politics, and in countless other areas. Her advocacy took her to small towns and cities throughout the South, to the urban North, and to the Midwest.[3]

Wherever she appeared, the striking and audacious Motley captivated and stunned onlookers. At that time, few had seen a woman lawyer or even a Black lawyer, much less the extraordinary combination of the two. The novelty of Motley and her courtroom talents made her an icon of equality. "She's a prime mover in the cause of civil rights across the nation," wrote one reporter, and "may justly be called 'The Civil Rights Queen.'"[4] Part heroine and part warrior, the moniker implied, she wielded the law like a sword of justice.

In bestowing the affectionate honorific, observers did not merely acknowledge her work inside the courtroom. The title implied that Motley had transcended her lawyerly role. She often created a "sensation." When "word got out that not only was there a 'nigra lawyer'" but "a 'nigra' woman lawyer," she recalled about her first trial in Jackson, Mississippi, it was "like a circus in town." "They were amazed at the way I spoke." Incapable of reconciling the lawyer's role with a Black woman's status in American society, some whites responded with tremendous hostility. In a federal courtroom during one trial, a white male lawyer, unwilling to call the imposing woman "Mrs. Motley," instead "pointed his finger" in his opponent's direction and called her "she." In a rare show of anger, Motley set him straight: "If you can't address me as Mrs. Motley, don't address me at all." A transformational lawyer, a trailblazing woman, and an exceptional African American, the Civil Rights Queen personified the extraordinary social change that she brought about through law.[5]

Few would have predicted her rise. Motley's own parents found her ambition to become a lawyer far-fetched. But she defied their expectations—something she did over and over again in her professional life. It was Thurgood Marshall, "Mr. Civil Rights," who gave the young lawyer her big break. Before meeting him, Motley had faced a string of rejections from Wall Street law firms led by white men. If Motley repelled these powerful white male lawyers, she fascinated Marshall. He offered her a job at LDF on the spot, and she happily accepted.

There, Motley flourished. "Connie just walked in, walked in and took over," Marshall recalled years later. She handled hundreds of civil rights cases over a twenty-year period that began in 1945 and continued through 1965—efforts that remade American law and society. In 1954, she played an invaluable role in *Brown v. Board of Education*, a singular case in twentieth-century American constitutional law. The unanimous U.S. Supreme Court decision outlawed state-mandated racial segregation in the nation's elementary and secondary schools. Motley desegregated flagship public universities in Georgia and Mississippi. She represented the Birmingham Children's Marchers, who were mercilessly attacked and thrown out of school for participating in antisegregation protests. She helped Dr. Martin Luther King Jr. escape the horrors of a jail cell in rural Georgia. Throughout the course of her work for the civil rights movement, Motley compiled an enviable record as a trial and appellate lawyer. One of just a few women lawyers and the first Black woman lawyer known to appear at the Supreme Court, she won nine of the ten cases that she argued before the nation's highest court. She summed up this work for the movement by saying, "We have wrought a miracle."[6]

But Motley's legacy does not only derive from her exceptional career as a civil rights lawyer. After garnering fame as an attorney, she found a different way to fight for social justice, embarking on an entirely new career—in politics. Again, she made history. In 1964, New Yorkers elected Motley to the state senate; she was the first Black woman to serve in that legislative body. In 1965, she made political history once more when New Yorkers elected her to the Manhattan borough presidency; she was the first woman to serve in the post.

Motley then pursued a third act. In 1966, President Lyndon B. Johnson appointed her to the U.S. District Court in Manhattan, making her the first African American woman to sit on the federal bench. During her more than thirty years on the court, Judge Motley decided numerous landmark cases in fields ranging from criminal law to civil rights and corporate law. The judge's rulings in civil rights cases defined her judicial career. Over the objections of lawyers who insisted that as a former civil rights lawyer and a Black woman she could not be "fair," Motley rendered decisions that implemented the Civil Rights Act of 1964 and opened the workplace to women lawyers, journalists, professors, and municipal workers. At the dawn of mass incarceration, she issued a historic ruling mandating due process rights and humane treatment for the incarcerated. And in a case involving low-level drug offenders, she struck down sentences mandated by a new regime of tough-on-crime narcotics laws that left millions of Americans behind bars. Motley's accomplishments, outstanding for any lawyer and unheard of among women attorneys, make her one of the most remarkable women of the twentieth century—a woman whose work created a "more perfect" union.

*

Motley's world-changing accomplishments, which made her a "queen" in her time, should place her in the pantheon of great American leaders. The feats of Martin Luther King Jr. and Thurgood Marshall are by now standard components of public memory and secondary school curricula. But far too few Americans today know Motley's name and deeds. Students do not routinely study her work and example—King's lawyer, Marshall's co-counsel, and a tactician praised by both as phenomenally talented. Despite her tremendous role in the effort to slay Jim Crow, most books and articles on the civil rights movement understate her importance. No television shows or movies imprint her name on the popular imagination. No boulevards bear her name. Her likeness is not even featured on a postage stamp.

There are many reasons why Motley's life and legacy have escaped examination—most obviously, it is because she was a woman. In Western societies, historical significance is coded male. The lives of men are deemed worthy of study and remembrance. By contrast, despite all she achieved, Motley has mostly been defined by Thurgood Marshall's mentorship. Certainly there is a logic to this, as Marshall served as the first Black justice on the U.S. Supreme Court and is rightfully celebrated for his singular achievements as a civil rights lawyer. Yet other men, much less prominent than Motley in the civil rights struggle and not nearly as accomplished, have also received more attention. Meanwhile, Motley's work at the bar, in the legislature, and on the bench is only beginning to draw significant interest.[7]

If simply being a woman explains partly why Motley is less known, her experience as a working woman also illuminates why she is less widely recognized by the public today than a person of her accomplishments should be. Her persona—reserved, honorable, imperial, and feminine—facilitated her professional breakthroughs in a world premised on masculine norms, steeped in gender stereotypes, and dominated by men habituated to both. But those same traits likely worked against her being widely perceived as a transformational leader in the mold of Marshall and King—talkative, limelight-seeking, charismatic, and masculine. These gender-linked differences in leadership style probably also contributed to the biggest professional disappointment of her career.[8]

In 1961, Motley was denied a promotion that would have given her a higher public profile, and that she chalked up partly to her gender and race. Following Marshall's resignation as director-counsel of the LDF, Motley was passed over for the top leadership post. Her frequent co-counsel, Jack Greenberg, a white man, succeeded Marshall. Motley—Marshall's longtime protégée—would not reach the pinnacle of power at the esteemed civil rights organization; she would remain a "number 2." As important as the second-in-command role was, history seldom remembers understudies. The snub boxed Motley into a club to which many other high-achieving women, both inside and outside the civil rights movement, belonged. "I am sure Thurgood thought, 'I am going to have all kinds of trouble if I put her up there,'" Motley said of the rebuff years later. "Women just didn't have the status" in the field at that time. And they did not fit most people's image of a leader. But women would gain prestige and power at least in part because of Motley's trailblazing electoral achievements and groundbreaking judicial decisions on behalf of professional women.[9]

In *Civil Rights Queen*, Motley's life and work take a turn in the spotlight. The book shows that hers is a story of a remarkable, and improbable, American life. As LDF's only woman lawyer for many years, the first Black woman elected to the New York Senate, the first female Manhattan borough president, and, most important, the first Black woman appointed to the federal bench, Motley had a tremendous impact on public life. She left an indelible mark on her time and bequeathed us a singular legacy. In various guises, across different eras of change, she helped remake the law and reconstruct America.

*

This book centers Motley's life not only to compensate for past omission, but also because her exclusion flattens history, and her inclusion thickens it. Through the lens she provides, we can better understand and interpret a host of subjects: pivotal moments in the civil rights movement, law versus political power as a tool of change, cultural diversity in the African American experience, and how gender—mediated by race and class—shapes life trajectories.

Motley's gender, embodied as Black and working class, makes her story of ascent especially intriguing. How did she manage that improbable climb from a humble neighborhood in New Haven to the top of her profession? How did her identity shape how she inhabited each role, and at what cost? What setbacks and glass ceilings did she encounter along the way? What can we learn from the stories of those who rise from humble beginnings, the "underdogs" of American society, whether they are African Americans who lived under Jim Crow or women before liberation? *Civil Rights Queen* engages these lines of inquiry.[10]

As it looks to Motley's story for answers to these questions, this book meditates on a theme embedded in James Baldwin's body of work: *"What is the price of the ticket"*?[11] The questions underpinning *Civil Rights Queen* are all about outsiders and power. How do outsiders—women, in particular—gain power, with what benefits, and at what costs? How does access to power shape and change individuals who initially sought it because of a commitment to social justice?

The book grapples with Baldwin's question by viewing Motley's life against the backdrop of distinct eras of activism. The young Constance Baker (Motley was her married name) came of age during the Great Depression, a period that generated a burst of civic activism.

She started her legal career as World War II ended and the Cold War began—an era of legal transformation. During this period, she and other Inc. Fund lawyers shook up both the legal profession and the nation by creating a new type of legal doctrine—civil rights law—and laying the groundwork for the landmark social changes of the era. When a new era of radicalism dawned during the mid-1960s—a time marked by dissent from liberal reform politics—Motley entered electoral politics, successfully serving as a legislator and borough president. She ascended to the bench in 1966 as the women's liberation movement dawned; during her years as a federal judge, she became an emblem of the liberal establishment. Motley retired from full-time judicial service during the Reagan Revolution, an era of retrenchment from interventionist government.

A changemaker and a "first," Motley was a path breaker who evolved in each new role, growing with the times and through her relationships with a circle of activist colleagues and friends. Her activism spanned generations that included some of the most compelling men and women of the twentieth century—Medgar Evers, James Meredith, Bella Abzug, Pauli Murray, Adam Clayton Powel Jr., Malcolm X, Shirley Chisholm, Martin Luther King Jr., John F. Kennedy, Robert F. Kennedy, Lyndon B. Johnson, and, of course, Thurgood Marshall. As a lawyer, as a politician, and as a judge she shaped struggles for equality and justice, sometimes in collaboration with, and at other times in competition with, some of these figures. In each role and era, Motley stood as a model of social change in America, and of its limitations.

The questions raised in *Civil Rights Queen*—about the purposes and limits of power when wielded by talented agents of change on behalf of marginalized people—remain relevant today. Ours is a turbulent age that has given rise to a new era of activism and dissent. The fanciful notion of a "post-racial" society ushered in by the 2008 election of Barack Obama to the U.S. presidency, the first African American to hold that office, gave way in 2016 to the presidency of openly-bigoted Donald J. Trump and mobilized a resistance to persistent inequities.

Many are hungry for inspiration. And many will find hope in this story of a woman who ascended from the bottom of society to the top of America's power structure, using her influence to fight for others and remake America. In fact, many have found her an inspiration. Kamala Harris, the first woman, the first African American, and the first South Asian vice president, is one important example. Motley inspired Harris "to fight for the voiceless and for justice," the vice president has said on several occasions.[12]

I started writing this book because I believe that Constance Baker Motley's life and legacy powerfully illustrate the peaks and valleys of the American struggle for a "more perfect" union, and I believe her story deserves a wider audience. In 2001, when I devoted a chapter of my book *Courage to Dissent: Atlanta and the Long History of the Civil Rights Movement* to Motley's work as lead counsel on the Atlanta school desegregation case, I was astounded by how little attention other writers had given her. The relative dearth of coverage struck me as not merely regrettable, but as a kind of historical malpractice. It deprived us of a more accurate and complete history. The invisibility of this fascinating woman in our public histories and popular culture distorts our sense of who rebuilt America. Motley's invisibility in our nation's history shortchanges us all. But her absence is especially detrimental to the sense of belonging of the many communities she visibly represented—African Americans, West Indians, women, girls, immigrants, and the working class. Like all people, members of these groups—historically excluded from power in the United States and often still marginalized—benefit from seeing themselves portrayed as significant, successful stakeholders in the national project. A shelf full of books—and my own life experience—teach me that.

In showing how Motley found her way into the American power structure despite the exclusion of Blacks and women from the spaces she dared enter, *Civil Rights Queen* offers insights not only about the struggle for equality and power in twentieth-century America, and into the still-unequal world in which we live today; her story also challenges the enduring fiction that pure talent best explains who succeeds in life, or that discrimination alone explains who does not. Motley's is a story about both talent and the structures of inequality, but it is not only about these critically important factors. It is a window onto how a woman's mindset in the face of inequality and her choices about how to publicly perform her identity positioned her in an unequal world. Some women leaders of the civil rights era—Pauli

Murray, the civil rights and women's rights lawyer; Ella Baker, the SCLC leader and mother of SNCC; and Shirley Chisholm, the first Black woman elected to Congress, come to mind—pushed their way into public life. Motley leaned in. She grabbed opportunities and endured challenges without making much fuss. Along the way, racism and sexism beset her, just as they linger and disadvantage women and people of color today. Motley benefited from good fortune and experienced bad luck. She cultivated male and female sponsors and encountered male and female detractors. Sometimes she grew weary, even sad. Through it all, Constance Baker Motley kept moving.

Motley's choices about her private life also profoundly shaped her professional opportunities. She chose a partner who was personally supportive and professionally successful, but unexceptional. She gave birth to only one child—a son whom she adored and made time for as best she could. On the road for work, she sorely missed her family. Preoccupied with the demands of her job, she relied on others for childcare and domestic help. A woman of extraordinary achievements, Motley faced problems universal to women who seek to advance a career and have a happy family life. In examining one life, *Civil Rights Queen* speaks both to a bygone era and to our own time, as women still try to balance work and family life.

Constance Baker Motley shook up the world. Her life fills out the picture of change in twentieth-century America, and it throws light on unfinished struggles.[13]

Part I

Beginnings

1

"The Base of This Great Ambition":
Nevis and New Haven

In her heart of hearts, Constance Baker was not like ordinary Black folks. Perhaps the most significant fact about her, she often said, was that her parents were not African Americans. My "parents were not Southerners, and their background and outlook were very different from the American Negroes," she insisted. "Their background was European."

Willoughby and Rachel, her father and mother, hailed from Nevis, a little island "paradise" in the West Indies that was until 1983 a British colony. They felt themselves cultured, cosmopolitan. Their hearts were with the British crown, and in their household "nobody . . . could speak against the King or Queen, because that was a sin."[1]

Baker's parents immigrated to the United States soon after the turn of the twentieth century and settled in New Haven, Connecticut. Born on September 14, 1921, Constance Juanita Baker grew up in the college town, a refuge for immigrants from all over Europe. New Haven was then home to about two thousand Black people, including a few hundred immigrants and a much larger group of African American emigrants from the South. Baker's father "couldn't stand American blacks." Growing up, she heard him denigrate them often, saying that they "allowed" themselves to be debased by Jim Crow and were content in their wretched condition. American Blacks were plainly inferior to those, like himself, of European stock.[2]

Her family's origins in Nevis, which was proudly touted as a "foundation of the British Empire," and their move to New Haven—a bastion of the white Anglo-Saxon Protestant elite—profoundly shaped the upbringing and identity of the girl who grew up to become the Civil Rights Queen.[3]

*

By the time Willoughby Baker and Rachel Huggins departed Nevis for the United States, hundreds of islanders had already fled the colony to find work along the eastern seaboard. As word of the earliest Nevisians' success in their new environment got back to the Caribbean, others followed suit. Edward Huggins, Rachel's brother, was the first in the family to leave the island for the States. He worked on vessels traveling between New York and the Caribbean for a while, briefly lived in New York and worked in construction, and settled in New Haven in 1905 after he crossed paths with some Yale students in the New York theater district who advised him of "easier service jobs" there. He eventually found work as the steward of the University Club at Yale. Willoughby, Edward's friend and Rachel's boyfriend, sailed to the United States in 1906 in pursuit of the same opportunity that Edward had found in New Haven. In 1907, Rachel, an eighteen- or nineteen-year-old then working as a seamstress and in a preschool, "gave up" her plans to "be a schoolteacher" and followed Willoughby to America; the passage to New Haven cost $25 and "the boat" ride took about a week, she remembered. The pair soon married.[4]

Just as for many other immigrants, for the Bakers the United States represented a chance to escape the misery that had enveloped Nevis following emancipation in 1834. A beautiful volcanic landmass, the island, along with its people, had lived through a tragic history.

During the seventeenth and eighteenth centuries sugar made Nevis one of Britain's most profitable colonies. Europeans lusted after sugar—the "white gold" that sweetened their coffee and tea and the confections that became staples of the wealthy Western diet. The market grew exponentially, and for a time, demand outstripped supply. The average English person's consumption of sugar rose from four pounds per year in 1700 to forty-seven in 1870.[5]

Sugar also made the island a center of the Atlantic slave trade, fueling planters' entanglement in human bondage. British planters developed a brutal system of forced labor in the West Indies to produce the sweet crystals after which Westerners so hungered. Enslaved Afro-Caribbeans (and, in an earlier era, white indentured servants) were put to the punishing work of sugarcane cultivation for as long as eighteen hours a day, six days a week. After the crop was planted and harvested, the production process shifted from the fields to the factories. Working in mills with crushing machinery, large metal kettles and furnaces, enslaved people boiled cane to yield a sweet, sticky syrup; and further boiling, curing, and refining produced a crystalline sugar that would be snapped up at market. The backbreaking toil of the enslaved brought immense wealth and status to Caribbean planters. Even as enslaved Afro-Caribbeans lost their lives and limbs operating the sugar works' heavy machinery, Nevis became known as "Queen of the Caribbees," home to the "best" sugar in the world. The island epitomized the link between slavery and European prosperity.[6]

In 1834, however, the island and its inhabitants set out on a new and uncertain course. That year, under abolitionist pressure, the British ended slavery in the colonies. The move freed nearly nine thousand Nevisians.[7]

Following emancipation, the island slid into economic depression. Social upheaval followed. Planters' unchanged racial attitudes and shifting economic fortunes choked the development of a truly free labor system. At the same time, manumitted men and women, along with white proprietors, discovered that years of sugar production had ravaged the soil. Floods, drought, and disease plagued the island, leaving the sugar industry to struggle. As life became increasingly wretched, most whites, including planters and merchants, fled, taking their economic and social capital, along with their political power. The few planters who remained and continued to grow sugarcane reaped meager profits, if any at all.[8]

By 1890, Nevis was in ruins. The island sat blighted by plantations that had run to seed. The British West India Royal Commission issued a report to the House of Commons that described the island's reversal of fortune: the sugar industry, once the envy of the slave-trafficking world, was at "the point of extinction." The value of land had fallen so far that estates could not be sold. Efforts to modernize the production of sugar, or develop alternative crops such as ginger, coffee, and tobacco, failed. A more promising venture—an effort to cultivate varieties of cotton typically grown in the South Carolina Sea Islands as a cash crop—struggled to take hold.

This state of affairs, the economic and social disorder that reigned after emancipation, put the Nevisian working class in dire straits. Job loss, irregular employment, low wages, labor strikes, poor working conditions, and abject deprivation were rampant. Although a small but significant Afro-Caribbean middle class managed estates for absentee whites, practicing trades and working as, say, shopkeepers, the great majority of Nevisians, unable to find good, steady work, fought to survive. Many islanders turned to subsistence farming.[9]

Others—squatters—settled on land that white landowners had abandoned. Most peasants lived in primitive thatched huts with mud walls and dirt floors, and under constant threat of dispossession. As many as twelve people were routinely packed into these one- or two-room, vermin-infested dwellings. Plumbing did not exist. People defecated into open pits carved into the earth. Filth and odor fouled daily life. People drank brackish water from wells and barrels. Poor diets stunted children well into their adult years, while infection and disease riddled many of the island's fourteen thousand inhabitants. Doctors were scarce and both preventable and curable diseases often went untreated. Children and adults routinely died before their time. There seemed little hope for a better life on Nevis.[10,11]

No wonder, then, that there was an exodus. Around the turn of the twentieth century, a steady stream of Afro-Caribbean Nevisians—hundreds annually—departed their homeland in search of employment and more hospitable surroundings. They found work in the construction, dockyard, and agricultural industries of the Panama Canal Zone, in Bermuda, Trinidad, St. Croix, and Costa Rica, in the oil fields and gold mines of Venezuela, and in the United States. Large numbers also found work at the New York City docks and in the service industries of New Haven.[12]

*

Despite the wretched conditions they had escaped, many immigrants, including the Bakers, held on to a romantic view of island life. Willoughby and Rachel treasured Nevisian history, traditions, folkways, and food, and associated the island with grandeur. Revising history, the Bakers erroneously opined to young Constance that slavery on Nevis had not been nearly as brutal as in the American South. The Bakers also reveled in the island's attractiveness to European elites. Nevis's Bath Hotel, with its thermal baths sourced from hot mineral springs reputed to cure numerous ailments, had long attracted Europe's wealthiest individuals. The springs advanced Nevis's reputation as a gem among the Caribbean isles. American founding father Alexander Hamilton, the first treasurer of the United States and architect of the American nation-state, was born on Nevis. All Nevisians, including the Bakers, took great pride in sharing a homeland with the American politician.[13]

But it was not only the connection with Hamilton that inspired this patriotic enchantment. The traditions of the English, of West Africans, and of native Carib Indians had interfused in the island's culture, and Afro-Caribbeans delighted in their creolized heritage. Willoughby and Rachel gloried, above all else, in being subjects of the British Empire. Like other islanders, they thought of England as their mother country and expressed allegiance to the Crown.[14] The colonial subjects' reverence for Britain sprang from deep cultural ties. In ways large and small, Nevis had long been an extension of British society. Nevisians carried British passports, fought in the British army, hailed the British monarch, and basked in the pomp and circumstance associated with official visits to the British territories by the royal family and its emissaries. The Crown appointed a governor, an administrator of the island, and officers of the court; all Englishmen, these officials observed and fostered English customs.[15]

The fixation on Britain and British culture might have inspired in Afro-Caribbeans a belief in white *racial* superiority, but generally it did not. With few whites on the island, Blacks experienced interpersonal forms of racism less frequently, and therefore escaped, to an extent, the sense of race-based inferiority that arises in more starkly segregated societies. Moreover, Afro-Caribbeans witnessed Blacks in every conceivable social role. Black people worked as both menial and skilled laborers, and as estate managers and administrators—at all levels of society. At the same time, the vestiges of colonial power clung on, and islanders were indoctrinated into European customs.

Their assimilation of British mannerisms occurred mostly by way of elite *Black* role models, and these same-race authority figures softened the significance of skin color as a marker of social status and heightened the importance of culture and class.[16]

The Afro-Caribbean middle class, composed of estate managers, landowners, administrators, and shopkeepers, happily cultivated English identities in their social inferiors. Nevis's colored elite believed they were duty-bound to play this role in much the same way that the "better" class of Blacks in the United States—W. E. B. Du Bois's "Talented Tenth"—believed they had a special obligation to advance the interests of African Americans. Upper-crust Afro-Caribbeans impressed on islanders who aspired to social mobility the need to display "respectable" traits. Strivers should marry well, embrace appropriate gender roles, attend church, enjoy the arts and discuss them over teas, and organize functions to promote good relations with neighbors. They should play sports (preferably cricket) and demonstrate refinement by dressing in well-made, embroidered garments. Such were the accepted trappings of proper acculturation.[17]

Yet because of the privileged position of the Afro-Caribbean middle class, color consciousness did take root on the island. More often than not, the middle class descended from racially mixed families and had lighter skin tones than other islanders. Thus, color, economic class, and social position were interwoven for the island's middle class. The economic and social domination of this colored elite created color hierarchies—though not, perhaps, a wholesale belief in white racial superiority. Color consciousness and loyalty to the Crown were, for both Willoughby Baker and Rachel Huggins, formative influences, which they carried with them to the United States.[18]

Born on Nevis in 1884, Willoughby Baker was the son of a Black man and a mother who had a white father. His racially mixed heritage and light skin meant he was marked as "colored" on the island and, according to his World War I and II draft registration cards, as "Indian" or "Native American" in the United States. He attended English Standard Schools through seventh grade, and while many other islanders toiled as menial laborers, he worked as a cobbler.[19]

Baker's racial classification and occupation, together with his ability to read and write, set him apart. Islanders such as Willoughby, who worked in nonagricultural positions—tradesmen, artisans, shopkeepers, and mechanics—held an elevated position in Nevisian society. Literally called "Special People," Baker and others of his rank took pride in having shaken off badges of slavery such as menial labor and field work. He possessed a sense of superiority that defined his politics, his values, and the attitudes he imparted to his children.[20]

Rachel Huggins, born on Nevis around 1886, was the daughter of a mixed-race father. She shared the surname of a notorious English planter, a man known for his cruelty toward those he enslaved. Rachel's father was a carpenter and had distinguished himself by building his own two-story home, a sanctuary in which the family took great pride. He also held stature in the community through activism in his church. Like Willoughby, Rachel attended the English Standard Schools and later worked as a preschool teacher. Much darker in skin color than Willoughby, she did not share her future partner's racially mixed appearance. But she was well aware of her heritage. Rachel did not denigrate other racial or ethnic groups, but she, like Willoughby, took pride in her education and her family's social standing.[21]

Willoughby and Rachel's mutual ability to afford the $25 passage to New Haven in the early twentieth century reveals the elevated status they enjoyed, which also helped ease their transition into life in the United States.[22]

*

Constance Baker Motley's parents, then, arrived in the United States a step ahead of many Black Americans. Their lot far surpassed that of the southern Black agricultural laborers who flooded New Haven and other northern cities during the Great Migration, which saw Black Americans move north and west to escape Jim Crow and find opportunity. However, as poorly educated menial laborers, Black migrants frequently found themselves on the back foot, competing for jobs and housing against immigrants such as the Bakers.[23]

Despite their relative advantage, Willoughby and Rachel both lost occupational status in the United States. Willoughby no longer worked in the skilled trades. Instead, he found work in the service indus-

try, which was not a kind of labor that Nevis's "Special People" performed. Rachel stayed home, birthing and raising twelve children,
precisely the same number of kids that her mother had given birth
to in the old country.

Willoughby and Rachel absorbed these losses while making
other gains. The pair wedded in New Haven at St. Luke's Episcopal Church on Whalley Avenue, whose membership included many
West Indian transplants. A family home came next. The Bakers
rented several houses, first on Day Street, then Garden Street, and
later on Dickerman Street, settling in racially integrated New Haven
neighborhoods.[24]

The West Indian community made up only a small portion of New
Haven's population. By the early twentieth century, thousands of
immigrants from many corners of the globe had planted themselves
in the seaport town. During the 1890s, Irish, Germans, Italians, and
Russian Jews flocked to New Haven to find work. During World War I,
about three thousand African Americans journeyed to the city from
the South. Both native-born Blacks and European immigrants substantially outnumbered the four hundred West Indians who inhabited
"Elm City" by 1930. The city's increasing cultural and racial diversity,
however, did not much improve race relations.[25]

Race constrained life for West Indians as well as African Americans. Vestiges of the city's involvement in the slave trade and the
remnants of earlier eras' discrimination remained intact. By custom,
some public venues refused to serve Blacks. And in an age when the
upwardly mobile jealously guarded their "heritage," coveted a place
on the "social register," and formed exclusive organizations to rein-
force hierarchy and "breeding," whites did not invite "Negroes" into
their homes or social clubs as equals.

At the same time, the lingering spirit of the antebellum period,
when Connecticut was a hotbed of abolitionism, still influenced
everyday race relations. Blacks could vote, attend neighborhood
schools without racial restriction, and find work in the city's service
industries and munitions factories. But employers practiced occupational segregation. The more lucrative manufacturing and industrial
sectors hired few, if any, Black people.[26]

If the discrimination bothered them, Willoughby and Rachel

Baker did not often acknowledge it. The family made little fuss about racism. Their daughter Constance in turn adopted their "more relaxed" attitude toward race. Later on in life, when she reflected on the New Haven of her youth, Baker recalled little racial bias. She could remember only one occasion when racism seemed grounds for her mistreatment. An attendant had refused, on account of her race, to admit the fifteen-year-old Baker to the municipal swimming pool in Milford. However, the young girl did not dwell on this disappointment; it was, she believed, an exception to the rule of racial détente that reigned in the town in which she grew up. "Fear and racial conflict were simply not a part of the landscape," she wrote.[27]

Baker remembered her childhood as a study in contrasts between North and South. To her, the social meaning of race in Connecticut and the South could not have been more different. She believed and frequently asserted that life in the South damaged the Black psyche in a manner unknown to northern Blacks. She trafficked, that is, in one of the enduring yet long-contested myths about American race relations. Contrary to the story that she spun, racial discrimination pervaded the United States. Racial caste systems operated in pre- and postwar New York, Chicago, Philadelphia, *and* New Haven, differing in degree from the Jim Crow of the South. Most tellingly, race limited Blacks' employment opportunities in New Haven, no less than it did in Birmingham. And she sometimes admitted as much. "When my father came over here, he couldn't get a job as a cobbler," she once recalled, "because that was a trade that Italians had a foothold in." "There were few blacks." On another occasion, she described the limited employment options available: "[Y]ou either worked as a domestic or you worked at Yale," she recalled, until World War II opened factory jobs to Blacks. Still, she downplayed the extent of racism in the North.[28]

Baker's memories about New Haven fit a family pattern. The city moderated the worst aspects of the American racial caste system, and that allowed her to grow into a person who "would not be put down." The experience of race in New Haven—geographically distant from the Jim Crow South—enabled a young Constance to believe in the power of personal agency.[29]

Economic disadvantage marked Baker's young life far more than racism. The ninth of her parents' twelve children, she knew deprivation early and often. Three of her siblings died in infancy, leaving nine mouths to feed: Olive, Joseph, Edna, Maxwell, Eunice, Marion, Edward, Cynthia, and Constance. "Poverty," she recalled, "was omnipresent" as her parents struggled to make ends meet. They often could not afford school supplies, and Constance, forced to accept charity from local schools, grew self-conscious.[30]

No one could blame the family's financial position on Willoughby's work ethic. He worked hard, but for low pay. He initially found employment as a dishwasher in a hotel on Chapel Street, across from Yale. Soon he landed a job as a chef at the university. Even though he always had stable employment, he took on side jobs to support the family, often working seven days a week to make a living. This hard work allowed him to buy the family's house and even invest in a restaurant on Dixwell Avenue, although it later failed. Given his steady employment and the fact that he owned a home, Willoughby could proudly claim the American success story told by so many immigrants. But money still ran short. Even in flush stretches, the Bakers never rose above the lower middle class.[31]

In the face of setbacks, Constance Baker's familial, geographic, and cultural context both shielded and bolstered her. The cluster of houses where the Bakers and their extended family resided were a "ghetto," but only "in the best sense of the word," she would later say. The extended Baker-Huggins clan, including aunts, uncles, and cousins who had emigrated from Nevis, nurtured a sense of belonging. The Baker siblings, with a twenty-year age gap separating the youngest and oldest, played with and protected one another. Constance and Eunice, just eighteen months apart, were companions and confidants. The clan visited each other daily, shared meals, traveled together, and went to social gatherings at the Antillean Society, a West Indian club that sponsored dances and other cultural activities. Tight-knit, the Baker-Huggins family and other West Indians enjoyed a sense of shared experience at the club. The networks formed inside the Antillean Society created opportunities for their members. Elders helped younger members find homes and employment. Neighbors celebrated weddings, births, communions, and confirmations at St. Luke's, a parish where members "embraced" all the community's children, blood relatives or not. The West Indians' cultural distinctiveness and apartness stirred resentment in the wider community, but the Bakers likely remained oblivious.[32]

*

For Constance, her parents' strong identification with Afro-Caribbean-English notions of respectability and social and political conservatism, and their pride in "being a part of the British Empire," remained powerful influences throughout her childhood. "God Save the Queen" frequently wafted out of the upright piano that sat in a corner of their tiny home. The Bakers practiced the conventions of the English middle class, baking them into Afro-Caribbean traditions, creating a worldview animated by the pursuit of upward mobility. In the Baker family, the saying "The Nevisians were simply more British than the British" rang true.[33]

Willoughby Baker carried himself in the manner of an English gentleman: pious, stern, hardworking, he ruled the roost. Barking orders in a British accent and brooking no resistance to his strict moral code, he spouted "conservative, Republican" views and saw himself as a "hard-working, law-abiding, self-respecting" person. He dominated his wife and children. Constance and her siblings were not permitted to be "mischievous." If the children got out of line, Willoughby would beat them with a leather belt. He expected Rachel to have the parlor "straightened up and ready for company," and she spent endless hours managing the household. Through dress and manner, Willoughby demanded respect. Handsome, tall, and "Hispanic" in appearance, he strutted around town in a top hat and tailcoat, as if he were "president of the First National Bank."

Like her husband, Rachel spoke with a British accent, dressed immaculately for public outings, and held her head high irrespective of her station in life. She accepted the patriarchal social order her husband imposed. Once married, she slipped into the role of homemaker. The mother of twelve kept the Baker home spotless, cooked, sewed, laundered and ironed clothing, instructed her large brood in their proper deportment, and handled all the other needs that her husband and children had.[34]

Outside the home, the Bakers demonstrated their social worth and cultivated an image of tranquil domesticity through displays of piety, courtliness, and refinement. Religion mattered a great deal; Willoughby and Rachel insisted that Constance attend weekly services at St. Luke's without fail.[35]

While the Bakers resided near the bottom of the social ladder, they taught Constance to think of herself as special and raised her to feel superior to others—to African Americans, in particular. Her father frequently aired slights about Black Americans and kept his distance, lest their social contagion affect him. In Willoughby's view, West Indians had proved themselves distinct from—better than—African Americans, who belonged to a lower caste. More often than not, he felt, Black Americans preferred leisure to hard work and reveled in ignorance. By contrast, Caribbean Americans worked assiduously to improve their fortunes through education and dignified labor.[36]

Willoughby's views reflected a concoction of beliefs and teachings: a large dose of West Indian cultural pride, more than a dash of class consciousness, a hint of British moralizing about "peasants," a shallow grasp of American history, and a strong measure of racist teachings that many immigrants imbibed during the process of Americanization. Willoughby seemed to have scant consciousness of how skin-color favoritism and plain luck figured in his relatively elevated position. The cartoonish picture he painted nevertheless served a psychologically important purpose: it instilled West Indian pride and fed middle-class aspirations in his children. The West Indians' embrace of the conceit of American exceptionalism and eager pursuit of the American dream proved to the Bakers that they were the so-called "Black Jews"—in other words, that they were special.[37]

*

Constance grew up in the shadow of the exclusive world of Yale University. Her childhood home and high school both stood a short distance from its campus. For many years, Willoughby cooked meals at Skull and Bones, the secret society at Yale that counts some of America's most powerful men among its members: presidents, cabinet officers, judges, publishers, and captains of industry and finance. It includes President William H. Taft, publishing magnate Henry Luce,

National Security Adviser McGeorge Bundy, Senator Prescott Bush, President George H. W. Bush, President George W. Bush, Supreme Court justice Potter Stewart, William F. Buckley Jr., and Secretary of State John Kerry.[38]

Willoughby grew to see himself as cut from the same cloth as the elites at Yale. He frequently mixed with the children of the wealthy and powerful and relayed stories to the family about these encounters. In fact, nearly all of Constance Baker's male relatives worked at the university's eating clubs, and all of them traded tales about the young white men of Yale. Constance was accustomed to such chatter. In his role as a chef, Willoughby believed he held tremendous sway over his young "charges": he "told the little white boys what to do." Visits by alumni he had served built his sense that he was beloved by his boys. And he felt himself fortunate to know these important people. The elite environment deepened his tendency to "identif[y]" with "upper-class whites." He read into himself the Ivy League college's prestige.[39]

Willoughby's affection for Yale also ran deep because it provided critical support to his family. Yale's food kept his family afloat. The Bakers survived the Great Depression by "literally eating the crumbs"—the leftovers—from the tables of Yale's wealthy sons. Even in good times, the extended Baker clan ate food from the university's table. The big family dinners that Constance fondly recalled years later were provisions available because of her father's position.[40]

In a different family, the dependence on Yale might have stirred resentment. In the Bakers, it inspired gratitude and loyalty. Willoughby, like all the Baker men, took pride in working for the university. He was pleased to play a role in the lives of the upper classes, and it increased his drive to succeed. The family connection to the university also left a deep impression on young Constance. "Yale was always visible," she said, referring to its literal and figurative presence in her life. The ambition she inhaled from her own community redoubled in the aristocratic environs of the university her father so cherished.[41]

2

"I Discovered Myself": The Great Depression, the New Deal, and the Dawn of a Political Conscience

Despite her family's pretensions and conceits, Constance Baker, like other children of the working class, expected to follow her father into a lifetime of low-status work. The period in which she came of age, the era of the Great Depression, made a humble life an especially likely fate. Notwithstanding a good academic record earned in fine schools, her place in the class hierarchy was plain.

Constance learned in racially integrated, economically diverse classrooms. Native-born whites went to school with Irish, Italian, Jewish, and Black immigrants, whether the students lived in single-family homes, multifamily dwellings, or tenements. Baker attended the better of the city's two public high schools. In fact, many counted Hillhouse High School as one of the best in the nation. In it, Baker earned grades that demonstrated her intelligence and diligence. Her senior year, she received As in English, biology, and geometry and Bs in French and physical education.[1]

Under the tutelage of sympathetic teachers and role models, Constance learned inside and outside of school. Once a month on Saturday afternoons, she and about seven other West Indian students had tea and cookies and enjoyed conversation around the dining table at the home of Alice Marsden White. Baker had met White, a well-traveled white teacher and daughter of a minister, at a "welcome hall" sponsored by the Congregational church. White had previously taught at a historically Black college and "realized" that the students "needed extra help," taking it upon herself to provide it. She would read to her students from great works of literature. With Miss White and Miss Genevieve Thompson, another white volunteer from the Congregational church, Constance also explored nature. She went on hikes, picking daisies along the way. The pair took her to places that Constance's parents were not able to because, as she put it, "my mother was always in the kitchen at home" and her father was off cooking for posh white boys at Yale. Baker called Miss White a "mentor" and the greatest influence on her life. To young Constance, White and Thompson were "saints" who taught her how "one individual" could "make a difference." The women "inspired" the group of West Indian students from modest backgrounds, she said, "to be something other than what we were."[2]

With the encouragement of White and other role models, Baker developed a keen interest in inequality. During her high school years, she discovered the writings of W. E. B. Du Bois and James Weldon Johnson; their works sparked in her an abiding interest in race relations. She learned about abolitionists Harriet Tubman and Sojourner Truth. And she read biographies of prominent figures in the American legal profession that fired her curiosity about the law. Three lawyers, in particular, made an indelible impression on Baker: Abraham Lincoln, the backwoods lawyer who became the Great Emancipator; George W. Crawford, a respected Black lawyer in New Haven; and Jane M. Bolin, the nation's first Black woman judge, an appointee to the Domestic Relations Court in New York City. The Alabama-born Crawford achieved remarkable success in New Haven after graduating from Yale Law School. An ally of the National Association for the Advancement of Colored People (NAACP), he also served as the city's corporation counsel and represented prominent clients in New Haven. Through Crawford, Baker learned about some of the NAACP's early cases that challenged segregation in higher education. In Bolin, also a Yale Law School graduate, she found the rare Black woman lawyer, one whose judicial appointment earned her a place in history. Based on these examples, Baker surmised that law could be a way to make a mark on society.[3]

Around the time that Baker first took special notice of race relations and of law as a profession, she also became immersed in community activism. She joined not just one but a long list of organizations, among them the New Haven Community Council and the

Dixwell Community Center. Many of her activities focused on economic class and the plight of the poor. "We were still suffering from
the effects of the Depression," she explained, and "all everybody ever
talked about was jobs and the economy." Baker's own background also
inspired her growing commitment to the problems of the working
class. Indeed, it would have been difficult for the daughter of a family whose livelihood depended, in part, on the university's noblesse
oblige to escape knowledge of class structure—and its winners and
losers.[4]

*

Baker came of age in the 1930s, an era of economic collapse and
flourishing Left-liberal coalition politics. This milieu inspired her
lifelong loyalty to the party of Franklin Delano Roosevelt, her belief
in government intervention to ameliorate inequality, and her dedication to reformist politics. These allegiances set her apart from her
father, "a true conservative" Republican "vigorously opposed to the
dole," or government benefits to aid the jobless. An intergenerational
and cultural conflict arose between father and daughter. The contrast
between his first- and her second-generation immigrant experience
only intensified as Constance grew older.[5]

Constance Baker saw firsthand the devastating impact of the Great
Depression. In Connecticut's small towns and villages, food, shelter,
and jobs disappeared, leaving thousands to suffer. Factory workers in
Bridgeport, New Haven, Waterbury, and Hartford lost their jobs. In
New Haven alone, sixteen thousand jobs were eliminated as manufacturing and arms companies laid off workers or closed down; Black
employees, the "last hired and first fired," suffered disproportionately. Nine of New Haven's banks failed, precipitating foreclosures
on numerous homes and the closure of many businesses. Hungry
people lined up at soup kitchens in search of food; others roamed
New Haven's streets, stealing to survive. Some beggars showed up at
the Bakers' home; her kindhearted mother fed them, no questions
asked, simply "because they were hungry." In 1934, three-fourths
of the residents in the city's poorest and most densely populated
wards lived on charity from social service agencies, and one-third
received public relief aid, the "dole." Buckling under the weight of

this tremendous need, New Haven declared itself bankrupt. President Roosevelt had inspired hope, but by the time Baker entered Hillhouse High School in 1936, the New Deal had not made a real dent in unemployment and desperate economic conditions. Recovery would not begin in earnest until Baker's senior year of high school, in 1939.[6]

In the meantime, while recovery lagged, reformers critiqued American capitalism and the institutions and individuals most identified with its broken condition: banks and bankers, stock and land speculators, big businesses and titans of industry, proponents of laissez-faire economics, and opponents of government regulation of financial markets. In newspapers, on the airwaves, and in public meetinghouses, commentators decried the joblessness, hunger, and humiliation occasioned by the failing American economic system. Labor unrest was common, and New Haven was a hotbed of strife. Workers went on strike to protest low pay and poor working conditions. Unions campaigned to organize the city's beleaguered factory employees.[7]

New and established organizations arose to demand alternatives to the broken system and urge policymakers to protect the interests of workers and ordinary people. In 1935, a "Popular Front" emerged, a coalition of leftist critics of laissez-faire economics in the United States and opponents of fascism in Europe. The Front, composed of Socialist, Communist, and Democratic party members, together with an array of unaffiliated liberals, sought to influence elections, and thus policy. The groups advocated trade unionism and worker-protective New Deal legislation and pushed for other socialist-oriented legislative initiatives. The Front's affiliates, including the Communist Party, staged mass marches demanding jobs and food for the unemployed.[8]

Trade union leaders also joined the fray. The Brotherhood of Sleeping Car Porters, the American Federation of Labor, the Congress of Industrial Organizations, and union locals championed workers' rights to bargain collectively, and endorsed political candidates.

Many of these critics of failing capitalism linked the struggle against economic exploitation to the battle against racial oppression. Spearheading the push for a labor-oriented campaign for civil rights was the National Negro Congress (NNC), an interracial Popular Front group backed by Communists and organized by prominent Blacks, including A. Philip Randolph and Ralph Bunche. The democratic socialist organization foregrounded the interests of the working class, promoted unions, and critiqued the New Deal for its shoring up of business interests and its failure to place human rights above property rights.[9]

Such leftist sentiment and organizing flourished in New Haven during the 1930s, as Baker grew up. The Communist Party USA (CPUSA) made special appeals to Black Americans and engaged in targeted outreach to New Haven's tight-knit West Indian community—with some success. Party leaders hoped that West Indian Blacks, as working-class and oppressed people of color, would enthusiastically join the worldwide interracial "revolutionary" struggle against "capitalist exploitation." The CPUSA appeared at a 1935 gathering of Nevisians in New Haven, which had been called to protest mistreatment of sugarcane workers still on the island: planters on Nevis had shot and imprisoned several striking workers. At the meeting, a leader of the CPUSA spoke out in support of fund-raising and legal-defense efforts for the islanders. The CPUSA's efforts yielded recruits, among them William Taylor, a second-generation Nevisian well known in New Haven; he signed on and began encouraging others to join the party struggle.[10]

A few years before, the Communist Party had rallied support in New Haven for the "Scottsboro Boys," nine young Black boys and men, aged thirteen to twenty-one, who were falsely accused in Scottsboro, Alabama, of raping two white women on a freight train car in 1931. An all-white jury sentenced eight of the defendants to death and the ninth to life in prison. The Scottsboro case became an international cause célèbre during the 1930s; as a flagrant miscarriage of justice, it illustrated the depths of racial oppression in the American South. Inside and outside the courtroom, the International Labor Defense (ILD), the Communist Party's legal arm, vigorously defended the youths.

The ILD launched a nationwide campaign to sway public opinion in the defendants' favor. The NAACP, the nation's oldest civil rights organization, was fervently anti-Communist and declined to besmirch its reputation by working with the ILD to defend the cause of the boys; it demanded exclusive control of the case. The NAACP's executive secretary at the time, Walter White, considered the Communists "dangerous" publicity-seekers out to "make martyrs" of the Scottsboro Boys for the Communists' ideological "gain." By the ILD's lights, the NAACP failed to grasp the true nature of Black oppression—at its core, a system of exploitation of the poor by capitalist "bosses," with the Scottsboro tragedy a case in point. The ILD's willingness to defend the accused, stressing that poverty made them and numerous other Black, working-class men and boys vulnerable to injustice and exploitation, attracted new converts and dealt a blow to the NAACP's public image. The NAACP, according to the ILD, was nothing more than "an instrument of the white capitalist class for the perpetuation of the slavery of the negro people."[11]

In 1932, at a CPUSA rally in New Haven, a Black woman named Janie Patterson, the mother of one of the Scottsboro Boys, took the stage. Despite criticism by naysayers and redbaiters, Patterson sang the praises of the ILD. The organization had defended her son and poor men like him nationwide. "They are the only ones who put up a fight to save these boys and I am with them to the end," she declared. In 1936, the CPUSA rallied again in New Haven, this time to promote James W. Ford, an African American candidate for vice president of the party and a chief organizer in Black communities.[12]

Constance Baker developed her political identity amid this left-leaning political tumult. A precocious girl with politically astute parents, she would have been aware of the socialist and communist organizing in her city during the 1930s. Her parents, especially her domineering father, would have spoken about communism, the Popular Front, and other leftist philosophies that threatened to overtake the country, if only to scorn them and their acolytes, such as Nevisian William Taylor. Baker was an adolescent in 1932 when Janie Patterson spoke in New Haven. But by 1936, when the CPUSA rallied on behalf of Nevisian sugarcane workers and in support of James W. Ford, the fifteen-year-old Baker had become an activist in her own right. It was around this time that she learned about the CPUSA's members in New Haven, including William Taylor, whom she knew as "a local soap box orator." The examples of the Communist Party's grappling with the "Negro Question" likely kindled her interest in reading the *Daily Worker*, the CPUSA's official news organ, whose pages were filled with discussions of Black rights during the late 1930s and into the early 1940s.[13]

By the age of eighteen, Baker had become involved with the National Negro Congress—the nation's most influential majority-Black Popular Front organization. She attended the NNC's annual meetings in 1938 and 1940. She also journeyed to the annual meeting of the NNC's youth group, the Southern Negro Youth Conference (SNYC), held in New Orleans in 1940. This meeting impressed her enough that she kept a remembrance of it: a copy of the *Daily Worker* that covered the meeting, including an address given there by then union leader John Lewis containing a proclamation in support of civil rights.

Although the precise extent of Baker's participation in the NNC and its youth division is uncertain, her dabbling in these Popular Front organizations does make clear that by early adulthood, she thoroughly identified as a Left-liberal. She could have made the SNYC's tagline, "Freedom, Equality, Opportunity," her own motto, for she wholeheartedly endorsed its quests for job security, peace, and racial equality. Moreover, influenced by civic leaders in New Haven such as lawyer George Crawford, Baker embraced the one issue that united Communists, Socialists, and leftists of all stripes during the 1930s: trade unionism, which appealed deeply and naturally to Baker. As a young woman growing up in a college town during the Great Depression, she was conscious of her family's place in the local hierarchy and was surrounded by relatives who all labored in low-status, if reliable, jobs at a university that was a bastion of the wealthy and privileged.[14]

*

Still a teenager, Baker had found a passion for social justice. Instead of engaging in lighthearted pursuits, she devoted much of her time to fighting disadvantage. Yes, she flirted with avowedly left-leaning national organizations, but she also volunteered for more conventional ones, specifically state and local groups that aided needy constituencies. She volunteered for the Connecticut Conference on Social and Labor Legislation (CCSLL), the New Haven Youth Council, and the

Dixwell Community Center. Her lasting commitments were to these community-based organizations, as opposed to the NNC and SNYC, both of which the House Un-American Activities Committee (HUAC) eventually tagged as "subversive."[15]

Baker wrote and edited position papers, newsletters, and speeches for the CCSLL, a lobbying organization that championed "progressive" legislation in telegrams, letters, and petitions to Congress. Through her work on CCSLL's Drafting Committee, she fortified her political commitments. Fervently pro-labor, the CCSLL condemned all proposals to limit the right of labor to organize, strike, and picket. And it opposed amendments to the federal law that sought to make it a "weapon for employers" by permitting greater employer influence over union elections. The group lobbied against cuts to the National Labor Relations Board's budget that were designed as a backdoor effort to gut the new minimum wage and maximum hour law. The CCSLL's advocacy for antilynching and anti–poll tax legislation and amendments to the Social Security Act (which they proposed should include domestic and agricultural workers) demonstrated its commitment to Black civil and voting rights. Its plea for affordable housing units signaled its commitment to low-income Americans.[16]

Baker helped craft the CCSLL's positions on foreign as well as domestic policy. The organization fervently opposed the United States' entry into World War II and questioned the motives of pro-war forces. The CCSLL lambasted defense appropriations on the grounds that pro-war "financial and industrial interests" would "reap profits and dividends" from American involvement in the conflict. "National defense means the creation of a nation of strong, healthy and well-fed people, employed at decent and substantial wages," it proclaimed. And the group did not cower before those who wielded the banner of national security as a weapon against political enemies. It took a stand against the Smith Act, a law meant to root out sedition by requiring the registration of aliens and alleged subversives. The CCSLL argued that in the hands of overzealous prosecutors, the Smith Act threatened freedom of speech, entrapped innocent people, and encouraged vigilantes "to report to the authorities any progressive" as a security threat. National defense should not be a tool for undermining civil liberties and civil rights, the group argued. Rejecting the suggestion that its progressive positions made it unpatriotic, the CCSLL declared itself a guardian of both American principles and the country's most vulnerable citizens.[17]

Baker honed her persuasive writing skills and learned how to transform white papers into policy change through the New Haven Youth Council (NHYC), an arm of the New Haven Community Council. As secretary of the council, and then as president, she wrote and spoke in service of the council's antiwar, antipoverty, and antidiscrimination causes. She advocated policies to combat unemployment and promote access to vocational and higher education for young people. She also argued for an increase in New Deal appropriations to aid the young and unemployed. Council members, including Baker, then planned and executed lobbying campaigns to promote these causes. It was quite "an educational experience" for her, "to be traipsing around Connecticut with adults, being only 15 or 16, and going to the Legislature" and meetings in Hartford to "lobby" for policy changes. She "learned a great deal" from these people "about the issues of the time" and how things worked.[18]

The Dixwell Community Center, a neighborhood meetinghouse supported by the Community Chest, served a different purpose. Constance came to the center, a social gathering place, for music and dancing with others her age. While there, she also encountered staff at the center who nurtured and guided her. The adults she met and social networks she created at the center profoundly shaped her personhood and path in life. She called the center an "anchor" in her world, and a refuge. At the Dixwell Community Center, Baker, who by then harbored ambitions far beyond her working-class background, found reassurance that she could and would one day "soar" in the wider world.[19]

Baker dreamt of a better life even as her reality suggested she would remain mired in poverty. Book-smart, charming, strikingly attractive, and with a wealth of community experience at seventeen, she found herself caught in the same plight as thousands of young Americans: unemployed despite graduating from a respected public high school. She considered and quickly dismissed the option of following an older sister into domestic service. She found such work "demeaning" and refused to do it.[20]

*

Adrift after graduation, Baker finally landed a job that she could bear to perform, courtesy of the New Deal. To spur recovery from the Great Depression, Congress, pushed by the Roosevelt administration, passed sweeping legislation to support agriculture, banking, and other industries, and to provide relief for the unemployed and especially vulnerable populations such as the elderly and youth. President Roosevelt established the National Youth Administration (NYA) in 1935 to prevent a "lost generation" of Depression-era youth. The brainchild of Eleanor Roosevelt, the agency provided jobs and education to people aged sixteen to twenty-five, who faced a 20 percent unemployment rate at the time, almost as high as the overall employment rate of 25 percent. The NYA sought to "raise economically disadvantaged youth" through federally funded student aid and on-the-job training established in cooperation with local nonprofits, community service organizations, and educational institutions. In 1940, the New Haven office of the NYA placed Baker in a "youth-opportunity" job.[21]

Baker worked as a seamstress for New Haven's St. Raphael Hospital, acquiring the kind of marketable skill the agency hoped youth might develop to better their standings. The job was practical, but the sewing work proved sporadic and inadequate, and lasted for only twelve weeks. Once it ran out, the NYA laid Baker off, forcing her to await another temporary position. In the next job provided by the agency, she refinished wooden chairs, a form of manual labor also performed by prisoners at the city jail. Although grateful for the work, Constance thought the job was beneath her.[22]

Baker's hit-or-miss employment pattern with the NYA continued for two long years and illustrated a problem endemic in the agency's work. While the NYA served a critically important purpose, the federal government had yet to commit the resources required for it to reach its full potential. Chronically underfunded, the agency was abolished in 1943. It did not and could not provide consistent and meaningful employment for the forty thousand youth who were out of work. In newsletters and working papers for the NHYC and the CCSLL, Baker had criticized the lack of funding allocated to the New

Deal's social service agencies. From 1939 to 1941, she lived that reality. It left her stressed and dejected.[23]

Baker feared a lifetime of drudgery. Three years after she had graduated with honors from Hillhouse High School, her talent, ambition, and political acumen had done little to elevate her circumstances. Her future looked not unlike that of Nevisian sugar workers, bricklayers, and cooks who had immigrated to New Haven during the early twentieth century in search of a better life, only to find themselves working in the United States as laborers. Baker wanted so much more.

3

"Like a Fairy Tale": Black Exceptionalism, Philanthropy, and a Path to Higher Education

Working menial jobs, Constance Juanita Baker yearned to attend college. The precocious young woman who had grown up in the shadow of Yale and in the company of Nevisian strivers longed for middle-class respectability and to make a mark on the world.

But in midcentury America, a college education made little sense to most people. In 1940, a majority of Americans had not even graduated from high school; most had completed no more than eighth grade. Only 6 percent of men and 4 percent of women could boast of completing college that year: a sliver of the American populace. Among African Americans, college graduates were an even smaller fragment.[1]

So their daughter's aspiration for a college education struck her parents, Willoughby and Rachel, as unrealistic and imprudent. The large family sometimes struggled to afford food and other necessities; they would never be able to raise the money to send Constance to college. Instead of dreaming of the unnecessary and impossible, Constance should secure a practical job, her parents counseled her, one with a steady income. She should become a hairdresser, Rachel advised. Every woman needed a good shampoo, cut, or style periodically; as a beautician, Constance would be indispensable in any community.[2]

If her family found Constance Baker's interest in college peculiar, they viewed her aspiration to attend law school as truly fanciful. In her junior year at Hillhouse High School, she had set her sights on becoming a "Fifth Avenue" lawyer. Yet without financial help, she stood no chance of realizing this dream.[3]

*

The intervention of Clarence W. Blakeslee—a Son of the American Revolution, a New Haven industrial magnate, a philanthropist, and a total stranger—changed everything for Constance Baker. Born in 1863, the civil engineer turned multimillionaire contractor exercised great influence in New Haven business and civic circles. A graduate of Yale, Blakeslee remained loyal to the university throughout his life. He demonstrated his ongoing interest in his alma mater by serving as a fellow of the Yale Corporation and by providing financial support to Yale students and programs. Among the university programs he especially favored was Dwight Hall, the public service center.[4]

Blakeslee did not limit his philanthropy to Yale. He also supported several local civic groups. He gave to the Young Men's Christian Association (YMCA), the New Haven Community Chest, the Chamber of Commerce, and—crucially for Constance Baker—the Dixwell Community House.[5]

He in fact built and subsidized Dixwell House, or Q House as it was more often called, for "the colored citizens of New Haven." It was there that Blakeslee, president of Q House and a member of its board of directors, first encountered Constance Baker.[6]

The occasion for their meeting was inauspicious. Disappointed to learn that few Blacks actually used Q House, Blakeslee had arranged a gathering to figure out how his good intentions had gone awry. George Crawford, the highly regarded Black lawyer who had been an influential figure for Baker, chaired the meeting.[7]

A nineteen-year-old woman, tall and poised, dominated the gathering. This young woman, the president of the New Haven Negro Youth Council, took the floor and unabashedly offered her explanation for the anemic interest. The Black community did not feel invested in Dixwell House, she said, because Blakeslee and others on the Yale-dominated board made all the programming decisions. Blacks felt like outsiders at "their" House. That young woman was Constance Baker.

Baker's words must have surprised Blakeslee. Perhaps they even stung him. Crawford, taken aback and annoyed by Baker's boldness, feared that the young woman's statement would alienate the philanthropist and weaken his and Yale's commitment to the community. New Haven could hardly afford such a setback.[8] Blakeslee had the opposite reaction. Baker's intellect and leadership ability made a tremendously favorable impression on him. Ironically, her forceful defense of Black community input at Q House laid the groundwork for her imminent escape from New Haven.

The day after the Q House summit, Blakeslee summoned the young woman to his office. He wanted to talk about the future—Baker's future. Blakeslee had been so taken with her remarks that he had looked into her background. He had learned that she had graduated with honors from the Hillhouse High School class of 1939, alongside two of his grandsons. Blakeslee inquired why Baker "was not in college." When she informed him that her parents could not afford the cost of tuition, the businessman made her an incredible proposal. He offered to bankroll her education, "as far as she wanted to go."[9]

Baker wanted to go very far indeed—all the way through college and law school. His bushy eyebrows arched, Blakeslee peered quizzically at the young woman. "I don't know much about women in the law," he said, "but if that's what you want to do, I'll be happy to pay your way." He even had a law school in mind for her. "I am sending my grandson to Harvard Law School. I guess if I can send him to Harvard, I can send you to Columbia." The young woman marveled at her "utter good fortune" and eagerly accepted. As she would later reminisce, Blakeslee's intervention in her life was "like a fairy tale."[10]

Blakeslee's support for Baker epitomized his philanthropic endeavor but departed from his usual practice in one respect. He had "helped a lot of kids," and yet had long favored young men. The philanthropist lavished attention on boys by sponsoring their memberships in the YMCA, a favored charity. He also subsidized summer camp fees for needy boys and bestowed charity on boys he encountered during his travels. Blakeslee sometimes happened upon young men of "fine character" and "apparent ability" and championed them for admission and scholarships to attend Yale. In still other instances, he subsidized scholarships that enabled "self-supporting" students who could not pay tuition to remain at Yale College.[11]

His sponsorship of Baker, whose anatomy, and skin color, set her apart from the typical beneficiaries of his support, said quite a lot. It pointed to the stellar impression that the nineteen-year-old Baker must have made on Blakeslee. But the wealthy stranger's unusual attention to the pretty, teenaged girl also raised questions in some people's minds about his true motives. "No one could quite believe his generosity," Baker recalled years later. By her account, however, Blakeslee wanted nothing more than to support her aspiration for upward mobility. "His wife's connection to academia and his two daughters, whom he had also sent to college, probably explain why Blakeslee would help a woman, in 1940, go to college and law school," she reflected in her autobiography.[12]

*

Within a few months of her conversation with Blakeslee, Baker set out for college in Nashville, Tennessee. Determined to delve more deeply into Black history and culture, she chose to attend Fisk University. A historically Black college, Fisk had been founded in 1866; the Freedmen's Bureau, aided by the American Missionary Society, had established the school as part of a concerted effort to elevate the Black community through education. In its early years, the school and its leaders endured financial struggles and hostility from the local white population. The townspeople, who had opposed emancipation and resented Reconstruction, could scarcely abide the sight of Blacks pursuing even a rudimentary education. They expressed their virulent disgust: as Fisk students journeyed to and from campus, onlookers jeered, hurled epithets, and threw stones. Black students sometimes retaliated. As unrest threatened the new educational experiment, the Freedmen's Bureau intervened to keep the peace.[13]

By the time Baker arrived at Fisk in 1941, the university had been transformed. No longer a fledgling school, it had become a thriving liberal arts institution with a multimillion-dollar endowment. It was called the "Negro Harvard." Students who came to Fisk could expect to study Latin, Greek, English, mathematics, history, and moral philosophy—a classical liberal education that mimicked the curricular offerings of leading colleges in the Northeast. Philanthropists considered Fisk the "capstone" of Black higher education.[14]

At the same time, Fisk had developed a reputation as a center for the study of race relations. An esteemed graduate, W. E. B. Du Bois (class of 1888), had helped make Fisk's national reputation. Fisk's leaders embraced Du Bois's concept of the "Talented Tenth": the college served as a training ground for the "exceptional" Black pupils charged with uplifting the race through community service. Moreover, under the leadership of Professor Charles S. Johnson, founder of the Fisk Institute of Race Relations, the university sponsored vitally important research on segregation's ill effects; the work laid the groundwork for racial reform in the postwar years.[15]

Fisk's prominence and expertise made it an attractive choice for Baker. She desperately wanted to be a part of the "Black Ivy League." Her matriculation at the southern Black college represented a trend: the number of students from the North on Fisk's campus more than doubled during the period from 1930 to 1943. Admissions officers welcomed students like Baker from the urban North. They tended to be better educated and less financially needy than southern students, who had endured the educational and economic harms imposed by Jim Crow.[16]

Despite her excitement about the education that awaited her at Fisk, Baker found the journey from New Haven to Nashville difficult. She boarded a New Haven Railroad train for New York City; there, at Pennsylvania Station, she took another train for her long-haul trip to Tennessee. On board the *Cincinnati Limited*, the Pennsylvania Railroad's popular New York–to–Ohio line, Baker surely enjoyed the breathtakingly beautiful scenery as the train wound over hilly terrain and through lush forests. The trouble started for her, as it did for so many Black people, in Cincinnati, where she connected to the *Pan American*.[17]

Sitting at the confluence of the Licking and Ohio rivers, the city of Cincinnati looked out over the neighboring state of Kentucky, which had chartered the Louisville and Nashville Railroad (L&N) in 1850. While Cincinnati was a site of abolitionist activism, Kentucky was famous for battles between pro- and anti-slavery factions. As the economic standard-bearer of the border territory and one of only a few north–south rail lines, the L&N straddled the line separating the racial politics of the North and the South. "Like the Union itself, the L&N was split down the middle," explained the author of a semi-nal history of the railroad.[18]

By the early twentieth century, the railroad had chosen sides. The L&N had staged a "southern invasion" and operated numerous pas-senger lines to the South—to Atlanta, Birmingham, Montgomery, Jacksonville, and Miami—and embraced a southern identity with train names such as *Southland*, *Dixie Flyer*, and *Dixieland*. Moreover, the L&N bowed to southern laws: when L&N trains heading south reached Cincinnati, the company required its workers and its pas-sengers to undertake steps intended to enforce Jim Crow. There—just before trains entered Kentucky and crossed into states where Jim Crow reigned—L&N workers ordered all "colored passengers" to disembark and board a segregated railcar.[19]

Baker experienced this humiliating L&N practice in 1941 on her way to Fisk. Ordered to disembark, she complied. She waited while L&N employees attached a special railcar—for colored people only—behind the train's engine. Like other Black passengers, she then boarded the rusty old car. The experience disturbed and angered her. In her forced removal to the segregated car, she came face-to-face with the closed society she had been shielded from in New Haven. As she traveled the three hundred miles from Cincinnati to Nashville, she must have agreed with Du Bois's observation: "There is not in the world a more disgraceful denial of human brotherhood than the 'Jim-Crow' car of the southern United States." Baker would never forget the indignity of the railcar. As a memento of the horrible incident, she took a placard that read "For Coloreds Only" from the segregated car: perhaps the would-be lawyer imagined a time when she would help end the insufferable practice. When her train stopped in Nash-ville, she disembarked, and once again she was filled with excitement and hope for her future.[20]

*

On Fisk's campus, Baker encountered students who expanded her conception of Black identity. She had come to Fisk to experience "majority-black culture"; what she encountered instead were stu-dents whose stories illustrated diversity, rather than sameness, in the African American experience. She became acquainted with Blacks from the South and from the North, and from wealthy families and from poor ones. The economic, social, and educational privilege of the peers who came from prosperous Black families impressed Baker. A first-generation college student from a struggling immigrant family, she was shocked to meet several Black students whose grandparents as well as parents had graduated from college. Moreover, she discovered that the parents of some Fisk students were professionals: doctors, lawyers, professors. This encounter with the Black elite broadened her understanding of Black history and fed her hunger for upward mobility.

In other ways, however, Fisk disappointed her. Notwithstanding Du Bois's hopes that Black collegians, the "Talented Tenth," would uplift the race, most Fisk students showed little interest in the pressing issues of the day. Baker found her peers' apathy astonishing. For most students, she observed, the struggles of the working class and of common Blacks took a backseat to social pursuits. Many students sought not to engage but to escape the harsh racial realities of the world off campus. Above all else, the students sought to build a cohesive on-campus community. Baker appreciated the social scene—she felt warmly welcomed on campus. At the same time, she wished more of her Fisk friends were as interested in pursuing social and racial reform as she was. Her thoughts anticipated the blistering critique that E. Franklin Frazier, the eminent sociologist, lodged in his groundbreaking 1957 book *Black Bourgeoisie*. Frazier lamented middle-class Blacks who coveted the material trappings and imitated the social behavior of whites; instead, well-heeled Blacks should lead a struggle for Black freedom, he argued.[21]

Baker's stay at Fisk did not last long. By the fall semester of 1941, just a few months after she had arrived, she had begun having second thoughts about her choice of college. The United States' preparation for and entry into World War II created new challenges at Fisk. Some of the college's most prominent faculty members answered the federal government's call for Americans to contribute to the Allies' effort to defeat the Axis powers. They resigned their teaching positions to serve in governmental agencies involved in war mobilization and national defense efforts. Meanwhile, Fisk's president took a leave of absence to aid the antiwar movement. The majority of Fisk trustees and faculty, by contrast, supported the war effort and urged others to do the same; many students followed suit by volunteering for the armed forces. This exodus pushed Baker to abandon her experiment with education in a majority-Black environment. At the end of the spring semester in 1942, she transferred to New York University's Washington Square College and continued her education in New York City, a world away from Nashville.[22]

*

Baker arrived at NYU during the summer of 1942 already familiar with life on campus. She had gotten to know the school the previous year when she enrolled in NYU's summer school courses. NYU was unlike Fisk in many ways, and it suited Baker.

Established in 1914 at the convergence of several New York City subway lines, Washington Square College, NYU's second undergraduate division, began as a commuter school and maintained that identity for decades. Unlike Columbia University, its rival, NYU consciously appealed to students from humble backgrounds. NYU's chancellor noted that during the Depression the school had seen an "upward surge of youth, ambitious, keen, hard-working, seeking, as America has always sought, for greater opportunities and wider horizons." People who hungered for social mobility flocked to what was at the time the nation's largest private university.[23]

At NYU, Baker found herself surrounded by thousands of students like herself—strivers from working-class and immigrant backgrounds. There, she found community. NYU's undergraduate college emphasized public service. Eleanor Roosevelt, the First Lady, frequently lectured on campus, and the college urged students to pursue careers of service. This was an ideal environment for Baker, and she thrived in it.[24]

Baker dabbled in different causes and organizations: "I was in everything," she recalled, and "enjoyed the excitement" of it all. But she remained most interested in laborers' struggles. She participated in groups that aided workers, enrolled in several courses related to labor issues, and majored in economics, a subject that attracted other students concerned with the plight of low-wage workers. She triumphed in debates with her peers about how to make capitalism work for all Americans. At Washington Square College, she nurtured her interests, her identity, and her abilities.[25]

The world around Washington Square College suited Baker as well. Whereas she had to risk trouble by venturing off the Fisk campus into segregated Nashville, she found New York City a welcoming place. While hardly a racial utopia, New York brimmed with alluring places and people. The bohemian artists and writers who populated the city lived unconventionally. Unlike segregationists, they posed no threat to Baker; rather, these free spirits stimulated, inspired, and sometimes even taught NYU students. She also met rabble-rousers. Most notably, NYU students staged several mass demonstrations against the war during the early 1940s, protests in which Baker likely participated.[26]

Baker lived in Harlem, the famed Black cultural mecca brimming with artists and intellectuals; there she found a social and political network that supported her and complemented her life on campus. She socialized with Louis Burnham, Edward E. Strong, and Benjamin Davis. These men, members of the Harlem-based Black intelligentsia and devotees of the American Left, impressed Baker and shaped her thinking about the struggles for class and racial reform.

She connected with Burnham and Strong in the spring of 1942 at a meeting of the Southern Negro Youth Conference. Both men—active in the SNYC and other organizations deemed "subversive" by the House Un-American Activities Committee—critiqued the oppression wrought by the American class system. Benjamin Davis, a lawyer and prominent member of the Communist Party USA, also took part in the lively political discussions Baker enjoyed with Burnham and Strong. The three, like others in Baker's circle, advocated for a Popular Front, a Left-center, populist alliance in support of initiatives for the working class and for oppressed people everywhere.[27]

Intellectually curious and politically aware, Baker eagerly conversed with these leftists and read the Communist *Daily Worker*. However, unlike many of her friends and associates, she probably did not join the Communist Party (notwithstanding spurious allegations to the contrary made decades later). She undoubtedly agreed with the Left's class- and race-based critique of the American system. She also welcomed the Popular Front's protests for structural change and planned to support these efforts through her legal work. But she devoted most of her time and energies to more mainstream, liberal organizations and planned a respectable career in the law.[28]

By October 1943, just over a year after arriving at NYU, Baker had completed her studies with a major in economics and a minor in government. Organized and resourceful, she had taken classes year round, skipping a summer break. The young woman from New Haven had been an exemplary student. She graduated with honors and joined, by invitation, the Justinian, NYU's pre-law honor society. She had taken a big, first step to escape her humble roots.[29]

*

Baker looked forward to enrolling in law school with great excitement. Legal education, she imagined, would transform her life. Law school could generate outstanding employment prospects, and through the practice of law she could contribute to the social good. She associated the legal profession with heroes and role models who had made outsized contributions to public life. If others recalled Abraham Lincoln's leadership in politics, Baker never forgot he was a lawyer. Moreover, she recalled the aphorism, attributed to Lincoln, that "an independent voice is God's gift to the nation."[30]

The Second World War proved to be a challenging period for law schools and universities overall, but it was also an auspicious time for women like Constance Baker to seek a professional education. With so many men participating in national defense efforts overseas and on the home front, enrollments at America's colleges and universities plummeted by 45 percent. Financial difficulties ensued, but within this dire context, the mission of higher education expanded. It became increasingly accessible to growing numbers of women.[31]

Out of patriotic duty and necessity, women had gone to work in naval yards, munitions factories, and construction sites. Iconic photos of "Rosie the Riveter" captured the public's admiration, and the wartime surge in employment eased women's acceptance in higher education. If women could assemble B-17s on production lines, administrators realized, they could also do the work of higher education. Moreover, the government needed women to fill strategically important technical and scientific positions as engineers, chemists, accountants, diplomats, statisticians, nurses, and stenographers. The proportion of female college graduates increased quickly and dramatically; during some of the war years, women constituted the majority of graduates.[32]

In 1944, Baker enrolled in Columbia Law School, which was just as altered by wartime dynamics as other schools around the country. When she arrived on the school's Upper West Side campus, she recalled, it "resembled a ghost town." With so many of America's ablest young men involved in the war effort, overall enrollments were low; whereas 505 students had been enrolled at the law school in 1940, only 116 attended in 1944. Campus life had deteriorated, and normal activities had been curtailed. The administration had suspended publication of ten law school journals, reduced the frequency with which the *Columbia Law Review* published, and ended the moot court competition. Ten of the twenty-five professors had left full-time teaching to serve in the military or in government. To make up for unavailable male matriculates, Columbia opened its doors to large numbers of women. In 1943, women constituted 43 percent of the class, and by 1944, they made up half.[33]

The presence of women made an immense difference to Baker. Ambitious and determined, she was capable of going it alone; but she had flourished in the kind of tight-knit community of politically like-minded friends that she had found during her days at NYU. At Columbia, she formed lasting friendships with a small circle of socially conscious women. Her closest law school friend was none other than Bella Abzug, the future congresswoman, who remained in her circle for years. Their friendship grew out of a shared commitment to social justice. Baker, who was opinionated but reserved, admired Abzug's brash personality. Long after graduation, when each had garnered fame for achievements in law and politics, the women continued to support, and occasionally commiserate with, one another.

Baker came to know several Black students, male and female, who had also gained a foothold at Columbia partly due to wartime exigencies. Elreta Alexander was the first Black woman graduate from Columbia Law School and a future state judge in North Carolina. Baker also crossed paths with Vertner Tandy, Almeric Christian, Edith Bornn, and other students who went on to successful careers in the law. Grateful for the camaraderie of her Black and female peers, Baker developed a much-needed sense that she belonged in the law, a profession that most everyone, including her own parents, deemed ill-suited to women. Peers like Abzug and Alexander, fellow outsiders, made the experience a little less lonely.

These friendships notwithstanding, Baker infrequently found inspiration inside the classroom. Unlike at NYU, where she had studied subjects that perfectly matched her interests, at Columbia she enrolled in traditional law school courses that bore little, if any, relation to her passions. At NYU she had taken courses on subjects she was fascinated by, such as "Government and Society," "Labor Problems," "Trade Unions and the Law," and "Elements of Public Law." At Columbia Law School, "Insurance," "Possessory Estates in Land," "Trusts and Estates," and "Business Organizations" were less captivating to a young woman drawn to law school in hopes of effecting social change.[34]

The field of civil rights had yet to emerge during Baker's time at Columbia. Thus, while constitutional law textbooks would have included *Plessy v. Ferguson*—the landmark 1896 case upholding segregated railcars—these texts did not cover the precedents that chipped away at and would eventually overrule the decision. Except in a few cases, the era's constitutional law precedents legitimized racial discrimination. Baker's constitutional law professor avoided the issue of race. Noel T. Dowling, the Harlan Fiske Stone Professor of Constitutional Law, hailed from Alabama and, outside of class, articulated support for Jim Crow. Nevertheless, inside the classroom, Baker remembered, Dowling behaved like a "gentleman," even as other students recalled the professor's discomfort around Blacks. By skipping the casebook's coverage of *Plessy* and other race-related cases, Dowling practiced a genteel form of racism. "Race, racism and American law," said Baker, "was not a part of the course of study" during her time at Columbia.[35]

Baker found herself underwhelmed in other Columbia Law School classrooms as well. Although the school accepted more women than ever during the 1940s, it had not taken steps to ensure that they felt welcome. Men dominated the ranks of professors; in fact, Columbia Law School did not tenure its first female law professor, Ruth

Bader Ginsburg, until 1972. A contingent of Columbia law professors hailed from the segregated South; in addition to Dowling, professors charged with teaching Baker conflict of laws (Elliott Cheatham), equity (Huger W. Jervey), and criminal law (Jerome Michael) were from the South. For many of these men, steeped in traditional gender norms, female students, not to mention Black females, made for profound awkwardness.

The customs of other professors also made it difficult for female students to feel as if they belonged. Professors routinely addressed class members as "gentlemen," even if a smattering of the students were, in fact, women. Law teachers frequently taught using hypothetical scenarios that denigrated women or recycled gendered stereotypes. The professors "did not treat us well," recalled Bella Abzug. "They were condescending" and "scoffing" and "they did not make it easy for us to function in law school." If, on a typical day, a professor ignored his female students, on another he might take pains to single them out. On "Ladies Day," the professor asked female students to stand and answer the probing questions characteristic of the "Socratic Method." These sessions put students on the spot, and on edge. Intimidating pedagogies and practices pervaded Columbia Law School during the 1940s and went unchallenged.[36]

The curriculum did include a few courses of interest to Baker. Two teachers in particular inspired her. She found civil procedure fascinating and developed a good relationship with Professor Paul Hayes, reputedly one of Columbia's most liberal. She enrolled in Labor Law and was shaped by a professor who had had a hand in developing the laws that granted workers new rights. She received her highest grade, an A-minus, on an essay that she wrote under the supervision of Professor Milton Handler. An antitrust expert, Handler served as the first general counsel to the National Labor Relations Board and drafted the National Labor Relations Act of 1935, a landmark law providing a guarantee of workers' rights, which resonated with Baker's core principles. Baker must have found studying with Professor Handler—a "model teacher" and an architect of one of the New Deal's signature laws—an invaluable opportunity.[37]

These good experiences aside, Baker would later claim she only "surviv[ed]" Columbia Law School. Although grateful for and proud of her admission, she did not fall in love with the law at Columbia. Rather, law school struck her as "esoteric" and "without practical application."[38]

Baker graduated from Columbia in June 1946. Clarence Blakeslee, the Yale alumnus who had made her undergraduate and law school education possible, attended the ceremony. It was a happy occasion for both benefactor and beneficiary. Blakeslee—who had frequently written Baker letters "encouraging" her to "go on," "just as a father would do"—expressed great pride that she had "gotten through" the ordeal of law school and had achieved her lofty educational goals. She had not only attained a college education but had also earned a law degree from one of the nation's most prestigious institutions of higher learning. Baker had defied tremendous odds.[39]

Most American workers at that time had not even set foot in college. If they were lucky, America's laborers toiled in blue-collar jobs in manufacturing, mining, or construction. Millions worked in service industries. Most women did not work outside the home. One-third of Black women did work, but in agriculture or domestic service—the most menial and least remunerative jobs. A minority among American workers, a member of a minority race, and a minority within her race and gender, Baker had catapulted herself into the halls of the American elite.[40]

Still, she faced tremendous professional challenges. Even as she graduated a member of the elite, she had faced discrimination, stereotypes, and low expectations throughout the years she spent in law school. And as she set out on her unlikely path, she was keenly aware of the mountain of disadvantages she faced in the workplace. Years later, Baker admitted that if at her law school graduation, "a poll had been taken of those least likely to succeed in the profession, I would have headed the list." No one expected a woman, particularly a Black woman from a modest background, to make it in the legal profession, which was, of course, dominated by a network of white men.[41]

4

A Fortuitous Meeting with "Mr. Civil Rights": Thurgood Marshall and an Offer Not to Be Refused

Several months prior to Baker's law school graduation a meeting that she would remember as "fortuitous" took place: her life in the law began to take flight in October 1945, during an encounter with Thurgood Marshall, then special counsel to the Inc. Fund. The LDF was already engaged in an ambitious campaign against racial discrimination. One day, over some hallway banter, a friend of Baker's named Herman Taylor mentioned that he had been working part-time as a law clerk for LDF; but with graduation approaching, he had decided to leave the position for full-time employment elsewhere. The LDF needed to hire a new clerk to replace him, and at Taylor's suggestion, Baker decided to apply. It would be far different from other experiences trying to find a job in the legal profession.[1]

Baker had once attempted to find work at a Wall Street firm, and the episode disheartened her. She visited one firm after accepting an invitation to interview by phone. Once she arrived at the law office and introduced herself as the job candidate, the partner looked at her as if he "had seen an unidentified flying object." The firm's receptionist turned her away. Other firms also shut the door in her face. Baker's search went nowhere.[2]

Her experience was hardly unique. Baker suffered much the same fate as other women law students, and in her case, race undermined her prospects, too. As World War II wound down, female law school graduates learned that their wartime access to and success in law school had not blunted the stereotypical thinking that had long relegated women to positions as law librarians, legal secretaries, and legal assistants. Women's opportunities diminished beginning in late 1945 and 1946 as a result of demobilization and the implementation of the Servicemen's Readjustment Act, commonly known as the GI Bill. Male veterans poured onto campuses and into law offices, displacing women. The vast majority of women in the field came to be shut out of jobs as "real" lawyers in corporate law firms—the most lucrative sector. Employers did not hide their distaste for women. Time and again, recruiters told women applicants, "We want a man."[3]

Baker's meeting with Mr. Civil Rights, after she applied for the role at LDF, alleviated the pain she felt over other firms' rejections. She had repelled powerful white male lawyers, but fascinated Marshall. And if partners in the Wall Street firms reveled in practiced formality, Marshall basked in folksy informality. During her interview, he heartily welcomed Baker to the office and regaled her with stories about other women professionals he had come across over the years. Despite his stature, Marshall accorded Baker both common decency and professional respect.[4]

Marshall also engaged in banter and behavior that had nothing whatsoever to do with Baker's professional qualifications, according to some. A tall and strikingly handsome "Romeo," well known for his extramarital affairs, he showed during the interview that he viewed Baker, no less than many other women, through a sexual prism. He reportedly asked her to climb a ladder next to a bookshelf; he wanted to inspect her legs and feminine form. Baker complied with the request.[5]

The alleged incident—grossly inappropriate by today's standards—would have been typical behavior of the era and not unexpected of Marshall, who was known to comment on the physiques of women he found attractive. In one poignant example, he boasted that his first wife, Vivian Burey, was "put together nicely"; she had acquired the nickname "Buster," he said, because she had large breasts. Considered in context, Marshall's supposed behavior toward Motley sounds entirely in character.[6]

Even if Baker found Marshall's behavior unwelcome, such objectification would probably not have surprised her: this conduct conformed to prevailing norms. Books, magazines, television, film, and advertising of the era condoned and even promoted sexual aggressiveness in men. The media obsessively discussed women's beauty, routinely depicted women as objects of men's sexual desire, and portrayed men's attention to women's physiques as a compliment. In 1950, a three-page spread in *Ebony* magazine pictured a woman's body alongside quotes by celebrity men appraising her form. And in 1955—a full decade after Baker's interview with Marshall—*Jet* magazine, in an article titled "Are Working Wives Less Moral," described women who worked outside the home as having invaded the "world of their husbands and boyfriends." In postwar America, Baker's job hunt was what transgressed gender norms; Marshall's objectification of her did not.[7]

The ingrained conception of gender roles that Baker challenged, first as a law student and then as an attorney, would not begin to give way until well after the dawn of the women's liberation movement in the late 1960s. Baker's own career, along with that of a handful of other high-profile women leaders, helped bring about the cultural change that today makes the Marshall incident cringeworthy.

In October 1945, Marshall wasted no time in offering the beautiful and brainy Baker the internship that she sought. And, spurning the advice of Columbia Law School faculty who counseled students to avoid employment during the academic year, Baker quickly accepted the position. Initially working without pay, she volunteered at the LDF after class in the afternoons, three to four days per week. When, several months later, she found the doors to Wall Street firms closed to her, she did not worry much. Thanks to the connection she had made with Marshall and the LDF months earlier, she could continue in a position that, it turned out, perfectly fit her interests.[8]

She would be forever grateful to Thurgood Marshall for giving her a professional break. Without Marshall's generosity of spirit and openness to hiring a woman, Baker often said, she "would not have gotten very far as a lawyer," for "women simply were not hired in those days." She never publicly accused Marshall of any impropriety; all that she could recall about their first meeting, she later wrote, was his "total lack of formality" and his "demand" for informality from "everyone in his presence." Whatever might have occurred during their initial meeting, it is easy to see why Baker felt so appreciative of the man who first hired her. Marshall had given her an opportunity she should and could not have refused.[9]

5

"They Hovered Over and Cared for Each Other": The Uncommon Union of Constance Baker and Joel Motley Jr.

I n 1945, the same year that she landed her dream job, Baker found the love of her life in Joel Wilson Motley Jr.

The pair first met in Harlem, the unparalleled center of Black political, social, and cultural life in the United Status. The "Harlem Renaissance," the period from roughly the 1910s to the 1930s of explosive literary and artistic output by Black writers—luminaries such as Claude McKay, Jean Toomer, Alain Locke, Langston Hughes, Zora Neale Hurston, and James Weldon Johnson—made Harlem the place to be for those who wanted to experience urban Black cultural and political life. The streets teemed with life; native New Yorkers mixed with thousands of migrants from the South, and everyday people walked side by side with writers, musicians, activists, and others eager to make a mark.

On street corners, preachers and politicos raised their voices on soapboxes, hoping to convert tenement dwellers to a new religion or ideology. The Cotton Club purred with the music of Louis Armstrong and Duke Ellington. Newcomers and longtime residents alike converged on the 135th Street branch of the New York Public Library, whose Division of Negro Literature, History, and Prints was later rechristened the Schomburg Center for Research in Black Culture. A cultural hub, the library hosted musical performances, book talks, theatrical productions, and political debates.[1]

Constance and Joel lived in two key Harlem meeting spots: the Young Women's Christian Association on 137th Street, and the Young Men's Christian Association on 135th Street at the intersection with

Lenox Avenue. Situated two short blocks from one other, the YWCA and YMCA, segregated by race until 1945, were a part of a national network of institutional counterparts dedicated to Christian fellowship among women and men in a family atmosphere.[2]

Black women sustained the YWCA, one of the city's most vital community-based organizations. The YWCA featured a cafeteria, meeting rooms, classrooms, an office, locker rooms, showers, and a pool, as well as residential spaces that women could rent for up to three years. Women engaged in study, recreation, and activism through the Harlem YWCA; the organization hosted lectures, provided job training, and offered classes in calisthenics, music appreciation, cooking, domestic arts, stenography, typing, hairdressing, dressmaking, and the trades, all to promote self-improvement, community service, and racial uplift. In addition to Constance Baker, who roomed there while attending NYU and Columbia Law School, Leontyne Price, the opera singer, and Dorothy Height, the activist, lived or worked at the Harlem YWCA.[3]

The YMCA, meanwhile, served as a center of Harlem's social and cultural life. It hosted art exhibitions, sponsored political workshops, offered academic and vocational courses, and staged sports matches, among other endeavors. Joel Motley lived at the YMCA along with other "new, young, dark male arrivals" to the city who followed in the footsteps of luminaries. The institution once hosted Ralph Ellison and Paul Robeson. Baker sometimes visited the YMCA to enjoy its cultural riches, ethnic cuisine, and the social life that made the neighborhood the "Negro capital of the world."[4]

On the weekends, residents of the YMCA and YWCA met and mingled on neighborhood streets and at dances and parties. At these social gatherings the young residents flirted with one another and enjoyed flings and courtships, yearnings that the war and its attendant worries heightened.

The twenty-three-year-old Baker and the twenty-two-year-old Motley—each young, good-looking, and available—crossed paths on a warm day in 1945. "Cruising for girls," Motley and two friends had walked the well-worn path from the YMCA to the YWCA. The trio happened upon Baker perched on a tripod stool in front of the building, along with two of her friends. She caught Motley's eye. He stopped to chat. The handsome pair soon began to date. As a Black American, Joel Motley would hardly have fit Willoughby Baker's idea of a proper suitor for his daughter, but his good looks and mild manner held tremendous appeal to his daughter.[5]

Born in 1923, Joel Wilson Motley Jr. had arrived in Harlem from Decatur, Illinois, known as the "heart of the heartland." Situated in the middle of the state, Decatur epitomized the nation's industrial and agricultural core. Cornstarch and glucose factories, grain and soybean processing plants, railroads and heavy manufacturing concerns dotted the landscape. So did the immense tanks and filters of a state-of-the-art sewage treatment facility. As a result of the waste that flowed from the city's factories and its sewage plant, an inescapable stench permeated the town. Driving into Decatur, one could see and smell both the promise and the peril of America's heartland.[6]

The city was also known for a more sinister reason. It was the site of the horrific lynching in 1893 of Samuel J. Bush, an African American day laborer. One of numerous unlawful killings of Blacks that led historian Rayford Logan to call the 1890s the "nadir" of Black history, Bush's lynching shaped the world into which Joel Motley Jr. was born. City fathers policed racial boundaries in Decatur, despite the town's connection to the lore of Abraham Lincoln: the future president and Great Emancipator had been nominated for president in Decatur, which had once been his home. Decades after Lincoln lived there, segregation was still pervasive, and separation of the races existed there in fact, if not by law, well into the twentieth century. Few of Decatur's restaurants served Blacks; theaters relegated Black moviegoers to balconies; and the minor-league baseball team barred Blacks until the 1950s. For a young man of color growing up there, Decatur afforded little opportunity. It is no wonder that Joel Motley left for New York.[7]

The young man's parents bequeathed him a complicated heritage. The family boasted an esteemed military past. Joel Jr.'s father, Joel Motley Sr., earned a Croix de Guerre from the French for valor during World War I. Even so, both before and after the war, Joel Sr. labored in low-wage and low-skill jobs. Initially, he worked as a cement finisher; later, he was a janitor. Nevertheless, in a sign of his ingenuity,

Motley had managed to purchase his own home, on North Monroe Street in Decatur.[8]

In 1922, Joel Motley Sr. married Della Wilson, also an Illinois native. Aged nineteen, Della became the bride of a man eleven years her senior. For a time, their lives proceeded as expected. Della worked as a domestic servant, a common occupation for Black women. The couple became active in the Antioch Baptist Church, where Della hosted the sewing circle. Joel Sr. helped to organize the American Legion post for local Black veterans. Children soon arrived. One year into their marriage, at age twenty, Della gave birth to the first of two sons, Joel Jr.; three years later, she bore a second son, Earl.[9]

It was during Joel Jr.'s grade school years that things took a turn for the worse. Mental illness plagued Della Motley. Little is known about her precise affliction; however, we do know her sickness proved so torturous and disruptive to her family that in September 1930, when Joel Jr. was seven years old, she was taken from her home and confined to an asylum. Della ended up as an inmate on the "female ward" of Jacksonville State Hospital for the Insane, Illinois's first state mental asylum.[10]

Like other patients at Jacksonville State, Della likely suffered there. Warehoused in poor and overcrowded conditions, subjected to surveillance and restraint, and administered potent and often dangerous drugs, inmates at Jacksonville State were given "treatments" now considered barbaric. Instead of getting better over time, many grew worse. Della, like most, never returned home. She died in the asylum after being confined there for twenty-five years.[11]

Della's commitment to an insane asylum—a source of shame in early-twentieth-century America—must have powerfully shaped Joel Motley Jr. As a result of his mother's illness, the seven-year-old Motley would have had to learn—having lost even her difficult presence—to live with his mother's absence. All this turmoil occurred while he was still a very young boy. Later observers described Motley as a "quiet," "unassuming," and "self-contained" man whose world revolved around his mate.[12]

Constance Baker's and Joel Motley Jr.'s backgrounds made them a fine match. As a young woman, Baker vowed never to marry a man like her father. Instead, she chose to make a life with the reserved son of a detached mother—a man who did not wish to dominate or need to compete with her.[13]

After dating for over a year, the couple became engaged and married. The ceremony took place at St. Luke's Episcopal Church on August 18, 1946. Dressed in a beautifully embroidered white wedding gown, Constance walked down the church aisle to Joel, decked out in a black tuxedo. Constance's mother and father, along with extended family and friends, surrounded the couple as they took their vows. Henceforth, Constance Juanita Baker would be known as Mrs. Constance Baker Motley.[14]

Mr. and Mrs. Motley made a handsome couple, fascinating to onlookers unaccustomed to highly educated, working wives. Constance Baker Motley, in her work as a lawyer, defied gender conventions. For his part, Joel Motley Jr. at once conformed to conventions and transcended them. He worked as a real estate and insurance broker, eventually becoming a partner in a successful Harlem firm; the position provided financial security and affirmed his status as man of the house. At the same time, he publicly supported his wife's career. From the outside, the couple appeared to have it all. They had created an uncommon partnership: an egalitarian marriage decades before the idea captured the American imagination and became the ambition of many working couples. In her marriage, as in so many areas, Constance Baker Motley set an example.[15]

To satisfy public curiosity—not to mention reporters'—articles about Baker Motley's professional exploits invariably included a paragraph about her husband. The reports advanced the idea that this was a marriage of equals. Constance Baker Motley, the accounts read, was "married to a lawyer" who "gave up the law for real estate." The pair reportedly met at law school. She had been a student at Columbia Law School, while he had supposedly studied law at New York University. Their paths had diverged, journalists reported, after graduation. In one article, Mr. Motley explained that "after he was graduated from New York University in 1946," he had left the law behind because he "just liked business" and had "always wanted to be in it." Law, he thought, would be too "confining."[16]

The premise of these stories about Joel Motley Jr.'s educational background was false. He had graduated from Decatur High School and then for a year had attended Millikin University in Decatur. Once in New York, he took a handful classes at NYU. But he had never graduated from college, much less from law school. His failure to obtain a college diploma "was a source of embarrassment." The shame was so profound that he repeatedly lied to the press.[17]

The deceit is, at first blush, exceedingly curious: decades would pass, after all, before the majority of Americans would graduate from college. Joel Jr.'s failure to get through college could hardly be called unusual: he was much like the average American, let alone Black Americans.[18] But Constance Baker Motley—rising from a working-class neighborhood in New Haven to Columbia Law School—had far exceeded the accomplishments of the average American. Therein lay the challenge. Joel Motley's embarrassment may well have derived in part from how he felt he compared with his exceptional wife. In view of her achievements, and the stature of the men in her professional circle, Joel Motley might not have felt he quite measured up. The dissemblance satisfied his need to be seen as his wife's social equal, but the hidden truth about Joel Motley Jr.'s education belied the egalitarian picture the couple presented to the world.

Notwithstanding the disparity between them in educational attainment and prestige, the couple thrived. Constance Baker Motley always offered her husband "support and encouragement," he said. And, friends noted, Joel Motley's "devotion" to his wife "had no parallel." "They hovered over and cared for each other," another friend said of them. In the years to come, Joel would support his wife as she made her way in a man's world.[19]

Part II

Becoming the Civil Rights Queen

COURTESY OF GETTY IMAGES

6

"A Professional Woman":
Breaking Barriers at Work and in the Courtroom

Constance Baker Motley lacked a fancy office and an impressive title in her first job at the Inc. Fund. Office space was tight at the organization's offices at 20 West 40th Street and Fifth Avenue in Manhattan. The staff worked in close quarters. Until the late 1940s, not even Thurgood Marshall had a private office in the seven-story redbrick building overlooking Bryant Park. Like everyone else, Marshall worked in a tiny space with a succession of colleagues, including, at one time, Motley. During Motley's initial years at LDF, six lawyers shared one large, high-ceilinged room. In addition to Marshall and Motley, the staff included lawyers Robert L. Carter, Franklin H. Williams, Jack Greenberg, and Marian Wynn Perry, as well as several secretaries.[1]

As in any organization, rivalries sometimes divided the attorneys. Carter, second in command in the office, won universal praise for his brilliant legal mind and skilled courtroom advocacy. But his personality sometimes clashed with his boss's; whereas Marshall was carefree and ebullient, Carter was bookish and intolerant of foolishness. Tall, handsome, "silver-tongued," and an outstanding lawyer, Williams matched his talent with an immense ambition. He argued with Marshall over the latter's "conservative" choices about which cases to take on; one blowup resulted in a shouting match that could be heard all over the office. Perry, a white woman lawyer with deep experience in labor and employment law and dedicated to the cause of racial justice, rounded out the small staff. Tensions over case assignments arose between Perry and Williams, as well as between

Perry and Motley. Racial politics shaped these dynamics. Perry and the other white women in the office were "walking on eggs," she once remarked.[2]

The lawyers did not always get along personally, but an unbreakable dedication to fighting discrimination united the group. The "boundaries" between "work and relationships" were "not very firm," recalled one Inc. Fund lawyer: they were "a team dealing with hostile forces." "We were like a family," Motley once observed. The us-versus-them mentality encouraged a close-knit, mission-driven community.[3]

Marshall's imposing presence and gregarious personality shaped the culture of the LDF. Informality reigned during and after hours. Even as he supervised the staff, raised funds to support the organization's endeavors, managed the increasingly long docket of cases, and argued cases in trial and appellate courts, Marshall exuded warmth and encouraged collegiality. He expected his staff to work on complicated legal tasks for long hours; each of them, secretaries included, complied. All the while, Marshall, in his playful manner, engaged his colleagues in lighthearted banter and regaled them with long stories.[4]

For some staff this casual, fun-loving atmosphere continued after work. A devotee of long dinners and alcohol, of card playing and partying, Marshall invited close colleagues to join him in these endeavors after the workday ended. The gatherings showcased Marshall's desire to "wear life like a very loose-fitting garment" and "worry about nothing." The lawyers sometimes talked legal strategy during these late-night sessions; on other occasions, officemates just played cards and drank. The men in the office frequently accepted the boss's after-hours invitations; sometimes their wives came along. Then, on Fridays, an end-of-the-workweek ritual occurred. "Every Friday afternoon someone got a bottle of Bourbon or Scotch and a poker game ensued," recalled Jack Greenberg. No women participated in the weekly poker games, where the men engaged in a lot of "locker room bragging" and race-inflected humor. Motley did not often take part in these social get-togethers, whether they took place during the workweek or on Fridays; most nights, she went home to Joel.[5]

Deeply committed to LDF's antidiscrimination mission, Motley mostly kept her own counsel. She concentrated on proving herself.

There was quite a lot for the young law clerk to do. In her earliest assignments, Motley battled discrimination against Black veterans. Requests for help poured into the Inc. Fund from servicemen who had experienced mistreatment on tours of duty and returned stateside motivated to challenge the unequal treatment. "Black servicemen," Motley recalled, "had been court-martialed for this, that and the other" and hit with "severe penalties." The alleged wrongdoing frequently involved sexual liaisons with white German women later labeled as "rape." The court-martial cases required Motley to plow through "stacks of service records" so voluminous that they "reached the ceiling almost." She also fought racially restrictive covenants; by banning the sale of property to Blacks (and Jews), these covenants perpetuated residential segregation. All of this work was tremendously satisfying to Motley, who joined her colleagues in helping to establish the burgeoning field of civil rights law.[6]

The field developed in fits and starts as the U.S. Supreme Court became receptive to cases demanding equal enforcement of the law. Motley learned the art of litigation by observing Charles Hamilton Houston, the NAACP special counsel and pioneer in the nascent field, in strategy sessions and in court. In 1948 Motley traveled with colleagues to Washington, D.C.; she entered the majestic U.S. Supreme Court for the very first time to watch Houston challenge state and federal enforcement of restrictive covenants. The lawyer stayed in a segregated rooming house, ate in segregated facilities, and rode in segregated cabs to see Houston attack the underpinnings of an insidious form of Jim Crow—residential segregation that confined Black Americans nationwide to crowded, substandard, ghettoized housing.[7]

Houston had prepared meticulously for the big moment, as Motley knew firsthand. In the run-up to his oral argument, she was thrilled to participate in a series of weekend strategy sessions and conference calls of "all the lawyers" across the country who were helping Houston and Marshall figure out how to argue their position. Houston prevailed, and in a series of cases that he and Marshall litigated, the lawyers established precedents that chipped away at residential segregation. Lorraine Hansberry would famously depict a Black family's difficult move from the inner city to a white neighborhood in her acclaimed play *A Raisin in the Sun*. These cases made such moves possible. The experience of listening to Houston, Marshall, Robert Carter, and others prepare and argue these important cases provided Motley "an amazing legal education."[8]

Before long Marshall decided that Motley was ready to try cases, and she transitioned from observer to participant in court hearings. In 1949 Marshall sent her to Baltimore to share the counsel table with Houston and assist him in a case that challenged inequality in education. This case, one in a series attacking discrimination by institutions of higher education, contested a Black student's exclusion from the School of Nursing at the University of Maryland. As Motley looked on, Houston peppered witnesses with well-phrased questions that unfolded in a sequence carefully chosen to push forward his legal strategy. Although he did not win at trial, Houston prevailed on appeal.[9]

In addition to observing experienced lawyers, Motley wrote pleadings and briefs in a variety of important cases, taking on assignments as needed. In one of her early efforts, she aided the Inc. Fund's successful challenge of restrictions on voting in the South Carolina Democratic Party primary (the so-called white primary). And in her first solo argument—made before the New York commissioner of education in 1949—she prevailed in an action that challenged racial gerrymandering of school district lines. Thurgood Marshall, pleased to see his protégée take this big step, accompanied her to Albany for the argument. Motley earned Marshall's confidence in this case and in other early endeavors. She was ready for greater challenges. Next, she faced her hardest test yet: her first trial.[10]

*

Motley's initial experience as a courtroom lawyer took place in Mississippi, the South's most racially repressive state and the scene of fierce and bloody resistance to the emerging struggle to overturn Jim Crow. In 1949, she journeyed to Jackson, the capital city, to prosecute a lawsuit on behalf of Black schoolteachers. The case constituted an opening salvo in a long-running battle against the racist state. In the lawsuit, Motley took her first turn as a field general in a two-decades-long war against white supremacy in Mississippi.[11]

She came on the scene in Jackson at an especially fitting time. Black veterans returning from World War II risked their lives and livelihoods by attempting to register to vote in the July 1946 Democratic Party primary. Mississippi U.S. Senator Theodore Bilbo, an ardent white supremacist, advocated Black voter suppression through all available means. The senator encouraged violent repression of Black voters by "red-blooded men" who could "keep the nigger from voting" by paying them visits the night before the election. It did not matter that in 1944, the U.S. Supreme Court had outlawed the "white primary," conferring upon Blacks the legal right to register and vote. The on-the-ground reality in Mississippi did not match law on the books.[12]

The Inc. Fund hoped to close the gap between social practices and legal ideals in the Magnolia State with the help of the state's Black teachers. The case that Motley had come to try in Mississippi—part of a legal strategy unfolding in several other states—advanced a simple yet novel idea: that regardless of race, teachers and administrators with equivalent education and experience should be paid equally. In Mississippi, Gladys Noel Bates, a Jackson science teacher and daughter of a local NAACP official, filed the lawsuit that attacked the school board's practice of using different salary schedules for Blacks and whites. The case, known as *Bates v. Batte*, was brought on behalf of all Black teachers in Mississippi. It exemplified the discrimination that plagued teachers, the backbone of the middle-class Black community: even when they held superior credentials, Black teachers invariably earned less than their white colleagues.[13]

As if the lawsuit itself were not enough of an affront to southern norms, LDF sent a co-counsel, Robert L. Carter, with Motley to Jackson. Not one but two Black lawyers from New York would invade the city, parade around the federal courthouse, sit at the counsel's table, cross-examine witnesses, and attack the school board's practice of assigning different values to the labor of Blacks and whites. The lawyers' presence stunned whites and fascinated Black locals. "No blacks or women had ever appeared in the court before," Motley recalled. The two—Carter, slim and bookish, and Motley, tall and stately—were a sight to behold.[14]

Motley and Carter arrived in Jackson ten days before the trial started and spent an extended period observing and participating in the southern way of life. The experience of living in Mississippi, if only for a short while, enlightened and frightened Motley. The three-day trial took place in August, the Mississippi summer hot and humid.

Historically, more Blacks had lived in Mississippi—by 1860 the capital of the cotton-producing, slave-trading economy of the plantation South—than in any other state of the Union. Brought to the state to labor on plantations and in the cotton fields, Blacks had comprised half of the state's population at the height of slavery and during the 1940s still constituted 40 percent. White planters constantly feared Black revolt, leading to the imposition of a brutally repressive racial regime, in a class by itself even by the standards of the Old South. The Mississippi state constitution disenfranchised Black citizens, who lived under "Negro law," a euphemism for the unequal application of laws, rules, and norms to African Americans. Law segregated them from whites in every imaginable sector of life. Sadistic racial violence—hanging, bludgeoning, dragging, drowning, dismemberment, and public burnings at so-called "Negro Barbecues"—and the threat of such brutality kept Blacks fearful and under white people's social and economic control. This degradation and violence made Mississippi the "state that was the South at its worst," according to a leading historian of the Magnolia State.[15]

During her time in Jackson Motley observed the vestiges of slavery and the ills of segregation. At the same time, onlookers gazed at Motley, the well-dressed "nigra woman lawyer," she recalled, as if she were a freak of nature. Never mind her occupation, Motley could not dine in the fine restaurants or sleep in the fine hotels on Capitol Street, even if they were far from the quality she had come to expect in New York. She and her co-counsel were relegated to a "rooming house" for blacks; "called a hotel," the place barely passed for proper overnight accommodations.

Even food was hard to find. The white owners of a grocery store refused to sell fruit to the lawyers, one of whom called Carter—a thirty-two-year-old lawyer and military veteran who had vowed to destroy Jim Crow after chafing at white officers' "raw, crude racism" in a segregated U.S. Army—a "boy." Showing tremendous restraint,

Carter held his tongue and defused the moment. "I felt Bob's hand pulling me out of the door," Motley remembered; incensed by the disrespect shown to her colleague, her first instinct was to defend Carter. He dissuaded her, saying, "Now, no point in getting upset when there is nothing we can do about it." For sustenance, the lawyers relied on the few Blacks in the community who did not depend on whites for their livelihoods: the Black doctor, dentist, insurance agent, or undertaker who could bear the risk of inviting the New Yorkers into their homes for lunch or dinner. On other occasions the pair ate at a restaurant in the city's Black commercial district. During those ten days in Jackson, Motley experienced the same racially charged indignities as her clients.[16]

Once in court Motley realized that locals considered her first trial an event not to be missed. As a rule, Mississippi's Black attorneys—there were only three—did not appear in court. They worked on legal matters, such as the drafting of wills and deeds, that did not disturb the racial order; when a case did call for a court appearance, white judges' and juries' hostility to Black lawyers demanded that litigants hire a white attorney to represent them. Motley and Carter's very presence in the courtroom was transgressive: they were the first Black lawyers to appear in a Mississippi courtroom since Reconstruction. The sight of two Black lawyers, one female, transformed the court proceeding into a spectacle. Hordes came to see them perform. The standing-room-only courtroom overflowed. Blacks "lin[ed] the walls," eager to bear witness to the attorneys' unprecedented assault on white supremacy. Motley recollected that "it was like a circus" had come to town.[17]

A first-time litigator in a new and hostile environment, Motley initially felt a "bit frightened." Locals' behavior justified her feeling ill at ease. The behavior of James Burns, one of the few Black lawyers in Mississippi and the Inc. Fund's local counsel, stunned Motley. Burns aided the New York lawyers in only the most perfunctory manner, making his arm's-length relationship to Motley and Carter clear to all. At the counsel's table he sat far away from the Inc. Fund lawyers. He did not participate in the trial, but instead "took notes the whole time, never looking up." And when he moved about the courtroom, Burns dramatically performed his subservience. He walked "completely bent at the waist," his back "never to the judge" when he exited the courtroom. At the end of the day he rushed away and refused to dine with Motley and Carter. "He was scared to death," Motley remembered. Burns's fear put her on notice: the case she had come to Mississippi to litigate might provoke violent white resistance.[18]

Motley did her best to ignore the racism of courthouse personnel. She felt anger but did not display it when the presiding federal judge, Sidney Mize, refused to call her "Mrs. Motley"; "Mrs." was an honorific denied Black women, regardless of status, in southern society. Instead of showing her the respect that married white women received, local whites referred to her as "that Motley woman." And she noticed a courthouse mural with "perfectly stereotypical" images. On one end appeared white women in hoop skirts escorted by white men in cutaway coats; on the other were Black men in work clothes and Black women in aprons beside bales of cotton, the cash crop of the plantation South, and symbols of Black bondage. Motley found the mural "emotionally agonizing," but did not dare say anything about its prominent placement in the federal courthouse. She focused on the task at hand.[19]

At trial Motley and Carter exposed the rank discrimination to which Jackson—and every other southern locale—subjected Black teachers and administrators. She called expert witnesses who demonstrated that Black teachers' credentials compared favorably with and sometimes surpassed those of whites, and that even when Black teachers held notably better qualifications than their white colleagues, the school board paid them less. The pair "relentlessly" cross-examined witnesses whom the school board called to justify its policies and practices. The state's witnesses squirmed. The LDF lawyers seemed to make headway in court. In fact, Motley dazzled many in the courtroom, who were "amazed" at the way she spoke. Even a court reporter praised her crisp questioning.[20]

In the end, however, Judge Mize dashed Motley and Carter's hopes of a win. The judge ruled against the lawyers on procedural grounds: he held that they needed to have "exhausted remedies" available in the Mississippi courts and administrative bodies before making claims in federal court.[21]

That legal doctrine, frequently invoked by courts troubled by the prospect of invading states' rights, doomed civil rights suits. Without a command from a federal authority few state courts or school boards in the Jim Crow South would concede discrimination. The federal court of appeals affirmed Judge Mize's order and the U.S. Supreme Court refused to consider the lawyers' petition for a hearing. Motley and Carter had to accept defeat. Motley had learned a tremendous amount about both law and culture during her first trial, but it had not ended with a legal victory. In fact, the Jackson school board fired the named plaintiff, Gladys Bates, from her position for complaining about discrimination, and she never found another job in her hometown.[22]

Still, Carter and Motley's challenge to Mississippi's white power structure impressed and emboldened the African Americans who had eagerly watched the civil rights lawyers' performance each day. The attorneys' confrontation with white authority made them beloved figures in Jackson's Black community. Robert Carter learned about the sensation the pair had caused when he entered one of the city's Black barbershops and happened upon Mississippians reenacting scenes from the trial. Community members also recalled the lawyers' courtroom drama at "beauty parlors, at parties, in backyards, wherever groups gathered." Motley and Carter provided hope that racial discrimination might soon end. The Jackson community's excited reaction convinced Motley that, both outside and inside the courtroom, lawyers functioned as translators of local people's grievances and catalysts for social change.[23]

However, as Motley's experience in Jackson showed, so-called merit-based policies could not ultimately be beaten by legal challenges. By the end of the teacher-salary campaign, although the pay gap between Black and white teachers had diminished, it had not closed. Whereas Black teachers had received 50 percent of whites' salaries in 1931, in 1946 they received 65 percent. At last, by the early 1950s, Mississippi and other southern states began the process of adopting merit-pay scales, ending the gross disparities that had existed between the salaries of Black and white teachers. The change occurred as cases challenging salary discrimination proliferated.[24]

Meanwhile, the broader scope of the Inc. Fund's litigation campaign came into focus. It would not end with teacher salaries. The campaign included suits over race-based disparities in school funding and the race-based exclusion of Blacks from institutions of higher education, not to mention cases that attacked discrimination in voting, transportation, and housing. By the early 1950s, the attention of southern legislatures turned toward averting court rulings on the most critical of all education-related issues: the legality of segregated education itself.[25]

*

Back at LDF's Manhattan offices, Motley mounted a more personal battle, one that illustrated the pervasive reach of gender pay gaps. A controversy erupted in 1949, the same year Motley traveled to Mississippi. Something was similarly amiss in her own workplace, which was not free of wage disparity. And if the lawyers of the Inc. Fund were "like a family," as Motley once said, then she, an underappreciated child, needed to rebel against its constraints.[26]

Like the Black teachers she had gone to bat for in Mississippi, Motley faced a salary discrepancy. The Inc. Fund, she believed, had neither offered her appropriate remuneration nor conferred on her a proper title. She had begun working at LDF before she had even graduated from law school; she started as an "intern." Her job title changed to "legal research assistant" after she graduated from Columbia Law School in 1946 and started working full-time at the Inc. Fund, making $2,400 a year. Three long years later she retained that title.[27]

The Inc. Fund referred to the other lawyers in the office as "assistant" or "assistant counsel," and the organization paid these attorneys more than Motley. Robert Carter, her co-counsel on the Mississippi case, had been hired in 1944. A recent graduate of Howard Law School with no prior legal experience, Carter quickly rose as Marshall's protégé. By 1945, within mere months of coming on board, he had earned Marshall's full confidence, along with the title "assistant special counsel" and a $3,000 annual salary. Marshall hired Jack Greenberg, a white graduate of Columbia Law School in 1949; in short order he received the "assistant counsel" designation and an annual salary of $3,200. Marian Perry, a "good-looking" "Anglo-

Saxon" woman who had graduated from Brooklyn Law School and had worked at the U.S. Department of Labor, joined the legal staff in 1945. She, too, had the title "assistant special counsel."[28]

Motley complained about the disparity in a sharply worded letter to Marshall. In a memorandum dated May 1949, she alluded to a prior conversation with Marshall about her title and pay. Previously, Marshall had declined to confer the "assistant special counsel" title, she noted, and had denied her a salary commensurate with that position, claiming that the Inc. Fund lacked the resources. Notwithstanding Marshall's decision, Robert Carter had recently ordered Motley to travel to the New Jersey State Conference of the NAACP Branches to discuss pending legal cases—a task typically performed by assistant legal counsel. Motley insisted she should not be asked to do the work of an assistant counsel while being denied the title and the pay. "In the past [four years] I have done everything and anything required of me for the Association," she wrote. "However, I do not feel I should be given the same assignments . . . [as] assistant special counsel when I am neither classified as such, nor paid the salary of an assistant special counsel."[29]

Marshall remedied, if not immediately, the disparate treatment that Motley had pointed out. The Inc. Fund's lead counsel could authorize a raise and title change for Motley; however, the board of directors, which managed the organization's finances, had to approve the changes. One month after her letter to Marshall, Motley submitted a formal application to Marshall and Roy Wilkins, acting executive director of the NAACP, for the position of assistant special counsel. Motley applied not for a new position, she noted, but for an existing one, in anticipation of another lawyer's resignation from the staff, evidently under Marshall's advisement. The only other female attorney in the office, Marian Wynn Perry, had resigned from the Inc. Fund's legal staff earlier that year. Marshall promoted Motley to a position the responsibilities for which she had evidently been performing all along. Because of her complaint, Motley not only gained a promotion, but by 1951 received the same salary as Jack Greenberg: $4,200 annually. One woman had made way for another. Motley would remain the only woman lawyer at LDF for over fifteen years.[30]

Motley lodged—and won—her personal complaint about her job

title and salary around the same time that she fought for salary equity on behalf of Gladys Bates and other African American teachers. Working on behalf of others in the courtroom, Motley questioned the often feeble explanations based on subjective assessments of experience and effectiveness school boards offered to justify the vast salary differences between Black and white teachers. She had also observed the profound implications of these disparities. The wage discrimination to which school boards subjected the educators undermined the living standards of a workforce—predominantly female—struggling to join or to remain in the middle class. She undoubtedly saw her own struggles in the troubles of her clients. The convergence of Motley's work and her personal life surely raised questions for her about whether the NAACP LDF always practiced what it preached.[31]

In reality Black women routinely faced exploitation and discrimination in many workplaces. They were at the very bottom of the economic ladder, behind even Black men, who were also regular victims of discrimination. During this era, many more Black women than white were in the workforce, but they labored in lower-status, less-well-paid jobs. In 1949, whereas 57 percent of Black women worked, only 37 percent of white women did so. Deprived of both education and the chance to acquire skills, and subject to gross discrimination, most Black women worked in menial, low-wage positions, as servants, laundresses, and factory workers. Even when Black women toiled in the same industries as white women, employers invariably paid them less. Only a very small number of Black women worked in semiprofessional and professional occupations—Blacks constituted 6 percent of women professionals overall. Protests were frequent. Black women objected to unequal wages—and the underlying assumption that they did not deserve advancement—through strikes, "Don't Buy Where You Can't Work" campaigns, and complaints made to the Fair Employment Practices Committee and filed in federal courts, as the teacher salary equalization cases show.[32]

Motley's difficulty at the Inc. Fund illustrates how a systemic problem can affect an individual's life—even a person of high status and exceptional achievement. The oppression faced by Black women in general made it difficult for any individual Black woman, no matter how talented or in what profession, to gain acceptance and earn respect. Work for civil rights or social service organizations did not exempt women—and certainly not Black women—from mistreatment.

After all, the Inc. Fund was not alone in undervaluing Black women workers; the pattern was the same in many well-regarded social justice organizations. The experiences of Motley's peers—Black female contemporaries such as Ella Baker, Rosa Parks, Septima Clark, Ruby Hurley, Fannie Lou Hamer, and Pauli Murray—made plain that gender shaped race in ways that limited professional opportunities and rewards. Like Motley, these women made important contributions to civil rights organizations, including the Southern Christian Leadership Conference (SCLC), the Montgomery Improvement Association, and the NAACP, but they all became embroiled in controversies over job titles, compensation, and public recognition. Male executives and predominantly male boards of directors consistently undervalued the work these women performed. Most famously, Dr. King never granted Ella Baker, a superb organizer and administrator in the SCLC, the title she believed she deserved. As a result, each woman had to fight against being relegated to the thankless role of "unsung heroine."[33]

Gender troubles within the NAACP, the Inc. Fund's parent organization, illuminate Motley's difficulties under Thurgood Marshall. At the time the two organizations shared board members and the NAACP exercised great influence over the Inc. Fund's decisions. But ultimate power rested with Marshall. Roy Wilkins, the acting executive secretary and de facto head of the NAACP from 1947 to 1949, played a critical role in the power structure of the two organizations.[34]

An effective leader in many ways, Wilkins also held a decidedly traditional perspective on gender roles—a stance that ran counter to women's advancement in the workplace. He viewed women as physiologically unsuited for work, let alone leadership, in prominent organizational posts. "Biologically," he once quipped, women "ought to have children and stay home"; after all, "God made them that way." "Quite a few" female staff members at the NAACP found that Wilkins did not "fully accept women as equals." He did not regard as peers the women who dominated the association's active membership and performed the lion's share of the "nitty-gritty" "organizational work." Wilkins's attitude affected their pay. "Men were more generously compensated than women," concedes Gilbert Jonas, a historian of the NAACP and its chief fund-raiser for many years. The disparity became so acute that the union representing employees urged some women staffers to file a formal protest. Yet an end to gender-based salary inequities was far off for many women who came after Constance Baker Motley.[35]

7

"We All Felt the Excruciating Pressure": Making History in *Brown v. Board of Education*

The *New York Times* offended Thurgood Marshall, Constance Baker Motley, and everyone else at the Inc. Fund. It was 1953. Marshall and his staff had worked day and night since the summer preparing legal briefs for a fast-approaching U.S. Supreme Court oral argument in the five cases that challenged racial discrimination in the public schools of Kansas, Virginia, Delaware, South Carolina, and the District of Columbia. The Inc. Fund's years-long legal campaign to undermine segregation in public education was going to culminate in a historic argument at the Supreme Court that fall; the justices had consolidated the five cases and set them for argument in October under the name *Brown v. Board of Education*. An interracial but predominantly Black law firm, the Inc. Fund took great pride in its efforts; the lawyers hoped to reshape American law and society by overturning *Plessy v. Ferguson*, the 1896 precedent upholding state-sponsored racial segregation.

But LDF's talented staff members were themselves undercut by the assumption of Black inferiority: In October 1953 Arthur Krock of the *New York Times* completely ignored the civil rights organization's work in a column about the ongoing cases. Prominent lawyers associated with the U.S. Department of Justice—all white—he wrote, were "doing all the research work" to overturn segregation. The lawyers of the NAACP Legal Defense Fund received no mention.[1]

The organization vigorously protested the omission. Arthur B. Spingarn, the organization's president, wrote a letter complaining about the *Times*'s grievous error. An unusually detailed press release followed. In preparation for the big day in court, the Inc. Fund's staff, "consisting of six lawyers, six secretaries and two clerks, swung into action," the release explained. The staff "put in shifts of fifteen to twenty hours a day, seven days a week, without requesting extra pay." The lawyers who worked on the cases had traveled "some 325,000 miles" and staff had gone through "1,000,600 sheets of copy paper, 2,700 stencils, more than 12,000,000 sheets of mimeograph paper and 115,000 sheets of carbon paper." The press release also emphasized how the Black press, Black organizations, and hundreds of Black individuals aided the campaign to overthrow Jim Crow. "We are overjoyed," Marshall said, "by the support we received from our own group." The public rebuke inspired a new article from the *Times*; the nation's paper of record now noted the uniformly "high-quality" legal work performed in the cases, including by the "Negro lawyers" who "predominate" on the "non-segregation side."[2]

Soon after this new round of media coverage, no honest professional or well-informed American could so cavalierly dismiss the Inc. Fund. The entire staff, along with a bevy of outside lawyers, historians, sociologists, and law professors, lent a hand in the concerted effort to overthrow Jim Crow launched in the *Brown* litigation. The LDF's offices hummed with activity as teams of lawyers prepared the cases from school districts in the four states and D.C. The presentation for each case had to be as polished and persuasive as possible, and the staff attorneys—all male except for Motley—worked at a feverish pitch. At the office until late in the evening and in weekend workshops, the team members debated strategy, conducted legal and historical research, and drafted legal briefs. "Our typical workday was from about 9 a.m. to 9 p.m.," Motley recalled, an extraordinary "load" that sometimes got the best of even the gregarious Marshall. He "curtailed" his "storytelling hours" and depended on his inner circle to buck him up. Motley, Marshall, and all the other lawyers "gave up their vacations," "went days without sleep," and "had not had a meal with their families for four full months," noted the Inc. Fund press release about the tireless preparations for the struggle against Jim Crow.[3]

The work had initially reached a critical point in December 1952, when the first oral arguments came before the U.S. Supreme Court. The Inc. Fund team, led by Thurgood Marshall and including Robert Carter, Jack Greenberg, Louis L. Redding, and Spottswood Robinson III, insisted that the Court reject *Plessy v. Ferguson*'s "separate but equal" rule. The mere fact of racial segregation harmed students, and therefore mandatory school segregation violated the Constitution. Carter argued that school segregation placed Black children "at serious disadvantage with respect to the opportunity to develop citizenship skills," relying on expert testimony that Jim Crow effectively placed Black children in a "separate caste" and "lowered" their "aspiration[s]," "instilled feelings of insecurity and inferiority," and "retarded their mental and educational development" in violation of the Equal Protection Clause. The team faced a formidable opponent: John W. Davis, an eminent lawyer and onetime Democratic presidential candidate. Marshall's "knees" had "buckle[d]" when he had learned he would face off against the famous constitutional lawyer.

Davis, nattily dressed in a "fine silk hat" and a cutaway "morning" coat that stopped at mid-thigh, the suit style common to the British aristocracy for horseback riding, exuded confidence. The lawyer was hardly timid in defending Jim Crow. He did not stop at arguing that the states' school segregation policies did not offend the Fourteenth Amendment as understood by Congress in 1868. "[E]qual protection in the minds of the Congress . . . did not contemplate mixed schools," he insisted. Davis warned that if the Court accepted the argument that states could not classify on the basis of race, it would open a Pandora's box:

> If the appellants' construction of the Fourteenth Amendment should prevail here, there is no doubt in my mind that it would catch the Indian within its grasp just as much as the Negro. If it should prevail, I am unable to see why a state would have any further right to segregate its pupils on the ground of sex or on the ground of age or on the ground of mental capacity.

The lawyers' argument against segregation threatened a whole range of social hierarchies long embedded in law and accepted in society. Despite making such a "totally offensive" argument, Motley, who was in D.C. to observe the oral argument, remembered that Davis had thought his performance in the cases "his finest hour."

Davis knew that his slippery slope argument might find a receptive audience among some of the justices. He was onto something: the prospect of reversing the long line of precedents upholding segregation troubled several justices. The Inc. Fund lawyers' argument required the Court to "face the fact," as Justice Felix Frankfurter put it, that the justices were being asked to upend "something written into the public law and adjudications of the courts" and repeatedly upheld by the Supreme Court, including esteemed jurists such as Oliver Wendell Holmes, Louis Brandeis, and Harlan Fiske Stone, all of whom, Frankfurter said, were "very sensitive to" civil liberties. Instead of relying on precedent, Marshall argued, the Court had to consider the "sociological facts," and those demonstrated that segregation, a relic of slavery, harmed Black children.[4]

In 1953, after Earl Warren, the former governor of California, joined the Court as chief justice, the Court asked the lawyers to reargue questions related to congressional intent. The Inc. Fund's team, aided by numerous scholars and outside lawyers, embarked on new rounds of debate, research, writing, and oral argument before the Supreme Court. In September 1953, Thurgood Marshall convened the entire "formidable" group of the "most brilliant" people in their fields, one hundred strong, in a three-day conference to present and test arguments. Bob Carter called the conference an "exhilarating intellectual experience." The feverish preparation culminated in a December 1953 oral argument before the U.S. Supreme Court. Motley looked on with pride as her colleagues argued, in turn, that the "separate but equal" principle should be overturned. The Court must reject segregation, Marshall argued, because the only thing that explained it was whites' "determination that the people who were formerly in slavery . . . shall be kept as near that state as possible." That rationale offended the Constitution.[5]

In the spring of the following year, the Court issued a unanimous decision in *Brown v. Board of Education*. Relying in part on social science data, the Court held that state-sanctioned school segregation violated the Fourteenth Amendment. The justices rooted their unanimous decision in a recognition of the vital role of education to success in American life. "Today, education is perhaps the most important function of state and local governments," the Court wrote. "It is the very foundation of good citizenship." States could not lawfully provide education of different calibers to students on account of race, the decision explained. "We conclude that in the field of public education the doctrine of 'separate but equal' has no place. Separate educational facilities are inherently unequal." The lawyers had achieved an astounding legal victory in a case that many would call the most important constitutional case of the twentieth century, and perhaps in U.S. history.[6]

The LDF attorneys and their allies celebrated into the wee hours. Motley recalled that she shared with her colleagues the "high" gained from "making history." Like them, she basked in both the professional stature that *Brown* conferred and the knowledge that the "original sin" of American law had been removed. Black Americans had attained a new freedom. Future generations, including Joel III, would reap the benefits of the work, an overjoyed Motley explained to her infant as he sat in his high chair that evening.[7]

Reactions to the decision by news commentators and ordinary people alike ensured the prominence of the Inc. Fund lawyers who had successfully argued the cases. Commentators called Thurgood Marshall a "brilliant" legal tactician and "defender of American democracy." The charming, earthy lawyer had made a powerful impression on the world as the standard-bearer for the argument against segregation. Marshall's entire team received praise. The Inc. Fund attorneys became "legal giants."

Constance Baker Motley had played an integral role on the legal team responsible for the landmark victory. As the five school cases wound through the federal courts and on up to the Supreme Court, she conducted invaluable legal research and helped write the legal pleadings and briefs needed to move the cases forward. In 1950, after the Court had paved the way for *Brown* by ordering the admission of a Black man to the flagship University of Texas School of Law who had been shunted off to a purportedly "separate but equal" Black law school (*Sweatt v. Painter*), Motley had drafted a blueprint for the coming frontal assault on segregation. She wrote and distributed to

NAACP-affiliated counsel a model complaint—the critically important document that instigates a lawsuit and, if well done, survives
defendants' efforts to get the case thrown out of court. The complaint
Motley drafted set forth the facts and the law that explained why segregation violated the Constitution and why the Inc. Fund's clients
were entitled to a remedy (in this case, a desegregated school). Thus,
when lawyers in Kansas and in the other *Brown* cases filed claims
attacking school segregation, they were building on Motley's intellectual handiwork.[8]

Following the Supreme Court's request for re-argument in the
five *Brown* cases in 1953, Marshall and Carter assigned Motley to
another vital task. They asked her to review legal cases relating to the
scope of congressional and judicial power to enforce the Fourteenth
Amendment—a decisive issue that the justices touched upon during
oral argument in the *Brown* cases. Could the framers have authorized
desegregation of the schools, something then unheard of, through
the open-ended language of the Fourteenth Amendment? The Inc.
Fund hoped to convince the justices that even if Congress had not
intended in the Fourteenth Amendment to end school segregation,
the Constitution authorized the Court to interpret the amendment
in that manner. Motley's legal research provided support for the Inc.
Fund's contention. She also proofread the briefs—"nightmare" work
that she, "the girl in the office," "endured," she recalled. In view of
her many contributions to the *Brown* litigation, the organization's
briefs to the U.S. Supreme Court credited Constance Baker Motley
as "of counsel." In a long list of over a dozen attorneys whose names
appeared on the briefs, her name stood out: she was the only woman
in the illustrious group.[9]

*

Nevertheless, Motley played a circumscribed, if critically important,
role on the legal team. Marshall had determined, through "delicate
negotiations," "who would argue which case in the Supreme Court."
The assignments brought glory and enhanced the chosen lawyers'
reputations. Numerous press materials highlighted the lawyers'
responsibilities in the cases. The men were the stars of the team.
Photographed on the steps of the U.S. Supreme Court after oral argu-

ment, they had their pictures plastered across newspapers nation-wide. Thurgood Marshall had shouldered the heaviest burdens of the historic cases, and, after winning, enjoyed the utmost adulation. For his leadership in the campaign against segregation that culminated in *Brown*, he became a household name—and "Mr. Civil Rights."[10]

Motley, by contrast, was part of *Brown*'s supporting cast—a vital team member who worked behind the scenes. Instead of participating in Supreme Court oral arguments of the cases, she observed them from the audience. The trial lawyer enjoyed a level of professional distinction supporting lawyers could not quite match. The exalted reputation of litigators rested on an attorney's ability to think "on his feet." The courtroom lawyer had to respond to questions from the bench and, during trial, pose pertinent questions to witnesses—all under the pressure of public scrutiny. Without the opportunity to demonstrate her prowess in the courtroom, Motley did not yet command the same level of attention and adulation as her colleagues.[11]

The slower track that Motley was on, likely related to her gender, was especially clear in comparison with the career path of Jack Greenberg. The Inc. Fund considered Greenberg Motley's closest peer in terms of rank and seniority. In reality, however, Motley had begun working at the Inc. well before Greenberg. He had joined LDF the same year, 1949, that Motley had won promotion to assistant counsel. Marshall had hired Greenberg, a World War II veteran, on the recommendation of Walter Gellhorn, an esteemed Columbia Law professor, who touted the young man's "brilliance." With these auspicious beginnings at LDF, Greenberg quickly earned Marshall's confidence.[12]

By 1954, Greenberg and Motley held the same rank, but Greenberg had gained more—and more significant—courtroom experience. In 1950 he was overjoyed when Marshall assigned him to handle his first big case: taking on segregation in the undergraduate program at the University of Delaware. He also aided Marshall in representing a defendant in the infamous Groveland case—the "worst case of injustice and whitewashing" Marshall had ever seen, in which four Black men had been wrongly accused of raping a white woman in 1949. A sheriff's posse murdered one of the men, and an all-white jury sentenced two of the remaining men to death, and sentenced the third, merely sixteen years old, to life in prison. In 1951 Marshall and Greenberg successfully appealed the conviction to the U.S. Supreme Court. Although an all-white jury again convicted the defendant after retrial, the lawyers' work on the Groveland case enhanced their reputations and deepened their relationship. (Seventy years later, the governor of Florida pardoned the four accused men, calling the case against them a "miscarriage of justice.")[13]

During the same period, while Motley had worked on significant cases, they were fewer in number and of a lower profile. The lawyers' disparate experiences culminated in 1954, when Greenberg argued one of the *Brown* cases in the U.S. Supreme Court, while Motley contributed to the research and writing of the Inc. Fund's legal complaint and briefs—and did "drudge" work.[14]

The pace and arc of Motley's career are better understood in light of a life-changing event. At the same time as she was seeking to advance professionally and support the Inc. Fund's bid to overthrow segregation, she became a mother. Joel Motley III was born on May 13, 1952, in New York City. At thirty years of age, Constance Baker Motley was much older than most other first-time mothers of her day. She had postponed childbirth to attend college and law school during her twenties, a decade of life when most women were marrying and starting a family.[15]

Motley worked until her baby was due to arrive and took a three-month leave of absence after giving birth. She returned to work full-time in mid-August, right in the middle of frenzied preparations for *Brown v. Board of Education*. A deadline hovered: the new mother helped to draft and revise briefs in the case, due to the Court in September, the month after she returned to the office.[16]

Even as she worked, motherhood altered the rhythms of Motley's life. Joel Motley III required constant attention during infancy and toddlerhood, and Constance Baker Motley happily devoted much of herself to caring for him; she ensured that her baby received the love prescribed by everyone from family members to Dr. Benjamin Spock, the widely read pediatrician whose advice on childrearing made an impression on the postwar generation. In his blockbuster 1946 book *Baby and Child Care*, Spock had advised parents to avoid harsh discipline and shower children with "love" and "affection," a recommendation that Motley eagerly followed.[17]

Yet, Joel Motley III's birth, infancy, and toddlerhood overlapped with a harried period in his mother's career. Motley experienced the tangle of emotions—joy and excitement, fear and anxiety—that all new parents feel, but unlike most young mothers of that time, she simultaneously faced the pressures that accompany a challenging professional career. By turns a sleep-deprived mother trying to placate an infant and a rising lawyer juggling an enormous workload, she would have struggled to meet the demands placed on an attorney, an especially difficult role to reconcile with raising young children—as it remains today.[18]

The Inc. Fund made enormous demands on its lawyers' time and energy, especially during the run-up to and following *Brown v. Board of Education*. Motley had to try to keep up with the fierce pace. During this whirlwind she dealt with difficult choices about how to organize her life and competing roles.[19]

Locked in a conflicted position unlike that of her male colleagues and up against the social expectation that women should raise their children full-time, Motley could not have followed the same ruthless schedule as the other attorneys. The three-month leave of absence following the birth of her child underscored that point, and the difficulties afterward of balancing her lawyer's schedule with childcare surely meant that she would have had serious concerns about meeting her dual obligations. And she must have been at least a little anxious about her colleagues' judgments about her unconventional choice to work at all, and certainly to return to work so soon after childbirth.

In the wake of *Brown*, the usually reticent and private Motley made a confession: she had experienced bouts of "depression." Her disquiet arose as she contemplated a coming reality. After enjoying the thrill of victory on May 17, 1954, the Inc. Fund lawyers confronted what would be a new challenge: litigation to implement the Supreme Court's landmark *Brown v. Board of Education* decision. The coming months and years promised more long hours filled with "day and night" discussions, more stress, as Motley and her colleagues began to prepare cases that would not just change legal precedent, but the

everyday lives of Black southerners. Motley wondered, "How will
we manage? The staff was small, our funds were meager, our plans
sketchy; thousands of school districts were involved." On top of these
profound challenges at work, she knew that she also had to meet the
countless essential responsibilities of childrearing.[20]

The tension between personal identity and professional aspirations that had been a part of Motley's life ever since she had declared
her interest in attending law school became more daunting after the
birth of Joel III. Defying the expectations of the many people who
warned her off law school, Motley had surmounted the problem that
Betty Friedan would write about so compellingly in *The Feminine
Mystique*, first published in 1963: escaping the dullness of house-
wifery. But as increasing numbers of women who participated in the
paid workforce would learn, mothers who worked faced a different
dilemma: how to reconcile labor outside the home and work inside
it. Who would take care of childcare, cooking, cleaning, and shopping
while women worked?[21]

As a professional Black woman, Motley confronted an especially
challenging social context. Black female professionals were often
objects of particular scrutiny, sometimes of scorn, in public and
private life. During the postwar era, as Motley struggled to make a
name for herself in the law and make a happy home, commentators
discussed the "deterioration" of the Black family, highlighted by a
divorce or separation rate four times that of white couples. Searching
to identify stressors, writers often excoriated, as a major source of the
Black family's ills, the "domineering" Black women who forsook family obligations to pursue careers. E. Franklin Frazier, the influential
Black sociologist and author of *The Negro Family* and *Black Bourgeoisie*,
chastised Black women for their ambition and "domineering" nature.
Wives who "seize the opportunity" to embark on a career, Frazier
wrote, "destroy the pattern of family life" that men expected. In this
environment, these women, frequent targets of criticism, felt "constant pressure" to be both career women and homemakers, explained
Paula Giddings, the noted historian of African American women.[22]

Raised in a household where her father was the "boss" of the
house, and keenly aware of her own unconventional path, Motley
navigated the demands of work and home as best she could. Through

practical and strategic choices, she endeavored to fill her dual roles as successfully as possible. Importantly, during a period when the average Black woman bore four children and the average white woman three, Motley gave birth to only one child.[23]

Household employees and the support of her extended family were indispensable to Constance and Joel. The Motleys employed a succession of housekeepers to perform the tasks in their Harlem apartment that to many women felt like drudgery. "[I] do not think that [a woman] should drown her talents . . . when someone else can do a better job in cooking and cleaning," she said in a 1961 interview. A woman who was "good enough at her job" and "earn[ed] enough to justify paying a housekeeper" should do so. Motley also turned to other women for childcare: for many years, she employed a live-in nanny/housekeeper. "Since Mrs. Motley may have to go off on a moment's notice on any of the cases she prepares," one reporter noted, "little Joel is often with a housekeeper." Joel recalls three such women who "looked after" him during his childhood. Constance Motley's sisters, who lived in New York and in nearby Connecticut, also pitched in to take care of Joel.[24]

Motley's use of paid, live-in childcare placed her in an elite group of women and a step ahead of the coming women's liberation movement. In 1950, only 2.5 percent of American families employed household help. Since the days of slavery, Black women had served as housekeepers for wealthy white women. During the 1950s they were still vastly overrepresented in domestic service. The household labor industry thus perpetuated a long-standing racial hierarchy, along with historically fraught mistress-servant relationships. An upper-class, professional Black woman who could afford to hire a domestic servant, Motley upheld many of the conventions of her new class, but at the same time she defied racial stereotypes—and pushed gender boundaries.[25]

Unlike many upper-class women, Motley hired household help not to gain leisure time but to make her work possible. She could only maintain her position in the professional labor force if a domestic assistant cooked, cleaned, washed and ironed clothes, shopped, and helped take care of Joel. Motley was unabashed that she required and paid for domestic service. The headline of one interview paraphrased her advice to women: "Work If You Can Pay the Maid." In the coming years, women's liberationists would agree with Motley that, for working women, childcare was a necessity; many activists would go even further to demand paid childcare as a right.[26]

Frequent out-of-state visits proved a particular challenge for Motley. Where possible, she kept her road trips short. She chose flights that let her travel back to New York in time for dinner with her family. "[R]unning around the country is not as bad as it sounds, as far as being with my family," she explained to an interviewer. "A jet plane gets you down [to the South] in two and a half hours . . . ; you've finished your case by the next afternoon, and you're back by suppertime." Other times, the family traveled with her. Even as a toddler, Joel III came with her on the road.[27]

Perhaps most important for her, Motley had married a man who supported his wife's career in word and deed. At a time when most men, following convention, relegated women to household tasks and childrearing, Joel Motley Jr. helped raise his son. Nell Moskowitz, a family friend, summed up the father's pivotal role in creating a stable family life and enabling his wife's career: "Joel was devoted to her and her ideals and was there to do whatever had to be done in order for her to keep doing what she had to do." Moskowitz continued, "She couldn't have been the kind of mother that she was without the husband that she had."[28] With this invaluable help, Motley performed a balancing act that would only grow more challenging as her career gained momentum and prominence.

8

"The Fight Has Just Begun":
The Decade-Long Slog to Desegregate
the University of Florida College of Law

In the wee hours of May 17, 1954, as the party celebrating the Inc. Fund's stunning success in *Brown v. Board of Education* began to wrap up, Thurgood Marshall warned his staff of the work ahead. "I don't want any of you to fool yourselves," he said. "The fight has just begun." He was right. The U.S. Supreme Court's May 31, 1955, decision, *Brown II*, which addressed how and when school districts would implement the Court's 1954 decision, made plain that Jim Crow schools would only be conquered after a long and drawn-out battle. *Brown II* dismayed advocates of school desegregation and buoyed its opponents.[1]

The *Brown II* Court refused to order immediate desegregation. Bending to pressure from President Dwight D. Eisenhower and those eager to assuage the white southern resistance to *Brown*, the justices instead endorsed gradualism. The Court left federal trial judges— products of local culture who often personally opposed the first *Brown* decision—to manage the desegregation process, and allowed local school boards latitude to exert significant influence. Desegregation should occur "with all deliberate speed," the Court decreed. For all intents and purposes, Marshall noted, "deliberate speed" meant "slow." Many commentators interpreted *Brown II* as an open invitation to delay or obstruct desegregation.

If Constance Baker Motley had not quite been at the center of *Brown*, she was a dominant force in efforts to implement the ruling in the months and years after *Brown II*. She doggedly fought the white power structure's resistance to desegregation in a series of lawsuits that challenged segregation in both elementary and secondary schools and in higher education. It was a slog. "We often found our best laid plans for speeding desegregation derailed," she remembered, as states and localities fought to keep separate schools for Blacks and whites.[2]

As part of this effort, Motley traveled to cities and towns all over the South, representing clients whose names history has mostly forgotten. Wherever she ventured, she was invariably the "only woman in the courtroom"—a one-liner that hints at the singularity and the loneliness of Motley's experience as she moved through the world as a civil rights lawyer during the 1950s.

*

In Florida Motley represented Virgil Darnell Hawkins, a "one-man civil rights movement." A middle-aged Black man, short, balding, and soft-spoken, Hawkins had first sought admission to the University of Florida College of Law in Gainesville in 1949, well before *Brown*. He had aspired to become a lawyer from a very early age, but little in his upbringing suggested that he stood a chance. The young man grew up in Okahumpka, in Lake County. As a rule, Okahumpkans did not become lawyers or professionals of any kind; born into a class of agricultural laborers, they were largely working-class people. Okahumpka natives farmed small plots that were often rented rather than owned. There, they harvested oranges and watermelons; for a time, the town was called the "watermelon capital of the world." A few locals worked in one of the town's two general stores, or at the Clarendon Hotel, or found other small-bore ways of eking out an existence.[3]

Okahumpka included a small community of desperately poor, wretchedly oppressed Black people. Virgil Hawkins's father picked citrus, serving as a minister on the side. Despite the family's bleak circumstances, young Virgil had long imagined a way out of Okahumpka and a better life for himself and his community. Hawkins knew the savagery of segregation through his own family experiences. His uncle had been murdered by a white man after an argument over a farm animal. His cousin had been lynched. Through the power of the law, Hawkins thought, he could aid and comfort the poor people who suffered appalling violence and discrimination under Jim Crow. He vowed "to help defend the Southern Negro through the courts." But Florida officials repeatedly dashed his hopes.[4]

The University of Florida College of Law had been established in 1905 for "white male students" only, and the flagship school's gatekeepers worked assiduously to prevent Hawkins from defiling its campus. Citing race, the Florida Board of Control, the university's governing body, denied Hawkins's application. Next, the state attempted to placate him and several other Black applicants by sending them elsewhere: in 1951 the state established a Blacks-only law school at the Florida Agricultural and Mechanical College (Florida A&M) and opened its doors wide to Hawkins. Instead of accepting the "separate but equal" accommodation, Hawkins asked the Florida Supreme Court to order his admission to the University of Florida College of Law. The court refused twice, despite local counsel's argument that, by virtue of *Sweatt* and other higher education cases that preceded *Brown*, Hawkins should be permitted to enroll in the college of his choosing. The court, disregarding federal law, rejected the argument on the grounds that Florida had made "substantially equal" facilities available to Hawkins and other Blacks at the Florida A&M law school.[5]

*

Constance Baker Motley made the long journey—eleven hundred miles—to Tallahassee, where the legal action was unfolding. Expecting to visit her brother, a Florida resident, during the trip, she brought the entire family along; with husband and toddler in tow, she set out by car for the seventeen-hour drive from New York to Florida. The year was 1955.[6]

Travel by car afforded the young family some flexibility, but it also created a host of challenges for them as African Americans heading south during the Jim Crow era. Below the Mason-Dixon line no hotel or motel would accommodate Blacks, no matter their profession, economic status, or upstanding character. Nor would restaurants or other white-owned establishments serve them. The Negro Motorist Green-Book, a travel guide that identified businesses in southern states that would serve Black people, lessened but did not eliminate the inconvenience and indignity that plagued Black travelers at the time.[7]

Unable to stay in a hotel, the Motleys did not stop overnight until they reached someone willing to take them in. After nearly nine hours on the road, they found friendship and protection in Durham, North Carolina, at the home of Conrad Pearson. A civil rights lawyer who had collaborated with the Inc. Fund, Pearson and his wife welcomed the Motleys and housed and fed them for a night.

But following this respite in Durham, the Motleys experienced a particularly cruel incident. In South Carolina a gas station attendant refused to allow Joel III—a three-year-old—to use the restroom because of his race. The episode infuriated Motley, and only strengthened her resolve to combat racism and segregation. It also taught her a lesson. "We learned . . . to ask to use the restroom first; if the answer was 'yes,' we would purchase gas; if the answer was 'no,' we would go to the next gas station."[8]

*

Once they made it to Florida, Motley's first assignment was to convince the Florida Supreme Court to order Virgil Hawkins's admission. As a matter of law the case could not have been more straightforward. A full five years earlier, in the *Sweatt* decision from 1950, the U.S. Supreme Court had rejected "separate but equal" accommodations for otherwise qualified Black law students. Then on May 17, 1954, the justices had issued the landmark *Brown v. Board of Education* decision, holding state-mandated segregation in schools unconstitutional. Just a few days later, in a May 24 decision, the Court had ordered the Florida Supreme Court to reconsider, in light of *Brown v. Board of Education*, its prior rejection of Hawkins's claim. Motley made her argument to the Florida Supreme Court in the fall of 1955; by then, Hawkins's entitlement to attend his state's flagship law school was clear.[9]

Nevertheless, when she rose to argue the case, Motley encountered a group of "stone-faced white male judges" unpersuaded by her references to legal precedents and unmoved by logical argument.

Since the U.S. Supreme Court had held that a makeshift law school established by Texas for Sweatt and other Blacks did not meet constitutional standards, it followed, Motley asserted, that a similar law school established by Florida for Hawkins and other Blacks was also unconstitutional. In a judicial sleight of hand, the Florida Supreme Court roundly rejected Motley's argument.[10]

The Florida Supreme Court's October 1955 opinion denied Hawkins's plea for admission to the University of Florida College of Law because, the court wrote, *Brown II* justified delay. The implementation decision of *Brown II* "does not impose upon the respondents a clear legal duty to admit" Hawkins immediately or at any particular point in the future, the five-justice majority wrote.[11]

Virgil Hawkins—and Constance Baker Motley—had collided with white resistance to desegregation. Indeed, one member of the court, Justice W. Glenn Terrell, openly trafficked in racism. Terrell wrote a separate opinion to explain why Hawkins should not attend the school. To justify delaying the "disaster" of desegregation, he cited "innate differences" in "self-restraint and cultural acuteness," as well as "moral, cultural and I.Q." differences between Blacks and whites. The justice also "ventured to point out" that segregation "is not a new philosophy." Nature itself supported Jim Crow, according to Terrell. "It is and always has been the unvarying law of the animal kingdom," he wrote. "The dove and the quail; the turkey and the turkey buzzard, the chicken and the guinea, it matters not where they are found, are segregated."[12]

Judicial resistance—and remarkable jousting back-and-forth between federal and state court judges—persisted in Hawkins's saga. In another decision in 1956, the U.S. Supreme Court made it clear that *Brown II* did not justify Hawkins's continued exclusion from the law school. Federal law authorized his "prompt" admission. Yet the Florida Supreme Court still refused to comply. After surveying local people, the court wrote, it had concluded that Hawkins's matriculation would result in "great public mischief." It predicted a boycott of UF by white alumni and prospective students, efforts by white parents and students to make life "unpleasant for Negro students," "violence" and "disruption," and a resulting "loss of revenue to our white institutions." The court also erected the "states' rights barrier" to desegregation, asserting its duty, as the judicial arm of a sovereign state, to avert the calamities that desegregation would precipitate. This latest salvo against desegregation caused Hawkins and the Inc. Fund to "give up on" the state court. Motley would no longer waste time arguing the finer points of law with state judges so obviously committed to defying the U.S. Supreme Court.[13]

Motley, along with Thurgood Marshall and Robert Carter, decided to try to end segregation at the University of Florida College of Law once and for all by filing suit in federal court. Initially, she suffered a startling defeat. Judge Dozier DeVane, to whom the case was assigned, rebuffed her when she attempted to present evidence in Hawkins's case. "Elderly and hostile," Motley recalled, Judge DeVane had been a member of the committee that had, in the face of Hawkins's application to UF in 1949, established the makeshift law school for Blacks at Florida A&M. In no way inclined to rule in Hawkins's favor, DeVane refused to hear the case entirely. The judge then "proceeded to lecture" Motley about all he had done to "help your people" in Florida. DeVane's "incomprehensible and irrelevant" hectoring of Motley continued despite her efforts to focus on legal precedents. "I do not consider any decision of the U.S. Supreme Court takes from me the right to control procedural activities in my court," the judge insisted. Motley could say nothing to appease him. Instead, she appealed his ruling to the U.S. Court of Appeals for the Fifth Circuit.[14]

After the appellate court ordered an end to his delaying tactics, Judge DeVane conceded defeat—in part. On June 18, 1958, he ruled that *qualified* persons could apply for admission to Florida's graduate and professional schools, including the University of Florida College of Law, without regard to race. At the same time, he ruled that Virgil Hawkins, who had posted a low score on a law school admission test, did not meet the requisite qualifications. Bitterly disappointed, Hawkins conceded that he had "wasted ten precious years of my life."[15]

Hawkins—who had launched his daring attack on Jim Crow in middle age—did eventually attend law school. In 1964 he enrolled at the New England School of Law in Boston and later graduated. At age seventy, Virgil Hawkins, Esq., hung out his shingle and began practicing law in his native Florida, which admitted him to the bar due to his "claim on [the court's] conscience."

Hawkins called his bar admission the "proudest day" of his life.[16] For Motley, now thirty-seven, the case marked the beginning of a series of high-profile cases in which she served as lead counsel. Her moment in the limelight had arrived.

9

"We Made a Mistake": "Poor Character," "Loose Morals," and Untold Sacrifices in Pursuit of Higher Education at the University of Alabama

Europe loves Lucy," proclaimed the *Afro-American* on February 25, 1956. Autherine Lucy—the daughter of an impoverished Alabama tenant farmer—had captivated the world. The shy and sensitive twenty-six-year-old Black woman had become an unlikely celebrity. Dozens of newspapers printed her photograph on their front pages, and readers worldwide knew Lucy's name.[1]

The events that had catapulted Lucy to stardom unfurled that winter. Already a college graduate, she had applied to the University of Alabama for an advanced degree in library science. Under federal court order, the university accepted her. The would-be librarian registered for classes. But within a few days, UA expelled her—for her own good, or so it claimed, and to preserve "law and order." Her presence on campus had unleashed fury. Whites protested her admission. This white uprising made Lucy a symbol of the Black American fight for equal rights.[2]

Everybody had something to say about the events that made her famous. Parisians praised the courage of the young American woman and lamented her plight. "Just because she is colored," a French story recounted, Lucy had been pelted with eggs, insulted with epithets, and expelled. Across the channel, Londoners warned that America would struggle to live down her mistreatment. Italians, Danes, and Swedes offered her scholarships. Filipinos lamented American racial prejudice. For years to come, Lucy's saga threatened the reputation of the United States abroad.[3]

In the treacherous Cold War geopolitical environment, foreigners made Lucy into an icon of the struggle between democracy and communism, good and evil. Communists alleged that the white backlash against Lucy illustrated American hypocrisy. In Moscow a leading Soviet newspaper ran a front-page story about her that dissected the matter. Discrimination against "Negroes" and "women"—endemic in America, the article maintained—along with the "profit motive," explained the vile resistance that met Lucy. American industrialists would rather relegate Negro women like Lucy to menial labor than let them attend college so they could qualify for higher-paying employment. "The sad story of Miss Lucy has torn off the mask of American democracy," the Soviet newspaper announced. Across South America people also supported Lucy. "In the United States they persecute colored people!" claimed a Venezuelan news report. By permitting the race-based harassment of Autherine Lucy, the United States—the world's self-proclaimed policeman—had forfeited its moral authority.[4]

In the United States commentators' opinions about the young woman differed widely. In her syndicated column, Eleanor Roosevelt, the former First Lady, praised Lucy's grace under pressure. Although Lucy had "apparently not enjoyed the publicity" that the NAACP's case had "thrust upon her," Mrs. Roosevelt said, the young woman nevertheless had acted with "quiet dignity." The National Council of Negro Women passed a resolution praising Lucy's defense of democratic principles and her courage. A *New York Times* opinion writer followed suit: "[A]nybody who respects moral courage" should "pay tribute" to the Alabama undergraduate.[5]

But down south views about what Lucy deserved differed. The majority of white southerners heaped scorn upon Lucy. "She's just a 'nigger,'" protested one white woman, and "should have stayed in her place." A former president of the UA alumni association congratulated "those students who resisted, and who will continue to resist the admission of a Negress named Autherine Lucy." Meanwhile, local Blacks reacted angrily to the hoodlums who had driven Lucy off campus and blasted the university's craven response to the mob. "I believe those white folks are losing their minds," said a Black schoolteacher. Another Black Alabamian cried, "The way they have treated that child makes me mad as hell."[6]

If her supporters reacted to her situation with righteous indignation, Lucy responded to the violent backlash with dignified compo-
sure and even defiance. Instead of shying away from adversity, she
stood her ground. Members of the mob "do not discourage me," she
insisted. She voiced her resolve in speeches to rapt audiences in several American cities. To a large group of well-wishers packed into a
Philadelphia church, she declared, "To God and country we owe the
right to be received as full first-class citizens everywhere." "I grew up
and paid my taxes," she said. "My taxes were feeding a state university
from which I was not getting benefits." Lucy felt compelled to fight
for the educational resources that she and other Blacks had earned.[7]

Despite this defiant rhetoric and her show of strength, Lucy's
resolve eventually crumbled. The pressure wore on her. Death threats
unnerved her. The egg-throwing, rock-hurling mob frightened
her. The epithets stung. The "hateful stares" of students on campus
weighed on her. The allegations of her being a Communist—a "blasted
lie," she called it—infuriated her. The insistence that she was merely
a tool of the NAACP exasperated her. Reports that Lucy's own parents
opposed her fight against segregation—that "mess," they called it—
saddened her. Criticism from Blacks who called her a troublemaker
wounded her. The university's law-and-order rhetoric justifying her
exclusion rankled. And finally, a few of the tactical mistakes that her
lawyers—Thurgood Marshall, Constance Baker Motley, and Arthur
Shores—made were devastating. Eventually, Lucy's role as the face of
an early civil rights struggle simply overwhelmed her, and she called
it quits. "I have done all that I can," she proclaimed in a moment of
candor and frustration.[8]

Relinquishing the role of a lifetime, Lucy departed the world stage,
moved away from Alabama, and recoiled into the conventions of the
1950s, building a life of middle-class domesticity. In front of a throng
of hundreds gathered at a Dallas church, under the glare of cameras
and flashbulbs, outfitted in a beautifully ornate gown, she married
a Dallas minister. Now Mrs. Hugh F. Foster, she soon gave birth to
twins. Autherine Lucy had freed herself from the unrelenting public
scrutiny that came with a life as a civil rights pioneer.[9]

Despite tremendous talent and heroic efforts, Constance Baker
Motley and her colleagues at the Legal Defense Fund did not always

win their battles. Lucy's case against segregation at Alabama's flagship university ended in spectacular failure. High-profile civil rights
cases, particularly high-profile setbacks, often came at the cost of
tremendous human suffering. Lucy was left to cope with the social
and economic fallout of challenges to Jim Crow on her own. Like
other plaintiffs before and after her, she bore a heavy burden.

*

Early on there were warnings that the AU case would exact unusually
high personal costs. Months before Autherine Lucy gave up on her
case, the litigation had brought embarrassment and pain to an early
companion in the fight to desegregate the university, Pollie Anne
Myers.

A hardworking and intellectually curious student with a mag-
netic personality, Pollie Myers was the one who instigated the effort
to bring down Jim Crow at UA. Long involved in the NAACP's youth
chapter, Myers hatched a plan while working part-time for Ruby Hurley, the NAACP's regional director. All Myers needed was a friend to
join the effort. To endure the inevitable pushback against her, Hurley
had counseled, Myers must not strike out alone.[10]

Myers found her ally in Autherine Lucy. The women, both farmers' daughters from modest backgrounds, became fast friends at the
historically Black Miles College where they had shared a class and
graduated in the spring of 1952. That same summer Myers asked Lucy
to join in her bid to attend UA. After some prodding from the far sav-
vier and more outgoing Myers, Lucy agreed to apply. Myers, already a
reporter for the *Birmingham World*, a local Black newspaper, wanted
to study journalism. Lucy, the introverted bookworm, chose library
science. The pair pledged to support each other through the sure-to-
be-arduous process in hopes of together pulling off a feat that neither
could accomplish alone.

On September 4, 1952, the women submitted their letters of
application to UA, making no mention of their race. The very next
day UA responded in a manner implying that admission was assured.
The university asked the women to submit $5 deposits, assigned both
students to the Adams-Parker dormitory, and asked each to submit
academic transcripts. The women complied with all requests, and on

September 13 received letters welcoming them to campus from the university's president and other officials. "We are so glad that you are to be a member of our student body," wrote Shaler Houser, the university's director of housing and women's counselor.

Once Myers and Lucy appeared on campus to finalize the admission process, everything changed. Discovering that the applicants the president had so recently and warmly welcomed to campus were Black, administrators backpedaled. "An error has been made," the dean of admissions said to the women. Administrators offered to return the women's deposits and directed them to Alabama State, the historically Black college in Montgomery.[11]

After AU bungled the women's applications, lawyers formally entered the case. Arthur D. Shores, the Birmingham lawyer who was one of the first African Americans to practice law in the state, appealed the rejection to the university's president, but to no avail. Ratcheting up the pressure, Shores filed a lawsuit on behalf of the women in July 1953; the case slowly wound through the courts, making little progress.[12]

Signaling the case's national importance and the sense that the time for action had arrived, Constance Baker Motley joined in 1955. If the action against UA had appeared premature in 1952, by 1955 *Brown v. Board of Education* had created a much more hospitable environment for the suit—at least in principle.

In a trial held in federal district court in Birmingham during the summer of 1955, Motley and Shores confidently argued that the university's policy of denying admission based on race violated the Constitution. They prevailed. On August 26, 1955, the court ruled in favor of Myers and Lucy. The women got ready to register for classes, set to begin in February 1956. That's when the real trouble began.[13]

Working with local lawyers, the university hired an agency to investigate the backgrounds of the two women. Detectives found information about Myers that cast her in an unfavorable light: she was married, and had become pregnant five months before the marriage. She had revealed neither her pregnancy nor her marriage to the university until forced to do so in open court. In a long string of questions, a lawyer extracted from Myers facts that she had not wanted to divulge. "Do you know Polly [sic] Anne Hudson?" the lawyer asked.

"Yes, I am she," Myers conceded. "Your name is not then Polly [sic] Anne Myers, is it?" "Well, it was," Myers answered. The lawyer forced Myers to admit that she had married in October 1952 and had taken her husband's surname, Hudson, one month after she had applied by letter to UA. But she had never informed the university of her marital status.

The implication of the questions was plain: Myers had lied about her name and fundamental elements of her life. She had evidently married in a hurry—just a month after she initially contacted UA—to avoid exposure of her "loose morals." Her misrepresentations and her misdeeds added to a picture of "poor character" and gave UA grounds to reject her application, the university later informed her.[14]

The justification played to the sentiments of the era. At the time, middle-class society, whether white or Black, frowned upon sexual activity before marriage. Women—and sometimes men—who engaged in premarital intercourse were deemed immoral. Single mothers, so-called fallen women, were shunned, and shunted to society's margins. In Myers's case, premarital sex, as revealed by childbirth early in marriage, reinforced a pernicious stereotype that was rooted in slavery and invoked to justify the sexual exploitation of Black women: innately promiscuous, Black women lacked moral virtue. Myers's personal life destroyed her credibility as both a representative of her race and a plaintiff in the case.[15]

As if this were not enough, the detectives turned up more damaging information. Myers's husband, Edward Hudson, had served time in prison for burglary. Hudson's lawbreaking stigmatized not only him; it also tarnished Myers through association with a Black man whose brushes with the law lent credence to the stereotype of innate Black criminality.[16]

UA admissions officials made the claim, superficially unrelated to race, that these two strikes, Myers's personal conduct and her marriage partner, proved her unfit to attend the university. Her reputation was sullied and her ability to persist in the case destroyed. Learning of her fate, she dissolved into tears.[17]

Myers's lawyers barely protested the airing of her dirty laundry. Rather than further jeopardize the case, Marshall, Motley, and Shores parted ways with her. Motley explained the lawyers' reasoning: "bad publicity," she said, would ruin the case. "In all these high-profile cases, we sought to avoid bad publicity regarding the plaintiffs because public support was critical." She continued, "We knew then what we know now: only exemplary blacks are acceptable." The brave woman whose activism and curiosity had instigated and propelled the suit found herself sidelined.[18]

The legal team's decision to drop Myers when the university attacked her character made strategic sense. Practically speaking, it allowed the lawyers to focus their energies on Lucy. The university had not turned up anything about her conduct or character that could be used to assail her. Thus it was Lucy's case rather than Myers's that could crystallize the issue of racial discrimination in admissions.

Politically, this decision also made sense. It reflected a Black middle-class commitment to respectable behavior. Middle-class Blacks had long advocated for conformity with white upper-class cultural norms as a strategy for blunting racial stereotypes and seeking racial uplift. Behavior that reinforced notions of Black inferiority, they believed, made it easier for whites to defend racial discrimination and harder for Black leaders to protest mistreatment. Middle-class Black women had long sought to combat claims of Black cultural inferiority, family pathology, and sexual immorality by endorsing and enforcing a strict social and moral code. Educated and upwardly mobile Blacks policed sexual modesty and urged conservatism in behavior, dress, and manners. These Black strivers ostracized promiscuous women and disapproved of nonmarital pregnancies. Conformity became a type of resistance. Pollie Anne Myers had not conformed to the orthodoxy. She had thereby made herself expendable.[19]

Constance Baker Motley's matter-of-fact assessment of Myers's situation—that she had to be "dropped"—surely rested on these social sensibilities as well as on the legal practicalities. Raised a striver in a socially conservative household, Motley had been acculturated to reject nonmarital pregnancy and premarital sex. From her standpoint, no less than that of other upwardly mobile Blacks, Myers's personal conduct and troubled marriage represented missteps.[20]

Myers was not the first standard-bearer whom the movement shunted aside, nor would she be the last. In pursuit of racial equality, civil rights lawyers and local leaders cut ties with individuals seen to have transgressed social norms. Claudette Colvin, who had been arrested for refusing to give up her seat to a white person on a segregated city bus in Montgomery, was cast aside as a representative of the race after she became pregnant by a married man. Instead of offering Colvin support, members of the local Black community branded her a troublemaker. Rosa Parks, an upstanding person, an older woman and happily married member of the local Black community, instead became the exemplar of the harms of discrimination during the Bus Boycott of 1955, a watershed in the history of the civil rights movement. Dr. King and other ministers relegated Bayard Rustin, a brilliant organizer, to a behind-the-scenes role in both the Bus Boycott and in subsequent efforts because of his homosexuality. In these instances and others, the implication could not be missed: civil rights organizations would not permit one individual's social nonconformity to impede an entire group's social progress.[21]

Despite her personal disappointment, Myers wanted to support Lucy, only to learn that her help was not wanted. Shores, who had initially claimed that he would sue for Myers's reinstatement, threw up roadblocks. When Myers visited his office one day, Shores seated her alone in an out-of-the-way room.

If Shores was unhelpful, Motley's deliberate indifference demoralized Myers. Once, at Lucy's request, Myers had tagged along to a meeting with Motley and Shores. Motley greeted Lucy warmly and with open arms, but she looked at Myers unsmilingly. She then turned away from Myers, escorted Lucy into Shores's office, and closed the door. Myers was heartbroken. She left Shores's office stricken by the realization that she had been cast aside, and that she was now, as Motley saw it, a liability. Ostracized by both the community and her former legal representatives, Myers left Alabama for Detroit, driving 725 miles north alone.[22]

*

Against the backdrop of Myers's public humiliation came the fateful events of February 1956. Autherine Lucy would be on her own in confronting segregation at UA. Frightened and exposed, she became the sole plaintiff in the case.[23]

Lucy attended her first classes at UA on Friday, February 3, 1956. She bravely entered the university's halls early that winter morning as a steady rain fell in Tuscaloosa. Sitting in the center of the front row during her very first course—a geography class—she had the entire row to herself. No one wanted to be near her. Throughout the day, most students ignored her, while some pointed and stared. A few openly showed their resentment. And in a sign that threats were lurking, a policeman trailed her as she moved about campus to each of her classes.[24]

Over the weekend, the situation became distinctly ominous as mobs started to riot on campus. On Monday, February 6, 1956, Lucy arrived at a university on edge: a restless crowd grew from three hundred to five hundred and then into the thousands. Members of the Ku Klux Klan prowled about. The hostile mob soon turned violent, hurling objects, burning a cross, waving Confederate flags. Some vowed to kill or "lynch" the twenty-six-year-old "black bitch." Others yelled, "Keep 'Bama white!" Full-scale rioting continued for several hours.

While she was exiting a building to reach a car waiting to take her to a class in a different building, eggs and stones rained down on Lucy. She later recalled when the rioting students caught sight of her car and broke its window. She "crouched to the floor." During another interaction, rioters threw a big rock that "just missed" her head. She had never "been so frightened" in "all her life" and "shook for five minutes" before she could "get control" of herself. She was trapped inside one of the campus buildings with no way to avoid the rioters. At last, state police rescued her. Lying facedown in a patrol car traveling at high speed, Lucy departed the university grounds for the safety of Birmingham.[25]

The university's response to the riots—and the civil rights lawyers' response to the university following the riots—made a bad situation even worse. Instead of punishing the mob, UA's board of trustees suspended Lucy indefinitely. For her own safety, the university explained, she had to go. The university's president, Dr. Oliver C. Carmichael, said someone might be murdered if she remained on campus. Another official agreed, citing the recent volatility: "There is no doubt in my mind that if the crowd had gotten to" Lucy, "they would have killed her." When campus rioters got wind of the decision, they "were cocky and bragging that they had won a victory," the *New York Times* reported.[26]

The danger that the university cited was real, as Motley well knew from her own experiences. She first saw men bearing firearms—shotguns and machine guns—during her visits to Birmingham and Tuscaloosa for the case. A group of Black men, eight to ten strong, wielded the weapons to protect her, Thurgood Marshall, and Arthur Shores, who housed the New York lawyers during their stay. Because of Shores's involvement in this case, among other civil rights actions, his home had been bombed repeatedly. The lurking hazards scared Motley: though she sorely needed rest during the litigation campaign, she was often unable to sleep and "stayed awake all night."[27]

*

Nevertheless, when the university and the district judge cited the danger to Lucy as the rationale for excluding her, Motley and Shores strenuously objected. In a federal district court appearance witnessed by numerous reporters and packed with spectators, Black and white, the lawyers argued that two sacred legal principles were at stake, and both had to be upheld. The university had to comply with court orders demanding Lucy's admission, and the state had to meet its obligation to ensure law and order. The lawyers went so far as to claim that the UA's board of trustees welcomed the violent uprising against Lucy. Ringleaders of the mob and university officials had conspired, Motley and Shores claimed, to drive Lucy from campus and crush court-ordered desegregation.[28]

On top of alleging in open court that the university had conspired with the mob against Lucy, Shores and Motley held a press conference. Dozens of reporters crowded into the regional NAACP office to hear them speak. Motley, who had evidently conceived of and crafted the conspiracy charge, took the lead. With news cameras rolling, she charged that four defendants unconnected to the university—one a former Klansman—had threatened Autherine Lucy with "bodily harm," "milled about on the campus in such a manner as to assimilate [*sic*] a mob," and "aided and abetted" UA's president and its board of trustees in a deliberate plan to prevent Lucy from attending classes. The entire episode, according to Motley, constituted a "cunning stratagem" and a "subterfuge."[29]

With the conspiracy claim, Motley had overreached. The press conference had gone awry from the start. The lawyers arrived more than an hour late. And in her exchange with reporters, Motley made a verbal slip, an unusual occurrence for the careful attorney. When asked to clarify whether she meant to use "assimilate" or "simulate" when referring to the mob, she repeated the error: the men had tried to "assimilate" a mob. Perhaps tired and confused, Motley had made an embarrassing mistake. The entire episode undermined the team's credibility. The lawyers had stumbled.[30]

In response, the university president called a press conference of his own. He rejected the "Negro woman's allegation" that AU had conspired with four random men—including Klan riffraff—to defeat Lucy. Motley's claims were "untrue, unwarranted and outrageous," he said.[31]

Thurgood Marshall conceded that AU had it right: the lawyers neither possessed any direct evidence of such a conspiracy nor could they marshal any. At a February 1956 hearing, Marshall stood before the federal court and retracted the explosive claims. After a "careful investigation," he admitted, "we are unable to produce any substantial—*any evidence*—which could support that allegation." He also withdrew the claim that Lucy's suspension amounted to a "cunning stratagem" and "subterfuge." The assertions Motley had made with such confidence just days earlier were unfounded.[32]

*

By the time Marshall abandoned the conspiracy allegations, the damage had been done. Incensed by the claim, the university's attorneys urged the court to penalize the lawyers for making false charges that had been disseminated "all over the world" in the press, on television, and on the radio. And adamant that the UA could not (and President Eisenhower's federal government would not) guarantee Lucy's safety, officials expelled her. The grounds for her expulsion drew on Motley's fateful claims at the conference. Her "false, defamatory, impertinent, and scandalous charges" justified Lucy's permanent exclusion.[33]

The federal court, which had sided with Lucy and her lawyers several times, would not side with the NAACP this time. While the court ruled that officials' safety concerns could not thwart the desegregation order, it would not second-guess the trustees' decision to banish Lucy for making, through her lawyers, the baseless conspiracy allegation. The trustees' preparation for Lucy's arrival on campus had been inadequate, the court found; nevertheless, the university had acted in "good faith." Shocked by the turn of events, Lucy declared herself "completely disheartened" and went into seclusion. Motley and the rest of the legal team had been defeated.[34]

This one misstep would have long-term implications. The dramatic turn in the UA litigation energized a years-long effort by Alabama officials—already resentful over the NAACP's "rabblerousing" and irate over the Montgomery Bus Boycott—to drive the NAACP from the state. It succeeded: in June 1956, the Alabama legislature banned the NAACP from operating there.[35]

The ordeal also "traumatize[d]" Lucy; a sensitive soul, she had floundered in the spotlight. Her decline became apparent when reporters and cameramen surrounded her at LaGuardia Airport in New York City, soon after she arrived on a flight from Birmingham. Marshall and Motley had spirited her to New York for rest and medical care following her harrowing experience in Alabama and the "terrific strain" it had imposed. At the airport, the lawyers greeted Lucy and led her through the expected jumble of journalists, cameras, and microphones. With the lawyers surrounding her like centurions, Lucy faced the inquiring crowd. Marshall's tall, bulky frame stood to her left; Motley, her face lined with anxiety, stood a little behind and to her right.

At first, Lucy's attire camouflaged her unease. Carrying a beige handbag in gloved hands, and wearing a fashionable felt pillbox hat and a long coat to protect her from the winter chill, she looked smart and collected. The façade soon crumbled. When Marshall urged her to read a prepared statement vowing to seek reinstatement at UA, Lucy's calm veneer dissolved. She refused to comply. Instead, she turned to Motley, who served not only as her lawyer but also as her companion and guide during the entirety of the trip. "Please get me out of here," she whispered. She repeated, *"Please* get me out of here."

Motley did so. She ushered Lucy off the stage. Autherine Lucy would not return to UA's campus; she was done.[36]

Marshall and Motley were forced to abandon the case—filed just after the *Brown II* decision—that they had hoped would be a landmark. Now they had no client, and each faced a $1 million defamation suit. The alleged ringleaders of the mob that terrorized Lucy turned the tables on the attorneys; they sued Marshall, Motley, and Arthur Shores, along with Lucy and Myers, for claiming they had conspired to deprive Lucy of her rights. Motley and Marshall departed Alabama under a cloud. They had been run out of the state.[37]

It was far from the civil rights lawyers' finest hour; it was a debacle. Even LDF's allies criticized the "tactical blunder." Autherine Lucy agreed. Days before her final expulsion from the university, she confessed, "We made a mistake."[38]

But Motley refused to admit the error or confess regrets. She deflected blame. The Montgomery Bus Boycott had incensed white Alabamians, she explained, creating an unfavorable environment for the lawsuit. President Eisenhower also deserved blame, she claimed, for refusing to provide federal protection for Lucy.[39] Motley's reluctance to acknowledge the misstep was not an atypical position for her and other lawyers in her line of work to assume. Her extraordinarily demanding job required her to regard the Inc. Fund's strategy as both heroic and just. She remained resolutely committed to the organization's legal strategy. Her duties bred an attitude of righteous indignation toward segregation and segregationists, along with a sense that the ends that the lawyers sought—equality under law for all Blacks—more than made up for troubles that individual Black plaintiffs endured. Moreover, as a woman lawyer, she fiercely guarded her appearance as a confident and tough attorney, no different from any other. Motley had never known Thurgood Marshall, Jack Greenberg, or Arthur Shores to apologize for mistakes, so why should she?

Part III

The Heights and Depths of Life as a Symbol and Agent of Change

10

The "Best Plaintiffs Ever": Desegregating the University of Georgia

In 1960, Hamilton Holmes and Charlayne Hunter filed a lawsuit attacking segregation at the University of Georgia at Athens (UGA)—the nation's oldest public university. Both Holmes and Hunter lived in Atlanta, the capital of the so-called New South, just seventy-five miles west of Athens. They were intelligent, ambitious, and far more poised than their ages might suggest.

Holmes descended from an elite, activist family. His father, the grandson of an esteemed physician, had made a mark in 1955 when he filed a lawsuit to desegregate the city's municipal golf courses. Athletic, handsome, and light-skinned, Holmes—in every sense other than his race—looked like a "clean-cut, all-American boy." Following the family tradition, he yearned to become a doctor and to fight for racial equality.[1]

Charlayne Hunter, meanwhile, had made a mark as editor-in-chief of the newspaper of Atlanta's Turner High School. Like Holmes, she had excelled academically at Turner; but unlike him, she was not an Atlanta native. The daughter of a chaplain for the U.S. Army, she had moved several times and endured long stretches apart from her father because of his job. Notably, following an assignment to a military base in Alaska in 1954, she spent nine months in America's "last frontier" state, and was at the time the only Black person in her entire school. The dislocations occasioned by her father's career meant she developed a high tolerance for change and uncertainty. With her petite figure, hazel eyes, auburn hair, and olive skin, Hunter was physically striking and garnered admiration from her high school peers, who voted her homecoming queen. Because of her looks, she long had been subjected to curious stares and racial taunts. The seemingly endless attention to her appearance and the experience of being a "military brat" toughened Hunter, preparing her for some of the challenges she would face.[2]

Together, Holmes and Hunter set out to accomplish a feat that had already failed once before. A 1950 bid for admission to UGA law school by a Black plaintiff, Horace Ward, had ended in defeat. However, Motley believed these two exemplary students were "among the best plaintiffs" the Inc. Fund had "had in any case," and had great faith that Holmes and Hunter could prevail years later.[3]

The Supreme Court's desegregation decision in *Brown v. Board of Education* had left the state of Georgia deeply polarized. In urban centers, Black leaders voiced support for *Brown*, which lagged in rural areas and among white teachers and administrators. Georgia's cadre of white politicians had denounced *Brown* categorically. Former Governor Herman Talmadge, who went on to represent Georgia in the Senate, had set the tone. He had promised the public that the state would deploy every conceivable tactic to avoid desegregating Georgia's schools. In 1956, the state legislature had followed through on that promise: it enacted a law allocating state funding only to public schools and colleges that provided "separate education for the white and colored races." In 1959, when Holmes and Hunter began their challenge at UGA, the state's elected officials remained defiant. Governor Ernest Vandiver had been elected in 1959 on a motto that pledged his resolve on segregation: "No, not one." Under his watch, no Black student would desegregate a white school or college. Or so he thought.[4]

In fact, the law was on the side of desegregation, and the law prevailed. *Brown*, Motley's 1958 victory in the University of Florida case (*Hawkins v. Florida*), and the Inc. Fund's 1950 win at the University of Texas (*Sweatt v. Painter*) foreordained the outcome of the battle over segregation at UGA. So did the U.S. Supreme Court's edict in *Cooper v. Aaron*, the 1958 Little Rock school desegregation case, which Motley also had helped litigate. Faced with violent white resistance to the integration of Little Rock's Central High School and Arkansas officials' defiance of a federal desegregation order, the justices had affirmed federal supremacy, holding that states could not nullify a federal court's authority to enforce *Brown*. All of this meant that the South's public universities would eventually have to comply with federal precedents that banned racial segregation. But it would take time for all the relevant stakeholders to resign themselves to that fact. In Georgia, the white resistance reached that inevitable conclusion only after a long-running, tension-filled legal and political drama had unfolded.[5]

*

The drama began with administrative gamesmanship. In July 1959, soon after Hamilton Holmes and Charlayne Hunter submitted applications to join UGA's freshman class, Registrar Walter N. Danner wrote a letter to the applicants explaining that he could not consider their requests for admission to UGA during the fall quarter of 1959 due to "limited facilities": the class had already been filled. Undaunted, the students requested admission for the winter quarter. Danner again turned them down.

Sensing that winning admission to UGA could take many months, Holmes enrolled at Morehouse College and Hunter matriculated at Wayne State University. The pair then applied to UGA as transfer students, seeking to begin classes during the spring quarter of 1960. Once again, Danner brushed them off. He offered a new rationale for his refusal to consider them: UGA stipulated that all applicants complete a formal interview, and neither Holmes nor Hunter had met that critical requirement.[6]

Eight months passed without progress, and a new admissions season had begun. Keen to demonstrate continued interest in UGA, Holmes and Hunter renewed their applications, now seeking entry in the fall of 1960. Months went by without a response. Then, on June 21, 1960, as spring turned to summer, Danner wrote to Hunter: the deadline for admission in the fall quarter of 1960 had again passed due to "limited facilities." With Holmes, Danner used a different tactic. His application remained incomplete, the registrar said, because he had not been interviewed. These latest retorts revealed that the entire process thus far had been bogus. UGA had no intention of dealing honestly with the students. For almost a year the university had done nothing but give Holmes and Hunter the runaround. While other states had blocked desegregation by immediately resorting to violence, Georgia had pursued a different but equally effective initial strategy: passive bureaucracy.[7]

In September 1960, Constance Baker Motley resolved to defeat Georgia's ploy. Together with Donald L. Hollowell—a respected Atlanta lawyer known as "Georgia's Mr. Civil Rights"—and Horace Ward—then a lawyer employed by Hollowell's firm, Motley filed a lawsuit in federal court. It sought to compel Danner to consider Holmes and Hunter's applications fairly and expeditiously. Hollowell, a tall, brown-skinned Army veteran known for his deep baritone voice, his commanding presence, and his powerful intellect, had made his mark by representing the likes of Dr. Martin Luther King Jr., student demonstrators, and other Black persons who found themselves caught in the crosshairs of Georgia's laws. Motley knew and admired Hollowell; he also served as her co-counsel in the ongoing Atlanta school desegregation case. Together with her colleagues, Motley made arguments in the suit before William A. Bootle, a federal district court judge, and succeeded. Bootle compelled UGA administrators to review and act upon Holmes's and Hunter's applications within thirty days.[8]

UGA's subsequent review process generated renewed controversy. After indicating that every student had to be interviewed prior to acceptance, the university subjected Holmes and Hunter to hourlong inquiries by Danner and two other administrators. Hunter's interrogators not only asked questions about her educational interests, but also queried whether "she had any apprehension about being the first Negro" to enter UGA. Hunter's able handling of the questions led officials to concede her "fitness" to attend the university. But her application still went nowhere. Following the interview, UGA advised her that, due to "limited facilities," she could not be admitted at that time. Her application would be reconsidered, the university claimed, the following April for admission in the fall quarter of 1961.[9]

Holmes fared worse. His hourlong interview amounted to a farce. Three officials peppered him with questions that ranged from the impertinent to the openly hostile. Instead of focusing on matters relevant to the educational process, administrators zeroed in on his moral character and racial views. They asked if he had ever been arrested. They wanted to know if he had ever visited "houses of prostitution" or the "red light district in Athens." They inquired about his attendance at "inter-racial parties" and his involvement in racial rabble-rousing—in particular, the sit-ins carried out by Atlanta students in March 1960. Holmes answered the questions as best he could. Following the interview, administrators denied his admission on grounds of his "evasive and contradictory" and, they implied, untruthful answers to their questions.

The university's continued recalcitrance set the stage for a trial focused on the merits of its admissions policies. The showdown took place at the federal courthouse in Athens. The marble building shadowed by magnolia trees looked much like the federal courthouse in Jackson where Motley had tried her first case. The atmosphere was redolent of that in Jackson, too. The courtroom "was packed": a swarm of people—most of whom were African American—gathered to see the Black lawyers challenge white supremacy and square off against an all-white and -male group of lawyers.[10]

Motley was joined by Hollowell, Ward, and Vernon Jordan, an intern in Hollowell's law firm and recent law school graduate. Holmes and Hunter sat with them at the counsel's table, dressed in their Sunday best. While all the Black lawyers were impressive to the crowd, Motley's presence caused a special stir, and inspired pride and delight. "Of course they had not seen a woman lawyer" in "those parts of the country," she recalled. Motley struck her client, Hunter, as serious, stern, and prepared—completely focused on the trial. She concentrated on the trial at hand, which "she seemed to regard as the most important mission of her life." "[S]he barely acknowledged my presence," Hunter recalled. "No one—be it defendant or plaintiff—was going to distract her from carrying her task to a successful conclusion."[11]

Once the trial began, the experience differed from Motley's previous desegregation cases in one vital respect: neither the university nor the court contested the by now long-settled legal principle that a taxpayer-supported university could not deny admission to an otherwise qualified candidate because of race. But, in a demonstrably false rendition of past and recent history, the university's president and chairman of its board of regents swore, in open court, that race did not factor into the school's admissions process. According to this fairy tale, UGA had not excluded or discriminated against any applicant on account of race. Admissions officials had applied the university's usual rules and procedures evenhandedly in considering both Holmes and Hunter. In response Motley launched pointed questions at the witnesses like "curve ball[s]" thrown "with so much skill and power that she would knock them off their chair[s]." They told a very different story.[12]

Motley, having reviewed thousands of application files and culled relevant evidence from them, showed that officials made exceptions to deadlines and procedures, but only for white applicants. During the precise period when Danner had denied Hunter's application due to "limited facilities," Motley's questions revealed UGA had admitted a white female student midyear. For the white female, Bebe Dobbs Brumby, daughter of a well-known Georgia family, UGA had made space despite its allegedly overtaxed facilities and the reputed difficulty of accepting students after the academic year had commenced. Motley also confronted administrators with university records showing that certain dormitories had numerous vacancies during the pendency of Holmes's and Hunter's applications; thus, the "limited facilities" rationale for their rejection was demonstrably false. Motley demonstrated that UGA had in fact admitted whites *after* informing Holmes and Hunter that they could not be accepted due to missed deadlines. Still other exchanges showed that while Holmes and Hunter had been required to sit for personal interviews, other students had fulfilled the requirement in different and less burdensome ways, or had not fulfilled it at all.[13]

Judge Bootle found her ability to wring out the truth so remarkable that it amused him. "I'd never seen a judge that giggled as much as Judge Bootle during that trial," Motley remembered. "[H]e was amused by the fact that here I was, a black woman, cross-examining . . . Georgia officials who were just squirming [and] making all kinds of statements that obviously weren't true." The whole thing was so ridiculous that Judge Bootle could not suppress his laughter.[14]

Near the end of the trial, having adduced ample evidence uncovering UGA's discrimination, Motley posed a question to Danner that she called the "old clincher": would he "favor the admission of a qualified Negro?" The registrar was caught. He could only answer one way, lest he belie UGA's claims of evenhandedness. Meekly, Danner answered in the affirmative: UGA would accept qualified Black applicants. Motley had made all the necessary points; the case now lay in the judge's hands.[15]

Bootle quickly issued a decision. The court's January 6, 1961, ruling—which came just weeks before the inauguration of John F. Kennedy as the country's youngest president—vindicated both the plaintiffs and the trial strategy adopted by Constance Baker Motley and Donald Hollowell. The judge ruled that UGA had rejected Hamilton Holmes and Charlayne Hunter "solely because of their race and color." "Had plaintiffs been white applicants for admission to the University of Georgia," Bootle wrote, "both plaintiffs would have been admitted to the University not later than the beginning of the Fall Quarter, 1960." The judge ordered the immediate admission of Holmes and Hunter to the university.

A native white southerner who had adhered to the segregationist ideology prior to *Brown*, Bootle became an unlikely force for legal and social change: he proclaimed a 175-year tradition of excluding Blacks from UGA unlawful and demanded an end to the practice. Holmes and Hunter were overjoyed. Motley, along with her co-counsel, had scored another major courtroom victory. Newspapers across the state and the nation covered the fall of segregation at UGA, the country's oldest publicly chartered college. The *Atlanta Daily World* called the decision "historic"; the *New York Times* noted that it "marked the first" time desegregation had occurred "at any level" in Georgia, a state whose leaders had once said racial mixing would "destroy" its public school system.[16]

If Bootle's decision brought jubilation to civil rights lawyers and their supporters, it generated scorn among most white Georgians, including those on UGA's campus. Within hours of the ruling, protesters gathered on campus to display their opposition, singing "Dixie" and screaming racial epithets. A group of about two hundred students hung a Black-faced effigy in the archway at the entrance to campus. As evening turned to night, the size of the crowd increased, along with the ferocity of their antics. Enraged students attempted to burn a gasoline-soaked, fifteen-foot cross on a lawn in front of the UGA president's home. Others set off firecrackers and threw eggs and rocks at passing cars. A journalist attempting to interview students was pushed to the ground and injured. One student summed up the sentiment, saying, "We don't like integration being crammed down our throats. It's unfair."[17]

The state's politicians agreed. Shortly after Bootle's decision was issued, Governor Vandiver and Eugene Cook, the state's attorney general, decided to fight the order to desegregate. The state announced plans to appeal the outcome to a higher court and requested that Judge Bootle temporarily delay his decision while the appeal was pending. The stay request set off a flurry of activity. Bootle ordered the state's attorneys, along with Motley and Hollowell and UGA's attorneys, to appear in his Macon courtroom at half past nine on the morning of January 9. When court convened, Motley and Hollowell argued vigorously that a delay would only embolden white resistance. But Judge Bootle had "no objection" to the state "testing the correctness" of his decision in a higher court. In a reversal of fortune, the landmark desegregation decision, only days old, came to a standstill.[18]

Disappointed by Bootle's about-face, Motley immediately phoned a higher authority—Chief Judge Elbert Tuttle of the U.S. Court of Appeals for the Fifth Circuit in Atlanta—and made an appeal of her own. Motley urged Judge Tuttle to reverse Judge Bootle's stay of the desegregation order—quickly. Time was of the essence; the students had waited more than a year for admission. Motley and Hollowell had driven the seventy-five miles from Atlanta to Macon to appear in Judge Bootle's courtroom that morning, and then back to Atlanta that afternoon to appear in Judge Tuttle's chambers. To reach his chambers in time, Hollowell drove at "ninety miles an hour," with Motley, "hair flying," in the passenger seat. They had to make a quick stop at Hollowell's law office in Atlanta, where Motley drafted the necessary legal documents. They arrived at Judge Tuttle's chambers at 2:32 p.m., two minutes after the scheduled start of the hearing. The media, local and national, swarmed, eager to know what new turn the dynamic case would now take.[19]

Judge Tuttle took less than an hour to make his decision. "Tuttle Boots Bootle," declared one news headline. On January 9, 1961, he reversed Judge Bootle's decision to stay the desegregation mandate because it had been "improvidently granted." "I am of the opinion that the quickest disposition that can be made of this case . . . is the best solution not only for [the plaintiffs] but for all others concerned," Tuttle wrote. This stunned the state's attorneys, but reversing the stay made Judge Tuttle a hero—the "chief jurist of the civil rights revolution." "At that moment," Hunter wrote in her memoir, "we all loved Judge Tuttle." After a dizzying sequence of events, the plaintiffs had won; an order by the U.S. Supreme Court affirmed the victory.[20]

But the drama continued to play out that day. Unaware that the stay had initially been granted by Bootle, Holmes and Hunter began the process of enrolling at UGA. An hour before they were to arrive on campus that morning, a crowd of about a hundred students assembled to protest. While Holmes and Hunter filled out paperwork in the registrar's office, a group of students pushed their way into the adjacent corridor. Lashing out against the pair's presence, the protesters chanted, "Two, four, six, eight, we don't want to integrate." "Nigger, go home," they shouted. Soon, hundreds more gathered on campus to boo and hurl epithets at Holmes and Hunter as they exited the registrar's office. Through it all, they remained calm. In a sport jacket and trousers, Holmes waded confidently through the crowd. Hunter, decked out in a beige cashmere coat, printed blouse, and pleated skirt, appeared stoical. She seemed to have "iron nerves." Both students strode behind Vernon Jordan, who had accompanied them for the enrollment process, and answered questions from a bevy of reporters as the rowdy crowd looked on.

Before the pair could leave campus, the news of the stay made its way to Athens. Students who wanted to hold on to segregation cheered Judge Bootle's stay. Escaping the scene, Holmes and Hunter entered a waiting vehicle. Several students surrounded their car and began violently to rock it. The two were shaken, but physically unharmed.[21]

While the trial put strains on Holmes and Hunter, the fast-moving case also placed significant physical and emotional demands on Motley, difficulties she endured with outward ease, making her stellar performance in the courtroom all the more remarkable. While conducting her tedious research poring over UGA's admissions records— work she needed to prove her case—she and Vernon Jordan drove back and forth between Atlanta and Athens every day for a "couple of weeks." "It took us two hours to drive down [to Athens] and two hours to drive back [to Atlanta]." "We'd leave at six o'clock in the morning," she remembered, "work . . . until six o'clock at night" and then "go . . . back the next day." They followed this especially grueling schedule because there was no place for them to stay in Athens, which was a small and segregated college town. Deprived of overnight accommo-dations, Motley and her colleagues had no choice but to make the long trip to and from Athens each day. Segregation also shaped their day-time movements. At lunchtime, "there was always a problem [about] where we were going to eat" because white-owned restaurants did not serve Blacks. In Athens, the lawyers found only one tiny restaurant that would serve them. Motley found herself suffering from "sheer physical exhaustion" by the end of each day, and even after winning the stay's reversal, her work still was not done.[22]

On January 11, two days after Motley's stupendous victory in Judge Tuttle's courtroom, a full-scale riot broke out on UGA's campus while rumors circulated that Governor Vandiver and state legislators would rather close the university than desegregate it. Up to two thousand people, a mixture of students, Ku Klux Klansmen, and other interlop-ers, converged. Some in the brewing melee carried loaded weapons. The mob targeted Charlayne Hunter's assigned dormitory, Myers Hall. As ringleaders urged the crowd to attack, the mob—waving Con-federate flags and yelling epithets, obscenities, and segregationist slogans—surged toward Hunter's room. They hurled rocks through the building's windows, shattering more than sixty panes of glass. Athens police, outnumbered fifty to one, attempted to control the crowd, to little avail. Protesters egged police cars and grabbed and launched some of the bombs of tear gas that officers were meant to deploy for crowd control.

When this unrest unfolded, Hunter was locked away in her first-story dorm at Myers Hall. But as the crowd became increasingly rau-cous and violent, officials moved her to a safe location, away from the flying shards of glass and the tear gas that had begun wafting into her living quarters. By midnight, law enforcement, now aided by slow-to-arrive state troopers, had contained the crowd. The troopers whisked Hunter—by now weeping and clutching a statue of the Madonna—back to her home in Atlanta. The officers also collected Holmes from his location off campus, where he had not directly experienced the disturbances, and took him back to Atlanta as well. Meanwhile, UGA's dean of students, J. A. Williams, made an astonishing announcement: UGA was to penalize the victims, rather than the perpetrators, of the campus riot. Williams suspended Holmes and Hunter from the university "in the interests of your personal safety and for the safety and welfare of more than 7,000 other students at the University of Georgia."[23]

The riot and the decision to suspend Holmes and Hunter sparked a tremendous backlash. Four hundred UGA faculty members signed a resolution calling for the students' speedy return to campus. The president of the University of Georgia, who had said little as the controversy swirled, now vowed to punish further rioting. Ten groups, civic and church organizations led by the League of Women Voters and the Georgia Council of Human Relations, issued a statement criticizing the university's suspension of Holmes and Hamilton and urging their reinstatement. The *Atlanta Journal* published an editorial condemning Governor Vandiver for condoning the inflammatory remarks that had given rise to the violence; the paper also lambasted UGA officials for failing to provide adequate security to Holmes and Hunter in the face of unrest. The Georgia Chamber of Commerce, perhaps the most influential group in the state, "denounced" the "wild demonstrations" and the politicians who had led Georgians to think that a court order could simply be defied. Violent segregationists had backed Governor Vandiver into a corner, but now, forced to choose between mob violence and law and order, the governor—who had earlier promised to defy the desegregation order—repudiated the violent resistance.[24]

Five days after the riot, Judge Bootle ordered Holmes's and Hunter's readmission; the two students returned to campus on January 16, 1961. But the end of flagrant resistance to desegregation did not mean they would have an uneventful everyday existence. Both courageously endured acts of hate and hostility as the days and months wore on. The university permitted some white girls to transfer out of the dormitory to which Hunter had been assigned on the grounds that her presence impeded their educational process. Other students were not so much openly hostile, but aloof, and predicted that Holmes and Hunter would do poorly in the demanding educational environment. "They'll never graduate," observed one white student.[25]

That prediction never came to pass. The students flourished academically, and ultimately thrived professionally. In 1963, both Holmes and Hunter graduated from UGA. Holmes earned a medical degree from Emory University, the first African American to do so, and went on to have a distinguished career. The chief of orthopedic surgery at the Veterans Hospital in Atlanta, he later served as head of orthopedic surgery at Grady Memorial Hospital. Hunter also realized her dream: she became a world-renowned journalist, best known for her roles as national correspondent for PBS's *MacNeil/Lehrer News-Hour* and as chief Africa correspondent for National Public Radio.[26]

*

While the case was ongoing for several months, Constance Baker Motley missed her family, but found ways to remain connected to her young son and husband. After each court appearance, she followed the same ritual. She made her way to the office of the clerk of court, where she requested to use the telephone and placed a collect call to her apartment in New York. For a few minutes at least, she heard the voices of her husband and eight-year-old, Joel III, and they of course heard her voice on the other end of the line. And on days when she was not scheduled to appear in court, Motley jetted back to New York to spend the weekend with her family. For her, it was all worth it.[27]

Through her leadership in the University of Georgia litigation, Motley cemented her standing. Her deft actions explained why it was that her colleague, Jack Greenberg, insisted she was a force to be reckoned with: "When she got ahold of a case, pity the lawyer on the other side."[28]

When Motley made her way back to New York after her triumph, it was as a rising star: she had earned a national reputation as an excellent civil rights lawyer. In keeping with the view that great talents are born instead of made, some observers chalked up her victory to "brilliance." But Motley, who had been working as an Inc. Fund lawyer for fifteen years by that time, credited the win to the collective endeavors of her colleagues, and stressed the importance of different traits. "It wasn't that we outsmarted the state," she insisted. "You win," she said, "by preparation and experience." "While they were looking up cases in the law books, we were calling them off by heart."[29]

11

A "Difficulty with the Idea of a Woman": The Setback of 1961

John F. Kennedy tried his best to avoid the subject of race during his campaign for president in 1960. Sit-ins and other protests against Jim Crow, meanwhile, proliferated nationwide, and polls showed he was facing declining support. The NAACP's Roy Wilkins warned the candidate not to take Black voters for granted, and Kennedy realized he needed to take decisive action to appeal to the community.

When Dr. Martin Luther King Jr. was arrested and detained on October 19, 1960, following a sit-in held in Atlanta, Kennedy found the opening he needed. A Georgia judge, treating King "like a hardened criminal," had sentenced him to four months' hard labor and ordered him to do his time at the maximum-security Georgia State Prison at Reidsville. Upon learning about this turn of events, Kennedy phoned Coretta Scott King, who was six months pregnant at the time, distraught, and fearful for her husband's life. In the phone call on October 26, just days before the election, Kennedy expressed sympathy for her husband's plight and promised to help gain his release. "I just wanted you to know that I am thinking about you and Dr. King," Kennedy told a stunned Coretta. King emerged from prison the very next day.

In a televised interview following his release, King praised Kennedy for being "courageous" and "a great force in making my release possible." King's father, Martin Luther King Sr., went further: the influential minister announced that he would be supporting Kennedy for president in light of the call he had so generously made to his daughter-in-law. This was the boost Kennedy needed over his opponent, Richard M. Nixon.[1]

In that presidential race, at the time the closest election in U.S. history, 68 percent of Black people voted for Kennedy; he had overwhelmingly won this critical constituency. At the same time, he had raised expectations that his administration would support civil rights. On the campaign trail Kennedy promised he "could integrate all federally assisted housing with a stroke of the Presidential pen." He also promised to speed up the process of school desegregation and to deploy the FBI to assist civil rights activists. A few months into his presidency, however, Kennedy had not done much to fulfill the promises, leaving Black people with little to show for their support.[2]

Once again needing to transform his standing with the Black electorate, in the summer of 1961, President Kennedy called Thurgood Marshall with a proposal that would serve both of their interests, as well as delight Black voters. Kennedy offered the country's most prominent civil rights lawyer a seat on the federal bench. Marshall, tired of the frequent travel and constant hustle that his position at the Inc. Fund demanded, had long lobbied for a judicial appointment; he believed he had earned it through his brilliant lawyering in *Brown v. Board of Education*. Under the pressure of litigating hundreds of civil rights cases nationwide, Marshall had "become more and more stressed out," Motley remembered. Now the man who had personified the courtroom struggle to end Jim Crow would command the courtroom as a presiding judge on the U.S. Court of Appeals in Manhattan.

Kennedy sent a clear message of support for civil rights by appointing Marshall. Burke Marshall, Kennedy's assistant attorney general for civil rights, noted that Marshall's appointment was "symbolic in a very important and useful way," as "Mr. Civil Rights" well knew. A master strategist whose "forceful personality usually allowed him to get his way," Thurgood Marshall had "drumm[ed] up support" for his nomination "in the black press and among civil rights leaders who had been crucial to Kennedy's narrow election as president," wrote one biographer. He had made it clear that Kennedy risked "angering the civil rights groups" if he was not appointed to the court. When the

White House announced Marshall's nomination on September 23, 1961, prominent Americans Black and white praised Marshall for his legal acumen and applauded Kennedy for his leadership in selecting him, which would undoubtedly provoke controversy and resistance in the South and in the U.S. Senate.[3]

Marshall's nomination to the court filled one void, but it created another at the nation's premier civil rights firm. With his elevation to the bench, Marshall would relinquish the reins of power at the NAACP's Legal Defense Fund. Who would become the Inc. Fund's new leader and the face of Black America's courtroom struggle for equal justice? Who could possibly follow Mr. Civil Rights? That question weighed on Constance Baker Motley, and on everyone else at the LDF.

*

By mid-1961, Constance Baker Motley had worked in the Inc. Fund office for fifteen years, and she viewed herself a worthy successor to her boss. She had earned the moniker the "Civil Rights Queen" in recognition of her major courtroom successes. That year she kept up her frenetic pace as a courtroom lawyer. As Marshall was preparing for his new role, she was on the road defending college students who had been arrested staging sit-ins against segregated lunch counters and restaurants. Black students at North Carolina Agricultural & Technical College in Greensboro initiated sit-ins on February 1, 1960, and the protests quickly spread throughout the South, igniting an exciting new, youth-led phase of the civil rights movement. But even as defense of the students and their "watershed" movement preoccupied her, Motley found herself thinking about her own career. She secretly hoped that in the coming months she would receive the nod to become Marshall's successor. Appropriately enough, Motley believed, the Civil Rights Queen would become the next standard-bearer of the civil rights movement's legal front. She was not alone. Medgar Evers, the NAACP field secretary in Mississippi, "was so certain" Motley "would be appointed Thurgood's successor," she recalled, that "he had posters printed to this effect."[4]

Back at the office, Marshall's imminent departure affected work-day rhythms. The director-counsel, whose larger-than-life personality had infused the office with chatter and laughter, was now scarcely present. Often on vacation in upstate New York, Marshall nonetheless maintained connection to the job by phone. Through conversations with staff members—Jack Greenberg, in particular—he kept abreast of happenings in the office. In strategy sessions with friends and supporters, he discussed the likely fight over his confirmation—and he handpicked the Inc. Fund's new leader.[5]

Marshall had in fact settled on his heir months before news of his judicial appointment went public. Secrecy and intrigue surrounded the choice, and because of a long-running professional rivalry between Marshall and his onetime chief assistant, Robert L. Carter, a personal grudge influenced his decision. Marshall's gregarious earthiness and penchant for whiskey-soaked partying contrasted sharply with Carter's introspection and love of wine and the Metropolitan Opera. Their conflict was exacerbated by an underlying current of competition over who was the better lawyer and who deserved credit for the Inc. Fund's victory in *Brown*. The two men also ranked the Inc. Fund's priorities differently. Carter groused about the amount of time Marshall spent out of the office, fund-raising and giving speeches to local communities; Marshall's absences increased Carter's workload. Marshall ensured that the Inc. Fund directorship did not go to Carter. The first blow to his chances occurred in 1955, when the charismatic public face of the Inc. Fund and a brilliant civil rights *leader* removed the perceived threat posed by Carter—an architect of *Brown* and brilliant civil rights *lawyer*. Carter was named general counsel of the NAACP, a partner of the Inc. Fund, but a separate organization with its own docket of cases; he was no longer directly in line to succeed Marshall at the Inc. Fund.

Carter was "furious." He felt "discarded" after his "vision and creative legal skills had produced these landmark race relations gains," he wrote in his memoir. Despite his banishment, he retained friends inside and outside the Inc. Fund. Given an opening, it was clear his supporters might try to make him the heir apparent. Indeed, some casual observers still expected Carter to succeed Marshall, while others thought he might anoint his mentee, Motley. By quickly settling on his successor and communicating his preference in private to his own enduringly loyal supporters, Marshall nipped in the bud any momentum that might make Carter, Motley, or other viable candidates the new chief. Marshall then waited for the summer to pass.[6]

Finally, in the fall of 1961, the news broke. Within days of the White House's September 1961 statement officially announcing Marshall's nomination, the Inc. Fund's executive committee had news of its own: Jack Greenberg would succeed Marshall as the general counsel of the NAACP Legal Defense Fund. Constance Baker Motley's beloved mentor had passed her over for the promotion of a lifetime.[7]

Although many respected Greenberg as an attorney, his appointment as Marshall's successor generated tremendous controversy. The selection process for such a high-profile role had been anything but transparent. Marshall alone chose his successor, and told the Inc. Fund's executive committee, which was largely loyal to him. On September 27, four days after the world first learned of Marshall's nomination to the bench and that he planned to leave the Inc. Fund, Dr. Allan Knight Chalmers, president of the Inc. Fund board, read Marshall's letter of resignation to the executive committee and conveyed "Marshall's hope that Jack Greenberg would be appointed" as the new director-counsel. Deferring to Marshall's wishes, the executive committee approved Greenberg's appointment. A few days later, at an "emergency" dinner meeting on October 4 at New York City's Hotel Roosevelt, the Inc. Fund's board of directors followed suit.

With Marshall, Greenberg, and Motley looking on, Chalmers urged the directors to appoint Jack Greenberg as director-counsel. He also recommended the appointment of Constance Baker Motley as associate counsel. In fact, Chalmers called the two appointments a "package" deal. Sizing up the racial politics of Greenberg's succession, Chalmers urged the organization to appoint an "aggressive, young, good-looking Negro man" to the post of administrator; that person, it was hoped, could take on externally focused, nonlegal tasks such as fund-raising and community relations—all responsibilities that no one expected Greenberg to handle successfully. After Greenberg and Motley left the room, the board voted and unanimously approved the arrangement, as well as the leaders' salaries; Greenberg would make $20,000 a year, and Motley $18,000.[8]

Greenberg and Motley then returned to hear Marshall's farewell address to the Inc. Fund and to make some remarks of their own. Marshall insisted that the organization's vital work would continue without him. He thanked Columbia University professor Walter Gellhorn, his mentor, and others "who had recommended young men to work with the Fund." Then Greenberg, "more than a little nervous" about the heady moment—the prospect of stepping into the shoes of a giant and thereby inheriting a docket of four hundred cases—thanked the board for the appointment; he also applauded the Inc. Fund's "wonderful" staff. Finally, Motley, gracious and succinct, expressed gratitude to the board for appointing her Greenberg's lieutenant; she also thanked Marshall for "making her a lawyer." Inside the board meeting, the transition seemed to go smoothly; but the formalities, and Motley's practiced collegiality, obscured her true feelings—anger and disappointment. "Greenberg's installation came with such swiftness that there was no time for the opposition to mobilize," Motley later said of the backroom maneuvering that led to Greenberg's selection. Tumult soon erupted.[9]

As the public would learn, the vote on October 4 had been merely perfunctory, the outcome predetermined. Hours before the scheduled dinner at which board members ostensibly approved Marshall's successor, an Inc. Fund press release had already announced Greenberg's appointment. To make matters worse, an afternoon edition of a local newspaper carried news of Greenberg's selection—all before the board of directors had been given a chance to vote. Editorials endorsing the decision soon followed. Marshall, adept at generating and managing publicity, had arranged for his friends at the major Black newspapers to publish editorials lauding the choice. Greenberg's ascension had been a fait accompli.[10]

Critics both outside and within the NAACP—the Inc. Fund's parent organization—decried the manner in which the decision had been made. The NAACP's board of directors held a meeting five days after Greenberg's appointment to allow people to air grievances over the selection process. Members complained that Marshall had not sought input about the monumental decision from the board of the NAACP. Separate legal entities since 1957, the institutions still shared a history and a mission; in these respects, the organizations remained a "family," particularly in terms of public perception. Given these long-standing ties, Marshall should have reached out to the NAACP's board, critics argued. The failure to consult the NAACP "perpetrated a fraud" on the public, said Oliver C. Sutton, a New York lawyer and NAACP member. According to critics, respect for the organizations' common mission demanded a collaborative, rather than a unilateral, selection process.[11]

The detractors made fair points about the process, its exclusiveness and lack of transparency, but behind closed doors, Marshall evidently *had* informed two key figures within the NAACP of his succession plan: Roy Wilkins, the organization's executive secretary and Marshall's long-time friend, and Bishop Stephen Gill Spottswood, the chairman of the board. Others lacked the power and the standing within the NAACP and Inc. Fund hierarchies to exert influence over the process. Wilkins made the point succinctly: the Inc. Fund "can act as it wishes irrespective of the wishes of the NAACP."[12]

But critics did not just condemn the selection process—many doubted that Greenberg was the right person for the job. No one questioned his talent; a skilled advocate, the attorney had handled his share of Inc. Fund cases and won numerous courtroom victories. But he reportedly lacked the passion for racial justice and connections in the Black community that many viewed as a prerequisite for heading the Inc. Fund as its lead lawyer. He "was not like the white liberals who are committed body and soul to advancing the cause of black Americans," Motley later observed. For some, Greenberg's lack of credibility as a passionate advocate of racial equality made his selection questionable, or, as Motley called it, "strange."[13] Marshall had been not only a civil rights lawyer, but a civil rights leader—a "symbol" of Black achievement and a "voice for his people." Greenberg—a dispassionate white man without a natural constituency in the Black community—struck many observers as an unlikely substitute.

Even Greenberg needed time to warm to the idea that he would succeed Marshall. Marshall's decision "astonished" him, he said. The lawyer acknowledged that he lacked the warmth and folksiness that proved such an invaluable asset to Marshall as he built support for the Inc. Fund's work. Greenberg confessed "ineptitude at making small talk." He knew, moreover, that some "fund-raisers" had counseled against his selection because he lacked Marshall's personal touch.

"My being white was not expected to be a plus with potential givers interested in giving to the black cause," he also conceded. But setting aside his anxieties, Greenberg rose to the occasion and took the Inc. Fund's helm.[14]

Despite his being caught in the crossfire of an intra-racial struggle, commentators also uniformly praised Greenberg's talent and experience. "I do not question Attorney Greenberg's ability neither do I object to him because he is Jewish," one letter writer reflected, expressing a sentiment that captured the viewpoint of most critics. "I have no quarrel with Greenberg's competence," another wrote. "I do not object to him because he is a white man," proclaimed many others. Even the most acerbic opponents of his selection promised to stand with Greenberg as he continued the Inc. Fund's good work.[15]

Nevertheless, Marshall's decision stung the small band of accomplished African American lawyers with whom he had worked so closely. "Naturally," Motley recalled, Blacks in the firm hoped that Marshall would select a successor to lead the nation's premier civil rights firm from among this pool of skilled "champion[s]" of Blacks.[16]

Motley's professional record had made her a strong contender for the post. By 1961, she had successfully argued numerous cases in federal appellate and trial courts. In the months preceding Marshall's decision, she had litigated and won a critical victory—the University of Georgia desegregation case. In Marshall's own estimation, Motley had demonstrated exceptional skills as a courtroom lawyer, and, given her outstanding qualifications, many observers felt his passing her over demanded an explanation. In fact, after Marshall's decision, during the period from 1961 to 1964, Motley argued before the U.S. Supreme Court and earned rave reviews. Her arguments induced Associate Justice of the Supreme Court William O. Douglas to call her one of the ablest appellate advocates he had yet seen, and led U.S. Attorney General Ramsey Clark to recommend her for a federal judicial appointment.[17] Besides Motley and Robert Carter, William T. Coleman, Loren Miller, and Spottswood Robinson III were all experienced litigators at the Inc. Fund, and could also have handled the job.[18]

Marshall's failure to seriously consider any of these Black lawyers offended many in the Black community. James Hicks, a writer for the

New York Amsterdam News, declared himself "puzzled" over the decision. He asked, "What the HELL happened?" Hicks, a longtime friend of Jack Greenberg, had nothing negative to say about him. However, Hicks asserted that the Inc. Fund—in particular its majority white executive board and board of directors—had perpetrated an injustice by denying an opportunity to a Black lawyer with greater seniority than Greenberg, especially because the Inc. Fund "spends half its time fighting for seniority rights of Negroes in jobs with whites."[19]

Others lamented the symbolism of the selection. The passing over of able Black lawyers suggested that after all these years and despite the NAACP's successes, Negroes still "are unable to represent ourselves." One writer complained, "Brilliant lawyers as Carter, Motley and others are over-looked completely." Wallace Hayes, a long-lived member of the NAACP, wrote, "In the beginning, when brilliant, militant Negro lawyers were few and unavailable, I could understand the advisability of accepting the services of an experienced, outstanding white lawyer. But today the situation is different." Congressman Adam Clayton Powell and other critics wondered if the Inc. Fund had caved in to pressure from white donors. A group of Black attorneys led by Lawrence R. Bailey, Esq., of New York, along with numerous letter writers, lamented the decision and the passing over of Robert L. Carter and Constance Baker Motley, who were both more experienced and senior to Greenberg in the NAACP's staff.[20]

All the critics made a similar point: by appointing a white man to lead the LDF, Marshall had sent the wrong message at the wrong time. Context mattered: as Marshall well knew, "Negro counsel" had been "shunned" for decades by white organizations, including labor unions, businesses, and law firms. Now, he had shunned his own people. And he had chosen a terrible time to make the mistake. In 1961, just six years after *Brown* was decided, Black civil rights still hung in the balance. During this still-early stage of the Black struggle for freedom, it was incumbent on supporters of the cause to express confidence in the talent of Blacks, as yet a much marginalized, maligned group.[21]

Privately, in conversations with the board of directors, Marshall quipped and hedged about Greenberg's shortcomings, saying, "It would be better if he was a nigger, but nevertheless . . ." At the same time, Marshall publicly championed the "eminently qualified" white lawyer, and pushed back against critics by alluding to the principles of nondiscrimination and integration. "As those who are fighting discrimination, we can't afford to practice it," he insisted.[22]

Marshall's own historic moment made the situation especially ironic. Just as he passed over worthy Black attorneys, Marshall found acclaim as the first Black man appointed to the prestigious U.S. Court of Appeals in United States history. Commentators—Black and white—had hailed Marshall's appointment not only because of his qualifications, but also because of his race. Yet whereas Marshall appreciated the racial symbolism of his own appointment, he responded cavalierly to critics' concerns about his choice of successor. His pose did not go over well, and many agreed with the observation of attorney Bruce Wright: "Judge Marshall's clever aphorism that those who fight discrimination cannot afford to practice it has the polish of sophistry and all of its faults." Another commentator made the point more simply and directly: Marshall's antidiscrimination justification for Greenberg's selection, when viewed in context, was "inane."[23]

More than a few people wondered whether Greenberg's appointment stemmed from self-interest. Perhaps Marshall hoped his endorsement of a white man for the Inc. Fund post would lessen opposition to his judicial appointment. Perhaps he felt that, in the face of Greenberg's stunning appointment and the opposition it engendered among Blacks, white power brokers who perceived Marshall's civil rights work as "anti-white" might relent, allowing Greenberg's selection to ensure the "smooth transition" that Marshall sought from the "mostly black NAACP family" to the "white world of federal courts and high-stakes politics." If true, such "realpolitik" did not endear Marshall to his Black family.[24]

*

While others dwelled on the racial politics surrounding Marshall's choice of successor, Motley felt slighted on an additional basis. Marshall had refused to champion her for the post, she believed, because of her gender.

"Women in those days [had] a hard time," she said in a 2002 interview, and lacked the professional stature that some of them would acquire in the late twentieth century. And in her 1998 autobiography, she asserted that her boss and mentor "had difficulty with the idea of a woman in a leadership role in a male world."[25]

Motley's claim might seem astonishing, because time and again over the years she had papered over the cracks in her experience as the Inc. Fund's only woman lawyer. In public, she expressed gratitude and admiration for Marshall; she portrayed him, that is, precisely as the public wanted her to. Yet Thurgood Marshall—the same man whom Motley praised for giving her a big break at a time when law offices systematically excluded women—was also responsible for the biggest setback of her career. Like all heroes, Mr. Civil Rights was imperfect. Motley was well acquainted with Marshall's failings, but had kept unflattering information about him to herself. Faced with the knowledge that he was paying her less than other Inc. Fund attorneys, she had protested and then soldiered on. This time it was different.[26]

Motley's decision to raise questions about Marshall's succession decision in her autobiography, after years of remaining silent about the gender discrimination she had faced, spoke volumes. She felt strongly that Marshall's choice merited public scrutiny. His passing her over for the promotion struck her as manifestly unfair. The normally stoic Motley was hurt, and for the first time, she let it show.

*

At the time of Greenberg's promotion, Marshall insisted he had chosen Greenberg as his successor entirely on merit. He had seriously considered only two candidates as the next director-counsel of the Inc. Fund, he claimed: Jack Greenberg and Constance Baker Motley. And he offered an exceedingly simple explanation for why Greenberg merited appointment instead of Motley: Greenberg was six months more senior than Motley within the firm.[27]

The seniority justification would make logical sense, except for one stubborn fact: Motley had worked at the Inc. Fund longer than Greenberg. He had begun working for Marshall in 1949—three years after Motley. Thus, in reality *she* had three years' seniority on him.

Marshall, Greenberg, Carter, and other colleagues judged Motley a superb lawyer; nevertheless, Carter, Marshall's chief lieutenant for many years, insisted that Motley had not been a part of Marshall's "inner-circle," where Marshall and Carter engaged in "conceptual analysis." In fact, *no* woman had been in Marshall's inner circle, Carter noted—a reality that only dawned on him years later. Motley's remove from the firm's central decision-making process could have led Marshall to conclude she was not ready to take over the reins of the organization.[28]

Marshall's attitudes and decision-making process would have been shaped by the broader context of women's place in American society in 1961. The appointment of Motley as successor would have been incredibly bold: in 1961, no comparable American institution had a woman as its head. Men led the most prominent public interest organizations of the era, including Americans for Democratic Action, the ACLU, and the National Lawyers Guild.[29]

Civil rights organizations, which strenuously argued that race should not be a barrier to opportunity, had not yet reached the same conclusion regarding gender. Men headed each of the major civil rights groups; women rarely, if ever, received national recognition for their contributions, no matter how significant. Jo Ann Robinson, the woman who organized the Montgomery Bus Boycott of 1955—the catalyst for later nonviolent direct action campaigns—received little public recognition as the architect of that signature event. Public recognition for Rosa Parks, whose defiance of a segregation ordinance gave rise to the famous boycott, hinged on depictions of her as a saint rather than as the leader and seasoned activist that she was. Dr. Martin Luther King Jr., who attained national prominence as a result of his role in the boycott, went on to lead the Southern Christian Leadership Conference. The most prominent women in SCLC, Ella Baker and Septima Clark, complained that King expected deference and fawning admiration and did not take women seriously. Both women worked closely with King and held mid-level management posts in SCLC, and both criticized the organization's "male chauvinism." King kept Baker at "arm's length." She never pierced the "inner circle" of King "confidantes." And when the job of executive director opened at SCLC, King never seriously considered her for the job.

Baker's experiences, in particular, dovetailed with Motley's. Before coming to SCLC, Baker had worked as national director of branches at the NAACP; there, too, she had been sidelined and passed over for promotion despite her considerable expertise and vital field work for the organization. Motley believed that she, like Baker and Clark, had encountered an insurmountable career roadblock: the assumption that womanhood and leadership were incompatible.[30]

Women's exclusion from leadership roles occurred even in groups nominally committed to egalitarian and communal forms of governance, as well as in staid ones such as the NAACP. Three years after Marshall passed Motley over for the position of Inc. Fund director-counsel, four women in the Student Nonviolent Coordinating Committee (SNCC)—the premier student group whose radicalism had spawned the nickname the "new abolitionists"—famously wrote a manifesto criticizing "male domination" at SNCC. It critiqued "widespread" and "deep-rooted" "male superiority" in the organization. "Consider why it is in SNCC," the authors wrote, "that women who are competent, qualified, and experienced, are automatically assigned to the 'female' kinds of jobs such as typing, desk work, telephone work, filing, library work, cooking, and the assistant kind of administrative work but rarely the 'executive' kind."[31]

Even when individual men believed in the principle of equal opportunity, social norms and traditional gender roles shaped women's opportunities and conspired to limit their professional prospects. Betty Friedan's 1963 book *The Feminine Mystique* identified the cultural and social roots of women's oppression. This "bible" of the women's liberation movement cited societal expectations that middle-class women should shake off professional hopes to seek fulfillment in the home as a major cause of educated women's discontent. While many Black women did work, prevailing gender norms still constrained their opportunities.[32]

Within this cultural context, it would be utterly unsurprising if gender colored Marshall's decision making. Nor is it surprising to find that gender influenced Motley's perceptions of Marshall and his decision-making process. After all, Marshall appointed his successor years before the advent of second-wave feminism had raised consciousness about women's right to equality in society, the workplace, and the home. During Motley's many years at the Inc. Fund, it is inconceivable that sex and gender had not shaped her working life—and in fact, they clearly did. From her very first interview with Marshall, which allegedly included allusions to her sexual attractiveness, through her battle with him over equal pay, and on through her pregnancy, which coincided with the Inc. Fund's preparations for *Brown v. Board of Education*, Motley's on-the-job experiences were profoundly shaped by gender.

Still, it is impossible to state with certainty that Marshall denied Motley the promotion *because of* her sex. The evidence in support of that view—Motley's statements about the promotion and circumstantial evidence that Marshall excluded her from the inner circle, coupled with plausible but unconvincing explanations for Greenberg's promotion—is merely suggestive. Gender more likely played an indirect role in Marshall's decision: Motley did not live up to the conventional, brash, masculine style of leadership. No woman could.[33]

Motley perceived Marshall's failure to support her promotion to lead counsel as a career setback that may indeed have had long-term consequences. Bill Coleman later speculated that the denial of the promotion might have cost her the greatest honor for which any lawyer can hope. "[I]t's highly possible if [Motley] had been head of the LDF, she may have ended up on the Supreme Court," Coleman conceded in hindsight, though the board of directors did not intend for Greenberg's success to undermine her. She had been *that* impressive. But at the time, Coleman "never thought of" how the decision would affect Motley's future prospects.[34]

*

"Marshall had more faults than one could shake a stick at," Motley wrote in a remembrance published just after his death in 1993, "but like other great men he had qualities which could only be described as noble."[35] That would be one of the few times that she offered a fuller and truer picture of the man. In the long run, her disappointment did not diminish her public and sincere adulation for Marshall, which persisted, seemingly unabated, well after 1961. She routinely gave him all credit for the victory of *Brown v. Board of Education* in her public remarks about the case: "Without Thurgood Marshall's legal ability and charisma, there would not have been a decision by the Supreme

Court in 1954 striking down segregated public education." "It was as if the gods were on his side." She also called Marshall "the voice of black America" and counted him at least as great as Dr. King.[36]

And Motley specifically acknowledged Marshall's role in the "advancement of women." In a 1991 *Yale Law Journal* tribute, which Motley penned after Marshall announced his retirement from the Supreme Court, she expressed her "personal debt to Thurgood Marshall." In 1946, he had aided her career "at a time when no one was hiring women lawyers." She was forever indebted to him for that opportunity.[37]

Motley's flawed mentor may have disappointed her, but the bond between the two remained strong. He had made her career. "If it had not been for Thurgood Marshall," she acknowledged, "no one would ever have heard of Constance Baker Motley."[38]

12

"That's Your Case": James Meredith and the Battle to Desegregate the University of Mississippi

It was 1964, and Nina Simone had just performed "Mississippi Goddam" at Carnegie Hall; the song became an anthem of the civil rights movement. A meditation on the mob violence and hard-core resistance that civil rights activists confronted in the most racially repressive of all states, the lyrics excoriated advocates of an incremental approach to Black freedom: "I don't trust you anymore / You keep on saying 'Go slow' / But that's just the trouble." The song lauded the courageous determination of those who stood up for "freedom now." Nina Simone's stark words captured the valleys and the peaks of activism in Mississippi, which had become notorious for an especially barbaric form of racism. Infamous the world over in 1955 for the brutal slaying of Emmett Till, a fourteen-year-old Black boy beaten, shot, and dumped naked in the Tallahatchie River for the "sin" of flirting with a white woman, the state symbolized racial violence and repression. A closed society with a populace that was largely poor, with little education, and known far and wide for its antipathy to Black lives, Mississippi was never going to take kindly to demands for racial change. Yet Constance Baker Motley sought precisely that in 1961.

*

"This man has got to be crazy!" Thurgood Marshall shouted to Motley in January 1961, not long before announcing his resignation from the Inc. Fund. "That's your case!" Marshall had descended upon Motley's office waving a letter from James Meredith. The missive contained such a preposterous idea that Marshall thought the writer must be out of his mind.

"I am submitting an application for admission to the University of Mississippi," Meredith wrote, and "I am anticipating encountering . . . difficulty with the various agencies here in the State." In view of the brewing trouble, Meredith requested Marshall's legal assistance. It was not only the contents of the letter but its matter-of-fact tone that convinced Marshall that Meredith must be "crazy," laboring under the delusion that he, or any Black man, could tear down the wall of segregation at Ole Miss. It had "long" been his ambition, Meredith claimed, on behalf of "my country," "my race," "my family," and "myself," to "break the monopoly on rights and privileges" held by Mississippi whites. The man fancied himself an envoy of God, sent to conquer segregation at the flagship university in the most racist state in the nation; he had a "Messianic complex." Despite Meredith's conceit and missionary zeal, Marshall believed he would be lucky to remain alive once whites caught wind of his plan.[1]

One of the Magnolia State's storied institutions, the University of Mississippi had been chartered in 1844 as a safe educational space for white sons of the South. With wealthy planters, slaveholding politicians, and future leaders of the Confederacy among its founders, the university consciously cultivated a distinct southern identity. Its nickname, Ole Miss, derived from the name given by slaves to the mistress of the plantation, "ol' miss." The school's mascot, the goateed, cane-toting "Colonel Reb," channeled a plantation owner, glorified the Old South, and romanticized the Lost Cause. A marble statue of a soldier—a memorial to 130 students killed during the Civil War—stood in the center of campus. Confederate flags dotted the grounds and white supremacy reigned: the university's southern identity turned on its whiteness—on excluding Black students. For 117 years, no Black American had matriculated to Ole Miss. That was until James Meredith, a man on a mission, came on the scene.[2]

Born to Moses and Roxie Meredith in Kosciusko, Mississippi, James Howard Meredith entered the world in 1933, during the throes of the Great Depression. He grew up on his father's farm, a patch of land located on the outskirts of his hometown, which was populated by no more than thirty-three hundred inhabitants. Under the tutelage of his father, one of the few Black landowners in town and a registered voter, Meredith developed a strong sense of self and an independent spirit, in spite of Jim Crow. He avoided many of the indignities of the caste system on the farm. Off it, he faced scarring encounters with racism.

One such traumatic moment occurred for fifteen-year-old Meredith on a southbound train from Detroit; as his train reached Memphis, the conductor demanded that Meredith and his brother move to the segregated car. Meredith "cried all the way home." The moral outrage engendered by that experience stayed with the young man, much as the indignity of changing to a Jim Crow railcar had riled a young Constance Baker. A good student with a curious mind, Meredith attended the segregated Attala County Training School. He graduated from a high school in St. Petersburg, Florida, where he had gone to live with a sister to gain a better education than he could find in Mississippi. In search of new surroundings and financial stability, Meredith then enlisted in the U.S. Air Force.[3]

Now nearing thirty, slender, religious, and patriotic, Meredith took great pride in his military service. The "soldier at heart" had served nine years, from 1951 to 1960. "Life was pretty good" in the military, he remembered. Assigned to racially integrated units, he lived for the very first time, he felt, without the scourge of racial oppression. The service also yielded a steady paycheck that rose with his promotions. And he saw the world. Meredith enjoyed an "amazing" three-year tour of duty in Japan, a country where he felt a great degree of personal freedom.[4]

In joining the Air Force and flourishing there, Meredith followed a well-worn path to social mobility and economic stability. In hopes of making something of themselves, members of America's poor and working class routinely joined the military. Service in the armed forces had also raised the political consciousness of many Black World War II enlistees who had fought against the Nazis in Europe, only to return to egregious violence and discrimination in the United States. Black veterans subjected to such abuse, angered by their mistreatment, demanded change by vaulting to the front lines of the nascent civil rights movement.[5]

For James Meredith, service in the newly integrated military deepened an already well-developed concern for race relations. He read about racial developments in the United States with passionate interest and vocally supported epochal changes such as the Supreme Court's decision in *Brown v. Board of Education* and the federally enforced desegregation of schools in Little Rock, Arkansas. His time in Japan set in motion a determined commitment to fight racism. There, he had experienced a personal freedom that he had never known, but desperately wanted, in his home state of Mississippi. Not long after he mustered out of the Air Force in 1960, Meredith wrote to the Inc. Fund proclaiming his desire to attend Ole Miss and fight a "war" against white supremacy. That was the letter that ended up in the hands of Thurgood Marshall and soon fell on the desk of Constance Baker Motley.[6]

After Marshall finished laughing about Meredith's proposal to sue Ole Miss for admission, he washed his hands of the case. Fresh off her victory in the University of Georgia case, Motley had demonstrated her ability to bring segregation to its knees. Marshall knew she had the smarts and courtroom skills to do the job; at the same time, he thought that in such a hard-fought case (if not at the Inc. Fund's office), her gender would be an advantage. A relative advantage, that is.

The fight to desegregate Ole Miss might get someone killed. But in the context of Mississippi's white supremacist yet chivalrous culture, as Marshall saw it, a Black woman would fare better than a Black man: any white supremacist, he opined, would scarcely think twice about murdering a Black man, but might hesitate to lynch a Black woman. The Black woman was a familiar presence to southern white men, Marshall insisted: all of them had been raised, after all, by "Black Mammies"—the stereotypical loyal nanny/housekeeper made famous by Hollywood films such as *Gone with the Wind* and *Birth of a Nation*. Given the white man's supposed soft spot for Black women, Marshall said, it was better for Motley to handle the Ole Miss case. Marshall made the claim in his usual teasing manner, but he evidently believed there was a truth nestled in his "joke."

Never mind that Marshall's "theory" perverted the truth in numerous ways. Motley, now an educated and elegant New Yorker, had little in common with the South's "Mammies." The Civil Rights Queen did not serve white men; she cross-examined them.

Marshall's "joke" also overlooked the rampant abuse—sexual and physical—that white male authority figures had visited upon Black women for hundreds of years. In fact, Motley had come in for her fair share of verbal abuse at the hands of white male Mississippians the last time Marshall had sent her to the Magnolia State to litigate a case. If her stories about being called everything but her rightful name had escaped Marshall, she could recall every last insult.[7]

But to give James Meredith the representation he needed, Motley once more left behind the comforts of her family life and well-appointed New York City apartment for the Deep South. Her son, now ten years old, would not see his mother for days at a time; she, no less than her client, was on a mission.

The Ole Miss case—*Meredith v. Fair* (so called after Charles Dickson Fair, the president of the Board of Trustees of State Institutions of Higher Learning in Mississippi)—was long, drawn out, and full of twists and turns. It would be a major turning point in the history of the civil rights movement—and it would boost Motley's career further still.[8]

*

Motley filed suit against Ole Miss on May 31, 1961. The action coincided with the unfolding of one of the most daring protests against Jim Crow to date: the Freedom Rides, a nationally electrifying event in which Motley also played a hand.[9]

Sponsored by the Congress of Racial Equality (CORE), the rides tested a U.S. Supreme Court ban on segregation in interstate transportation. To gauge compliance with the decision, an interracial group of activists traveled together by bus from Washington, D.C., through the Deep South. At designated stops along the way, Black riders supported by white allies attempted to use segregated facilities in bus and train terminals.

The Freedom Rides created excitement among civil rights activists, but segregationists viewed the protests as an appalling affront to their way of life. While the rides had proceeded without incident in

the Upper South, white mobs in Anniston, Birmingham, and Montgomery, Alabama, attacked activists with clubs, rocks, and pipes. For
the Kennedy administration, which continued to cultivate support
among African Americans without offending white southerners,
the rides were a hassle—a movement to be managed rather than encouraged. The president, battling fallout from the failed Bay of Pigs
invasion and keen to avoid confrontations with his southern white
supporters, wanted the rides "called off." President Kennedy feared
being drawn into a standoff over segregation and forced to provide
federal protection to the riders. That is exactly what happened.[10]

As the Freedom Riders approached Jackson, Mississippi, tensions
mounted. The prospect of dealing simultaneously with the riders and
a suit to desegregate Ole Miss infuriated white Mississippians and
irritated the Kennedy administration. Hoping to head off disaster,
Attorney General Robert F. Kennedy brokered a deal with officials:
if the state could ensure the riders safe passage to the state capitol,
the administration would not grumble if police arrested the riders for taking part in the protest. Thus on May 24, 1961, just a few
days before Motley headed into court to overturn segregation at Ole
Miss, hundreds of Freedom Riders passed into the state, attempted
to use a whites-only restroom at a bus terminal, and were promptly
arrested for breach of peace. For the next thirty-nine days, many of
the riders would remain locked away in a jail in Jackson, where some
began a hunger strike to protest their arrests. Enter Constance Baker
Motley.[11]

On behalf of the state NAACP, Motley sued the state of Mississippi
for continuing to enforce segregation laws in transportation that the
U.S. Supreme Court had long before ruled unlawful. She won hand-
ily, while waging a double-barreled attack. Both of the lawsuits she
handled—one on behalf of the Freedom Riders and the other against
Ole Miss—made the Civil Rights Queen an unwelcome, not to say
detested, presence in the Magnolia State.[12]

"Why did you have to come now?" Judge Sidney Mize of the U.S.
District Court asked Motley on May 31, 1961, as she arrived at the
federal courthouse in Meridian to file suit. Mize did not hide his displeasure at seeing the rabble-rousing lawyer in his courtroom. The

judge's query marked an ominous beginning to the most audacious case of Motley's career.[13]

"I don't choose my cases or my clients," Motley parried wryly. This was only partly true. She did not let on that Thurgood Marshall had misgivings about representing James Meredith. Nor would she admit a fact widely known at the Inc. Fund: the organization had been reluctant to engage Mississippi in a fight over segregation. Resistance would be greatest in this state infamous for its vicious brand of racism and violent opposition to change. Another unacknowledged yet critically important detail animated the March 31 conversation between Motley and Mize: they had a history.[14]

Mize and Motley first tangled in 1949. Mize could hardly forget Motley: the person now standing before him was the same lawyer— the same Black woman—who in *Bates v. Batte* had accused the state of discrimination against Black teachers. Motley recalled Mize with a contempt for his segregationist beliefs that rivaled his disdain for her courtroom activism. Moreover, she could never forget how Mize had insulted her in open court. Over and over again, Judge Mize had refused to call the lawyer "*Mrs.* Motley." The indignity of the experience was etched in her mind. Thanks to Mize, Motley had lost in her very first trial, and her client was forced out of town. For feats such as these, the judge who presided over one of the South's most "unreconstructed" courtrooms had gained a reputation as an "accomplice" of the white resistance to the Black freedom struggle.[15]

Judge Mize's beliefs sprang from his upbringing. Born in rural Scott County in 1888, he had been taught to believe that genetically fixed differences made Blacks inferior to whites. Mixing injured both races, he claimed. His racial worldview—the same ideology that James Meredith's father had taught his son to defy—facilitated his professional ascent as a young lawyer. Mize had graduated first in his class from the Mississippi College School of Law, practiced in Gulfport for several years, and then worked in state government as a district attorney and a county judge. He acquired a fine reputation; colleagues and neighbors viewed him as a man of learning and character. Over time, he made connections with powerful men, including James Eastland, U.S. senator from Mississippi, whom he counted as a close friend.

An ally of southern Democrats and segregationists and well versed
in the region's racial norms, Mize was chosen for a prized lifetime
judicial appointment in 1937. A man of the nineteenth century, Judge
Mize would have to deal with the twentieth's most pressing social
problems.[16]

Mize was not the only defender of white supremacy that Motley
would have to face in the coming trial. Dugas Shands, Esq., proudly
safeguarded segregation, a system in which he manifestly believed,
and defended Ole Miss during the Meredith case. In fact, in his capacity as head of the so-called civil rights division of the state attorney
general's office, Shands represented Mississippi in the vast majority
of cases filed against it by advocates for Black freedom—including
the Freedom Riders case, where he also opposed Constance Baker
Motley.[17]

Shands defended an institution that he and his family knew well.
His grandfather and namesake, G. Dugas Shands, was a Civil War
veteran and had taught at Ole Miss's law school and served as its
first dean. Shands's father, Audley Shands, followed his father to the
School of Law; after graduation, he became a well-known member
of the bar and twice served as vice president of the state bar association. Dugas Shands followed in the footsteps of his father and,
more tellingly, of his grandfather, who liked to refer to the Civil War
as the "War of Northern Aggression." The youngest Shands had also
received his law degree from Ole Miss and had served as a founding editor of the *Mississippi Law Journal*. At the start of his career, he
had worked in the family firm; he later became a government lawyer, and in that sector established his own professional identity. He
had served as city attorney for Jackson, had represented its public
schools, and had worked briefly for Senator Eastland on the Senate
Judiciary Committee.[18]

Shands worked longest—eighteen years—for the state attorney
general's office, during which time he earned plaudits from locals.
He could be counted on, one columnist noted, as a "veteran defender
of the southern way of life." Whites knew that by reputation and association he "stood between" Mississippi and integration. He was a
member of the White Citizens' Council—a network of men committed to preserving segregation through legal obstruction, social and

economic intimidation, and violence. The organization was born in the wake of *Brown v. Board of Education*. Upper- and middle-class citizens populated the group, distinguishing the Council from the Klan, which was the domain primarily of working-class ruffians. Motley's opponent was thus a staunch and well-known racist.[19]

Shands performed his job with skill and dramatic flair. No mere states' righter, he exhibited personal bigotry throughout his courtroom battles. The tall, thin, white-haired, slow-speaking fifty-five-year-old man made a show of his racial hatred. The very idea of a Black woman lawyer violently clashed with his racial worldview. At first he ignored Motley altogether. But this strategy could not succeed. Shands had to accept Motley's personhood in the context of the trial. His second way of trying to consign her to a subordinate position, where he believed all Blacks belonged, worked better. He refused to address the Inc. Fund lawyer in the customary manner as "Mrs. Motley." Instead, he used only indirect references, calling Motley "her" or "she."[20]

At one point early on, Motley jumped to her feet in a bid to put an end to the charade. But the tipping point occurred when Shands called her "Constance." Motley immediately objected. "I would like for Mr. Shands *not* to call me by my first name," she insisted. Judge Mize had his own troubles with language when managing trials with Black lawyers, but he did maintain a modicum of professionalism, and cautioned Shands. Henceforth, the lawyer referred to Motley as the "New York counsel." Although an improvement over the alternatives, this regional reference revealed Shands's ongoing contempt not just for Motley but equally for all the "northern aggression" that she represented. He continued to call Motley's local co-counsel, Jesse Brown, one of the few Black lawyers in Mississippi, "Jesse."[21]

Motley found Shands's racism bewildering. A proud woman taught not to dwell on racism and the limitations it might impose upon her, the Inc. Fund lawyer found it difficult to accept that Shands perceived all Blacks—including her—as innately inferior. "Having been born and raised in Connecticut," she had not encountered "that kind of hostility" before. So profound were his white supremacist convictions that Shands refused to shake hands with Blacks. Motley became aware of this particular rule during an airport encounter with the lawyer, when she had "gone over and extended" her hand, but "it stayed out there," the gesture unreturned. Evidently, Shands feared contagion. How could an educated man, even one from the Deep South, hold such unscientific and irrational views, Motley wondered. And how could Shands not appreciate that her achievements disproved his belief that Blacks constituted "an inferior species of human being"? "Even if you had gone to Columbia Law School and had a college degree," Motley mused, Shands still believed in your inferiority. Years later, she still had not "ceased to be amazed" that the lawyer "honestly believed that I was an inferior person."[22]

Once in court, Shands and other lawyers from the Mississippi attorney general's office sought to defeat Meredith's claim through delay and obstruction. This was the one play that was available to the state. Even the most optimistic segregationist could recognize that in the long run the state would not prevail on the merits of the case, thanks to Motley's past litigation and victories in several high-profile cases that made the underlying law perfectly clear. A state could not exclude a student from a public institution of higher education on account of race. The legal battle in *Meredith v. Fair* thus turned on the state's denial that race could explain why Ole Miss had rejected Meredith.

Shands, with Judge Mize's help, relied on delay as a first line of defense, and for months that tactic worked remarkably well. In early June 1961, the initial false start occurred. Supposedly because of the judge's busy calendar, Mize delayed further proceedings in the case until July 10, which ensured that Meredith could not enter Ole Miss during the summer term, as he had hoped.[23]

Then on July 10, with the hearings set to continue, the attorney general's office requested another delay in proceedings. Dugas Shands had taken ill, and the ailment of the state's star attorney justified another postponement. Motley objected, calling the state's request for additional time nothing more than a ruse. Shands could be replaced, she argued; surely other lawyers in the office could handle the case. In fact, she quipped, given the many similar cases that had preceded Meredith's suit and the limited defenses available to the state, "a first-year law student" could replace the ill attorney. Moreover, if the judge countenanced postponement of the hearings until

Shands regained his health, the case could be delayed indefinitely. The court should not tolerate foot dragging, Motley argued, when a man's constitutional rights hung in the balance. "We have to press our case. We can't sit back and say, 'well anytime you get ready to hear it' is fine with us," she contested.[24]

Unconvinced, the judge granted the state's request to postpone the hearings, this time until August 10. Mize expressed sympathy for Shands; the numerous civil rights cases he had handled for Mississippi had evidently caused his blood pressure to rise. Motley and Meredith would have to await his recovery from an illness that they—litigious rabble-rousers—had probably caused, the judge implied. If the case continued, it would "endanger the life" of the state's leading counsel. Going further, Judge Mize rejected Motley's requests to take the testimony of the registrar at Ole Miss. He also partly rejected her request to review records of applicants both denied and accepted to the university during the period when Meredith had applied. Motley had hoped to defeat Ole Miss by exposing inconsistencies between the registrar's testimony and evidence culled from the records, just as she had done when representing Holmes and Hunter against the University of Georgia. But Judge Mize limited her review. The court had stopped Motley in her tracks, at least for the time being.

Not at all surprised that she had gotten nowhere in Judge Mize's courtroom, Motley—known for her persistence as well as for her acumen—resigned herself to a prolonged battle and several visits to the court of appeals, a bench composed of judges more sympathetic to the cause of civil rights.[25]

Once court reconvened in August 1961, Motley finally subjected the single most important witness, Robert Ellis, the registrar of the University of Mississippi for more than a decade, to one of her withering examinations. Testy and defensive under questioning, Ellis attempted to justify his claim that from the very first glance, Meredith's application did not pass muster. It was a "problem application," incomplete and unacceptable. Meredith's race did not give rise to the problem, Ellis insisted; his color had absolutely no impact on the admission decision.[26]

The registrar claimed he had rejected Meredith's application for two perfectly legitimate reasons. First, the historically Black college from which Meredith sought transfer had not attained the proper accreditation. The other sticking point was that no University of Mississippi alumni had endorsed Meredith's candidacy. He had not secured the five letters of recommendation from alumni that Ole Miss required of applicants. In a cover letter to Ellis, Meredith had written, "I will not be able to furnish the . . . alumni letters because I am a negro and all your graduates are white." His explanation exposed Ellis's hypocrisy. If no white alumnus could be expected to support a Black man's admission to Ole Miss, it was precisely because of his race that Meredith could never meet the requirement. Moreover, under further questioning from Motley, Ellis conceded that many white applicants had gained acceptance without submitting alumni letters. She had uncovered critical evidence that James Meredith *had* been treated differently because of race.[27]

Despite Motley's arguments and the evidence to the contrary, Mize found "as a fact" that Ole Miss had not discriminated against any student, and "particularly not" against James Meredith. Therefore, the main contention of Motley's complaint had "utterly failed." Mize ruled that he was persuaded that Meredith had been refused admission because he had not turned in a complete application. He had not even tried to obtain the letters, even after Ellis had supplied him with a list of (white) local alumni.

The judge denied Motley's motion for a temporary injunction that, pending trial, would have stopped the university from excluding Meredith. But Mize, as a trial judge, did not have the last word in the matter; Motley appealed to a higher court.[28]

*

After hearing arguments from Motley and Shands, the U.S. Court of Appeals for the Fifth Circuit issued a critical ruling in the case. Judge Minor Wisdom—a white man born and raised in the segregated South who became an "unlikely hero" after issuing ruling after ruling that undermined Jim Crow—wrote the January 12, 1962, opinion that categorically rejected the version of facts offered by the registrar and accepted by Judge Mize. The Magnolia State had insisted that Meredith's application had not been denied on account of race because the state had no such policy: the state did not mandate Jim Crow at its institutions of higher education. Ellis had taken the point still further, claiming that Motley, who had not researched the genealogical records of all Ole Miss graduates, could not prove that there had never been a Negro graduate of Ole Miss.

Alluding to *Peter Pan*, the appellate court called the state's version of the facts "never never land" claims, myths invented solely for purposes of litigation. In reality, Mississippi did practice Jim Crow and vigilantly patrolled racial boundaries in every facet of life—in schools, parks, playgrounds, and on transportation, among other places where Blacks were kept separate from whites. This was a "plain fact known to everyone."[29]

The defects in Meredith's application—the prerequisites that Mize concluded had "nothing in the world" to do with race—had to be viewed in light of the state's racial caste system. For Blacks who had been denied access to the university since the beginning of its history, the alumni recommendation requirement amounted to an insurmountable burden. "The traditional social barriers" made it most unlikely, if not impossible, "for a Negro to approach alumni with a request for such a recommendation," the court concluded. Moreover, the court took note that the requirement had been invented only a few months after the U.S. Supreme Court had decided *Brown v. Board of Education*. The alumni recommendation requirement, innocuous on its face, posed little difficulty for white applicants and violated the equal protection of the laws when imposed upon Blacks. The court also noted that Jackson State, the historically Black college from which Meredith sought to transfer credits, had indeed achieved the proper accreditation. Therefore, the university could no longer refuse Meredith on that basis. Repeating a dynamic from the case against the University of Georgia, the appeals court sided with Constance Baker Motley and her client at a critical juncture.[30]

But Motley had not achieved complete victory with this ruling. Because of the "muddy" trial court record, the appeals court had settled only a few issues in the case. To be sure, Judge Mize had been rebuked on a central question—whether Ole Miss practiced segregation. But the other critical question of whether Ole Miss had a good reason for denying Meredith's entry had not been answered during the initial proceedings. So, despite recognizing that the university could not reject Meredith's application on the basis of his failure to produce recommendations from alumni, the appeals court let stand Mize's decision refusing to require Ole Miss to admit Meredith. Another trial would have to take place in Judge Mize's courtroom, during which he would need to determine whether or not Ole Miss had in fact turned Meredith away for legitimate, nondiscriminatory reasons.

Motley and Meredith could only hope that Mize would follow the higher court's directive: to hold a trial as soon as possible on that question, giving Meredith a "fair, unfettered and un-harassed opportunity to prove his case." He should not have to take "roads through the woods" and "follow winding trails through sharp thickets" to attain an education, the appeals court wrote. But that was merely wishful thinking.[31]

During the next round of litigation, a ten-day period in mid-January 1962, punctuated by yet more delays at the state's behest, Judge Mize took another trip to "never never land." Deprived of relevant university records, in a courtroom filled with spectators, virtually all Black, Motley questioned eleven individuals—members of the Board of Trustees of State Institutions of Higher Learning, Ole Miss deans, and other administrators—about the role of race in admissions. With one exception, the witnesses testified that race played no role whatsoever in their decision making.

"I do not think of students in regard to race," said an admissions committee member. The head of personnel argued that race could not be a factor in decisions because the committee's discussions did not include a study of the applicants' "genealogical background." Moreover, he noted, "We have students whose appearances run a wide range of color and physical characteristics." When Motley asked Trustee Tally Riddell whether he had ever seen Negroes on campus, Riddell claimed not to know what a "Negro" was. "Tell me what you mean by Negro and I'll try to answer." Riddell simultaneously insisted that he had seen people "darker than" Motley herself roaming the Ole Miss campus. Meanwhile, the judge disregarded as immaterial the testimony of the one witness who conceded that racial "gossip" had crept into a conversation about a Black applicant to the law school. But if the sworn testimony of these upstanding Mississippians was to be believed, officials never even thought about applicants' race—and certainly did not enforce a segregationist admissions policy.[32]

Even as the state's witnesses peddled their myth that race neither defined nor limited social relations at Ole Miss, the state's customary, racist social norms were on vivid display in the courtroom. A fifty-foot-wide mural depicting the plantation South, complete with Blacks picking cotton, loomed large over the proceedings. Dugas Shands, a man of advanced age and ill health, continued his campaign of disrespect toward his opposing counsel, still refusing to call Motley by her name. As one reporter noted, Shands "could hardly restrain his seething racial contempt for the tall, stately Black woman attorney who dared to oppose him." Edwin Cates, another Mississippi attorney general, repeatedly made what sounded like racial slurs: he pronounced "Negro" as "Nigguh," explaining that he had spoken that way "all his life."[33]

Meanwhile, James Meredith's actions, personality, and character became focal points after the court entered into evidence his August 1961 testimony about his application to Ole Miss. Motley had asked Meredith to read from the series of letters he had written to Ole Miss's registrar, Robert Ellis, and those he had received in return. In one letter, Meredith had revealed that he was not a typical applicant. "I am an American-Mississippi-Negro," Meredith had written; he expressed hope that his application "would be handled in a manner that will be complimentary to the state and to the University of Mississippi."

In response, Ellis, who had expressed his delight that Meredith wished to join the student body only a week earlier, now sent him a telegram that ground the admissions process to a halt. As it turned out, Ellis's telegram claimed, Meredith's application had been filed too late and could no longer be considered. For months Ellis did not respond to Meredith's subsequent correspondence requesting consideration during later semesters. He eventually wrote to inform Meredith that he had been denied admission. Meredith's long effort to become the first Black man to attend Ole Miss had thus begun with Ellis's swift about-face—evidence of the university's whites-only admission policy, as Motley had argued earlier and now reiterated.[34]

Shands, during a blistering cross-examination, which Meredith later called "the Nigger Treatment," had in the previous trial painted the plaintiff as an academically unprepared, untrustworthy neurotic driven by bad motives. He now rehashed his invective and recast his aspersions on the character of Meredith—a soldier to whom the U.S. Air Force had awarded a Good Conduct Medal. Referring again and again to "James" rather than "Mr. Meredith," Shands lambasted the motives of the twenty-nine-year-old, honorably discharged veteran.

The "Nigra's" problem was not race, howled Shands, but character. Shands accused "James" of lying about his residence during the voter registration process, of lying to individuals who had endorsed his application to Ole Miss, and of lying about his motives for applying. A "troublemaker," "James" had not applied to Ole Miss out of a genuine interest in pursuing an education. Rather, "James" wanted "special treatment" and desired "to make trouble simply because he is Negro." Meredith—defiant and mercurial, according to Shands—had sought to antagonize the state of Mississippi and had filed his application in "bad faith," just as Robert Ellis, the Ole Miss registrar, had claimed. To hammer home the point, the state introduced Meredith's Air Force medical records; the documents proved, Shands argued, that Meredith had no credibility, but rather an "unstable" and "nervous temperament" and a desire to "fight authority."[35]

During the initial proceedings, Motley had vigorously objected to the state's efforts to malign her client's character, and she reiterated her objections now. She decried the state's attempt to "entrap" her client, Shands's implication that Meredith had "something to hide," and Shands's haranguing tone. She also objected, for one simple reason, to the so-called evidence contained in Meredith's Air Force medical records. Ole Miss could not cite the Air Force reports to justify Meredith's exclusion because the state had only recently acquired the information. The registrar had not had access to the records when he had rejected Meredith; the state could not therefore months later cite the records to explain its rejection of his application. As for the state's attempt to label her client a "troublemaker," Motley retorted that "any Negro who seeks admission to any white school in the South was a troublemaker" because he flouted Jim Crow.[36]

Turning the court's attention to the law, Motley marshaled evidence to show that Mississippi had in fact mandated segregation at its institutions of higher education and that, moreover, after *Brown v. Board of Education*, the state legislature had enacted a statute mandating that the state resist desegregation. Mize dismissed the statute as insignificant, claiming the state had undertaken to maintain segregation through "legitimate," as opposed to illegal, means.[37]

When Judge Mize issued his February 3, 1962, decision on the merits of Meredith's claim, the outcome had long been inevitable. Mize's mind was not going to change, and for the second time in less than a year, the judge concluded that Ole Miss had done nothing wrong. The evidence "overwhelmingly showed" that Meredith had not been subjected to racial discrimination. "The proof in the instant case on this hearing fails to show that the application of any Negro or Chinaman or anyone of any other race has been rejected because of his race or color." Motley had "failed entirely" to prove her case, wrote Mize. And, yet again, Motley appealed.[38]

On June 25, 1962—"Judgment Day in Mississippi"—the U.S. Court of Appeals for the Fifth Circuit, in its second go-round on *Meredith v. Fair*, finally gave Motley and Meredith the victory they had sought for over a year. By a vote of two to one, the appeals court concluded that Ole Miss had in fact discriminated against James Meredith solely on account of race.

The record, Judge Minor Wisdom wrote, "leads the Court inescapably to the conclusion that from the moment the defendants discovered Meredith was a Negro they engaged in a carefully calculated campaign of delay, harassment, and masterly inactivity," all designed "to discourage and to defeat" him. The court mocked the "troublemaker" label that Ole Miss had cited as a nondiscriminatory rationale for denying Meredith's application. The state's objection to Meredith on grounds of his "defiant" personality amounted to nothing more than an aversion to "just the type of Negro who might be expected to try to crack the racial barrier at the University of Mississippi: a man with a mission and with a nervous stomach." The state's "Fabian" tactics—its war of attrition against Meredith—had finally failed. The court ruled that Ole Miss's tacit policy of excluding Blacks violated equal protection under the law, and ordered the all-white university to admit Meredith at the start of the fall semester.[39]

13

"I Am Human After All": Trauma and Hardship in the Long Battle at Ole Miss

Whether despite, or because of, this astounding court victory, an additional setback in the case nearly broke James Meredith's will to fight. In a desperate, last-ditch series of legal maneuvers, Ben F. Cameron—an ardent segregationist, a friend of Dugas Shands—who could not accept that Motley ("she") had bested him in court—and a U.S. Court of Appeals judge who had not even participated in the proceedings—tried to "stay" his colleagues' desegregation order.

Around the same time, in June of 1962, a Mississippi attorney general filed frivolous voter fraud charges against Meredith. This, along with the open defiance of the appeals court's favorable decision by one of its own members, was unprecedented. Motley had to think and act quickly to save Meredith from arrest for "fraud." She urgently turned to the court of appeals, which enjoined Mississippi's transparent attempt to create a new basis for foiling Meredith's matriculation to Ole Miss. But the process of beating back Judge Cameron's efforts to frustrate the mandate of his colleagues would take a lot longer and require more court maneuvering.[1]

After months of struggle and endless delays, Meredith had had enough. Browbeaten by these ominous displays of white resistance, he wrote to Motley, resigned. He wanted to give up on his bid to enter Ole Miss. "I will not attempt to obtain an undergraduate degree from the University of Mississippi," the letter proclaimed. Keenly aware that Motley, who had poured herself into the case, would be disappointed in his decision, Meredith pleaded for understanding. "I am human after all," he wrote.

Meredith had grown tired of waiting for a deliverance that never came. Life had passed him by; his peers had graduated from college, begun careers, and moved on with their lives. Instead of getting his degree from Jackson State—he was only six credits short of completing all his requirements—Meredith was still waiting for Ole Miss to accept him. In the meantime, he and his family had endured a high cost, literally and figuratively, fighting to integrate the University of Mississippi, whose gatekeepers wanted neither him nor his kind. "[M]y family is giving up much more in this fight than I am," he said. "I am never able to forget," he wrote, "that my wife could have had her a twenty- or thirty-thousand-dollar home" and other "luxuries" by now "had I not decided to come to Mississippi to fight white folk." In sum, he said, the battle had been "hell." Like any soldier, he needed "rest" before continuing the fight.[2]

Motley was stunned by this message. For years, from well before he had contacted the Inc. Fund, Meredith had planned to break the racial barrier at Ole Miss. He considered himself a "Chosen One"—someone in the same league as the Reverend Martin Luther King Jr. He believed his fight to integrate Ole Miss was an assignment ordained by God Almighty. But now that he had reached the threshold of victory, he was flailing, bereft, and adrift.[3]

In order to salvage her case and support her client, Motley morphed from lawyer to counselor, a role she often played in high-stakes civil rights cases. To get a handle on the fraught situation, she first removed her client from the site of his pain and suffering. She called Meredith and summoned him to New York. Instead of discussing the matter while surrounded by hostile whites and in the middle of a muggy southern summer, the pair would talk in Motley's New York City apartment, where Meredith could taste freedom. She hoped the change of environment would help the young man look into the new future he had imagined.[4]

Talking with him in her own living room, Motley—a no-nonsense person, a woman of action, and a steely lawyer with no time for handwringing—cajoled Meredith. She persuaded him, she later wrote, that "he had gone too far and that too much had been invested in the case" by the Inc. Fund and the federal appeals court to "abandon" the litigation.[5]

Motley's pleading and coaxing anticipated the refrain of a song published two years later—a ballad of hope and frustration that told the story of Black freedom fighters and became an anthem of the civil rights movement. The song was released in 1964 by the recording artist Sam Cooke, a Mississippi native, a few months after he was turned away from a hotel in Shreveport, Louisiana, because of his race, and then arrested for disturbing the peace after he objected to the mistreatment. The ballad articulated the injustices that Blacks—activists and everyday people alike—regularly encountered. One line in particular—"It's been too hard living / But I'm afraid to die"—spoke to the constant stress and the "real threat of death" that hung over Meredith's case. Despite such heartaches, the song promised a positive resolution to the long movement's travails in the future. "A Change Is Gonna Come," the title indicated. In New York that summer, a battle-hardened Motley sang a sweetly similar tune into Meredith's ear.[6]

Just as Meredith reached his breaking point, support arrived, precisely as Motley had promised. On September 10, 1962, U.S. Supreme Court justice Hugo Black intervened in the drama playing out in the court of appeals: together with other justices, Black voided the rogue orders of Judge Cameron. Justice Black had been born in a small Alabama town in 1886 to a father who had served as a Confederate soldier and had been a onetime member of the Ku Klux Klan. Yet after President Franklin Roosevelt appointed him to the Supreme Court, Black distinguished himself as a staunch proponent of civil liberties and civil rights. An outspoken advocate of the decision to strike down state-mandated school segregation in *Brown v. Board of Education*, he played a critical role ending Jim Crow in higher education.

Just nine days before the beginning of fall classes, Black halted any further action preventing James Meredith's matriculation to Ole Miss. At long last, the soldier was going to be able to enroll at the university, and the long-sought transformation in Mississippi's race relations appeared to be on the horizon. Motley summed up where things stood after Justice Black intervened: "This is the end of the road."[7]

*

Like so many among the state's elite and political class, Mississippi's governor, Ross Barnett, was the son of a Civil War veteran, an Ole Miss law school graduate, and a plaintiffs'-side lawyer known for his folksy style. Barnett had won the race for governor on his third try by pledging to fight integration. And during the fight over James Meredith's admission, he made good on his promise. A day after Justice Black issued the Court's final desegregation mandate, Barnett vowed to defy it.[8]

Meredith's struggle was already into its seventeenth month, and still not over. He now had to make his way onto campus and into the classroom of Ole Miss against the wishes of a powerful coalition of politicians, as well as run-of-the-mill racists, who held tight in every corner of the state. A violent and fanatical white resistance, drummed up by Governor Barnett, redoubled efforts to maintain white supremacy at the university, and a terrifying drama unfolded a mere week before the start of Meredith's first semester, on September 19, 1962.

Repurposing the states' rights arguments his forebears had invoked to preserve slavery, Barnett insisted that the federal government had no authority to disrupt Mississippi's policies and practices. Justice Black's order was "illegal"—null and void—the lawyer turned governor proclaimed. Pursuant to the U.S. Constitution's Tenth Amendment, Mississippi could control its schools free of federal interference. The governor would rather close Ole Miss than let Meredith defile the institution's racial integrity.[9]

It did not matter to the governor that the U.S. Supreme Court had repeatedly rejected his view of federal-state relations. The Court had repudiated his position in *Brown v. Board of Education*, which banned state-mandated school segregation. It had asserted federal supremacy in *Cooper v. Aaron*, its 1958 landmark decision ordering desegregation of the Little Rock schools in the face of state officials' refusal to implement a federal court order. And in *Hawkins v. Florida*, the Court had required desegregation of a taxpayer-supported law school, notwithstanding resistance by a federal judge.

Nonetheless, to Barnett and his many acolytes, local social norms, as enshrined in state law long before *Brown*, trumped the federal court's interpretation of the Constitution. According to the long-

discredited idea of "interposition and nullification," states retained
sovereignty under the Tenth Amendment to the U.S. Constitution,
which reads, the "powers not delegated to the United States" nor
"prohibited by it to the States" are "reserved to the States respectively, or to the people." Invoking antebellum arguments, Barnett and
like-minded racial demagogues argued that the Tenth Amendment
conferred power on the states to block enforcement of disfavored
federal laws.[10]

On September 13, in a twenty-minute speech televised and aired
on the radio across the state, the governor repeated his pledge to
block Meredith's matriculation. The "day of reckoning is upon us,"
Barnett proclaimed, and it was time to stand up for the rights of
white Mississippians. Despite the court orders, "No school in our
state will be integrated while I am governor." He would make any
and every "sacrifice" to "preserve the racial integrity of our people
and our institutions." "We will not drink from the cup of genocide,"
he said. Barnett also promised to protect southern "patriots" who
stood with him and against the federal government. Those patriots
included civic insiders who supported Barnett's pro-segregation
stance—state legislators, all but one of the congressional delegation,
journalists, educators, and members of the White Citizens' Coun-
cils. Ole Miss students hailed the governor's rhetoric and, in a show
of support, burned an effigy of James Meredith. The Ku Klux Klan
and other white supremacists converged in Oxford to stand with the
governor in a fight to preserve white racial integrity. In the face of the
hysteria whipped up by Barnett, a few dissenters called for calm, if
not for integration.[11]

Reluctantly, President John F. Kennedy entered the fray. Justice
Black had pulled the government into the case in early September;
at his behest, the administration confirmed that it would enforce the
desegregation order. In response to the Department of Justice filing,
Mississippi's attorney general quipped that the "House of Kennedy
is wholly incapable of resisting pressure from the NAACP and other
radical groups." But civil rights groups took a decidedly different view
of the administration: its reluctance one year earlier to protect the
Freedom Riders disappointed activists and "erased" what one bi-

ographer called the "aura" of "infallibility" that had surrounded the Kennedys. Now, a year and a half later, the administration had a second chance: it could at once advance the national interest and prove its commitment to civil rights by ensuring that Ole Miss admit James Meredith.[12]

U.S. Attorney General Robert F. Kennedy at first took a conciliatory approach. He sought to coax Ross Barnett into compliance. The Kennedys' political fortunes hung in the balance. They could "kiss Mississippi and the Deep South goodbye," as the head of the state Democratic Party had said, if the federal government forced Ole Miss to desegregate. Hoping to work out a "compromise," one that would both permit Meredith to enter the university and Governor Barnett to save face, the attorney general engaged Mississippi's governor in diplomacy by phone.

The series of calls in which the Kennedys attempted to negotiate compliance took place the weekend following Black's issuance of the court mandate to desegregate. Robert Kennedy concocted a plan that would allow Mississippi to continue stonewalling Meredith. When Meredith appeared at the university to register for classes the following Thursday, Ole Miss would refuse him. The administration would then return to federal court seeking an order to secure Meredith's registration; the unfolding court process could last up to a year. Barnett agreed to the face-saving plan. However, just days after his initial phone conversation with Kennedy, he asked to postpone the staged registration effort. In the interim, the state legislature had urged Barnett to continue to defy the federal government. Given the state's changing positions and a divided board of trustees at the university, no one, including Bobby Kennedy, knew what would come to pass when James Meredith actually showed up to register for classes.[13]

Meredith arrived at the University of Mississippi to register at 3:15 p.m. on September 21, accompanied by law enforcement personnel. He rode with three U.S. marshals, and the commissioner of public safety drove the lead car in the caravan. Many more cars preceded and trailed the vehicle in which Meredith and the marshals sat. Some one thousand people, mostly students, had gathered in anticipation of Meredith's arrival, to scorn their would-be classmate. The mass of white faces jeered, hissed, and cursed Meredith—a slight, brown-skinned, bespectacled man of five feet six inches and 135 pounds—as he emerged from the vehicle. "Nigger, nigger, nigger," the students chanted. Rebel yells echoed through the air. Meredith did not flinch. He remained poised and resolute, and appeared emotionally detached in the face of the crowd's hostility. As state troopers ringed the campus building, a patrolman and an attorney from the U.S. Department of Justice, John Doar, accompanied Meredith inside.[14]

Governor Ross Barnett awaited Meredith in a grandstanding show of defiance. The state's chief executive had personally assumed the duties of the university's registrar. When the young man made his request to register, the governor-registrar refused. He proclaimed Ole Miss a whites-only institution and turned Meredith away. Barnett then marched outside and made a triumphant announcement to the gathered throng: "James Meredith has been denied admission" to the University of Mississippi. The crowd roared. Barnett emerged as the savior of white supremacy.[15]

The week following the first attempt to register, Meredith tried twice more to enroll at Ole Miss; each time, Barnett or his lieutenant governor personally blocked Meredith's entry, eliciting uproarious approval from the gathered whites. The effort to desegregate Ole Miss had morphed into a full-fledged standoff between the federal government and the recalcitrant governor of the nation's most racist state—a place that led the nation in the lynching of Black bodies. Barnett had the full backing of the people of Mississippi and the state legislature, where leaders proclaimed the governor a "brilliant" statesman. In other southern states, whites met Barnett's racial fanaticism with open arms, welcoming a national crisis.[16]

In a series of legal maneuvers, Barnett first attained a state court order banning Meredith's enrollment at Ole Miss, and issued an executive order mandating the arrest of anyone who sought to impede state officials' enforcement of state law. Harkening back to Civil War–era legal theory, Mississippi had "interposed" its law and authority against those of the federal government.

In short order, the feds struck back. The U.S. Court of Appeals again ordered Ole Miss to enroll Meredith and held Governor Barnett in contempt of court for disobeying its prior desegregation order. The conflict between the federal and state governments could not have been clearer. The struggle had to end, and it could end in only one way.[17]

President Kennedy sought to bring the crisis to conclusion. He took over negotiations with Barnett, which Robert Kennedy had until then handled. On the phone, Kennedy pleaded with Barnett for an "amicable" solution that would avoid bloodshed and permit the enforcement of federal orders. In those private conversations with President Kennedy, Barnett struck a conciliatory note and agreed to a deal. But when Meredith sought to enroll once more, the governor went back on his word again. With the Mississippi public so inflamed by the example of Barnett's defiance, Attorney General Robert Kennedy aborted Meredith's fourth attempt to enroll at Ole Miss; the Kennedy administration feared "extreme violence and bloodshed," and rightly so. Barnett had made inevitable the "federal invasion" he had long decried; the forces of white resistance that the governor had primed would surely fight back.[18]

The president finally took dramatic and definitive action. On September 30, 1962, he signed an executive order directing the secretary of defense to "take all necessary steps to enforce" the court orders and "to remove all obstructions of justice" in Mississippi. He then federalized the state's National Guard and mobilized both the Army and the U.S. Marshals Service to enforce the orders of the Fifth Circuit Court of Appeals. Around Oxford, as word of the mobilization spread, tension hung heavy in the air. Informed that Meredith would arrive on campus that Sunday afternoon, Barnett refused to guarantee local law enforcement's cooperation in maintaining law and order. Danger loomed.[19]

Sunday came, and hundreds of armed U.S. marshals descended upon Ole Miss. C-130 transport aircraft rimmed the Lyceum building, the center of campus. The appointed delegation of Department of Justice lawyers drove in, while Motley waited off campus for word of her client's fate. James Meredith arrived that evening in a procession of cars and military vehicles; marshals escorted him to a dormitory,

Baxter Hall, where he was meant to remain under guard until the next morning.[20]

   The crowd swelled. As the sun set and the presence of U.S. marshals interspersed with soldiers—some of them Black—increased, onlookers became more hostile. Some hissed and booed at the marshals and soldiers. State troopers, the only local presence there, stood around, choosing to observe rather than control the crowd; many eventually departed the scene. By sunset, the crowd had swelled to a thousand or more. Journalists milled and mingled and occasionally flashed cameras. The restive crowd turned from hostile to unruly. "Get the nigger out," "Burn Kennedy and the niggers," and other such threats rose from the crowd. Violence soon erupted.

   The mob, a mix of students, locals, out-of-towners, and Klansmen, rioted. It directed its venom toward the marshals and journalists. In the middle of the chaos, Barnett went on television and radio and made equivocal remarks—decrying the federal invasion but urging peace—which did little to calm the crowd. In the chaos that ensued on campus that night, the angry crowd more than doubled in size, property was damaged, objects flew, gunfire erupted, numerous marshals and participants sustained injuries, and two men died. The violence went on and on, lasting for hours into the evening. It took thousands of National Guardsmen, military police, regular Army troops, U.S. marshals, and the repeated firing of tear gas to force the mob's retreat and restore order.[21]

   At 8:00 p.m. President Kennedy took to television and radio to comment on the unfolding events. Consistent with his obligations under the Constitution and the statutes of the United States, he had, he said, ordered the National Guard to begin to carry out court orders to desegregate Ole Miss. Americans are "free to disagree with the law," Kennedy allowed, "but not to disobey it." The president expressed "regret" for federal intervention, but also stated plainly why it needed to occur:

   If this country should ever reach the point where any man or group of men, by force or threat of force, could long deny the commands of our courts or our Constitution, then no law would stand free from doubt, no judge would be sure of his writ and no citizen would be safe from his neighbors.

In light of these high stakes, the federal government took the necessary steps to secure Meredith's rights. "Mr. James Meredith is now in residence on the campus of the University of Mississippi," the president proclaimed.[22]

The next morning—after the campus melee had been contained and more than two hundred people arrested—James Meredith matriculated at Ole Miss. Under the protection of federal marshals and accompaniment of Department of Justice lawyers, Meredith paid his tuition and fees with $230 in cash and registered for classes. Registrar Robert Ellis, a critical figure in the state's efforts to keep Meredith out, handed him his class schedule. With that, James Howard Meredith, the grandson of a slave, became the first Black person ever to attend the University of Mississippi, bastion of the rebel South.[23]

Tear gas lingered in the air in the classroom where Meredith attended his first class. The professor lectured on colonial American history. Meredith sat at the back of the room. U.S. marshals waited outside the classroom, ready to intervene if a troublemaker moved from taunts ("We'll get you nigger!") to action.[24]

Meredith had discovered a truth that the generations of Black students who followed this pioneer into historically white institutions would also find: desegregation itself sometimes gave rise to racial harms, academic experiences shadowed by social isolation and hostility.

*

Constance Baker Motley called the swirl of events surrounding Meredith's matriculation the "last battle of the Civil War." The injury, death, and destruction that accompanied the desegregation of Ole Miss sustain this metaphor. The rhetoric deployed by Ross Barnett and other Mississippians also summoned a comparison with the Civil War: to defend Jim Crow, mid-twentieth-century southern leaders asserted the same southern and state sovereignty invoked a hundred years before to defend slavery.

With this violence and wartime rhetoric came trauma. Like so many other veterans, James Meredith had "returned fighting." In the course of his war to enter Ole Miss, he experienced anxiety, fear, and loneliness. Motley, too, a lawyer who undertook the profound responsibility of translating into law the goals of a client at the cutting edge of the Black freedom movement, experienced anger, fear, and bouts of depression. The pair's tribulations were hardly unusual. Arduous and unending, activism exacted a heavy toll on all freedom fighters. Thurgood Marshall, Dr. King, and many student activists agonized over the physical and emotional demands of the work they were doing. Meredith summed up the situation in his characteristically direct way: "Social change," he said, "is a painful thing."[25]

Meredith muddled through an array of hardships that followed his arrival on the Ole Miss campus. U.S. marshals and military police hovered over his every move. Officers accompanied him to and from his dorm and to class; communicating via two-way radios, the agents, faithfully fulfilling their duty to protect and defend him, code-named him the "package" or "cargo." His residence, a two-bedroom apartment with a kitchen and bathroom, located in Baxter Hall, had enough space to accommodate the bodyguards, affording privacy and alleviating danger. But these special living arrangements exacerbated his separation from his peers. With Meredith confined to a room of his own, white students could avoid the company of a Black man. Excluded from the dining halls, Meredith ate most of his meals alone in his apartment and stayed out of white students' way.[26]

He continued to live in a state of siege. Federal agents protected him for the duration of his education in Oxford, Mississippi. Marshals guarded him even as he slept. During daylight hours, as he made his way to class across campus, students either ignored or insulted, harassed, and threatened him. Other "classmates" threw rocks and bottles, set off firecrackers, banged on doors, threw eggs, and otherwise tormented Meredith. Hate mail poured in. One envelope contained a singed rope. Another letter writer sent Meredith a poem of sorts:

> Roses are red, violets are blue.
> I've killed one nigger and might as well make it two.[27]

The onslaught of hatred affected Meredith deeply, although his distress did not always show on his face. In fact, to many onlookers, he appeared hollowed out—a robotic shell of a man. When angry whites hurled their invective—a chorus of voices yelling "nigger," "Black bastard," and whatever other vile language trailed him—he stared ahead blankly. The officer in charge of his security detail marveled at his reserve. He "wears no expression on his face," the officer commented, despite the "palpable" hatred that surrounded him. Instead of answering the troublemakers, he ignored them; he remained "detached" and did not visibly take the insults personally.[28]

Observers witnessed the performance of a lifetime: on a mission that had gripped him in his youth, Meredith approached his role in the desegregation of Ole Miss like the good soldier he had been for nine years. Focused and resilient, he would not be deterred from his assignment, however daunting. Fear did not show on his face because he had determined not to walk in fear. He even donned a "uniform" for his mission: every single day, he wore a suit and tie as he braved the hostilities on campus. The outfit, together with his dignified bearing and unfailing politeness, concealed his inner anguish from strangers.[29]

Constance Baker Motley saw through Meredith's mask—the detachment that shielded him from a world of hurt. Despite appearances, the attorney knew he experienced profound anxiety. "[T]he whole experience was pretty devastating" for him, she recalled. Motley had represented Black students in desegregating universities in Georgia, South Carolina, Florida, Louisiana, and Alabama. But Meredith, she concluded, had "suffered personally more than any other individual that we ever dealt with in any of these cases." All of these plaintiffs faced hardship and harassment. But besieged by the racial fanaticism of Mississippi, Meredith faced tribulations of a different order of magnitude.[30]

"There was always the real threat of death in his case," Motley said. From the start, Meredith feared for his and his family's safety. "Whenever a Negro questioned the status quo in Mississippi," he knew, "he just simply disappeared." Through disappearances, banishment, and extrajudicial killings, the state and its agents purged dissidents who threatened the dominant ideology. Meredith jeopardized white supremacy, and in recompense for that violation of social norms, he knew that he might lose his life. A murder for hire, likely committed by a paid Black informer, he surmised, was a distinct possibility.[31]

As his grueling first semester at Ole Miss drew to a close, the weight of the situation threatened to overtake him. All semester, Meredith had found it extraordinarily difficult to focus on his studies. By December, he was worn down and unable to concentrate. He started to skip classes. Motley, who had kept close tabs on her client throughout the ordeal, worried that he would "flunk out," and conceded that both his mind and his body needed "rest." The proud soldier denied that he was on the brink of collapse, but at Motley's prodding, he agreed to seek respite up north over the winter break.[32]

Once again visiting Motley in New York, away from prying eyes, Meredith could live in "seclusion" and devote long hours to study, doing what was necessary to pass his courses that semester. Along with Motley, Louis Pollak—the esteemed lawyer, Yale law professor, and longtime friend of the NAACP Legal Defense Fund—made arrangements for tutors to aid Meredith in his study. The plan was that for the duration of the break, Meredith would live rent-free in a New Haven apartment, where tutors would coach and drill him until he had mastered the relevant subjects. Motley, in an act of concern and devotion, personally drove him to New Haven.[33]

Lawyer and client "talked all the way up" on the two-and-a-half-hour drive from New York to New Haven. Comforting each other, they talked about the travails of the past months and shared their hopes for the future. Once they arrived in New Haven, Motley helped Meredith settle in. Having ensured that her client had all he needed for a successful stay, Motley departed. The encounter left her with new hope that Meredith could complete his mission—a victory that would be a powerful fillip for Motley and the entire civil rights movement.[34]

Three days after she returned to her apartment in New York, alarms set in. "At three o'clock in the morning," Motley recalled, "the doorbell rang. My husband and I were frightened because who comes at three o'clock in the morning? Except trouble," that is. Opening their door, Constance and Joel Motley saw the agitated face of James Meredith. Explaining, Meredith said that he "just couldn't study." He had decided to leave New Haven and return to Jackson. "I decided that what I wanted to do is to go back to Jackson and meet my friends and dance and have a good time and relax." He continued, "I just feel like dancing."[35]

Motley, astonished and not a little angry, was resigned. She could not force Meredith to focus; she could not make a grown man study. In the face of his decision, she "just gave up." The next morning, she called Louis Pollak. "Now, look, we're going to have to face reality, Lou," she told him. "Meredith is not going to make it." Frustrated and at the same time sympathetic toward her client, she proclaimed, "We've failed." The grand social experiment had not worked out as the LDF had intended. Notwithstanding her own disappointment and the delight segregationists would take in Meredith's leaving campus, Motley insisted that the time had come to end his suffering: "We cannot ask him to do more than he's done."[36]

In the end, however, the worst-case scenario did not come to pass. Back in Jackson, in familiar environs, surrounded by family and friends, Meredith did something that he had not been able to do during the upheaval at Ole Miss: he took a break. He went to parties. He chatted with friends. He did not think about colonial American history; he ignored political science. And he danced. For a few winter weeks in 1962, James Meredith—the small man with the nervous stomach whose suit to desegregate Ole Miss had made him an icon of the civil rights movement—relaxed.[37]

His weeks of freedom and rest, of partying and socializing, revitalized him. Meredith returned to school for the spring semester of 1963 with his mind restored and his ability to concentrate intact. And although he had not spent the winter recess studying, he passed his courses. That spring he graduated from the University of Mississippi. Like other activists, Meredith had buckled under pressure, but he had not broken.[38]

*

Meredith was not alone in faltering. While Motley had focused her energies on ensuring that her mentally exhausted client stayed on track, Meredith had noticed that the fight was wearing her down too. The steely lawyer could not hide her worry and anxiety. Even

as she counseled him on the drive from New York to New Haven, he
noticed that Motley "was visibly shaken by the sustained pressure of
the ordeal." All along, as he well knew, Motley had been "emotionally
involved" in the case. Without her "personal interest," he recognized,
the case "would never have come this far."[39]

Motley worried about making winning arguments, of course. But
in the eighteen months that she was litigating the Ole Miss case,
concerns about physical safety weighed on her too. She feared that
Meredith's role as the face of the struggle would lead to his death.
She ruminated over the possibility that "he'd be shot someday." She
also lived with nagging fears over her own safety. She realized she was
"taking a chance" with her life by working in Mississippi and staying
there overnight with Black families supportive of the struggle for civil
rights. Her fear was not abstract, but based on concrete incidences.
The White Citizens' Council routinely subjected the NAACP and its
affiliates to surveillance. The state police tailed Motley and Medgar
Evers, the courageous NAACP field secretary tasked with fetching her
from the airport, driving her to and from court, finding her housing,
and schooling her in local customs. They had endured threats and
harassment on their own. "We had no protection, no F.B.I. and no
U.S. Marshals," Motley reflected. That only changed when Meredith
moved onto the Ole Miss campus.[40]

The federal government's actions, and especially its inaction, angered Motley. The Kennedy administration had not provided her with
security until very late in the evolution of the case. She recalled a
moment of fury when she "slammed the phone down on Burke Marshall," the assistant attorney general for civil rights at the Department
of Justice. Motley was, she recalled, "outraged that the department
had not offered me, Meredith, or any other lawyer protection during
our dangerous mission." She was incensed that the Department of
Justice waited and waited before becoming involved in the pivotal
case. Motley and her colleagues had filed the action in May 1961, but
the federal government did not intervene until late September 1962—
after Motley and LDF had prevailed in the court of appeals and laid
the groundwork for a successful appeal to the U.S. Supreme Court.
For all those months, while Motley and Meredith faced down the

threat of death, the Kennedy administration withheld both protection and unequivocal public support.[41]

Despite its late entry into the case, the federal government became an acclaimed protector of the civil rights movement once it had muscled in. This development left Motley exasperated. The magnanimous view of the Kennedy administration and its lawyers was unmerited, she believed; the administration had entered the Meredith case not out of deep concern for the rights of Black Americans, but to preserve the stability of the republic.[42]

Motley's interactions with Judge Harold Cox, a Kennedy appointee and one of the least sympathetic justices she faced on the court of appeals, deepened her anger at the administration. When all but the dullest or most hate-obstructed person could see that Mississippi had lost its fight to preserve Jim Crow, Motley appeared before Judge Cox. The embittered segregationist judge, who could barely contain his disdain for her, grabbed the motion papers from her hand and threw them back at her. Cox's action was so egregious that Judge Mize intervened on her behalf. "Judge Cox, it's over," Mize had urged. The interaction encapsulated the disrespect that Motley had endured in Mississippi, both at the hands of putative friends—such as the Kennedy administration—and evident foes such as Cox, a man Motley called the "most openly racist judge to sit on the federal bench."[43]

Like Meredith, Motley wore a mask. Her steely exterior matched her taciturn personality, and her serious demeanor matched the professional manner typically associated with lawyers. She shielded herself from the assumption—steeped in stereotyping—that as a member of the "weaker sex," she did not belong in the legal profession, a world dominated by hard-charging men.

Occasionally, Motley went alone to sit along the banks of the Mississippi River. The state had declared the riverbanks hallowed ground: a memorial to the Battle of Vicksburg, which famously marked a turning point in the Civil War for the Union. Wrapped as she was in racial history, Motley still remembered learning about the battle during her days as a student at NYU, when she was so full of commitment to social justice.[44]

Staring into the wide expanse of the mighty Mississippi River,

Motley contemplated the past—the nation's and the state's bloody racial history—and how the Inc. Fund's work had reshaped the national story. She could sense that "history was being tested in a way that it must have been during the days of our Founding Fathers." History was being rewritten by the Meredith case and others like it, and because of her own work and sacrifice. Motley's knowledge that she played a starring role in redeeming America's tortured racial history enabled her to press on despite her mental and physical exhaustion. There, among the grass and trees that lined the Mississippi, she found calm as she contemplated history and her part in it.[45]

Motley also built community with a small band of lawyers, activists, and community members who took part in LDF's effort to end Jim Crow in the state. She became a mentor to Inc. Fund lawyer Derrick Bell. Never one to engage in flattery, Motley later said that she "could not have made it through . . . without Derrick's able assistance."[46] She also leaned on Medgar Evers, the NAACP's most prominent operative in Mississippi. Evers had himself applied to the Ole Miss law school in 1953. Unsuccessful in his own bid against Jim Crow and a fellow military veteran, the NAACP field secretary had enthusiastically supported James Meredith. He eagerly chauffeured Motley between the Jackson airport and the court, accompanied her to public meetings, directed her to Black-owned cafés and corner markets where she could purchase food and sundries, and found locals to host her rent-free during her stints in the state. He also provided her with moral and emotional support. The pair spent long days with each other. Evers often invited Motley to his home; there, the lawyer enjoyed home-cooked meals and fellowship with Evers, his wife, their three children, and whoever else was passing through.[47]

Whenever court recessed, Motley commuted back to New York. She longed, in particular, to see her young son, Joel, who grew accustomed to glimpsing his mother's face from a distance—on television, as journalists reported on her exploits in the Deep South. During her many trips to Mississippi, Motley often wondered if she would hold her son and husband again.

A string of terrifying events justified her anxiety. During one incident, a Mississippi state police car tailed their vehicle as she and Evers drove the hundred miles from Jackson to Meridian, to the federal courthouse. "Medgar kept checking the rearview mirror," Motley recalled. The lawyer habitually worked on legal papers during long commutes, and she tried to focus on the work at hand. But she could not concentrate, and soon Evers instructed her to hide her work. "Don't look back," he said. "Put that yellow [legal] pad in *The New York Times*." Scarcely breathing, her head "straight forward," Motley followed Evers's instructions. She would never forget her fear that day, and the relief she felt when the officer abandoned the tail.[48]

At night Motley was keenly aware that when staying with allies in their homes, she and her hosts were endangered. On one occasion, she and her secretary, Roberta Thomas, shared a bedroom at the front of a small wood-frame house owned by an NAACP leader in Meridian. "With no fence or sidewalk separating it from the dirt road it abutted, you might as well have been sleeping on the sidewalk because that's how near you were" to the road, she said. "You were left with absolutely no protection." That night she could not rest. She and Thomas "stayed up all night, frightened to death."[49]

Motley kept up her harried pace for eighteen months, making twenty-two trips to Mississippi in the course of the James Meredith case. That she departed alive was, she believed, "due to sheer luck." "I felt my nine lives had been used up." After all, she mused, "How many times can you be lucky?"[50]

Only one month after Motley left Mississippi for the last time, Medgar Evers was assassinated. Byron De La Beckwith, a well-known member of the Ku Klux Klan and the White Citizens' Council, hiding behind a honeysuckle bush, gunned Evers down with a high-powered hunting rifle in the early hours of June 12, 1963, just as he emerged from his car and was about to walk in the door of his home. Indefatigable, Evers had arrived after midnight, following a church meeting about the ongoing struggles over civil rights. His wife, Myrlie, and their children were impatiently awaiting his return; the family had gathered earlier that evening to watch President John F. Kennedy's televised address. The same night that Kennedy finally offered a full endorsement of the Black freedom struggle, an endorsement that even Motley could praise, a white supremacist killed Evers—the face of the civil rights movement in the nation's most racially repressive state. He was just thirty-seven years old.[51]

Motley had warned Evers about the honeysuckle bush many times; she had insisted that a "political foe" intent on doing him harm could lie there in wait. Motley's worst fear had been realized.[52]

Evers's assassination devastated her. For two years he had been her constant companion in Mississippi. Traumatized and despondent, she could not get out of bed for weeks following his death. Grief-stricken, she could not even bring herself to attend his funeral. Motley decided then that the "price we were paying to end segregation was too high," and she vowed never to return to Mississippi.[53]

Nevertheless, she left the state victorious. Constance Baker Motley emerged as one of the most respected lawyers in America after the Meredith case. A story in the *New York Times*, titled "Integration's Advocate," captured the professional heights to which she had soared. "A tall striking woman with piercing dark eyes is almost always in the courtroom in the eye of the hurricane surrounding the struggle for civil rights in the South." Motley's successful fight to desegregate Ole Miss had brought her public esteem and professional success—along with devastating loss and profound pain.[54]

14

An "Eye-Opening Experience": The Birmingham Civil Rights Campaign

The stench of urine and feces emanating from the jail latrine knocked the stylishly dressed Constance Baker Motley back on her heels. Assaulted by the odor, holding her nose, she turned and ran from the jail. Meanwhile, the men who had accompanied her to this desolate stretch of earth calmly entered the detention center, apparently unbothered by the stink.[1]

Motley had come to rural Americus, Georgia, on a sultry summer day in late July 1962 to speak to a client. As a rule, she knew, her poise impressed observers. This time was different. The usually unflappable lawyer showed weakness. Running from the malodorous prison laid bare a gender-linked failing, she felt. After all, her male companions, lawyers Donald L. Hollowell and C. B. King, both Army veterans, had breezed right past her into the penitentiary's bowels.[2]

In fact, the whole scene frightened her. The jail, a cinder-block building plunked down in a clearing in the middle of the country-side, stood alone on its remote patch of land, with no businesses or residences nearby. Anything could happen here in the backwaters of Georgia. History had already shown how things could go wickedly wrong in these parts. In July 1946—not nearly long enough ago—a rural boondocks in Georgia not unlike the place where she now found herself had given rise to "history's worst lynching": a quadruple murder. The four victims included a pregnant Black woman and her boyfriend—a veteran of the U.S. Army—as well as another Black couple. The "Moore's Ford Lynching" had made national headlines and precipitated rallies against mob violence in New York City and Washington, D.C. The NAACP had offered a $10,000 reward for information about the perpetrators of the gruesome crime, still unsolved today and etched in the collective memory of Black Americans. On this fallow southern ground, the attorney was scared to death. Motley called the jail visit the "most horrendous experience" of her life. Given the many travails she endured, that statement spoke volumes.[3]

Motley endured the peril and the smell to see a legendary client—Dr. Martin Luther King Jr.—a man she wanted to help not only from professional obligation, but also out of personal pride.

Dr. King—at once one of the most beloved and most hated men in America—faced a dreadful situation. At the invitation of local activists, he had come to nearby Albany in December 1961 to reinvigorate a stalled campaign against segregation. But cunning public officials and infighting among civil rights activists snarled the campaign as it was again getting under way. The chief of police, Laurie Pritchett, had responded calmly and nonviolently to the demonstrations. The police arrested activists, but not for violating Jim Crow laws. They had charged the protesters with run-of-the-mill petty offenses such as parading without a permit and disobeying police orders.

King had already been arrested twice during the Albany campaign. Now, in late July, he sat locked away in jail for a third time; there, separated again from his wife, his children, and his public, the minister sweltered in hundred-degree heat and grew weak from fasting. On prior occasions, King had chosen to remain in jail in hopes of attracting publicity to the cause and putting pressure on officials to end segregation, but this time, on his third confinement to the jail, he wanted out. The Albany movement had not worked according to plan; in fact, the city fathers had grown increasingly resistant to change since King's arrival. His continued confinement served no purpose, and he had work to do on the outside.[4]

Once Motley made her way inside, Dr. King greeted her warmly. "I was informed that Connie Motley was here," King recalled, "and I was very happy." Motley got right to work. After a series of legal maneuvers, King was released by his captors.[5]

This "harrowing" visit to King was but the first of a series she would make to represent him in the two years following the disappointing outcome of the Albany campaign, routinely called a "stunning defeat" for King.[6]

*

In the spring of 1963, the eyes of the nation turned to Birmingham, Alabama, then known as the home of a thriving iron and steel industry. In April and May of that year, Birmingham, a land trapped in a "Rip Van Winkle" slumber on issues of race, and the nation's "chief symbol of racial intolerance," according to Dr. King, became a flashpoint in the Black struggle for equality.[7]

In his inaugural address, George C. Wallace, elected governor of Alabama in 1962 on a pro-segregation and states' rights platform, rebuked the civil rights movement. "I draw the line in the dust and toss the gauntlet before the feet of tyranny," the governor had said. He vowed to maintain "segregation now, segregation tomorrow, segregation forever." Theophilus Eugene "Bull" Connor, the Birmingham commissioner of public safety and an unapologetic racist who controlled the police and fire departments, also vowed to defend white supremacy. The civil rights movement had encountered two of its fiercest foes.[8]

For five weeks, beginning April 3, 1963, Dr. King's Southern Christian Leadership Conference and a coalition of grassroots activists led by Rev. Fred Shuttlesworth of the Alabama Christian Movement for Human Rights (ACMHR), a "firebrand" known for his invincible courage and confrontational leadership style, staged a mass civil disobedience campaign and squared off against the ardent segregationists. Through sit-ins, demonstrations, and boycotts, protesters sought to expose the cruelty of Jim Crow and draw attention to the value of Black purchasing power; ultimately, they hoped to desegregate the city and increase Black employment opportunities.

The campaign was the brainchild of Rev. Wyatt Tee Walker of SCLC, who called it "Project C." The "C" stood for "confrontation"— nonviolent confrontation. "If we could crack Jim Crow in Birmingham, known as the nation's most segregated city," Walker said, "then we could crack any city." Shuttlesworth, who had been brutalized and nearly blown to bits in retaliation for his efforts to desegregate

Alabama's schools and buses, agreed that a successful drive against Jim Crow in Birmingham would reinvigorate the movement. He warned that the campaign would be extremely dangerous, but could be extremely rewarding: "You have to be prepared to die before you can live in freedom," he said.[9]

Project C involved forms of protest—sit-ins and selective buying campaigns—that by 1963 were conventional. Yet in its early days, the meticulously planned campaign had generated little community support; many middle-class Blacks actively opposed it, and casual observers largely ignored it. "[O]ur community was divided," King conceded. Small numbers of activists—a mere seven at a local cafeteria and eight at Woolworth's—turned out to stage sit-ins on April 3. Instead of contending with the demonstrators, workers took the day off. Only a smattering of the protesters were arrested. Even Rev. Fred Shuttlesworth generated little enthusiasm when he led a sit-in on April 6; only a few dozen people came to join him. Officials eventually arrested forty people, far too few to disrupt civil order or threaten merchants' bottom lines. The abysmal turnout validated Shuttlesworth's fear that SCLC had arrived in Birmingham ill-prepared to lead a broad and massive civil disobedience campaign.[10]

The very next day, on April 7, there was another small demonstration involving about twenty people, an embarrassingly small number, but this time it ended differently. Bull Connor unleashed police dogs and fire hoses on protesters. The modest numbers did not stop Connor from overreacting. At Connor's behest, police used German shepherds and wielded clubs to clear out the peaceful and prayerful protesters marching toward the town center. In the chaos, several barking police dogs pinned a nineteen-year-old Black man to the ground, and officers kicked the man—a bystander otherwise uninvolved in the movement—as he lay there helpless. News reports and public attention highlighted this incident of police brutality. The spectacle grabbed the attention of those who previously had ignored the protest, and SCLC found the "key" to motivating the Black community and garnering press coverage: demonstrations that precipitated violent confrontations with Bull Connor's police.[11]

A few days later, on April 10, Dr. King, Rev. Shuttlesworth, and the other ministers leading Project C defied a court order, which had

A young Motley—always dressed to the nines—as a young lawyer. *(Courtesy of the Motley family)*

Clarence W. Blakeslee, a New Haven philanthropist, who, after seeing Motley speak at a community event, offered to pay for her college and law school education. *(Courtesy of Yale University Library)*

Motley *(second from right)* "night clubbing" with her husband, Joel *(fifth from left)*, and family and friends in New York in the 1940s. *(Courtesy of the Baker Royster family)*

Motley outside of court with Roy Wilkins *(left)*, director of the NAACP; Jack Greenberg, her LDF co-counsel *(far right)*; and a client. *(Courtesy of the Motley family)*

Motley with James Meredith after the LDF team that she led sued for his admission to the University of Mississippi. *(Courtesy of the Motley family)*

Second-in-command at Defense Fund as Associate Counsel, Mrs. Motley interrupts dictation of speech to secretary Roberta Thomas to discuss brief with Fund Atty Norman Amaker. Suit sought desegregation of Albany, Ga., recreation facilities.

Brief in Albany case receives characteristic painstaking study by attorney above. She reads some of mail (right) received by her most celebrated client, James Meredith. Meredith shipped Fund two large boxes of mail he received about Ole Miss case.

Only woman lawyer at Fund, Mrs. Motley chairs conference in Greenberg's office of staff attorneys (l. to r.): Derrick Bell, Frank Heffron, Norman Amaker, Leroy Clark, Michael Melsner, George Smith and James Nabrit III. She once admitted working with men presents "special problems as many men honestly believe that women are inferior."

(Top left) Motley works on a brief with LDF secretary Roberta Thomas and attorney Norman Amaker. *(Middle left)* Motley works on a case at the LDF offices. *(Right)* Motley prepares papers at the LDF offices. *(Bottom)* Motley heads a conference of LDF staff attorneys including *(from left to right)* Derrick Bell, Frank Heffron, Norman Amaker, Leroy Clark, Michael Melsner, George Smith, and James Nabrit. *(Courtesy of Columbia University Library)*

Motley and Mississippi NAACP field secretary Medgar Evers. (*Courtesy of the Motley family*)

Motley with James Meredith (*center*), the first black student at the University of Mississippi, and LDF attorney Derrick Bell (*left*). Motley led the LDF's efforts to sue for Meredith's admission at the segregated university. (*Courtesy of AP Images*)

Motley with James Meredith after the LDF team that she led sued for his admission to the University of Mississippi. (*Courtesy of the Motley family*)

Photographed outside the Supreme Court, Motley and her LDF co-counsel Jack Greenberg on the cover of *Jet*. (*Courtesy of Columbia University Library*)

Motley with Donald Hollowell (*center*), her co-counsel in the University of Georgia case. (*Courtesy of the Motley family*)

Motley with LDF colleagues Jack Greenberg *(left)* and Thurgood Marshall *(right)*. *(Courtesy of the NAACP Legal Defense and Educational Fund)*

Motley with Dr. Martin Luther King Jr., who was then president of the Southern Christian Leadership Conference (SCLC), and his wife, Coretta Scott King, at an SCLC banquet in Birmingham, Alabama, in 1965. *(Courtesy of AP Images)*

Motley shaking hands with civil rights leader Rev. Fred Shuttlesworth. After Shuttlesworth was arrested during a protest in Birmingham in 1962, Motley helped him challenge his conviction, arguing his case in front of the Supreme Court in 1965. *(Courtesy of Birmingham Library)*

Motley at her apartment in New York City, circa 1962. *(Courtesy of the Motley family)*

Motley circa 1963, the year before she was elected to the New York State Senate. *(Courtesy of Columbia University Library)*

Bella Abzug *(left)*, who was Motley's law school classmate and was later a member of Congress, and Shirley Chisolm *(right)*, who served with Motley in the New York State Senate and later was the first Black woman elected to Congress. *(Courtesy of AP Images)*

Motley; her son, Joel III; and her husband, Joel Jr., at her swearing-in ceremony for Manhattan borough president. *(Courtesy of the Library of Congress)*

been a part of city officials' plan to halt the movement. First, officials refused to issue the protesters a permit to parade; next, they secured a court order enjoining unlicensed protests. King called the injunction nothing more than a "pseudo-legal way of breaking the back of legitimate moral protest." Nevertheless, because of the authority vested even in courts that issue erroneous rulings, the situation posed a dilemma.[12]

Dr. King and his movement had come to a crossroads. Out of respect for the U.S. Supreme Court's stand against segregation in *Brown v. Board of Education* and other federal court decisions that aided the movement, King had vowed never to violate a federal court order. At the same time, the ministers concluded that the movement owed no deference or loyalty to state and local courts, where, more often than not, proud racists presided.[13]

In the face of the command to stop engaging in civil disobedience without a permit, King held a press conference. "Injunction or no injunction," he said, "we are going to march tomorrow. . . . I am prepared to go to jail and stay as long as necessary." Unlike federal courts, "recalcitrant forces in the Deep South," King said in his statement, deployed the law "to perpetuate the unjust and illegal system of racial separation." In light of the corruption of the judicial system, SCLC would go on with Project C, "out of great love for the Constitution notwithstanding the court's demand."[14]

Project C had made a radical move. It was justified, King insisted, because the court's order was "unjust, undemocratic, and unconstitutional." "I've got to march," King said, and "if we obey it, then we are out of business," he explained to naysayers who tried to dissuade him from violating the order.[15]

On Good Friday, during the Easter weekend, one of the busiest shopping periods of the year, King, Shuttlesworth, and Abernathy set out to march. The ministers, dressed casually in blue jeans and gray work shirts, led a group of about fifty from the Zion Hill Baptist Church toward town. Hundreds of spectators lined the street to witness the procession. Bull Connor and his police force came out to meet them, standing in the middle of the street to block their way and barking orders: "Don't let them go any further!" Connor ordered King and Abernathy arrested, while the crowd of protesters jeered.

Pushed and prodded by the officers, the protesters sang freedom songs. Meanwhile, at the Birmingham city jail, officers booked King and Abernathy and placed each man in solitary confinement. Held incommunicado and alone, King worried about the fate of the movement, feeling demoralized and afraid in the "utter darkness" and "brutality" of the dungeon that confined him. The experience was no less than "holy hell," Abernathy later said.[16]

The protests continued, and in the days following King's solitary confinement, friends called on President Kennedy to end the "reign of terror" in Birmingham. In his "Letter from a Birmingham Jail," King eloquently defended civil disobedience, countering criticism by white clergymen who called Project C "unwise and untimely." His letter rejected the pleas to end demonstrations in the city. "I am in Birmingham," King wrote, because "injustice is here." The minister proclaimed that "injustice anywhere is a threat to justice everywhere." The letter would become the movement's most celebrated manifesto and a vital part of the twentieth-century American literary canon.[17]

Motley watched the events in Birmingham unfold with pride and awe. Unlike her mentor, Thurgood Marshall, who had a frosty relationship with Dr. King and was skeptical about whether street protests were an effective means of securing civil rights, Motley saw the value of the demonstrations. Although she frequently cited the "spectacular" civil rights cases in which she played a role as the "single most important factor" in social change, she deeply appreciated the courage and the hunger for equality that motivated King and his followers. Thus when King—a man she called an "American hero"—called for her in May 1963, she did not hesitate to answer or support the Birmingham campaign.[18]

Motley had been fighting for change in the state of Alabama since 1955. In *Brown*'s wake, she had traveled to that "scary place" to aid in a case that sought to desegregate the University of Alabama. That effort ended in failure when, following a riot, the university expelled Motley's client. Years later, the battle to desegregate the state's flagship institution of higher education continued, and Motley remained a part of it. She also represented students fighting for admission to public schools in Birmingham, Mobile, and Huntsville. At the same time, she litigated the 1963 case that desegregated South Carolina's Clemson University. The many other assignments notwithstanding, Motley brought lawsuits to assert the constitutional rights of the Birmingham activists to protest segregation. Her efforts were vital to the movement's continued momentum.[19]

Following the fateful Good Friday protests in April 1963, Motley and three other lawyers were called upon to assist Dr. King. Released from the Birmingham jail on April 20, King was in legal jeopardy, facing a trial for contempt of court because of his decision to defy the order enjoining protests. Constance Baker Motley and Jack Greenberg, together with two local Black lawyers, Arthur Shores and Ozell Billingsley, defended Dr. King and Rev. Shuttlesworth, Wyatt T. Walker, Ralph Abernathy, Andrew Young, and other leaders of SCLC named in the injunction. Along with King and his team of activists at the Black-owned Gaston Motel—the headquarters of the Birmingham movement—Motley and her co-counsel strategized about how to fight the corrupt judicial system.[20]

In room 30 of the Gaston Motel, which sat in the heart of Birmingham's Black ghetto, Motley observed how the weight of leadership wore on King. Up close she could see King's complexities and humanity, just as she had observed the full personhood—warts and all—of Thurgood Marshall while working at his side. Strong and steady in public appearances, in private King was often mired in doubt and indecision. He frequently felt low in spirit and "alone," even in a crowded room. Motley also experienced the lively social life that bound civil rights activists together; amid the tribulations, the freedom fighters bonded and shared a sense of community. A naturally reserved person, Motley nevertheless exuded warmth and had a "twinkle in her eye" as she chatted with other luminaries. She could not help but feel a great deal of satisfaction in coming to Birmingham to fight the good fight.[21]

In late April 1963, walking alongside King, Shuttlesworth, Walker, Abernathy, Young, and other prominent ministers, Motley made her way to the courthouse, the sole woman leader in a pack of alpha males. The dignified lawyer entered the Jefferson County Courthouse and stood tall.[22]

The courtroom teemed with spectators. Like so many others

across the South, Black Alabamians had come to see the woman
lawyer confirm the reputation that preceded her: when "Constance
Baker Motley walked into the court, she was superb, and she took no
prisoners."[23] Courthouse employees—white women—also "deserted
their desks" and piled into the court to witness the famous woman
lawyer. Motley's presence and her command of the room represented
something rare and different: a woman in a male environment, exert-
ing intellectual authority and challenging sex-role stereotypes. In the
Deep South of 1963, some years before the advent of the women's
liberation movement, Motley symbolized women's emancipation.[24]

When her turn came to speak, Motley enunciated every syllable
and spoke in her low and steady voice. The judge assigned to hear the
case did not give her much hope for victory. She was arguing before
Judge W. A. Jenkins—the very same judge who had entered the vaguely
worded injunction against the demonstration to begin with. "There
is not a shred of evidence," Motley informed the judge, "that these
defendants engaged in unlawful activity of any kind." Peaceful protesters, King and his allies had made every effort to comply with the
law, but had been thwarted by the city.[25]

Bull Connor slipped into the courtroom while Motley spoke. King's
lawyers had called the volatile man as a witness. The personification
of white resistance, Connor could answer critical questions about the
circumstances leading up to the Good Friday conflict. As he sat waiting his turn on the witness stand, in a dramatic display of disdain for
Motley, the public safety commissioner closed his eyes. Rather than
acknowledge Motley and her presentation, he pretended to sleep.
By now accustomed to such juvenile displays of intolerance, Motley
ignored Connor and his slight. His childish antics only strengthened
her resolve. She called him to the stand.[26]

Motley lobbed questions at Connor about his machinations in the
run-up to the demonstrations. She observed that, as a known antago-
nist of the civil rights movement, Connor had personally ensured the
movement's fate when he and the police chief had refused to respond
to Project C's requests for a parade permit.

When Judge Jenkins abruptly cut short her questioning, she pursued a different path. She called Lola Hendricks, a participant in the
Birmingham movement, to the stand. The witness testified that Con-

nor had been personally involved in the decision to deny a permit to Project C. In fact, Connor had scoffed at the request. "No, you'll not get a permit in Birmingham," he had told Hendricks. Instead, he said, he would see the demonstrators in the city jail.[27]

A third witness lent credence to the narrative that Motley sought to develop. Under her questioning, W. J. Haley, chief inspector for the Birmingham Police Department, conceded that the city had targeted movement leaders for punishment on specious grounds. The mass arrests of Project C participants constituted the "first time in 20 years" the city had enforced the law against parading without a permit. Haley could not recall a single other arrest for that infraction.[28]

Motley insisted on King's innocence. Because the leaders of Project C had duly sought a permit and could not force the city to issue one, the ministers could not lawfully or logically be held in contempt of court. In a different courtroom, presided over by a fair judge, Motley's legal strategy would have held sway. In Judge Jenkins's court, the logic and facts adduced utterly failed to persuade. Jenkins was interested only in the question of whether the injunction had been *violated*, not whether it complied with the Constitution.[29]

In fact, Judge Jenkins did not take kindly to *any* of the defense attorneys' arguments. Jack Greenberg's references to the sanctity of the freedoms of speech and assembly did not sway him. But the judge listened intently to the city attorney's plea to "put these troublemakers in jail until they learn their lesson." The court should make it clear to the preachers, the city attorney insisted, that "they can't get away with" stirring up "mob violence."[30]

Following the conclusion of the three-day trial, the judge found each of the named leaders guilty as charged. The ministers' actions constituted "obvious acts of contempt" and "deliberate and blatant denials of the authority of this court and its order," Jenkins ruled. In addition to personally violating the order, he maintained, the accused had "used" their positions as ministers "to encourage and incite others" to do so. The judge imposed a $50 fine on each minister for criminal contempt of court and sentenced each to five days in jail. The defense attorneys immediately appealed Jenkins's decision, postponing the jail sentences.[31]

While the appeal went forward, King, Abernathy, and other Project C leaders regrouped to continue the battle against segregation in Birmingham. "We will march again, again, and again as long as we are denied our constitutional rights," King promised.[32]

*

The appeal failed, and despite King's brilliant rhetorical defense of mass civil disobedience in his letter, the movement sputtered while he and its leaders sat in jail, and it continued to lag even after the ministers' release. Not even Dr. King could draw the volunteers—the "troops"—needed to sustain the protests or gain major national attention. The press lost interest, and volunteers were dwindling. Defeat loomed. Some of King's advisers began whispering that he should resign himself to the loss and quietly leave the city.[33]

Others, however, suggested that if they lacked protesters, Project C should recruit school-aged children. While youth activists previously had participated in sit-ins and demonstrations, SCLC had never recruited children en masse. King expressed deep skepticism about the idea; the Birmingham city jail was "no place for children." Others inside and outside of SCLC and ACMHR agreed, and when Birmingham's Black middle-class leaders caught wind of the idea, they angrily rejected it. How, they asked, could any respectable person approve of the idea of serving up little Black boys and girls to Bull Connor?[34]

But the movement's impending collapse eventually compelled King and others to relent and try enlisting youth. Movement veterans James Bevel, Wyatt T. Walker, Andrew Young, and Dorothy Cotton quickly got to work. Focusing on high school students, they set out to conscript prom queens and kings, athletes, academic standouts, and other school leaders to join Project C's marches. Under the guidance of Rev. James Bevel of SCLC—the strongest proponent of children's participation in the protests—organizers recruited youngsters through visits to area high schools. The recruiters distributed leaflets about the movement's goals, and encouraged participation over the objections of parents, principals, and other administrators. Students enthusiastically joined.[35]

Thousands of them—some elementary-school-aged—skipped

class on Thursday, May 2, and gathered at the 16th Street Baptist Church. After talking and mingling with classmates, the students listened to Rev. Bevel's exhortations and instructions. A charismatic speaker, he urged the youngsters to take a stand for freedom.

Then, just after noon that day, at Bevel's urging, throngs of students spilled out from the imposing redbrick church across from Kelly Ingram Park and into the street. With picket signs in hand, the students marched the eight blocks toward city hall and the business district, all the while singing freedom songs. The lyrics to "We Shall Overcome," "Oh Freedom," and other hymns tamped down their fear and inspired feelings of joy and calm, remembered Audrey Faye Hendricks, one of the participants—only nine years old and a third-grader at the time. "We shall overcome / We shall overcome / We shall overcome some day / Oh, deep in my heart / I do believe / We shall overcome some day," they sang, arms locked together. When the students reached town, happy and excited, they approached select merchants and municipal buildings. The young activists, carefully following instructions, remained peaceful.[36]

Before long the inevitable occurred: the children's march encountered Bull Connor, together with city police officers and firefighters. The sight of the uniformed officers wiped the smiles off the faces of some children and stopped others in their tracks. Although flustered by the presence of so many people—so many children—Connor ordered his men to arrest and confine the students. Officers carted dozens of youngsters to squad cars. After the cars filled, Connor called for police wagons. Then he called for school buses to transport the children to jails as more and more of them arrived on the scene.[37]

Hundreds of children were arrested that day. While held, the youths endured questioning about the mass movement. After police took Audrey Hendricks to Juvenile Hall, five or six white men surrounded the third-grader and queried her about the mass meetings and, in particular, whether leaders had forced her and others to participate. Nervous and afraid that "they might kill" her, Hendricks revealed all that a nine-year-old could about the movement's tactics. For seven long days, the little girl remained in jail, deprived of contact with her parents. The children slept on mattresses piled on the floor, and survived on peanut butter sandwiches and milk. Larry Russell, then sixteen, remembered that officers fingerprinted him and treated all of the young people "like common criminals."[38]

News of the youths' activism and their arrests garnered national attention and widespread condemnation. Attorney General Robert F. Kennedy called what became known as the Children's Crusade "a dangerous business" that risked innocent life. But the federal government had "no authority," he insisted, to intervene in the local battle. So despite the criticism, youth-led demonstrations continued in the coming days.[39]

In the face of new protests, Connor escalated his response, ordering firemen and police officers to violently suppress the demonstrations of children. Chaos ensued. As video cameras rolled and photographers snapped pictures, the Birmingham Fire Department pummeled children with high-pressure hoses as Connor yelled, "Let 'em have it." Hit with the force of the water, children fell to the streets, some spinning under its power. Officers unleashed snarling dogs on the kids. Connor delighted in the fright caused by police dogs; he liked, he said, to see the "niggers run." Policemen also attacked the children with clubs. These men brutalized scores of children at Connor's command, some of whom lost flesh as a result of the water pressure, while others sustained bites and gashes from the dog attacks. Many onlookers responded to this violence with more violence, pelting officers with bricks and rocks. Amid the bedlam, Connor ordered hundreds of arrests. Police cars, police wagons, and school buses again carted hundreds of children off to jails and juvenile detention facilities. When the pens at these facilities overflowed, Connor held the young activists at the local fairgrounds. The same scene played out again later that week.[40]

Over the airwaves and on live television, in domestic and foreign newspapers, journalists disseminated the scenes and sounds of children mowed down, clubbed, and dragged off to jail. The images from Birmingham—pictures of state-sponsored violence against children as young as six, who had come together to demand equal rights— shocked the world. Photographs and video footage showed the depth to which human beings would sink to defend white supremacy. By focusing a harsh light on the severity of the problem of American racism, the Children's Crusade marked a turning point in the civil rights movement.[41]

The travails of the child activists did not end there. In a stunning act of retaliation, Birmingham's school superintendent, Theo R. Wright, in a May 20 letter to principals, ordered the immediate expulsion or suspension of all students who had joined the Children's Crusade. Three members of the board of education—each of whom had been appointed by Bull Connor—had endorsed the superintendent's decision at a meeting specially called for that purpose.[42]

Wright's order dispensed with the due process requirement found in the same policy he relied on to oust the students. In the case of the Children's Crusade, Wright observed, the board members had made an exception to the rule that entitled students to hearings prior to suspension or expulsion because "there is not enough time remaining during the present school session to have trials of all of these students." The school year was set to end on May 30, 1963, ten days after the superintendent's fateful letter. The students would not only be deprived of their due process rights: by making the suspensions and expulsions a part of their permanent academic records, the board of education ensured that the punishments would forever haunt them and imperil those who planned to graduate in the spring. Wright was making an example of the children.[43]

The school district's actions angered and frightened parents and students alike. Many students had joined the movement without the knowledge or approval of their parents. Uninvolved in the protests themselves, parents fretted. Many had warned against the participation of children in Project C, and now their fears had been realized. In a community with limited access to education and historically low high school graduation rates, many worried over what would become of their families' livelihoods. Given all that the families and children had to lose, Motley recalled, "everybody" was "upset." And Dr. King's decision to involve the children drew intense criticism.[44]

At this precarious moment, Motley—working once again with Jack Greenberg and local counsel Orzell Billingsley Jr. and Arthur D. Shores—filed a lawsuit in federal court arguing that the board's action violated the rights of all 1,080 students who had been penalized. Motley contended that by suspending or expelling participants in the

Children's Crusade, the superintendent and board of education had made the legal process an instrument of racial discrimination. She requested the reinstatement of every student.[45]

*

A lawsuit required plaintiffs, and Motley found brave representatives of the cause and the case in Rev. Calvin Woods Sr. and his daughter, Linda. Rev. Woods was a singular man. Called to the ministry while in elementary school, steeped in social activism, and a strong believer in "speaking to social issues," he was a Baptist minister and a Birmingham native. He had been beaten, arrested, convicted, and sentenced to six months in prison for protesting the desegregation of Birmingham's buses in 1956, although his sentence was eventually overturned. He cofounded, with Rev. Fred Shuttlesworth, the Alabama Christian Movement for Human Rights, which was a cosponsor of Project C. Integrally involved in the campaign, Rev. Woods had also been beaten and arrested by the Birmingham police during the protests, and Ku Klux Klan members had spat in his face.[46]

That Rev. Woods's daughter joined the struggle for civil rights surprised no one. Hidden away in the backseat of the reverend's Cadillac, Linda and her sister, both still in grade school, had traveled to protests with their father for years. Linda grew up watching her father's brave exploits, and what she saw left an indelible impression on the young girl. The sight of whites "treating my dad so bad" when "all he was trying to do was to make things better for Blacks" "made" her "want to get involved." Inspired by her father's example, Linda seized the opportunity to do her part.[47]

Linda Woods's moment in the sun arrived that May day in 1963, when, at the tender age of eleven, she joined the Children's Crusade. Birmingham police officers arrested her and charged her with parading without a license, just as officers had arrested her father, Dr. King, and other adult protesters. Linda had joined a family protest tradition.[48]

With that family tradition came consequences. Like her father, Linda faced repercussions for daring to defy Jim Crow. The fallout of her participation in the Children's Crusade occurred when, like over a thousand others, she brought home a letter from the highest official in the school district informing Rev. Woods that his daughter could no longer attend the Washington School. Motley had found her ideal plaintiff for the trial.[49]

The judge, Clarence W. Allgood—a native of Birmingham and one of several segregationists whom President Kennedy chose for lifetime appointments to the bench—was disinclined to side with the children. That was clear to Motley soon upon arriving in his courtroom at eleven o'clock in the morning. Allgood waited until late in the afternoon to deny Motley's request for the injunction. In the interim the judge mused aloud on subjects entirely unrelated to the issue of the children's rights.[50]

Allgood's first unnerving comment was in reaction to Motley—to her presence at the lawyers' table in the federal courtroom—in patently sexist terms. Judge Allgood "wanted to know," Motley recalled, "how it was that I, a woman lawyer, was the only one arguing the proposition" when several male lawyers, including Billingsley and Shores, had accompanied her to the hearing. Motley deflected the remark, employing a tactic that Thurgood Marshall had long urged Black lawyers to use in the face of bigoted comments. Instead of directly engaging the judge's insult, Motley retorted in a way that did not even acknowledge it: "Well, because I am the Legal Defense Fund attorney assigned to the case, and I have had prior experiences in issues of this kind, and these local lawyers are not experienced in these matters." Of all the lawyers in the courtroom, Motley insisted, she, in fact, had the greatest claim to belong there.[51]

Sharpening his point, the judge blurted, "You're a woman. Would you want your child marching in some parade?" "Well," a steely Motley countered, "we're not here to discuss the morality of it or whether I would have my child here, but whether we are going to enjoin the school board from keeping these children out." Cool as ever on the outside, Motley seethed on the inside.[52]

Allgood next commented on another topic not at issue. He volunteered that he bore no "racial hatred" toward Blacks. In fact, he said, for the past twenty-five years, a Black man had worked for him.

As Motley watched the time pass, she grew agitated. She had no illusion that the court would side with the plaintiffs and planned to appeal the judge's adverse ruling. Time was of the essence if she was to appeal that same day and spare the parents and children another day of anxious uncertainty. Allgood's musings—nothing more than a stalling tactic—stood in her way. At 3:00 p.m., after endless extraneous talk, Judge Allgood finally announced his decision, and it was exactly what Motley had expected.[53]

In his written opinion ruling against Linda Cal Woods and the hundreds of other students, Judge Allgood expressed his profound disapproval of their activities and truancy. "This Court was shocked," wrote Allgood, "to see hundreds of school children ranging in age from six to sixteen running loose and wild without direction over the streets of Birmingham and in the business establishments." Under the circumstances, Birmingham's police officials understandably exacted punishment on the students who "ran wild" for forty-five minutes. The court would not interfere in the workings of the board of education, and it trusted that its officials—"dedicated, courageous, honorable men"—would not have imposed punishment as a result of "prejudice, anger or retaliation." Motley believed that Allgood had deliberately waited until the late afternoon to deliver this predictable ruling. He had hoped to deprive her of the ability to appeal to the Fifth Circuit, and to deprive the appellate court of the chance to immediately rule on the matter.[54]

Yet Motley was one step ahead. She had been so certain that Allgood would rule against her clients, and so determined to immediately appeal the decision, that she had taken an extraordinary step: she had alerted Chief Judge Elbert Tuttle of the Fifth Circuit to expect to receive her legal papers challenging Allgood's decision. Judge Tuttle, who by now had witnessed Motley try numerous cases, agreed to hear the appeal later that same afternoon. Motley planned to depart Birmingham for Atlanta, the location of the federal courthouse, on the last flight of the day in the afternoon. Allgood's stalling made her afraid that she would be too late.[55]

Shortly after 3:00 p.m., Motley rang Tuttle's chambers to inform him that she would not be able to make it to Atlanta in time after all. "I'm afraid we won't be able to get there today because the last plane has left." But Tuttle's next words surprised and delighted Motley. "No," he said, "*I checked the schedule* and there is one at 5 o'clock that will get you here by six." Tuttle promised Motley that he would hear her appeal at 7:00 p.m. The conversation—and the extraordinary deference the chief judge showed to Motley—illustrated the tremendous respect and goodwill the civil rights lawyer had earned. Motley arrived on time, and Tuttle vindicated the students—all 1,080 of them.[56]

Just hours after Allgood, in the long and meandering hearing, had justified the children's punishment, Judge Tuttle ordered the school superintendent to halt the suspensions and expulsions of the students involved in the Children's Crusade. In comments from the bench, Tuttle chastised Allgood for ignoring clearly relevant U.S. Supreme Court precedent. In decisions issued earlier that same week, the justices had reversed the convictions of activists who had been arrested while staging sit-ins at segregated lunch counters. Given the High Court's decision, Tuttle—visibly angry and exasperated with the school board's attorneys—said the students had been illegally arrested for doing nothing more than exercising their constitutional rights. Tuttle called it "shocking" that they had been thrown out of school, particularly at a time of national alarm about school dropouts. The *New York Times* called Tuttle's decision a "sharp rebuke" of the Birmingham judge and, by extension, of the superintendent of schools.[57]

Following Tuttle's initial decision, a three-judge panel of the Fifth Circuit issued an opinion formally reversing Allgood's decision. The court had sided with Motley. The Crusaders would not be punished for protesting Jim Crow and would return to school.[58]

Motley called her advocacy on behalf of the Children's Crusaders her greatest "professional satisfaction." The critically important case laid the groundwork for attorneys' demands in the years to come that students subjected to disparate punishment in schools receive full constitutional protections.[59]

But Motley did not tout her victory merely because of its legal significance. The case also held personal importance. Motley was moved by it partly because the case involved the lives of young and vulnerable children, and partly because of her nearly religious belief in education as an engine of social mobility. Education had propelled her out of the working class, and she was deeply committed to ensuring that others could turn to it as a tool for advancement. She never forgot that Linda Woods, eleven years old, cried when the superintendent expelled her. The little girl protested that she had marched on a Saturday, and thus had been wrongly accused of skipping school. Although Motley would never admit it in open court, the case surely brought to mind her own son, Joel, who was about the same age as Linda at the time.

Motley had imparted her love of learning to Joel. A precocious boy who enjoyed school, he had trouble fathoming "why whites were so mean and kept Negroes out of school." When Motley explained that in Birmingham, "I'm helping these kids go to school," Joel had been "very pleased." Through her representation of the Birmingham Crusaders, Motley had forged a special connection not only to her clients, but also to her son, hundreds of miles away.[60]

Motley's successful advocacy for Linda Woods and the other Crusaders made a tremendous contribution to the Birmingham campaign, helping to keep afloat a movement that had nearly foundered at several points that spring. Long a proponent of the view that Inc. Fund's lawyers had been the primary catalysts of change in the civil rights movement, in Birmingham, Motley understood more than ever the tremendous importance of civil disobedience. While there, she chose not to impose any legal strategies created by the Inc. Fund in New York upon her clients; instead, in collaboration with King, Shuttlesworth, and Abernathy, she formulated legal strategies consistent with the movement's priorities.[61]

Motley ended up handling several cases for Birmingham's activists that left indelible marks on the law and shaped the movement's course. Two others that she handled on behalf of sit-in demonstrators and for Rev. Shuttlesworth ended up in the U.S. Supreme Court. In *Gober v. Birmingham* and *Shuttlesworth v. Birmingham*, the justices ruled in favor of Motley and her clients, deciding that activists could not lawfully be arrested merely for exercising a constitutionally protected right to assemble and protest segregation. And in *Shuttlesworth*, the Court confirmed what the editor of the *Afro-American* had written back in 1963: Judge Jenkins's order forbidding civil rights demonstrations was "obviously unconstitutional."[62] As a result of Motley's advocacy in these cases, activists were able to return to the streets, where the struggle for the soul of America played out.[63]

*

While Motley's role in the Birmingham campaign is barely remembered today, Dr. King repeatedly and publicly recognized her vital role in the movement for civil rights. In a 1965 column published in the *New York Amsterdam News*, King wrote of the lawyers who played their parts to bring about social chance: "There have emerged leaders of great renown," King said, citing "Clarence Darrow, Wendell Willkie, Thurgood Marshall, Charles Houston, Jack Greenberg, and that Portia, Constance Baker Motley," alluding to the beautiful, intelligent, and witty heroine of Shakespeare's *The Merchant of Venice*. To King, Motley was one of the few lawyers who had helped to redeem this country.[64]

Motley reciprocated King's admiration. She thought of him as a saint and an American revolutionary. She greatly admired his courageous willingness to "subject himself to personal suffering and even die" for the cause of changing America. Moreover, King charmed Motley by being a "gentleman." He took pains, she recalled, to "guard her reputation": King, a known womanizer, insisted that the door remain open and the room accessible whenever Motley met him in a hotel.[65]

The close and respectful relationship that King and Motley shared is striking, even surprising. Few knew King to possess enlightened views about women and gender norms. The minister believed that the "primary role" of his wife, Coretta, "was to stay home and raise the children," and he had a well-earned reputation as a philanderer. The FBI, hostile to his civil rights agenda, threatened on numerous occasions to expose his many affairs. King's messy private life and "compulsive sexual athleticism" worried even his friends.[66]

King and SCLC's board of directors, mostly ministers, also enforced traditional gender roles as well as a "sexist culture" within the organization. The SCLC employed few women, and the handful who did join the staff served as "helpmates"—in background roles. Dorothy Cotton, director of SCLC's citizenship education program, adored

King but complained that he expected her to make coffee. Ella Baker, the SCLC associate director who organized its national headquarters and spearheaded its voter registration campaigns, openly criticized King and his colleagues for failing to take seriously women and their ideas. James Lawson, a proponent of nonviolent direct action who helped King formulate strategy, observed that King "had real problems with having a woman in a high position." Bernard Lee, another aide, agreed that King "was absolutely a male chauvinist."[67]

Motley had managed to gain King's respect and admiration despite being a woman. But there was a catch. The minister recognized her not as a woman who was his equal, but as a woman who was exceptional. For King, Motley's professional role defined her, placing her in a class by herself. Her work in the customarily male legal profession eclipsed her gender identity. Her law degree and splendid performance as a legal strategist sheltered her from the treatment typically accorded women of the era. Motley and King's relationship made a critically important and still relevant point: structural gender inequality can thrive notwithstanding an individual man's capacity for a collegial relationship with a particular and extraordinary woman.

King's interactions with Motley do not indicate that he generally accepted women as peers and leaders; but he did experience personal growth as a result of the relationship. Because of his relationship with Motley, he recognized the possibility that a woman might have more to offer than prevailing notions of womanhood indicated. It was an "eye-opening and learning experience" for the minister to see "a woman lawyer of her caliber," recalled Clarence Jones. A personal attorney for King who counseled him throughout the Birmingham campaign, Jones conceded that King admired Motley despite "rampant male chauvinism" in the civil rights movement, including in SCLC. In King's eyes, Motley "walked on water," Jones remembered. He never dismissed or condescended to her; he listened to her and followed her counsel. And for Motley, King's praise helped to raise her already vaunted professional profile.[68]

The two women's leadership roles in the movement led Clarence Jones to call Motley the "lawyer equivalent" of Ella Baker. But Jones's comparison obscured a key point: the women experienced gender bias—and King—differently. Motley's law degree and superior professional status elevated her in King's eyes. Moreover, her good looks and the care she took with her attire and overall self-presentation certainly did not escape Dr. King, a man known for his "love of beautiful women," or other men in SCLC. Baker, on the other hand, lamented that her lack of an advanced degree, her confrontational personality, and her antipathy to being a "fashion plate" limited her prospects with King and therefore in SCLC. By 1965, deeply disappointed with King and his personal failings, Baker had left SCLC behind.[69]

That same year, SCLC invited Motley to speak at its annual convention in Birmingham. Onstage, she feted Dr. King as an "American hero." "We are fortunate," Motley said in her presentation, "that Dr. King came to us to serve and to lead." But not long before, Baker had lambasted the same man as an inauthentic and often ineffective leader with "feet of clay."[70]

Motley's address elided a missing link: the attorney had represented clients who participated in the struggle not only because of King's heroism, but also because of the community organizing of Ella Baker and many others, little known, and mostly women. Organizing in homes, on the streets, and in community meetings, Baker and others who shared her commitments laid the groundwork for Dr. King's community mobilization and for Motley's legal strategizing. As a translator of the cause, Motley worked in courtrooms—sites that were outside of and largely hostile to Black communities—to defeat charges leveled by the white power structure against movement activists. Both Motley and Baker, among countless other women, made vital contributions.[71]

*

In the end, the Birmingham campaign did in fact win fundamental social and legal change. Following the standoff in April 1963, white city fathers and businessmen remained largely reluctant to accede to the movement's demands, but some nevertheless agreed to desegregate lunch counters and increase Black employment opportunities.

Bull Connor and numerous white vigilantes rejected this state of affairs and mounted a barbarous show of resistance. Mobs bombed the residences of prominent Blacks, including the home of Rev. A. D.

King, brother of Dr. Martin Luther King. The terrorism was meant to communicate that no one could escape white power and its wrath.[72]

The violence backfired. After the bombings, President Kennedy pronounced his unequivocal support for the movement's goals, if not its tactics. "The events in Birmingham," said the president in a televised address one month after the demonstrations, "have so increased cries for equality that no city or state legislative body can prudently choose to ignore them." In an ironic twist, Bull Connor had proved so vital to the movement's success in raising consciousness worldwide about the evils of Jim Crow that President Kennedy later quipped, "The civil rights movement should thank God for Bull Connor. He helped it as much as Abraham Lincoln."[73]

Within weeks of the Birmingham standoff, lawyers working for the Kennedy administration began drafting a piece of comprehensive civil rights legislation. The early drafts evolved into the landmark Civil Rights Act of 1964. Congress passed the act during Lyndon B. Johnson's presidency, one year after the climactic events that transpired in Birmingham in the spring of 1963. Observers rightly credited the confrontations on Good Friday and the Children's Crusade as two of several key developments that gave rise to the landmark law. Constance Baker Motley had embodied and been an agent of momentous social change.[74]

Part IV

A Season in Politics

15

"An Ideal Candidate":
The Making of a Political Progressive

On August 28, 1963, thousands gathered at the Lincoln Memorial in Washington, D.C., to demand justice for Black Americans. The March on Washington for Jobs and Freedom was being held one hundred years after the issuance of the Emancipation Proclamation. The event brought together a gamut of civil rights leaders. Black veterans were there along with labor organizers like Bayard Rustin, who planned the march, and A. Philip Randolph, who had protested Black exclusion from federal defense contracting during the 1940s. Black southerners who were wrung out by brutal, racist regimes and the meager living conditions under Jim Crow, as well as a contingent of actors, singers, and other celebrities—Marian Anderson, Bob Dylan, Joan Baez, Harry Belafonte, Ruby Dee, and Ossie Davis—were out in force, too. Young children played about the ankles of their parents. White northerners awakened to the brutality of segregationists by the images newspapers ran from the Children's Crusade in Birmingham were in attendance. Representatives from the NAACP, CORE, SNCC, the National Urban League, and SCLC were among the large numbers of activists there. Martin Luther King Jr. came to urge Congress to enact a comprehensive version of the civil rights bill proposed by President Kennedy; he delivered a speech that would later be inscribed in national history books: "I Have a Dream." John Lewis, then chairman of SNCC, took the stage to speak out against the political moderation of the Kennedy administration and to demand the strongest possible remedies for Black suffering.[1]

Constance Baker Motley, just months removed from her work in

Birmingham, also joined the gathering in Washington that day. Her attendance bore witness to her evolution. She had transformed from a lawyer wholly devoted to a courtroom-based strategy for social change, much like her mentor, Thurgood Marshall, into a movement lawyer who zealously defended the rights of nonviolent protesters. The Montgomery Bus Boycott and the 1963 march, in Motley's eyes, showed that African Americans were "politically aroused," "politically active," and ready to aid the struggle in the courts to defeat Jim Crow.[2]

Motley began to endorse direct action publicly. At a speaking engagement held just one month before the March on Washington, she called direct action "essential." "[P]ressure must be brought to bear on Congress" to enact antidiscrimination legislation, she told the audience, emphasizing the power possessed by ordinary citizens to exert that pressure through mass demonstrations.[3]

Nevertheless, when the day of the March on Washington arrived, Motley hesitated. Often weary because of the demands of her job—intellectual, physical, and with a relentless travel schedule—she was not inclined to make the trek to D.C. "Oh, I don't know whether I want to go to that," she had said to her husband. "I really feel so tired." She had gone on a trip to Cape Cod with him and their son; there she planned to rest and to escape, at least for a time, the frenetic pace of work and her grief over the recent loss of her dear friend Medgar Evers, who had helped her so much during James Meredith's fight to desegregate Ole Miss. For weeks after Evers's murder, Motley had found it exceedingly difficult to muster the energy to rise from her bed and go about her daily activities. With so many burdens on her time and psyche, she thought she might best be served by skipping the march and finding rest. But in the end, duty called.[4]

Motley's prominent role as a lawyer for the movement obligated her, she decided, to leave the warm breezes of Cape Cod for the muggy heat of Washington in late August. She would attend, but without any expectation that much would come of the endeavor. While she hoped the march would be successful, she doubted that Bayard Rustin, its chief organizer, could pull off the mass assembly he imagined. Motley expected few people to show up. "For something like that to be successful would require a great deal of money and organization," she mused, "which everybody knew this movement didn't have."[5]

But watching television reports about the march as they ate breakfast in their hotel room, the Motleys' expectations rose. By eight o'clock in the morning, reports indicated that as many as twenty-five thousand people would attend the march—far more than Motley had imagined. The figures quickly grew. Within half an hour, journalists revised the number upward: based on the people already on the Mall and those disembarking from the buses rolling into town, they estimated that as many as fifty thousand people would attend. An hour later reporters again readjusted the number to one hundred thousand. As the size of the crowd grew, so did Motley's excitement: she and her husband "ran to the march." Little Joel was in tow. When the family arrived at the Lincoln Memorial, she knew for certain that it would be "quite an occasion."[6]

Motley witnessed the march from a privileged vantage, a raised platform reserved for the movers and shakers of the civil rights movement. In the hours before the program started, she had the splendiferous experience of happening upon people whom she had met in her travels. She reacquainted herself with old friends and clients from the small towns and rural backwaters she had visited in Alabama, Mississippi, Georgia, South Carolina, and the many other places she had sojourned in her career. "Plain ordinary people" she had represented in the Deep South came up to her, shook her hand, and remarked upon her role in getting the movement to this high point at the Lincoln Memorial. Through their eyes, Motley saw herself anew. She appreciated more than ever the immensity of her role in the unfolding Second Reconstruction. The adoration of throngs of admirers felt good. The entire day—the coming together of hundreds of thousands of Black people, many previously politically inactive, to protest Jim Crow—amounted, Motley concluded, to the "20th century's finest hour."[7]

Energized by the March on Washington, after that long, hot summer of 1963, Motley, like the nation and the movement, began a new chapter. Just months after the march took place, President John F. Kennedy was assassinated, shaking the nation to the core and further galvanizing racial change. Legislators and voters alike were jolted awake, and the assassination helped pave the way for the passage of the Civil Rights Act of 1964.

Lyndon B. Johnson, the twentieth century's first southern president, played a decisive role. Eager to prove himself by securing the passage of a stronger civil rights bill than Kennedy would have supported, Johnson championed equality in an address before Congress just five days after Kennedy's assassination. "We have talked long enough in this country about equal rights," Johnson urged. "We have talked for 100 years or more. It is time now to write the next chapter, and to write it in the books of law." Defying the segregationist delegation that had defeated civil rights legislation so many times before, a bipartisan Congress passed the landmark bill, which banned racial discrimination in public accommodations, education, and employment, and transformed Black Americans' legal and social status. But this giant step in federal law, taken nearly one hundred years after the Thirteenth Amendment banned slavery, would not address, much less remedy, the economic subjugation of Blacks, nor would it banish inequity in the political system.

*

The next phase of the freedom struggle—the pursuit of political power—and the next phase of Motley's career—a bid for electoral office—were to converge in the months just before and after the passage of the Civil Rights Act in 1964. Few people, and still fewer Black Americans, could claim to be as widely known as Motley, particularly across racial lines. Motley had a nationally recognized name as well as a sterling reputation. New York politicos spied a golden opportunity.

Manhattan power brokers sought Motley out during a time of extraordinary progress and change. That year the city hosted the World Series, the Beatles' "British Invasion," and the World's Fair—opened by President Johnson. The six-hundred-acre, "international" extravaganza was held at Flushing Meadows. Corona Park in Queens featured hundreds of pavilions, as well as restaurants, pools, fountains, attractions, and corporate exhibits, all organized around the theme of "Peace Through Understanding"—apt for this age of strife and fracture. New York reveled in its brimming cultural resplendence, while voices demanding racial justice grew louder and louder. The same year, riots in Harlem broke out over the murder of a fifteen-year-old boy at the hands of the NYPD. Malcolm X, the charismatic minister who surged to national prominence after breaking away from the Black nationalist Nation of Islam, led a chorus of people who condemned racism in the North as well as the South. Motley, as a widely respected proponent of incremental, court-based racial change, was perfectly positioned for her political fortunes to rise in this context.[8]

The Tammany Hall political machine—synonymous with the Democratic Party and known as much for its entrenched corruption as for its progressive policy stances—dominated New York's political landscape. It controlled nominations to elective office, and party loyalty topped the list of qualifications. Tammany's influence extended to Black politics through its standard-bearer, J. Raymond Jones, the so-called Harlem Fox. Jones had migrated from the Virgin Islands to New York in 1918; he discovered the potential power of the Black vote during the 1920s as a follower of the flamboyant Black nationalist Marcus Garvey. During the 1930s, Jones set out to build a base of power in the Tammany machine, the once-powerful voter-turnout group that was at that time dominated by the Irish and in decline after a press campaign exposed its corruption. By the late 1940s, Jones, known as the "eyes and ears of Harlem," had helped Tammany woo Harlemites and rebuild its power; in the process he became an expert on arcane election procedures, a master campaign strategist, and the most highly paid, highest-ranking Black political appointee in New York. He established himself as a "new breed" of Black politician: leaving Black nationalism behind, he sought to build influence within the white power structure rather than outside of it. In 1964 he made history when he was appointed the first Black chief of Tammany Hall. In that role, he was to play kingmaker for the Democratic Party. A sought-after supporter of national party figures such as John and Robert Kennedy and Lyndon B. Johnson, Jones also exerted significant influence over local and state elections. Now, only a few months after ascending to his post, the Harlem Fox courted Constance Baker Motley to run for office.[9]

Despite the prominence of her figure, Motley was a political novice, and Jones's outreach to her was prompted by an unexpected and, to him, undesirable situation. State Senator James Watson had newly resigned his seat to accept a nomination as a civil court judge. In response, the "reform" wing of the Democratic Party endorsed a candidate, Noel Ellison, whom Jones and other Black power brokers deemed unsuitable for leadership. On the surface, Ellison, a Black small business owner, looked respectable enough. But a little digging turned up serious concerns: Ellison had been convicted of "numbers running"—illegal betting—on four separate occasions. The would-be senator's first arrest and conviction had occurred in 1934, soon after he arrived in the United States from Jamaica as a fifteen-year-old. The most recent conviction happened just two years prior to his endorsement, in 1962.

Jones, who during his term as leader of Tammany Hall hoped to free it from the perception—and the reality—of corruption, including office-selling, bribery, and mob ties, found Ellison an embarrassment, an "unacceptable" standard-bearer for the party. It was "obvious" to Jones that the whites among the local reform party leaders, a racially mixed group, had assumed that any Black candidate, no matter his rap sheet, would do for the Upper West Side assembly district that included predominantly Black central Harlem. The Fox was "furious," and set out to replace Ellison with someone of impeccable credentials and high moral fiber.[10]

Motley had risen to the top of the heap of possible candidates when James Watson, who knew Motley from their time at NYU, recommended her as a candidate to replace him. This immediately struck Jones as a brilliant idea. Motley possessed an extraordinary combination of education, experience, and community standing, plus, she was an excellent public speaker and "was very tall and stately" in her bearing. Jones, who had been dreaming about achieving Black political power since the 1920s, saw Motley as a breakthrough candidate. He could imagine it all coming together: Motley could begin her political career in the state senate, then become the first female (and first Black female) Manhattan borough president, and eventually win election as New York City's first Black and first female mayor![11]

Jones marshaled prominent Blacks to support Motley's candidacy, and to convince her to run for the office. James Watson, now Judge

Watson, was the first to approach his old classmate. "Why don't you run for my senate seat," he whispered in her ear at a luncheon meeting. Motley demurred: "I don't have the stomach for it," she said.[12]

A long list of African American luminaries who objected to Ellison as the party's candidate pressed her to reconsider. Dorothy Height—president of the National Council of Negro Women, a member of the President's Commission on the Status of Women, and a longtime advocate of women's participation in electoral politics not only in "ornamental" roles but as party leaders and public officials— headed the civil rights activists who urged Motley. Height, one of the few other women who had also been on the platform at the March on Washington, had known Motley for decades. Sara Fleming, the founder of a women's civic group in New Haven, had first introduced the young activist to Height thirty years before. Dr. Kenneth B. Clark, the psychologist whose influential, if controversial, doll study had been cited by the Supreme Court in *Brown v. Board of Education*, and Robert C. Weaver, an economist and authority on housing discrimination later appointed the first secretary of health and human services, also supported Motley's bid for office.[13]

If Motley attracted Height, Ellison repelled him. Height "feared" that Ellison would be manipulated by "the least desirable forces" in the district. Clark agreed. "Dorothy Height and I grew up here in the streets of Harlem," Clark said, "and we never heard of this man." Edward R. Dudley, a friend of Motley's ever since they were students together at Columbia Law School and the person who urged her to apply for an internship with Marshall, was now the Manhattan borough president and a close ally of Jones. He, too, endorsed Motley's run. After learning that the part-time senate seat would not interfere with her ability to continue her work at LDF, Motley relented. She would run.[14]

Eighteen years into her career at LDF, Motely welcomed the change. After litigating so many cases that brought about so much change, she had concluded that "most of the civil rights problems in the North can be only improved by legislation." She would continue to handle select cases for LDF, but her focus would shift to politics for a season, beginning in 1964. Even before the passage of the Civil Rights Act, she believed that the period, the mid-1960s, had ushered in a time of rebirth and reward for elite Blacks. "[F]or educated blacks," she noted in her memoir, "our time had come." She believed that, because of the social standing she had earned through her career as a civil rights lawyer, her political career would be "jet-propelled." Recalling Du Bois's notion of the "Talented Tenth," Motley felt that by virtue of her intellect and experience, she deserved to lead. But not everyone felt the same way.[15]

Adam Clayton Powell Jr., the pastor of the historic Abyssinian Baptist Church, civil rights activist, flamboyant personality, and representative of Harlem in the U.S. House of Representatives since 1944, was a force to be reckoned with. An unapologetic critic of American hypocrisy, the congressman was also an indefatigable proponent of Black access to affordable housing, fair employment, and political power. Powell did not defer to J. Raymond Jones, to Tammany Hall, or to anyone else. In fact, he and Jones competed for influence. The congressman jealously guarded his position as community power broker.

Also born in New Haven, Powell had known Motley since the war years. They had met in Harlem when Motley was attending Columbia Law School. By that time, Powell, the first person of African descent elected to the New York City Council, had already made a name for himself in politics. After Motley graduated, their paths crossed often, and, as members of the small band of well-educated Blacks who held the reins of leadership in the postwar struggle for racial equality, the two were driven by a common purpose.[16]

But the pair had taken different paths to leadership, and to Powell, their differing forms of activism mattered. Motley rose to prominence as a courtroom intermediary for Blacks' civil rights and had gained legitimacy by making persuasive legal arguments to uniformly white panels of judges. By contrast, Powell had won renown through on-the-ground organizing and had gained legitimacy by building close personal relationships with Blacks in Harlem. And so it was in keeping with his community-based brand of activism that Powell preferred the head of the Harlem Lawyers Association—a local man—to Motley for the open state senate seat. Sure, Motley knew civil rights law, but what did she know about the concerns of the local community?[17]

The nomination for the senate seat turned into a battle. Motley

initially lost the Democratic Party nomination to Ellison. Unaccustomed to losing, and in so public a manner, the lawyer got cold feet;
she quickly regretted her decision to enter electoral politics. But
influential supporters intervened. Claiming that the vote had been
"rigged," the Democratic Party and Mayor Robert F. Wagner, among
others, filed a lawsuit arguing that Motley's loss had resulted from
"irregularities." They argued that Ellison had prevailed because his
backers had manipulated the proxy voting process. The state supreme
court agreed, and ruled Ellison ineligible to stand for election. A
majority of the committee on vacancies supported Motley, and they
flipped the result, instating her as the party's nominee in a special
election that was to be held in February 1964. Motley had won the
skirmish, but the resistance to her candidacy exposed a real vulner-
ability: her reputation and credentials alone would not win her the
seat.[18]

Motley—a woman who had found fame in formality-steeped
courtrooms under a penetrating white gaze—did not scream "authentic Black," "natural leader," or whatever people conjured when they
thought of Black power brokers. She projected a reserved and dignified image, a persona consistent with the upper-class British cultural
conventions that her parents had taught her. This mask helped her
fit into a legal profession controlled by men and by white people, a
culturally conservative climate, sometimes hostile to her, but more
often indifferent. She was pleasant and witty, but she was not known
for approachability, or for her ease with workaday people—key ingre-
dients to political success. To win the confidence of voters, she would
have to reinvent herself.

Motley needed to appeal to voters who included the people of central Harlem, an area famous for its link to the Harlem Renaissance.
The neighborhood's culture—vibrant and heterogeneous—comprised
a spectrum of people and proclivities. Southern migrants and Carib-
beans, Puerto Ricans and whites, artists and laborers, doctors and
lawyers, Democrats and Republicans, Socialists and Communists,
Black nationalists and Black Power enthusiasts comingled there. If
any single cultural strain held the neighborhood together, it might be
described as earthy, edgy, artistic, proletarian, and mediated by the
Black experience. Certain matters rose to the top voters' priorities.

They cared about access to affordable housing and gainful employment, about public safety, and about education reform. Some but not
all prioritized school desegregation—the fight that had made Motley
famous. Notwithstanding her qualifications, Motley had her work cut
out for her.[19]

*

For nearly twenty years, from 1942 to 1961, Motley had lived in
Harlem in an apartment located at 2181 Madison Avenue, a building known as the Riverton, which was the counterpart to Stuyvesant
Town, at 420 East 23rd Street. The two collections of redbrick high-
rise apartment buildings looked the same, with one big exception:
only Blacks lived at the Riverton, and only whites lived at Stuyvesant
Town. The irony was profound: by day, Motley fought segregation,
including residential segregation, and by night, she lived its reality. In 1961, she and her family, following a path trodden by other
middle-class Blacks, moved to 875 West End Avenue, an otherwise
all-white apartment building in an affluent neighborhood outside
of Harlem, at the intersection with West 103rd Street. Despite her
profession and status, the Motleys "had a little trouble getting into
the building at first," but it did not take long for the gatekeepers to
realize the folly of trying to exclude one of the nation's foremost civil
rights lawyers.[20]

Motley had viewed Harlem as a Black "cultural mecca" when she
had moved there in 1942, but by 1961 she was eager to leave behind
the neighborhood that she had come to think of as a "ghetto." The
family's ability to "afford the move" told everyone she had arrived.
The move "allowed me to escape the psychological stigma that every
ghettoized person endures," Motley recalled. Yet it was the very same
neighborhood she left behind that, three years later, she was vying
to represent.[21]

In a bid to reconnect Motley to Harlem—and reintroduce Harlem
voters to Motley—Dorothy Height, Kenneth Clark, and other well-
known figures suggested she take "walking tours" of the district.
Walking alongside her, the respected figures introduced the candidate to local people and vouched for her authenticity. While she
walked the streets and shook hands with locals, campaign literature

was circulated that depicted her at home with her family and with famous clients in southern courtrooms. And during its final days, the campaign received a big boost: Mayor Robert Wagner and James Meredith, Motley's most famous client, endorsed her candidacy and joined her on the campaign trail.[22]

The tactic worked. Motley promised locals that she would represent their interests. She vowed that if elected she would fight for laws and policies that would yield "more jobs, better housing and better schools" for Blacks. She would continue to seek equal opportunities in housing, education, and employment, much as she had throughout her career; but now she would seek those imperatives from the legislature.[23]

Voters turned out to meet Motley, and then they turned out for her at the polls. In February 1964, she won. On the morning of the election, she stood on Broadway in the mild, sunny weather, shaking the hands of passersby—an election day ritual—but few even knew that the election was taking place; only the most engaged voters paid attention to off-cycle elections. In announcing Motley's victory, the *New York Times* noted that she had won in "one of the quietest political campaigns in many years." Nevertheless, she won. She captured about 60 percent of the 5,950 votes cast. And then, a few months later, aided by the Johnson landslide, voters turned out for her again. She won a full two-year term in the state senate in the regular election held that November.

It was a historic win; she was the first Black woman to hold a seat in that body. Notes of warm congratulations poured in from friends and luminaries in the movement. Motley's election made national news and generated special headlines. Riffing on her name as if she were royalty, the *Chicago Daily Defender* called her "Constance the First." Meanwhile, the *Philadelphia Tribune* offered this description of the first "colored woman" in the New York Senate: "Tan Woman Senator Takes Seat in New York," a headline boasted.[24]

Right out of the gate, Motley cast herself as a liberal lioness. Within a month of taking her seat, she introduced dozens of bills, all tailored to insights she had gained from the neighborhood and her years in the courtroom.[25]

Each and every one of Motley's legislative proposals sought to advance civil rights and equal opportunity. Several sought to open the workplace to New Yorkers regardless of their background. These initiatives went to the heart of the 21st senatorial district voters' concerns. The proposed bills sought to help end discrimination in apprenticeship and training programs, gateways to skilled employment and union jobs that paid well and enabled middle-class life. Motley also proposed to ban employment discrimination at volunteer fire departments and hospitals, long the preserve of white ethnic groups. She introduced a bill to end the requirement that marriage license applications list the "color" of each party. At a time when nineteen states still banned interracial marriage, the initiative sought to unyoke race and marriage. The U.S. Supreme Court would not get around to decriminalizing interracial marriage until 1967.[26]

Senator Motley often used her voice to address the unfinished business of racial inequality in criminal law. In 1964, amid concerns about organized crime, urban riots, and narcotics abuse, and at the urging of a tough-on-crime governor, Nelson A. Rockefeller, the New York legislature debated, and then enacted, "no-knock" warrant and "stop and frisk" laws. The no-knock bill authorized police who suspected the presence of narcotics and possessed a special warrant to forcibly enter a home without knocking; the stop-and-frisk law permitted an officer to stop, question, and search a person in a public place if he reasonably suspected that the individual had committed or was about to commit a crime. The New York State Association of Chiefs of Police called the no-knock warrant a "necessary tool" to stamp out the "rising narcotic trade." The idea that an officer executing a search warrant "must stand at the door and tell the people inside who he is and what he wants" was, the association claimed, "silly." The stop-and-frisk law ended the "sad state of affairs" that prevented officers from "accosting" the suspicious persons who purportedly roamed around at night in a "neighborhood where he does not belong." Officers' ability to stop and frisk suspects would protect, the association said, the "multitude" against "the minority groups who carry dangerous weapons, dope peddlers," and people who worked "only at crime."[27]

While law enforcement loved the no-knock and stop-and-frisk bills, many New Yorkers—including civil libertarians and civil rights activists—hated them. During the legislative debate over the bills, New Yorkers worried about police brutality and abuse of power sent letter after letter to Motley's office. In a handwritten note, Edgar Hayes of West 29th Street wrote, "These two bills are aimed directly at the harassment and intimidation of minority groups!" The Harlem Lawyers Association agreed. The group expressed unwavering opposition to the bills on grounds that the provisions would worsen the already bad experiences that Black and Puerto Rican New Yorkers had in their encounters with police. The Harlem lawyers, alongside others, argued that the bills contravened the logic of a landmark 1961 U.S. Supreme Court decision, *Mapp v. Ohio*: the case had banned states' use of evidence obtained in searches and seizures by the police that violated the Fourth Amendment. The proposed New York laws appeared to encourage the disregard of individual rights that the Court had so recently outlawed. Many who urged Motley to vote against the bills appreciated the frustrations of law enforcement officers. But Edward F. Flynn, like other New Yorkers, expressed "extreme apprehension" about the "additional arbitrary power" that the bill would grant the police at the expense of individual citizens' rights.[28]

Governor Rockefeller—a member of a moderate Republican family whose "support for blacks and black colleges was legendary"—had warmly greeted Motley's election to the senate. The governor "had seemed more thrilled than I by my election to the New York Senate," Motley recalled in her memoir. Just after her election, Rockefeller's aides "arranged for a photo opportunity," signaling the governor's recognition of her historic achievement. Despite her acquaintance with Rockefeller, Motley did not hesitate in voting against the bill he championed.[29]

The racism she had witnessed in the nation's criminal legal system informed her decision. In fact, she had grappled with injustice in the criminal law system in her debut argument at the U.S. Supreme Court in 1961. Best known for her victories in civil cases, in *Hamilton v. Alabama* she convinced the justices to reverse the criminal conviction of Charles Clarence Hamilton, an illiterate and mentally disabled Black man. Hamilton had been accused, arrested, twice indicted, and ultimately convicted of breaking and entering at night "with intent to ravish"—rape—an elderly white woman. An all-white, six-man jury in Jefferson County, Alabama, rendered the verdict and sentenced Hamilton to death by electrocution. Not only had the evidence been flimsy, Motley had argued, but the state of Alabama had violated the Constitution by depriving Hamilton of the right to counsel during arraignment. Motley had won, saving a man's life. She had also seen police corruption, compounded by racial bias, infect the criminal legal system in New York. For as long as she could remember, Blacks in Harlem had been protesting police harassment and corruption. In light of these searing experiences, how could she support legislation that expanded the discretion of law enforcement and increased the criminal legal system's grip on American citizens? She could not.[30]

Motley knew that the no-knock and stop-and-frisk bills would undermine individual rights and have perverse consequences for the poor and for communities of color—the most vulnerable of her very own constituents. "I certainly will vote against any bill which permits policemen to search persons without due requirements of law," she responded in a short but pointed letter to an American Legion post vice commander who had lobbied her to oppose the bill. "It is my opinion," she wrote to another legislator, that the bill clearly infringed upon the constitutional rights of citizens. The law was passed by a majority of her colleagues, but by rejecting the expansion of police power that sowed the seeds for what is now called mass incarceration, Motley nurtured her legacy as a fierce proponent of racial equality.[31]

Motley's experiences also motivated her legislative advocacy against unfairness in the housing market. The inadequate housing available to working-class people and people of color had been a point of contention for countless years. Through laws, policies, pacts, and practices, landlords, sellers, real estate agents, city planners, and governmental agencies confined Blacks to specific neighborhoods away from whites, particularly middle-class whites. In the South, it was not uncommon for Blacks and the working poor to live in shacks that lacked indoor plumbing. In the North, in cities such as Chicago, Detroit, Cleveland, Philadelphia, and New York, the have-nots suffered in overcrowded neighborhoods and unsafe high-rise tenement buildings that sometimes lacked heat and hot water, reliable electricity, and proper ventilation. Regardless of class background, Blacks, Latinos, and other groups deemed undesirable faced flagrant housing discrimination. In Harlem there were few affordable and safe apartment units for the mostly Black residents crammed into its city blocks. The neighborhood, a mere 3.5 square miles, housed more than 232,000 people in 1965—more than 100 per acre—in old, dilapidated, and deteriorating buildings.[32]

Motley knew all about these conditions. She had lived in Harlem both as a student and, later, as a rising Black professional. Married to a Harlem real estate agent, she had heard her husband's stories about the local housing market, including how race figured into the price of rental units and influenced landlords' responses to tenants. She had fought deplorable housing conditions as a civil rights lawyer, repeatedly suing to end residential segregation. But the ghettos remained largely impervious to lawsuits, particularly in the North, where segregation did not exist by law. In a 1963 address to the Women's City Club of New York, Motley had called "Black ghettos" the "prime symbol of American racism," profoundly harmful to Blacks' educational and employment opportunities. She spoke of how the isolation of Black children in ghettos produced "social and cultural poverty," burdening them with handicaps they passed along to their own children, who repeated the "same frustrating cycle of low-level existence."[33]

For decades, tenants had withheld rent payments until landlords fixed housing code violations. In extreme cases, when "slumlords" repeatedly jeopardized the safety and welfare of low-income tenants, tenants organized mass strikes to withhold rent. As early as 1934, a rent strike forged by middle-class Blacks in the Sugar Hill section of Harlem helped to popularize the strategy and create strong tenant advocacy organizations that laid the groundwork for rent control legislation.

Rent strikes were held on several occasions in 1963 and 1964, as Motley was beginning her legislative career, but they had never been declared lawful. Motley introduced a bill, favored by housing activists, to legalize such strikes. Partly because of her efforts, in 1965 the legislature relieved tenants who abandoned unsafe dwellings of the legal responsibility to pay rent.[34]

Motley also took a stand in an ongoing struggle against school segregation and for educational reform. Just prior to her election, in February 1964, she had endorsed a massive one-day school boycott of New York City schools by 460,000 students—half the system's pupils. Staged by Black and Latino activists, the boycott both dramatized and protested the inferior facilities, overcrowded conditions, and inadequate education provided by schools predominantly attended by students of color. Pickets marched at 300 of the city's 860 schools, crossed the Brooklyn Bridge, and ended up in front of the board of education in downtown Brooklyn.

Observing all this, Senator Motley introduced legislation to promote school equity; her bill required school authorities to draw district boundaries and select school sites in a manner that avoided the segregation of pupils by race, color, or national origin. The measure constituted a clear extension of her past advocacy. In 1961, she had won a judgment against the board of education of New Rochelle, New York; the court found that the board had perpetuated unlawful segregation through school site selection choices and attendance zones. In the New York Senate, Motley introduced bills to ban de facto school segregation perpetuated through precisely these same means. She also advocated free college tuition and supported scholarship programs for needy students.[35]

With initiatives such as these Motley made a point and proved skeptics wrong, all in just a few short months. The courtroom warrior against inequality in education, housing, and criminal law had become a legislative champion for equality in those same areas. Motley had taken an unexpected foray into politics, and she had made an impact. One of just three African American members of the New York Senate at the time, she had shaken things up in Albany.

While Motley's stint in the legislature would be brief, she paved the way for other Black women to seek and win political office and advance progressive legislative agendas. Shirley Chisholm followed directly in Motley's footsteps when she won election to the New York State Assembly in 1965, and three years later, made history as the first Black female member of the U.S. Congress. Once again, Motley had been an agent of change, this time by making a risky move to politics.[36]

16

"Crisis of Leadership": A Clash Between Radical and Reform Politics

When Lyndon Johnson ascended to the presidency, he was seen as illegitimate in the eyes of the Kennedys and many of the Washington elite. Johnson desperately wanted to prove them all wrong.[1]

The president found his issues in poverty—in the privation and hardship, the hunger and rags, the illiteracy and humiliation that the born-poor son of a Texas farmer knew all too well. In his first State of the Union address, Johnson championed the greatest expansion of the welfare state since the New Deal. He declared an "unconditional war" on poverty and unemployment—a bid to end the era's soaring 19 percent poverty rate and related social ills. Race profoundly shaped the incidence of poverty in America; dogged by discrimination and its vestiges, Blacks lived at the bottom of society. Statistics clearly showed this racial divide. In 1959, 18.1 percent of whites lived in poverty, compared to a staggering 55.1 percent of Black Americans. Children fared worse—and Black children had it worst of all. In 1965, poverty trapped a whopping 65.6 percent of Black children, compared to 20.6 percent of white children.[2]

With Medicaid, Job Corps, Head Start Legal Services, Volunteers in Service to America, food stamps, and the Community Action Program, among other initiatives, Johnson empowered the thirty million destitute Americans who did not share in the nation's prosperity. Through the "better schools," "better health," "better homes," "better training," and "better job opportunities" the president had called for in an address to Congress, Johnson sought to "replace despair with opportunity" and give all Americans a "fair chance to develop their own capacities."[3]

The president's antipoverty policies and his commitment to upward mobility held tremendous allure for Motley. Johnson's proposal to give the poor a "hand up" rather than a "handout" spoke to her. His rhetoric appealed to her populist instincts and her personal history. Having gained opportunity through New Deal–era antipoverty programs, Motley eagerly supported Johnson's commitment to new policies that would ensure every citizen had a chance to "advance" to the "limits of his capacities."[4]

Just as Franklin Delano Roosevelt's New Deal programs had grown out of the economic calamity that had overtaken the country during the 1930s, desperate need and social unrest in the 1960s helped give rise to Johnson's War on Poverty. These same fraught conditions spurred Motley's initiatives in the New York legislature. But for many striving for Black freedom, these liberal, reformist policies did not meet the moment.[5]

A civil rights protest led by the Brooklyn chapter of the Congress of Racial Equality, planned for the televised April 22 opening of the 1964 World's Fair in Queens, cast a spotlight on Black activists' growing antipathy to the white establishment and its Black allies—people like Motley. Mayor Robert F. Wagner and Governor Nelson Rockefeller hoped that the fair would stimulate spending and therefore economic growth. Instead, disgusted by the government's lavishing millions on the event while many people of color in the city faced devastating poverty, the CORE chapter planned to disrupt the event. It organized a "stall-in" of automobiles along the highways leading to the fair—extraordinarily busy throughways such as Grand Central Parkway and the Brooklyn-Queens Expressway—to obstruct traffic.[6]

The planned protest spurred a vehement backlash; government officials and law enforcement condemned it as a dangerous stunt. Mayor Wagner mobilized more than a thousand police officers and dozens of tow trucks to prevent it. President Johnson, scheduled to speak at the fair's opening ceremonies, warned that such "extreme measures" hurt the cause of civil rights. Roy Wilkins, the head of the NAACP, mocked the bush-league scheme. The media castigated the "extremists" who supported it. James Farmer, CORE's national director, announced that the tactic was antithetical to the movement's aims, and he suspended the chapter responsible for it. The local CORE chapter's threatened stall-in did not materialize. But chanting protesters still made a point; they drowned out President Johnson's remarks at the fair's opening. The thwarted stall-in showcased growing tensions between reformers and radicals. During her foray into politics, Motley found herself caught in the middle of the ideological battle between the likes of President Johnson, Governor Rockefeller, and Mayor Wagner, and radical provocateurs like Malcolm X.[7]

*

When the civil rights movement—the integration-oriented crusade from which Motley had emerged—achieved its greatest victory yet in the Civil Rights Act of 1964, Malcolm X's influence was skyrocketing. The leader of the Organization of Afro-American Unity, a Harlem-based offshoot of the Nation of Islam, Malcolm X advocated Black racial pride and self-sufficiency. He did so as Martin Luther King's wing of the civil rights movement lost ground as a guiding force, particularly in urban, working-class Black communities.

Malcolm X ridiculed King's devotion to nonviolent civil disobedience; in the context of violent white resistance to Black liberation, he insisted that fidelity to nonviolence made little sense. Blacks under attack should defend themselves, he argued. When asked about the Birmingham protests, Malcolm said, "If anyone sets a dog on a Black man, the Black man should kill the dog, whether he is a four-legged or a two-legged dog." Instead of pleading for integration and allowing the white establishment to co-opt demonstrations, such as what he considered the "Farce on Washington," Blacks should adopt tactics that destabilized the social order. "Revolution is bloody, revolution is hostile, revolution knows no compromise," X proclaimed in his "Message to the Grassroots." Malcolm X also called Thurgood Marshall a "twentieth century Uncle Tom" and dismissed the NAACP's legal strategy as beneficial only to "the middle-class so-called Negroes, who are in the minority." "[W]hat to them is an American dream to us is an American nightmare," he said. Blacks, according to Malcolm, should instead demand self-determination, political power, and an end to white cultural dominance.[8]

*

In 1961, Malcolm's searing critique of the NAACP's legal strategy—a campaign that had taken down Jim Crow in education, public transportation, parks, playgrounds, and so many other areas—had ensnared Motley, the future state senator, presaging the coming ideological clash she encountered in New York politics. Following the lead of other prominent figures who sought to defend the quest for integration, Constance Baker Motley agreed to appear on a panel with Malcolm X. Like many others, she underestimated him. The minister relished appearances with the likes of Motley. He viewed these debates as opportunities to advocate for his political philosophy and gain the upper hand over the Black establishment. In preparation for them he famously practiced scoring points through dramatic confrontations; his performances were scattered with barbed rhetoric and personal insults. Little did Motley realize, but X's opponents—and foils—could rarely best him.[9]

Malcolm and Motley were to debate on October 15, 1961, at the "Open Mind Roundtable," televised by NBC News. One of many such events held at the time, the discussion comprised a moderator, academics, veterans of the civil rights movement, and Malcolm X. The moderator framed the discussion with the question "Where Is the Negro Headed?" Motley had just returned to New York from her crusade against Ole Miss, and seemed well positioned to answer the question. Dr. Kenneth B. Clark, whose research on segregation's psychological harms the justices had favorably cited in *Brown v. Board of Education*; Richard Haley, field secretary for CORE; and Professor Monroe Berger, a Princeton University sociologist, were also on the stage.[10]

Without mincing words, Malcolm X called Black Americans "disillusioned" and "very angry." Motley—the only woman on the panel and the last person to speak—steered the discussion toward what she evidently perceived as an uncontroversial point through a series of leading questions. "You recognize, don't you," she queried, that the struggle for racial equality had yielded "some progress" and "greater dignity" for the "American Negro"? "We don't disagree on that, do we?" she pressed. "Don't you think the Negro today is substantially

better off than he was at the end of slavery," that "we have made progress, and we are continuing to make progress?"

Malcolm retorted, speaking of the millions of Blacks imprisoned
at the time: "Now you have 20 million black people in America who are
begging for some kind of recognition as human beings and the average white man today thinks we're making progress."[11]

The sharp rejoinder registered his pleasure in critiquing the
worldview and achievements of integration's icons, and equated
the Civil Rights Queen's guarded optimism about racial change with
the naïve, paternalistic musings of the "average white man."[12]

The exchange could only have left Motley, who was accustomed to
admiration and deference, stung. She proudly touted the Inc. Fund's
"historic" win in *Brown*, with its "tremendous" social impact, and
she frequently called her eighteen-month-long battle to desegregate
Ole Miss "the last battle of the Civil War." She carried herself like
Black royalty. How dare Malcolm X—a man she would have considered
an uneducated convict turned sidewalk preacher—disrespect her, a
tireless, tested advocate for social justice who had created tangible
improvement in the lives of millions of Black Americans?[13]

But instead of showing her displeasure, Motley took the high road
during the television appearance. She insisted that she and the minister were in "basic agreement" that the condition of the Negro "has
been bad and is still very bad in many areas." Yet her second attempt
to reach consensus failed, just like the first. Malcolm did not even
bother to respond to the Civil Rights Queen. He rejected the idea
that Blacks and whites, rich and poor, could ever "integrate." And
he continued to disparage the achievements of the "traditional black
leadership" class.[14]

*

Three years later, Motley again had to contend with Malcolm X, now
a world-famous foe of the mainstream civil rights movement. This
time Motley steered clear of any direct confrontation. Nevertheless,
she could hardly avoid the reality that he and his radical beliefs had
put her in a bind. By the mid-1960s, Motley—a civil rights lawyer
once considered a transformational figure—looked weak and accommodationist. The rise of the Muslim minister and his organization,

right there in Harlem, the neighborhood that Motley represented
in the state senate, put her on the defensive and pushed her, out of
political necessity, even further to the left.

Malcolm X and Congressman Adam Clayton Powell Jr., a confirmed
skeptic and a vocal critic of Motley's despite her legislative efforts,
enjoyed a cozy relationship, and together reinforced the view that
her brand of politics was deficient. Malcolm praised the congressman's independence from the Democratic machine and viewed him
as an authentic and effective representative of the people of Harlem,
a leader able to extract concessions from the white establishment
on behalf of his constituents. The pair also shared a bombastic rhetorical style, a belief in Black self-determination, and a flamboyant
masculinity. Motley, one of few women in the male-dominated world
of New York politics, could not share in the masculinity that bound
Malcolm X and Congressman Powell together. By comparison, her
politics and style looked tamer—and they were.[15]

A Democratic Party loyalist, Motley believed in the American
dream and in the possibility of integration. Her life and work rested
on faith in the progress that could be made through whites' good faith
and Black excellence. She looked to the rule of law—including antidiscrimination laws—and the welfare state to ensure equal opportunity regardless of race. By contrast, according to Malcolm X and
Congressman Powell, unrelenting white racism was an omnipresent
fact of life. Nevertheless, Powell shared Motley's basic commitment
to the American political system and to the Democratic Party, and
Malcolm X also endorsed the ballot as a path to Black power. However,
amid the social division and political turbulence of the mid-1960s,
the contrast between the two points of view was stark. And during the
time of Black nationalism's dominance, Motley—forever associated
with integration, by now passé in some quarters—found herself on
the defensive.[16]

Motley had made her name as a social justice warrior in the courtroom, as a progressive in the legislature, and stood her ground against
the radicals. She dismissed Black nationalism as a tired, emotional
response to racism in which leaders routinely deployed inflammatory
nationalistic rhetoric to stoke the grass roots. Malcolm X masterfully
whipped up crowds by castigating "white devils" and "Uncle Tom" civil

rights leaders, but he offered no real program for social change. Powell "play[ed] the Black Nationalism card" throughout his career, using it to gain and maintain power in Harlem. In several public addresses, Motley alleged that the new "militant" Black leadership had caused a "crisis" in the Black community through its "abandonment" of the "traditional techniques of achieving opportunity"—tried-and-true practices such as "conference, persuasion and conciliation" in the courts and legislatures. The turn away from the methods that had delivered concrete wins for the movement toward fiery rhetoric had led the public astray, Motley claimed. Activists had turned to "startling" tactics that included demonstrators chaining themselves to bulldozers and blocking the entrances to Mayor Wagner's and Governor Rockefeller's offices. It was all wrong.[17]

*

The riots that took place in Harlem just two weeks after the passage of the landmark Civil Rights Act proved to Motley that her fears were justified. A white police lieutenant had killed a Black teenager—James Powell, only fifteen years old—during a confrontation on East 70th Street; Powell had been loitering and misbehaving in the predominately wealthy, white neighborhood. The off-duty officer said he had fired three shots after the young man, who was armed with a knife, refused to obey his order to halt. Back in Harlem many residents dismissed the officer's account. The shooting fit a pattern of brutality and overreaction by the New York Police Department. Seething with anger, the community mobilized to protest the killing. Over a thousand people attended a rally on 125th Street organized by local chapters of CORE. Speaker after speaker chastised the NYPD. Critics also charged whites with a wider pattern of racial oppression: Blacks endured terrible schools, overcrowded housing, and unskilled low-wage employment.[18]

A few peaceful days followed the initial protest, but violence erupted during a demonstration at a police station on West 123rd Street in Central Harlem. Thousands of angry Harlemites flooded the streets. A senior officer emerged from the station and promised that an investigation had been launched into the shooting of James Powell, but the demonstrators were not mollified. The police tried to disperse the protesters, firing rounds into the air while the crowd grew angrier. Some demonstrators threw rocks or pulled fire alarms. Others looted businesses. Several tossed Molotov cocktails and set fires. Many stood observing and applauding the chaos and destruction. Some yelled, "Killer cops must go!," "Police brutality must go!"

Amid the violence, Jesse Gray, leader of a housing council and the recent rent strikes, urged Blacks to seek revenge on wrongdoers and oppressors; they should kill police officers and other whites on sight, he said. "Blood for blood" was the mantra. Several Black leaders called for the resignation of the police commissioner, Michael Murphy, for failed leadership—his officers incited violence by excessively using force, by firing live ammunition for crowd control, and through indiscriminate brutality.[19]

A swarm of additional officers converged on the fracas. Seeking to regain control of the neighborhood, Mayor Wagner ordered more than five hundred policemen to Harlem. Sirens screaming, officers patrolled in black-and-white cars, and firefighters were deployed. Police guarded the streets on foot, revolvers drawn. Some officers, wearing riot gear, manned rooftops, while another contingent of patrolmen wearing military-style tactical gear guarded the area. Eventually the National Guard took charge—the same branch of the military that President Eisenhower had called on in 1957 to quell the violent white backlash against the nine Black students who sought to desegregate Little Rock's Central High School. Mobilized by Governor Rockefeller, the guardsmen restored order, but not before significant damage had been done.

During what turned out to be a six-day melee in Harlem, 450 people were arrested, over 100 were injured, and one person died. And the protests spread to other parts of the city and state. A "night of Birmingham horror" had hit New York City, home of the most sophisticated and progressive population in the United States, or so it was believed.[20]

The charged episode laid bare the chasm between the civil rights activists and the new generation of Black liberation advocates. Mayor Wagner had called in Dr. Martin Luther King, who just months earlier had led the world-famous Birmingham campaign against segregation, to restore calm. But Harlem's leaders rejected King out of hand;

they were "mad as hell" at Wagner for trying to "import Dr. King from Atlanta to discuss problems in Harlem." In other corners of the city, however, King and his nonviolent philosophy of reform remained popular. A survey published in the *New York Times* one week after the riots indicated that the overwhelming majority of residents considered Dr. King the most effective Black leader; Congressman Powell and Malcolm X came in a distant second and third, respectively. And residents counted the NAACP the most effective civil rights organization.[21]

As one of only a handful of Black officials, and the first Black woman state senator, Motley was an authoritative voice during the riots, and she sided with the forces of reason and reform. She condemned police brutality, urged calm, and insisted on the rule of law. Playing the role of racial mediator and moderate, she sought to both serve her Black constituents and appease her white colleagues while assiduously avoiding assessments of blame. "Whether or not it's true," she said, "Harlem believes the police are the enemy" and "not there for their protection." She did not comment on Black Harlemites' demands for the firing of the police officer involved in the shooting, but she did endorse a civilian review board of police misconduct. "Police in Harlem often use more force than is necessary in arresting suspected criminals or disorderly persons," she explained on a television segment called "The Police and the People."[22]

Motley also took the opportunity to point a finger at provocateurs all around her. "There is only one word which completely characterizes the Civil Rights picture in New York State today," she declared. "That word is 'Crisis.'" Chaos had devolved, she insisted, because "the traditional techniques for achieving equal opportunities—conference, persuasion, and conciliation—have been abandoned." These have been replaced, she said, "by more and more dramatic and more and more bizarre protests."[23]

The senator laid the blame for the leadership crisis at the feet of radical protesters, as well as those who condoned them. Their actions would only prolong the moment when "public acceptance" of the changes that had been achieved in the law would result in equality on the ground, she believed. "A monumental bridge of understanding must be created in all areas of our country," Motley said, "so that the minority of dark skin may follow other minorities into the main-stream of American life." The outlandish protest tactics used by con-temporary activists would never create the interracial harmony she believed was needed for real social change.[24]

In addition to endorsing a civilian review board, Motley insisted that solutions to Harlem's challenges lay in early childhood educa-tion, social services, and government-subsidized jobs—the kind of policies President Johnson championed. She viewed her mission as a legislator, a local newspaper reported, as the elimination of the "dire living conditions" that had "prompted" the "bitter Harlem riots." The "Negro in Harlem" and in other ghettos lived in a state of "frustration, despair, and deprivation," she said, and "until he is promised brighter opportunities, the danger of future riots will exist." Her position aligned with the President's legislative priorities at the time.[25]

Only one month after the Harlem riot, President Johnson deliv-ered on his promise. In August 1964, he signed into law the Eco-nomic Opportunity Act, the centerpiece of the "War on Poverty." It served partly as a response to the civil rights movement's demands that the federal government address the needs of the millions of Americans—especially African Americans—trapped in poverty. The groundbreaking legislation established a federal job corps, work training, community action, preschools, and community health and legal services programs, alongside a host of other signature social welfare programs still with us today. A coalition of civil rights, labor, and antipoverty activists praised these vital initiatives. Dr. King called the Economic Opportunity Act the "twin" of the Civil Rights Act, a law that would help to eliminate the racialized poverty that sty-mied opportunity in New York, Chicago, Detroit, and Atlanta. Motley sang the praises of these programs; to her, they answered demands in Harlem and beyond for equality and opportunity, and participation.[26]

But even to some of her friends in the civil rights movement, much less the radicals, the programs fell short of the full-scale com-mitment needed to ensure economic security and opportunity for impoverished Americans. Martin Luther King, a partner with John-son in efforts to enact civil rights legislation, called for an expanded social contract and a more generous redistributive package of entitlements for poor Americans. King supported a guaranteed income for all Americans, an imperative backed by a coalition of labor and civil rights organizations. Labor leader and civil rights organizer Bayard Rustin agreed; in the months after the Economic Opportunity Act passed, he advocated for a more ambitious program—nothing less than full employment, the abolition of slums, a massive public works program, and the reconstruction of the educational system to dismantle the root causes of urban poverty. In the coming years, Rustin and King would describe the necessary investments and reconstruction efforts as a "Marshall Plan for the Cities." Their proposals were much more expansive than the poverty programs that Motley supported.[27]

But the middle ground that Motley staked out during the racial travail and conflict of the mid-1960s paid dividends that neither King and Rustin, nor Malcolm X and Adam Clayton Powell, could ever claim or desire. Motley's star shone even brighter. The path of moderation made her an even more attractive political candidate and an absolute favorite of the liberal, Democratic establishment. Popular with power brokers, Motley was on her way to becoming one of New York City's chief spokespersons and policymakers.

17

"Not a Feminist":
The Manhattan Borough Presidency

A resignation created the golden opportunity Motley needed, and seized, to become Manhattan borough president, the "boss" of New York City.

In early 1965, standing borough president Edward R. Dudley stepped down from his post to become a justice on the New York Supreme Court. Dudley's departure left a vacancy. It was a coveted position: the Manhattan borough president advised the mayor, appointed local officials, voted to approve the New York City budget, and thus influenced critically important municipal priorities. Motley's authority would far outstrip the influence she could exert as one of many state senators, who, she said, lacked "real power." As the "Beep," as the borough president was called, Motley could promote the interests of underresourced and disaffected people, including people of color.[1]

Mayor Robert F. Wagner, a friend of Motley's, headed the city council that was to fill the position on an interim basis. At the New York Democratic State Committee's 1964 conference, the mayor praised Motley as a "fearless, fighting woman," a "champion of human rights," and one of the state's "brightest stars." Wagner himself aspired to a career in the U.S. Senate, where his father, Robert F. Wagner Sr., had served for two decades. Through his support of Motley, Wagner burnished his standing among prospective voters, particularly among women and people of color. He also respected Motley personally and shared her politics. Her pragmatic racial politics appealed to him and other white liberals—never more so than in light of the perceived threat to the social order posed by Black radicalism. In fact, the more Malcolm X berated the "traditional Black leadership," the more the white establishment was drawn to traditional Black leaders—those who shared Wagner's belief that "prophets of despair" and "peddlers of hate" only worsened the racial crisis.[2]

Taken by her many virtues and egged on by the "Harlem Fox," J. Raymond Jones, Wagner urged the city council to select Motley as Dudley's successor. She would hold the post until the next election for the full four-year term, when she would run on a slate with Wagner. Initially, some of the councilmen balked; three of the eight instead voted to elevate Earl Brown, the acting borough president, whom Wagner had previously promised to support upon Dudley's resignation. Brown was a desirable candidate. A Harvard-educated journalist, he had gone into politics after making his mark at the *New York Amsterdam News* and *Life* magazine, and serving as chairman of the New York Commission on Human Rights. Observers worried that Motley did not really want the job, and yet would push out a perfectly fine candidate if she took it.[3]

These skeptics feared that Motley intended to exploit the borough presidency to advance her own ambitions, that her aspirations went far beyond the world of New York City politics, and that the post would be a mere stepping-stone to a more coveted career. By early 1965, rumors swirled that she would be nominated to a federal judgeship. The prediction found its way into the *New York Times*, where an editorial writer who complimented Motley as a woman of "talent and distinction" also expressed "hope" that she would not use the borough presidency "merely as a momentary stop-over point."

This buzz was based in fact. Motley knew that the Johnson administration was considering her for an appointment. When Mayor Wagner first proposed the borough presidency post to her, she "told him no" because "her name had been submitted for a seat on the federal bench." She agreed to go for the post only after the Johnson administration, bowing to pressure from New York Democrats, including the Harlem Fox, slowed down the judicial process to lend credibility to her political bid. In the meantime, Motley—while waiting for the judicial appointment to materialize—publicly denied that any such appointment was in the offing. Instead, she touted her commitment to a long career in politics.[4]

Motley claimed she planned to run for the interim borough presidency and then to stand for reelection to a full four-year term. Her assertion was not completely insincere; she had been recommended for a judgeship and had submitted relevant paperwork to officials, but the nomination could not be taken for granted. While she waited to see if the nomination would lead to a seat, she did not want to pass up the opportunity to rise to a higher political office. The borough presidency would solidify her reputation as "Constance the First," as some had taken to calling the high achiever.

Other members of the city council complied with the mayor's wishes. After a second vote, Motley was selected by a unanimous decision. The political novice had vaulted over the veteran who had been considered next in the line. Commentators did not mince their words in reporting on the about-face. One news headline about Motley's ascension summed it up neatly: "Rookie Wins Political Plum." Another journalist spelled it out in more unflattering terms: "The councilmen in their wisdom and judgment" had been "all set to give the job to Earl Brown," the reporter wrote, but the mayor had "forced them, with neat parliamentary footwork and a little arm-twisting, into electing Mrs. Motley." Manhattan's new "champion" of the "people," as Wagner called Motley, had gained office through a backroom deal, one that left her open to the criticism that the white power structure had cherry-picked her for the post. The criticism had the virtue of being true, as Motley herself conceded. Nevertheless, through her selection, she had once again made history.[5]

Just thirteen months after she first sought elective office, Constance Baker Motley had become the "boss of New York," and the first woman to hold that position. As a result of her election to the borough presidency, she also joined the powerful New York Board of Estimate. A policymaking body composed of the mayor, the city comptroller, the president of the city council, and the five borough presidents, the board held tremendous sway. Its members put together the New York City budget, determined land-use policy, and entered into contracts, among other city-wide responsibilities.

In a stunningly short period of time, Motley had gained tremendous political power in the nation's most populous city. She had captured the highest-profile office ever held by a Black woman in the United States, and with its $35,000 annual salary—the highest-paying. The *New York Times* reported her selection as borough president in a front-page story. The paper referred to the political rise of Motley—the "comely and statuesque" forty-three-year-old lawyer, wife, and mother of a thirteen-year-old son—as "meteoric."[6]

It spoke volumes about Motley that while other prospective Black and female candidates encountered indifference from power brokers, a bevy of influential men had sought her out for office and orchestrated her victory. Powerful men who admired Motley recognized that support for her would be personally advantageous. Wagner trumpeted his role in her career at every turn. He traveled to New Haven in 1965 for a dinner, attended by seven hundred, celebrating her achievement as the first female borough president. He declared himself "very proud" of the interventions he had made on her behalf, and lavished her with praise. Wagner used adjectives that many who knew Motley well would also reach for: "independent-minded, hard-working, sharp-witted," entirely "free of discrimination," and "painstakingly conscious" of her role as a representative of both her race and all the people of Manhattan.[7] J. Raymond Jones also continued to champion Motley, not only because he despised Earl Brown, but also because of his "secret ambition" to "engineer" her election as the first Black and first female mayor of New York City.

These connections, partly professional, partly social, revealed something paradoxical about Motley: even as she suffered setbacks on account of her race, her sex, and her background, her singular identity and achievements, and her elegance and even temperament gained her favor with powerful male insiders interested, for one reason or another, in anointing an outsider to an important role.[8]

But in other quarters Motley's rise continued to stir suspicion and stoke controversy. Brown's supporters staged a last-ditch unsuccessful effort to defeat her. They galvanized thousands of voters to sign a petition to list Brown, rather than Motley, as the Democratic Party's candidate for the post. Francis Adams, a former police commissioner, called Motley's selection a "cynical political maneuver" by the mayor. Robert B. Blaikie, an independent candidate for mayor, claimed Motley was "deceiving the voters into believing" that she would remain in the post for the full term. That fall, while she campaigned for office, the judiciary committee of the New York County Lawyers Association interviewed Motley—a prerequisite to the judicial nomination. Confronted with Blaikie's allegation, Motley refused to comment at first. After the association confirmed the screening interview, Motley protested that she had "no promise or assurance of an offer" of a judgeship. And she quipped, "I may decide to run for Governor next year but that's no reason why I should not run for Borough President." Blaikie did not find that funny. Motley's stint in the post amounted to a "gimmick," he said, and a "fraud on the people." Voters deserved a borough president fully committed to remaining in office instead of using the position as a stepping-stone, he pronounced.[9]

Congressman Adam Clayton Powell Jr. greeted news of Motley's ascendency to the borough presidency with scorn and reiterated his long-held opinion that she was a pawn of the white establishment. The manner in which she had won the post and the identity of her main champion, Mayor Wagner, confirmed for Powell what he had been saying all along: Motley was illegitimate. In a stinging public rebuke, the Harlem representative called Motley a "white man's Negro." Other Harlem leaders also sent telegrams to Wagner making their disapproval known, including Hulan Jack, the first Black Manhattan borough president, and Percy Sutton, an on-the-rise state assemblyman. Their opposition was for naught.[10]

*

As Motley's political star rose, the civil rights movement's ongoing campaign for a free and unfettered right to vote accelerated. For years a bevy of civil rights organizations had spearheaded protests against poll taxes, literacy tests, hostile voting registrars, intimidation, and violence—the prongs of Black disenfranchisement in the South. The pace of activism for the vote increased after the NAACP's successful suits against white primaries, and culminated in 1965—the same year Motley ran for a full term as Manhattan borough president.[11]

Milestones in the struggle toward political power had occurred before Motley's personal breakthrough, and more would follow. In 1957, Dr. Martin Luther King Jr., in his address "Give Us the Ballot," had envisioned how the Black vote would transform American democracy. If you "give us the ballot," "we will fill our legislative halls with men of good will," he declared, and "we will no longer have to worry the federal government about our basic rights." In 1965, Dr. King and the Southern Christian Leadership Conference had joined forces with SNCC to dramatize white resistance to Black political participation in Selma, Alabama, and throughout the South. In March of that year, the groups organized a fifty-four-mile march from Selma to Montgomery, hoping to persuade Congress to enact voting rights legislation. "We will bring a voting rights bill into being on the streets of Selma," King promised.[12]

The famous march was met with violent police attacks, which inspired its ignominious name—"Bloody Sunday"—and turned the tide in the struggle for the right to vote. Television footage evoked shame and anger. In eighty American cities, including Boston, San Diego, and Detroit, people outraged by Bloody Sunday staged more demonstrations demanding federal action.[13]

After the melee that greeted the first march, protesters reconvened a few weeks later in Selma; they returned with a federal court's protective order, and Constance Baker Motley, in tow. This time hundreds of FBI agents, U.S. marshals, U.S. troops, and military policemen watched over the marchers. Dr. King led it, together with locals, celebrities, and civil rights legends—including A. Philip Randolph, Rosa Parks, and Motley herself in the procession. Again, violence broke out.

Motley had stopped practicing law in the Deep South partly to avoid situations like Selma, and she had not been in a hurry to return to a place where the threat of bodily harm hung over every action. But at Mayor Wagner's urging, she attended the second Selma march as a representative of New York City. As she walked alongside Burke Marshall, the assistant attorney general for civil rights, her worries for her safety abated; federal agents shielded them from harm. When the marchers finally made it to Montgomery, King gave a triumphant speech praising the protesters' fortitude. But not everyone could celebrate the finish. Three voting rights activists were murdered—Jimmie Lee Johnson before the march, James Reeb during it, and Viola Liuzzo afterward—and their deaths drove home to Americans the reality long known by locals and activists such as Motley: in the Deep South, those who dared advocate for equal rights risked their lives. Nevertheless, these tragic deaths had an unintended consequence: they quickened President Johnson's and Congress's resolve to pass federal voting rights legislation.[14]

Enacted on August 6, 1965, the Voting Rights Act banned racial discrimination, mandated compliance through federal oversight, and promised to transform American democracy. President Johnson invited Martin Luther King Jr., Thurgood Marshall, and Constance Baker Motley, among others, to join him at the U.S. Capitol for the ceremonial signing of the bill. With these luminaries looking on, Johnson signed the bill into law, and sealed what John Lewis called the "movement's finest hour."[15]

With greater access to the ballot, Blacks could elect their own representatives—officials who would advocate for Black interests in government. The civil rights movement could turn from "protest to politics," as civil rights organizer Bayard Rustin urged. The transformation from outsider to insider politics could now upset the American political order. Rustin hoped it could enable the movement to achieve policies for better jobs, schools, and housing. In the months and years after the law's enactment, other civil rights leaders called on Black Americans to vote and to elect Black officials in hopes of realizing the promise of democracy.[16]

In the vanguard of the new era of Black political power, Motley enthusiastically endorsed the idea that the vote paved the way to opportunity in American society. A sense of urgency infused her public addresses. At the Southern Christian Leadership Conference's 1965 convention, held just a few days after the Voting Rights Act became law, she exhorted the crowd, "I believe that wise exercise of the right to vote" is the "keystone" to the achievement of "actual equality," including "an equal share in the state's revenues" and the "elimination of poverty and illiteracy." On this occasion and on many others, she touted the role that could be played by electing Black officials who would seek substantive policy changes for disadvantaged communities. "A Negro who does not vote is not helping to make a better world for his or her children." This conversation about the urgent need for Black political power redounded to her favor.[17]

Despite the grumblings of Powell and others, Motley's popularity and fame grew and grew. By virtue of her role as the incumbent Manhattan borough president, she was a constant presence in New York, and her heavy schedule made her a high-profile figure. She attended galas, "women's day" events, and "ladies' night" programs. She gave keynote addresses at luncheons and dinners organized by an array of civic organizations. Trade groups, social clubs, and community service organizations honored her with citations and awards. As the Salvation Army band played holiday tunes, she pulled the switch that lit the forty-five-foot white spruce Christmas tree in Union Square. She shared the stage with celebrities such as Ossie Davis and Sammy Davis Jr. The press covered many of these events, and anyone who was paying attention knew Constance Baker Motley's name.[18]

Motley's political reputation also grew because of her initiatives and work. She supported an expanded role for Americans in government. She proposed that the number of citizens on the Community Planning Board, an advisory body that offered advice to city officials, should increase from nine to twenty-five. She championed a plan to revitalize Harlem from 110th to 155th Street through the construction of new mixed-income and integrated housing, commercial establishments, and industrial areas. She eventually prevailed in her bid to win city approval for the plan, but not without enduring considerable criticism of her wish to "desegregate" the inner city. She insisted, however, that "the time has come for Negroes to select between the security of the ghetto and the challenges of the open society." And she offered a spirited defense of the plan: "In my judgment there is an inherent incompatibility between the existence of racial ghettos and the achievement of equal rights for Negroes." She continued, "I fought long and hard for desegregation in the south. I shall not now condone it [segregation] in the north."[19]

To some, Motley's framework spelled disaster for Black Harlem. But she rejected opponents' claims that her plan for a "quality, inte-

grated" Harlem would undercut Black representation in the legislature. "Negroes should reach these positions," she argued, "as
American citizens of integrity and ability," and should not be "propelled there by a ghetto vote." And whereas some criticized the scope
of her ambitions, she insisted that history proved her right to think
big:

> This is a nation which sacrificed immense human and eco-
> nomic wealth to maintain the Union.... This is the nation
> which developed the Marshall and Truman doctrines to protect
> civilization and revive the economy of Western Europe. This is
> a nation that has provided billions in assistance to other coun-
> tries in the last 20 years. This is a nation that has reached a
> new pinnacle in prosperity.... To ask whether America can
> desegregate the inner city and reclaim the ghettos is merely an
> exercise in rhetoric; of course it can.

Her optimism about social change recalled her heady days as a civil
rights lawyer, when she and her colleagues had achieved successes
once thought impossible.[20]

Motley's win in the regularly scheduled election in November 1965
surprised no one: she ran unopposed for the four-year term as Manhattan borough president. By the time election day arrived, all three
major parties—Democrats, Republicans, and Liberals—endorsed her,
a major feat. It was the first time in living memory that the Republican Party had endorsed a Democrat. The editorial page of the *New
York Times* praised the "Tripartisan Mrs. Motley." She is a "person
of such unusual character that color becomes an irrelevancy in her
candidacy," the *Times* wrote, noting that Motley had served "with distinction" during her brief political tenure.[21]

*

A symbol as well as a flesh-and-blood woman, Constance Baker
Motley and her ascent to the borough presidency evoked strong and
contradictory reactions—love and hate. Dr. Martin Luther King Jr.,
Rev. Ralph Abernathy, and Fred Shuttlesworth sent a joint telegram
praising her when she won the election in November. These men,

icons of the civil rights movement, described her political ascent as a harbinger of racial progress, and they took a bit of credit. "We have been in many battles together," they said, and "we wish to share a small part in this additional stride toward freedom." Her client James Meredith wrote to "congratulate" her on "her latest victory." A press release by the NAACP Legal Defense Fund, meanwhile, extolled her as "an attractive wife and mother" and recalled her career as the "chief courtroom tactician for the entire civil rights movement."[22]

Others called Motley a racial fraud. "Your skin is smooth and bronze," one letter from a stranger began. This observation about her looks then segued into a vicious accusation: "[Y]ou are not a Negress." Her derivation from the "culture and civilization of the West Indies," the writer said, made the politician a member of the "brown race." Motley had based her "ambitious life on a hoax." Similar allegations, sometimes whispered, sometimes shouted, persisted.[23]

Complete strangers lashed out at Motley's success, slamming her in terms both sexist and racist. Why, asked one angry writer, identifying herself only as female, "should a Negress be given a $35,000 a year job?" "Don't we have white Americans who can do such jobs?" she asked. Another postcard writer blamed Motley and other civil rights agitators for the "discrimination" that "white middle class Christians" now suffered; Motley's rise to power proved that "integration is race suicide," a social death caused by that mélange of "Liberals-Jews-Niggers."[24]

People loved to publicly dissect Motley—assessing her racial authenticity, her standing as a woman, her looks, her attire, and her family life—throughout her career. But the critiques escalated when she became the Manhattan borough president.[25]

That Motley was a Black woman profoundly shaped skeptics' reactions to her political rise. She accumulated political power just as debates about women's place in American society gained renewed prominence as a social and political issue. By 1960, 30 percent of women worked, a trend that represented a shift away from the stereotype that women were to serve as mere housewives. Women were a significant part of the workforce and demanded the attention of governmental officials. In 1961, John F. Kennedy, under pressure from both his administration's Women's Bureau and women in the

Democratic Party, established the first Presidential Commission on the Status of Women. Chaired by Eleanor Roosevelt, the commission issued a highly publicized report in 1963 that documented widespread sex-based discrimination in the workplace and demanded an end to it. Signature legislation followed. The Equal Pay Act of 1963 mandated that men and women receive equal pay for equal work. The Civil Rights Act of 1964 banned discrimination in employment on account of sex, as well as race, color, religion, and national origin. The pressure to demonstrate commitment to these measures, including by appointing women to government posts, fell to the Johnson administration. The attention to women's rights would only grow in 1966, after the founding of the National Organization for Women (NOW), dedicated to lobbying, legislation, and litigation for women's equality. Several of Motley's activist friends, including Pauli Murray and Dorothy Height, played leading roles in these early struggles for women's equality.[26]

Many observers counted Motley's political successes as victories for women and for Blacks, while others questioned her suitability for politics at all. Some praised her and touted her as a role model for social and political change. But nearly every commentary noted her sex. Many reporters called her a "lady." In one article, she was the "brilliant lady lawyer," while in another, she was the "City's Top Lady." Another reporter proclaimed that "political power" now "rested" in the "hands of a lady." Several journalists called her the "woman lawyer." Others wondered how a woman—a married woman and mother of a young child—could hold political office.[27]

Guarded and disinclined toward public self-reflection, Motley seldom acknowledged the stress that went with her high-profile role. But with a few friends and peers, she did admit the strain. She commiserated with Shirley Chisholm, the pioneering Black female legislator from New York and a historic figure herself. When Motley served in the New York Senate, Chisholm served in the state assembly. After Motley became borough president, Chisholm wrote to congratulate her friend and to express how much Motley's "presence is missed on the Albany scene." "I am feebly attempting to fill the vacuum," Chisholm said. Motley responded by describing the worries and responsibilities that came along with the borough presidency and called her new post a "most demanding position." She found the many constituencies, interests, and problems presented, together with the nonstop "mandatory after-hours events," a tremendous challenge.[28]

Exchanges with Dorothy Kenyon, an attorney, a friend, and a dinner companion, also provide a glimpse into Motley's inner world. The women were separated by differences of birth: Kenyon hailed from a wealthy New York family. But their shared support of liberal causes, experiences as women in the legal profession, and a history of activist lawyering brought them together. The pair became friends when Kenyon, the sole female board member of the American Civil Liberties Union, collaborated with the NAACP Legal Defense Fund. A former New York municipal judge and mid-level bureaucrat, Kenyon supported Motley's political career through financial contributions and volunteer service.[29]

Motley and Kenyon confided in each other. In the run-up to the primary election in September 1965, when controversy had swirled over whether Motley would jettison the borough presidency for a judgeship, the two commiserated. Public scrutiny and criticism pierced Motley's calm and steady veil. In a letter to Kenyon, Motley conceded that "the borough presidency of Manhattan is a difficult job" and the "most challenging post for me" yet. "I am working diligently to be effective." Following her win, she expressed her "surprise" and relief that she had prevailed by such a wide margin. "I never really doubted your success," Kenyon responded. "But I'm awfully happy that you can now relax and sleep well" at night.[30]

With an expertise formed over a lifetime in the spotlight, Motley trod carefully to manage public perceptions. She took care not to offend either those who supported women's equality or those who were skeptical of women's entry to public life. At civic gatherings, churches, in front of predominantly female audiences, and at predominantly Black or white gatherings, she tailored her talk about gender and race to the audience. She discussed political and social matters and chatted about family and personal life in ways that engaged the audience's preconceptions, preferences, and prejudices.

Motley accepted speaking invitations from many women's groups. When in 1965 the American Association of University Women

(AAUW), a group of predominantly white college-educated women dedicated to women's advancement through research and education, bestowed her with its "Woman of the Year" award, she spoke as if she felt at home. She proclaimed her "deep honor" and "pride" in receiving the commendation from a group of like-minded, working women. Before this group that had championed equal pay and rank for women since 1945 and welcomed women of all races since 1949, Motley emphasized a shared commitment to an equal and democratic social order. Saluting the AAUW, she remarked upon the "genius and glory of the American system" and noted that the belief in equality for all should be as "self-evident as the truths in the Declaration of Independence."[31]

In front of Black women, she excluded uncritical talk of American exceptionalism. Motley instead stressed community, service, and race and gender inequities. During a speech on Women's Day at the Abyssinian Baptist Church in Harlem, she extolled the unsung service of women in the community, commiserated that their battle to better the Black community went underappreciated, and endorsed equal rights for women. She began with praise for the concrete steps the church women had taken to "promote more stable community life." And in a bow toward respectability, she touted the women's service as a "counterforce to the disruptive elements" in the community.[32]

Motley then acknowledged the numerous roles African American women played in society, at home, and in the workplace. She invoked a pleasing proverb: "Men may work from sun to sun, but women's work is never done." She continued, "The woman of the home remains wife, mother, cook, nurse, seamstress, tutor, house cleaner, adviser, and hostess," despite the fact that women now worked outside the home more than ever. A full third of married women were now "breadwinners," she told them. She ended her address by condemning workplace discrimination against women and concluded with hope for a better day. Citing the Equal Pay Act and the Civil Rights Act and noting the increasing numbers of Black women in the professions, in sales, and in clerical work—as opposed to menial labor—she encouraged her audience to "take advantage of the slow but sure breakdown in discrimination in employment."[33]

The Beep sometimes spoke in contradictory terms: she invoked stereotypes in the same breath as she attacked stereotypes and praised women's achievements. At a luncheon sponsored by the National Association of Negro Business and Professional Women's Club, she complimented the crowd of "handsome, well-dressed" women and referred to women as the "weaker sex." At the same time, she congratulated the women for having the "brain power to overcome the double handicap of sex discrimination and color discrimination." She lauded the audience by comparing them to the other sex: men were as likely to be found "at the racetrack" as in the office, she said. She relied on tropes about females' incompetence too. In one speech she invoked the secretary who ended a dictation session by asking her boss to "please tell me what you said between 'Dear sir' and 'Yours truly.'" She closed by applauding the talented women in the club for undermining racist and sexist assumptions. By demonstrating "excellence" in white-collar professions, these women helped to "kill" the myth that Blacks were by nature a "blue collar" class, as well as the idea that women should not "venture outside the kitchen." When these women demonstrated "superiority" in the workplace, Motley asserted, it prompted the "white observer" to rethink race and gender stereotypes.[34]

Wherever she ventured in public, Motley encountered the era's embedded social expectations of gender, race, and class politics, often through journalists' questions or accounts about her activities. Every report about her appointment to the borough presidency mentioned that the $35,000 salary made her—a woman—the highest-paid municipal official in the country. While a note of skepticism ran through some of those accounts, the Black press took pride in Motley's salary. Many stories also remarked on her appearance. She is "tall and handsome," read countless articles. The trappings of her position—limos, drivers, and endless dinner parties—set her and her family apart from most other New Yorkers. Journalists scrutinized how she handled herself, her family, and the affairs of the City of New York. "Who is the boss in her house?" they wanted to know. When faced with such questions, Motley routinely deflected by turning the attention back to her family. My son "likes my big office" and "the big car" (a city-provided Cadillac), she once mused.[35]

Motley's leadership and rhetorical style distinguished her from many women activists in her social circle. As part of a new generation of women leaders, she enjoyed friendly relations with several of the most influential female opinion makers of the era. She frequently encountered Betty Friedan, the feminist icon, during coffee klatches at the exclusive Manhattan private school their children attended. She had maintained her friendship with Bella Abzug, the first woman U.S. representative from New York, since their days at Columbia Law School. She also crossed paths with Pauli Murray, the iconoclastic Black feminist lawyer whose early advocacy for women's equality antagonized the civil rights establishment. And she knew Shirley Chisholm from the world of New York politics. Motley respected each of these women, all dynamic agents of change, but set herself apart.[36]

Unlike Shirley Chisholm and Pauli Murray, who both insisted that Black women faced "double discrimination," Motley downplayed sex-based discrimination. "I am convinced that womanhood is no obstacle in elective office," she claimed while speaking at the YMCA. "I can truly say that, although I am the first woman to serve on the Board of Estimate in this city, I have never heard the question of sex discussed." The trailblazer welcomed greater numbers of women in government because she believed that women possessed talent, just like men. But she generally declined to speak about her personal feats as steps forward for her sex. Society urgently requires our "very best talents in office," she said. "To the extent that women have such talents and desires," she continued, they should serve in government. Qualifications trumped sex.[37]

Motley steered clear of the women's movement, whereas Friedan and Abzug embraced it. She repeatedly rejected being called a "feminist." As one memorable headline blared: "I'm Not a Feminist Says Madame Borough President." Motley explained her position to one reporter: she had been "too busy fighting discrimination on the basis of race *for men and women* to become a feminist." She laid claim to a role in the continuing struggle for racial justice, but she would not publicly proclaim herself an ally in the struggle for women's equality. It was a strategic choice for a pathbreaking Black woman politician.[38]

In fact, Motley played up her femininity, did not shun attention to her appearance, and dwelt on her roles as wife and mother. Repeatedly described as "soft-spoken," she avoided the strident tones associated with "mannish" and "aggressive" women. For the cameras, she embraced domesticity. On the evening when she won the Democratic primary for borough president, her husband and son surrounded her and showered her with affectionate hugs and kisses, putting their love and support on full display. Photos of her at home with her husband and son dotted her news profiles. In interviews, she interspersed talk of her professional life with stories about her home life. "One of the compensations Constance Baker Motley finds in her new job as borough president," a *Newsday* profile noted, is that, unlike during her career as a civil rights lawyer, "she can come home every night to her husband and son." Reporters peppered her with questions about household management, cooking, and caretaking; she answered gamely. The borough president extolled spending her free time at home with Joel Jr. and Joel III, listening to classical music and preparing meals.[39]

Motley also dressed the part of a respectable woman. A celebrity about town and on call day and night, she did New York City's business in fashions popular during the 1960s. With her short hair immaculately coiffed, sometimes topped off with a wide-brimmed or pillbox hat, she liked to wear a strand of pearls around her neck, medium-height heels, and fitted-silhouette dresses or skirt suits. She never wore pantsuits—a chic choice favored by more and more women. Motley thought pants—a style that exposed the "bulging thigh" and the "wiggling posterior"—inappropriate for work; she avoided the monstrosity. For formal events, she donned sheath cocktail dresses made of chiffon, and accented those with rose-shaped brooches or corsages. Her stylish look suggested that her impressive professional exploits had diminished neither her womanliness nor her "pride" in being a woman. Reporters gushed, calling her "stately," "handsome," "comely," and "attractive," with "piercing brown eyes." Even her political supporters called her "our glamour girl."[40]

Motley's self-presentation aided her career, but her image sometimes clashed with reality. Skeptical of feminism and opposed to radical racial politics, she nevertheless championed many of the progressive causes backed by feminists and radicals. She advocated social and economic reform for women, people of color, and the working class; full employment, decent housing, quality schools, urban renewal, and antipoverty initiatives topped her legislative agenda. But she touted these initiatives in the name of New Deal–style government interventionism.[41]

Motley's public disdain for feminism was mostly a pose. No less than self-proclaimed women's liberationists, she appreciated that when a woman rose to a high-profile position such as the Manhattan borough presidency, it was a step forward for women everywhere. She occasionally conceded that her electoral success advanced a goal of the progressive social movements of the 1960s—that Blacks and women had arrived as a "political force" not to be ignored. She did not care to publicly embrace women's liberation, but she understood that she embodied its new face.[42]

The reality of Motley's life also jarred with the glamorous, easy-going image that the media promoted with her help. In private she stressed the position's endless demands on her time. The borough presidency required her not only to attend countless daytime meetings, hearings, lunches, and ribbon cuttings, but also to "say a few words" at countless dinners, banquets, award ceremonies, and holiday parties. Night after night, she was not, in fact, home with her son and husband; she was working, and someone else—a housekeeper, her husband, or a relative—was preparing the family's meals. Joel III, who had been a student at the famed Dalton School in New York, enrolled at New Hampshire's Phillips Exeter Academy, the exclusive boarding school, during her demanding stint in politics. Later, after her political career had ended, the truth emerged. Motley conceded that she "didn't see her family too often" during the whirlwind period when she became one of "the most powerful woman" in the U.S. government. Powerful male officeholders might have admitted the same thing. But nobody asked.[43]

Part V

On the Bench

18

"First": The Judicial Confirmation

The women's dress shop in Lord & Taylor, the New York City land-mark and the nation's oldest department store, was Constance Baker Motley's longtime preferred retailer. Fifth Avenue's iconic flagship store specialized in ready-to-wear garments that gave customers the "American Look": classic clothing that signified social status, confidence, and glamour. When she needed a new handbag or an outfit for a special occasion, Motley visited Lord & Taylor. In January 1966, just such a need arose. The president of the United States had summoned her to the White House.

For months, Motley had been expecting a call about her application for a judicial appointment, but discussions had dragged on, and after waiting so long, she could not be certain that the plum prize would ever materialize. The president's summons meant that perhaps her time had finally come. With Lord & Taylor's help, she planned to look her best for the meeting.[1]

Accompanied by her husband, Joel, and her cousin, Dr. Shirley Williams, Motley arrived at the East Gate of the White House at ten o'clock in the morning on January 25, 1966. She wore a knee-length black boat-neck dress, dainty pearl earrings rimmed with gold, a flower brooch with golden leaves and a pearl center, and a cream woolen pillbox hat encircled by a felt ribbon. A smile so broad that it crinkled the corners of her eyes adorned her face. She waited perched on a plush chair in the Oval Office, on the brink of achieving even greater heights.[2]

Lyndon Baines Johnson greeted Motley, seated his large, imposing frame across from her, and told her the news she was hoping to hear: "Well, we're going to announce your appointment to the bench today." The president planned to nominate Motley to a federal judgeship— the honor of a lifetime.[3]

Johnson famously hated leaks, and he had sworn everyone to se- crecy about the announcement, so Motley experienced the news as something of a surprise, just as the president had intended. "Today?" she first asked, a little stunned. She soon recovered herself and came to her senses: it would be foolish to delay for one minute the an- nouncement of her nomination to the bench. "Oh no," she said, "it's all right; we'll do it today." She thanked Johnson, the president she would credit with finally "tak[ing] the bull by the horns" to make monumental strides in support of Black freedom. She beamed with gratitude and pride.[4]

The full significance of the moment continued to dawn on Motley as Johnson described how thoroughly her nomination had been vet- ted. He had, he told her, discussed her qualifications with luminaries from all walks of life, each of whom had backed her appointment. In his decision to nominate her for the bench, Johnson had received enthusiastic support from every civil rights leader in the country, a U.S. Supreme Court justice, and other federal judges. Johnson wanted full credit from these leaders and all other onlookers for his pathbreaking achievement. His desire to live up to the transforma- tional reputation of his political idol, Franklin Roosevelt, motivated his appointment of Motley, but so did the lobbying of many activist groups.[5]

"Passionate" about appointing "qualified" Blacks, Mexican Amer- icans, and women to prominent posts in government, Johnson also felt pressure from many quarters to back his promising rhetoric about equality with action. The pressure came from "liberal eastern- ers" who thought of him as just another "southern bigot" despite his pivotal role in the passage of the Civil Rights Act. Demands for action also came from women's rights activists who refused to accept the notion that women did not "measure up" to the men who routinely snagged important positions in government. Critiques of Johnson's hiring practices ran in newspapers at the time. A 1965 article in the women's section of the *Washington Post* kept a tally of the gender breakdown of Johnson's appointments; despite claims by the admin-istration that its talent scout sought out female candidates, the article noted, the president had appointed "only two" women to "top jobs" by mid-1965. Women deserved better.[6]

Blacks clamored for representation, as well. Louis Martin, a vet-eran reporter for the *Chicago Daily Defender* and the deputy chairman of the Democratic National Committee, with close ties to the Kenne-dys and to Johnson himself, helped scout Black appointees. Martin compiled a list of "well-trained, well-qualified Negroes" and then "agitat[ed]" for them to be "given appointments in the federal estab-lishment." Johnson knew Roy Wilkins at the NAACP and Whitney Young at the National Urban League, and he reached out to both when vetting prospective Black nominees. All three had enthusiastically supported Motley's judicial nomination, just as they had been thrilled months earlier with Johnson's nomination of Thurgood Marshall to be the U.S. solicitor general. Against this clamor for representation, Johnson's appointment of Motley helped him advance a desirable narrative: the president wanted to make "absolutely clear to Negroes" and other Americans that his administration prioritized civil rights.[7]

Johnson was also competing to best John F. Kennedy, his prede-cessor. Kennedy's appointees to the bench in the South had be-smirched his already mixed civil rights record. Under pressure to support a strong civil rights bill, President Kennedy had claimed that the Department of Justice—led by his brother, U.S. Attorney General Robert F. Kennedy—preferred civil rights litigation to civil rights legislation. President Kennedy vowed to appoint judges who would fairly weigh the hundreds of cases involving school desegregation, voting rights, public accommodations, and more that the LDF had filed in federal courtrooms across the Jim Crow South.[8]

But Kennedy's Justice Department had broken its promise. In a bid to appease Senator James Eastland of Mississippi, the powerful chairman of the Senate Judiciary Committee, and other segregation-ists who could block his legislative priorities, Kennedy appointed several openly racist judges to federal courts in the heart of the South. A quarter of the judges that John Kennedy had nominated and Rob-ert Kennedy had supported—men such as Harold Cox of Mississippi, Clarence Allgood of Alabama, and Robert Elliott of Georgia—were

well-known segregationists and opponents of the legal campaign
for racial equality. Far from advancing the objectives of civil rights
litigators or even fairly considering the cases before them, Kennedy's judges rigged the system against civil rights, invariably rejecting
claims of racial discrimination no matter how clearly the law favored
Black plaintiffs.[9]

Constance Baker Motley had squared off against many of these
Kennedy-appointed jurists. Several of them had ruled against her,
only to be overturned on appeal in case after case. During the litigation to desegregate Ole Miss, she had faced Harold Cox. The first and
the worst of Kennedy's racist judicial appointees, Cox was handpicked
by Senator Eastland. "Openly hostile," Judge Cox "despised blacks,"
Motley recalled. From his seat in the federal courthouse, he called
Blacks "niggers" and "chimpanzees." The judge had lashed out at Motley so viciously during the Ole Miss trial that a judicial colleague—a
more genteel segregationist—had intervened to admonish the judge.
Finally, thanks to Lyndon Baines Johnson, the tables were turning.[10]

Johnson waited to notify Senator Robert F. Kennedy, brother of the
slain, beloved president, and a powerful member of the Senate, until
after he had announced Motley's nomination. "[H]e had the newspaper people come in" and invited a crowd of photographers armed
with flash cameras to capture the moment. Only then did the president contact the Democratic senator from New York, Motley's home
state. Mistrust and a sense of grievance shadowed the conversation
Johnson needed to have with Kennedy about Motley's nomination. A
thorn in Johnson's side because of Kennedy's elitist "portrayal of him
as a southern bigot," Kennedy had also earned Motley's ire because
of his halfhearted support of the civil rights movement. Moreover,
Motley had angered the newly elected senator in 1964 when she had
opposed his preferred candidate for majority leader of the New York
Senate. Kennedy, in turn, had slow-walked her nomination. Because
of his fickle attitude toward Motley, among other slights, Johnson did
not pay Senator Kennedy the usual respect of advance notice about
the date of the announcement.[11]

Instead, minutes after he had divulged the news to the press,
Johnson asked his secretary to "get me Bobby Kennedy on the phone."
When he picked up, the president taunted him. "You know what,

Bobby, I have Judge Motley here," Johnson drawled, "and I thought you might want to be the first to congratulate her." President Johnson then "put the telephone in my hand and pushed it up to my face," Motley recalled, "so that I could then thank the Senator for help- ing me." During the brief exchange between Motley and Kennedy, "Johnson had just roared" with laughter. Here they were; she a newly nominated federal judge, and Kennedy beaten. Following the phone call, Johnson whisked Motley away to a White House luncheon hosted by Mrs. Claudia "Lady Bird" Johnson in honor of "women doers."[12]

The next day, a picture of Motley and Johnson appeared on the front page of the *New York Times*. "Mrs. Motley Is Chosen for a Federal Judgeship Here," the headline blared. She would be the first Black woman nominated to the federal bench. The accompanying story observed that the selection of the then–borough president for the judgeship "had been some time coming" and that there was "little doubt" that the U.S. Senate would confirm her for the post. The writer wrongly cited Senator Robert F. Kennedy as the champion of Motley's nomination. The senator had worked with Motley during his service as attorney general, the paper noted, and "had been impressed with her." The other senator from New York, Jacob K. Javits, a Republican, also backed Motley; he called her a "breakthrough." "The greatest tribute to her is that she would have rated" the appointment regard- less of her race and gender because of her "talent and training," Javits remarked. Despite this high praise, the article's certainty that Mot- ley's confirmation would be a cinch proved wrong.[13]

The perfect optics of that day at the White House concealed what was happening behind the scenes. Motley's stellar record as a civil rights litigator and her prominent role in New York politics had not insulated her nomination from criticism. Kennedy's support for her was lackluster. Prominent members of the bar had questioned the narrowness of her qualifications. And a powerful southern senator opposed her outright. The confirmation process proved arduous. If Motley's ascent symbolized the rise of women and Black people, her battle for confirmation was a harbinger of the fits and starts that out- siders would encounter as they sought access to power in America.[14]

Remarkably, it was Motley's famed career as a civil rights lawyer that slowed her bid for the Senate's confirmation. Wielding the power

of his chairmanship of the Judiciary Committee, Senator James Eastland held up her nomination for months. A wealthy plantation owner
known by the "trademark" cigar that dangled from his lips, Eastland
was also known for his daily consumption of scotch. He defended
white supremacy like his life depended on it. From the floor of the
Senate, his tall frame erect, his too-tight spectacles pinching the
temples of his large, round head, his thinning hair combed to the left,
he railed against the "mongrelization" of the races. Whites should
never mix with Blacks, an "inferior race." The "greatness of America"
depended, he said, on white "racial purity" and the "maintenance
of Anglo-Saxon institutions." These rants had earned Eastland a
reputation as "The Voice of the White South," as had his adamant
opposition to *Brown v. Board of Education*, which had "destroyed the
Constitution." Eastland "proudly affixed" his name to the Southern
Manifesto, the vow taken by southern congressmen to defy the U.S.
Supreme Court decision through every legal means. He was not going
to let the Black woman who desegregated his alma mater, Ole Miss,
slide quietly to confirmation as a judge on the federal bench.[15]

Practiced in the tactics of delay and obstruction, Eastland also had
led Senate opposition to the judicial appointment of Thurgood Marshall, Motley's mentor and former boss. In 1966, he recycled a tactic
that he had deployed, unsuccessfully, before. Rather than directly
attacking Motley's race or specifically raising the Ole Miss controversy, Senator Eastland tried to kill Motley's nomination by smearing
her name.[16]

The drama played out on the floor of the U.S. Senate. The nomination had been approved by a bipartisan subcommittee during a
hearing in April, only to encounter public resistance from Eastland.
The senator had been working unflaggingly against the nomination
behind the scenes, aided both inside and outside the Senate. In an
extended speech on August 30, 1966, Eastland proclaimed his opposition to Motley. He cried:

> Mr. President, I cannot approve this nomination. . . . The
> Internal Security Subcommittee received a phone call from a
> witness who . . . pledged under oath and she placed this nomi-
> nee in the Communist Party.[17]

By 1966 individuals could no longer be criminally prosecuted for Communist Party affiliation. But Congress could and did designate Communist Party members or sympathizers as security risks. Given the real threat posed to the United States by spies and collaborators of the Soviet Union, the U.S. Supreme Court upheld the mandatory registration of Communists, as well as the government's right to interrogate, blacklist, deport, and otherwise penalize suspected subversives. In the 1960s, the Cold War was raging, and the charges Eastland had leveled against Motley, if true, could sink her nomination.[18]

The witness Eastland found, Estella Sgritta—a high school teacher and a "very high-class lady"—had initially made the allegations against Motley to the Senate Internal Security Subcommittee, charged with investigating Communist activity in the United States, years prior to Motley's judicial nomination. In a sworn statement to the subcommittee, which Eastland led, Sgritta alleged that she had firsthand knowledge of Motley's activities. Sgritta herself had been active in the Communist Party, alongside then–Constance Baker, she alleged. Sgritta had driven young party members, including Baker, to meetings of the Young Communist League and the Connecticut Youth Conference, a known Communist front. The witness supported her allegations with detailed information. She remembered that she had fetched Baker from a certain house in New Haven on Dickerman Street; Baker had lived at 54 Dickerman. Sgritta alleged that she had observed Baker's efforts to organize a "Communist study group" at New York University during the summer of 1943, when Baker had lived in New York and been a student there. Baker had solicited advice about setting up the group from Sgritta's husband, Leonard Farmer, at the time also a confirmed Communist. These accumulated facts, Eastland said, painted a clear picture: a young Constance Baker Motley had been "an ardent Communist."[19]

In a concerted effort to destroy the civil rights movement, Eastland—the "quintessential southern red- and black-baiter"—frequently called those who sought to end segregation "Communists," regardless of whether the accusations were based in reality. By his biographer's estimation, Senator Eastland, as head of the Senate Internal Security Subcommittee, "spent hundreds of hours probing whether . . . critics of his semi-feudal Delta homeland were acting on behalf of Stalin or his agents."[20]

The evidence marshaled against Motley fell short of proving her a "Communist," but an investigation ordered by the White House in 1965 did uncover inconvenient facts about her political past. She had come of age during the Great Depression, an era of flourishing Left-liberal coalition politics in which socially engaged people demanded aid for working-class victims of the cratering economy and for all victims of racial discrimination. She had moved in the same circles as critics of capitalism and advocates for radical reform of the failing economic system. Under questioning by special agents for the Federal Bureau of Investigation in 1966, Motley described her place in the milieu:

> I recall that during the period 1939–1941, when I was active in . . . youth groups in the New Haven area, communism was discussed freely as it was an issue of the day. I may have discussed communism with Sidney Taylor or Leonard Farmer [known CP party members]. . . . Although I may have discussed communism, I do not now . . . recall Leonard Farmer or Sidney Taylor attempting to induce me to join the Young Communist League or the Communist Party. . . . I never cooperated in any way with the Communists even though . . . they were interested in Negro problems.[21]

Beginning in the 1930s, Motley, along with Dorothy Height, Paul Robeson, A. Philip Randolph, Adam Clayton Powell, and others who later became prominent civil rights leaders, had joined left-wing organizations that sought both working-class solidarity and racial equality. Some were attracted to socialism or communism for pragmatic reasons: at the time, major American political parties did not support racial justice, and the Communist Party USA was one of the few committed to the pursuit of economic and racial justice for African Americans. It organized cells in Black neighborhoods and attracted activists, artists, intellectuals, and workers who sought to advance Black liberation, economic justice, and world peace. The CPUSA also stood out because of the activism of trailblazing Black women—journalist Claudia Jones, professor Dorothy Burnham, community organizer Audley Moore, professor Louise Thompson Patterson, and others—who populated the leadership and the rank and file.[22]

Intrigued, the young Constance Baker had read the *Daily Worker*, the official news organ of the Communist Party in the United States. A few groups with which she affiliated—the National Negro Congress, the Southern Negro Youth Conference, the American Labor Party, and the American Peace Mobilization—later landed on a list of organizations that included known Communists. In 1942, while enrolled at NYU and living in Harlem—a hub of Communist organizing and political activism of all stripes—Motley had associated with men she described as the "leading left-leaning" Black intellectuals and activists, which included Communists or Communist sympathizers. Baker had been a staunch leftist; there was no question about it.[23]

In her bid to attain a judgeship, Motley went through several interviews about these political activities. The White House sought a "complete and detailed statement of her version of events." It came to light that the young Constance Baker, her actions, and her associates had attracted the attention of hunters of subversives. Investigators had scrutinized every nook and cranny of her life and compiled a thick file of evidence made up of information from informants, photographs, marriage licenses, handwriting analyses, voting registration records, intelligence reports, military records, and interviews with teachers, colleagues, associates, judges, clergy, and civic leaders.[24]

The Federal Bureau of Investigation summarized the "derogatory information" in the file and presented it to the White House. One informant claimed that Baker had attended "open and closed" meetings of the Young Communist League in New Haven and in New York. Another advised that persons who attended these meetings were not necessarily members of the YCL. But he said that "Connie Baker," whom he recalled as "a young, attractive colored girl in her early 20s, who was fairly light skinned," could have been a "sympathizer." A third person, Leonard Farmer, a "card-carrying Communist" who had renounced his membership and then volunteered to cooperate with the government, claimed that Motley had been a member of the party in New Haven and New York during the 1940s. Sidney

Taylor, also a confirmed Communist, alleged that Baker was "once with us" and had even headed a youth group in New Haven. Internal security forces located Baker's voting records in New York in 1943 and learned that she had stated a preference for the American Labor Party, later listed as subversive. In 1943, Military Intelligence in New Haven advised that "one Connie Baker" of 54 Dickerman Street "was reported to have been training to be a Red organizer among the Negroes." The government recovered a telegram Baker had signed from the Emergency Peace Mobilization, another organization later designated a Communist front. The investigators even uncovered that Clarence Blakeslee, the philanthropist who had bankrolled Baker's education, had taken part in a program sponsored by the New Haven Committee on American-Soviet Friendship, also a cited organization.[25]

In interviews with FBI special agents in March 1966, Motley responded to the trove of information and substantiated—up to a point—the narrative that Eastland hoped would deprive her of a seat on the bench. Motley admitted that she had known and associated with Sgritta and Farmer during the 1940s. But she equivocated about the most explosive allegation made against her—that she had inter-acted with Farmer and his wife during the summer of 1943 in New York City, where she supposedly engaged in youth organizing for the Communist Party. Although she did not "presently remember it" or "recall" it, Motley said in her 1966 statement, she may well have met the Farmers in New York City in 1943. (Remarkably, thirty-two years later, in a 1998 memoir published after she had retired from active status on the U.S. District Court, Motley did *not* equivocate about whether she had known the couple in New York. "When I was an undergraduate at NYU, I met a number of community activists," she wrote, "including James Farmer and Estelle Sgritta, whom I had known in New Haven.") The nominee also hedged about whether she had been involved with certain allegedly Communist front organiza-tions. Motley conceded that someone may have given her a "lift from my home to some of the meetings" under contention, but she did not "presently recall any of these occasions." She admitted to being a part of a political circle that included Communists. Sgritta's statement had contained elements of truth.[26]

In fact, the only significant discrepancy between Motley's account of her activities and those offered by Sgritta and the two other informants concerned Motley's formal membership in the Communist Party. No real evidence established that she had gone so far as to join the party. And she adamantly denied membership in her 1966 statements to the FBI. "As I have stated before I was never a member of the Young Communist League," she averred. The FBI's investigation had not proved otherwise: "it could not be determined," the Bureau had concluded, whether Baker had joined the Young Communist League or the Communist Party. Otherwise, the picture was clear: like many Depression-era liberals, Motley had, for a season, embraced the radical Left. That, alone, was not a crime.[27]

Senator Eastland's efforts to block Motley's appointment as a federal judge backfired. In an auspicious development for Motley, by the mid-1960s, anti-Communists' focus had largely shifted to the New Left, urban rioters, and proponents of Black Power. She looked innocuous compared to these elements, who were perceived as dangerous, present-day threats to the social and political order by liberals and conservatives alike. To true leftists, Motley represented the establishment. Whether Marxists, Socialists, or Black nationalists, they considered her more of a foe than an ally. In the face of her reputation as a middle-of-the-road Democrat and a lawyer who had only changed America case by case, Eastland's attempt at character assassination failed.[28]

President Johnson did not pull Motley's nomination. The attorney general did not advise him to do so. The Judiciary Committee did not change course. Numerous respected legal and political heavyweights remained in Motley's corner. Thurgood Marshall topped the prominent insiders who vouched for her. In his signature folksy style, Marshall—then a judge on the U.S. Court of Appeals—confirmed that he had known Motley for decades and could "guarantee" her allegiance to the United States. He cited their shared experience at the dawn of the Cold War. Inside the NAACP, he said, they both had worked to root out Communists. Motley had "worked as hard as he" had at the NAACP to "kick out" "left wingers." "[I]f there is anyone who hates communists more than Mrs. Motley," Marshall declared, "he would like to see him." Jack Greenberg, Motley's co-counsel, agreed. He had

"not the slightest doubt" of Motley's "loyalty to the United States."
Robert F. Wagner, New York City's mayor, who had worked alongside
Motley in the New York Senate and during her term as Manhattan
borough president, proclaimed her "thoroughly loyal."[29]

With the backing of public figures intact, New York's senatorial
delegation stood behind Motley's nomination, albeit without disput-
ing the facts that Eastland had brought to light. Senator Jacob Javits,
the Republican who had gotten to know Motley when she served as
Manhattan borough president, threaded the needle in his statement.
"I do not challenge at all what the Senator from Mississippi has said,"
Javits pronounced. "I do not say that this fact should not be considered. I only say it should be weighed against the record of Mrs. Motley in the subsequent 24 years." Continued Javits, "Mrs. Motley is a
woman of great capacity, one of the principal counsels" to Thurgood
Marshall, and a woman who had fought a "great legal battle" for equal
rights. Her stellar record outweighed the relevance of the allegation
that years ago she had been a Communist. Senator Kennedy closed
ranks: Motley's good works in recent decades dwarfed the evidence
uncovered by Eastland. He personally vouched for Motley. She had
shown great "courage" and "integrity" and had earned the respect of
lawyers at the Department of Justice. Notwithstanding his maneuvers
against Motley's nomination, Kennedy did strongly support her during the confirmation vote in August 1966—though, admittedly, by that
time it would have been scandalous not to defend her.[30]

*

The judicial nomination also revealed that there were limits to Motley's white, liberal support. As rumors swirled of her imminent
nomination to the bench, liberal Democrats and their mainstream
institutions also voiced skepticism. During an interview with the
local bar association, a routine occurrence for judicial nominees,
members of the Association of the Bar of the City of New York point-
edly asked Motley whether she had "made a political deal to get the
appointment." Her legal experience, they implied, could not explain
her nomination.[31]

The American Bar Association—known to this day for systematically rating people of color and female lawyers lower than white and

male lawyers, regardless of education, age, ideology, or the length and nature of their experience—also proved a stumbling block. The ABA hesitated to approve Motley's nomination on the grounds that she lacked trial experience in New York—a patently ludicrous suggestion given her extensive experience in courts nationwide. The ABA ultimately rated her merely "qualified," as opposed to "highly qualified," its highest rating for the post. Others in the profession questioned whether Motley's representation of plaintiffs in civil rights suits posed problems: Was she really qualified for the job, given the supposedly narrow field of her practice? And would she be fair to all sides, particularly in cases alleging racial discrimination?[32]

Notwithstanding his public support, Senator Robert F. Kennedy was worried, he said in private, that constituents might perceive Motley's appointment as too "political" given her race and her background as a civil rights lawyer.[33] Kennedy made these arguments in July 1965 when President Johnson announced to his inner circle that he sought to appoint Motley to a judicial position even more prestigious and coveted than the U.S. District Court. Johnson wanted Motley to succeed Thurgood Marshall, a judge on the Second Circuit Court of Appeals since 1961. Marshall's seat on the appeals court would become vacant when Johnson promoted him to U.S. solicitor general. Johnson hoped to make a big splash through dual appointments of Motley and Marshall. It would be a sensation, bolstering Lyndon Johnson's legacy as the twentieth century's leading presidential champion of racial equality.[34]

In a phone call to Attorney General Nicholas Katzenbach on July 9, 1965, Johnson discussed how best to move forward. "When we go with Marshall, how [do] we get Motley at the same time?" Johnson asked. Aware that senatorial support for his historic nomination would be critical, the president needed to know about contingencies: "Is there a way you can check with the senators?" At the same time, he needed to know that Katzenbach himself "would not object to Motley." The attorney general personally supported the nomination. Johnson insisted that Katzenbach double-check that "she is not objectionable" to power brokers. The president also wanted assurances that "she has been checked" by the ABA. "She was checked for the district court vacancy. She has not been checked for the court of appeals," Katzenbach said. "Is it conceivable that they wouldn't qualify her?" Johnson asked.

Katzenbach, who would have known that ABA ratings could trip candidates up, particularly women, and particularly Black candidates, continued: "Umm . . . it's conceivable, but highly unlikely on the court of appeals."[35]

Johnson's initial plan did not come to pass. Just days after the president set the proposal in motion with the announcement of Marshall's nomination to the post of solicitor general, Senator Kennedy called Attorney General Katzenbach. Johnson's simultaneous appointment of Motley and Marshall—two Blacks and two NAACP lawyers—to prestigious federal posts would be too risky and would appear to be motivated by political interests, Kennedy said. A "political and public relations viewpoint" drove his conclusion. In a memo to the president, the attorney general documented Kennedy's concerns. While Kennedy had previously acceded to the president's wish to appoint Motley to a lower court seat, "he had not, of course, known of the pending nomination of Marshall at the time he indicated he would approve Mrs. Motley." In the senator's "judgment," Katzenbach's memo noted, "it would be preferable to replace Marshall with an outstanding District Court judge, Edward Weinfeld," a white man.

Kennedy argued that Weinfeld would be the safer, superior successor to Marshall. The "liberal New York Jewish community," an important constituency, would applaud the selection of the Jewish candidate," said Kennedy, as would the "whole of the New York bar" and "lawyers throughout the country." The American Bar Association would "probably" rate Weinfeld "exceptionally well qualified." Kennedy—soon to earn a reputation as a sure friend of civil rights when he ran for the presidency in 1968—had revealed his limitations. Regarded as political problems rather than political allies, in his eyes, Blacks were expendable.[36]

The attorney general's memo to the president ended with his assessment of the senator's position:

I think there is merit in Senator Kennedy's assessment and that it is worthy of consideration. Clearly, he would prefer this [Weinfeld] alternative and seriously believes it is preferable.

Committed to groundbreaking appointments but worried about the political risks, Johnson would not defy Kennedy's wishes.[37]

It did not help Motley's prospects that Democratic Party pols, operatives at the state and local level, also implored Johnson to postpone her nomination to a federal judgeship, whatever the court. If Motley, then the borough president, received a judicial appointment before November, "chaos" would ensue for the New York Democratic Party. "Please don't touch Motley until after the election," one person begged Johnson on a phone call.[38]

Johnson surrendered over the idea of appointing Motley to the court of appeals, but he held his ground on the district court. The president made a historic appointment, even if it was not the one he originally hoped to make.

*

On August 30, 1966, after a seven-month delay, the Senate confirmed Motley's appointment as U.S. district judge in New York, over the objections of Senator Eastland.[39]

Motley had achieved her most impressive feat. The first African American woman appointed to the federal judiciary and the first woman appointed to the prestigious U.S. District Court in New York City, Motley joined the federal judiciary, a club that was, until her appointment, practically all-white and all-male. Only four other women, all white, had been appointed federal judges by 1966.[40]

A White House memorandum announced Motley's appointment. Its one-word header simply said: "First." "Constance Baker Motley was the first Negro woman ever appointed to a lifetime federal judgeship," read the memo. The appointment symbolized that "[t]he Negro is on his way" and that "doors are opening on every side." Along with Motley, the narrative implied, all of society's African Americans and women rose, too.[41]

Newspapers all over the country covered Motley's appointment. Many emphasized her rise from working-class New Haven to the pinnacle of the legal profession. A Virginia daily vividly described the wonder of her achievement: "Lady Lawyer's Cinderella Story Comes to Happy End." A photo in the center of the article pictured the new judge Motley chatting with President Johnson.[42]

Motley's story offered the hope of interracial and cross-gender harmony. The autumn of 1966 swirled with seemingly unending resistance to school desegregation, turbulent civil rights protests and civil disorder, the revolutionary political rhetoric of the Black Power movement and the Black Panther Party, the founding of the National Organization for Women, and the full emergence of the women's liberation movement. The prominence of politicians such as James Eastland and George Wallace was a measure of the staying power of segregationist ideas. And the juxtaposition of Lyndon Johnson's anti-poverty policies and Black rage in poor communities demonstrated the diminishing efficacy of white liberals and their policies. Through Constance Baker Motley's appointment, Johnson sought to bridge the divide between the reform-minded, integrationist activism of the postwar years and the radicalism of the mid- to late 1960s. To President Johnson and many other idealists, Motley's ascent affirmed American beliefs that opportunity abounded and social mobility was available to those with luck and pluck.[43]

This hopeful spirit was on full display on September 9, 1966, when two hundred political luminaries, federal judges, and family and friends gathered for Motley's formal induction to the judgeship. Solicitor General Thurgood Marshall—who had his own bruising battle with Senator Eastland and other segregationists during his confirmation process to the U.S. Court of Appeals—had "held her hand" during the months-long process and stood there beaming during the short ceremony.[44] Motley's proud husband, her fourteen-year-old son, her mother, and four of her siblings also looked on as the forty-four-year-old lawyer, wearing a dark blue dress and a single strand of pearls, took the oath of office. She raised her right hand as the chief judge of the U.S. District Court asked her:

> Do you, Constance Baker Motley, solemnly swear that you will administer justice without respect to persons, and do equal right to the poor and to the rich, and that you will faithfully and impartially discharge and perform all the duties incumbent upon you . . . agreeably to the Constitution and Laws of the United States?

After Motley's pledge, a U.S. marshal invested her with her judicial robe and escorted her to the bench.[45]

For civil rights and women's groups that hailed her achievement, Motley's personal triumph also signified that oppressed groups would have a friend on the court. At the headquarters of the NAACP Legal Defense Fund, Motley's workplace for twenty years, staff members cheered. With one of their own on the bench, supporters were sure the quality of justice meted out in the courts could only improve. Motley herself had encouraged this kind of thinking. During her wait for confirmation, she had told a reporter for an African American newspaper that with her appointment to the bench, "America is about to make good on its promise of equal opportunity for all."[46]

But right away, letters questioning Motley's suitability poured into the White House—a harbinger of the persistent skepticism she would encounter.[47] Attorney Cecile L. Piltz, a little-known New York lawyer, wrote to President Johnson to express her dismay. "The Federal District Court has heretofore been reserved for our legal scholars," she said. "It had been graced by men . . . with . . . outstanding abilities, breadth of experience and catholicity of views." Motley was not in the same league, Piltz claimed. In her mind, Motley was inexperienced in the law and undistinguished. She wrote:

> To appoint Constance Motley to the Bench because she is a negro . . . is an affront to every attorney in this country and particularly . . . the many women who have spent a lifetime in the law and because they were women, have received no recognition.[48]

The White House shot back with a letter of its own. Mrs. Motley "was not nominated because she is a Negro," staffer James E. Marsh Jr. wrote. President Johnson appointed her "only after the most painstaking evaluation of her qualifications." She "is indeed well qualified for the post."[49]

19

"A Tough Old Bird": Judge Motley's Court

Judge Motley's workday at the federal courthouse in lower Manhattan followed a steady rhythm. It began promptly at 9 a.m. and ended as late as 9 p.m. Driven to work each day by her husband, Joel Jr., she took the judge's elevator to her chambers on the twentieth floor of the federal courthouse. Her office walls were pink, and she decorated the room with a floral chintz sofa and matching draperies. It made a statement: Constance Baker Motley had arrived at the storied U.S. District Court for the Southern District of New York—"the greatest" trial court "in the country, bar none."[1]

Usually the first person to reach the office, Motley began her work in the mornings quietly. Once her judicial clerks and other staff had arrived, she drank a cup of coffee. A running "joke," one of her male clerks—it was always a man—prepared coffee for everyone else. "It was my job to make coffee for the chambers," remembered law clerk Howard Fischer, "since, according to the judge, no one else made it like I did." Later in the morning, Motley departed chambers for the courtroom, at least one clerk in tow. From her perch on the bench, she presided over trials and hearings. After a quick break for lunch in chambers, usually a sandwich, she returned to the courtroom; work there went on through the afternoon. She then returned to her chambers to write legal opinions and orders into the evening.

The weekends offered little respite. Motley worked on most Saturdays, save in summer, when she spent time at her country home in Connecticut. But even when on "vacation," she took along several cardboard boxes filled with work. "For this job, you need a lot of endurance," she said. Given the endless stream of cases on the nation's largest and busiest federal trial court, "You can never feel, I'm caught up."[2]

*

Despite her workload, Motley mentored a new generation of lawyers. She hired women and people of color as her clerks—prestigious positions awarded to new law school graduates. These candidates, highly qualified and all from elite schools, nevertheless often would have been overlooked by other judges. Motley's "background as a non-affluent, black woman played a major role in opportunities she was denied and opportunities she was given," and those experiences inspired her to "create opportunities for others." Motley often found clerks through the recommendation of her former LDF colleague Derrick Bell, then a professor at Harvard Law School. Except for a few who found the "intensity" of the work overwhelming, Judge Motley's clerks enjoyed working in her chambers; of great value personally and professionally, these clerkships launched promising careers in government, law firms, public interest organizations, and academia.[3]

Many students applied to work for Motley because of her legendary professional achievements. "I had gone to law school to do women's rights and civil rights," explained Elizabeth Schneider, and "the fact that . . . I ended up working for her really was like, oh my God!" Schneider "felt blessed" to have landed the job with Motley and "felt so lucky" to be "in her presence." Lynn Huntley, who came to the clerkship committed to a career as a civil rights lawyer, considered Motley a hero. Huntley "wanted to walk in her footsteps, to learn everything from her."[4]

Motley's "intelligence," "integrity," and "generosity" impressed her clerks. They admired her even though, as many attested, "[s]he was a workaholic." Her clerks worked the same long hours she did; they stayed in chambers until she had left for the evening. "Everybody was very serious about the work," recalled clerk Dorothy Roberts. Keenly aware of the high stakes of Motley's turn on the bench, the clerks "wanted to do the best job possible" and help her reach the right outcomes in the numerous cases on her docket. "[I]t was work, work, work, work, work, all the time, at a very intense pace," recalled

Laura Swain. Joel Jr. endured the pace, too. Having driven the judge to work each day, he faithfully came to collect her, patiently waiting for her at the day's end, reading newspaper after newspaper until she was ready to go home. He would arrive around 7 p.m. and "try to get the judge to come home," but "usually" it would be 8 or 9 p.m. before they would leave. Joel then drove his wife to their apartment on the Upper West Side.[5]

As the first Black woman federal judge, Motley faced special inspection, and she knew it. "[O]f course there is more scrutiny," she once said. "Some people just cannot imagine a federal judge being anything but a white man." Inside and outside the courtroom, Motley took pains to demonstrate classic judicial virtues such as fairness, competence, and intellectual preparedness. "You win," she emphasized after one of her landmark courtroom victories, through "preparation . . . and experience." The judge was always well prepared and displayed extraordinary mastery of the job.[6]

Motley also wore a mask. Presiding in court, she had a stern and commanding presence. "Formal and reserved," Judge Motley still practiced the politics of respectability, conforming to middle-class norms of appearance, speech, and behavior. As a child, she had learned to embrace respectable attributes and mannerisms; as an adult, she performed respectability to shield herself from discrimination, and now, she clothed herself in it on the bench. She wore a black judicial robe while in court, and practiced cautious speech and impeccable behavior. She was impenetrable, and "a formidable presence on the bench," recalled Pierre Leval, who practiced in her courtroom while an assistant U.S. attorney. "She was scary," remembered John Gordon, another lawyer who tried cases in her courtroom. Lynn Huntley summed up the judge's demeanor: "She was a tough old bird."[7]

Judge Motley adopted a steely persona to command respect. Her presence—the first Black woman federal judge in American history—"provoked complicated reactions" and required an "extreme adjustment" from lawyers used to seeing a white man presiding, remembered Elizabeth Schneider. Some of these lawyers "tested her," another clerk recalled. They spoke out of turn or otherwise attempted to dominate a trial or court appearance. "Plenty of lawyers in major criminal cases," Motley later said, were "harassing and baiting," typically "when their clients had no defense." Simon Procas, who also clerked for Motley, remembered the fate of a lawyer who "just didn't get it." The judge "repeatedly admonished" the lawyer "to stop speaking over her." Motley ultimately "stunned the lawyer into silence": she held him in contempt of court, imposing a $1,500 fine.

On retreating to chambers, Motley looked at Procas and said, "Men! They always think that if you're a woman they can interrupt you, no matter what the circumstances!" Another lawyer called her "Mrs. Motley" rather than "Judge Motley," shocking her clerks. Huntley, who worked for Motley during her early years on the bench, remembered that the judge "sat there like a stone." Motley's response to such antics "was quite intimidating"; she never allowed herself to lose her temper. Without exception, she admonished lawyers without emotion. Anger would have undermined her authority, she believed. Laura Swain, a clerk who went on to become a federal district court judge herself, observed, "She was very good at being the 'alpha dog.' " "I was sometimes surprised that lawyers were disrespectful to a federal judge," said clerk Sara Moss, "but she never seemed fazed by it." Motley would not "cut off" or "belittle" people, but she would insist on proper deference and decorum. "She had no tolerance whatsoever for lawyers who were unprepared, inarticulate or inappropriate in demeanor," recalled yet another clerk. She always remained in control.[8]

If she looked on the occasional disruptive attorney dimly, Motley set at ease young attorneys, male and female, who were low in the pecking order. She particularly encouraged the handful of women lawyers who appeared before her in court. At the same time, she frequently took women to task and instructed them on how to be good advocates.[9]

Most of all, by forcing all of her observers to bear witness to her professional competence, Motley gave no one legitimate grounds to question her. And following a politicized confirmation process, she was aware that some people would always view her as an activist lawyer rather than a great judicial mind. So she sought to write opinions that the gatekeepers on the appellate court would affirm. Nevertheless, when the situation called for it, she did not shy away from innovation. "The ultimate court is not last because it is right, it is right because it is last," she once told a clerk, half smiling. But even in these circumstances, the judge hewed as closely as possible to the law as it had been interpreted by the court of appeals. Motley, no less than other judges, wanted to protect her professional reputation and preserve the possibility of promotion to a higher court.[10]

*

Motley liked being a judge. "I get great satisfaction out of my work," she noted. Her work on the court "affect[s] people's lives intimately." She also enjoyed the deference and admiration her position on the prestigious federal court stirred from colleagues, lawyers, court-house staff, and everyday people on the streets of New York. Clerks witnessed this public adulation when they accompanied her to her favorite Italian or Chinese restaurants, or to purchase fruit on Chambers Street. One clerk described walking through the courthouse with the judge and seeing people fawn over her; it was "like being with a Queen," recalled Daniel Steinbock.[11]

Motley's clerks shared meals with her and fetched them, too. Anticipating a break in a trial, she once sent clerk Scott Optican on a breakfast errand: the judge "snapped her fingers" and "handed me a note." It said: "Sausage McMuffin with egg, orange juice, hash browns, in the robing room in 15 mins." Clerks also fetched the judge's go-to lunchtime meal—a tuna sandwich on wheat with a slice of egg—from the courtroom cafeteria. After an early experience taught her to avoid the lunchroom, she rarely, if ever, went there herself. One clerk remembered that "there was one judge, in particular, who did not want to have a woman there. And let it be known that she was not welcome." Her clerks were protective of her, and their gofering shielded her from these kinds of indignities. They not only grabbed her lunch for her, but also brought her special treats. Knowing she "loved Jewish food," Steinbock would sometimes "get blintzes" for her from Wolf's Delicatessen, or as she fondly called it, "Wolfies." She broke her endless dieting for such indulgences.[12]

In addition to being aided by her clerks, Motley was also helped by her trusted and beloved assistant, Roberta Thomas, who had worked as her secretary since her days at the Inc. Fund. Thomas would help

Motley select new attire when her personal shopper visited from Lord & Taylor. More important, "Roberta . . . interpreted the judge's actions for the law clerks (she doesn't mean that; that's just the way she is)," said one clerk, who recalled the judge's "partnership" with her secretary. "The Judge and Roberta were a wonderful 'odd couple' with great respect and affection for each other." Everyone in chambers worked as a team to help support their "tough" boss.[13]

Judge Motley treated her clerks with respect and built relationships with them. She often drew them in through war stories. Motley shared memories of working with Thurgood Marshall under harrowing circumstances in the Deep South. "I was stunned that someone who argued the [James] Meredith case was not able to eat in restaurants with Jack Greenberg," remembered Susan Davis. "It was a window into a generation of civil rights leaders."

A compassionate if demanding supervisor, Motley also cared for her clerks; she helped them through personal and professional challenges. Clerk Lan Cao was born in Vietnam and arrived in the United States when she was five without her parents; they remained in Vietnam until the country collapsed after the war. Cao "bonded" with the judge over shared experiences of discrimination that were both "unjust and humiliating," the clerk remembered. Motley permitted another clerk, Barbara Botein, to leave work by 6:30 p.m. every evening to spend time with her young children. On another occasion, the judge encountered a clerk in distress. Susan Davis was sitting at her desk with "tears streaming down" her face, "wondering if I was cut out for the task." Davis had realized, she told Motley, "that I had spent many years using my wit and humor to get by, fooling people into thinking I was up to a particular task, and that I finally had been 'found out.'" Motley "stood quietly for several minutes" and then retorted, "[H]oney . . . I'm *still* waiting for people to find *me* out!" Davis took the judge's words to heart. "That bit of self-awareness, candor, humor and empathy never left me, and became part of my professional and personal foundation in the decades that followed," she said.[14]

The judge's dry sense of humor and her "girlish laugh" lifted the mood of her clerks, if not the workload. "You could kid around with her," remembered one clerk. The judge laughed uproariously with

her clerks after a well-known lawyer—a very "handsome" one at that—
who was trying a case in her courtroom attempted to "flirt" with her.
The group got a kick out of his silly idea that "flirting" would sway,
of all people, Judge Motley. She was quick-witted and poked fun at
her staff. When a newly engaged clerk introduced his fiancée, Motley
promptly turned to the young woman, whom she had just met, and
said, "Are you sure you want to do that?" Still another clerk held the
door for her and recalled her good-natured ribbing: "You hold the
door for me," said Motley, "*not* because I am older, but because I am
smarter." The judge once autographed a book, addressing it "To my
favorite law clerk," one remembered. "When I told her how much
that meant to me," the judge deadpanned, "Oh, I write that to *all* of
my law clerks." Scott Optican remembered that during a discussion
of some aspect of race and the law, "at one point she turned to me,
laughing, and said: 'What do *you* know about it, White boy . . . ?'"
Motley's sense of humor endeared her to those who worked for her,
but it was also a survival tool: "One of the most critical lessons" that
she "learned from Thurgood," Motley once explained, was "to laugh
off slights," "conceal" the "pain and anger" generated by racial injustice, and adopt a carefree attitude toward life.[15]

Motley also set her clerks at ease by inviting them to her country
home in Chester, Connecticut. The Motleys purchased their historic
1745 home, located at 99 Cedar Lake Road, in 1966. They spent weekends, holidays, and summers in their eleven-room residence in the
quaint, rural, and overwhelmingly white small town that had branded
itself the "place to experience old New England." Her love of the quiet
life in the picturesque hamlet reflected a pride in New England, its
history, and in the region's reputedly genteel race relations. When
in Chester, Motley shed her "very forbidding" public and courtroom
persona, trading her dresses and suits for blue jeans and Timberland
boots. She spent hours working in the family's large vegetable garden
and walking in the woods on the eight acres of land that surrounded
the house. "I come here to get away from it all," she explained. The
matriarch of the beloved dwelling, she entertained family, friends,
and law clerks in a sanctuary from the hurried pace and clamor of
New York City.[16]

During those weekends in Chester, Motley's clerks relaxed over informal dinners. The judge seemed to like cooking—it was "the sport of the weekends" for her. She prepared delicious dinners for her team. "I still remember how proud she was of her homemade lasagna and of her vegetable garden in Connecticut," a clerk reminisced. Over homemade meals, they talked about anything other than the work that awaited them back in the office.

Most of all, people remembered that Motley treated her colleagues and employees like they were family. And it was as a family that Motley and her clerks faced down the many cases she handled as a trailblazing judge on the powerful U.S. District Court.[17]

20

"The Weeping and the Wailing": The Black Panther Party, the FBI, and the Huggins Family

Just three years after Constance Baker Motley reached the pinnacle of her career, a tragedy struck her family. It would reverberate in her jurisprudence about crime, punishment, and mass incarceration.

John Huggins Jr. was the son of John Huggins Sr., a first cousin with whom Motley was close. Motley spent time with both John Sr. and John Jr. at family events, at St. Luke's Episcopal Church, and at her summer home. John Jr. was twenty-three years old, a campus activist and a U.S. Navy veteran who had served a tour in Vietnam, when he was murdered. Judge Motley deeply felt the loss. In fact, the death devastated and marked the entire clan. Tribulations, including the hardships in the old country that had driven them to America, of course had beset the family before. But the death of Huggins had no equal in memory: it stood out as the "most excruciating thing that ever happened."[1]

The young man's funeral took place on a blustery January day in 1969, just a few days after the inauguration of Richard M. Nixon, a man who had won the presidency by castigating white liberals, slamming campus radicals, and appealing to "law and order." Nearly five hundred mourners crowded into St. Luke's in New Haven to grieve. "Shooting Victim New Haven Native," blared a news headline; the picture printed alongside the article showed the handsome, unlined face of the young man from a "respected New Haven family" with long ties to Yale University.[2]

The mix of people in the chapel registered the long distances, literal and figurative, that Huggins had traveled in his short life, the details of which belied the crude stereotypes that Nixon deployed about student activists. Nixon called them "unpatriotic" "bums." John Jr. and those who mourned him defied this binary vision. Veterans, peaceniks, civil rights activists, Black revolutionaries, teachers, preachers, Californians, New Yorkers, and people of all races came together at his funeral. Amid this diverse array of humanity, members of the Black Panther Party—dressed in waist-length black leather jackets and black pants—stood out, their fists raised in salute. The Panthers had come to bury one of their own: John Huggins Jr. had died a "martyr for the cause," shot to death in Los Angeles, where he had been the "brains" of the Panthers' local chapter.[3]

Huggins's youth and the shocking circumstances of his death floored the people assembled. The world's troubles had landed on their doorsteps. Waves of grief passed through the flock. Some mourners silently wiped away tears. Others cried out loudly. Family members—who had every reason to expect his life to be long and triumphant—wept and wailed. Motley, then a newly appointed judge, could not attend in light of her position, a choice the family understood. The judge was there in spirit, a "presence" hovering over the assembled mass, remembered Huggins's sisters, Joan and Carolyn.[4]

That cold January day in 1969, controversies swirled throughout the nation over the rise of political revolutionaries and law enforcement's efforts to suppress them. This touched Motley personally. The civil rights movement had evolved from nonviolent protests for civil and voting rights into demands for Black economic and political power. These aims were increasingly being articulated with revolutionary rhetoric borrowed from the global movement for Black decolonization. Stokely Carmichael of the Student Non-Violent Coordinating Committee popularized the phrase "Black Power" at a protest march in Lowndes County, Alabama, in 1966. The Black Panther Party, founded by Huey P. Newton and Bobby Seale in Oakland, California, in October 1966, provided an organizational structure for the ideology of Black nationalism. John Jr. lived and died in this critical moment of Black awakening and ideological transition.[5]

He had grown up with expectations of success. The social status of his parents showed in the five-bedroom colonial where John Jr. was raised. He joined the Boy Scouts, enrolled in the Hopkins School, one of the nation's oldest and toniest prep schools, and welcomed white friends into his home. Smart, soft-spoken, and well connected, he was headed for a bright future.[6]

Trouble crossed his path during his seventh and eighth grades. A strong sense of racial and class identity set in among white students, and "Johnny started running into blatant discrimination," his sister Joan recalled. Whites at the prestigious school uttered dreadfully offensive things. One white boy's taunt—"Hey Huggins," I "smelled your father," at a Yale football game—stung the boy deeply. After the onslaught of this racist bullying, Huggins left the school, transferring to the local public high school. But problems followed him there, too. "He quickly got on the wrong side of the principal," said his sister. Disillusioned, "Johnny" left without graduating and, against the wishes of his parents, joined the Navy. After service as a radarman in Vietnam and in the Philippines, Huggins Jr., discharged with a commendation, returned stateside now wiser to the world, and capable of taking the fight to anyone.[7]

In 1966, John Jr. became involved in antipoverty activism in his home state of Connecticut. He joined a raucous demonstration at the state welfare office in Hartford, where his mother had long served on the board. Police arrested him and several others for breaching the peace. He pled guilty and paid a fine.[8]

After this run-in with the law, John decided to finish his education. He enrolled at Lincoln University, the historically Black college in Pennsylvania, through a family connection. During his freshman year, he met his future wife, Ericka Jenkins, a fellow student who shared his passion for justice. Jenkins came from a different world. A native of working-class Washington, D.C., she grew up "living between the housing projects and the petit-bourgeoisie," she remembered. Ericka was strikingly good-looking, with light brown skin, a big, dark, "frizzy" mane, and long limbs. The nineteen-year-old's political consciousness had fully developed by high school: an intellectually precocious poet angry about poverty, oppression, violence, and the "bullshit that Black people survive," she attended the March on Washington in 1963 and found it a "transformative" experience. She "watched in amazement that African Americans and other poor people were coming together to say no to further oppression." In that moment, Ericka remembered, she "made a vow to serve the people." Disenchanted with tradition-bound institutions, she left her hometown after graduating high school. Now more than ever, Washington, D.C., "reminded her of a plantation," she said, with the White House standing in for the "big house." Still in her teens, she called herself "an existential rebel."[9]

At Lincoln, Ericka and John, both members of the Black student congress, despaired over how quiet their campus was. Elsewhere, Black students had "awakened" to the Black nationalist teachings of Malcolm X. Ericka was "looking for something real," and "so was John," she said. "I've got to do something for my people," John said in a phone call to his father. Ideologically simpatico, John and Ericka "became friends, then lovers," she recalled years later. "At first we were just friends. Then I realized that our hearts were quite alike, that we thought alike and wanted the same things for the most marginalized and oppressed people in this country." John's political sensibility and his empathy for others drew her to him. Together, the couple set out to join the revolution.[10]

Leaving Lincoln University behind in November 1967, they packed up the Chrysler John's father had bought him and drove cross-country. Their journey took them to the Golden State, the epicenter of the newly formed Black Panther Party for Self-Defense, which Ericka had read about in *Ramparts* magazine, a widely popular radical publication. The couple settled in Los Angeles and joined the Panthers.

A revolutionary political organization, the Black Panther Party (BPP) analogized Black Americans to colonial subjects. The party's "Ten-Point Program" called for self-determination: Blacks should decide whether to remain in the United States or find a new homeland. The BPP also advocated for socialism to redress the oppressions of class and race, and urged Blacks to arm and defend themselves against white aggressors. The party's charismatic founders attracted tremendous attention: Huey Newton and Bobby Seale were handsome and cool. They wore black berets and showed off their weapons. In 1967 they gained worldwide fame when Seale led a group of heavily armed party members into the California state capitol building to protest a bill that would have limited the right to carry loaded weapons on city streets. Passionate and idealistic, the Hugginses found the Panthers exciting.[11]

John Jr.'s alliance with the Panthers took many by surprise. Because he came from a Black "establishment" background and his manner was soft-spoken, family members and friends were astonished. It "did not compute," recalled Constance Royster, Constance Baker Motley's niece and a keeper of family history. Everybody knew that John held strong political beliefs, but in the late 1960s civil disobedience was considered edgy behavior in some households, if no longer an unusual part of many young people's lives. Judge Motley, the family's most prominent member, spent part of her illustrious career fighting to protect civil rights protesters. Nonviolent civil disobedience—practiced by Gandhi and King, labor and civil rights activists, women's libbers, and peaceniks—shocked no one. The Panthers, however, stood for beliefs far outside the mainstream. Such views were unexpected of any Huggins or, indeed, of any Black man who had grown up in a five-bedroom colonial-style house.[12]

John and Ericka had no patience for racial liberals and talk of reform and voting rights. White terror reigned as the civil rights movement inched toward Black freedom. By 1968, both Malcolm X and Martin L. King Jr. had been assassinated. American cities convulsed and burned. Tired of brutal poverty and police brutality, young Black men and women rose in rebellion. The Panthers spoke to the pain of these disillusioned young people.[13]

Deeply affected by the social unrest, Ericka and John became "prime movers" in the Panthers' Los Angeles chapter and John the party's "area captain." He started sporting a bushy beard, and let his close-cropped hair grow into an Afro. Ericka, too, pregnant with their child, wore her hair natural. Life in the party engulfed them.[14]

*

Not long after the couple embraced the Panthers, the FBI got involved. J. Edgar Hoover, then director of the FBI, in 1969 labeled the Panthers the "greatest threat" to the "internal security of the United States." This assertion justified his effort to destroy the BPP through a counterintelligence program, called COINTELPRO, that aimed to sow discord within political organizations, and thus dismantle them. Hoover specifically targeted Black nationalist organizations and instructed all local offices to disrupt them. Following the FBI's lead, federal, state, and local law enforcement agencies made the infiltration and eradication of the Panthers a top priority. Mayhem ensued; law enforcement pursued the organization and its members through often-illegal surveillance, raids, and brutality. Many Panthers fell at the hands of the police. Three days after the assassination of Dr. King on April 4, 1968, the police killed seventeen-year-old Bobby Hutton—bullets blew off the boy's face. The death provoked an enormous outcry and deepened the loyalty that many, including John and Ericka, felt to the Panthers.[15]

In 1969, an FBI-fueled campaign of chaos, fear, and violence against the Black Panthers ensnared Motley's family. Enrolled in UCLA's "High Potential" program, designed to recruit promising Black students to campus, John and Ericka used the campus as a base from which to organize students and "street brothers" in support of the Panthers. John rallied college students to "get their heads out of the sand" and "care" about the "problems of the ghetto." The Panthers would collaborate with anyone committed to their economic and social justice program. One rival group, US, a Black nationalist organization led by UCLA graduate Ron Karenga, was after Black solidarity, and competed with the Panthers for recruits. Intent on destroying the BPP, the FBI tried to exploit the groups' ideological differences.[16]

A government file, hundreds of pages long, documented the agency's scheme. The FBI relied on informants, surveillance, wiretapping, tax investigations, and the tracking of property and weapons purchases, all undertaken in collaboration with state and local law enforcement. In a September 25, 1968, memo to FBI director Hoover, special agents in the Los Angeles field office noted that "there is considerable friction between the Black Panther Party (BPP) and the 'US' organization headed by Ron Karenga." At that point, the bad blood was limited to vitriolic talk. The FBI's L.A. bureau promised to ratchet up the conflict in order to "further this schism." Two months later, in a memo dated November 29, 1968, FBI agents detailed a plan:

The Los Angeles Office is currently preparing an anonymous
letter for Bureau approval which will be sent to the Los Angeles
Black Panther Party (BPP) supposedly from a member of the
"US" organization in which it will be stated that the youth group
of the "US" organization is aware of the BPP "contract" to kill
RON KARENGA, leader of "US," and they, "US" members, in
retaliation, have made plans to ambush leaders of the BPP in
Los Angeles.

It is hoped that this counterintelligence measure will result
in an "US" and BPP vendetta.[17]

In January 1969, the student director of UCLA's new Black studies
program was being selected. John Huggins Jr., well liked, intelligent,
and known for his passionate commitment to poor communities, was
a strong candidate for the post. But US supported a different candidate. On January 17, during a lunchtime meeting about the issue held
in the student center, three armed, dashiki-wearing US men walked
into the center. John and another well-known Panther leader, deputy
minister of defense Alprentice Carter, had just adjourned a meeting
attended by about 150 students. The US gunmen opened fire, and
John Jr. fell in a hail of bullets. He had been shot in the back; a bul-
let had severed his aorta in broad daylight, on the UCLA campus. A
lethal combination, ideological rivals and FBI-backed "goons," the
US members killed Carter as well. The men's deaths made national
news and shocked the community in New Haven.[18]

Local news reports noted that Huggins came from a "respected
New Haven family" that was active in civic organizations and the civil
rights movement. Writers cast John Jr. as a prodigal son. The young
man had been a civil rights activist, the *New Haven Register* noted,
before moving to Los Angeles and joining the "extremely militant
Black Panthers." It quoted the pastor of the Dixwell Avenue Congregational Church, the longtime spiritual home of some members of
John's family, who described the young man as "an extremely bright
person who was well liked by many around here." His death was nothing short of a "tragedy," and all the more so because it "involved" a
three-week-old daughter, now deprived of her father. "The shocking
thing is that the Huggins family is so clearly social class Number One

black," said an upstanding white community member. His parents had given him so much, yet he still "couldn't make it," the person opined. One of John's sisters later explained that "it was kind of jolting for some people in Connecticut to think that our brother would be a member" of BPP and "wind up getting shot in the back."[19]

While the family reeled, his sisters, Carolyn and Joan, blamed the FBI's COINTELPRO program: that "nasty business" had inflamed tensions and led to Johnny's death. Judge Motley, only in her third year on the bench, quickly received word of the death. Despite her hectic schedule, the judge had always remained close to her extended family, regularly visiting her relatives in New Haven. John Jr.'s death was "terribly wrenching." It also left an indelible mark on the Black Panther Party, which celebrated John Jr. as a "martyr"—a man who had died a "courageous, revolutionary" death at the hands of the United States. At his funeral, the party presented a Panther flag, folded into a three-corner pillow much the same as the American flag at military funerals, to the members of the Huggins family.[20]

*

The murder of John Huggins Jr. shook Motley, and the FBI's documented role in "stirring up" the conflict that gave rise to the assassination must have disturbed her as well. The incident illustrated that any Black man, no matter how noble his cause or respectable his background, could become mired in police intrigue and violence. To be sure, Judge Motley had taken a dim view of the Panthers; the party was ideologically "over the top," she believed. In fact, Motley found all strands of Black nationalism—from followers of Marcus Garvey to Malcolm X and the Panthers—reflective of the way that racism could "crush" the "spirit" and instill the belief that the "white man would never accept Black people." She often criticized the "shrill" voices of the "radical Left," including the Panthers, and minimized their achievements next to the towering accomplishments of stalwart organizations such as the NAACP and the National Urban League. And she eschewed violence and knew that the Panthers had not been blameless in a number of interactions with law enforcement that ended in carnage. But Motley also knew how overzealous and unethical the FBI had been.[21]

On the very evening that John was killed, Los Angeles police officers raided the apartment Ericka shared with John and their infant daughter, Mai, and seized an "arsenal of weapons and ammunition" including an M1 rifle, shotguns, and pistols. Claiming that they feared the Panthers would retaliate after the murder of John and Alprentice, the officers arrested Ericka and several other Panthers for possession of deadly weapons and conspiracy to commit murder. Following a dreadful, if brief, stint in jail, the police dropped the charges and Ericka abandoned Los Angeles.[22]

The young widow relocated to her husband's family home in New Haven and emerged within months. Relying on the aftermath of John Jr.'s martyrdom and the strength of her own leadership and charisma, Ericka founded the Connecticut chapter of the Panthers and managed it. New Haven was fertile ground for activism. Angry at local officials' indifference to the poor and urban renewal projects that displaced populations, members of the Connecticut Panthers disdained mainstream society. They distributed leaflets around town that called "[p]istols, rifles, shotguns, machine guns, and grenades" the only "symbol of justice the pigs know." These provocations did not go unnoticed.[23]

In May 1969, the now twenty-three-year-old Ericka was arrested again, this time in a raid by the New Haven police. She was charged with kidnapping, torturing, and murdering a suspected FBI informant, nineteen-year-old Alex Rackley, who was described as possessing a "child-like intelligence and demeanor." Evidence gleaned from an audio recording she had made showed that Ericka had undeniably been present at the Panthers' New Haven headquarters while three other Panthers had beaten and tortured Rackley for two days, before leading him away from headquarters at gunpoint and later killing him in a nearby swamp. The gunmen pleaded guilty, but Huggins disclaimed responsibility. She insisted again and again that despite her presence at headquarters, she "didn't know what was happening." Black Panther Party chairman Bobby Seale was also implicated in the killing; Seale was in New Haven to give a speech at Yale, and the prosecution claimed that he ordered Rackley's execution. Huggins and Seale were to stand trial together.[24]

Behind the scenes, Judge Motley played a pivotal role. First, she intervened by connecting Ericka Huggins with Catherine Roraback, a well-regarded civil liberties lawyer and one of just a few prominent female criminal defense lawyers at that time. Roraback had made her name representing Estelle Griswold in *Griswold v. Connecticut*, the first successful challenge to a state's ban on contraception and a crucial legal building block for *Roe v. Wade*, the abortion rights case. Keenly aware of how gender shaped women's experiences, especially their ability to be heard in a man's world, Roraback was the perfect lawyer to defend Ericka's interests, as Judge Motley would have concluded.[25]

*

The case that followed in 1972 was a cause célèbre that attracted worldwide attention and vividly illustrated both the excesses of the Black Panther Party and corruption of the FBI and local law enforcement. Prosecutors insisted that the case was about a simple murder. But the public interpreted the goings-on in New Haven as tied to growing tension between the police and the Panthers, between whites and Blacks.

The trial divided the community and the Yale campus into pro- and anti-Panther factions. Many Yale students, bearing "Free Bobby, Free Ericka" signs, rallied to the Panthers' cause. Under pressure, the president of Yale, Kingman Brewster Jr., declared that he was "skeptical of the ability of Black revolutionaries to achieve a fair trial anywhere in the United States." Vice President Spiro T. Agnew in turn called for Brewster's ouster for his support of the "criminal left." Throughout what turned out to be a six-month trial, John Jr.'s mother, Elizabeth, then working as a librarian at Yale University, asked permission from President Brewster to attend the proceedings, and he encouraged her to do so. A "force of nature," Joan Huggins remembered, Elizabeth made her way to the proceedings "every single day" for six months. She also cared for Mai, her young granddaughter, while Ericka languished at the Connecticut Correctional Institution for Women waiting for the trial to begin and then conclude.[26]

The jury ultimately failed to reach a verdict, and the court dismissed all the charges against Huggins and Seale and ordered the two of them released from jail. Roraback had been indispensable to the outcome: she emphasized Huggins's sex and downplayed her decision-making authority within the BPP, which was widely known for the machismo of its gun-toting leaders. Huggins, who had cowritten a position paper on sexism in the BPP, helped Roraback craft the strategy centered on gender. It had worked. Copious evidence also implicated federal agents and local police in unlawful wiretapping; through illegal surveillance of the Panthers' headquarters, officers had their hands on a blow-by-blow account of Rackley's torture and kidnapping. But they had failed to intervene and rescue him.[27]

Like numerous other Panthers committed to revolutionary politics and armed self-defense, Ericka Huggins endured a terrifying saga. And despite the hung jury and dismissal of charges, the murder of Alex Rackley backfired on the party's members. The Panther-on-Panther murder led to increased law enforcement raids on party chapters across the country. Dozens of members were arrested.[28]

*

At the same time, the period that Ericka and Bobby Seale spent in jail threw a harsh light on FBI and police practices. The pair's incarceration brought increased national attention to the plight of inmates. Ericka campaigned against "oppressive" conditions during her confinement. The Panthers also blasted repressive prison conditions. Both galvanized a prisoners' rights movement that would also be bound up with the judicial legacy of Constance Baker Motley.[29]

Months after John Huggins Jr.'s death and a few weeks after Ericka Huggins's trial, the judge was on the brink of a pivotal moment in her professional life. Just as the Huggins drama unfolded, Motley authored the most socially progressive—and controversial—decision of her judicial career. Like the family saga, the groundbreaking case involved injustices in the criminal legal system.

21

"Pawns in a Very Dangerous Game": Crime, Punishment, and Prisoners' Rights

In 1976 inmates 20727 and 212582 at Stormville Prison, located in New York's Hudson Valley, wrote to Judge Motley seeking her help. The two men complained about the swelling population, "repressive" penal practices, and public "indifference" to inmate rehabilitation. The letter's writers, David Daloia and William Randall, attributed these problems to the "mandatory jail sentences" required by the "Rockefeller drugs laws."[1]

Enacted in 1973 by then-governor Nelson Rockefeller—who had been a friend and supporter of Judge Motley's for many years—the strict new laws promised relief from crime and drug abuse. In New York City during the 1970s, open-air drug bazaars dotted the streets, addiction to heroin and cocaine devastated neighborhoods, and violent crime soared. Eager for solutions, Rockefeller, a moderate Republican and longtime proponent of rehabilitation, took a hard right turn. "Life sentence, no parole, no probation" for "drug pushers," Rockefeller told his aides. The governor championed and the legislature passed new laws that required judges to give those convicted for the possession and sale of narcotics lengthy prison sentences. Popular with legislators in both parties and with much of the public, tough-on-crime laws like Rockefeller's saw quick results. Tens of thousands of people were thrown into the criminal legal system. Prisons swelled with the bodies of Black and brown men. New York had inaugurated a phenomenon known as "mass incarceration," which soon went nationwide.[2]

The two inmates who wrote to Motley in 1976 felt like "pawns" in "a very dangerous economic game." Correctional agencies and police departments reaped financial incentives from the wars on crime and drugs. They had bought "more guns," arrested more people, built more prisons, and crammed ever larger numbers into existing facilities. The public in the meantime was eager to punish perceived wrong-doers, and ordinary people were oblivious to the darkness of life inside, Daloia and Randall wrote. Cast off from society, the prison-ers desperately wanted a chance for "real change."[3]

The inmates had not written to Judge Motley by accident. By 1976, prisoners in and outside New York knew her name: Motley had earned a reputation as a judge who would listen and who presided over a courtroom where inmates' voices could be heard. It fell to courts like hers to address the claims of the burgeoning prisoners' rights movement and its challenges to the logic and machinery of mass incarceration.

The social, political, and cultural changes wrought by the civil rights movement created the environment in which courts were first able to recognize that all people, whether they lived inside or out-side of prison walls, deserved civil and human rights. *Cooper v. Pate*—a landmark 1964 U.S. Supreme Court case establishing that prisoners can sue to avenge the rights guaranteed in the Bill of Rights—laid the groundwork. The case "permitted, indeed obligated" federal courts to provide a "forum where prisoners could challenge and confront prison officials," explained a noted authority. But it was a narrow decision. *Cooper* established inmates' right to challenge practices; it did not disturb the overarching legal framework that granted cor-rectional officials tremendous discretion.[4]

Tasked with maintaining security and order in dangerous circum-stances, wardens and their staff took whatever steps they deemed appropriate to ensure law and order. They could censor mail, refuse visitors, and conduct searches of inmates. Except in extreme circum-stances and notwithstanding *Cooper*, the law obligated courts to avoid interfering with internal prison management. It fell to trial courts to determine the actual scope of inmates' rights.[5]

From her perch on the federal bench, Motley played a command-ing role in the prisoners' rights movement. Her part in the struggle reflected a lifetime of professional and personal experiences. From her time as a civil rights lawyer, a politician, a resident of Black communities, and a matriarch of the Huggins family, she understood more about the causes of Black and brown communities' tortured relationship with the police, their skepticism of the court system, and the distrust of local government than most people who donned judicial robes. She thus insisted on weighing the claims that prisoners made in her courtroom with fairness. One particular inmate's shocking allegations about life inside New York's prisons grabbed Motley's attention and resulted in the most daring decision of her judicial career.

*

By the time Martin Sostre filed a civil rights claim in Motley's courtroom, he had already achieved notoriety within the New York prison system. An Afro-Cuban native of Spanish Harlem born into abject poverty in 1923, Sostre was incarcerated in 1952, at age twenty-eight, for the sale of narcotics; he wound up in the Attica Correctional Facility in western New York State. During his imprisonment, Sostre converted to the Nation of Islam, developed a new "social and political awareness," became a yogi, and transformed himself from "a street dude, a hustler" to an activist and a superb jailhouse lawyer. Sostre was an "extraordinary personality" who operated somewhere on the line "between brilliance and genius," recalled one of his lawyers.[6]

While at Attica Sostre hoped to buy a Koran and form a religious study group with other inmates. Officials denied his requests; they questioned the sincerity of his beliefs and claimed that his organizing efforts threatened order in the prison. Officers placed him in solitary confinement; for four of the twelve years he spent at Attica, he languished there, allegedly for disruptive behavior arising from his desire to exercise his religious faith. Having educated himself on the law with books borrowed from the prison library, Sostre sued. He asserted that the state's actions violated his religious liberties and civil rights, and in 1964 he prevailed.[7]

Sostre's audacious suit, filed prior to the Supreme Court decision in *Cooper v. Pate*, resulted in one of the earliest legal precedents protecting inmates' religious and civil rights. A "building block" for *Cooper*, Sostre's successful religious liberty case constituted the "*Brown v.*

Board of Education of the prisoners' rights movement," according to a noted historian.[8]

In 1968, out of Attica, Sostre was again arrested for the sale of narcotics—$15 worth of heroin. Nothing more than political animus had landed him behind bars, he insisted. He charged that, in line with its COINTELPRO initiative, the FBI, working with police in Buffalo, New York, had set him up to remove him from the community because of his political beliefs and activities. Sostre's Afro-Asian Bookshop, located in the Buffalo ghetto, had sold texts by James Baldwin, Richard Wright, Stokely Carmichael, Malcolm X, and Mao Zedong; and it had become a gathering spot for politicized young Black men and white student leftists—the sort labeled "disorderly" and "subversive." The FBI surveilled him. And local police visited the shop on several occasions, warning him against selling "commie" literature—"the kind of stuff" that "can get you in trouble." Sostre ignored the harassment.[9]

The context, national and local, shaped what ensued. Law enforcement's surveillance and harassment of Sostre took place during the explosive summer of 1967, the year that civil disorder broke out in over a hundred American cities. Police believed that Sostre, a mentor to local activists fighting police brutality, could stir up trouble in Buffalo, a racial hotspot soon expected to explode. And before long, it did. In July, a three-day-long riot, replete with looting and burning, broke out in the city. In its aftermath, police and newspapers claimed that Sostre—characterized as a violent and anti-white drug dealer— had been a major instigator of the riots. Two weeks after the uprising, federal agents and local police beat him, "wrecked" and raided his bookstore, and arrested him on two counts: inciting a riot and selling narcotics. Sostre insisted that he had done nothing wrong; in a show of solidarity with oppressed people in and beyond Buffalo, he had merely exercised his First Amendment rights.[10]

But an all-white jury convicted Sostre, who had been brought into court in chains. The presiding judge ordered him bound and gagged, and noted the inmate's putative "connections" to "the Viet Cong and Black Power." The judge sentenced him to thirty to forty-one years, plus thirty days for contempt of court, again to be served at Attica prison. At the time, Sostre was forty-four years old, and the term amounted to a life sentence.[11]

The warden at Attica "did not want him back." Immediately upon Sostre's second arrival, the deputy warden sent him to solitary confinement, and then "pleaded" with the state corrections department to transfer him elsewhere. The very next morning, a department official transferred him to the Green Haven prison in Stormville, New York. At Green Haven, Sostre was again immediately placed in solitary confinement; he remained there for several days before joining the general prison population. At no point did he give up on his legal activism.[12]

Undaunted, Sostre set out to prove that he had been wrongfully convicted. With his days as a drug user and peddler long behind him, he denied that he had sold anyone heroin and questioned the credibility of the alleged witness to these supposed acts. He insisted on his right to join community protests against injustice. From prison he sent a letter to supporters that eloquently explained his position:

> I greet you from prison and thank all of you who are supporting me in the defense against this frame-up designed to destroy me and the bookshop . . . which they, the power structure, say is inflammatory and Marxist.
>
> My position is that, although the literature may be objectionable to some, . . . I have the constitutional right to sell all literature which promotes freedom of thought and discloses facts which are hidden from us by the controlled news media.
>
> If this is a crime, then I must always be a criminal.[13]

The self-taught "lawyer" set out to reverse his conviction, and handwrote legal petitions for himself and a co-defendant, a woman who had also been arrested at his bookstore. But when he sought to mail the papers to lawyer Joan Franklin at the NAACP, a prison guard refused his request. The warden again sent Sostre to solitary confinement. During a brief period out of solitary, Sostre again attempted to mail his legal papers. But prison officials confiscated his correspondence, and the warden called him into his office to interrogate him about the contents of the proposed mailing. After questioning Sostre, officials returned him to "punitive segregation," another name for solitary confinement. Held there without notice, he remained segregated in a six-by-eight-foot cell with only a bed and a locker—no personal belongings, newspapers, or books of his choice—from June 25, 1968, to July 2, 1969, more than a year.[14]

Sostre filed suit against the wardens of Attica and Green Haven prisons, the state commissioner of prisons, and the governor of New York, Nelson Rockefeller. In a complaint dated October 15, 1968, written in neat block handwriting, Sostre alleged that his relegation to solitary confinement constituted "cruel and unusual punishment."

*

Judge Motley was randomly assigned Sostre's case. After reading all the material, she issued a temporary court order demanding his transfer from solitary confinement back into the general prison population. Cheering his release, the *Black Panther*, the party's official newsletter, approvingly called attention to Motley's history-making status as the first Black woman federal judge. Maybe Sostre, who often lambasted courts as "racist" and "tyrannical," would now have a fair chance in court, given the arbiter of his case.[15]

Under a watchful public gaze, Judge Motley presided in the subsequent trial. Proceedings began on October 29, 1969, lasted more than a week, and attracted tremendous attention. People crowded the sidewalks in front of the federal courthouse in lower Manhattan. Several hundred pickets and activists wearing "Free Martin Sostre" buttons hoisted banners. Self-professed "revolutionaries" "all over the country were watching" the case, a journalist reported. The court stationed extra armed security guards around the courthouse and the courtroom. Spectators, including many Black Panthers, packed the stately courtroom. Represented by Victor Rabinowitz, a civil liberties lawyer well known for representing dissidents Julian Bond, Paul Robeson, Alger Hiss, and Daniel Ellsberg, among others, and co-counsel Kristin Glen, a recent law school graduate, Sostre also played a strategic role in the trial.[16]

In his testimony, Sostre humanized inmates and explained the horrendous conditions detailed in his complaint. On the witness stand and under oath, Sostre—in a show of solidarity with Black nationalism—held up a clenched fist instead of an open hand. In testimony that lasted a whole day, he painstakingly described what had happened to him when he spent over a year in "the hole," a lonely place wholly apart from the "society of brothers" in the general prison population. He said that guards "stripped me, they searched me," and "they gave me cast-off clothing" "without buttons" that exposed his otherwise naked body. The guards then confined him to Cell 17. The cramped quarters had only the basics—a bed without sheets, a locker, a toilet, and a face bowl that ran only cold water. A "bare electric light bulb" hanging from the ceiling remained on all day and night. The solitary block itself had no newspapers or magazines, and "no library," save a few "shoot-'em-up" books that were of no interest to Sostre. A prisoner confined to solitary could earn the "privilege" of one hour's exercise per day—but only if he submitted to strip searches and rectal exams. Sostre refused the "humiliation." "They will never dehumanize me," he said.[17]

Solitary confinement deprived Sostre of intellectual stimulation and communication with the outside world. Most significantly, guards confiscated a box of his legal materials, including minutes, notes, and law books that he had painstakingly gathered over time to aid his defense against unjustified charges. Sostre and his lawyer entered into evidence more than twenty letters that had been tampered with or censored by prison officials.[18]

Sostre saw, heard, and experienced awful things. Racism colored every interaction, he testified. An overwhelmingly white correctional force ruled over the inmates, 80 percent of whom, like him, were Black or Latino. "It is a white-run concentration camp for black and brown people," he said. The guards routinely beat him, and he overheard the "screams" of another inmate subjected to a "savage beating." Among other indignities, he described how every half hour of every night during his thirteen months in solitary, a guard woke him up by shining a powerful flashlight into his eyes. "If your head is covered," the guard "will kick the wall to wake you," or "come into your cell" and "shake the bed or take your blanket away to punish you." Sostre described the desperation that conditions in the "box" created. He testified that Ray Broderick, an inmate briefly confined in nearby

Cell 13, did not last long. Distraught over indefinite confinement to the "tank," the inmate "hung up"—he committed suicide. Ray's death distressed Sostre. "I saw him alive and well before he hanged up. I saw him alive and well before he hanged up," he repeated. Silence enveloped the courtroom.[19]

Many others gave evidence at the trial. Expert witnesses testified that solitary confinement was "degrading, dehumanizing," and "conducive to mental derangement." Dr. Seymour Halleck, a professor of psychiatry and a consultant to the state's prison system, testified that the conditions Sostre had described could "destroy the spirit and undermine the sanity of the prisoner." Two inmates confirmed Sostre's account.

State prison officials testified that Sostre had been punished for a variety of serious infractions and deserved the treatment he received. He had practiced law without a license, a deputy warden testified, and boasted of an escape plan in a letter to his sister. He possessed "racist" literature written by Black Panthers and other radicals that officials considered "contraband," and he had corresponded with a "revolutionary" organization. In one letter, Sostre wrote, "If the law will not free me, I shall eventually be freed by the universal forces of liberation," a statement that officials interpreted as a threat of insurrection.[20]

In her decision, issued on May 14, 1970, Judge Motley held that Sostre's relegation to solitary confinement offended the Constitution. In sixty-six thorough pages, she marched through the many ways that Sostre's mistreatment violated that charter of liberties, the Bill of Rights. An indefinite length of punishment exceeded constitutional boundaries. "But for the intervention of this court," Motley wrote, "Sostre would, in all likelihood, still be in punitive segregation for this alleged offense." Recalling despotic regimes, she noted that prison guards punished Sostre without informing him of what his wrongdoing had been. Since he was initially denied both a lawyer and a hearing, it was only as a result of the trial, precipitated by his suit against the Attica and Green Haven wardens, that Sostre had learned which prison rules he had allegedly broken to merit punitive segregation. Moreover, some of the supposed infractions did not actually violate prison directives. And Motley noted that Sostre had not been charged with "violence, attempting to escape, incitement to riot," or similar charges.[21]

Crucially, Motley also held that the horrid conditions of Sostre's confinement constituted "cruel and unusual punishment." During the entirety of his stay in the segregated group of cells, only one other human being was held near him. Guards rationed and limited Sostre's food supply. They allowed him a hot shower only once a week. "But, as Plaintiff and Plaintiff's counsel put it, the crux of the matter is human isolation," Motley wrote. She concluded:

> This court finds that punitive segregation under the conditions to which Plaintiff was subjected at Green Haven is physically harsh, destructive of morale, dehumanizing . . . needlessly degrading, and dangerous to the maintenance of sanity when continued for more than a short period of time.

In line with the testimony of Dr. Seymour Halleck, Motley wrote that inmates could not be expected to survive psychologically more than fifteen days in punitive segregation. Longer terms risked their sanity.[22] The "totality of the circumstances to which Sostre was subjected for more than a year," Motley concluded, "was cruel and unusual punishment when tested against 'the evolving standards of decency that mark the progress of a maturing society.'" The conditions "could only serve to destroy completely the spirit and undermine the sanity of the prisoner." Among other authorities in support of her conclusion, she cited a 1958 U.S. Supreme Court opinion holding that the Eighth Amendment protects "the dignity of man" and limits punishment to "civilized standards."[23]

In passages confirming that prison officials pursued a vendetta against Sostre, Motley held that Green Haven's warden and staff "retaliated" against him because of his "legal success." One day after his court-ordered release from solitary confinement, officials had again disciplined him, this time for "having dust on his cell bars." Then officials punished him for having "racist literature" in his cell—namely, Sostre's own handwritten political documents called "Revolutionary Thoughts" comprising a list of officers of the Black Panther Party and articles on political topics. Moreover, the warden censored his correspondence with his attorneys and others. The Green Haven warden waged a campaign against Sostre, partly for political and partly for personal reasons. "There is no room for doubt that Sostre's troubles with defendants stem not from his acts or threats to prison security, but from his political thoughts and beliefs," Motley wrote. She continued:

> Sostre was being punished specially by the Warden because of his legal and Black Muslim activities during his 1952–1964 incarceration, because of his threat to file a lawsuit against the Warden to secure his right to unrestricted correspondence with his attorney . . . and because he is, unquestionably, a Black militant who persists in writing and expressing his militant and radical ideas in prison.[24]

Sostre's exercise of his First Amendment rights could not be grounds for claims he posed a threat to prison security. The censorship of his correspondence violated his rights under the Constitution's First (free speech) and Sixth (speedy trial) amendments.[25]

The most audacious ruling of Motley's entire judicial career, the decision vindicated both Martin Sostre and the prisoners' rights movement. It decisively weakened what was left of the "hands-off" doctrine—the idea that judges should invariably defer to the expertise and judgment of correctional officials—that had hobbled so many other inmates' suits. Taking the unusual step of expressly inserting herself into the opinion, Motley wrote, "I believe that courts should look behind" the "shibboleth of prison discipline" that was "offered up as [an] excuse for ignoring or abridging the constitutional rights" of inmates. This was a bombshell opinion.[26]

To many observers, the most noteworthy aspect of Motley's ruling was about money. In an utterly unprecedented move, she awarded Sostre a financial settlement. She applied a 1961 U.S. Supreme Court decision establishing that individuals could sue police officers who violated their civil rights to the state correctional officials in Sostre's case. She calculated the damages for each violation of his rights. The court awarded Sostre $25 per day for every day that he had spent in punitive segregation (a sum total of 372 days), adding up to $9,300 in compensation for the injuries inflicted by the two prisons. In addition, she awarded him compensation to redress the "bad faith and malice" that the wardens had shown toward him. For this "reprehensible" conduct, the court awarded Sostre the additional sum of $10 per day, or a total of $3,720 in "punitive" damages. Martin Sostre had won resoundingly.[27]

Because aspects of Motley's opinion applied broadly, it promised legal protection to many other inmates. She ordered prison officials to establish rules and procedures governing future disciplinary proceedings. Lawyers who represented other inmates could and did cite Motley's opinion—parts of which the court of appeals upheld—on behalf of men and women locked up nationwide. Because of what Motley wrote, prisoners everywhere were able to demand the protections of the Bill of Rights and sue over inhumane conditions of confinement.[28]

In law enforcement and correctional offices across New York, Judge Motley sparked outrage. Prison guards reportedly felt "powerlessness," reported the *New York Times*. They nursed a sense of "outrage," said one guard, that "this Black motherfucker" had managed to "get all he wanted" from the judge. The state attorney general called Motley's order a "federal invasion of state prison management." "Unprecedented in almost every aspect," the attorney general insisted, in a letter to the judge, that the decision had caused "unrest" at the state's prisons and threatened the already "fragile" condition of prison discipline. Motley's opinion had sparked chaos at the Wallkill state prison, a medium-security prison to which Sostre had been transferred after the judge ordered his release from solitary confinement. The state complained that the judge had given "judicial protection" to Sostre's "inflammatory writings"—words that threatened prison security because of the jailhouse lawyer's vast influence over "less aggressive and less intelligent inmates." The attorney general's office further noted that "white inmates are very resentful because they feel Sostre is getting special treatment." They were "jealous" of his success, particularly his monetary compensation. Motley saw the letter as a ploy to shape the narrative and influence the outcome of the case on appeal.[29]

Meanwhile, prominent media outlets celebrated Motley's verdict and Sostre's victory. The *New York Times* hailed the decision as a "startling" and "historic" win for prisoners' due process rights. The *Afro-American*, a premier historically Black newspaper, wrote that the "far-reaching decision" held the "potential of changing life for the better in prisons around the nation." Because of the *Sostre* decision, another commentator wrote, "prisons in America and particularly in New York can never again be quite the dark pits of repression and despair they once were." Law reviews and civil rights lawyers wrote Motley asking for copies of the opinion. Sostre himself and other advocates of prisoners' rights celebrated Motley's decision as a watershed moment that ensured dignified treatment for inmates.[30] And he soon became known internationally as an advocate for human rights, one beloved by the activists and lawyers who joined the prisoners' cause.[31]

The ruling not only changed the law, but also mobilized inmates. A front-page story in the *New York Times*, written just months after Motley vindicated Sostre's rights, was titled "Rising Protests and Lawsuits Shake Routine in State Prisons," and told the story of the decision's nationwide impact. "Disquiet has been seeping through the stone-walled fortresses," with inmates protesting overcrowded, dirty, and dangerous conditions. "Our prisoners read the newspapers," complained a retired deputy warden. "What you've got now," said the commissioner of the New York prison system, "are prisoners who are much more conscious of their civil rights than they ever were before." Unbowed, politically aware, and without their freedom to lose, inmates no longer felt cowed to submit to the authority of the state or its representatives.[32]

An avalanche of cases and work stoppages followed as inmates sought to vindicate the bundle of rights asserted by Sostre and affirmed by Motley. In Boston, Puerto Rican inmates sued a 122-year-old facility, the Charles Street Jail, arguing that the conditions there "affront[ed]" "basic human dignity" and violated the Constitution. In other cases, prisoners sought the due process protections to which Motley held inmates were entitled. Those subject to disciplinary procedures sued for the assistance of counsel. Prisoners at Walpole prison in Massachusetts sued for damages, claiming that guards had beaten them and segregated them in "the hole" for months at a time.

In other suits inmates sought to gain more counselors, psychiatrists, and Black and Puerto Rican prison guards.[33]

Most famously, in 1971, a thousand inmates rose up at the Attica Correctional Facility in New York in a standoff with state officials. Inspired by Motley and Sostre, they demanded civil and political rights, as well as improved conditions. During a days-long standoff, which left forty-three people dead, the prisoners sought out Judge Motley. Seeing her as a fair-minded representative of the state, they asked her to serve as an "observer" in negotiations between themselves, then-governor Rockefeller, and other state officials. But Motley would play no such role; after many "closed-door" conferences and phone calls with trusted advisers, she concluded that her involvement would be inconsistent with her role as a judge.[34]

*

Some effects of the decision struck closer to home. Motley issued her opinion in the Sostre case right in the thick of Ericka Huggins's trial and imprisonment. In the midst of the excitement generated by her opinion, the increased protests and activism to redress unjust imprisonment and inhumane prison conditions, Huggins too complained that correctional officials had violated her civil and political rights.[35]

Building on claims made by Sostre, other Black Panthers, and assorted revolutionaries before her, Huggins's lawyer, Catherine Roraback, sued officials for censoring letters to counsel, limiting her reading material, restricting access to visitors, denying telephone access, preventing access to the press, and subjecting Huggins and her belongings to invasive searches. Black Panther Party chairman Bobby Seale joined the lawsuit.[36]

Citing Motley's opinion, the presiding judge ordered prison officials to provide relief to the inmates. Administrators were made to stop opening Huggins's and Seale's correspondence with counsel, and to permit the two Panthers to read "inflammatory" materials. The prisoners had triumphed based in part on the strength of Motley's opinion.[37]

*

On appeal a year later, all nine of the judges on the U.S. Court of Appeals for the Second Circuit heard the Sostre case—an extraordinary treatment reserved for the thorniest or most consequential cases. Exemplifying how difficult the appeals court found the issues presented, the judges failed to speak in one voice on many of them. Instead, five of the court's nine judges issued their own individual opinions.[38]

In a partial victory for Sostre and others, the majority of the judges presiding sustained a key element of Motley's groundbreaking decision, affirming her holding that inmates, like all others, possessed the constitutional right to free political expression and communication with attorneys or court officers. Sostre could neither be punished for his political beliefs or legal activities, nor prevented from mailing documents to his lawyer. That said, to promote discipline and keep order, the court held, correctional authorities could regulate mail and censor some material—even if it pertained to political beliefs or legal activities.[39]

But the majority of the nine judges rejected the epic central judgment of Motley's decision. The court overruled Motley's holding that the conditions of Sostre's confinement constituted "cruel and unusual punishment." The judiciary lacked the power to contravene state law and correctional policy. "Even a lifetime of study in prison administration," the court wrote, "would not qualify" a judge "to command state officials to shun a policy that they have decided is suitable" because "the choice may seem unsound or personally repugnant." Motley had, in other words, exceeded the boundaries of her authority.[40]

The court also mostly rejected Motley's financial award to Sostre; it upheld the damages award against only one of the two prison officials Sostre had sued, the warden of Green Haven prison. By this point, however, the warden had died, and thus Sostre would receive no compensation for the wrongdoing he had experienced.[41] The appellate court's opinion had managed, wrote one columnist, "simultaneously to nod to the progressive and genuflect to the primitive."[42]

The court of appeals dashed the promise held out to inmates by the most innovative element of Motley's decision. The U.S. Supreme

Court declined to hear the appeal. Motley's affirmation of inmates' right to free political expression and to due process before punishment stood, but the fight to better the lives of incarcerated people by ending indefinite solitary confinement would have to wait for another day.[43]

Yet Motley stood by her decision and continued to value the daring of those involved in the prisoners' rights movement. She explained:

> The issue was whether it was "going too far, too fast." . . . Well, of course, somebody always has to start it, and you have to be willing to be criticized for that kind of thing. [S]omebody has to have the courage.[44]

She drew an explicit parallel to the experience of civil rights lawyers and activists. Back then, observers repeatedly exhorted those fighting for social change to do so incrementally. Motley took from her civil rights movement days fortitude in the face of resistance, even from a higher court. One of her clerks explained her position: "She told me that . . . her job [was] to decide cases the best she could." She took pride in reaching the outcome she believed was justified by the law.[45]

The saga ended with a measure of justice for Martin Sostre. On Christmas Eve 1975, Governor Hugh Carey of New York granted him clemency, mercy born of new evidence that raised profound doubts about the drug conviction that had landed him in prison. In 1973 the key witness against him recanted; in a sworn affidavit, he admitted that he had not, in fact, bought heroin from Sostre, and had, in fact, worked with police to frame him. This illustrated a pattern of government frame-ups of politically active Black men across the country, according to experts who supported Sostre's bid for clemency. And it called into question the legitimacy and integrity of the entire criminal legal system.[46]

Finally freed in February 1976, Sostre praised Governor Carey's courage. But the fifty-two-year-old had spent more than twenty years of his life in prison, and five of those in caged isolation. He expressed bitterness about the injustices that he had experienced in the so-called justice system. "I am a human being," he said at a news conference held at 777 United Nations Plaza in New York City. "I have feelings. . . . I am not happy that all this can happen in a so-called civilized society." Conjuring the mantra of the movement he had led, Sostre said, "Human rights do not end at the prison gates."[47]

*

For Motley, her sweeping decision in the *Sostre* case was a beginning, not an end, to the stand she took against the machinery of mass incarceration. In 1977, she ruled in a case with two women plaintiffs that penalties imposed by the Rockefeller drug laws violated the Eighth and Fourteenth amendments. The case involved only two of the hundreds of thousands of people who found themselves embroiled in the criminal legal system. Martha Carmona pleaded guilty to possession of a controlled substance, three and three-eighth ounces of cocaine, and was sentenced to somewhere between six years and life in prison. Her co-plaintiff, Roberta Fowler, was similarly convicted of the criminal sale of a controlled substance—one individual dose of a substance containing cocaine, or 0.00455 of an ounce—and was sentenced to between four years and life. Citing the draconian sentences, Martha and Roberta challenged the constitutionality of New York's sentencing scheme for drug offenses.[48]

In her opinion about the case, Motley humanized the two women. She described the background of each, stories that would have been familiar to those who knew anything about the lives and labors of working-class women, particularly women of color emigrées living in New York. Born in Puerto Rico, Carmona, forty-one years old, grew up in the United States. For thirteen years, she had worked as a sewing machine operator for a garment manufacturer. Most recently, she had worked part-time in a Manhattan beauty salon. Motley also noted details that described Carmona as an exemplar of "respectable womanhood and diligent motherhood." "Though presently unmarried (she was married at age eighteen and divorced a year later), she has a daughter approximately twenty-one years old whom she was supporting until her arrest on the instant charges in 1974. The daughter subsequently had to resort to public assistance," Motley recounted. Before 1974, when she was arrested on drug-related charges, Motley noted, Carmona had never been convicted of a crime. After her arrest, she had tried to cooperate with police and prosecutors, but without success.[49]

Fowler was twenty-three years old and a mother of two. The plaintiff's own mother had died "while she was a teenager," a traumatic event that had led to her "receiv[ing] psychiatric counseling for some time thereafter," Motley wrote. A high school dropout, Fowler had found employment at places like the New York State Department of Labor, the Eden Park Nursing Home, and the New York Telephone Company. Motley noted that since her imprisonment, Fowler had been trying to better herself. She had "taken the high school equivalency examination," and she "made diligent efforts to maintain close contact with her children," who frequently visited her at the Bedford Hills prison.[50]

In her ruling, Motley held that a life sentence for possession of a small amount of drugs was grossly out of proportion to the crime: such sentences violated the Eighth Amendment's ban on cruel and unusual punishment, as applied to the states by the Fourteenth Amendment. The sentences were "significantly more severe" than those imposed for the same offenses in other states, she wrote, and were "more severe than those imposed for many serious and violent crimes in the State of New York itself." Motley ordered the women released from prison if the state did not decide a constitutionally appropriate sentence within ninety days. The decision "opened the way for hundreds of narcotics offenders to petition" the federal court for review of their sentences, the *New York Times* reported. Motley had "cast serious doubt on the continued validity of every sentence imposed under the Rockefeller drug laws," wrote an attorney for the Legal Action Center, a nonprofit focused on "restoring opportunity" for people convicted of crimes.[51]

But the state instead appealed, and a three-judge panel of the court of appeals reversed Motley's decision. A few years' imprisonment with the likelihood of parole was not too severe a punishment for participating in the "socially destructive" narcotics trade, the majority held, by a two-to-one vote. The dissenting judge emphasized that the women were not "wholesalers, importers, dealers, or distributors" of the banned substances.[52]

Carmona and Fowler appealed to the U.S. Supreme Court, but to no avail. The justices declined to hear the appeal. Thurgood Marshall, then a justice on the country's highest court, joined by Justice Powell, dissented. In an opinion that cited the protections of the Magna Carta and the Bill of Rights, along with the reasoning of Motley's opinion, Marshall argued that the justices should not "abdicate" their responsibility to assess punishments imposed by legislatures.[53]

*

History vindicated Motley. The Rockefeller drug laws, which she had opposed since her days as a New York senator, failed in their purpose. By the 2000s, the prison population had exploded to absorb millions of people, the overwhelming majority of whom were low-level drug offenders like Carmona and Fowler, not to mention the thousands like Martin Sostre, who were wrongfully imprisoned on drug charges before and after the laws' enactment. Communities of color, particularly African American men, were hit hardest of all. The law had made little tangible difference, as the international drug trade remained profitable, while high rates of both substance abuse and drug-related crime persisted. Bowing to pressure from experts and activists, policymakers in New York finally conceded what Judge Motley had known all along: the drug laws led to grave injustices.

In 2004, New York Governor George Pataki, a Republican, signed the Drug Law Reform Act. The law increased the quantities of narcotics required for a drug offense to be classified a felony, and it reduced sentences for those convicted of drug-related offenses. The legislation also permitted inmates serving life sentences for drug offenses to petition for resentencing.[54]

Forty years earlier, in both the *Carmona* decision and a public address, Judge Motley had warned that the "severe" system of punishments for addicts and drug dealers would cause extraordinary harm to individuals "deprived of life and liberty." She argued that it would undermine the criminal system as a whole because it "stripped" judges of the discretion to weigh and impose sentences. And, she added, alluding to the disparities of race and class in drug arrests, "The full force of this new criminal justice mandate will come to bear only on those few who are unlucky enough to be arrested, prosecuted and convicted." The legitimacy of the system itself "deserves as much attention, if not more," she insisted, than "crime in the streets."

If only Motley's words had been heeded, the nation might have escaped the devastation caused by draconian criminal laws and sentences during the four-decade-long and futile War on Drugs.[55]

22

A "Woman Lawyer" and a "Woman Judge": Making Opportunity for Women in Law

Pauli Murray's note of congratulations to Constance Baker Motley nearly jumped off the page. "Dear Connie," she wrote, "I cannot let this day go by without saying Bravo! Well deserved!" "Hooray for our side!" The pathbreaking feminist lawyer's *Peanuts*-themed notepad, complete with a sketch of Patty—a female character from the comic strip's early days—channeled the satisfaction and joy that animated Murray's message. Dorothy Kenyon, another of Motley's feminist activist friends, felt the same way. "Marvelous," Kenyon wrote in a telegram to Motley. "I always wanted you to be on the bench," she added. "I only wait to welcome you on the Supreme Court bench one day and—perhaps—argue a case before you." The greetings from Murray and Kenyon expressed the hopes of many progressives as Motley joined an all-male, all-white federal court. Having fought for equality since the postwar years, by the late 1960s these women were ready to win.[1]

The sense of possibility created by Motley's rise occurred against the backdrop of the full emergence of the women's liberation movement. Owing to the ingenuity of leaders such as Murray, who had coined the term "Jane Crow" and eloquently described the simultaneous impact of sex and race discrimination, the landmark Civil Rights Act of 1964 had banned both sex and racial discrimination. In 1965, Mary King and Casey Hayden wrote a memo that indicted the sexism prevalent in both the civil rights movement and the New Left. The authors, young women who were active in the Student Non-Violent Coordinating Committee and Students for a Democratic Society, complained that men in these organizations deprived women of leadership positions, consigned them to housework and secretarial tasks, and induced them to engage in sexual relations. While the picture the writers painted did not describe the experience of all women in these organizations, their critique catalyzed a social awakening in younger women in much the same way that Betty Friedan's 1963 publication of *The Feminine Mystique* had articulated middle-class housewives' dissatisfaction with traditional sex roles.[2]

In 1966, Pauli Murray, Shirley Chisholm, Betty Friedan, and other prominent women founded the National Organization for Women (NOW), dedicated to equality under law for women, including reproductive rights and equal opportunity in the workplace. NOW touted the role of law in the struggle for women's liberation. "WE BELIEVE that the power of American law . . . must be effectively applied and enforced to isolate and remove patterns of sex discrimination, to ensure equality of opportunity in employment and education, and equality of civil and political rights and responsibilities on behalf of women." Women also sought increased political power. In 1968, New Yorkers elected Shirley Chisholm to the U.S. House of Representatives: the first Black woman ever elected to Congress, Chisholm unabashedly advocated equality for women and people of color.

Building on the momentum of her historic win, in 1971, Chisholm helped to establish the National Women's Political Caucus. The founders of the NWPC included, in addition to Chisholm, Betty Friedan; Gloria Steinem, a writer who later started *Ms.* magazine; and Bella Abzug, a labor lawyer who was elected to Congress from New York in 1970. The NWPC engaged in collective action: the group held seminars and workshops and staged sit-ins and mass protests. Activists demonstrated against sexism and racial inequality and for more generous welfare benefits, held antiwar and antinuclear rallies, and went on strike to support the Equal Rights Amendment. In 1972, for the first time in history, women held a protest for abortion rights. And in 1974, a group of Black women formed the Combahee River Collective, and brought new attention to the intersecting forms of oppression based on race, gender, class, and sexual orientation that they faced. By the 1970s, these organizations and upheavals in politics, society, and culture heralded the arrival of the movement for women's liberation.[3]

Litigators, among them Pauli Murray, Dorothy Kenyon, Florynce Kennedy, and Ruth Bader Ginsburg, translated activists' demands into legal claims. On several occasions, these lawsuits wound up in the courtroom of the Honorable Constance Baker Motley.[4]

Very few of the cases the judge decided in her early years on the court presented any opportunity to reconsider the gender status quo. But a handful did. One unprecedented case, filed in 1975 over the place of women in the legal profession, tested the reach of the Civil Rights Act, particularly its ban on employment discrimination. The lawsuit shook the legal profession, yielding headlines about a world turned upside down: a "prestigious, old-line Wall Street firm" had been "stung" by a suit "filed by a woman lawyer and heard by a woman judge," screamed the *Wall Street Journal*.[5]

*

Founded in 1879 by Algernon Sydney Sullivan and William Nelson Cromwell, Sullivan & Cromwell was one of New York's oldest and most prestigious law firms. Its reputation had been built on representing the masters of the financial sector. Calling himself the "physician of Wall Street," Cromwell gained renown for his ability to rescue failing companies. Sullivan & Cromwell advised the developers of America's railroads and the owners of the nation's industrial and commercial interests; it counted companies with household names such as General Electric and U.S. Steel among its clients. Politically connected men, including Allen Dulles and John Foster Dulles, numbered among its partners, and they raised the firm's profile higher still.[6]

Like every other top-tier firm in the lucrative New York market, Sullivan & Cromwell effectively excluded women from its ranks. Apart from a few exceptions, women who sought employment at these firms, particularly in litigation departments, told the same story of rejection. And on the rare occasions when firms broke that rule, the women did not last long.

Many female candidates rejected by firms like Sullivan & Cromwell later earned recognition as excellent lawyers. Constance Baker Motley was turned down by a partner at a New York law firm who "took one look at" the 1946 graduate of Columbia Law School and refused to interview her. Sandra Day O'Connor could only find work as a legal secretary despite graduating at the top of her class from Stanford Law School in 1952. "I declined that," O'Connor noted sharply in an interview after she was appointed a justice on the U.S. Supreme Court. Ruth Bader Ginsburg, who graduated first in her class at Columbia Law School in 1959, suffered a similar fate; none of the twelve firms with which she interviewed offered her a position—rejections that the superbly credentialed lawyer found "depressing."

The pattern of sex discrimination that deprived Motley, O'Connor, Ginsburg, and countless other meritorious women of lucrative opportunities persisted well into the 1970s. During the 1960s, even as Congress banned discrimination in employment, law firms brazenly refused to change their practices. In one survey taken at that time, law firm respondents deemed women unsuitable for the law, particularly litigation. "Women can't keep up the pace," they are prone to "emotional outbursts," and their "responsibility is in the home," the male lawyers explained. But in the 1970s, that would finally change.[7]

Much as World War II had opened the doors of Columbia Law School to Constance Baker and a handful of other women, the Vietnam War created educational opportunities for women during the late 1960s. Women filled the seats left by men entering military service. The percentage of women in law school climbed steadily over the decade, rising from about 3 percent in the early 1960s to nearly 9 percent by 1970. Many of these women entered law school after taking part in civil rights, student, and antiwar movements. They viewed law as a tool of social change.[8]

New York University's School of Law attracted such reform-minded women. After graduating from the law school, Diane Serafin Blank, Susan D. Ross, and Janice Goodman found—as Motley, Ginsburg, and O'Connor had before them—that they were not going to be welcomed into the legal profession. To fight the yawning gap between their expectations and their experiences, Blank, Ross, Goodman, and several others founded the NYU Women's Rights Committee (WRC).[9]

Vital in the struggle to open access to women in the legal profession, the WRC raised awareness about the unequal opportunities for women in the law and pushed to correct the disadvantages. To publicize the unfair treatment, the committee conducted a survey documenting a litany of challenges faced by women lawyers. What they found was that there were only three women partners among the thousands of lawyers at twenty leading Wall Street law firms. In April 1970, WRC members held a two-day conference at NYU about sex discrimination; at the invitation of the committee, female law students from more than a dozen law schools across the country shared their experiences and resolved to fight for equality.[10]

In their highest-profile step yet, the WRC traveled to Congress during the summer of 1970 to testify about women's inferior status in law and expose the adverse effects of discrimination. Armed with anecdotes, social scientific evidence, and statistics, Blank, Ross, and others described a "vicious cycle" of unfair treatment in law school admissions and activities, in job placement services, and in employment. Ross described a "disturbing pattern" of law professors who failed to take a firm stand against women's mistreatment; instead of sanctioning men for discrimination, they cautioned women against "being too sensitive." "The low status of women in the legal profession is not accidental, but rather, part of an institutional structure designed to keep women down," Blank testified. The WRC members demanded federal action against sex discrimination in the legal profession. To ensure success, Blank and other women at NYU and Columbia law schools "took notes" during "their interviews" and "developed extraordinarily damaging" material about law firms. Their revelations formed the basis of formal discrimination complaints, first made to the New York City Commission on Human Rights, and then to its federal counterpart, the Equal Employment Opportunity Commission.[11]

Ultimately, these women turned to the courts. On January 15, 1975, Diane Blank sued Sullivan & Cromwell. A fitting plaintiff, Blank had, by that time, gained notice for founding an all-female law firm conceived to challenge discrimination. The suit replicated the logic and legal claims women made in a dozen lawsuits filed against major New York law firms around the same time. Blank alleged a "pattern and practice of sex discrimination" by Sullivan & Cromwell. She claimed that the firm systematically discriminated against women in its employment policies. It refused to hire well-qualified female attorneys. The firm subjected the few women whom it did hire to less favorable working conditions. It paid women lower salaries; excluded or marginalized women associates in the firm's culture; denied them opportunities to advance; and relegated them to "behind-the-scenes" legal specialties such as trusts and estates.[12]

Known as a "factory," Sullivan & Cromwell reveled in working its lawyers long, hard hours. Attorneys boasted about staying at their desks until midnight for several weeks in a row. The firm's chairman in the 1970s also frequently "bragged" to young lawyers that he had "missed his wedding anniversary" and the "birth of a child" because of his duties at work. The firm came first. Over drinks and meals, often at men-only clubs, the attorneys who worked there bonded and enjoyed their "life at the top," wrote a historian of the firm. Within this professional ethos, a woman lawyer did not fit; it was ridiculous to think that any woman, responsible as she was for bearing children, would want to be a lawyer, much less actually work as one.[13]

The cold numbers affirmed that women could scarcely be found in major New York City law firms in 1970. The fifty largest firms employed 3,900 attorneys, and there were only 151 women among them. Sullivan employed 140 lawyers, only three of them women. Every single one of the firm's fifty partners was a man. Representing Blank against them was a formidable opponent, Harriet S. Rabb—an attorney who had served as counsel in employment discrimination actions against several other high-profile employers, including *Newsweek*, *Reader's Digest*, and the *New York Times*.[14]

A modest, soft-spoken white woman, Rabb grew up in Houston during the era of Jim Crow. Despite her privileged upbringing, her religion marked her. A "teen-aged Jewish over-achiever," as she called herself, she developed a strong commitment to equality despite the racism prevalent in her hometown. Her mother was a practicing physician, and Rabb grew up hearing stories about the indifference she encountered in medical school. "She told me that when she was in the lab, professors used to walk by, stop and see what people were doing with their research," Rabb remembered. But "whenever they came to a woman," the "professor simply walked behind and moved on to the next man." Rabb's mother—one of only two women in her medical school class at the University of Texas—kindled in her daughter a commitment to social justice. "Whatever gumption I had in my life," Rabb said, "starts with my mom."[15]

Rabb attended Barnard College in New York City, where "everything was unlike anything in Houston, Texas." And she chose Columbia for law school; there she formed friendships with "other young people [who] were really committed to civil rights and human rights." The death and despair of the Vietnam War shadowed Rabb's law school experience. In this milieu, progressive students bonded, joined ongoing protests for peace and human rights, and committed themselves to repairing the world. Rabb knew in her "heart" that she wanted to use her law degree to fight injustice.[16]

Under the tutelage of William Kunstler and Arthur Kinoy—brash "movement lawyers" famous for their defense of leftist causes—Rabb "learn[ed] how to be a lawyer." She acquired formidable skills as a litigator representing civil rights and antiwar activists affiliated with the Student Non-Violent Coordinating Committee and Students for a Democratic Society. By 1971, Rabb—who looked like the average "Upper West Side mommy you might stumble across in Zabar's"—had made her mark. This unassuming woman earned a reputation as a skilled and tireless civil rights lawyer. She got involved in the Sullivan litigation at the behest of lawyer Eleanor Holmes Norton, then chair of the New York City Human Rights Commission, the trailblazing Black woman lawyer who was the first female to lead that body.[17]

Rabb sued Sullivan & Cromwell in the U.S. District Court for the Southern District of New York. *Blank v. Sullivan & Cromwell* ended up with Judge Motley by the luck of the draw. The clerk of court assigned cases by spinning a drum, a decades-old practice. Locked and placed in open court, the drum contained index cards affixed with the names of the twenty-seven judges of the court. After the drum had been spun and ground slowly to a halt, the clerk pulled out the fateful card; it bore the name of the only woman and the only person of color on the court. Constance Baker Motley, the famed civil rights lawyer, would preside in one of the first cases testing the antidiscrimination principles of Title VII of the Civil Rights Act of 1964—a landmark statute for which she and her colleagues at LDF had laid the groundwork. Motley's assignment to the case came as dire news to Sullivan & Cromwell.[18]

The law firm's primary attorney, Ephraim London, protested. To defend against the high-profile sex discrimination suit, Sullivan & Cromwell had opted not to rely solely on its usual counsel, steeped as he was in corporate practice. Instead, the firm undoubtedly believed it was shrewd to hire London, a Jewish attorney from a well-known family of progressive lawyers. Over four decades of practice, London had earned a reputation as a respected civil liberties lawyer; in several successful arguments at the U.S. Supreme Court, he had fought the censorship of films. As an authority on constitutional law, he had taught at NYU law school and knew one of the women on the suit's opposing side. London could lean on his progressive reputation during his vigorous defense of the firm against discrimination allegations. That fall of 1975, he pressed his advantage by making an audacious claim.[19]

In an extraordinary personal letter written to Motley, London urged the judge to withdraw from the case because, as an African American and a woman, there was every likelihood she had experienced workplace discrimination. London cited a past statement that Motley had reportedly made regarding "the crippling effects of discrimination." Given her identity and experiences, Motley would identify strongly with other women who claimed discrimination, the attorney alleged. "I believe you have a mindset that may tend, without your being aware of it, to influence your judgment," London asserted.[20]

He also made a formal request for Motley's removal. The lawyer sought her disqualification from the case following her decision to certify *Blank v. Sullivan & Cromwell* as a class-action lawsuit. A crucial decision, class-action certification meant that Blank's suit would cover not just her own claims, but those of hundreds of other unsuccessful female job applicants; under questioning, the firm would have to reveal how it had handled all these women's applications, and if it lost the case, it would owe thousands of dollars in damages to each woman.

During a June 2, 1975, pretrial conference, Motley explained her reasoning. She wanted to ensure that the case moved swiftly to trial and did not get bogged down in needless court filings. A judicial colleague, citing a binding appellate court decision, had just granted class certification in a nearly identical case, and it followed that she should do the same in *Blank*. Motley's determination came three days after Blank requested class-action status, and weeks before the official due date for defendant's response to the motion. "Stunned," London protested. He was "not prepared to respond to the motion," but argued that "there were substantial reasons for denying the class certification," most of which turned on Diane Blank's alleged mis-representations about her qualifications to work at the firm. Motley's hasty class-certification decision proved, London argued, that because of her race, gender, and practice background, there was no way she could be fair. By implication, he argued, only a white man could properly preside in a sex discrimination suit.[21]

Motley was enraged. She refused to remove herself from the case. Rabb recalled that "in one of the more humorous and satisfying moments" she had ever witnessed in court, Motley asked London if his request for recusal implied his wish for "a man with no civil rights experience"?[22] In a short and forceful opinion, she spelled out why she would not leave the case. Sullivan had no actual evidence to support its claim that she could not be impartial. Motley denied that anything in her nine years on the court supported London's claim. She had often ruled *against* plaintiffs in civil rights cases, including women in workplace discrimination actions. Sure enough, Motley's judicial record showed that she, like every other judge, was more likely to rule *against than for* alleged victims of discrimination. In fact, she sided with defendants in 56.5 percent of the sex and race discrimination cases she ruled in over the course of her career. Instead of favoritism, her rulings proved her impartiality.[23]

After analyzing the black letter law on judicial recusal, Motley directly addressed the heart of London's allegation. "It is beyond dispute that for much of my legal career I worked on behalf of Blacks who suffered race discrimination," she said. "I am a woman, and before being elevated to the bench, was a woman lawyer." But these facts did not and could not, by themselves, rise to the level of "bias" within the meaning of relevant law. "[I]f background or sex or race of each judge were, by definition, sufficient grounds for removal, no judge on this court could hear this case," Motley wrote. The judge had turned London's argument on its head. The court of appeals upheld her judgment.[24]

For years after she initially wrote, commentators cited Judge Motley's opinion in *Blank* for the proposition that neither sex nor race alone can disqualify a judge from presiding in a case, and lauded it. The *Blank* principle, as it came to be called, along with other precedents, established that while the appearance of impartiality and actual impartiality are important, no party to a lawsuit has the right to a judge "free" of identity or ideology—as if such a person existed. A judge's background or experience in a certain field, such as workplace discrimination or civil rights, will not automatically disqualify her or him from a case. Like Motley, all judges come to the bench "with a background, experiences, associations, and viewpoints."[25]

Yet London continued to besmirch the motives and reputations of all the women involved in the suit. He accused Diane Blank of engaging in "guerilla tactics" against the firm, and berated her during her deposition, a pretrial interview meant to suss out the evidence in a case. London denigrated Blank's law school grades and insulted her membership in a "second-string" law review. He also went after her lawyer, Rabb. In one striking incident, London wrote a letter that insulted Rabb personally. In response to a request for his signature on a routine document, he refused. He accused Rabb of "behaving like a 'Yahoo.'" The allusion, he conceded, was to Jonathan Swift's *Gulliver's Travels*: a "very crude kind of people who behaved in an uncontrolled manner." He also called Rabb "obtuse" and "puerile."

Motley upbraided London for such "strong language," calling it conduct unacceptable from a lawyer in her courtroom. In her nine years on the bench, no lawyer had behaved so inappropriately. The "yahoo" accusation could not have been wider of the mark; Rabb's courtroom genius lay not only in her knowledge of the law, but also in her famously unflappable, "unthreatening and tactful style." Nevertheless, London frequently resorted to calling Rabb and her client unprofessional. Instigated by Blank, a self-described "feminist" lawyer, executed by Rabb, a lawyer for women's causes, and presided over by Motley, the case amounted to a radical attack on Wall Street firms orchestrated by and for women, London insisted. These tactics did not work.[26]

The case ended just as counsel for the prestigious law firm had apparently feared: the lawsuit and the resultant settlement reshaped the workplace. A pivotal evidentiary ruling set the suit's climactic conclusion in motion. Motley held that the plaintiffs could cite the firm's decades-long record of failing to hire women partners as evidence of a pattern of sex discrimination in the selection of associates. This, coupled with the class-certification decision, sank the firm's chances of prevailing.[27]

Sullivan agreed to settle the case to avoid both the expense and the damaging revelations that a trial might divulge. The firm did not admit it had discriminated against women in the past, but it did agree to adopt new policies and practices for the hiring, assignment, and promotion of lawyers in order to ensure that it did not "discriminate on the basis of sex." Going forward, Sullivan would take affirmative steps to recruit and hire women associates at a percentage "comparable" to the percentage of women applicants.[28]

The Sullivan settlement proved a watershed moment in the history of women in the law and "marked a turning point in Big Law." The agreement put all firms on notice that Title VII applied to high-status and traditionally male occupations. *Blank* signaled the far-reaching impact of the employment title of the Civil Rights Act. Diane Blank, who had set these changes in motion by insisting that the firm's failure to hire her had resulted from discrimination, was "delighted" with the settlement. "It is important for women to know they have an equal opportunity to obtain these kinds of jobs," she said.[29]

The suit created opportunities for professional women that earlier generations had only imagined. Greater numbers of women began to enter law school: by 1980, women constituted 12.4 percent of the profession. True, by 1980, Sullivan & Cromwell still had not made a single woman partner, but the number of female associates at the firm had grown steadily over the course of the previous decade. A giant among Wall Street law firms had been made to change, even if gender equity remained elusive at Sullivan & Cromwell and, indeed, among all major law firms. Not infrequently, newly hired women attorneys found firms' work cultures inhospitable. Work norms proved particularly challenging for mothers, and women of color faced what commentators dubbed a "double bind" of race- and sex-based disadvantage that gave rise to professional isolation and high attrition rates.[30]

Although an imperfect remedy, the resolution of the Sullivan & Cromwell case proved unsettling to some. The sex of the judge and the plaintiff's lawyer remained key elements of the narrative spun to explain the decision. "Sullivan & Cromwell Settles Female Class-Action Suit Assigned a Woman Judge," a *Wall Street Journal* headline blared. "Two women lawyers and a woman judge have brought Sullivan & Cromwell, one of the most conservative and prestigious old-line Wall Street firms, to its knees," the story went.[31]

But none of the critics of the outcome focused on the fact that the 1964 Civil Rights Act prohibited sex discrimination in employment, and none spoke of the need for workplace equality. Instead, coverage was dominated by the groundless accusation that a biased judge and a radical feminist attorney posed a threat to tradition. Printed in publications like the *Wall Street Journal*, the resilient narrative showed that the backlash against efforts to achieve equal opportunity in American institutions—heralded by the election and reelection of Richard M. Nixon, and his rants against "leftists" and "liberal bias"—had gained traction, even among New York elites.[32]

*

Motley had the last word, but the brazen effort to remove her from the high-profile case signaled continuing resistance to her authority and how foreign the notion of a "woman judge" was. Like the world of elite firms that Motley's decision in *Blank* shook up, the federal judiciary remained a male domain as late as 1977, the year that Motley approved the landmark *Blank v. Sullivan & Cromwell* settlement.

Eleven years after Motley's appointment to the bench, remarkably little had changed; the number of women working as federal judges across the country had increased by just two. Acutely aware of the public scrutiny that any jurist's words drew, Motley nevertheless spoke out in favor of increasing the number of women and persons of color on the bench. In a speech to a bar association on Law Day in May 1977, she insisted that the federal judiciary "must now change." "No system can call itself fair if major groups" that the system "purports to serve" are not represented. She described the federal judiciary in the South—still all white—and the virtually all-male judiciary nation-wide as "simply indefensible." Several more years would pass before federal officials answered her call.[33]

Women's share of federal judgeships did not begin to grow appreciably until the later years of Jimmy Carter's presidency. Elected in 1976, Carter came under pressure from the National Women's Political Caucus, a nationwide organization that launched a Judicial Appointments Project in 1977, as well as other civil rights groups. By the time he left office in 1981, Carter had changed the face of the nation's judiciary: forty women were by then serving on the federal bench. The Carter White House of course encountered vigorous opposition to its effort to make these lifetime judicial appointments. Critics frequently made the charge that female nominees and nominees of color lacked the requisite qualifications, including practice experience in private law firms. They conveniently ignored the fact that those same private law firms had refused to hire women, not to mention people of color, until Diane Blank sued in Judge Motley's courtroom and won.[34]

*

The outcome in *Blank* confirmed the hopes of Motley's allies. Pauli Murray, Dorothy Kenyon, and Bella Abzug had rejoiced when Motley ascended to the bench because they believed that the legendary civil rights lawyer, cloaked with judicial power, could and would advance the collective cause. The *Blank* result confirmed that the presence of progressive allies on the federal bench could make a fundamental difference. With judges such as Motley presiding, women and people of color could now make claims that would be heard by impartial arbiters, and they would have a fair chance of leveraging the law to their benefit.

But Motley's identity ran like a fault line through her courtroom. The conflict surfaced with special poignancy in *Blank*, but it was not the last time it reared its head. On many more occasions across her career, lawyers questioned Motley's purported liberal "bias" and sought her recusal from litigation involving civil rights laws.

Motley's experience exemplified the scrutiny and skepticism encountered by many judges who are women, people of color, or otherwise differ from the white male judiciary of old. Her plight presaged that of A. Leon Higginbotham, Robert Carter, Nathaniel Jones, and Damon Keith—all civil rights lawyers appointed to the federal judiciary during the 1960s and '70s. Like Motley, these men faced motions for recusal from litigants. In response to questions during confirmation proceedings about whether he could "be fair to white people," an "annoyed" Judge Carter turned the tables. Following the logic of *Blank*, he asked if "white candidates were asked whether they could be fair to Blacks," a "more pertinent question," he believed, "considering the history of brutal suppression and victimization of Blacks by whites" and "data showing that white judges were consistently less generous towards Black defendants than toward white defendants." The reality, Carter observed, is that "no white candidate is asked that question."[35]

Despite objections by Motley, Carter, and so many others, identity-based attacks persist. Women, people of color, and other judges whose background marks them out as "different" have often endured the same skepticism as the first generation of female jurists and judges of color. In 2016, the president of the United States attacked the evenhandedness of a Mexican American judge solely because of his heritage. During litigation over gay rights, some commentators called for the removal of a judge presiding in a case about gay marriage because of his sexual identity. "If a gay judge is disqualified, how about a straight judge," a legal ethicist responded, echoing Motley's powerful argument forty years after *Blank*, and not for the last time.[36]

23

"For a Girl, You Know a Lot About Sports": The New York Yankees Strike Out in Judge Motley's Courtroom

In 1977, the same year that she presided over *Blank v. Sullivan & Cromwell*, Constance Baker Motley encountered Melissa Ludtke—another woman with unusual professional aspirations given her sex. They were brought together by the World Series.[1]

For fans of America's pastime, the 1977 World Series proved to be among the most thrilling in recent memory. The best-of-seven series pitted the archenemies the New York Yankees and the Los Angeles Dodgers against one another. The Yankees arrived at the fall classic ready to avenge their loss the previous year to the Cincinnati Reds. The Yankees had not merely lost; they had been swept, a humiliating turn of events for the baseball dynasty. Their hopes now largely rested on a recently acquired superstar slugger, Reggie Jackson. Despite the pressure of the 1976 sweep and acrimony during the regular season between the egotistical rightfielder, Jackson, and the club's volatile manager, Billy Martin, the "Bronx Zoo" felt poised to win. Without a doubt, the Dodgers' Dusty Baker and other strong hitters threatened the Yankees' ambition. But with the strong lineup that Martin had assembled, the pinstriped team expected to come out of the series as champions for the twenty-first time after a fifteen-year drought. The drama surrounding the series made it one of the most anticipated in several years, and *Sports Illustrated* reporter Melissa Ludtke leapt at the chance to cover the goings-on.[2]

A longtime baseball fan, Ludtke grew up in Amherst, Massachu-setts. A love of competitive games—volleyball, baseball, football, you name it—ran deep in her family. The eldest of five children, Ludtke recalled that she had "a childhood that was filled with sports and competition in sports." She "loved," "knew," and "could talk sports"; what was more, she played them. Luckily for Ludtke, the college town—which she felt was "a wonderful place to grow up"—was years ahead of Title IX, the federal law that demanded equal opportunity regardless of sex, and her high school offered both girls' and boys' teams. Taking full advantage, Ludtke, a "tom-boyish" blonde and a onetime cheerleader, played volleyball in the fall, basketball in winter, and tennis in the spring. During summers on Cape Cod, she sailed. Ludtke's mother "had a passion for baseball," and nurtured the same love of the game in her daughter. Mother and daughter went to Fenway Park together, where the whole family rooted for the Red Sox. All this set Melissa Ludtke, a graduate of the well-known women's college Wellesley, on her ineluctable professional path to sports journalism.[3]

But women had barely pierced the field of journalism, much less the specialized domain of sports journalism at the time, making Ludtke's career choice a peculiar one. At *Newsweek*, the *New York Times*, and other industry leaders, women who aspired to journalistic work heard the refrain telling them, "Women don't write here." As recently as 1970, women had had to file a sex discrimination complaint against *Newsweek* to break away from the usual roles to which print media companies assigned them: secretary, researcher, fact-checker, "mail girl," and other ancillary roles. The women who sued *Newsweek* prevailed in a settlement that forced the magazine to accelerate the hiring and promotion of women. Similar suits against the *New York Times* and other publications followed, prying open the doors of opportunity, if ever so slightly.[4]

It was in the face of this daunting professional reality that Ludtke set her sights on a career in sports journalism. In the fall of 1974, she got her break when Time Inc. hired her as a "researcher reporter," which was another way to say that she was to be a fact-checker, the lowest position on the editorial hierarchy. The job required seventeen- or eighteen-hour days—in the office during the day and at sporting events in the evening—but offered interesting assignments. Before long, Ludtke earned a promotion, and she began to learn the arts of interviewing and reporting. Soon she began writing columns about baseball, the sport she had the most "affinity for," and over time she rose to the rank of junior baseball reporter. The job required her to "basically liv[e] in baseball parks"; she spent long hours in Shea and Yankee stadiums. When Time Inc. asked her to cover the 1977 World Series for one of its flagship publications, *Sports Illustrated*, Ludtke knew she had landed a tremendous opportunity: on the biggest stage in Major League Baseball, she was poised to make her mark.[5]

Yet Ludtke faced a big disadvantage—a problem that hindered her from the start of her career on the baseball beat. She could only have access to players on the field during batting practice or in the dugouts—never in the clubhouse locker rooms. Players found batting practice an inconvenient time to talk, so her contact with them on the field was not always useful to her stories. In the intimate setting provided by the locker room, reporters had the latitude to ask players questions that shed light on game-day analyses and allowed them to witness the athletes' personalities off the field. The clubhouse locker room was for courting good publicity, and that was where Major League Baseball urged players to make themselves available.[6]

But while MLB permitted male reporters to enter the clubhouses to seek out interviews, women were barred by order of Commissioner Bowie Kuhn. In 1975, the commissioners of the National Basketball Association and the National Hockey League opened their clubhouses to women reporters, but Kuhn refused. In a letter to the managers of all MLB teams, the commissioner demanded a "unified stand." Kuhn—a bespectacled lawyer widely viewed as a "pompous" "stuffed shirt," as one obituary described him—considered the clubhouse a "private domain" in which women did not belong. Not unlike segregationists who espoused a doctrine of "separate but equal" to justify racial segregation, Kuhn limited female reporters to "interview facilities adjacent to the teams' dressing quarters."[7]

*

The first game of the 1977 World Series was held at Yankee Stadium on October 11, in front of a live crowd of more than fifty-six thousand excited fans and with sixty million more people watching at home. The highly anticipated match took place on a cool fall day in a recently renovated Yankee Stadium. The $100 million makeover had turned the old, architecturally distinctive Bronx arena—fondly known as the "House That [Babe] Ruth Built"—into a plush modern structure that contained a computerized 565-square-foot scoreboard, enormous luxury boxes, corridors studded with photos of Yankee greats, and an upgraded clubhouse where the athletes enjoyed a spacious players' lounge that had Yankee-blue carpets, recessed lighting, saunas, and lockers painted in red, white, and blue.

At a match this highly anticipated, Ludtke decided to make a stand. She made plans to interview the players after the first game, not in the corridors to which she was usually relegated but in their new, deluxe clubhouse.[8] In the past, Ludtke had "never forced the issue of her admittance to locker rooms," but the World Series beat demanded that she eliminate any disadvantage. She considered it "essential" that she have the chance to work "in the same manner as other writers." Otherwise, a frustrating and awkward scenario, one she had experienced all too often as a sportswriter, would repeat itself: denied access, she would be forced to plead with athletes to talk to her. Sometimes she would have to go home empty-handed, without completing an interview if the players chose to ignore her. At other times she would enlist one of the male reporters to ask a few of the athletes to come out of the locker room and talk to her. There were times when she would wait outside in the corridor for hours and no one would show.[9]

With such a consequential assignment at hand, Ludtke was not about to let herself be sidelined again. Before the game started, she approached the Dodgers' manager, Tommy Lasorda, and asked for permission to interview the team in the locker room. Her request ended up going to the players themselves, and, bucking the commissioner, the majority voted to let her into their sanctuary. Ludtke already had limited access to the Yankees' clubhouse thanks to a preexisting relationship she had built with Billy Martin. Having worked out "solutions" with both teams, Ludtke felt confident she would be able to cover the series up close.[10]

But on the evening of the first game, after the actress Pearl Bailey sang her way through the national anthem and the twelve innings of the game culminated in a 4–3 victory for the Yankees, Ludtke's workaround was foiled. The commissioner learned about her request and intervened. During the fifth inning of the first game, a lieutenant of Kuhn's found Ludtke in the press box. "I was told that the commissioner had overruled the Dodgers and nullified whatever their vote had been, and that I was not to enter either locker room that night or any other night," Ludtke recounted later. Upset and angry, she inquired why the commissioner had nixed the players' decision. Kuhn offered two extraordinary rationales: first, he said, "the players' wives had not been brought into the decision-making"; and second, the commissioner "thought that the children of the ballplayers would be ridiculed in their classrooms" if Ludtke spent time with them in their locker room. In other words, potential harm to women and children, an age-old justification for discrimination, was put forward to explain Ludtke's plight.[11]

After game six of the series, it was apparent how much she lost by being deprived of access to the players on one of Major League Baseball's most magical nights. The game ended with a stupendous win for the Yankees. In a historic highlight, Reggie Jackson hit three home runs—becoming only the second player to do so in one game of the series since Babe Ruth, the Yankees' most legendary player, pulled it off in the 1930s. Jackson won the title "Mr. October" that night. Ecstatic fans chanted his name over and over—"Reg-gie," "Reg-gie," "Reg-gie." After the Yankees won 8–3, reporters swarmed the field for reactions from Jackson and others to their come-from-behind victory. Once he made it through the crowds, off the field, and into the clubhouse, Jackson was still surrounded on all sides; print and television reporters and their cameras followed him into the locker room. Unable to enter, Ludtke stood in the crowded hallway, where people pushed and yelled and celebrated. Illustrating the absurdity of the situation, Ludtke could in fact glimpse the pandemonium inside the locker room, in the same way that television viewers at home could: "I could watch on a monitor what was happening in there, but I was forbidden from being in there," she recounted.[12]

Ludtke waited and wended her way to the back door until a staff member came out and informed her that she "was not allowed in," and then closed the door in her face. More time passed in the loud and crowded hallway; Ludtke managed to talk briefly to two players, even as people continued to mill about, calling for Jackson and other team members. Midnight came and went. At 12:10 a.m., Ludtke was "still waiting outside the Yankee clubhouse door for Reggie Jackson, watching as men [some without press credentials] passed freely in and out." Sal, a guard, patrolled the clubhouse, ensuring she did not enter. Over an hour and a half after her male escort had requested that Jackson speak with her, the star appeared. He was too tired for an interview. Humiliated as well as disappointed, Ludtke left the stadium; she didn't have the information she needed to fully and accurately report the story at the caliber that *Sports Illustrated* required.[13]

In December of that year, Melissa Ludtke, with Time Inc.'s backing, sued Bowie Kuhn, the New York Yankees, and the mayor of New York City over her experience during the series, calling it unjust and alleging that it violated the U.S. Constitution. Ludtke, an accredited reporter, had been barred from the locker room solely because of her sex, a bald-faced contravention of the nondiscrimination mandate of the Equal Protection Clause. As a limitation on the freedom of the press, they argued that the policy also violated the First Amendment. Frederick A. O. Schwarz Jr., a great-grandson of the founder of the famous toy store, a lawyer in private practice with Cravath, Swaine & Moore, and a friend of the civil rights movement, represented these claims on behalf of his client. The Yankees were his "passion"; but Schwarz represented Ludtke at the behest of an important corporate client—and because he believed in "fairness and equality." He also liked Ludtke "a hell of a lot"—she was, he said, a "spunky woman."

The suit created a stir. National news networks and papers covered the case and revealed a deeply divided public view of the issue. Many people did not think the case presented a "serious" instance of sex discrimination; instead they felt Ludtke exhibited a shameful desire to break social norms. "We think her suit idiotic," declared one editorial. "[T]his sex discrimination business has gone too far." The "simple fact is that some people, male and female, prefer not to expose themselves in mixed company," wrote a columnist. Several commentators accused Ludtke of simply wanting to see nude players, whether it was "Reggie in the buff" or "Thurman Munson in the shower."[14]

Even Jane Pauley, the trailblazing television host only two years older than Ludtke, reacted frostily, and lent credence to the objections made in the name of male "modesty." During an interview with a visibly anxious Ludtke on NBC's *Today Show* in January 1978, Pauley surprised her by bringing up the journalist's offhand comment about a photo of a shirtless Reggie Jackson hanging (oddly) in the studio's hallway. Ludtke had referred to Jackson's "chest" and, Pauley insisted, had been interested in "leering at athletic bodies." Flustered, Ludtke tried to explain that her remark was a feeble attempt to "get loose" from the pressure of the situation. She "wanted to do [her] job," she said—not unlike the barrier-breaking Pauley herself. The interview, watched by millions, underscored how well the privacy argument played with many Americans, including women. In the coming federal court proceedings, the debate centered around whether it was male privacy or women's equality that properly framed the dispute over Ludtke's demand for access.[15]

*

If knowledge about sports had been a factor in assigning the case, Judge Motley would have been the last judge let near it. She was not the least bit interested in baseball. But a spin of the assignment drum in the U.S. District Court handed the case to Motley.

Many observers believed that Schwarz, Ludtke's lawyer, "had it in the bag," given the judge's background and her landmark ruling for Diane Blank. As a woman whose "life had been in civil rights," they told Schwarz, "all her instincts will be clearly on your side." Confident in the strength of the case on its own merits, Schwarz counted Motley's expertise in civil rights law an advantage, but he did not assume she would see the case through Ludtke's eyes. Instead, after familiarizing himself with the judge's background, Schwarz concluded that in fact she might be especially ill-suited to the case in one critical respect: "she knew very little about sports."[16]

Because sports were considered a mere pastime rather than big business, Schwarz worried that the judge might, like other observers, underestimate the significance of Ludtke's complaint. The lawyer set out to blunt this assumption. In addition to marshaling legal precedents, he introduced evidence adducing the connection between change in society and in sports—baseball especially. He submitted two affidavits meant to "demonstrate that baseball . . . had been a vital part of American history," particularly for labor and civil rights. The affidavits called out how significant Jackie Robinson's integration of baseball in 1947 had been, noting that this occurred even before the desegregation of the U.S. Army via executive order in 1948, and well before the desegregation of schools by the U.S. Supreme Court in 1954. He thought this evidence might "convince Judge Motley that she should care about these questions, not just abstractly"; the evidence about the importance of baseball, he hoped, would help her understand that the case mattered for social change, much as cases involving schools or public accommodations did. Schwarz also introduced evidence to try to disabuse Motley of the idea, implicit in much negative commentary about the case, that locker rooms and nudity had to go hand in hand. He brought diagrams of the Yankees' clubhouse to show that it was not a "grimy place," that showers were removed and hidden from view, and that curtains were available to any players who should want them for privacy in the cavernous professional space.[17]

But for Motley, the law surpassed all. The suit required her to consider two major issues in constitutional law. She had to determine whether New York City's involvement with Yankee Stadium constituted state action within the meaning of the Fourteenth Amendment. If so, she had to confront an underlying issue: whether the blanket exclusion of female sportswriters violated the Fourteenth Amendment's guarantees of equal protection and due process of law.[18]

First, Motley determined that MLB did qualify as a state actor. A precedent had been set in a case that she and her own LDF colleagues had won. *Burton v. Wilmington Parking Authority* (1961) established that state action could be premised on the "entwining" of activity by a private party and a state agency. MLB was a state actor, she concluded, because of the organization's financial relationship with the city. However, the city had not endorsed the Yankees' exclusionary policy, so Schwarz needed to establish that the policy violated the law.[19]

New York City had acquired the site on which Yankee Stadium was built through eminent domain (the government's right to take private property and convert it into public use) and by claiming the property would be used to advance the city's cultural, recreational, and economic vitality. Then, nearly bankrupt, the city had leased the stadium to the Yankees under contractual terms that made it the team's financial partner. As a business partner and a municipal authority, the city was involved in the team's practices and regulated numerous aspects. Most important, it had known of the Yankees' blanket ban on women reporters in the locker room, but failed to either question or end the policy. These facts made the MLB a "state actor" within the meaning of the Constitution, Motley held, and subject to suit for violating Ludtke's constitutional rights. Motley's analysis hewed closely to the law, but nevertheless revealed judicial innovation.[20]

Motley's ruling on the merits of Ludtke's case was likewise innovative. Following a two-hour hearing, she found that the Yankees' treatment of women journalists was a violation of Ludtke's constitutional rights, and that the privacy justifications for the discriminatory policy were inadequate. Relying on the landmark abortion-rights case *Roe v. Wade* (1973), Motley conceded that privacy could be a constitutionally legitimate objective. But citing another landmark case, *Califano v. Goldfarb* (1977), a sex discrimination suit that had been won by Ruth Bader Ginsburg, Motley interrogated and rejected the argument applied in this case. *Califano* required courts to determine the *actual* purpose of a policy at the time it was created, instead of accepting a purpose applied to defend the policy against a lawsuit after the fact. Motley accepted that players were entitled to privacy, but rejected it as a legitimate reason for banning female journalists from the locker room entirely. The organization could easily protect its ballplayers' privacy without "maintaining the locker room as an all-male preserve," the judge concluded. The Yankees had struck out.[21]

The lawyers for the defense had not helped the team's case: counsel had conceded during one hearing that the team could use less restrictive means to protect the players' privacy while "enabling female sportswriters to enjoy precisely the same conditions of employment as their male colleagues." The lawyer had made the concession under insistent questioning by Motley. "[I]sn't it possible for [the players] to use curtains in front of this cubicle . . . to undress and hide [themselves] from these women," she had inquired. "Or put [up] swinging doors" or "curtains" for a player to hide behind if a woman came in? "It's possible, your Honor," the lawyer had answered, but requiring the men to conceal themselves in this way would disrupt their usual manner of interacting after a game, he went on. They had grown accustomed to walking around the locker room naked. In her decision, Judge Motley held that the players' "custom" "surely could not stand against constitutional attack." Again citing a case that Ginsburg had won—this time *Reed v. Reed* (1971)—Motley reasoned that "mere administrative convenience" could not justify discrimination on account of sex.[22]

Finally, Motley held that the sex-based exclusion unjustifiably violated Ludtke's substantive due process rights. It inhibited her right to pursue her profession, a bedrock principle of individual liberty protected by precedents extending back to the nineteenth century.[23]

*

The *Ludtke* decision inspired ferocious pushback, perhaps the most of any case in Motley's career. Bags of hate mail attacking the result arrived at her chambers. Editorial writers responded harshly. One began his attack on Motley's decision with a candid confession of bias: "Call me a male chauvinist pig. Have a bra burning on the front lawn of my house. Shred my wife's copy of *Ms.* magazine," he raged. "Women do not belong in the Yankee clubhouse! No. No. No. A thousand times no." As for Judge Motley herself, he spewed, "How ironic that SHE would rule." Her opinion was a "joke" on baseball—and an unfunny one at that. Another writer, in an article entitled "Men Have a Right to Keep Fig Leaf," argued that disrobed ballplayers had a right to privacy from prying female eyes. He called the fig leaf an "inalienable right," and cited an "embarrassing episode" in which the eyes of a female reporter, a "Yalie" no less, had wandered toward the crotch of a bare-bottomed Yankee during an interview. There is, he argued, a "difference between men and women that cannot be legislated out of existence." He continued, "I'd like to see Judge Motley's reaction if I wanted a few brilliant quotes while she was changing robes in her chambers."[24]

Sympathetic to the players and their custom of walking naked around the clubhouse unobserved by women, Motley came up with a cheeky yet practical remedy in her exchanges with Schwarz. "Let them wear towels," she decreed. She had toppled another bastion of male dominance and exclusion.[25]

From the outset of the case, the defendants bet that if Motley ruled against the Yankees, she would easily be reversed by the appeals court. According to Schwarz, "being a woman and an African American judge, they thought her decision would maybe be taken more lightly by the Court of Appeals." That assumption proved wrong. At a hearing before an all-male panel of the U.S. Court of Appeals, one of the judges quipped back at Kuhn's remark that Ludtke did not belong in the locker room because "baseball is a family game": "The last I heard, the family includes women as well as men." The commissioner and his lawyers dropped the appeal. The "strategy"—to bet against Judge Motley—had failed.[26]

The decisions that Motley made in a handful of cases, before and after *Ludtke v. Kuhn*, cemented her reputation as a friend of civil rights on the bench. In *Monell v. Department of Social Services* (1972), she created a framework for female employees of New York City agencies to challenge unpaid pregnancy leave. Motley decided in favor of a woman in a 1990 sexual harassment case against New York Telephone Company, the facts of which made for good newspaper copy. The plaintiff, a Frances Danna, alleged that a hostile work environment and certain egregious acts proved her case: photographs depicting anal and oral sex were posted in the workplace, and colleagues called Danna "an ungrateful cunt."

Together, these high-profile decisions confirmed that Constance Baker Motley's selection for the bench had been good for people of color, and good for women—just as activist lawyers Pauli Murray, Dorothy Kenyon, and Bella Abzug had hoped, and as Senator James Eastland and so many other powerful men had feared. But judgments based on these high-profile cases did not tell the whole story about Motley and her judicial record on civil rights.[27]

24

No "Protecting Angel": Blacks, Latinos, and Ordinary People in Judge Motley's Courtroom

In addresses to the NAACP, the Urban League, and women's groups, President Jimmy Carter boasted that he had appointed more Black and female judges than all previous presidents combined. "No President has done as much for Black people," he and his representatives claimed. Many of the Carter appointees, like Johnson appointees Constance Baker Motley and Thurgood Marshall, hailed from public interest practice or other "nontraditional" backgrounds. These appointments reinforced to a public unaccustomed to outsiders in the power structure an association between judges' identities and the realization of Black and female interests through the courts.[1]

Constance Baker Motley preceded Carter's wave of appointments and, as the first Black woman appointed to the federal bench, was something of a test case. Allies who fought on behalf of people of color and the working class sought validation, fairness, and justice in her court. "Women and Negroes everywhere" had taken "a significant step" forward through her appointment, Bella Abzug had written her when she was nominated. In Motley, bystanders thought, the movements for racial and social justice now had a mouthpiece; oppressed people would gain a voice, and their causes would receive a fair hearing with her on the bench. With her there, they believed they were more likely to prevail.[2]

But in the rush to celebrate the new complexion of the judiciary, few questioned whether the hoped-for association between a judge's personal identity and judicial outcomes would always pan out in practice. A handful of commentators cautioned that the appointment

to the bench of the civil rights movement's most talented lawyers—
including Marshall, Motley, and Robert Carter—might have the perverse effect of undermining the movement, but little heed was paid
to them. They had argued that, deprived of its best and most experienced lawyers, the legal struggle for equality might be less successful.
Nor did many recall the warnings of Ralph Bunche, the pioneering
Black political scientist and Nobel Peace Prize–winning diplomat,
who, during the Great Depression, amid debates about the best path
toward equality for African Americans, cautioned against overreli-
ance on the courts. The law did not hover like a "protecting angel,"
Bunche wrote. It invariably reflected the dominant order, he insisted,
and judges' sympathy for minority interests could never be assumed.[3]

Reality bore out the warning about overconfidence in the courts
and oversimplification of the judicial role. Outcomes in Motley's
courtroom belied the cartoonish assumption that identity determines
how judges decide cases. That supposition rests on the wrongheaded
idea that judges are perfectly free to impose their personal preferences. In fact, judges—trial court judges especially—are constrained
by prior decisions and by professional norms. This was as true for
Motley as it was for others.

More than any other factor, Motley's best understanding of the
law guided her decision making. Of course, her values and experiences influenced how she saw and interpreted facts and the law, just
as they do for all judges. And because of her commitment to equal
justice, she was always open to the claims made by people of color
and working-class people—the "little guys"—in her court. Moreover,
the "enormity of the responsibility" she bore as the first Black woman
federal judge "was always on her mind" and "weighed on her"; and
as she understood it, that responsibility required her to perform her
job skillfully and with impartiality.[4]

But her understanding of racial discrimination, formed in the
crucible of the fight against Jim Crow in the South, did not inexorably
lead her to an expansive conception of the Civil Rights Act in many
race-related employment discrimination cases. De jure segregation
framed her response to many contemporary claims of discrimination, as illustrated by her remark "My God, people . . . don't know
what *real* discrimination is." Motley never denied the persistence of

racism, but she had little patience for those who did not concede how far the country had come since the days of Jim Crow. She considered the changes that had occurred in race relations since *Brown* and the enactment of the Civil Rights Act, a "revolution in society" that had made African Americans "the newest in-group," following successive waves of immigrants. "The fact is that racism, despite all the doomsayers, has diminished," she wrote in 1998. "With the elimination of official segregation and some private discrimination," she insisted, "there is no longer a single common impediment to blacks emerging in this society." She conceded that some Blacks "did not rise into the middle class, as most African Americans have." But she had a ready explanation for that outcome: "The African Americans who have succeeded," she observed, "were prepared to do so."

Plaintiffs in her courtroom who alleged discrimination faced a sympathetic but also critically engaged listener. With her presiding, the more that instances of alleged discrimination looked like segregation-era practices—clearly arbitrary decisions based on unfounded racial stereotypes or racist attitudes revealed through epithets and a paper trail—the better for a worker suing under the new civil rights law.[5]

But many allegations of workplace discrimination turned on evidence that was thin when compared to the common forms of racial exclusion under segregation; the bits of evidence that plaintiffs brought to court rarely incontrovertibly showed overt, or "real," racism. In the process of deciding cases, Judge Motley, like any other trial court judge, had to draw inferences about the available material, weigh both sides of a controversy, and interpret the law. And the governing law increasingly cut against plaintiffs.

Moreover, because of her identity, Motley faced continuing scrutiny and criticism. With so many eyes upon her, she took special care to demonstrate evenhandedness. She always cited ample evidence to support an outcome, particularly one that might favor an alleged victim of racism. In the Sullivan & Cromwell case, she had defended her impartiality by pointing to decisions in which she "ruled against civil rights plaintiffs." In truth, the assumption that a civil rights claimant would "automatically win" in her courtroom irritated her.

As a Black woman judge, Motley labored under the pressure to

show that her judgments did not come from a perspective sympathetic to victims of discrimination; in reality, her standpoint was
based in professional expertise, but critics dismissed it as "bias." She
"listened to the evidence" and decided cases as she saw them, without
fear or favoritism, recalled a colleague. She had "all her experience,
her knowledge, her strong beliefs, but she approache[d] everything
with receptivity," a clerk said. And yet the outcomes in many of the
race discrimination cases—the suits that brought Motley's civil rights
background into special focus—disproved her so-called bias.[6]

The plaintiffs who prevailed in these cases were themselves
special: they tended to be virtuous folks who had suffered obvious
wrongs. The winners were people like Harold F. Evans Jr.

*

A thirty-eight-year-old Black man, Evans filed a suit against the Connecticut State Police in 1990. The facts he alleged evoked the long,
fraught history of strained police-community relations in American
cities. Evans came of age at a time when civil rights activists stepped
up efforts to root out what the Guardians, a Black police organization founded to promote fairness in the criminal legal system, called
a culture of discrimination within the Hartford Police Department.
Eight out of every ten police officers charged with keeping law and
order in Hartford were white—and this at a time when African Americans and Latinos comprised fully half of the city's residents.[7]

Allegations of racial bias plagued the system. In 1979, the Hartford
Human Relations Commission determined that discrimination may
have contributed to the police force's racial composition. The commission urged the city to correct the mismatch between Hartford's
diverse inhabitants and its overwhelmingly white police force. The
hiring of a more racially representative police force was "crucial" to
the "effectiveness" of law enforcement, it said. Its reasoning followed
the logic of a 1967 federal advisory commission report on civil disorders, written in the wake of riots in Watts, Harlem, Newark, and
Detroit. The report explained that "to many Negroes police have come
to symbolize white power, white racism, and white repression." Following a lawsuit, the Connecticut State Police "conceded" in 1982 that
its hiring policies had an "adverse impact on minorities," reported

the *Hartford Courant*. To remedy the situation, the state police agreed to federal oversight and promised to increase the number of Black and Latino troopers to constitute 10 percent of the force, commensurate with the percentage of Black and Latino residents in the state. The changes should have created opportunity for Evans.[8]

He developed a deep interest in a law enforcement career amid the national conversation about equity in policing. After he earned a bachelor of science degree in administration of justice from American University, he returned to his home state to look for work in law enforcement. His bachelor's degree not only prepared him for a career in law enforcement, it overqualified him; at the time, few officers had earned college degrees.[9] In 1985, the Connecticut State Police Academy accepted Evans for state trooper training. Some months later, he graduated from the training academy, seventeenth in his class, with an 89.5 average. He then entered a six-month stint as a trainee trooper, and received generally strong reviews for his work. Nonetheless, before his probationary period even ended the state police discharged him and detailed a laundry list of grounds for his firing. Evans filed suit, alleging discrimination.[10]

The issue before Motley, as the judge overseeing the case, was whether the state had terminated Evans for a legitimate reason. Many signs pointed to race as a factor. A court-appointed expert witness—law professor Burke Marshall, whom Motley knew from his days as assistant attorney general for civil rights during the Kennedy administration—sought evidence about Evans's trainee class.[11] Marshall found damaging facts. He wrote a report that detailed a high attrition rate among racial minorities in Evans's trooper trainee class. Five out of nine Black trooper candidates and two of seven Latinos did not make it through the probationary period. By contrast, only one white candidate had failed. These statistics suggested a pattern consistent with decades-long complaints about police hiring practices: African Americans and Latinos could scarcely make their way onto police forces in the first place, much less win promotions to positions of authority. While Marshall's findings did not alone prove that racial discrimination caused high Black attrition rates, other evidence made it difficult for Motley to discount race as a contributing factor.[12]

The state's own witnesses harmed its case. They couldn't keep their stories straight. Across their testimony, the witnesses offered inconsistent rationales for Evans's dismissal. His commanding officer contradicted the state's claim that it had fired him for "poor performance and productivity."[13] There were only two remaining justifications: his "purportedly deficient report writing skills" and his "bad attitude." Motley called the rationales "disingenuous" and a mere pretext for discrimination; not one shred of evidence supported either claim, she found.[14] She offered a scathing response to one justification, which she had heard many times before. The "bad attitude" rationale was nothing more than a "stereotype" and a "euphemism," she wrote, for the "plaintiff was Black."[15]

It was little surprise that Judge Motley ruled in Evans's favor. The state's reasons for terminating him "were hardly free from discriminatory animus," she concluded. The judge awarded Evans significant monetary relief for the discriminatory discharge, nearly $900,000 in back pay and attorneys' fees. The court of appeals affirmed Motley's decision.[16]

Harold Evans and his lawsuit had presented a rarity: a straightforward case. Judge Motley applied settled law in favor of an overqualified and model plaintiff who had squared off against a recalcitrant defendant. Other cases involved more complex legal controversies and imperfect litigants—Blacks and Latinos, women, and workaday people trying to eke out an existence in New York.[17]

*

The fate of African American communities had often risen or fallen in tandem with the fortunes of African American teachers, especially women. Making up a large and influential segment of the Black middle class, these teachers, underpaid and underappreciated by whites, played a vital role in Black communities during segregation. They imparted knowledge and cultivated in their charges a sense of belonging. They served as role models and "ambassadors of racial uplift" for their students. W. E. B. Du Bois, the renowned sociologist, praised the manifold contributions of Black teachers under profoundly challenging circumstances and demanded "decent wages, decent schoolhouses and equipment, and reasonable chances for advancement" on their behalf. The LDF and its lawyers, well aware of the vital role teachers played, devoted significant time and resources to salary equalization cases in schools.[18]

Motley had begun her career as a civil rights lawyer in 1949 with a groundbreaking case she brought on behalf of Gladys Noel Bates, a teacher in Jackson, Mississippi, in the heart of the Deep South. While Motley and her colleagues did not prevail in the case, the threat of litigation prompted the state to raise Black teachers' salaries. But the problem of their unequal treatment did not cease. As Motley explained in a reflection made years later in 1974, many white people "viewed Black teachers as inferior" regardless of their credentials.[19]

Faced with civil rights lawsuits, school districts in Mississippi and other southern states started using less obviously discriminatory criteria: professional licensing requirements and exams. These requirements heightened the pay disparity between Black and white teachers in the wake of *Brown v. Board of Education*, when Black institutions closed and qualified African Americans lost their jobs in droves as districts transitioned Black students and staff, selectively, to formerly all-white schools. By 1965 districts had dismissed or demoted thousands of Black teachers, using restructuring for "desegregation" as a pretext.

Desegregation had resulted, the *Chicago Daily Defender* wrote, in a "veritable reign of terror" against Black educators. The pattern continued into the late twentieth century: between 1980 and 2003, the proportion of public school teachers across the country who were Black fell from 12 percent to 6 percent. In 1996, the controversy over who could and should teach in public schools surfaced in the New York City courtroom of Judge Motley. Now a septuagenarian, Motley no longer had anything to lose or anything to prove.[20]

On behalf of African American and Latino educators, mostly women, Elsa Gulino attacked the fairness of the state and city's mandate that teachers pass exams before receiving their licenses. Overall, Blacks and Latinos passed the exam at a lower rate than whites. The teachers argued that this racial disparity, perpetuated by reliance on an exam that had not been shown to measure preparedness to teach, constituted unlawful discrimination under Title VII of the

Civil Rights Act. Lawyers from the Center for Constitutional Rights—a premier public interest law firm founded by civil liberties attorneys William Kunstler and Arthur Kinoy—took up the teachers' case.[21]

Gulino, a Latina who had earned a bachelor's and a master's degree in education, landed a position in the New York City public school system, where she began her career as a substitute teacher in 1983. Gulino was determined to improve her status in the profession and wanted to work as a bilingual education teacher. She pursued advancement through coursework, field work, and more. Having completed this curriculum, she received a promotion to the position of bilingual special education teacher at Public School 159 in the Bronx. There, she earned the highest performance ratings possible, and was widely considered an effective and dedicated teacher. She received tenure in 1991.[22]

But before she had a chance to get accustomed to her new responsibilities in a tenured role, Gulino ran into a problem. In order to retain her license and position, district officials informed her that she had to take and pass a new national teachers' exam. Eager to remain in her position, Gulino sat for the exam. She took it three times and failed it three times. Notwithstanding her excellent reputation, the district revoked Gulino's license to teach in the New York City schools, drastically cut her salary, demoted her back to substitute teacher, and revoked her pension. Other teachers who joined her lawsuit told similar stories. Well-educated, dedicated, and obviously good teachers, they thrived professionally by all but one measure: satisfactory test scores on the newly imposed national teachers' exam.[23]

The State and the City of New York told a different story. Officials argued that the facts of the case exemplified the "savage inequalities" that plagued urban American schools: low test scores, high dropout rates, low graduation rates, and subpar teaching were rife in schools that served African American and Latino children. These schools, where the teachers who brought suit largely taught, were little more than factories for failure and cried out for intervention. The newly required exam that the teachers had failed, the officials claimed, constituted a praiseworthy attempt to reform a broken system.[24]

New York wanted to improve the quality of teaching in the city's schools and thereby better the performance of students who were primarily from low-income and disadvantaged backgrounds, of African American and Latino descent, and often recent immigrants and English-language learners. The policy of awarding licenses only if educators passed national exams in communication and their teaching subject sought to ensure uniform minimum teacher qualifications and, by extension, teacher quality. These underlying realities were a dreadful, nationwide phenomenon. Failing school systems, segregated by race and class and defined by inequalities, persisted despite the gains won in *Brown v. Board of Education*.[25]

Judge Motley initially decided for the plaintiffs: she permitted the Black and Latino educators to file their case as a class action, a step that made it easier for the plaintiffs to discover and amass evidence of discrimination. The teachers' lawyers would be able to show how the testing requirement harmed Elsa Gulino and the other plaintiffs. The judge also concluded that the plaintiffs had marshaled enough evidence to establish a preliminary ("prima facie") case. Data adduced by statisticians showed that only 45 percent of the certified class members passed the relevant tests, compared to 85 percent of whites.[26]

The numbers required interpretation, and the two sides competed to imbue the statistics with different meanings. The plaintiffs' attorneys focused on the "staggering effect" of the tests on the employment prospects of teachers of color; the results "screen[ed] out" hundreds of otherwise-qualified candidates. Meanwhile, New York officials argued that reasonable people could in fact read the exam questions and would readily appreciate that the test measured the academic skills necessary for teacher competency.[27]

The state's officials ultimately convinced Motley that a legitimate rationale justified use of the test. A specific component of the exam, an essay portion said to measure a teacher's communication skills, persuaded her of the test's legitimacy and won the case for New York City.[28] As she put it:

> Teachers who are unable to write a coherent essay without a host of spelling and grammar errors may pass on that deficiency to their students, both in commenting upon and grading the work they turn in.[29]

Motley's own background likely inclined her to a deep skepticism of a teacher or would-be teacher who lacked what she considered proper communication skills. She was an accomplished daughter of a West Indian family that prized British culture—including mastery of the "King's English"—and regarded itself as superior stock. The judge set high standards for herself and for others. Education had been her path out of the working class, and her linguistic prowess had been key to her ascent. As a student, Motley had written a poem that her English teacher found worthy of publication in a textbook, and she had once won a prize for an essay on tuberculosis. And she told and retold the dramatic story of her journey to college, a route out of poverty that revolved around her powers of persuasion.[30] "My big break came" when Clarence Blakeslee, a wealthy New Haven contractor and member of the Yale Corporation, "heard me speak at a meeting at the Dixwell Community House." On the basis of a single speech—and her academic record—the generous donor had offered to finance her way through college and law school. Motley's oratorical brilliance had significantly altered the course of her life.[31]

The judge took great pride in having excelled academically in "overwhelmingly white" schools in New Haven. She took "all of the courses for college-bound students as well as three years of Latin and two years of French," and graduated with "senior-year honors."[32] One white teacher in particular had mentored Motley, and nurtured her academic development and her interest in civil rights activism. The only Black woman she encountered in school had worked as a "teacher's assistant," not unlike some of the demoted plaintiffs in the Gulino case.[33]

Motley had represented many meritorious Black teachers and fought for deserving Black students during her more than twenty years as a civil rights lawyer. Gladys Bates, the Black educator from Jackson, Mississippi, personified excellence. She merited higher pay, but was denied by racist white officials. The pay differential was transparently based "solely on skin color." Undoubtedly, Bates deserved her position, as did others whom Motley had represented in Jackson. But these clients, sometimes overqualified, had little in common with the teachers whose suit against education reformers in New York City Motley presided over decades later.[34]

Motley's sympathies in the Gulino case—framed by the defendants as a battle pitting the interests of educators against those of students—lay with the pupils. All her life, Motley had championed young people from disadvantaged backgrounds who might possess the talent and resolve to rise above them—students who reminded her of her younger self. Until the end of her days, she fondly recalled the "Black school children and their parents" who served as her plaintiffs. She was their champion. As a legislator she had introduced bills to ban de facto school segregation. And decades before the current movement, she advocated free college tuition and supported scholarship programs for poor students.[35] She demonstrated an ongoing commitment to the needs of disadvantaged students through the care she took, despite her busy legislative and judicial schedules, to respond to the numerous letters she received from students. She also peppered her public addresses with words endorsing educational equity. In a talk she gave in 1979 at a judicial luncheon, she lamented the plight of "children struggling against the ravishes of poverty in America." But in the Gulino case, Motley's sympathies betrayed her.[36]

In 2006, the Court of Appeals for the Second Circuit reversed the most important element of Motley's decision. The judge had erred, the appeals court held, in her conclusions about the legitimacy of the teachers' exams. Motley had found the essay portion of the exams valid despite the state's failure to conduct a study to formally validate its effectiveness. Her approach had "lowered the bar for defendants." Motley's position that employers did not need to conduct validation studies was wrong, and the court of appeals panel unanimously reversed her verdict on that point.[37]

Many commentators were taken aback by Motley's ruling in the Gulino case given her career as a noted civil rights lawyer. Members of the civil rights bar expressed disappointment that Motley—who had once represented Black teachers in antidiscrimination suits—sided with the defendants in this important case. That her longtime employer, the NAACP's Inc. Fund, had litigated the landmark cases establishing a "disparate impact" theory of employment discrimination worsened the disappointment. Unlike the disparate *treatment* theory of discrimination—which required plaintiffs to prove an employer's intent—plaintiffs could prove disparate *impact* discrimination through evidence showing that, regardless of intent, African Americans or Latinos fared significantly worse than whites in hiring or promotion.[38]

Motley's decision in Elsa Gulino's case may have disappointed some onlookers, but it vividly confirmed that she would not give plaintiffs alleging discrimination preferential treatment. Once, in response to a defense lawyer who questioned whether a former civil rights lawyer could be fair in discrimination cases, Motley pointed to her record. Her performance on the bench vindicated her, she said: numerous adverse decisions demonstrated that, like other judges, she frequently ruled against plaintiffs. Her decision against the Black and Latino schoolteachers thoroughly proved her point.[39]

*

Many other cases also demolished the myth that people of color found an uncritically receptive arbiter of the law in Judge Motley. Lawsuits brought by Black and Latina workers who earned a living through "pink-collar" jobs—positions "caring, cashiering, catering, cleaning, clerical," or other support positions stereotyped as "women's work"—stand out.

In New York, women in these jobs toiled in the office towers housing the investment banks, law firms, businesses, and other corporate giants that powered the city and the nation's economy. Given the high cost of living in New York City, many had to spend hours and hours every week just trying to make it in to work, commuting from afar on whatever forms of transit available. The women reported to supervisors who were overwhelmingly male and usually white. And they performed repetitive "drudge" work for long hours. Stuck in what scholars called a "pink-collar ghetto," many filed lawsuits about the additional troubles they met on the job: sexual harassment, poor working conditions, low pay, and a lack of opportunity for promotion.[40]

These women, everyday people in comparison to Diane Blank and Melissa Ludtke, seldom prevailed in Motley's courtroom. Fior D'Aliza Minetos's suit against Hunter College of the City University of New York (CUNY) illustrated the difficulties such women encountered, and still do, in workplace discrimination suits, even when open-minded judges like Motley preside.

Minetos, a Dominican American, worked for ten years as an office assistant in the music department at Hunter College. In 1995, she sued several professors and the college, alleging employment discrimination in violation of Title VII. Minetos was represented by Ralph B. Pinskey, an experienced employment lawyer who had, up until this point, never tried a case in New York, and Barbara A. Rosenberg, a newly minted member of the New York bar. The office of the attorney general of New York defended Hunter College, an institution known for its egalitarian history and mission.[41]

Minetos alleged that she had suffered mistreatment on multiple fronts, making her experience illustrative of intersectional discrimination, or marginalization that is not confined to a single form of oppression—say, sexism. She claimed that she had been subjected to discrimination because she was Hispanic, Dominican, spoke with an accent, and was older than forty. Women of color have often talked about experiencing discrimination along multiple axes—for instance, for their race and sex, or their national origin and race. But intersectional discrimination proved a difficult concept for the courts to comprehend, let alone handle to the satisfaction of those who alleged suffering it, as Minetos soon learned.[42]

Five music professors, four white men and one white woman, conspired to deny her a promotion to "head secretary," Minetos said, despite her seniority and good performance evaluations. Hunter College, she claimed, customarily promoted the most senior worker from within, except in her case. All the professors conceded that they wanted, indeed actively sought, to have her ousted from the department. But they denied having any illegal motive, even though a few of them had allegedly made racial slurs in Minetos's presence. When Minetos inquired as to why she would not be promoted, one of them told her that "her communication skills were not good enough for the job." In court, they alleged that Minetos had not been promoted simply because the department faced impending budget cuts, and she was frequently absent on the job.[43]

But what doomed Minetos above all else, they said, was her attitude. They found her "impolite and curt" rather than "courteous and helpful"—both to visitors and to themselves. The entire music department staff disliked her, so much so that there was a chance they would resign en masse were she promoted. No faculty member would have agreed to be chair of the department; the only candidate for that position refused to take it on if Minetos became head secretary.[44]

This final—and it was the chief—explanation for the decision not to promote Minetos sounded a lot like the "angry woman" stereotype. Because they are perceived to be ill-tempered, many women, especially Black women, can have limited employment prospects. Observers, noting Minetos was Dominican American, would likely have lumped her in with other women of African extraction and considered her "Black," despite the fact that she didn't identify as such. Far less likely to be promoted to management positions, Black women are also far more likely than other workers to report on-the-job discrimination. Judge Motley would have spotted the "bad attitude" trope right away and understood its racial connotations; it was a stereotype often applied to African Americans generally, and Motley explicitly noted its adverse impact on Harold Evans's career with the Connecticut State Police.[45]

Whether or not the explanation resonated with Motley, the law required her to lend credence to Minetos's claims. Obliged to review the facts in the light most favorable to the plaintiff, the judge did so, in spite of the state's request to dismiss the lawsuit. Motley permitted all but Minetos's age discrimination claim to proceed to trial. Minetos, who said she had suffered problems with her heart and mental health after learning she would not be promoted, finally had something to celebrate: she had scored an early win.[46]

But her victory did not last. A jury returned a verdict for Hunter College. Minetos claimed that the jury, made up of eleven white citizens and one Latina, had been rigged to favor the defendants by the attorney general's office during the selection process.[47]

As a matter of course each party in a lawsuit assists in the selection of an "impartial" jury. Toward that end, each side is entitled to "strike," in moves that are called peremptory challenges, prospective jurors from the pool. But the process is not meant to be a free-for-all.

Motley at a City Hall budget hearing with Randolph Rankin in 1965. *(Courtesy of the Library of Congress)*

Senator James Eastland of Mississippi was a staunch segregationist who opposed the integration of the University of Mississippi. *(Courtesy of the United States Senate)*

Motley with President Lyndon B. Johnson in the Oval Office on the day he nominated her to the U.S. District Court for the Southern District of New York. *(Courtesy of the Library of Congress)*

The judges of the U.S. District Court for the Southern District of New York. Motley *(center back)* stands out in a sea of white men in black robes. *(Courtesy of the Motley family)*

Motley on the cover of *Jet* after her nomination to the court. *(Courtesy of Columbia University Library)*

Protestors demanding freedom for prisoners' rights activist Martin Sostre, along with the release of Black Panther Party leaders Huey Newton and Bobby Seale. *(Courtesy of Getty Images)*

Motley pouring coffee at home. *(Courtesy of the Motley family)*

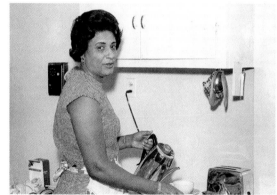

Motley having a meal at home with her husband, Joel Jr., and son, Joel III. *(Courtesy of the Motley family)*

Motley with her husband and son.
(Courtesy of the Motley family)

Motley playing chess at home with her son. *(Courtesy of the Motley family)*

Motley and her husband. *(Courtesy of the Motley family)*

John Huggins Jr., activist and leader of the Los Angeles chapter of the Black Panther Party, photographed in the summer of 1966 in New Haven, Connecticut. (*Courtesy of the Huggins family*)

Sports Illustrated writer Melissa Lutdke, who sued to allow women reporters into men's locker room, in her office in 1978. Motley decided the case in Lutdke's favor in 1972. (*Courtesy of AP Images*)

Harriet Rabb, a professor at Columbia Law School, who litigated a landmark sex discrimination case before Motley regarding a hiring practice at a top New York law firm. (*Courtesy of The Rockefeller University. Photograph by Lubos Stepanek*)

Motley (*left*) with her sisters Eunice and Marion at their annual summer gathering in Chester, Connecticut. (*Courtesy of the Baker Royster family*)

Motley, family, and friends in Chester, Connecticut, circa 1968. (*Courtesy of the Baker Royster family*)

Motley and her husband in Chester, Connecticut, at the celebration of their fiftieth wedding anniversary in 1996. (*Courtesy of the Motley family*)

Motley receives the Presidential Citizens Medal from President Bill Clinton in 2001. *(Courtesy of the William J. Clinton Presidential Library)*

Motley with family members and President Clinton upon receiving the Presidential Citizens Medal. *(From left to right)* Motley's son, Joel; daughter-in-law, Isolde; granddaughter, Hannah; husband, Joel; grandson, Ian; President Clinton; Motley; niece, Connie Royster; and cousin, Dr. Shirley Williams *(Courtesy of the William J. Clinton Presidential Library)*

Motley and her husband with President Clinton upon receiving the Presidential Citizens Medal. *(Courtesy of the William J. Clinton Presidential Library)*

Motley with *(from left to right)* former LDF counsel Derrick Bell, Julian Bond, and Representative Kweisi Mfume. *(Courtesy of the Motley family)*

Motley as photographed by Timothy Greenfield-Sanders in 2004. *(Courtesy of Timothy Greenfield-Sanders)*

The law requires litigants to strike jurors only on nondiscriminatory grounds; race cannot motivate challenges to the seating of a juror.[48]

The attorneys for the state had violated the law, Minetos's attorney, Pinskey, argued, by striking racial and ethnic minorities from the pool. They had rejected two African American and one Latino juror for pretextual reasons. What was more, Judge Motley had witnessed the unlawful behavior, he said. Questioned over why the three people of color had not been seated, the defendants' lawyer gave careful explanations detailing his reasoning.[49]

Pinskey objected. He argued that the attorneys for Hunter College "had purposefully attempted to exclude minorities from the jury," and the judge "agreed with me." At that point in the process, Motley had intervened, after which time the "defendants had allowed a Hispanic female" to sit, making her the sole person of color on the jury. "We then discussed the remedy" for the harm, Pinskey recalled. But while Motley agreed that the defendants had violated the law against race-based jury selection, she had denied Minetos's request that all the people of color wrongly rejected be seated on the jury. Motley offered a different solution: "If Minetos lost," she stated in open court, she "would be entitled to a new trial." But when Minetos did lose, and Pinskey requested a new trial, Motley denied it.[50]

The judge explained her decision in a long and impassioned opinion. It was remarkable for its acontextual application of the principle of nondiscrimination in jury selection, first enunciated in an 1880 Supreme Court opinion that struck down a statute limiting jury service to white Americans. Motley's opinion chided "both sides" for impugning the judicial process. Each party had violated the law against race-based jury selection, she said. Even as Minetos complained that defendants had deployed peremptory strikes so as to seat an all-white jury, the state alleged that Minetos's attorney sought to rid the jury of all white men. Pinskey had struck jurors on the grounds, as he explained it, that they were likely to be "pro-management" and were thus unlikely to side with Minetos in her challenge to Hunter College faculty and administrators.

During the trial, when Pinskey sought to justify the peremptory strikes, an impatient Motley had barely permitted him to speak, interrupting him without allowing him to finish his thought.[51] Motley insisted that peremptory strikes should be forbidden from the selection process entirely. In her opinion, she explained why she found Pinskey's rationale unpersuasive: taking into consideration the city's demographics. She wrote, "In New York City the business community is overwhelmingly and disproportionately white. Thus the 'pro-management' excuse offers easy cover for those with discriminatory motives in jury selection." The plaintiff's "discriminatory use of her peremptory challenges" had been unlawful, "irrespective of the final racial makeup of the jury," Motley determined.[52]

She went on to elaborate on the point that was of most interest to her: the destructive consequences of race-based juror selection strategies. In Motley's eyes, the practice "corrupt[ed]" the judicial process. Although she did not say so in her opinion, she had encountered this issue firsthand. During her time as a civil rights lawyer, she had lost only one of the ten cases that she had argued before the U.S. Supreme Court: the 1965 case *Swain v. Alabama*.[53]

Robert Swain was a nineteen-year-old Black man convicted of the rape of a seventeen-year-old white girl in Talladega, Alabama. The jurors on that case, all white, found Swain guilty and sentenced him to death by electrocution. Appealing the case before the U.S. Supreme Court, Motley had argued that the use of an all-white jury—selected from a pool absent of Blacks—had corrupted the prosecution. No Blacks served on juries in the county because, she said, "Negroes are consistently struck from trial jury panels by the prosecutor." Faced with this rank discrimination, Motley claimed that her client had been unconstitutionally deprived of a jury made up of his peers, and thus he deserved a new trial. But by a 7–2 majority vote, the Supreme Court rejected her argument: while the Constitution barred intentional racial discrimination in the empaneling of juries, it did not entitle a defendant to same-race jurors, or even to a racially proportionate jury. Because Motley was not able to prove *intentional* discrimination, the argument failed. Robert Swain remained on death row at Kilby prison in Montgomery.[54]

Some twenty years later, the Supreme Court vindicated Motley, if not Swain. In a rare move, the Court reversed its previous ruling. In 1986, in *Batson v. Kentucky*, the justices conceded that peremptory challenges could constitute a significant source of harm to the administration of justice. If strikes were deployed on a racial basis, the Court found that they violated the Fourteenth Amendment's guarantee of equal protection under the law. It then pronounced a legal test to determine whether race had been an unlawful motivating factor in jury deselection, which required a defendant challenging a strike to object with sufficient details showing discrimination. If a defendant were to do that successfully, the burden shifted to the prosecutor to articulate "neutral" reasons for striking the juror. Then the burden would shift back to the defendant to show that the stated "neutral" reason was in fact a pretext for discrimination, or a lie. Should the court agree that the reason was pretextual, known as a Batson challenge, the struck juror had to be seated. And if the court improperly denied a Batson challenge, it could be grounds for the reversal of a conviction and for a new trial. The complicated maneuvers and countermaneuvers by defendants and prosecutors could be all for naught.[55]

This test proved unworkable, Motley wrote in her *Minetos* opinion. "We have now had enough judicial experience with the Batson test to know that it does not truly unmask racial discrimination." The test failed because, as in the *Minetos* case, "lawyers can easily generate facially neutral reasons for striking jurors and trial courts are hard-pressed to second-guess them." The problem plagued employment discrimination cases "particularly," the judge said, noting the frequency with which she had witnessed parties who "are tempted to exclude jurors on the basis of race or sex or national origin alone." Reaching the conclusion that peremptory strikes should not be permitted to begin with, Motley added her voice to that of Justice Thurgood Marshall, who had argued the same in several of his opinions.[56]

Motley's professional loss in *Swain* informed the strength of her views about peremptory strikes, but the lesson she had learned backfired against Fior D'Aliza Minetos. Minetos's bid for a new trial was doomed. Under pressure to apply the rule against race discrimination to "both sides," Motley found the plaintiff's actions just as blameworthy as the defendant's—an example of a corrupt system. Motley's opinion elevated legal principle above Minetos's interest and the context provided by the socioeconomic conditions at play.

The judge discerned no distinction between the college professors' strategy of eliminating people of color from the jury and Minetos's bid to assemble a group that would include at least some of
her peers. Minetos believed that a fair jury would have people on it
capable of seeing the world through her eyes—the perspective of a
working-class Dominican American woman who spoke with a "distinct accent." While she was bound to follow the law, no one expected
a judge with Motley's experience to do so little in the way of appre-
ciating the underlying class, racial, and gender dynamics.[57] To top
it all off, Motley also held that Minetos had "completely failed" to
demonstrate that she had been discharged because of her Hispanic
background.[58]

The Minetos case illustrated how Motley's experience as a civil
rights litigator and the depth and breadth of her knowledge in the
field could just as easily work against plaintiffs as it could work for
them. Minetos and her lawyer left the court bewildered and upset
with the judge's about-face on the promised retrial. "Forgive me,"
Pinskey said later, "but I feel like that was BS." Minetos wanted to
challenge this outcome, feeling she was wronged by the system. But
she "did not have the money to appeal to the Second Circuit," and
so "the case ended there." It had been misguided to presume that
Motley—simply because she was a Black woman and had a background as a civil rights lawyer—would see the world through the eyes
of a marginalized person of color, or rule in her favor.[59]

Motley pushed the law's boundaries in high-profile sex discrimination cases, ones involving elite lawyers and journalists, famous law
firms, and sports teams. But in employment discrimination cases
that featured racial and ethnic minorities—everyday people engaged
in ordinary work in urban America—the judge seldom issued favorable rulings. Appellate courts had erected a high bar to successful
claims for race discrimination in the workplace. And Motley's record
showed little inclination to try to break new ground in these cases.
Like her judicial colleagues on federal trial courts, Motley most often
favored employers over employees in these cases. She followed the
rules, however tilted they sometimes were.[60]

Legacies

Being a "First" is always both an honor and a burden.

—CONGRESSWOMAN BELLA ABZUG
TO CONSTANCE BAKER MOTLEY, 1966

P resident Lyndon Baines Johnson did not get to nominate Constance Baker Motley to the U.S. Court of Appeals, as he had initially hoped to. "The opposition to my appointment was so great," Motley explained years later, that "Johnson had to withdraw my name." Her sterling credentials did not count for much: it did not matter that she had prevailed in nine of ten Supreme Court oral arguments, winning cases that remade American law and society. "I wasn't wanted on the Second Circuit," she reflected. But even as Johnson made history by appointing Motley to the U.S. District Court, he held out hope of a promotion for her. "Work your way up" to the court of appeals, he advised her. Unfortunately, no such position opened for her during his presidency.[1]

Still, others continued to expect that Motley would be elevated to a higher court. During the 1970s, the National Women's Political Caucus and other advocacy groups eager for the appointment of the first woman justice touted Motley as a nominee to the U.S. Supreme Court, calling her "an obvious choice" given her accomplishments and dedication to "human rights." News outlets reported that her name appeared on the Supreme Court short lists of President Richard Nixon and his successor, President Gerald Ford. "Black Woman Proposed for Supreme Court," excitedly proclaimed a front-page story in the *Pittsburgh Courier* in 1971. A more realistic chance for promotion was afforded by the election of a Democrat, President Jimmy Carter. But Motley was never tapped.

U.S. Attorney General Griffin Bell—who had tangled with Motley when she was a lawyer—reviewed every potential appointment "case-by-case, state-by-state and circuit-by-circuit." Bell had veto power over nominations, and evidently he opposed her promotion. The many admirers who believed Motley deserved to be appointed to the U.S. Court of Appeals or the Supreme Court were deeply disappointed. She "didn't get her chance," observed one such colleague, an African American woman, "and we're still waiting." Perhaps Ramsey Clark, the U.S. attorney general from 1967 to 1969, best summed up the situation: "History sometimes misses its chances."[2]

The Civil Rights Queen would never sit on the same appellate court as her mentor, and it was "one of Thurgood Marshall's biggest disappointments," as Motley tells it. It was hardly a crushing defeat, given Motley's historic appointment to the powerful federal district court, as well as her successful service as the first female chief judge of the U.S. District Court between 1982 and 1986; through this administrative role she secured funding to build a majestic new federal courthouse and reinforced the fairness-promoting system of random assignment of cases to judges, among other achievements.

Still, the resistance to her nomination to the court of appeals—where her decisions could only be reviewed by the U.S. Supreme Court—or to the Supreme Court itself, illustrated the enduring paradox of her career. After her record of extraordinary achievement, she hit a roadblock that illustrates the broader dynamic of exclusion amid access in her life, and the ongoing challenges faced by outsiders. Motley "made it," but whatever her talents, she advanced professionally only when it suited powerful gatekeepers. She never coasted on "easy street," and her identity always shadowed her achievements.[3]

Critics offered a long list of reasons why Motley should not be promoted to a higher court. Some raised her sex or race explicitly. Others claimed—falsely—that she had a high reversal rate, erroneously stating that she frequently issued wrongheaded decisions that the appeals court reversed. Still others called Motley "too liberal" for the court of appeals or Supreme Court, and, more than others, that criticism stuck.[4]

True enough, Motley issued decisions in favor of plaintiffs in several high-profile civil rights cases during the mid- to late 1970s, around the same time that she had the best chance of promotion to a higher court. But, like her ruling in Harold Evans's case, virtually all of these decisions implemented the employment antidiscrimination provisions of the Civil Rights Act, which was enacted by an overwhelming bipartisan vote. Motley's decisions opened the professional workplace to women: she granted women lawyers, journalists, professors, municipal workers, and a host of others equal access to the workplace. In cases of flagrant sexual harassment, she also issued rulings favorable to women; when men groped women's bodies or used crude language, she saw the significance of that behavior for women's workplace access and equality. She issued groundbreaking opinions that advanced the basic liberties of the homeless, gays and lesbians, and, most remarkably of all, prisoners. Her decisions in most of these cases should not have been perceived as so controversial.[5]

Moreover, Motley decided more than twenty-five hundred cases during her judicial career, and in only a handful did she reach outcomes that truly pushed the law in favor of the disadvantaged. Her overall judicial record did not justify the perception that her past as a civil rights lawyer, her race, or her gender predetermined outcomes in her courtroom. In most discrimination cases litigated before her, Judge Motley, like most other federal judges, sided with defendants. In cases to do with questions over racial discrimination, she seldom decided in favor of people of color. She found most claims of workplace discrimination weak, and in the cases where plaintiffs did win in her courtroom, they tended to be white women. And yet these outcomes that contradicted the stereotypes about who she was—the many instances in which she ruled against plaintiffs in civil rights cases, for instance—garnered little or no press attention.

Her high-profile cases involving civil rights and civil liberties—the decisions that defined her judicial legacy and that this book highlights—crowded out the attention that might have been paid to more mundane cases, many involving business and commerce. Television networks, book publishers, airlines, celebrities, and owners of Major League Baseball teams squared off in Motley's courtrooms. In a bid to maintain a tight grip on the logos and merchandising potential of all professional teams, Major League Baseball sued the Brooklyn Dodger Sports Bar, a small business, for trademark infringement.

When Motley sided with the sports bar, New Yorkers hailed her for "avenging" the city. Her decision compounded the image of her as the liberal judge who looked out for the "little guy." Yet when all was said and done, her supposed sympathy for consumers and small businesses did not usually translate into victories for the underdog in her courtroom.[6]

She readily enforced the property rights of business owners; in her courtroom, no less than in any other, larger corporate entities with greater resources—big business—prevailed. In most corporate cases, there was no obvious underdog: titan faced off against titan. The U.S. Supreme Court vindicated her in one of her highest-profile decisions, involving a powerful corporation and a leader in the television industry, the Columbia Broadcasting System: in 1974, the Court affirmed Motley's ruling against CBS and in favor of cable broadcasters who retransmitted copyrighted content, resulting in an amendment to the federal Copyright Act. Pleased, the judge "held a little celebration in chambers." The decision "laid the foundation for" the expansion of the cable TV industry, a clerk explained. It also showed that in the context of business-related cases, Motley did not merely hold her own. She defied the unfounded but perpetual aspersion—also leveled against Thurgood Marshall—that a civil rights lawyer was not prepared to handle important business disputes.[7]

Neither the breadth of Motley's judicial record nor her actual performance on the bench satisfied naysayers. Constance Baker Motley never escaped her reputation: being the "Civil Rights Queen" was a double-edged sword. It defined her. In every phase of her career, observers expected her to channel the views of those wedded to social justice. That reputation propelled her stint in politics. Should success be defined as promotion to a higher court, however—whether to the U.S. Court of Appeals or the Supreme Court—that same reputation sabotaged Motley's prospects. Because of her association with the civil rights movement, some believed she made judgments with her eyes open wide to reality, rather than upholding the fabled principle that justice is blind. Critics and admirers, plaintiffs and defendants, elites and everyday people—the whole throng—assumed Motley likely to favor victims of discrimination, no matter how flimsy their cases. This was the expectation despite abundant evidence to the contrary:

the idea that female judges and judges of color "actively promote the interests of those groups as they perform the duties of their office," researchers have established, is based not in fact, but in stereotyping and beliefs engendered by enduring social divisions.[8]

The backlash generated by decisions in which Motley truly pushed law and society were cases in point: they revealed far more about the social divisions, racial hostilities, and economic dynamics that prevailed in America within a given moment than about Motley herself. In 1976, she prohibited the use of isolation and physical or pharmaceutical restraints as punishment for youths held at Goshen Annex for Boys, a state-run institution for juvenile delinquents. Guards had bound and handcuffed Joe Pena, the sixteen-year-old lead plaintiff, in a "strip room" and then held him in isolation for five days. Reprising precepts from Martin Sostre's case, Motley held that the Eighth Amendment's ban on cruel and unusual punishments barred such actions.

In 1985, over the objections made by factions of the Catholic Church, New York City mayor Edward Koch, and the NYPD, Motley cited First Amendment freedoms in ruling that gay Catholics could demonstrate peacefully in front of St. Patrick's Cathedral during New York City's annual Gay Pride Parade. The demonstrators, part of the parade, sought to step out of line in front of the cathedral briefly to convey the "message that homosexuals can be and frequently are practicing Catholics" and "to protest the Roman Catholic Church's anti-gay position." Antigay prejudice at the time framed public perceptions of Motley's ruling in the case. The *New York Times* headline about Motley's decision captured the underlying dynamics: "Judge Rebuffs Police on Homosexual Rally." A year *after* Motley's decision protecting the protest rights of gay people, the U.S. Supreme Court *upheld* a statute criminalizing consensual gay sex. Was Motley's protection of First Amendment freedoms "too liberal"? Or were the Supreme Court's antigay outcomes in fact "activist"? History has vindicated Motley: in recent years, law on the status of people who identify as LGBTQ in society, as well as on mass incarceration and prison conditions, has moved toward the positions that she embraced decades ago.[9]

Nevertheless, public abuse rained down on Motley after such decisions. The most vicious attacks occurred after headline-grabbing rulings related to crime and punishment, particularly, but not only, following the case of Martin Sostre. In 1985 Motley mandated that a hearing should take place before a neutral magistrate within twenty-four hours of an arrest; neutral arbiters would determine if police had a legally sufficient reason to arrest someone. The decision affected the more than two hundred thousand people then arrested each year by the City of New York, and it garnered a fiercely negative reaction. One letter writer accused Motley of being a "cop hater" who had "let the boys in blue down." More hate mail containing thinly veiled threats poured in after her 1995 decision that the police could no longer arrest people who either were or looked homeless without evidence they had committed a crime. The decision ended "homeless sweeps" of Penn Station by Amtrak police and incensed some New Yorkers. A self-described "taxpayer" wrote:

> As someone who was forced by homeless on two occasions to give them money, I say you are a fucking piece of shit. Judges like you should be put out to hang from a lamp post. Drop Dead you fucking Democrat. . . . Your day will come.

Another writer angry about the Amtrak ruling called her a "god damn nigger FREAK" in receipt of an "undeserved salary" from the "honest working people using Penn Station." The venomous hatred of angry New Yorkers bore more than a passing resemblance to the threats of violence that Motley had experienced years before as a civil rights lawyer, when men with shotguns had stood guard protecting her from harm.[10]

*

What do Motley's experiences before, during, and after her appointment to the court tell us about the underlying questions animating *Civil Rights Queen*: the relationship between individual success and group advancement, and the price of the ticket for American outsiders who make it inside? We learn that context—and role—matter. An outsider's background and identity also matter. Observers repeatedly flattened Motley's identity, but she experienced it in multiple dimensions. It encompassed race, gender, class, place—and occupation.

Motley's ability and inclination to push for social change for others varied greatly according to her career phase and professional role. She made her name as a civil rights lawyer, and in doing so she effected change for many others. Her historic wins in case after case—achieved in the context of the Black freedom movement's direct action campaigns and reactions to it by government and white decision makers at the state and local levels—fundamentally altered American law and the lives of all Americans.

Because of Motley African Americans gained access to higher education, a key lever of social mobility, in the South. Because of Motley thousands of African American students were able to access better schools and prepare for higher education. Thousands of young activists who had engaged in peaceful protests for equal rights escaped unjust punishment. Many other concrete examples, from fields as varied as education, housing, and voting rights law, illustrate how her civil rights lawyering transformed life for so many. In spite, or perhaps because of, her father's callous views, Motley's work was devoted to improving the lives of the very people Willoughby Baker had spent a lifetime castigating as shiftless, worthless, inferior people of color.

Motley's successes in the courtroom laid the foundations for the second phase of her career. Her stint in politics proved advantageous to her constituents, including residents of Harlem. As a New York state senator and Manhattan borough president, she pursued policies meant to increase opportunity and equity for low-income people of color. "She always brought the civil rights issue with her," critics said. She supported greater resources for social programs and urban revitalization. At the same time, elected to office in a multiracial, multiethnic city, she cultivated white constituents and championed pluralism. Not everyone was impressed with her racial politics, which looked decidedly middle-of-the-road next to the Black Power movement. Adherents of that philosophy critiqued the belief that integration into white power structures was a solution to racial oppression. Motley, elected because she had been a transformational figure as a civil rights lawyer, looked weak and accommodationist in the eyes of radicals. That perception does not alter the fact that during a mere two years in office, she achieved more concrete social change through her policy, budgetary, and legislative initiatives than many critics ever managed.[11]

Motley's experience in politics illustrates a reality that has become increasingly clear over time and has been most obvious following the election of Barack Obama, the nation's first Black president. The election of same-race politicians may—but does not necessarily—translate into policies helpful to underresourced, minoritized communities. People of color are ideologically heterogeneous and have competing interests; elected representatives accountable to multiracial constituencies risk losing support if they push policies that prioritize the interests of the least powerful constituents. The right to vote for representatives of one's choice, deemed fundamental to full citizenship by civil rights activists, was, it turned out, insufficient to achieve political and economic empowerment for Black communities. Motley's experience as a barrier-breaking Black politician illustrated both the potential and the limitations of voting as a strategy for Black liberation.

The third phase of her career—her judgeship—promised greater rewards. Both opponents and champions of Motley's appointment to the bench expected her to vindicate the struggles of the 1960s social movements for change. Reality often belied this expectation. The closer Motley came to the pinnacle of American power, the less unconstrained was her ability to advance the imperatives of the disadvantaged. The judicial role conferred power, but also limited her capacity to advance the vision—nurtured since her youth and throughout the first two trailblazing phases of her career—of substantive justice premised on equal opportunity for all.[12]

Mindful that she had twice been deprived of a seat on the court of appeals and convinced that many in the legal world—including some judges—viewed her as an activist rather than a great judicial mind, she wrote careful opinions that the appellate court would be unlikely to reverse. She chafed at those who praised her skills as a civil rights lawyer but underestimated her judicial prowess. Through her unrelenting preparation, her respectable identity performance, and her

meticulous work, Judge Motley fought back against those who underestimated her judicial talent.[13]

But Motley did not sacrifice her principles or beliefs about certain
legal subjects in a bid for respect or promotion. When the facts and
the law demanded it, she issued decisions that advanced progressive
causes; but she did not openly or purposefully use the law to advance
those agendas. Her decisions for or against, say, Title VII plaintiffs
or criminal defendants, reflected her genuine assessment of what the
law demanded. As the Honorable Miriam Cedarbaum, Motley's longtime judicial colleague, explained, Motley was a "very honest person"
and a "stern judge"; she "listened to the evidence" and decided cases
as she saw them.

A judicial clerk agreed that the judge was "very open-minded."
In high-profile criminal cases, Motley "listened to all the evidence"
without a "pre-disposition" one way or the other. She had "all her
experience, her knowledge, her strong beliefs, but she approache[d]
everything with receptivity," an attitude the clerk found singular
among judges. "I'm not interested in judging people," Motley once
said to her clerks. "I want to learn about what makes them" who "they
are." For her, judging was not an "intellectual game."[14]

However she decided cases, the judge's race, sex, and background
as a civil rights lawyer made her an influential symbol of social, political, and legal change. Once she ascended the bench, Motley powerfully represented the end of the era of bald race- and gender-based
exclusion. She stood for two abstract but powerful concepts: equal
opportunity and the rule of law. Her symbolism and achievements
galvanized many who followed in her path.

A legend among her colleagues, Motley inspired many women
and people of color who joined the federal judiciary long after her
own historic appointment to the bench. The Honorable Ann Claire
Williams of the U.S. Court of Appeals marveled at Motley's talent for
setting "at ease" the junior colleagues who were "intimidated" by
her presence. Motley taught these women to "laugh off" the many
"affronts" that women and of-color judges faced. Motley treated the
Honorable Kimba Wood, newly appointed to the U.S. District Court
in Manhattan, to lunch. "Charming" and "gracious," she imparted

knowledge and disarmed her junior colleague with her "sense of humor," leaving Wood "in awe." To "me and other female judges and black judges," Wood remembered, "she really was just a delightful mentor." The two struck up a friendship. Later, Motley even helped alleviate the pressures of Wood's job by taking on part of her caseload. Wood remembered:

> She didn't preach about how to be a judge, but she would listen to you if you had a problem. And she frequently came to me saying, "Now, I know how busy you are . . . ," and I was fairly new . . . and she would say, "Give me your longest case. Give me your worst trial."

After Judge Anne Thompson's appointment to the judiciary in 1979, Motley reached out to congratulate her, the first Black woman on the federal bench in New Jersey. Motley offered to "answer any questions." Over time, they grew close and enjoyed "walks through the woods" and dinners at the Motleys' summer home. The judge also supported the career of William Kuntz, a talented young African American lawyer from a "very humble" background. She introduced him to influential attorneys and judges—including Justice Thurgood Marshall—and helped him develop the professional network that later facilitated his appointment to a federal judgeship. "She made things happen for me," Kuntz remembered. Because of all the ways she encouraged and befriended judicial colleagues, "[w]e all looked up to her and respected her, admired her . . . almost worshiped her," Thompson recounted.[15]

"She was one of my favorite people," Justice Sonia Sotomayor enthused in a 2015 interview. The pair met during Sotomayor's induction ceremony to the U.S. District Court for the Southern District of New York. Motley was, by then, a dean of the court. She had entered "senior status," or semiretirement, in 1986, at age sixty-five, but continued to hear a reduced load of cases. She warmly welcomed Sotomayor to the court, helping the new judge acclimate to her responsibilities. The pair developed a bond. They chewed over matters both serious and light over lunch. Sotomayor caught glimpses into Motley's ideals. "She had great expectations of herself and others,"

Sotomayor observed; she believed that talented people of color, especially those from modest backgrounds, had "an obligation to show the world what we can do" and "give back to the community" by reaching "as high a position as you're capable of reaching." And "you don't complain."

But for all that they shared, the younger judge never doubted that generation and approach—if not their deeper values—set them apart. Sotomayor described Motley as a woman who had a strong "sense of belonging," but without "changing tradition." In one anecdote, Sotomayor described how Motley once admitted that "she still did not like women coming into the courtroom in pants." So, Sotomayor said, she "always" wore a "dress or suit . . . whenever I met her for lunch." The justice admired Motley's intelligence and the self-assurance she projected—"nothing was impossibly hard for her"—and at the same time respected the different ways they moved through the world.[16]

The judicial colleagues differed in their conception of how race, ethnicity, and other background factors affected the work of judging. Whereas Justice Sotomayor wrote of her hopes that a "wise Latina" judge "would more often than not reach a better conclusion than" a white male judge without her experiences,[17] Motley stressed that *all* judges were rich in experience. She thought of herself as multidimensional, as having been shaped by the many facets of her background. But she did not claim that women or people of color gained special insights because of their identities.

Women, Motley argued, did *not* have a different voice. She supported the appointment of women, especially women of color, to the bench, but not because she thought "they bring something totally different to the bench than white men." She advocated for judicial diversity because, she believed, inclusion reinforced democracy. By affirming openness and fairness, the mere presence of women and racial-minority judges would build confidence in government. Motley rested her case for an inclusive bench on the promise of American democracy and its key feature—the representation of all people, and thus the full spectrum of American voices.[18]

Motley's great faith in the American system of governance was rooted in experience. Her tremendous power as a representative of American opportunity animated her career. New York's Democratic political establishment recognized how mightily she symbolized the nation's transformation into a racially inclusive democracy when it first encouraged her to run for office in 1964 and made her the "boss" of New York in 1965. President Johnson saw her as an emblem of his own active commitment to Black freedom when he appointed her to the judiciary in 1966.

Despite the stardom Motley had achieved, she remained tightly connected to her humble roots. A story shared by her judicial colleague and friend Anne Thompson about a chance meeting one summer on Martha's Vineyard in the early aughts illustrates how humble and gracious Motley remained more than half a century after she had shot to fame. Thompson recounted:

> I remember when President Clinton came to the Vineyard. . . .
> We were guests at the golf club and . . . Vernon Jordan came
> over and greeted us. . . . And, lo and behold we looked up and
> saw this tall, sandy haired guy coming toward us. I said, "Oh,
> my God. Here comes the President."
>
> And, she said, "Stand up, stand up, stand up." So, we all
> stood up and [the president] said, "You don't have to stand." . . .
> And, she being so humble, just the way she always was, put her
> hand out and said, "I'm Constance Baker Motley," introducing
> herself like she was just anybody. And he gave her the big Bill
> Clinton charm and he said, "I know who you are, you don't ever
> have to tell me who you are. I know who you are."[19]

Indeed, he did. In 2001, President Clinton awarded Constance Baker Motley the Presidential Citizens Medal, an honor awarded to individuals who perform "exemplary deeds" for "country or fellow citizens."

Throughout her multifaceted career, Constance Baker Motley had helped advance the ideals of American democracy to form a "more perfect union," the president told the audience assembled at the White House pavilion for the ceremony. Before a crowd that included a U.S. Supreme Court justice, members of Congress, and other dignitaries, Clinton listed Motley's contributions. "As advocate, lawyer, public servant, and judge," the president proclaimed,

Motley had been not merely "capable," but "superb." All Americans "are in your debt." By remaking the law, Motley had reconstructed society. The judge added the medal to the collection of awards that she had earned in her later years: honorary degrees from numerous colleges; recognition from scores of civic groups; induction into the National Women's Hall of Fame in Seneca Falls, New York; and the NAACP's Spingarn Medal, awarded to her in 2003 for "extraordinary" achievement. Yet these tokens of a lifetime's achievements do not capture the woman in full.[20]

Keenly aware of her historic accomplishments and her role in helping to move American democracy forward, Motley looked inward and toward home when asked to reflect on her life. A strong believer in the importance of family, she called her son, Joel, "her greatest accomplishment." A graduate of Exeter, Harvard College, and Harvard Law School, Joel III made a career in the financial services industry, while simultaneously working to promote human rights. He married and established a family of his own. He was never "resentful, overawed or burdened by her fame, reputation, or presence." Motley was proud that Joel "turned out well," she said, "even though his mother was always working."[21]

This last comment surfaces Motley's strained relationship with traditional conceptions of wifedom and motherhood. Her relentless work to redeem the nation took her away from her family. "Joel [Jr.] was devoted to her and her ideals and was there to do whatever had to be done in order for her to keep doing what she had to do," explained a close friend. Throughout her career, her husband played the roles of caretaker, protector, and supporter.

The couple defied traditional gender roles in many respects, but not all of them. Joel consistently out-earned his wife, and his economic dominance preserved a conventional balance of power in the relationship, Judge Motley herself conceded. It explained his willingness to go through life as "Mr. Constance Baker Motley." "Had I been economically successful," Judge Motley once asserted, "that would have been a problem for my husband." "But I wasn't any threat because I wasn't making any money," she reflected in an interview. Nevertheless, love and companionship defined her marriage.[22]

Motley took pride in the life she had made with her husband. Their "partnership" lasted more than fifty years, until the judge's passing in 2005. Joel Jr.'s death followed only a few months later. This surprised no one: he "could never live without Connie," people said.[23]

Throughout her life, Motley not only held close her immediate family, but also embraced the traditions and network of kin that came from Nevis, her ancestral homeland. She praised the courage and culturally conservative values imparted by her West Indian parents and her extended family, and she devoted considerable time to tracing her roots, disseminating genealogy, and organizing family reunions. Every year, she traveled to Nevis, where she bought a home, to "relax," to be "anonymous," "to be quiet" and to be herself. Long after her parents had passed away, she visited family and spoke with community elders who had known them.[24]

New England—her idealized American home—also held pride of place. Motley never lost touch with New Haven, where, beginning in the early twentieth century, the Huggins clan had settled, gained employment, bought property, and built relationships. She enjoyed the church, community, and family relations she still found there. "Revered" by family members who took "tremendous pride" in her accomplishments, she stayed in touch. She bought her relatives a "family home": located at University Place in New Haven, the house served as a "base" for the clan, her mother and siblings. Motley had "an amazingly close" relationship with her sister Eunice. She "took a particular interest in" Eunice's daughter, her namesake, Constance (Connie) Royster, who spent her youth playing with Joel III, three years her junior. A member of the first class of women to matriculate to Yale, Connie lived with her aunt in her New York apartment when she attended Rutgers School of Law. The judge "tutored" and "mentored" her niece before, during, and after law school, subsidized her living expenses, introduced her to important people and places, offered career advice, and even gave Connie's law school commencement address.[25]

Motley's enduring connection to New Haven rooted her in her modest beginnings. Conscious of her working-class background, she believed she had mostly escaped racism by virtue of life in New England. The most humiliating experience of her young life—the forced move to the Jim Crow railcar during her 1942 trip to Fisk University—

scarred her precisely because of its stark contrast with the absence of state-enforced racial segregation in Connecticut. But race and racism had been a destructive force in her life, and in the lives of family members, despite the relative safety she enjoyed in New Haven.

The racism her young cousin John Huggins experienced, his driving ambition to combat discrimination within and beyond his home state, and his murder left the whole family bereft. In the end, the family's proximity to whiteness could not save John from the ravages of American racism.

*

Motley personified "Black Excellence," and her presence in the power structure reassured onlookers that America's promise of equal opportunity was true. Her appointment to the federal court marked her personal success as well as her symbolic importance. As the only woman, moreover the only Black woman, on the most prestigious federal trial court, she was a powerful emblem of social change in and for America. When the "civil rights trailblazer, lawmaker, and judge," as her *New York Times* obituary described her, died on September 28, 2005, at eighty-four years of age, the U.S. Senate passed a resolution "recognizing and honoring" her lifetime achievements. Highlighting what he called her greatest achievement, then-Senator Barack Obama of Illinois praised Motley for "drafting the complaint that would become *Brown v. Board of Education*." Summing up her impact, Senator Charles Schumer of New York proclaimed, "Her passing is a great loss to New York, as well as the country, and for this reason her life must be remembered and celebrated."

Numerous other dignitaries mourned her passing. A "woman of valor," Motley "never quit on America," wrote President Bill Clinton. Instead, "she showed us what America could become" and "demonstrated by example how much we have to gain by embracing the energy and talents of all our people." In a remembrance titled "My Human Rights Hero," Associate Justice Ruth Bader Ginsburg, who had long admired Motley, just as Motley admired her, perhaps best captured her legacy and her humanity. Ginsburg wrote, "I count it my great good fortune to be among the legions whose lives Judge Motley touched. She taught me and others of my generation that law and courts could become positive forces in achieving our nation's high aspiration—as carved above the entrance to the U.S. Supreme Court—Equal Justice under Law."[26]

But Motley gained access to power through law without ever enjoying all its privileges. After years of being the "girl in the office" at the Inc. Fund, she earned a reputation as a brilliant civil rights lawyer. Yet she failed to secure promotion to director-counsel of the premier public interest law firm partly because decision makers, including Thurgood Marshall, her beloved mentor, did not seriously conceive of a Black woman as the leader of such a critically important national organization. That outcome, although disappointing to Motley, is also utterly unsurprising given the context.[27]

Reserved by nature and culturally conservative, Motley developed her self-contained persona, monotonal voice, "lady-like" manner, and unperturbable demeanor out of the often unfriendly, if not downright hostile, environments she encountered as a result of being a first. Through these qualities, she protected herself; only a select few could peek behind her mask. Admired by strangers and beloved by clerks and colleagues who did glimpse the woman behind the public persona, she earned a reputation as a talented judge, one deeply committed to fairness, to truth, and to her craft.

Meanwhile, Motley's race, gender, and practice background deprived her of recognition as one of the judicial greats. She never achieved that standing, although she deserved acclaim for several deeply impactful and farsighted decisions. As a lawyer she had paved the way for the Civil Rights Act of 1964; as a judge, she had implemented it in these pivotal cases. But ironically, these groundbreaking opinions diminished her judicial reputation among critics who discounted her hard-earned expertise.

Ultimately, Motley's career reveals a paradox of opportunity for insiders in the American power structure. She was a remarkable and historic figure who both made and embodied change for and by African Americans and women. She had sought and achieved the American dream of individual and family success. And as a lawyer, politician, and jurist, she had created opportunities for the many other able competitors who were vying for success within the boundaries of America's political, legal, and economic systems. She had come closest to disrupting the power structure during her years as a civil rights lawyer, when Motley shook up the system by demanding compliance with American ideals.

Yet once she ascended to a federal judgeship, this singular woman was not, by her own admission, a gladiator who could or would fundamentally upend the rules of the system. She had become a part of the system. Her life on the bench illustrates a critically important phenomenon: when icons of opportunity and diversity take the reins of power in American institutions, the structure envelops them.

That is the price of the ticket. The system admits outsiders who play by its rules, fits them into its logic, and permits incremental reform. The power structure does not fundamentally transform; at best, it accommodates difference. It positions agents of change, like Constance Baker Motley, to "do what they can with what they have." That's how Thurgood Marshall described the challenge of working through the law to change an unjust society.[28]

Acknowledgments

The writing of this book has been a labor of love. It has been an enormous challenge and an absolute joy to bring to life on these pages the life and work of Constance Baker Motley. I am grateful to the many people who made invaluable contributions to this work.

I have benefited immensely from the diligent research assistance of librarians. Melinda Kent of Harvard Law School Library was particularly helpful; she tracked down numerous vital records, including court documents, archival papers, articles in obscure journals, and West Indian legal codes, among other sources. Jon Ashley, John Roper, and Benjamin Doherty of the University of Virginia Law Library collected years of data on Motley's judicial and litigation dockets. Cathi Palombi, also of UVA, tracked down FBI files critical to understanding Motley's difficult judicial confirmation process. The collections of the Schlesinger Library on the History of Women in America at Harvard's Radcliffe Institute for Advanced Study were uniquely helpful, enhancing my ability to tell a story about the relevance of gender to Motley's professional life and social networks. I found a treasure trove of vital documents and photographs at the Sophia Smith Collection of Women's History at Smith College and at Columbia Law School. Marta Daniels of the Chester Historical Society, and many dedicated professionals at the Library of Congress, the National Archives of the United States, the National Archives of St. Kitts and Nevis, the Jimmy Carter Presidential Library, New York University, the University of Texas, and Yale University, also helped me locate immensely important records.

I could not have completed this book without my students. I gained critical insights from students who participated in my research seminars and critical support from students who worked as my research assistants. Thanks to Akua Abu, Cathi Choi, Emma Costa, Kelsey Hazzard, Emily Graham, Louis Fisher, Alisha Jarwala, Jyoti Jasrasaria, Elizabeth Katz, Emma Leibowitz, Tim Lovelace, Catherine McCord, Thaddeus Kennedy, Hannah Motley, Katie Renzler, Dominick Rolle, Kamika Shaw, Matthew Shaw, Connie Sung, Elena Vazquez, and Samuel Weiss for your sleuthing and data collection in support of *Civil Rights Queen*.

Intellectual exchange with scholars at several universities improved this project. I am indebted to colleagues at Harvard, particularly at the law school, in the history department, and at Radcliffe. I also am grateful to faculty at Columbia, Michigan, Chicago, Princeton, Stanford, Virginia, and Yale, as well as at Boston College, Boston University, and the Graduate Center at CUNY. The Radcliffe Institute Fellowship class of 2018 offered invaluable insights, as did members of the "Writing Black Lives" panel, Robert Reid-Pharr and Imani Perry. Participants at meetings of the American Society of Legal History, the Organization of American Historians, and the Association of American Law Schools proved helpful, as did members of the National Association of Women Judges and audiences at the U.S. District Court for the Southern District of New York.

I owe special thanks to those who read and commented on book chapters, or helpfully discussed the book concept: Barbara Babcock, Constance Backhouse, Felice Batlan, Nancy Cott, Lani Guinier, Jane De Hart, Annette Gordan-Reed, Ken Mack, Randall Kennedy, Martha Jones, Jane Kamensky, Michael Klarman, Kevin Kruse, Pnina Lahav, Serena Mayeri, Daniel Nagin, Martha Minow, Nancy MacLean, Mark Tushnet, and Ted White.

Joel Motley III, Isolde Motley, Constance Royster, Joan and Shirley Williams, Joan and Carolyn Huggins, Mai Huggins Lassiter, and friends and professional colleagues of Constance Baker Motley enriched this work by sharing memories and photos that helped me fill out the picture of her.

Numerous publishing industry professionals helped bring this book to fruition. Gloria Loomis, my agent and my advocate, believed in the book and ensured its placement with the right publisher. Maria Goldverg, my editor at Pantheon Books, earned my trust from day one. She immediately appreciated that Motley both embodied and made social change and recognized that her story deserved the full treatment and the widest possible audience. Maria shepherded *Civil Rights Queen* through the publication process with great enthusiasm. Juliet Frey and Phoebe Braithwaite provided extraordinarily helpful editorial assistance.

My colleagues at the Harvard Radcliffe Institute created space and snatches of time for me, amid the demands of my role, to finish this book. Many thanks to Alex Hall, Jane Huber, Nisha Mongia, and Dami Seung for your generous support, and to Ryan Mulcahy and Jess Brilli for your good judgment.

Above all else, I am grateful for the love and support of my family. Daniel, my partner and best friend, read chapters and kept me going through the decade-long process of writing *Civil Rights Queen*. Julius and Avi, our dear sons, brought humor and purpose to our home, and proper perspective to my work outside of it. I found my number one fan in Faith, my sister and my friend. And I am eternally grateful to my parents, for everything. Special thanks to my mother for helping me choose a cover photo that captures the fierceness and the joy of Constance Baker Motley.

Notes

INTRODUCTION

1. Clipping, n.d., "Negro Fatally Shot in Jail at Manchester," NAACP Papers, Legal File, 1940–55, Library of Congress, Police Brutality, 1949–50, Sam Terry folder; Roy C. Wright to Walter White, March 1, 1949, NAACP Papers, Terry folder.

2. Roy C. Wright to Walter White, March 1, 1949; Albert Riley, "Shot in Jail: Manchester Vet Dies of Pistol Wounds," *Atlanta Constitution*, February 28, 1949, Terry folder; "Same Terry Case: Minnie Kate Terry's Statement," Terry folder.

3. Constance Baker Motley to Tom C. Clark, March 4, 1949, NAACP Papers, Legal File, 1940–55, Library of Congress, Police Brutality, 1949–50, Sam Terry folder; Thurgood Marshall to Maceo Hubbard, March 17, 1949, Terry folder; Alexander M. Campbell to Thurgood Marshall, March 22, 1949, Terry folder; Roy C. Wright to Walter White, March 1, 1949, Terry folder; Constance Baker Motley to J. Howard McGrath, May 9, 1950, Terry folder; James McInerny to Constance Baker Motley, June 15, 1950, Terry folder.

4. See "NAACP's 'Portia' Tackles S.C. Segregation Wall," *Journal & Guide* (Norfolk, VA), November 24, 1962; "Civil Rights Queen," news clipping, record group 2, box 3, newspaper clippings folder, Constance Baker Motley Collection, Columbia Law School (hereafter cited as Columbia Motley Collection).

5. Thurgood Marshall Reminiscences, Columbia Oral History Project, 28; Cole and Greenaway, "Judge Constance Baker Motley and the Struggle for Equal Justice."

6. Motley quote from *Atlanta Constitution*, July 30, 1964. Marshall quote from Thurgood Marshall Reminiscences, Columbia Oral History Project

(1994), 29. On Motley in Supreme Court history, see Cushman, *Supreme Court Decisions and Women's Rights*, 224.

7. The most extensive treatments of Motley's life to date include Tomiko Brown-Nagin, *Courage to Dissent: Atlanta and the Long History of the Civil Rights Movement*, 308–56; Brown-Nagin, "Identity Matters: The Case of Constance Baker Motley"; and Ford Jr., *Constance Baker Motley*.

8. On leadership style and gender, see, for example, Eagly and Johnson, "Gender and Leadership Style."

9. Cole and Greenaway, "Judge Constance Baker Motley and the Struggle for Equal Justice." For comparable experiences, see, for example, Ransby, *Ella Baker and the Black Freedom Movement*.

10. For other works that illuminate these and related questions, see Theoharis, *The Rebellious Life of Rosa Parks*; Ransby, *Ella Baker and the Black Freedom Movement*; Chana Kai Lee, *For Freedom's Sake*; Rosenberg, *Jane Crow*; Charron, *Freedom's Teacher*; also see De Hart, *Ruth Bader Ginsburg*.

11. See Baldwin, *The Price of the Ticket*.

12. "Another Excellent Appointment," *Call and Post* (Cleveland), February 5, 1966, 9B; see Kamala Harris, tweet, August 30, 2018.

13. For comparable figures, see Lewis, *W. E. B. Du Bois, 1868–1919*; Juan Williams, *Thurgood Marshall*; Tushnet, *Making Civil Rights Law*; Garrow, *Bearing the Cross*; Giddings, *Ida*; Painter, *Sojourner Truth*; Theoharis, *The Rebellious Life of Rosa Parks*; Ransby, *Ella Baker and the Black Freedom Movement*; Chana Kai Lee, *For Freedom's Sake*; Rosenberg, *Jane Crow*.

1. "THE BASE OF THIS GREAT AMBITION": NEVIS AND NEW HAVEN

1. See Oral History Interview of Constance Baker Motley, conducted by Peggy Lamson, ca. 1967, p. 5, Lamson Papers, Schlesinger Library, Radcliffe Institute, Cambridge, MA.

2. Motley, *Equal Justice Under Law*, 40, 16.

3. See Aspinall, *The British West Indies*, 1; Oral History Interview of Constance Baker Motley, conducted by Peggy Lamson, p. 5.

4. See Frucht, "Emigration, Remittances and Social Change," 196; Motley, *Equal Justice Under Law*, 13, 14.

5. See Goucher, LeGuin, and Walton, "Commerce and Change"; Eric Williams, *Capitalism and Slavery*, 98; Hubbard, *Swords, Ships and Sugar*, 61, 84–85, 153–54; Rich Cohen, "Sugar Love: A Not So Sweet Story," *National Geographic*, August 2013, 78–97.

6. Dunn, *Sugar and Slaves*, 189–191; Dyde, *Out of the Crowded Vagueness*, 49–50, 97; Hubbard, *Swords, Ships and Sugar*, 85; Aspinall, *British West Indies*, 1, 160.

7. Aspinall, *British West Indies*, 160.

8. See "Proceedings, Evidence, and Documents Relating to the Windward Islands, the Leeward Islands, and Jamaica," *Report of the West India Royal Commission*, vol. III, appendix C (1897), p. 214, National Archives of St. Kitts and Nevis, Basseterre, St. Kitts; *Colonial Report to the House of Commons on the Leeward Islands*, colonial report no. 337 (1900), p. 43, National Archives of St. Kitts and Nevis, Basseterre, St. Kitts (hereafter cited as NASKN); *Colonial Report to the House of Commons on the Sugar Industry in Antigua and St. Kitts-Nevis, 1881 to 1905*, colonial report no. 35 (1906), pp. 4–5, NASKN; Hubbard, *Swords, Ships and Sugar*, 173, 174; Dyde, *Out of the Crowded Vagueness*, 172.

9. "Extinction" from *Report of the West India Royal Commission* (1897), 209, 213; *Annual Report to the House of Commons on the Leeward Islands*, colonial report no. 445 (1904), p. 25, NASKN; *Colonial Report to the House of Commons on the Leeward Islands* (1900), 43; Bonham C. Richardson, *Caribbean Migrants*, 20. On the poor conditions of labor, see Richards, "The Pursuit of 'Higher Wages' and 'Perfect Personal Freedom,' " 280–83.

10. See *Report of the West India Royal Commission* (1897), 232; *Annual Report to the House of Commons on the Leeward Islands* (1904), 15; Richards, "Pursuit of 'Higher Wages,' 6, and 'Perfect Personal Freedom,' " 279, 280–83, 285, 290; Dyde, *Out of the Crowded Vagueness*, 177; Frucht, "Emigration, Remittances and Social Change," 197.

11. See "Nevis Improvement Schemes: Water Supply," Colonial Development Act of 1929, discussing how a water supply had been under consideration for a long time but had not materialized due to a lack of funds, NASKN. The problem persisted into the mid-twentieth century. See "Charlestown Water Crisis," *Nevis Recorder*, August 1, 1959; see also *Annual Medical and Sanitary Report, St. Christopher and Nevis* (1928), preface, which shows significant incidence of syphilis, whooping cough, gonorrhea, tuberculosis, flu, yaws, and malarial diseases; *Annual Report to the House of Commons on the Leeward Islands* (1904), 16; *Report of the West India Royal Commission* (1897), 219, 220, 235; *Annual Report to the House of Commons on the Leeward Islands* (1904), 16.

    As late as 1958, Nevisians complained that the Crown provided only one doctor to treat the island's inhabitants. See "One Doctor for 14,000 People in Nevis," *Nevis Recorder*, February 8, 1958.

12. See Richards, "Pursuit of 'Higher Wages' and 'Perfect Personal Freedom,' " 281–82, 287; Hubbard, *Swords, Ships and Sugar*, 192; *Report of the West India Royal Commission* (1897), 219; Richards, "Pursuit of 'Higher Wages' and 'Perfect Personal Freedom,' " 281–82; Richardson, *Caribbean Migrants*, 21.

13. See Aspinall, *British West Indies*, 79; Chernow, *Alexander Hamilton*, 3–5, 6, 7–10.

14. See Waters, *Black Identities*, 27; see also Motley, *Equal Justice Under Law*, 9–11.

15. See "My England," *St. Kitts-Nevis Daily Bulletin*, March 29, 1916, and "Passport Regulations," *St. Kitts-Nevis Daily Bulletin*, April 27, 1916. Past royal visits are discussed in "Loyal Address to Her Majesty," *The Democrat* (Charlestown, Nevis), December 5, 1953.

16. Waters, *Black Identities*, 27.

17. See Olwig, *Global Culture, Island Identity*, 119, 207; Waters, *Black Identities*, 27–28. Du Bois famously wrote, "The Negro race, like all races, is going to be saved by its exceptional men." See Lewis, *W. E. B. Du Bois, 1868–1919*, 288.

18. Olwig, *Global Culture, Island Identity*, 118.

19. See *Records of the Selective Service System, 1926–1975*, National Archives at St. Louis, St. Louis, MO; Military State: *Connecticut*; NARA Series: *M1962*; NARA Series Title: *World War II Draft Cards (Fourth Registration) for the State of Connecticut*; ARC Number: *2555449*; ARC Title: *Registration Cards of the Fourth Registration*; Creator: *Selective Service System. Connecticut State Headquarters (1940–1947)*; Record Group Number: *147*; United States, Selective Service System. *World War I Selective Service System Draft Registration Cards, 1917–1918*. Washington, DC: National Archives and Records Administration. M1509, 4,582 rolls. Imaged from Family History Library microfilm. See also Motley, *Equal Justice Under Law*, 13–14.

20. Frucht, "Emigration, Remittances and Social Change," 197.

21. Motley, *Equal Justice Under Law*, 10–11, 12–13. See *Sixteenth Census of the United States, 1940*, Enumeration District 11–129, New Haven, New Haven County, Connecticut (National Archives Microfilm Publication T627, roll 542, p. 6A).

22. Motley, *Equal Justice Under Law*, 12–13; Model, *West Indian Immigrants*, 16–17.

23. Model, *West Indian Immigrants*, 17; on migration, see Warner, *New Haven Negroes*, 122, 123.

24. See Waters, *Black Identities*, 151. See also Motley, *Equal Justice Under Law*, 26; Caplan, *Legendary Locals of New Haven*, 29; Model, *West Indian Immigrants*, 22, 25. See also Warner, *New Haven Negroes*, 182–83, and Lassonde, *Learning to Forget*, 15.

25. U.S. Census Reports, Vol. 1, 1900, p. 980 (Washington, DC: U.S. Census Office, 1901); Sletcher, *New Haven*, 8–9; Warner, *New Haven Negroes*, 124.

26. Sletcher, *New Haven*, 50–53, 117; Warner, *New Haven Negroes*, 5–6, 8, 11, 17–18, 39–41, 46–47, 182–84, 240–46, 253–54; Motley, *Equal Justice Under Law*, 21.

27. Anna Quindlen, " 'Ordinary Woman' Makes History," *New York Times*, Au-

gust 31, 1977; Motley, *Equal Justice Under Law*, 15, 46; "Constance Baker Motley," in Gilbert and Moore, *Particular Passions*, 137.

28. "Constance Baker Motley," in Gilbert and Moore, *Particular Passions*, 137; Kitty Gellhorn, "The Reminiscences of Judge Constance Baker Motley," Oral History Research Office, Columbia University (1978), 32, 35 (hereafter cited as "Motley Reminiscences"); see also Warner, *New Haven Negroes*, 230–44.

29. Motley, *Equal Justice Under Law*, 41.

30. Motley, *Equal Justice Under Law*, 33, 41; Motley, Constance Baker. Oral History Archive, National Visionary Leadership Project (last accessed August 25, 2020).

31. Motley, *Equal Justice Under Law*, 14, 27, 30; see Olwig, *Global Culture, Island Identity*, 7, 116–17, and Richardson, *Caribbean Migrants*, 32.

32. Joan and Shirley Williams, in discussion with the author, November 1, 2012, p. 4 (transcript on file with author). The Williamses are sisters and relatives of Constance Baker Motley and are familiar with family history; Constance Royster, in discussion with the author, June 24, 2014, p. 3, June 25, 2014, pp. 2–3 (transcript on file with author); Warner, *New Haven Negroes*, 193.

33. Motley, *Equal Justice Under Law*, 40.

34. Motley, *Equal Justice Under Law*, 20; Gilbert and Moore, "Constance Baker Motley," 137.

35. See Motley, *Equal Justice Under Law*, 21–27; Frucht, "Emigration, Remittances and Social Change," 201; Olwig, *Global Culture, Island Identity*, 7, 21.

36. Motley, *Equal Justice Under Law*, 26. See Constance Royster, in discussion with the author, June 24, 2014.

37. Motley, *Equal Justice Under Law*, 53.

38. Harry Negher, "Yale Chef's Daughter New Borough Chief," *New York Herald*, March 7, 1963. See Thornton McEnery, "The Fifteen Most Powerful Members of 'Skull and Bones,'" *Business Insider*, February 20, 2011; James C. McKinley Jr., "Geronimo's Heirs Sue Secret Yale Society over His Skull," *New York Times*, February 19, 2009; Robbins, *The Secrets of the Tomb*; and Sutton, *America's Secret Establishment*.

39. Motley, *Equal Justice Under Law*, 14, 26; Constance Royster, in discussion with the author, June 24–25, 2014. See Warner, *New Haven Negroes*, 247.

40. Motley, "Remarks," Women's Forum, Yale University, May 6, 1979, Constance Baker Motley Papers, Sophia Smith Archives, Smith College, Northampton, MA (hereafter cited as Smith Motley Papers); Joan and Shirley Williams, in discussion with the author, November 1, 2012.

41. "Personal Profile: Constance Baker Motley," *New Haven Register*, Febru-

ary 11, 1979; Joan and Shirley Williams, in discussion with the author, November 1, 2012; Motley, *Equal Justice Under Law*, 16.

2. "I DISCOVERED MYSELF": THE GREAT DEPRESSION, THE NEW DEAL, AND THE DAWN OF A POLITICAL CONSCIENCE

1. Grade report, senior year, New Haven High School, 1938–39, record group 1, box 1, Columbia Motley Collection. On Hillhouse, see Lassonde, *Learning to Forget*, 6, 23, 123–24, 137–39.
2. Motley Reminiscences, 86–87, 92.
3. Motley, *Equal Justice Under Law*, 91–92. See also J. Clay Smith, *Emancipation*, 127, 162; Caplan, *Legendary Locals of New Haven*, 40; and McLeod, *Daughter of the Empire State*, 59.
4. Motley Reminiscences, 100.
5. Motley, *Equal Justice Under Law*, 26.
6. Connecticut's munitions industries eagerly rose to Roosevelt's challenge to make the United States the "arsenal of democracy." See Sletcher, *New Haven*, 126, 129; Warner, *New Haven Negroes*, 1, 265–66; Anthony V. Riccio, *The Italian American Experience in New Haven*, 202; Joseph F. Nunes, "After Roaring Twenties, a Great Depression," *Hartford Courant*, October 18, 2014; and Lassonde, *Learning to Forget*, 21. Quote from Motley, *Equal Justice Under Law*, 33.
7. See Storrs, *The Second Red Scare and the Unmaking of the New Deal Left*, 9; McDuffie, *Sojourning for Freedom*, 91–93; and Glenda Elizabeth Gilmore, *Defying Dixie*, 307–11.
8. McDuffie, *Sojourning for Freedom*, 91–93.
9. Jervis Anderson, *A. Philip Randolph*, 229–35.
10. On Blacks and race relations in Communist Party theory, see Harris and Spero, *The Black Worker*, 415–17.
11. D'Amato, "The Communist Party and Black Liberation in the 1930s"; Dan T. Carter, *Scottsboro*, 143–44; Goodman, *Stories of Scottsboro*, 28, 36, 38, 84; McDuffie, *Sojourning for Freedom*, 57, 61–62; Harris and Spero, *The Black Worker*, 415–17; Murray, "The NAACP versus the Communist Party."
12. D'Amato, "The Communist Party and Black Liberation in the 1930s."
13. Motley, *Equal Justice Under Law*, 36, 216–17. See also "Lewis Demands Full Negro Rights; Lashes Warmakers, Denounces FBI," *Daily Worker*, April 27, 1940.
14. See *Program*, Fourth Annual Southern Negro Youth Conference, New Orleans, LA, 1940, Columbia Motley Collection *Working Program*, Third Annual National Negro Congress, April 1938, Columbia Motley Collection; Motley, *Equal Justice Under Law*, 36. See also Hughes, "'We Demand Our Rights.'"
15. Hughes, "'We Demand Our Rights,'" 49. See also Seventh American Youth

Congress, July 1941, record group 1, box 1, conference memorabilia 1941, Columbia Motley Collection.

16. See "Memorandum on the Achievements and Prospects of the Connecticut Conference on Social and Labor Legislation," 1943, Elizabeth Wade White Papers, box 16, Connecticut Conference folder, New York Public Library; David Hedley to Constance Baker, December 30, 1940, box 1, Columbia Motley Collection; Connecticut Conference on Social and Labor Legislation, "Legislative Facts," n.d., pp. 1–4, Sterling Library, Yale University; Robert Calhoun et al. to Constance Baker, December 27, 1940, record group 1, box 1, conference memorabilia 1940, Columbia Motley Collection; David Hadley to Constance Baker, 20 December 1940, record group 1, box 1, conference memorabilia 1940, Columbia Motley Collection.

17. Connecticut Conference on Social and Labor Legislation, "Legislative Facts," n.d., pp. 1–4, Sterling Library, Yale University; Connecticut Conference on Social and Labor Legislation, "What Is National Defense?," pp. 1–5, Sterling Library, Yale University; Connecticut Conference on Social and Labor Legislation, *Draft Declaration on National Issues*, December 1940, record group 1, box 1, conference memorabilia 1940, Columbia Motley Collection.

18. Motley Reminiscences, 100.

19. Constance Baker Motley to Dixwell Community Center, n.d., box 1, Columbia Motley Collection; Motley, *Equal Justice Under Law*, 44–45.

20. *Sixteenth Census of the United States, 1940*, Enumeration District 11–129, New Haven, New Haven County, Connecticut (National Archives Microfilm Publication T627, roll 542, p. 6A); Motley, *Equal Justice Under Law*, 43.

21. Abramowitz, "Eleanor Roosevelt and the National Youth Administration, 1935–1943"; Wiesen Cook, *Eleanor Roosevelt*, 269–72.

22. Motley, *Equal Justice Under Law*, 42–43.

23. Motley, *Equal Justice Under Law*, 43; Robert Frank, Antiwar Speech Draft, n.d., record group 1, box 1, memorabilia 1941–42, Columbia Motley Collection.

3. "LIKE A FAIRY TALE": BLACK EXCEPTIONALISM, PHILANTHROPY, AND A PATH TO HIGHER EDUCATION

1. See National Center for Education Statistics, *120 Years of American Education*, 8–9.

2. Motley, *Equal Justice Under Law*, 43.

3. Motley, *Equal Justice Under Law*, 41, 43; "Constance Baker Motley," in Gilbert and Moore, *Particular Passions*, 138.

4. See "Clarence Blakeslee," *Who's Who in Commerce and Industry*, 2nd ed.

(1938); "Local Man Named in S.A.R. Election," *Bridgeport Telegram*, June 15, 1927; "Local YMCA. Man Honored at New Haven," *Bridgeport Telegram*, November 4, 1921; "Approved Application for Membership, The Connecticut Society of the Sons of the American Revolution, Sept. 30, 1914," available at Ancestry.com. *U.S., Sons of the American Revolution Membership Applications, 1889–1970* [database online]. Provo, UT: Ancestry.com Operations, Inc., 2011.

5. "Clarence Blakeslee," *Who's Who in Commerce and Industry*, 2nd ed. (1938); "Community Chest Rift in Elm City," *Bridgeport Telegram*, October 7, 1926, 8; "Chamber of Commerce Will Ask Official Support for Park Measure," *Bridgeport Telegram*, February 18, 1927.

6. "Clarence Blakeslee," *Who's Who in Commerce and Industry*, 2nd ed. (1938).

7. Motley, *Equal Justice Under Law*, 43–44.

8. Motley, *Equal Justice Under Law*, 45.

9. Motley, *Equal Justice Under Law*, 45.

10. Motley, *Equal Justice Under Law*, 43.

11. See Dr. James R. Angell to Clarence Blakeslee, January 10, 1933, James Rowland Angell Records, box 34, folder 372, Yale University Manuscripts and Archives; Fay Campbell to Clarence Blakeslee, October 15, 1925, Dwight Hall Records, folder 113, box 4, Yale University Manuscripts and Archives; Dr. James R. Angell to Clarence Blakeslee, January 10, 1933, Angell Records, box 34, folder 372; Clarence Blakeslee to Dr. James R. Angell, March 30, 1932, Angell Records, box 34, folder 372; "Local YMCA Man Honored at New Haven," *Bridgeport Telegram*, November 4, 1921, 6; Wallace, *Yale's Ironmen*, 41 ("helped a lot of kids").

12. Motley, *Equal Justice Under Law*, 46.

13. See Joe M. Richardson, "Fisk University: The First Critical Years." The university was incorporated as "Fisk University" in 1867; Joe M. Richardson, *A History of Fisk University, 1865–1946*, ix.

14. See James D. Anderson, *The Education of Blacks in the South, 1860–1935*, 244–45, 251, 263–64; Cohen, *Fisk University*, 9 (the term "Negro Harvard" bestowed by the *New York Herald Tribune* in 1947); Richardson, *A History of Fisk University*, 82, 124–25.

15. See Gilpin, "Charles S. Johnson and the Race Relations Institutes at Fisk University"; Anderson, *The Education of Blacks in the South*, 251, 263–64; Richardson, *A History of Fisk University*, 53, 113–14, 126–27, 131, 137, 140–42.

16. Motley, *Equal Justice Under Law*, 42; Richardson, *A History of Fisk University*, 131.

17. See Weller, *The New Haven Railroad*; "A Brief History of the New Haven Railroad," available at www.nhrhta.org/htdocs/history.htm (last accessed

August 30, 2016); "'New Haven' Traffic Is Still Rising," *Hartford Courant*, July 2, 1944, A4; Motley, *Equal Justice Under Law*, 47.

18. See Turner, "Abolitionism in Kentucky"; Griffler, *Front Line of Freedom*. The quote is found in Klein, *History of the Louisville and Nashville Railroad*, 27.

19. See Klein, *History of the Louisville and Nashville Railroad*, 102–3.

20. See Motley, *Equal Justice Under Law*, 47; Du Bois, *Darkwater*, 176–77; Louisville and Nashville Railroad Menu, May 1941, record group 1, box 1, conference memorabilia, 1941, Columbia Motley Collection.

21. See Motley, *Equal Justice Under Law*, 49–51. In a landmark and controversial work originally published in 1957, Professor E. Franklin Frazier, a Fisk sociologist, discussed and condemned the materialism and anti-intellectualism of middle-class Blacks. See Frazier, *Black Bourgeoisie*.

22. See Richardson, *A History of Fisk University*, 132–35; Motley, *Equal Justice Under Law*, 51–52. Washington Square College was the undergraduate unit of NYU, established in 1914. See Frusciano and Pettit, *New York University and the City*, 151.

23. See Frusciano and Pettit, *New York University and the City*, 149, 162–63. The quote is found at 181.

24. See Frusciano and Pettit, *New York University and the City*, 151, 159, 162–63; Motley, *Equal Justice Under Law*, 55; see also Transcript of Constance Juanita Baker, New York University, October 1943 (on file with author). Distinctions should be made among the various NYU colleges and schools. For example, whereas NYU used selective admissions in the early to mid-twentieth century to weed out undesirable elements, particularly Jews, Washington Square College did not follow such a policy and its student body was disproportionately Jewish and immigrant. See Frusciano and Pettit, *New York University and the City*, 167, 184.

25. Baker's recollections are found in Motley Reminiscences, 149, 150, 161.

26. See Frusciano and Pettit, *New York University and the City*, 143, 170–73, 184.

27. See Motley, *Equal Justice Under Law*, 52–53; McDuffie, *Sojourning for Freedom*, 93, 138, 140, 141–43, 145; Gerald Horne, *Black Liberation/Red Scare*, 114–16. For a discussion of the CPUSA and its appeals to Black Americans, see Woods, *Black Struggle, Red Scare*, 22, 53, 88–89, 132–33, 161–64.

28. See Motley, *Equal Justice Under Law*, 52–53; "Lewis Demands Full Negro Rights; Lashes Warmakers, Denounces FBI," *Daily Worker*, April 27, 1940.

29. See Motley, *Equal Justice Under Law*, 53; see also Transcript of Constance Juanita Baker, New York University, October 1943 (on file with author).

30. See Motley, *Equal Justice Under Law*, 34; J. Clay Smith, *Emancipation*, 127, 162.

31. See Cardozier, *Colleges and Universities in World War II*, 116, 211–12.

32. See Cardozier, *Colleges and Universities in World War II*, 116, 211–12. The federal government helped keep many colleges afloat during the war by subsidizing defense-related educational efforts. See Kandel, *The Impact of War upon American Education*, 168. On women's participation in higher education, see National Center for Education Statistics, *120 Years of American Education*, 68, 75–76. On women's work during World War II, see Honey, *Creating Rosie the Riveter*.

33. "Ghost town" quote is from Motley "Reflections." *102 Columbia L. Review* 6 (2002), 1449. Figures are from "Report of the Dean," Columbia Law School (hereafter cited as "Report of the Dean"), 4–5; see also "Constance Baker Motley," in Salkin, ed., *Pioneering Women Lawyers*, 43–52, and Goebel, *A History of the School of Law, Columbia University*, 348, 352. The first few women had been admitted to Columbia Law School in 1927. See Whitney S. Bagall, "A Brief History of Women at CLS: Part II" (2002), http://web.archive.org/web/20030920070540/http://www.law .columbia.edu/law_school/communications/reports/Fall2002/brief2.

34. Conceding that this traditional curriculum was in fact a problem, the Columbia Law School faculty sought to reform it during the 1940s on grounds that it did not effectively convey critical information about the substance and procedures of law. By the time these changes fully took root, Baker was long gone. See Record in the School of Law, Columbia University, Constance Juanita Baker, May 31, 1946 (on file with author); "Report of the Dean," 14–22.

35. See Whitney S. Bagall, "A Brief History of Women at CLS: Part II" (2002), http://www.law.columbia.edu/law_school/communications/reports /Fall2002/brief quoting the Law School News; Record in the School of Law, Columbia University, Constance Juanita Baker, May 31, 1946 (on file with author); Motley, *Equal Justice Under Law*, 95. On Dowling, see Slauter, "From 'Equality Before the Law' to 'Separate but Equal,'" 15; Robert L. Carter, *A Matter of Law*, 31.

36. See Motley, *Equal Justice Under Law*, 95; Barbara Aronstein Black, "Something to Remember, Something to Celebrate," 1457. Bagall, "A Brief History of Women at CLS: Part II" (2002), http://www.law.columbia.edu/law _school/communications/reports/Fall2002/brief quoting the Law School News; Abzug quote is from Oral Histories of Women Graduates: 1930s and 40s, available at https://web.archive.org/web/20140605063027/www .law.columbia.edu/alumni/highlights/articles/oralhistory/experience.

37. See Record in the School of Law, Columbia University, Constance Juanita Baker, May 31, 1946; Motley Reminiscences, 172–73; see also "Milton Handler, 95, Is Dead; Antitrust Expert Wrote Laws," *New York Times*, November 12, 1998; Fuld, "Professor Milton Handler."

38. See Record in the School of Law, Columbia University, Constance Juanita

Baker, May 31, 1946 (on file with author); quotes are found in Motley, *Equal Justice Under Law*, 59.

39. Motley, *Equal Justice Under Law*, 59; Motley Reminiscences, 148.

40. Motley, *Equal Justice Under Law*, 59. For labor statistics, see U.S. Department of Commerce, Bureau of the Census, *Bicentennial Edition: Historical Statistics of the United States, Colonial Times to 1970* (1975), 131–32, 139, available at www.census.gov/library/publications/1975/compendia/hist _stats_colonial-1970.html (last accessed September 30, 2016). Women's labor force participation rose to 38 percent during the war years, but by 1950 had dropped to 34 percent. See Mitra Toossi, "A Century of Change: The U.S. Labor Force, 1950–2050," *Monthly Labor Review* (May 2002): 15–16, 18. On Black women and work, see Giddings, *When and Where I Enter*, 232–33.

41. See Motley, *Equal Justice Under Law*, 49–51; see also Salkin, ed., *Pioneering Women Lawyers*, 44.

4. A FORTUITOUS MEETING WITH "MR. CIVIL RIGHTS": THURGOOD MARSHALL AND AN OFFER NOT TO BE REFUSED

1. Motley, *Equal Justice Under Law*, 58. In 1939, the NAACP and its legal affairs department became separate organizations; the legal side of the organization became known as the NAACP Legal Defense Fund (LDF).

2. Lawrence Alexander, "Early Days Recalled by Judge, *Times-Picayune*, March 31, 1985, A34. Several prominent Black male graduates of Columbia Law School also could not find jobs. See Motley, *Equal Justice Under Law*, 52–53.

3. See "Report of the Dean," 6; Goebel, *A History of the School of Law, Columbia University*, 358.

4. See Motley, *Equal Justice Under Law*, 58–59.

5. Author interview with Mark Tushnet, March 30, 2016; Juan Williams, *Thurgood Marshall*, 190–91, 230; Zelden, *Thurgood Marshall*, 88–89.

6. See Zelden, *Thurgood Marshall*, 19; Juan Williams, *Thurgood Marshall*, 50.

7. See "Are Working Wives Less Moral?," *Jet* 7, no. 13 (February 3, 1955): 25; Catherine Marshall, "An Introduction by Mrs. Peter Marshall," *Life* 41, no. 26 (December 24, 1956): 2–3; Robert Coughlan, "Changing Roles in Modern Marriage," *Life* 41, no. 26 (December 24, 1956): 115; Cott, *Public Vows*, 157.

8. Thurgood Marshall to Walter White, November 7, 1945, NAACP Papers, LOC, box III: J-6, folder 14; Motley, *Equal Justice Under Law*, 58; Motley Reminiscences, 171.

9. "Constance Baker Motley," in Gilbert and Moore, *Particular Passions*, 138; Motley, *Equal Justice*, 58.

5. "THEY HOVERED OVER AND CARED FOR EACH OTHER":
THE UNCOMMON UNION OF CONSTANCE BAKER AND JOEL MOTLEY JR.

1. See David Levering Lewis, *When Harlem Was in Vogue* (New York: Oxford, 1981), 27.

2. Motley, *Equal Justice Under Law*, 55.

3. On the YWCA, see Height, "The Adult Education Program of the YWCA Among Negroes"; Weisenfeld, "The Harlem YWCA and the Secular City, 1904–1945."

4. The quote "new, young, dark" is from Sarah A. Anderson, " 'The Place to Go,' " 384; "Negro capital" is from Lewis, *When Harlem Was in Vogue*, 27. See also Mjagkij, *Light in the Darkness*, 119. The Harlem YMCA also served as a safe space for homosexuals. See Schmidt, "White Pervert."

5. Email from Joel Motley III to author, September 2, 2020.

6. See Guillory, *Decatur, Illinois*, 19, 46, 72; Agersborg and Hatfield, "The Biology of a Sewage Treatment Plant."

7. See Guillory, *Decatur, Illinois*, 62; Cha-Jua, "A Warlike Demonstration"; Chicoine, "One Glorious Season."

8. See *Decatur Daily Review*, November 23, 1928; Year: *1940*; 1923 Decatur City Directory, 369; Census Place: *Decatur, Macon, Illinois*; Roll: *T627_843*; Page: *61A*; Enumeration District: *58-4;* Year: *1930*; Census Place: *Decatur, Macon, Illinois*; Roll: *538*; Page: *10B*.

9. See *Decatur Daily Review*, April 1923.

10. Year: *1940*; Census Place: *Jacksonville, Morgan, Illinois*; Roll: *T627_861*; Page: *34A*; Enumeration District: *69-25;* Enumeration District: 0017; Image: 22.0; FHL microfilm: 2340273; Joel Motley Sr., U.S. Census, 1930; see also author interview with Joel Motley III, June 27, 2015; Mehr, *An Illustrated History of Illinois Public Mental Health Services, 1847 to 2000*, 28, 300, 338, 355–56, 398, 436. For background on Jacksonville State and mental health reform in Illinois, see Lighter, *Asylum, Prison, and Poorhouse*, 13–30, 109–11.

11. See Illinois Department of Public Health, *Della Motley, Medical Certificate of Death*, Springfield, December 11, 1955. On conditions in facilities, see Lighter, *Asylum, Prison, and Poorhouse*, 109–11; Mehr, *An Illustrated History of Illinois Public Mental Health Services, 1847 to 2000*, 28, 300, 338, 355–56, 398, 436; Grob, *The Mad Among Us*, 1–2, 113–15, 130–31; Grob, *Mental Illness and American Society, 1875–1940*, 101–5.

12. For discussions of the impact on children of maternal mental illness, see Walsh et al., "Attachment and Coping Strategies in Middle Childhood Children Whose Mothers Have a Mental Problem"; Grunebaum, *Mentally Ill Mothers and Their Children*; also author interview with Joel Motley III, June 27, 2015.

13. Motley, *Equal Justice Under Law*, 26.

14. Motley, *Equal Justice Under Law*, 55.

15. See "Nine Agents Will Attend Seminar in Atlantic City," *New York Amsterdam News*, July 18, 1959, 8; "Record Month in Realty Transactions," *New York Amsterdam News*, September 10, 1949, 25; Motley, *Equal Justice Under Law*, 55.

16. See Joseph Wershba, "A Fight for Justice Gets Harder as It Becomes More Successful," *New York Post*, March 8, 1961, 48; "World Elks Plan Award to Mrs. C. Motley," *New Haven Register*, August 18, 1963; "She Reached Her Goal," *Afro-American*, February 11, 1961; "1st Negro Woman Attorney Appears in Mississippi Court: Bit Scared, but Enjoys Experience," *Chicago Defender*, February 11, 1950. The quote from Joel Motley Jr. is found in Bill Berry, "Five Strong Black Men Support and Encourage Famous Wives," *Ebony*, April 1978, 154–58.

17. "Embarrassment" from author interview with Joel Motley III, June 27, 2015; see also *1942 Decatur City Directory*, 297; email from Melinda Kent to author, November 18, 2016.

18. Statistics found in National Center for Education Statistics, *120 Years of American Education*, 7–8.

19. "Devotion" quoted in author interview with Hon. Anne Thompson, January 19, 2015.

6. "A PROFESSIONAL WOMAN":
BREAKING BARRIERS AT WORK AND IN THE COURTROOM

1. While Motley worked at the Inc. Fund, the organization twice moved, first to West 43rd Street and then to 10 Columbus Circle. See Greenberg, *Crusaders in the Courts*, 154; "NAACP Legal Defense and Educational Fund: A Finding Aid to the Collection in the Library of Congress," Library of Congress, revised March 2018, http://rs5.loc.gov/service/mss/eadxmlmss/eadpdfmss/2015/ms015025.pdf.

2. See Williams, *Thurgood Marshall*, 93, 178; Greenberg, *Crusaders in the Courts*, 27, 30, 32, 33. "Walking on eggs" from Kluger, *Simple Justice*, 273.

3. See Williams, *Thurgood Marshall*, 93, 178; Tushnet, *The NAACP's Legal Strategy Against Segregated Education, 1925–1950*, 29; Sullivan, *Lift Every Voice*, 298. "Hostile" from author interview with Michael Meltzer, May 9, 2013. "Family," from Cole and Greenaway, "Judge Constance Baker Motley and the Struggle for Equal Justice," 6.

4. Ball, *A Defiant Life*, 62; Zeldon, *Thurgood Marshall*, 39.

5. See Williams, *Thurgood Marshall*, 164, 190–93; Greenberg, *Crusaders in the Courts*, 24–25. "Wear life" quote from Zeldon, *Thurgood Marshall*, 16.

6. Motley Reminiscences, 170–72.

7. Motley, *Equal Justice Under Law*, 66–68.

8. Motley, *Equal Justice Under Law*, 66–67, 69; Motley Reminiscences,

420; Tushnet, *Making Civil Rights Law*, 27, 35–36; see also Steele v. Louisville and Nashville Railroad, 323 U.S. 192 (1944) (holding that union owed Blacks duty of fair representation); Morgan v. Virginia, 328 U.S. 373 (1946) (state segregation statute unlawfully burdened interstate commerce).

9. Motley, *Equal Justice Under Law*, 70–71; see also McCready v. Byrd, 73 A.2d 8 (1950), cert. denied, 340 U.S. 827 (exclusion of Black student violated equal protection).

10. Motley, *Equal Justice Under Law*, 66–67, 265 n. 21; Rice v. Elmore, 165 F.2d 387 (4th Cir. 1947), cert. denied, 333 U.S. 875 (1948) (exclusion of Blacks from primary unlawful); Shelley v. Kramer, 334 U.S. 1 (1948) (judicial enforcement of racially restrictive covenants unlawful).

11. Motley, *Equal Justice Under Law*, 71.

12. On the significance of the state and the city and of Black soldiers' voting rights efforts, see Dittmer, *Local People*, 1, 2, 3–19. In Smith v. Allwright, 321 U.S. 649 (1944), the U.S. Supreme Court outlawed nominally private organization's perpetuation of discrimination in the electoral process (the racially restrictive "white primary").

13. See Bates v. Batte (5th Cir. 1951); Dittmer, *Local People*, 20, 36; Tushnet, *The NAACP's Legal Strategy Against Segregated Education*, 5–6, 88–89. Bates was fired in retaliation for participation in the case and replaced by a new plaintiff, who also was fired. Motley, *Equal Justice Under Law*, 72.

14. News clipping, n.d., Columbia Papers, Record Group 2, Series 5; Robert L. Carter, *A Matter of Law*, 77–78.

15. Lawrence Alexander, "Early Days Recalled by Judge," *Times-Picayune*, March 31, 1985, A34; Motley, *Equal Justice Under Law*, 71; Dittmer, *Local People*, 9, 12–15. "Everybody's choice" was McMillen, *Dark Journey*, 2, 202, 233–34.

16. News clipping, n.d., Columbia Papers, Record Group 2, Series 5; see also Motley, *Equal Justice Under Law*, 71–74; Dittmer, *Local People*, 19–20; O'Brien, *We Shall Not Be Moved*, 15; Robert L. Carter, *A Matter of Law*, 36; Motley, *Equal Justice Under Law*, 75; Motley Reminiscences, 466.

17. Motley, *Equal Justice Under Law*, 72–74; news clipping, n.d., Columbia Papers, Record Group 2, Series 5; see also Meier and Rudwick, "Attorneys Black and White"; Marie Brenner, "Judge Motley's Verdict," *New Yorker*, May 16, 1994.

18. Motley, *Equal Justice Under Law*, 77–78; "First Negro Woman Attorney Appears in Miss. Court: Bit Scared but Enjoys Experience," *Chicago Defender*, February 11, 1950. "Scared" from Brenner, "Judge Motley's Verdict."

19. Motley, *Equal Justice Under Law*, 75–76, 77; news clipping, n.d., Columbia Papers, Record Group 2, Series 5.

20. See "First Negro Woman Attorney Appears in Mississippi Court"; Robert L. Carter, *A Matter of Law*, 78.

21. See Bates v. Batte, 187 F.2d 142 (5th Circ. 1951).

22. See Bates v. Batte, 342 U.S. 815 (1951) (denying certiorari); Motley, *Equal Justice Under Law*, 78.

23. Robert L. Carter, *A Matter of Law*, 78.

24. Tushnet, *The NAACP's Legal Strategy*, 96–97, 103.

25. Tushnet, *The NAACP's Legal Strategy*, 104.

26. "Family" from Cole and Greenaway, "Judge Constance Baker Motley and the Struggle for Equal Justice."

27. See Tushnet, *Making Civil Rights Law*, 36; Motley Reminiscences, 178.

28. See Tushnet, *Making Civil Rights Law*, 35–36; Robert L. Carter, *A Matter of Law*, 57–58; Greenberg, *Crusaders in the Court*, 27–29; "Marian P. (Perry) Yankauer, Urban Planner and Civil Rights Activist, at 79," *Worcester Telegram & Gazette* (Massachusetts), January 31, 1994, B5.

29. Constance Baker Motley to Thurgood Marshall, May 25, 1949, NAACP Papers, Library of Congress, Administrative File, box III: J-6, folder 14.

30. Constance Baker Motley to Thurgood Marshall and Roy Wilkins, June 20, 1949, NAACP Papers, Library of Congress, Administrative File, box III: J-6, folder 14.

31. Minutes, Meeting of the Executive Committee of the Board of Directors, NAACP Legal Defense and Educational Fund, Inc., May 7, 1951, p. 2. The salaries for the pair remained equal in 1955: $7,000 per year. Meeting of the Executive Committee of the Board of Directors, NAACP Legal Defense and Educational Fund, Inc., December 7, 1955, p. 2. On teacher salary equalization cases, see Brown-Nagin, *Courage to Dissent*, 90–91.

32. See Giddings, *When and Where I Enter*, 232–34, 237, 245, 256–57; Jacqueline Jones, *Labor of Love, Labor of Sorrow*, 201–5, 209.

33. See, for example, Ransby, *Ella Baker and the Black Freedom Movement*, 106, 146, 173–74, 183–84, 297; Giddings, *When and Where I Enter*, 258; Theoharis, *The Rebellious Life of Mrs. Rosa Parks*, 116–22, 141–44; Chana Kai Lee, *For Freedom's Sake*, 43, 116–19; Glenda Elizabeth Gilmore, *Defying Dixie*, 320–21, 324–26; MacLean, *Freedom Is Not Enough*, 119–23; Brown-Nagin, "The Transformation of a Social Movement into Law?"

34. See Williams, *Thurgood Marshall*, 261; Jonas, *Freedom's Sword*, 73.

35. The "Biologically" quote is from Marilyn Bender, "Black Woman in Civil Rights: Is She a Second-Class Citizen?," *New York Times*, September 2, 1969, 42. The "nitty-gritty" quote is from Jonas, *Freedom's Sword*, 341–42; see also Jonas, *Freedom's Sword*, 26, 46, 61, 304–5; MacLean, *Freedom Is Not Enough*, 122–23. Black women generally are paid less than other women and men; they earn 65 cents for every dollar earned by a white male. The wage gap persists even when these women are college-

educated. See Patten, "Racial, Gender Wage Gaps Persist in U.S. Despite Some Progress."

7. "WE ALL FELT THE EXCRUCIATING PRESSURE": MAKING HISTORY IN *BROWN V. BOARD OF EDUCATION*

1. Arthur Krock, "Supreme Court's Questions on School Segregation," *New York Times*, October 27, 1953, 26.

2. See Arthur B. Spingarn, Letter to the Editor, *New York Times*, November 6, 1953, 26; NAACP LDF Press Release, "Filing of Brief Ends 22 Hectic Weeks for N.A.A.C.P. Lawyers," November 16, 1953; Arthur Krock, "High Quality of Briefs in Separate School Cases," *New York Times*, December 1, 1953, C2.

3. See NAACP Legal Defense and Educational Fund, Inc., Monthly Report, June 15–September, 15, 1953, p. 2; NAACP LDF Press Release, "NAACP Intensifies Drive Against School Jim Crow," June 11, 1953; NAACP LDF Press Release, "Filing of Brief Ends 22 Hectic Weeks for N.A.A.C.P. Lawyers," November 16, 1953; Motley, *Equal Justice Under Law*, 85.

4. See Kurland and Casper, eds., *Brown v. Board of Education (1954 & 1955)*, vol. 49, pp. 3, 11, 317, 322, 333. "Finest hour" from Cole and Greenaway, "Judge Constance Baker Motley and the Struggle for Equal Justice," 10.

5. See Kurland and Casper, eds., *Brown v. Board of Education (1954 & 1955)*, vol. 49, pp. 3, 11, 317, 322, 333, 523. See also Greenberg, *Crusaders in the Courts*, 168–94; Kluger, *Simple Justice*, 617–19, 624–26. "Formidable," "brilliant," and "exhilarating" from Robert L. Carter, *A Matter of Law*, 126; Motley Reminiscences, 419.

6. See *Brown v. Board of Education*, 347 U.S. 483, 493 (1954).

7. See "Drive Urged to Back School Bias Decision," *New York Times*, September 6, 1954, 15; Motley, *Equal Justice Under Law*, 84; Kluger, *Simple Justice*, 709–10; Marie Brenner, "Judge Motley's Verdict," *New Yorker*, May 16, 1994, 65.

8. Motley, *Equal Justice Under Law*, 103. For a discussion of *Sweatt v. Painter* and its relationship to *Brown*, see Tushnet, *The NAACP's Legal Strategy*, 125–37; Lavergne, *Before Brown*, 5–6.

9. See NAACP Legal Defense and Educational Fund, Inc., Monthly Report, June 15–September, 15, 1953, p. 2; Brief for Appellants in Nos. 1, 2 and 3 and for Respondents in No. 5 on Further Re-argument, Brown v. Board of Education (October 1954); Motley, *Equal Justice Under Law*, 103; "nightmare" at ibid., 85. "Girl" from Brenner, "Judge Motley's Verdict."

10. See NAACP LDF Press Release, "Filing of Brief Ends 22 Hectic Weeks for N.A.A.C.P. Lawyers," November 16, 1953; Juan Williams, *Thurgood Marshall*, 230–31, 234; "delicate negotiations" from Motley, *Equal Justice Under Law*, 110.

11. See NAACP LDF Press Release, "NAACP Attorneys Tell Justices That Dixie Education Pattern Violates 14th Amendment," December 12, 1952.

12. Greenberg, *Crusaders in the Courts*, 27–28, 43–44.

13. Greenberg, *Crusaders in the Courts*, 86–90, 93–102. A practical consideration partly motivated the Delaware assignment; Greenberg's in-laws lived in Delaware, which meant that he would have housing when he traveled to the state, saving the Inc. Fund money. It also helped that Marshall had hired Greenberg on the recommendation of a friend, who called the young Columbia Law School graduate "brilliant." Forever after, Marshall called him brilliant, too. The masterwork on the Groveland case is Gilbert King, *Devil in the Grove*. "Worst case" is from ibid., 256; see also Jacey Fortin, "Florida Pardons the Groveland Four, 70 Years after the Jim Crow–era Rape Case," *New York Times,* Jan. 11, 2019.

14. "Drudge" from Marie Brenner, "Judge Motley's Verdict."

15. See Constance Baker Motley to Thurgood Marshall, n.d., NAACP Papers; author interview with Joel Motley III. On delayed childbirth, see Forest et al., "Cohort Differences in the Transition to Motherhood."

16. Motley's leave of absence was not called "maternity leave," as that did not yet widely exist; maternity leave was introduced as a national policy in 1993. See Berger and Waldfogel, "Maternity Leave and the Employment of New Mothers in the United States."

17. See Spock, *Dr. Spock's Baby and Child Care*; see also Eric Pace, "Benjamin Spock, World's Pediatrician, Dies at 94," *New York Times*, March 17, 1998.

18. See, for example, Harrington, *Women Lawyers*, 24, 31, 196–97, 236.

19. See NAACP LDF Press Release, "Filing of Brief Ends 22 Hectic Weeks for N.A.A.C.P. Lawyers," November 16, 1953, and sources cited above.

20. Motley, *Equal Justice Under Law*, 106, 110.

21. See Friedan, *The Feminine Mystique*; also Meyerowitz, "Beyond the Feminine Mystique"; Vandenberg-Daves, "Teaching Motherhood in History."

22. See Giddings, *When and Where I Enter*, 217, 248–49, 251, 256; see also Frazier, *The Negro Family in the United States*, 288.

23. See Giddings, *When and Where I Enter*, 248.

24. See Joseph Wershba, "A Fight for Justice Gets Harder as It Becomes More Successful," *New York Post*, March 8, 1961, 48; Ann Geracimos, "Mother on a Wing," *New York Herald Tribune*, 1962; author interview with Joel Motley III, June 27, 2015; author interview with Constance Royster, June 24–25, 2014; electronic message from Constance Royster to author, December 8–9, 2016; electronic message from Joel Motley to author, December 11, 2016.

25. See Jacqueline Jones, *Labor of Love*, 21–22, 24–25, 110–16, 210–11; Palmer, *Domesticity and Dirt*, 8. On the role of Black working women in creating

more egalitarian family structures, see Landry, *Black Working Wives*, 75, 80–81.

26. See Okin, *Justice, Gender, and the Family*; Stoltzfus, *Citizen, Mother, Worker*; Dinner, "The Universal Childcare Debate." For Motley's admission, see "Work If You Can Pay the Maid, Says Woman Judge to Women," *Hartford Courant*, January 27, 1966, D23.

27. Wershba, "A Fight for Justice Gets Harder as It Becomes More Successful," 48.

28. Author interview with Nell Moskowitz, April 17, 2012; Motley Reminiscences, 121; "She Reached Her Goal," *Afro-American*, February 11, 1961.

8. "THE FIGHT HAS JUST BEGUN": THE DECADE-LONG SLOG TO DESEGREGATE THE UNIVERSITY OF FLORIDA COLLEGE OF LAW

1. "Fight has just begun" quoted in Juan Williams, *Thurgood Marshall*, 229. On *Brown II*, see Greenberg, *Crusaders in the Courts*, 203–6.

2. See Motley, "Twenty Years Later: My Personal Recollections of Brown and Some Personal Comments on Its Impact and Implementation," University of Notre Dame, March 21, 1974, Smith Motley Papers, box 14, folder 2, p. 16.

3. See Burhop, *Okahumpka*, 17–18, 47–48, 49, 51, 54.

4. See "South's Most Patient Man: Virgil Hawkins Tells 10-Year Fight to Study Law in Florida," *Chicago Daily Defender*, November 5, 1959, A11; Dubin, "Virgil Hawkins," 915–18.

5. See Hawkins v. Board of Control, 60 S.2d 162 (1952).

6. Motley, *Equal Justice Under Law*, 113.

7. See Motley, *Equal Justice Under Law*, 113; see also Green, *The Negro Motorist Green-Book*.

8. Motley, *Equal Justice Under Law*, 113.

9. Hawkins v. Florida Board of Control, 347 U.S. 971 (1954).

10. Motley, *Equal Justice Under Law*, 113; Hawkins v. Florida Board of Control, 347 U.S. 971 (1954).

11. See Hawkins v. Board of Control, 83 So.2d 20, 24 (1955).

12. See Hawkins v. Board of Control, 83 So.2d at 25 (Justice Terrell, specially concurring).

13. See "Florida Rebuffs Supreme Court on Bias Decision," *New York Times*, March 9, 1957, 1; Hawkins v. Board of Control, 350 U.S. 413, 414 (1956); Hawkins v. Board of Control, 93 So.2d 354 (Fla. 1957); Motley, *Equal Justice Under Law*, 116–17.

14. See "One Judge Still Leads to Another," *Afro-American*, February 8, 1958, 3; Hawkins v. Board of Control, 162 F. Supp. 851 (N.D. Fla 1958); Motley, *Equal Justice Under Law*, 116–17.

15. See Motley, *Equal Justice Under Law*, 117; "Nine-Year Florida Fight Won,"

Afro-American, June 28, 1958, 1; "South's Most Patient Man: Virgil Hawkins Tells 10-Year Fight to Study Law in Florida," *Chicago Daily Defender*, November 5, 1959, A11. Starke left school after three semesters, owing in part to the pressure associated with being a pioneer. George Allen was the first Black graduate of the University of Florida School of Law. See Taylor, "A History of Race and Gender at the University of Florida Levin College of Law, 1909–2001."

16. See "Admitted to Florida Bar After 28-Year Fight," *Afro-American*, February 26, 1977, 8.

9. "WE MADE A MISTAKE": "POOR CHARACTER," "LOOSE MORALS," AND UNTOLD SACRIFICES IN PURSUIT OF HIGHER EDUCATION AT THE UNIVERSITY OF ALABAMA

1. Ollie Stewart, "Europe Loves Lucy," *Afro-American*, February 25, 1956, 1; Autherine J. Lucy, "Miss Autherine Lucy Tells of Hectic Alabama U. Crusade," *Atlanta Daily World*, February 9, 1956, 1.

2. See James, "Alabama U. Girds for Trouble: Two Negroes to Enter— Governor Defiant," *Southern School News*, n.d.; E. Culpepper Clark, *The Schoolhouse Door*, 163, 180–88, 194; Motley Reminiscences, 292–93; Greenberg, *Crusaders in the Courts*, 225–26.

3. Stewart, "Europe Loves Lucy," 1; "Lucy Story Makes Front Pages All over World," *Afro-American*, April 7, 1956, 5.

4. "Soviet Press Play Up Autherine Lucy Case," *Plain Dealer*, March 23, 1956, 1; "South Americans Show Great Interest in Lucy Incidents," *Afro-American*, March 24, 1956, 8.

5. "Supporting Miss Lucy: The NCNW Passes Resolution," *Washington Post*, February 28, 1958, at 30; "A Salute: World's Best Loved Lady, Mrs. FDR Has Praise for Autherine and Boycotters," *Chicago Daily Defender*, March 24, 1956, 8; "Miss Lucy Goes to College," *New York Times*, February 6, 1956, 22.

6. "Alabama U. Alumnus Urges Ban on Co-ed," *New York Times*, February 22, 1956, 14; Peter Kihss, "Negro Co-ed Is Suspended to Curb Alabama Clashes," *New York Times*, February 7, 1956; Peter Kihss, "Negro Co-ed Asks End of Suspension," *New York Times*, February 8, 1956, 1; "Nobody's Neutral About Lucy," *Afro-American*, March 10, 1956, 8.

7. Autherine J. Lucy, "Miss Autherine Lucy Tells of Hectic Alabama U. Crusade," *Atlanta Daily World*, February 9, 1956, 1; Ruth Rolen, "Miss Lucy Steals Philadelphia's Heart," *Afro-American*, January 23, 1956, 18.

8. "Marshall Hits Red Report on Autherine Lucy," *Atlanta Daily World*, March 8, 1956, 5; Ethel L. Payne, "Autherine Lucy Youngest of 9 in Alabama Family," *Chicago Daily Defender*, February 8, 1956, 5; Robert H. Denley, "Relative, School Aide Say Miss Lucy Should Give Up," *Chicago Daily*

Defender, March 10, 1956, 3. "Mess" quote is from Lee and Shores, *The Gentle Giant of Dynamite Hill*, 164.

9. Samuel Hoskins, "She'll Always Be Our 'Miss Lucy,'" *Afro-American*, April 28, 1956, 6; "Miss Lucy Gives Up Her Fight to Enter Alabama U. During Current Semester," *Washington Post*, March 8, 1956, 1. After her expulsion, Lucy ended her effort to attend AU that same semester and eventually entirely ended her role in the case. See "Autherine Lucy Calls It Quits," *Chicago Daily Defender*, March 27, 1957.

10. E. Culpepper Clark, *The Schoolhouse Door*, 3–7, 17; Lee and Shores, *The Gentle Giant of Dynamite Hill*, 155.

11. University of Alabama Summary, Columbia Motley Papers, p. 2.

12. University of Alabama Summary, Columbia Motley Papers, p. 2.

13. University of Alabama Summary, Columbia Motley Papers, p. 3; Tushnet, *Making Civil Rights Law*, 238.

14. See Transcript, Lucy v. Adams, U.S. District Court, Birmingham, Alabama, June 29–30, 1955, 122–24. The transcript mistakenly refers to the child as five months old; in the press of court, the lawyer may have miscalculated the child's age and Myers did not correct him. Or the transcriptionist may have mistakenly referred to the child as "five" rather than "two" months old. See also Peter Kihss, "Negro Co-ed Asks End of Suspension," *New York Times*, February 8, 1956, 1; "God Help Alabama!," *Chicago Daily Defender*, February 22, 1956, 11; E. Culpepper Clark, *The Schoolhouse Door*, 54, 56, 105–6. Notably, well before and long after the UA desegregation case, UA cited nonmarital sex or pregnancy as a basis for disqualifying candidates. Clark, *The Schoolhouse Door*, 42–43.

15. White, *Too Heavy a Load*, 52–54, 69–72, 128–31.

16. See Muhammad, *The Condemnation of Blackness*.

17. Peter Kihss, "Negro Co-ed Asks End of Suspension," *New York Times*, February 8, 1956, 1; "God Help Alabama!," *Chicago Daily Defender*, February 22, 1956, 11; E. Culpepper Clark, *The Schoolhouse Door*, 54, 56, 105–6.

18. See Transcript, Lucy v. Adams, U.S. District Court, Birmingham, Alabama, June 29–30, 1955, 123. Shores made but quickly withdrew a contempt motion predicated on the university's rejection of Myers. See E. Culpepper Clark, *The Schoolhouse Door*, 85. See also "God Help Alabama!," *Chicago Daily Defender*, February 22, 1956, 11; Clark, *The Schoolhouse Door*, 54, 56, 105–6. "Bad publicity" from Motley, *Equal Justice Under Law*, 122.

19. Giddings, *When and Where I Enter*, 45, 151–52, 256; Higginbotham, *Righteous Discontent*, 14–15, 145, 189–90, 185–229; see also Kunzel, "White Neurosis, Black Pathology," 306. Notably, Black communities tended to accommodate the children born of nonmarital relationships, whereas as social norms compelled single and pregnant white women to place such children up for adoption. See Solinger, *Wake Up Little Susie*, 6–7, 12–13.

Nevertheless, Black single mothers remained objects of scorn within and outside of Black communities. See ibid., 63–65, 187–88.

20. Email interview with Constance Royster, December 22, 2017; "God Help Alabama!," *Chicago Daily Defender*, February 22, 1956, 11; E. Culpepper Clark, *The Schoolhouse Door*, 54, 56, 105–6. "Dropped" from Motley, *Equal Justice Under Law*, 122.

21. See Colvin, *Twice Toward Justice*; Margot Adler, "Before Rosa Parks, There Was Claudette Colvin," NPR, March 15, 2009; Garrow, *Bearing the Cross*, 67, 69, 139–40.

22. E. Culpepper Clark, *The Schoolhouse Door*, 85–87.

23. Shores, *Gentle Giant*, 159.

24. James, "Alabama U. Girds for Trouble: Two Negroes to Enter—Governor Defiant," *Southern School News*, n.d.; E. Culpepper Clark, *The Schoolhouse Door*, 163, 180–88, 194.

25. "Miss Autherine Lucy Tells of Hectic Alabama U. Crusade," *Atlanta Daily World*, February 9, 1956, 1; James, "Alabama U. Girds for Trouble: Two Negroes to Enter—Governor Defiant," *Southern School News*, n.d.; E. Culpepper Clark, *The Schoolhouse Door*, 163, 180–88, 194; Motley Reminiscences, 292–93; Greenberg, *Crusaders in the Courts*, 225–26.

26. Peter Kihss, "Negro Co-ed Asks End of Suspension," *New York Times*, February 8, 1956, 1; "Courageous Miss Lucy Denies Being High-Handed," *Pittsburgh Courier*, March 3, 1956, 2.

27. Motley Reminiscences, 282–84; Motley, *Equal Justice Under Law*, 123.

28. See Arthur Carter, "Lucy Sues for $3000, Right to Enter Ala. U.," *Afro-American*, February 18, 1956, 1; E. Culpepper Clark, *The Schoolhouse Door*, 96–97, 104–5; Hollars, *Opening the Doors*, 1–2, 9, 41; Motley Reminiscences, 282–84.

29. See Carter, "Lucy Sues for $3000, Right to Enter Ala. U.," 1; E. Culpepper Clark, *The Schoolhouse Door*, 96–97, 104–5; Hollars, *Opening the Doors*, 1–2, 9, 41; Motley Reminiscences, 282–84.

30. See Carter, "Lucy Sues for $3000, Right to Enter Ala. U.," 1; E. Culpepper Clark, *The Schoolhouse Door*, 88, 96–97, 104–5.

31. "Coed's Charges on College Rioting Are Denied by Alabama U. President," *Washington Post*, February 11, 1956, 19; E. Culpepper Clark, *The Schoolhouse Door*, 87–88, 97–98, 104–5.

32. See Transcript, Lucy v. Adams, U.S. District Court, Birmingham, Alabama, Feb. 29, 1956, 9–10; Carter, "Lucy Sues for $3000, Right to Enter Ala. U.," 1; E. Culpepper Clark, *The Schoolhouse Door*, 88, 96–97, 104–5.

33. UA's lawyers urged sanctions during the February 29, 1956, hearing. See Transcript, Lucy v. Adams, U.S. District Court, Birmingham, Alabama, Feb. 29, 1956, 13. Quote from "Miss Lucy Sad over Expulsion," *New York Post*, n.d. "On Lucy Expulsion: Full Statement of U. of Ala. Trustees," *Afro-*

American, March 10, 1956, 6; "Miss Lucy in Seclusion to Shun Racists," *Atlanta Daily World*, February 15, 1956, 1; Al Sweeney, "'Shocked' Says Lucy of Ouster," *Afro-American*, March 10, 1956, 1; "Court Ignored; Coed Expelled," *Atlanta Daily World*, March 2, 1956, 1; Bem Price, "Miss Lucy Expelled by Alabama U.," *Washington Post*, March 2, 1956, 1; E. Culpepper Clark, *The Schoolhouse Door*, 96–97, 104–5; Hollars, *Opening the Doors*, 1-2, 9, 41; Motley Reminiscences, 282–84.

34. "Court Ignored; Coed Expelled," *Atlanta Daily World*, March 2, 1956, 1; Bem Price, "Miss Lucy Expelled by Alabama U.," *Washington Post*, March 2, 1956, 1; E. Culpepper Clark, *The Schoolhouse Door*, 96–97, 104–5; Hollars, *Opening the Doors*, 1–2, 9, 41; Motley Reminiscences, 282–84.

35. E. Culpepper Clark, *The Schoolhouse Door*, 96–97, 104–5, 112; Hollars, *Opening the Doors*, 1–2, 9, 41; Motley Reminiscences, 282–84.

36. "Terrific strain" from "Miss Lucy Sad over Expulsion," *New York Post*, n.d.; see also Motley Reminiscences, 282–84; Greenberg, *Crusaders in the Courts*, 226.

37. "Suit Hits Lucy," *Afro-American*, March 10, 1956, 8; "'Outsiders' Seek Four Million Dollars from Miss Lucy, Marshall," *Atlanta Daily World*, March 3, 1956, 1.

38. See "Made a Mistake, Miss Lucy Says," *Washington Post*, June 20, 1956, 21; "'Tactical Blunder' Blamed in Lucy Case," *Washington Post*, March 5, 1956, 2.

39. See "Made a Mistake, Miss Lucy Says," 21; "'Tactical Blunder' Blamed in Lucy Case," 2; "Miss Lucy and NAACP Sued for $4 Million," *Washington Post*, March 3, 1956, 2; Motley, *Equal Justice Under Law*, 124; Motley Reminiscences, 284–85; Greenberg, *Crusaders in the Courts*, 226.

10. THE "BEST PLAINTIFFS EVER":
DESEGREGATING THE UNIVERSITY OF GEORGIA

1. "Clean-cut, all-American boy" is from "Athens Story Told by Lawyers for Students," *Atlanta Daily World*, January 17, 1961, 3, quoting attorney Donald Hollowell. See also Pratt, *We Shall Not Be Moved*, 72–73; Brown-Nagin, *Courage to Dissent*, 115–18.

2. See Barbara Milz, "Charlayne Learns from News, Too," *Atlanta Constitution*, January 12, 1961, 15; Pratt, *We Shall Not Be Moved*, 72–73; Hunter-Gault, *In My Place*, 19–20, 33–34, 36, 57, 64, 68, 72, 88, 91–92.

3. In 1950, Horace Ward had unsuccessfully sued for admission to UGA. See Ward v. Regents, 172 F. Supp. 847 (N.D. 1959). In addition, in 1956, six Black Americans sued unsuccessfully to enter the Georgia State College of Business. See Hunt v. Arnold, 172 F. Supp. 847 (1959). See also Pratt, *We Shall Not Be Moved*, 72–73.

4. See Brown-Nagin, *Courage to Dissent*, 105–6; Bruce Galphin, "U.S. Court Demands Desegregation Now," *Atlanta Constitution*, January 7, 1961, 1.

5. See Brown-Nagin, *Courage to Dissent*, 136, 319, 323; Motley, *Equal Justice Under Law*, 130.

6. See Holmes v. Danner, 191 F. Supp. 385, 388–89 (1960).

7. See Holmes v. Danner, 191 F. Supp. 385, 388–89 (1960).

8. "2 Seek to Mix Georgia School," *Chicago Daily Defender*, September 10, 1960, 10; Holmes v. Danner, 191 F. Supp. 385, 393 (1960). On Hollowell, see Daniels, *Saving the Soul of Georgia*; Brown-Nagin, *Courage to Dissent*, 235–36.

9. See Holmes v. Danner, 191 F. Supp. at 393, 407–8; "Asked Opinions on Race Matters, Student Testifies," *Atlanta Daily World*, Dec. 15, 1960 at 1.

10. See Holmes v. Danner, 191 F. Supp. at 393, 407–8; "Asked Opinions on Race Matters, Student Testifies," *Atlanta Daily World*, December 15, 1960, 1.

11. See Motley Reminiscences, 274; Hunter-Gault, *In My Place*, 156–57, 160.

12. Holmes v. Danner, 191 F. Supp. at 396–400. The "curve ball" allusion is from Hunter-Gault, *In My Place*, 161.

13. See Motley Reminiscences, 270.

14. Motley Reminiscences, 273.

15. Holmes v. Danner, 191 F. Supp. at 396–406; Bruce Galphin, "Negroes Challenge College Deadline," *Atlanta Constitution*, December 14, 1960, 1; Lamson, ed., *Few Are Chosen*, 146; Pratt, *We Shall Not Be Moved*, 82; Hunter-Gault, *In My Place*, 157–58. The "old clincher" reference is from Trillin, *An Education in Georgia*, 41.

16. "Georgia University Told to Admit Negroes," *New York Times*, January 7, 1961, 1; Claude Sitton, "2 Negro Students Enter Georgia U." *New York Times*, January 11, 1961, 1; "Historic Decision," *Atlanta Daily World*, January 11, 1961, 6; Holmes v. Danner, 191 F. Supp. at 402. On Ward's participation in the litigation and reconciliation with UGA, see Pratt, *We Shall Not Be Moved*, 81–82, 146–48.

17. Claude Sitton, "Two Negro Students Enter Georgia U.," *New York Times*, January 11, 1961, 1; "200 Students Hang Effigy on Campus," *Atlanta Constitution*, January 7, 1961, 1; Pratt, *We Shall Not Be Moved*, 87.

18. See Holmes v. Danner, 191 F. Supp. at 411.

19. "Ninety miles an hour" and "hair-flying" from Motley, *Equal Justice Under Law*, 137–38; see also Emanuel, *Elbert Parr Tuttle*, 184–85.

20. See Emanuel, *Elbert Parr Tuttle*, 184–85, 192; see also Nick Taylor, "The Judge Who Changed Your Life," *Atlanta Constitution*, June 18, 1972, SM8; Hunter-Gault, *In My Place*, 175.

21. Cliff Mackay, "Charlayne's Beauty Stuns at University of Georgia," news

clipping, n.d., Motley Columbia Papers; Kathryn Johnson, "Negro Girl Sat Quietly in Her Dorm During Rioting," *Macon Telegraph*, January 13, 1961; Hunter-Gault, *In My Place*, 173.

22. Motley Reminiscences, 270, 271, 272.

23. Bruce Galphin, "2 Negroes Enroll at University," *Atlanta Constitution*, January 11, 1961, 1; Jack Nelson, "2 Students, 3 More in Klan Indicted at Athens," *Atlanta Constitution*, January 20, 1961, 20. "C of C Here Backs Pupil Placement," *Atlanta Constitution*, January 19, 1961, 33; Reg Murphy, "Vandiver Asks Open-School Laws; Governor Warns of U.S. Force," *Atlanta Constitution*, January 19, 1961, 1; Marvin Wall, "University Pledges to Prevent Rioting," *Atlanta Constitution*, January 14, 1961, 1.

24. "C of C Hits Flareup at University," *Atlanta Constitution*, January 14, 1959, 24; "Negroes Reinstatement Urged by 10 Groups," *Atlanta Journal*, January 13, 1961, 1; "Shameful Morning After," *Atlanta Journal*, January 13, 1961, 4; Emanuel, *Elbert Parr Tuttle*, 189.

25. Bruce Galphin and Barbara Milz, "Coeds Can Leave Negro's Dorm," *Atlanta Constitution*, January 16, 1961, 1.

26. Bruce Galphin and Barbara Milz, "Coeds Can Leave Negro's Dorm," *Atlanta Constitution*, January 16, 1961, 1.

27. Emanuel, *Elbert Parr Tuttle*, 183.

28. Greenberg Columbia Oral History, 128.

29. Quote about "calling them off by heart" from Nan Rosenthal, "A Knowledge of Law Helped at Georgia U.," *New York Post*, February 5, 1961, at 12. "Preparation and experience" from Peggy Lamson, ed., *Few Are Chosen*, 147.

11. A "DIFFICULTY WITH THE IDEA OF A WOMAN": THE SETBACK OF 1961

1. See Transcript after Release from Georgia State Prison at Reidsville, October 27, 1960, available at https://kinginstitute.stanford.edu/king-papers/documents/interview-after-release-georgia-state-prison-reidsville; Steven Levingston, "John F. Kennedy, Martin Luther King, Jr., and the Phone Call That Changed History," *Time*, June 20, 2017.

2. See Navasky, *Kennedy Justice*, 109–10; Ryan, *Roy Wilkins*, 88–89, 98–99; Juan Williams, *Thurgood Marshall*, 289–90; Garrow, *Bearing the Cross*, 142–45.

3. Davis and Clark, *Thurgood Marshall*, 235; "Marshall Named to Appeals Court: NAACP Counsel Is Picked by Kennedy," *New York Times*, September 24, 1961, 54; "stressed out" from Motley, *Equal Justice Under Law*, 149; "forceful personality" from Juan Williams, *Thurgood Marshall*, 5, 290–92.

4. Thurgood Marshall Reminiscences, Columbia Oral History Project (1994), 28; see Brown-Nagin, *Courage to Dissent*, 139–40; Motley, *Equal Justice*, 151.

5. Williams, *Thurgood Marshall*, 294.; Greenberg, *Crusaders in the Courts*, 294; Robert L. Carter, *A Matter of Law*, 136–37.

6. Greenberg, *Crusaders in the Courts*, 294–95; Juan Williams, *Thurgood Marshall*, 294–95; Jonas, *Freedom's Sword*, 75–79, 413 n. 11; Robert L. Carter, *A Matter of Law*, 136–37. Whiskey and wine references from Jonas, *Freedom's Sword*, 77.

7. Juan Williams, *Thurgood Marshall*, 294.

8. Minutes of NAACP Legal Defense Fund Board of Directors Meeting, October 1961, pp. 4–5, William Hastie Papers, Harvard University; "NAACP Unit to Elect General Council," *New York World-Telegraph*, October 4, 1961; James Booker, "His Greenberg Appointment," *New York Amsterdam News*, October 14, 1961, 2; Greenberg, *Crusaders in the Courts*, 294–95; Jonas, *Freedom's Sword*, 79.

9. Minutes of NAACP Legal Defense Fund Board of Directors Meeting, October 1961; Motley, *Equal Justice Under Law*, 151.

10. See "NAACP Unit to Elect General Council," *New York World-Telegraph*, October 4, 1961; Greenberg, *Crusaders in the Courts*, 294–95; Jonas, *Freedom's Sword*, 79.

11. See Oliver C. Sutton, Esq., to *New York Amsterdam News*, October 15, 1961; Jonas, *Freedom's Sword*, 78, 413 nn. 11–12; Greenberg, *Crusaders in the Courts*, 297; Meeting of the Board of Directors of the NAACP Legal Defense and Educational Fund, October 4, 1961.

12. Jonas, *Freedom's Sword*, 78, 413 nn. 11–12; Greenberg, *Crusaders in the Courts*, 298.

13. Motley, *Equal Justice Under Law*, 152–53.

14. Greenberg, *Crusaders in the Courts*, 294.; Juan Williams, *Thurgood Marshall*, 294.; Greenberg, *Crusaders in the Courts*, 295; Wallace S. Hayes to NAACP Board of Directors, October 13, 1961, NAACP Papers, General Office Files, 1956–1965; Hicks, "Why??," *New York Amsterdam News*, October 14, 1961, 13.

15. Greenberg, *Crusaders in the Courts*, 295; Wallace S. Hayes to NAACP Board of Directors, October 13, 1961; Hicks, "Why??"

16. Motley, *Equal Justice Under Law*, 151.

17. Motley, *Equal Justice Under Law*, 195, 213.

18. Juan Williams, *Thurgood Marshall*, 297.

19. Hicks, "Why??"; Morton Cooper, "White Leader in the NAACP," *Chicago Daily Defender*, April 2, 1963, 11; letter from "Disgusted" to Roy Wilkins, October 6, 1961, NAACP Papers, General Office Files, 1956–1965; Wallace S. Hayes to NAACP Board of Directors, October 13, 1961.

20. James L. Hicks, "Why??," *New York Amsterdam News*, October 14, 1961, 13; Cooper, "White Leader in the NAACP"; letter from "Disgusted" to Roy Wilkins, October 6, 1961, NAACP Papers, General Office Files,

1956–1965; Wallace S. Hayes to NAACP Board of Directors, October 13, 1961.

21. Hicks, "Why??"; Cooper, "White Leader in the NAACP"; Evelyn Cunningham, *Pittsburgh Courier*, October 21, 1961, A1.

22. "Jack Greenberg Replaces NAACP Counsel Marshall," *Atlanta Daily World*, October 6, 1961, 1.

23. James Booker, "Hit Greenberg Appointment," *New York Amsterdam News*, October 14, 1961, 2; Oliver S. Hutton to *New York Amsterdam News*, October 15, 1961; Juan Williams, *Thurgood Marshall*, 295.

24. Juan Williams, *Thurgood Marshall*, 295.

25. Motley, *Equal Justice Under Law*, 151; Cole and Greenaway, "Judge Constance Baker Motley and the Struggle for Equal Justice," 12.

26. Marshall went on to become a "liberal lion" on the Court, including in sex discrimination cases. One scholar has called him a "pragmatic feminist." See Taunya L. Banks, "Justice Thurgood Marshall, the Race Man, and Gender Equality in the Courts." To the extent that Mark Tushnet, Marshall's biographer, discusses sex discrimination cases, he counts the justice favorable to women's claims of discrimination. See Tushnet, *Making Constitutional Law*, 107–8. Notably, Justice Brennan, another liberal lion, also issued decisions favorable to women, and also personally espoused views that contradicted his legal liberalism. See Stern and Wermiel, *Justice Brennan*, 386–87, 399, 400–401, 405–6.

27. See Juan Williams, *Thurgood Marshall*, 295. Marshall may have believed that Motley had conspired with Robert Carter, both his lieutenant and his rival, to have him removed as head of the Legal Defense Fund. If so, then Marshall's unfounded assumption that Motley had been disloyal would also have been a factor in her failure to obtain the director-counsel position. Williams, *Thurgood Marshall*, 294–95. William Coleman, Esq., an Inc. Fund board member in 1961, confirmed the "seniority" justification. Author interview with William T. Coleman, January 13, 2011, 2, 6, 7, 8, 13, 14.

28. Robert L. Carter, *A Matter of Law*, 99; Greenberg, *Crusaders in the Courts*, 159–62.

29. See, e.g., Fleishman, *The Foundation*, 299; Rabinowitz and Ledwith, *A History of the National Lawyers Guild: 1937–1987*, 35; United States Congress, House, Committee on Internal Security, *Hearings, Reports and Prints of the House Committee on Internal Security* (Washington, DC: Government Printing Office, 1973), 1303; see also Douglas Martin, "John Pemberton Jr., Civil Rights Crusader, Dies at 90," *New York Times*, October 29, 2009, www.nytimes.com/2009/10/30/us/30pemberton.html; "Patrick Murphy Malin, 61, Dies; Headed the Civil Liberties Union; Left Crusading Agency in 1962 for Presidency of College in Istanbul," *New York Times*,

December 14, 1964, www.nytimes.com/1964/12/14/patrick-murphy -malin-61-dies.html;"Preliminary Inventory of the National Lawyers Guild Records, 1936–1999," Online Archive of California, http://pdf.oac .cdlib.org/pdf/berkeley/bancroft/m99_280_cubanc.pdf.

30. See Ransby, *Ella Baker and the Black Freedom Movement*, 173, 183–84, 106– 7, 110, 121, 137, 297; Robinson, *Montgomery Bus Boycott and the Women Who Started It*; Theoharis, *The Rebellious Life of Rosa Parks*. On Clark and sexism within the SCLC, see Brown-Nagin, "The Transformation of a Social Movement into Law?"

31. Evans, *Personal Politics*, 83–101; Student Nonviolent Coordinating Committee Position Paper: Women in the Movement (Fall 1964).

32. Friedan, *The Feminine Mystique*.

33. That is, under current law, the evidence described above would be insufficient to support a sex discrimination claim on a theory of disparate treatment in a court of law. See, e.g., Price Waterhouse v. Hopkins, 490 U.S. 228 (1989) (discussing sex stereotypes); McDonnell Douglas Corp. v. Green (1973). "Sex-plus" discrimination can be a basis for liability under Title VII of the Civil Rights Act. See Philips v. Martin Marietta, 400 U.S. 542 (1971).

34. Author interview with Bill Coleman.

35. Motley, "Thurgood Marshall," 208, 209.

36. Motley, "Standing on His Shoulders," 23, 26, 34–35.

37. Motley, "Standing on His Shoulders," 21–22.

38. Motley, "My Personal Debt to Thurgood Marshall," 24.

12. "THAT'S YOUR CASE": JAMES MEREDITH AND THE BATTLE TO DESEGREGATE THE UNIVERSITY OF MISSISSIPPI

1. Motley, *Equal Justice Under Law*, 162, 315.

2. See Sansing, *The University of Mississippi*; Eagles, *The Price of Defiance*, 15–19.

3. James H. Meredith, "I'll Know Victory or Defeat," *Saturday Evening Post*, November 10, 1962, 14–17; Donna Ladd and Adam Lynch, "A Soldier's Story: The JFP Interview with James Meredith," *Jackson Free Press*, September 24, 2008; Doyle, *An American Insurrection*, 18–20.

4. Meredith, "I'll Know Victory or Defeat."

5. See Knauer, *Let Us Fight as Free Men*.

6. Meredith, *Three Years in Mississippi*, 4.

7. Motley, *Equal Justice Under Law*, 163. On stereotypes about and abuse of Black women, see Clinton, *The Plantation Mistress*, 201–2; Bogle, *Toms, Coons, Mulattoes, Mammies and Bucks*, 6–7; McGuire, *At the Dark End of the Street*.

8. Motley, *Equal Justice Under Law*, 172–73.

9. The definitive work is Arsenault, *Freedom Riders*.

10. Tye, *Bobby Kennedy*, 206–7; Arsenault, *Freedom Riders*, 86, 114–15, 118–19, 122, 135.

11. "King Vows: Freedom Rides to Continue," *Chicago Daily Defender*, June 5, 1961, 1; Tye, *Bobby Kennedy*, 211; Doyle, *An American Insurrection*, 33–34.

12. Motley, *Equal Justice Under Law*, 132, 149, 167–68; Bailey v. Patterson, 369 U.S. 31 (1962) (holding that Court had declared segregation in interstate and intrastate transportation unlawful and the issue was settled).

13. Motley Reminiscences, 303.

14. Johanna Neuman, "Meredith's Lawyer: It Was Mississippi or the Constitution," *Clarion-Ledger* (Jackson, MS), September 26, 1962, 63; Motley Reminiscences, 302.

15. See Motley Reminiscences, 302; Dierenfield, *The Civil Rights Movement*, 72 (unreconstructed); Mason and Smith, *Beaches, Blood, and Ballots*, 126.

16. See "Mize, Sidney Carr," Federal Judicial Center, www.fjc.gov/history /judges/mize-sidney-carr (last accessed April 11, 2017); Goldman, *Picking Federal Judges*, 19–20; Smead, *Blood Justice*, 189; Banks, "The United States Court of Appeals for the Fifth Circuit," 278; Motley, *Equal Justice Under Law*, 75.

17. Transcript of Proceedings on Certain Matters, July 15, 1961, United States District Court for the Southern District of Mississippi, pp. 3, 5, 6.

18. See News Brief, "Twenty Years Ago Today," *Clarion-Ledger*, January 2, 1958, 20; Landon, "The Origins of the University of Mississippi Law Journal"; "Shands Rites Wednesday," *Clarion-Ledger*, April 22, 1975, 4; "For the Defendants," chapter 8 in Martin, *Count Them One by One*, 77; Landon, *The University of Mississippi School of Law*, 41.

19. See "Shands Rites Wednesday," *Clarion-Ledger*, April 22, 1975, 4; "For the Defendants," chapter 8 in Martin, in *Count Them One by One*, 77; Bill Minor, "Woman Lawyer Beat Segregationists," *Clarion-Ledger*, October 13, 2005, 4.

20. Transcript of Ruling on Motion to Require Defendants to Produce Certain Records and to Take the Deposition of Robert Ellis, August 4, 1961, United States District Court for the Southern District of Mississippi, p. 20.

21. Motley Reminiscences; Bill Minor, "Constance Baker Motley Spent Her Lifetime Ensuring Civil Rights," *Clarion-Ledger*, October 16, 2005, 65.

22. Oral History Interview of Motley by Lamson, pp. 5–6.

23. Transcript of Proceedings on Certain Matters, July 15, 1961, United States District Court for the Southern District of Mississippi, pp. 3, 5, 6.

24. Transcript of Proceedings on Certain Matters, July 15, 1961, United States District Court for the Southern District of Mississippi, pp. 3, 5, 6.

25. Transcript of Proceedings on Certain Matters, July 15, 1961, United States District Court for the Southern District of Mississippi, pp. 8–9, 13; Docket Sheet, Meredith v. Fair, June 27, 1961, Order Suspending and Staying the Deposition of Robert B. Ellis; Testimony of Robert E. Ellis, Meredith v. Fair, August 17, 1961, United States District Court for the Southern District of Mississippi, pp. 389–414; Meredith v. Fair, 199 F. Supp. 754, 755 (S.D. Miss. 1961).

26. Transcript of Ruling on Motion to Require Defendants to Produce Certain Records and to Take the Deposition of Robert Ellis, August 4, 1961, United States District Court for the Southern District of Mississippi, pp. 5–6; Testimony of Robert E. Ellis, Meredith v. Fair, August 17, 1961, United States District Court for the Southern District of Mississippi, pp. 332–33, 395.

27. Transcript of Ruling on Motion to Require Defendants to Produce Certain Records and to Take the Deposition of Robert Ellis, August 4, 1961, United States District Court for the Southern District of Mississippi, pp. 6, 8, 255–86.

28. Meredith v. Fair, 199 F. Supp. 754, 756–758 (S.D. Miss. 1961).

29. Meredith v. Fair, 298 F.2d 696, 698, 701 (5th Cir. 1962); "Attorneys Argue in Mixing Case," *Clarion-Ledger*, January 10, 1962, 1; see also J. M. Barrie, *Peter Pan* (1904).

30. Meredith v. Fair, 298 F.2d 696, 701–2 (5th Cir. 1962).

31. Meredith v. Fair, 298 F.2d 696, 701–2 (5th Cir. 1962); "Meredith Case Studied by U.S. Appeals Court," *Clarion-Ledger*, April 21, 1962, 1; Tommy Herrington, "Judge Begins Meredith Suit," *Clarion-Ledger*, January 17, 1962, 1.

32. Meredith v. Fair, 202 F. Supp. 224 (U.S. District Court, S.D. Miss., 1962); Tommy Herrington, "UM Officials Deny Talking Meredith Bid," *Clarion-Ledger*, January 25, 1962, 1; Herrington, "NAACP Side Rests in Meredith Hearing," *Clarion-Ledger*, April 18, 1962, 1.

33. "Seething" from Bill Minor, "Woman Lawyer Beat Segregationists," *Clarion-Ledger*, October 13, 2005, 4; see also Tommy Herrington, "UM Officials Deny Talking Meredith Bid," *Clarion-Ledger*, January 25, 1962, 1; Transcript of Testimony, Meredith v. Fair, U.S. District Court, January 16, 1962, pp. 281–83.

34. Testimony of James Howard Meredith, Meredith v. Fair, United States District Court for the Southern District of Mississippi, August 1961, pp. 12, 17, 40–44, 60.

35. Testimony of James Howard Meredith, Meredith v. Fair, United States District Court for the Southern District of Mississippi, August 1961, pp. 80–95, 96–115; "Meredith Evidence Under Advisement," *Clarion-Ledger*,

January 28, 1962, 1; "Character Statute Cited in James Meredith Case," *Clarion-Ledger*, February 2, 1962; Tommy Herrington, "NAACP's Side Rests in Meredith Hearing," *Clarion-Ledger*, January 26, 1962, 1; Eagles, *Price of Defiance*, 242; see also Meredith v. Fair, 298 F.2d 696, 700 (5th Cir. 1962).

36. Testimony of James Howard Meredith, Meredith v. Fair, United States District Court for the Southern District of Mississippi, August 1961, pp. 95–96, 97, 99–223; "Meredith Evidence Under Advisement," *Clarion-Ledger*, January 28, 1962, 1; "Character Statute Cited in James Meredith Case," *Clarion-Ledger*, February 2, 1962; Motley, *Equal Justice Under Law*, 165. During the January 1962 trial, the judge entered into evidence testimony given by Meredith and Ellis during the August 1961 preliminary hearing. During the 1962 proceedings, litigants referenced the prior testimony. See Herrington, "NAACP's Side Rests in Meredith's Hearing," *Clarion-Ledger*, January 26, 1962, 1.

37. Meredith v. Fair, 202 F. Supp. 224, 227 (U.S. D. Ct., S.D. Miss. 1962).

38. Meredith v. Fair, 202 F. Supp. 224, 227 (U.S. D. Ct., S.D. Miss. 1962); W. C. Shoemaker, "Judge Rules Ole Miss May Reject Meredith," *Clarion-Ledger*, February 4, 1962, 1.

39. "Meredith Appeals; Wants Quick Entry," *Clarion-Ledger*, February 6, 1962, 1; "Meredith Case Studied by U.S. Appeals Court," *Clarion-Ledger*, April 16, 1962, 1; Meredith v. Fair, 305 F.2d 343, 345–61 (5th Cir. 1962); "Ole Miss Ordered to Take Meredith," *Clarion-Ledger*, April 29, 1962, 1; Motley, *Equal Justice Under Law*, 175–76.

13. "I AM HUMAN AFTER ALL": TRAUMA AND HARDSHIP IN THE LONG BATTLE AT OLE MISS

1. "Ole Miss Ordered to Take Meredith," *Clarion-Ledger* (Jackson, MS), April 29, 1962, 1; "State to Postpone Trial of Meredith," *Clarion-Ledger*, June 14, 1962, 4; "Legal Battle Shapes Up Between Federal Judges," *Clarion-Ledger*, July 30, 1962, 14; "Meredith to Seek Aid of High Court Justice," *Clarion-Ledger*, August 7, 1962, 1; "Judge Ben Cameron, 73, Dead," *New York Times*, April 4, 1964, 27; Motley, *Equal Justice Under Law*, 174.

2. On the stays, see Meredith v. Fair, 305 F.2d 341 (5th Cir. 1962); "Appeal to be Pushed: Attorney General Patterson Hopes Court Will Be Willing," *Clarion-Ledger*, June 27, 1962, 1; Motley, *Equal Justice Under Law*, 175–78.

3. Motley, *Equal Justice Under Law*, 179; Motley Reminiscences, 315.

4. Motley, *Equal Justice Under Law*, 179.

5. Motley, *Equal Justice Under Law*, 179.

6. Sam Cooke, "A Change Is Gonna Come" (RCA Victor, 1964); see also "Sam Cooke and the Song That 'Almost Scared Him,'" *All Things Considered*, National Public Radio, February 1, 2014 (last accessed May 4, 2017).

7. "Meredith to Seek Aid of High Court Justice," *Clarion-Ledger*, August 7, 1962, 1; "Hugo Black Orders Meredith Admitted," *Clarion-Ledger*, September 11, 1962, 1; Meredith v. Fair, 83 S.Ct. 10 (1962).

8. Eagles, *Price of Defiance*, 281–82.

9. "Governor Vows Negro Won't Enter Ole Miss," *Clarion-Ledger*, September 11, 1962, 1.

10. "Governor Vows Negro Won't Enter Ole Miss"; see also Motley, *Equal Justice Under Law*, 179; U.S. Constitution, Amendment X.

11. "Governor Vows Negro Won't Enter Ole Miss"; James Saggus, "Crucial Racial Fight Scheduled This Week," *Clarion-Ledger*, September 16, 1962, 1; Eagles, *Price of Defiance*, 282–85.

12. On Kennedy, see Tye, *Bobby Kennedy*, 211–18; Eagles, *Price of Defiance*, 274–75, 278, 281. "Aura" from Tye, 212.

13. Eagles, *Price of Defiance*, 288–93.

14. "Governor Barnett Rejects Meredith," *Clarion-Ledger*, September 21, 1962, 1; "Resolute Mississippian: James Howard Meredith," *New York Times*, September 21, 13.

15. "Governor Barnett Rejects Meredith"; see also Eagles, *Price of Defiance*, 304–5.

16. See "Hundreds More Were Lynched in the South Than Previously Known," *Atlanta Journal-Constitution*, June 14, 2017 (citing the Equal Justice Initiative, *Lynching in America: Confronting the Legacy of Racial Terror* [2017], https://lynchinginamerica.eji.org/report/).

17. Claude Sitton, "Meredith Rebuffed Again Despite Restraining Order," *New York Times*, September 26, 1962, 1; "Senators Back Ross," *Clarion-Ledger*, September 27, 1962, 1; "Ross Halts Negro for Second Time," *Clarion-Ledger*, September 26, 1962, 1; Eagles, *Price of Defiance*, 281–88.

18. Edmond Lebreton, "JFK Takes Over Guard as Army Enters Crisis," *Clarion-Ledger*, September 30, 1962, 1; Eagles, *Price of Defiance*, 338–39.

19. "JFK Takes Over Guard as Army Enters Crisis"; "Kennedy Telegram and Executive Order," *New York Times*, October 1, 1962, 22; Eagles, *Price of Defiance*, 343–44.

20. "JFK Takes Over Guard as Army Enters Crisis"; "Kennedy Telegram and Executive Order"; Eagles, *Price of Defiance*, 343–44.

21. "JFK Takes Over Guard as Army Enters Crisis"; "Kennedy Telegram and Executive Order"; "Eastland Orders Probe of Events at Ole Miss," *Clarion-Ledger*, October 2, 1962, 1; Eagles, *Price of Defiance*, 352–70.

22. "President's Talk on Mississippi Crisis," *New York Times*, October 1, 1962, 22; "Kennedy Telegram and Executive Order."

23. "Eastland Orders Probe of Events at Ole Miss"; "Resolute Mississippian, James Howard Meredith," *New York Times*, September 21, 1962, 13; Eagles, *Price of Defiance*, 371.

24. James H. Meredith, "I'll Know Victory or Defeat," *Saturday Evening Post*, November 10, 1962, 14–17.

25. W. E. B. Du Bois, "Close Ranks," *The Crisis* (July 1918): 111; John Hope, "The Negro College, Student Protest and the Future." "Social change" from McGee, *James Meredith*, 71. On the toll of activism, see, for example, Berg, "Trauma and Testimony in Black Women's Civil Rights Memoirs."

26. Meredith, *Three Years in Mississippi*, 211, 230; Motley, *Equal Justice Under the Law*, 183.

27. The poem is quoted in Meredith, *Three Years in Mississippi*, 226. See also Junius Bonds, "Meredith Will Need Guard for 2 Years, Mrs. Motley Tells Tribune," *Philadelphia Tribune*, October 30, 1962, 3; Motley, *Equal Justice Under Law*, 183; Henry T. Gallagher, *James Meredith and the Ole Miss Riot*.

28. Meredith, "I'll Know Victory or Defeat"; Meredith, *Three Years in Mississippi*, 230; Henry T. Gallagher, *James Meredith and the Ole Miss Riot*, 100–101; Bonds, "Meredith Will Need Guard for 2 Years, Mrs. Motley Tells Tribune."

29. On respectability and dress, see, for example, Wolcott, *Remaking Respectability*, 56–57; Randall Kennedy, "Lifting as We Climb," *Harper's*, October 2015.

30. Motley Reminiscences, 312.

31. Motley Reminiscences, 312; Meredith, *Three Years in Mississippi*, 79, 217–18.

32. Motley Reminiscences, 317; Motley, *Equal Justice Under Law*, 183; Meredith, *Three Years in Mississippi*, 232–33.

33. Motley Reminiscences, 316–17.

34. Motley Reminiscences, 316–17.

35. Motley Reminiscences, 317–18.

36. Motley Reminiscences, 319.

37. Motley Reminiscences, 318.

38. Motley Reminiscences, 319, 325; Eagles, *Price of Defiance*, 371–424. On Motley's recommendation, Meredith later was accepted to (and graduated from) the Columbia University School of Law.

39. Meredith, *Three Years in Mississippi*, 233.

40. Motley Reminiscences, 328; Johanna Neuman, "Meredith's Lawyer: It Was Mississippi or the Constitution," *Clarion-Ledger*, September 26, 1962, 63.

41. Motley, *Equal Justice Under Law*, 179. On Kennedy's intervention, see "Kennedy Telegram and Executive Order"; Navasky, *Kennedy Justice*, 259.

42. Motley, *Equal Justice Under Law*, 179; Neuman, "Meredith's Lawyer: It Was Mississippi or the Constitution."

43. Neuman, "Meredith's Lawyer: It Was Mississippi or the Constitution"; Motley, *Equal Justice Under Law*, 180–81; see also "W. Harold Cox, Federal Judge in Mississippi, Dies," *Washington Post*, February 28, 1988.

44. Motley, *Equal Justice Under Law*, 172.

45. Neuman, "Meredith's Lawyer: It Was Mississippi or the Constitution"; Motley, *Equal Justice Under Law*, 172.

46. See Derrick Bell to Constance Baker Motley, April 24, 1989, Smith Motley Papers, Personal Correspondence; Motley, *Equal Justice Under Law*, 172–73; Doyle, *An American Insurrection*, 24.

47. See Motley, *Equal Justice Under Law*, 172, 188; Eagles, *The Price of Defiance*, 72–79, 241; Doyle, *An American Insurrection*, 24; "Meredith to Seek Aid of High Court Justice," *Clarion-Ledger*, August 7, 1962, 1.

48. Motley, *Equal Justice Under Law*, 180. Police habitually followed Evers. See Michael Vinson Williams, *Medgar Evers*, 284–85.

49. Motley, *Equal Justice Under Law*, 180; Motley Reminiscences, 310.

50. Neuman, "Meredith's Lawyer: It Was Mississippi or the Constitution."

51. Motley, *Equal Justice Under Law*, 188; Williams, *Medgar Evers*, 3–4, 276–77, 281, 283.

52. See Michael Vinson Williams, *Medgar Evers*, 4, 276; Motley Reminiscences, 311; David Stout, "Byron De La Beckwith Dies; Killer of Medgar Evers Was 80," *New York Times*, January 23, 2001.

53. Motley, *Equal Justice Under Law*, 189.

54. "Integration's Advocate," *New York Times*, September 11, 1963, 30.

14. AN "EYE-OPENING EXPERIENCE":
THE BIRMINGHAM CIVIL RIGHTS CAMPAIGN

1. See Motley, *Equal Justice Under Law*, 158.

2. Motley, *Equal Justice Under Law*, 158.

3. "Horrendous" from Motley, *Equal Justice Under Law*, 159. On the lynching, see Brown-Nagin, *Courage to Dissent*, 46, and Wexler, *Fire in the Canebrake*.

4. See "Martin Luther King's Diary in Jail," *Jet*, August 23, 1962, 18. On the Albany movement, see, for example, Fairclough, *To Redeem the Soul of America*, 86–90; Jackson, *From Civil Rights to Human Rights*, 148–154.

5. Comments about Motley are from Martin Luther King Jr., "The Law Is Majestic," *New York Amsterdam News*, July 31, 1965, 16.

6. Historians cite the professionalism of the local police force and dissension within the movement to explain the failure of the Albany movement. See Garrow, *Bearing the Cross*, 217–18. King agreed that the Albany movement had not achieved its goals, but emphasized that the movement learned invaluable lessons from the struggle. See Martin Luther King Jr., *Why We Can't Wait*, 34–35.

7. Martin Luther King Jr., *Why We Can't Wait*, 39, 47.

8. Richard Pearson, "Former Ala. Gov. George C. Wallace Dies," *Washington Post*, September 14, 1998, A1; "Eugene 'Bull' Connor Dies at 75; Police Head Fought Integration," *New York Times*, March 11, 1973.

9. See Eskew, *But for Birmingham*, 3–5, 112–13, 210–11. Eskew notes that a Project X, a selective buying campaign designed to put pressure on the white merchants, preceded Project C, a broader protest movement that directly engaged city officials; ibid., 211–12. On Shuttlesworth, see Manis, *A Fire You Can't Put Out*, x, xi, 122; Jon Nordheimer, "Rev. Fred L. Shuttlesworth, an Elder Statesman for Civil Rights, Dies at 89," *New York Times*, October 5, 2011. "Crack" from McWhorter, *Carry Me Home*, 307. The Shuttlesworth quote "prepared to die" is from Martin Luther King Jr., *Why We Can't Wait*, 52.

10. Eskew, *But for Birmingham*, 214–15, 217, 219, 225, 227, 230–31. "Divided" from Martin Luther King Jr., *Why We Can't Wait*, 64.

11. Eskew, *But for Birmingham*, 227–28.

12. Walker v. Birmingham, 279 Ala. 53, 56 (1965) (citing news bulletin and upholding contempt conviction); "Pseudo-legal" from Martin Luther King Jr., *Why We Can't Wait*, 68.

13. See Andrew Young, *An Easy Burden*, 231.

14. See Foster Hailey, "Negroes Defying Birmingham Writ," *New York Times*, April 12, 1963, 1; Andrew Young, *An Easy Burden*, 231; Greenberg, *Crusaders in the Courts*, 304; Walker v. Birmingham, 279 Ala. 53, 56 (1965) (citing news bulletin and upholding contempt conviction). The Inc. Fund appealed the decision in the case to the U.S. Supreme Court, which ruled against King and SCLC. In Walker v. Birmingham, 388 U.S. 307, 308, 323 (1967), the U.S. Supreme Court upheld the criminal contempt conviction of King and several others on grounds that the activists had deliberately violated the injunction.

15. Young, *An Easy Burden*, 237–40; Martin Luther King Jr., *Why We Can't Wait*, 68.

16. Hailey, "Negroes Defying Birmingham Writ," *New York Times*, April 12, 1963, 1; "60 Are Arrested in Birmingham: Martin Luther King Among Those Held After March," *Baltimore Sun*, April 13, 1963. Descriptions of King (and Abernathy) in jail from Martin Luther King Jr., *Why We Can't Wait*, 73; Jones and Connelly, *Behind the Dream*, 68–69; "Rev. Abernathy Tells 3,000: Jail Was Holy Hell," *Philadelphia Tribune*, April 27, 1963, 1.

17. Martin Luther King Jr., *Why We Can't Wait*, 78–79, 83; Young, *An Easy Burden*, 240–41, 244; see also Foster Hailey, "Birmingham Jails Six More Negroes," *New York Times*, April 14, 1963, 1.

18. "Spectacular" quoted in "Constance Baker Motley Interview," in Lanker, *I Dream a World*, 65. "American hero" from Remarks by Constance Baker

Motley, Southern Christian Leadership Conference Banquet, August 5, 1965, Smith Motley Papers, box 14, folder 2.

19. "Scary place" from "Constance Baker Motley Interview," in Lanker, *I Dream a World*, 65; see also "Blocked Desegregation Delay," *New Journal and Guide* (Norfolk, VA), February 2, 1963, 9. The Birmingham, Mobile, and Tuskegee schools desegregated in September 1963, with the aid of the National Guard. See "Wallace Ends Resistance as Guard Is Federalized," *New York Times*, September, 11, 1963, 1.

20. Young, *An Easy Burden*, 231; see also "Birmingham Curb Asked in U.S. Suit," *New York Times*, April 20, 1963, 12; Martin Luther King Jr., *Why We Can't Wait*, 101.

21. "Twinkle" from author interview with Clarence Jones, Esq., October 3, 2017, p. 7; see also Young, *An Easy Burden*, 231; "Birmingham Curb Asked in U.S. Suit," *New York Times*, April 20, 1963, 12; Martin Luther King Jr., *Why We Can't Wait*, 48. "Alone" from King, *Why We Can't Wait*, 71.

22. "Rev. King Faces Contempt Rap in Court Trial," *Philadelphia Tribune*, April 23, 1963, 1; "Contempt Trial of Rev. King Opens in Birmingham Court," *Chicago Daily Defender*, April 23, 1963. On Black lawyers, see Mack, *Representing the Race*.

23. "Superb" from author interview with Clarence Jones, Esq., October 3, 2017, p. 9; see also "Rev. King Faces Contempt Rap in Court Trial"; "Contempt Trial of Rev. King Opens in Birmingham Court." On Black lawyers, see Mack, *Representing the Race*.

24. Cliff Mackay, "Birmingham Sidelights," *Afro-American*, May 4, 1963, 12.

25. "Contempt Charges Groundless, Motley Says at King Hearing," *Afro-American*, May 4, 1963, 15; "Contempt Trial of Rev. King Opens in Birmingham Court."

26. "Contempt Charges Groundless, Motley Says at King Hearing"; "Contempt Trial of Rev. King Opens in Birmingham Court"; "I'm Still Commissioner, Explodes Bull Connor," *Afro-American*, May 4, 1963, 15.

27. "Birmingham Conviction of Dr. King and Associates to Be Appealed," *Call and Post*, May 11, 1963, 4C; "Contempt Trial of Rev. King Opens in Birmingham Court"; "Contempt Trial of Dr. King Opens," *New York Times*, 1963, 20; "Judge Weighs Rev. King's Fate," *Chicago Tribune*, April 25, 1963, 16; "Rev. Abernathy Tells 3,000: Jail Was Holy Hell," *Philadelphia Tribune*, April 27, 1963, 1.

28. "Birmingham Conviction of Dr. King and Associates to Be Appealed"; "Contempt Trial of Rev. King Opens in Birmingham Court"; "Contempt Trial of Dr. King Opens"; "Judge Weighs Rev. King's Fate"; "Rev. Abernathy Tells 3,000: Jail Was Holy Hell."

29. "Contempt Trial of Rev. King Opens in Birmingham Court"; "Contempt

Trial of Dr. King Opens"; "Judge Weighs Rev. King's Fate"; "Rev. Aberna-thy Tells 3,000: Jail Was Holy Hell."

30. "Contempt Charges Groundless, Motley Says at King Hearing."

31. "Contempt Charges Groundless, Motley Says at King Hearing"; "Rev. King Faces Contempt Rap in Court Trial"; "Contempt Trial of Rev. King Opens in Birmingham Court"; "11 Ministers Sentenced," *Baltimore Sun*, April 27, 1963, 6; "Dr. King Sentenced," *New York Times*, April 27, 1963, 9.

32. "Contempt Charges Groundless, Motley Says at King Hearing"; Emory Jackson, "Showdown Nears in Birmingham Fight," *Call and Post*, May 11, 1963, A1.

33. Young, *An Easy Burden*, 259–61; Branch, *Pillar of Fire*, 76.

34. Young, *An Easy Burden*, 261–65. "No place for children" from Branch, *Pillar of Fire*, 76.

35. Young, *An Easy Burden*, 261–65; Manis, *A Fire You Can't Put Out*, 367.

36. Young, *An Easy Burden*, 264–65. Recollection about importance of sing-ing is from an interview with Audrey Faye Hendricks. See Levin, *Free-dom's Children*, 78; Rochelle, *Witnesses to Freedom*, 55.

37. Eskew, *But for Birmingham*, 266–67.

38. Hendricks's account found in Levin, *Freedom's Children*, 79; see also inter-view of Judy Tarver in ibid., 80, and of Larry Russell in ibid., 84.

39. See "Contempt Count Sought on Martin Luther King, Jr.," *Los Angeles Times*, April 14, 1963, 1; Eskew, *But for Birmingham*, 266–67.

40. Emory Jackson, "Showdown Nears in Birmingham Fight," *Call and Post*, May 11, 1963, A1; Eskew, *But for Birmingham*, 266–70, 280–81; see also Levin, *Freedom's Children*, 80.

41. Eskew, *But for Birmingham*, 266–75, 281–92, 293.

42. Theo R. Wright to Sir, May 20, 1963, Record of Appeal, U.S. Court of Appeals, Fifth Circuit, Woods v. Wright, No. 20875; Claude Sitton, "U.S. Appeals Judge Orders Birmingham to Reinstate Pupils," *New York Times*, May 23, 1963, 1.

43. Theo R. Wright to Sir, May 20, 1963.

44. "Mary Gadsen Interview," *Freedom's Children*, 85; "anxious" from Rochelle, *Witnesses to Freedom*, 62; Motley Reminiscences, 430.

45. Woods v. Wright, 334 F.2d 369 (5th Cir. 1964).

46. See David M. Halbfinger, "Birmingham Recalls a Time When Children Led the Fight," *New York Times*, May 2, 2003; Representative Terri A. Sewell, Honoring Bishop Calvin Woods Sr., *Congressional Record*, E277, February 28, 2014; Joseph D. Bryant, "Longtime Birmingham Civil Rights Figure Honored with Marker at Kelly Ingram Park," Al.com, September 14, 2014; "Reverend Calvin Wallace Woods, Sr.," The HistoryMakers, www.thehistorymakers.org/biography/reverend-calvin-wallace-woods -sr; Motley, *Equal Justice Under Law*, 135.

47. See Halbfinger, "Birmingham Recalls a Time When Children Led the Fight."

48. See Halbfinger, "Birmingham Recalls a Time When Children Led the Fight"; Andrew Manis, Rev. Calvin Woods Interview, Birmingham Public Library Digital Collections, pp. 1–5; Rev. Abraham L. Woods, University of Alabama, Mervyn H. Sterne Library, Oral History Interview, October 28, 1975.

49. Woods v. Wright, 334 F.2d 369, 370–71 (5th Cir. 1964).

50. See Woods v. Wright, 334 F.2d 369, 372 (5th Cir. 1964); James Barron, "Clarence Allgood, 89, Federal Judge Since 1938," *New York Times*, December 2, 1991; Motley Reminiscences, 431 (referencing "Judge Armstrong" but meaning "Judge Allgood").

51. Motley Reminiscences, 431.

52. Motley Reminiscences, 431–32.

53. Motley Reminiscences, 432.

54. Woods v. Wright, No. CA 63-249 at *2 (U.S.D.C. Ala., May 22, 1963).

55. Woods v. Wright, 334 F.2d 369, 373 (5th Cir. 1964); Motley Reminiscences, 432.

56. Woods v. Wright, 334 F.2d 369, 371–73; Motley Reminiscences, 432; Emanuel, *Elbert Parr Tuttle*, 250.

57. Claude Sitton, "U.S. Appeals Judge Orders Birmingham to Reinstate Pupils," *New York Times*, May 23, 1963, 1; Order, Woods v. Wright, No. 20875 at 2–4 (Tuttle, J.).

58. Woods v. Wright, 334 F.2d 369 (5th Cir. 1964).

59. Woods v. Wright, 334 F.2d 369, 371–75 (5th Cir. 1964).

60. Ernestine Cofield, "Predicts Most Schools in South Will Be Mixed in Five Years," *Chicago Daily Defender*, July 20, 1963, 9.

61. On the difference between movement lawyers and conventional civil rights lawyers, see Brown-Nagin, *Courage to Dissent*, chapter 7; Motley, "The Roles of Women in Civil Rights Struggles," University of Virginia, Carter G. Woodson Institute, May 31, 1989, Columbia Motley Papers, record group IX.

62. "Dr. King vs. Bull Connor," *Afro-American*, April 20, 1963, 1.

63. See Motley, *Equal Justice Under Law*, 196; Greenberg, *Crusaders in the Courts*, 311–12. The cases are Gober v. Birmingham, 373 U.S. 374 (1963); Shuttlesworth v. Birmingham, 373 U.S. 262 (1963).

64. "Played their part" is from Martin Luther King Jr, Address to the Association of the Bar of the City of New York, April 21, 1965, p. 7. Comments about Motley are from Martin Luther King Jr., "The Law Is Majestic," *New York Amsterdam News*, July 31, 1965, 16.

65. See "Martin Luther King's Diary in Jail," *Jet*, August 23, 1962, 18.

66. On King's strained marriage and infidelity, see David J. Garrow, *Bearing*

the Cross, 164–65, 236, 285, 308, 328, 339, 361–62, 374–76, 586. "Compulsive" in ibid., 375.

67. See Ransby, *Ella Baker and the Black Freedom Movement*, 183–92; Morris, *The Origins of the Civil Rights Movement*, 114–15; Garrow, *Bearing the Cross*, 103, 107, 111, 113, 115, 120–21, 141, 150, 188, 311. Lawson quoted in Garrow, *Bearing the Cross*, 141. "Sexist culture" by Cotton, 376. "Chauvinist" from Garrow, *Bearing the Cross*, 375. See also Brown-Nagin, "The Transformation of a Social Movement into Law?"

68. Author interview with Clarence Jones, Esq., October 3, 2017, pp. 10, 11.

69. Author interview with Clarence Jones, Esq., October 3, 2017, p. 5. For a discussion of the women and the NAACP, see chapter 4.

70. See "Remarks by Mrs. Constance Baker Motley at the Opening Banquet at the Annual Convention of SCLC," August 9, 1965, p. 1; see also Ransby, *Ella Baker*, 173, 184. "Beautiful" from Garrow, *Bearing the Cross*, 375.

71. Motley also defended civil rights protesters in Rock Hill and Columbia, South Carolina, Nashville, Tennessee, and Montgomery, Alabama, among other locales, during the 1960s. See Abernathy v. Alabama, 375 U.S. 963 (1964); Edwards v. South Carolina, 369 U.S. 870 (1962); Fields v. South Carolina, 375 U.S. 44 (1963); Henry v. Rock Hill, 375 U.S. 6 (1963); Hamm v. Rock Hill, 377 U.S. 988 (1964); Thompson v. Virginia, 374 U.S. 99 (1963); Bouie v. Columbia, 378 U.S. 347 (1964); Mitchell v. South Carolina, 378 U.S. 551 (1964); Bell v. Maryland, 374 U.S. 805 (1963); Shuttlesworth v. Alabama, 373 U.S. 262 (1962); Gober v. Birmingham, 370 U.S. 934 (1962); Peterson v. Greenville, 370 U.S. 935 (1962); Zellner v. Lingo, 334 F.2d 369 (5th Cir. Ala. 1964), Morrison Cafeteria Co. of Nashville, Inc. v. Johnson, 344 F.2d 690 (6th Cir.).

72. Sitton, "50 Hurt in Negro Rioting After Birmingham Blasts"; Eskew, *But for Birmingham*, 299–303.

73. Eskew, *But for Birmingham*, 3–5.

74. Sitton, "50 Hurt in Negro Rioting After Birmingham Blasts"; Young, *An Easy Burden*, 230.

15. "AN IDEAL CANDIDATE": THE MAKING OF A POLITICAL PROGRESSIVE

1. See Brown-Nagin, *Courage to Dissent*, 226–27; Garrow, *Bearing the Cross*, 281–82.

2. Motley Reminiscences, 489–90.

3. Billye Oliver, "Mrs. Motley Speaks," *New York Amsterdam News*, July 27, 1963, 27.

4. Motley Reminiscences, 444–45.

5. Motley Reminiscences, 445.

6. Motley Reminiscences, 446.

7. Motley Reminiscences, 446–47, 451; March on Washington Organizing Manual No. 1 (1963), NAACP Papers, Group III, Series A, Administrative File General Office File, pp. 31, 37, 43, 261, 265.

8. See John Steele Gordan, "The World's Fair," *American Heritage* 57, no. 5 (October 2006).

9. See Walter, *The Harlem Fox*, 3, 4–6, 8, 10.

10. See Walter, *The Harlem Fox*, 166–67; Peter Kihss, "Ellison Opponent Receives G.O.P. Bid," *New York Times*, January 16, 1964, 21.

11. Walter, *The Harlem Fox*, 167.

12. Motley, *Equal Justice Under Law*, 203.

13. Interview with Dorothy Irene Height, Black Women Oral History Project, 1976–1981, pp. 111–12; Dorothy Height, "A Woman's World," *New York Amsterdam News*, February 5, 1966, 21; Motley, *Equal Justice Under Law*, 206.

14. Interview with Dorothy Irene Height, Black Women Oral History Project, 1976–1981, pp. 111–12; Dorothy Height, "A Woman's World," *New York Amsterdam News*, February 5, 1966, 21; Motley, *Equal Justice Under Law*, 204.

15. Peter Kihss, "Ellison Opponent Receives G.O.P. Bid," *New York Times*, January 16, 1964, 21; Richard P. Hunt, "Ellison Replaced by Mrs. Motley," *New York Times*, January 24, 1964, 13; Motley, *Equal Justice Under Law*, 205.

16. See Haygood, *King of the Cats*, 1–4; Hamilton, *Adam Clayton Powell Jr.*, 425.

17. Motley, *Equal Justice Under Law*, 206; Walter, *The Harlem Fox*, 167, 170.

18. Interview with Dorothy Irene Height, Black Women Oral History Project, 1976–1981, p. 112; Walter, *The Harlem Fox*, 167. The fight between Motley and Ellison also represented a struggle between the reform and regular wings of the Democratic Party. See Hunt, "Ellison Replaced by Mrs. Motley."

19. See Gallagher, *Black Women and Politics in New York City*, 38–39, 41–42, 102, 107, 121–33, 187; Motley, *Equal Justice Under Law*, 204.

20. Motley, *Equal Justice Under Law*, 203.

21. Motley, *Equal Justice Under Law*, 203.

22. Interview with Dorothy Irene Height, Black Women Oral History Project, 1976–1981, p. 112; "Mrs. Motley First Negro Woman Senator," *New York Amsterdam News*, February 8, 1964, 1; Donald Drake, "A Child Turned Away," *Newsday*, February 6, 1964, 31; Walter, *The Harlem Fox*, 167; Hunt, "Ellison Replaced by Mrs. Motley"; Campaign Pamphlets, Smith Motley Papers, box 10, folder 3.

23. James Booker, "Weaver, Motley in Senate Race," *New York Amsterdam News*, February 1, 1964, 1; Donald Drake, "A Child Turned Away," *Newsday*, February 6, 1964, 31; Motley, *Equal Justice Under Law*, 206.

24. "Constance the First"; Booker, "Weaver, Motley in Senate Race"; Drake, "A Child Turned Away"; "Tan Woman Sen. Takes Seat in N.Y."; "New State Senator Takes Her Seat"; Motley, *Equal Justice Under Law*, 206. Motley's bid for election to the Senate was helped when the Liberal Party candidate, Cora Alexander, bowed out of the race during the special election. See "Mrs. Motley Runs for State Senate," *Afro-American*, February 1, 1964, 2.

25. "Sen. Motley Introduces 7 Rights Bills," *New Journal and Guide* (Norfolk, VA), March 7, 1964, 8; "Senator Motley Says Legalize Rent Strikes," *New York Amsterdam News*, March 21, 1964, 23. On landlord and tenant relations and conflict in New York City during the era, see *St. John's Law Review*, "Rent Strike Legislation."

26. An Act to Amend the Domestic Relations Law, Senate of New York, February 25, 1964, Smith Motley Papers, box 10, folder 8; Constance B. Motley to A. W. Rawlings, February 11, 1964, Smith Motley Papers, box 10, folder 13; Constance B. Motley to Hon. Lloyd E. Dickens, February 17, 1964; "Sen. Motley Introduces 7 Rights Bills"; Gallagher, *Black Women and Politics in New York City*, 117.

27. Constance B. Motley to A. W. Rawlings, February 11, 1964, Smith Motley Papers, box 10, folder 13; Constance B. Motley to Hon. Lloyd E. Dickens, February 17, 1964; New York Association of Chiefs of Police, Smith Motley Papers, box 10, folder 13; also see *St. John's Law Review*, "The No-Knock and Stop-and-Frisk Provisions of the New York Criminal Code."

28. Josephine M. Smith to Constance Motley, February 26, 1964, Smith Motley Papers, box 10, folder 13; Edgar Haynes to Constance Baker Motley, Smith Motley Papers, box 10, folder 13; Andrew R. Tyler to Constance Baker Motley, February 16, 1964, Smith Motley Papers, box 10, folder 13.

29. Motley, *Equal Justice Under Law*, 211.

30. See Hamilton v. Alabama, 368 U.S. 52 (1961).

31. Constance B. Motley to A. W. Rawlings, February 11, 1964, Smith Motley Papers, box 10, folder 13; Constance B. Motley to Hon. Lloyd E. Dickens, February 17, 1964. On mass incarceration and its history, see Hinton, *From the War on Poverty to the War on Crime*.

32. See Kenneth B. Clark, *Dark Ghetto*, 21, 30–34; Spear, *Black Chicago*, 23–25; Lewis, *When Harlem Was in Vogue*, 25–26; Thomas J. Sugre, *Sweet Land of Liberty*, 203–7.

33. Motley, "Speech Before the Women's City Club of New York," Smith Motley Papers, box 13, folder 1, item 1, p. 4; "Senator Motley Says Legalize Rent Strikes," *New York Amsterdam News*, March 21, 1964, 23.

34. "Sen. Motley Introduces 7 Rights Bills"; "Senator Motley Says Legalize Rent Strikes." On landlord and tenant relations and conflict in New York City during the era, see *St. John's Law Review*, "Rent Strike Legislation."

35. Constance B. Motley, March 3, 1964, Smith Motley Papers, box 10, folder 17; Print. 3117, Intro. 2905, Senator Motley, An Act to Amend the Education Law, State of New York, March 3, 1964, Smith Motley Papers, box 10, folder 17; Taylor v. Board of Education of New Rochelle, 195 F. Supp. 231, aff'd 294 F.2d. 36, cert. denied 368 U.S. 940 (1961).

36. See Gallagher, *Black Women and Politics in New York City*, 1, 176–77.

16. "CRISIS OF LEADERSHIP":
A CLASH BETWEEN RADICAL AND REFORM POLITICS

1. Caro, *The Passage of Power*, 179–80, 184–87, 197–200, 204–5, 410–11.

2. Caro, *The Passage of Power*, 3–4, 17–21, 537–42; Robert F. Clark, *The War on Poverty*, 1–20. Statistics from United States Bureau of the Census, *Historical Poverty Tables, 1959–2016*, Tables 2, 3, and 4.

3. See Lyndon B. Johnson, Annual Message to the Congress on the State of the Union, January 8, 1964; Robert F. Clark, *The War on Poverty*, 1–20. Statistics from United States Bureau of the Census, *Historical Poverty Tables, 1959–2016*, Tables 2, 3, and 4.

4. Kotz, *Judgment Days*, 27, 89.

5. For context, see United States Bureau of the Census, *Historical Poverty Tables, 1959–2016*; Kotz, *Judgment Days*, 27, 89.

6. See "CORE Plans World's Fair Traffic Jam," *Boston Globe*, April 10, 1964, 36; "CORE Group to Blockade World's Fair," *Chicago Daily Defender*, April 14, 1964, 3; see also Samuel, *New York City 1964*, 180.

7. See "Johnson Critical of Fair Chanting; Mayor Ashamed," *New York Times*, April 24, 1964, 1; "CORE Plans World's Fair Traffic Jam"; "CORE Group to Blockade World's Fair"; "CORE Suspends Chapter for Urging Tie-Up at World's Fair," *New York Times*, April 11, 1964, 1; see also Tirella, *Tomorrow-Land*.

8. See Marable, *Malcolm X*, 133–35, 203–4, 238, 252–54, 264–65, 336–37, 480, 483, 485; Joseph, *Dark Days, Bright Nights*, 65; Malcolm X, "Open Mind Roundtable" (October 1961), in *Malcolm X: Collected Speeches, Debates and Interviews (1960–1965)*, 60.

9. See Branham, "'I Was Gone on Debating,'" 119–23, 130.

10. Transcript, "Open Mind Roundtable," NBC News, October 15, 1961.

11. See Malcolm X, *Malcolm X: Collected Speeches, Debates and Interviews (1960–1965)*, 58.

12. See Marable, *Malcolm X*, 133–35, 203–4, 238, 252–54, 264–65, 336–37, 480, 483, 485.

13. See Clarke, *Malcolm X*, 147–48. Motley quotes from Blackside Interview, November 2, 1985, 12 (Ole Miss), and Motley, *Equal Justice Under Law*, 60 (*Brown*).

14. See Transcript, "Open Mind Roundtable."

15. Hickey and Edwin, *Adam Clayton Powell and the Politics of Race*, 166; Marable, *Malcolm X*, 55–56, 108–9, 126, 133, 204, 210, 262; Haygood, *King of the Cats*, 160; Joseph, *The Sword and the Shield*, 142–43.

16. See "Powell Says Mrs. Motley Wants Out of 35G Post," *Philadelphia Tribune*, June 22, 1965, 6; Motley, *Equal Justice Under Law*, 53–54, 84, 207, 211–12, 244; Hickey and Edwin, *Adam Clayton Powell and the Politics of Race*, 294–96. Motley quote about Powell in *Equal Justice Under Law*, 53–54.

17. See "Malcolm X Termed Stimulus to Action," *New York Times*, March 1, 1965, 17; Motley, "The Civil Rights Crisis," Smith Motley Papers, box 13, folder 1; Motley, *Equal Justice Under Law*, 53–54, 84, 207, 211–12, 244.

18. Paul L. Montgomery and Francis X. Clines, "Thousands Riot in Harlem Area; Scores Are Hurt," *New York Times*, July 19, 1964, 1; Peter Kihss, "Harlem Riots Spread over Three Decades," *New York Times*, July 20, 1964, 17; Hickey and Edwin, *Adam Clayton Powell and the Politics of Race*, 267.

19. "Malcolm X Lays Harlem Riot to 'Scare Tactics' of Police"; Peter Kihss, "Harlem Killings Report Urged," *New York Times*, July 28, 1964, 1; Peter Kihss, "Police in Harlem Reduce Patrols," *New York Times*, July 27, 1964, 1; Hickey and Edwin, *Adam Clayton Powell and the Politics of Race*, 267, 269; Baruch College, "Disasters: Harlem Riots of 1964," https://baruch.cuny.edu/nycdata/disasters/riots-harlem_1964.html.

20. Kihss, "Harlem Killings Report Urged"; Kihss, "Police in Harlem Reduce Patrols." President Eisenhower "federalized" the Arkansas National Guard, placing it under the control of the U.S. Army at a time when the state government had not tamped down a violent mob's attack on the students.

21. Hickey and Edwin, *Adam Clayton Powell and the Politics of Race*, 275.

22. Montgomery and Clines, "Thousands Riot in Harlem Area: Scores Are Hurt"; "N.Y. Race Riots Aimless; Birmingham's Well Planned," July 24, 1964, *Oneonta Star* (New York), 1; "Brutality Board, Pro and Con," *Daily News*, May 18, 1964, 1.

23. "The Civil Rights Crisis," Statement Prepared for the State Democratic Committee Campaign for Schools by Senator Constance Motley (Democrat of Manhattan), Smith Motley Papers, box 13, folder 1, pp. 1, 3–4.

24. "The Civil Rights Crisis," p 2. "Public acceptance" from Motley, "Address by Manhattan Borough President Motley at Luncheon of the Women's Division of American Jewish Congress," May 17, 1965, p. 2. Although Motley gave that address one year after the events described in this paragraph, she repeated themes already on her mind by mid-1964.

25. "The Unique Triple Life of Constance Baker Motley," *New York Herald Tribune*, August 23, 1964.

26. Kotz, *Judgment Days*, 182–83; Brown-Nagin, "The Civil Rights Canon"; "The Unique Triple Life of Constance Baker Motley."

27. See Jackson, *From Civil Rights to Human Rights*, 189, 204; Bayard Rustin, "From Protest to Politics: The Future of the Civil Rights Community," *Commentary*, February 1, 1965; Brown-Nagin, *Courage to Dissent*, 258–60, 266–67; Ashmore, *Carry It On*, 21.

17. "NOT A FEMINIST": THE MANHATTAN BOROUGH PRESIDENCY

1. "Real power" from Motley Reminiscences, 609. Clayton Knowles, "Mrs. Motley Wins Manhattan Post," *New York Times*, February 24, 1965, 1; Motley, *Equal Justice Under Law*, 205.

2. See Remarks by Mayor Robert F. Wagner, Women's Division 13th Annual Political Conference, New York State Democratic Party, March 2, 1964, Robert F. Wagner Documents Collection, Speech Series, box 060053W, folder 12, pp. 1–2; Clayton Knowles, "Mrs. Motley Inducted by Mayor," *New York Times*, February 25, 1965, 1; James F. Clarity, "Robert Wagner, 80, Pivotal New York Mayor, Dies," *New York Times*, February 13, 1991, A1; Motley, *Equal Justice Under Law*, 205. "Prophets of Despair" from Peter Kihss, "Wagner Asserts Disorders Harm Negroes' Cause," *New York Times*, July 23, 1964, 1.

3. "Top Manhattan Post Goes to Motley," *Pittsburgh Courier*, March 6, 1965, 4; Knowles, "Mrs. Motley Wins Manhattan Post"; Thomas P. Ronan, "Mrs. Motley Given G.O.P. Endorsement," *New York Times*, August 13, 1965, 1; Motley, *Equal Justice Under Law*, 205.

4. See Bill Moyers to Lyndon B. Johnson, July 20, 1965, Lyndon Johnson Papers, White House Central Files, Constance Baker Motley folder; Lyndon Johnson and Nicholas Katzenbach, Presidential Recordings Program, Miller Center for Public Affairs, WH6507-03-8326, July 9, 1965; "Manhattan's New President," *New York Times*, February 24, 1965, 40; Marvin Sleeper, "A Lady's Protest to City Hall," *New York Journal-American*, February 19, 1965, 1; "Constance Baker Motley: Judgeship in Borough Post," *New York Amsterdam News*, February 27, 1965, 15; Motley Reminiscences, 624–25.

5. Lillian S. Calhoun, "Confetti," *Chicago Daily Defender*, March 2, 1965, 4; "Rookie Wins Political Plum," *New Journal and Guide* (Norfolk, VA), February 27, 1965, B1; Clayton Knowles, "Mrs. Motley Wins Manhattan Post," *New York Times*, February 24, 1965, 1; Motley, *Equal Justice Under Law*, 205.

6. Knowles, "Mrs. Motley Wins Manhattan Post"; Clayton Knowles, "Mrs. Motley Inducted by Mayor; Brown Is Extolled at Ceremony," *New York Times*, February 25, 1965, 28.

7. Robert F. Wagner, "Dinner in Honor of Mrs. Constance Baker Motley,"

May 17, 1965, pp. 4, 13, 15, 19, 20; Robert F. Wagner Documents Collec., Speeches Series, box 060033W, folder 4, Wagner-LaGuardia Archives, LaGuardia Community College; Knowles, "Mrs. Motley Inducted by Mayor; Brown Is Extolled at Ceremony."

8. Robert F. Wagner, "Dinner in Honor of Mrs. Constance Baker Motley," May 17, 1965, pp. 4, 13; Robert F. Wagner Documents Collec., Speeches Series, box 060033W, folder 4, Wagner-LaGuardia Archives, LaGuardia Community College; "Constance Baker Motley: Judgeship in Borough Post," *New York Amsterdam News*, February 27, 1965, 15; Knowles, "Mrs. Motley Wins Manhattan Post"; Knowles, "Mrs. Motley Inducted by Mayor; Brown Is Extolled at Ceremony." On Jones's aid to Wagner, see Walter, *The Harlem Fox*, 11.

9. James Booker, "Brown v. Motley in Dem Primary," *New York Amsterdam News*, August 14, 1965, 1; Edward C. Burks, "Borough President Race: Mrs. Motley May Turn Judge; Blaikie Hates the Post," *New York Times*, September 12, 1965, 81; Alvin E. White, "$64 Question: Is Ray Jones Seeking Borough Presidency," *Afro-American*, September 4, 1965, 12; "Top Manhattan Post Goes to Mrs. Motley," *Pittsburgh Courier*, March 6, 1965, at 4; "Don't Call Her a Shoo-in," *Miami Herald*, February 24, 1965, A8; "Motley Candidacy Opposed by Adams," *New York Times*, February 20, 1965, 26.

10. Powell opposed Motley's candidacy for both the interim and full-term position. See James W. Sullivan, "Mrs. Motley for Borough Chief?—Rep. Powell Objects," *New York Herald Tribune*, n.d.; "Top Manhattan Post Goes to Mrs. Motley"; "Don't Call Her a Shoo-in" ; "Motley Candidacy Opposed by Adams"; Walter, *The Harlem Fox*, 192–93.

11. On Black campaigns for voting rights, see, for example, Lawson, *Black Ballots*; Lawson, *Running for Freedom*.

12. See May, *Bending Toward Justice*, 54; see also Martin Luther King Jr., "Give Us the Ballot," Martin Luther King Jr. Papers, vol. 4, Stanford University.

13. May, *Bending Toward Justice*, 90–91.

14. May, *Bending Toward Justice*, 130–47; Motley, *Equal Justice Under Law*, 207–8; Motley Reminiscences, 385, 387.

15. See Telegram from Lawrence F. O'Brien to Constance Motley, August 5, 1965, Lyndon B. Johnson Papers, White House Central Files, Constance Baker Motley folder.

16. See Bayard Rustin, "From Protest to Politics: The Future of the Civil Rights Movement," *Commentary*, February 1, 1965.

17. See Remarks by Constance Baker Motley, Borough President of Manhattan, at the Opening Banquet of the Convention of the Southern Christian Leadership Conference, Birmingham, Alabama, August 9, 1965, Smith Motley Papers, box 13, folder 3; Lawrence Alexander, "Early Days Recalled by Judge," *Times-Picayune*, March 31, 1985, at A34.

18. "Borough President Cited for Outstanding Achievement," *New Journal and Guide* (Norfolk, VA), September 25, 1965, B8; Elizabeth Shelton, "Phi Delta Kappa to Honor Constance Motley," *Washington Post*, August 10, 1965; "Luncheon to Honor Constance B. Motley," *Call and Post*, November 13, 1965, at B7; "First Park Yule Tree Is Lighted in Union Sq.," *New York Times*, December 4, 1965, 33; "NBPW List Sammy Davis for Awards Luncheon," *New York Amsterdam News*, May 1, 1965, 17.

19. Remarks by Manhattan Borough President Constance Baker Motley Before the Second Borough President's Conference of Community Leaders, January 21, 1966, Smith Motley Papers, box 13, folder 5; Samuel Kaplan, "Mrs. Motley Urges Broadening of Citizen's Role in Government," *New York Times*, July 1, 1965, at 17.

20. Remarks by Manhattan Borough President Constance Baker Motley Before the Second Borough President's Conference of Community Leaders, January 21, 1966, Smith Motley Papers, box 13, folder 5; "Mrs. Motley Seeks Plan for Harlem," *New York Times*, September 7, 1965, 36; "Mrs. Motley Battles for a Better Harlem," *New York Amsterdam News*, September 11, 1965, 4; Samuel Kaplan, "Mrs. Motley Urges Broadening of Citizen's Role in Government," *New York Times*, July 1, 1965, 17. Block quote is from Lyn Shepard, "Candidates Given 'New Harlem' Goal," *Christian Science Monitor*, October 4, 1965, 6.

21. "Tripartisan Mrs. Motley," *New York Times*, August 14, 1965, 22; "Motley Winner," *New York Amsterdam News*, November 6, 1965, 2; "Borough President Cited for Outstanding Achievement."

22. Telegram to Constance Baker Motley from Martin Luther King Jr., Ralph Abernathy, Fred L. Shuttlesworth, and Wyatt T. Walker, n.d., Smith Motley Papers, box 8, folder 28; James Meredith to Constance Baker Motley, Smith Motley Papers, box 8, folder 28; NAACP Legal Defense Fund Press Release, Columbia Motley Collection.

23. Alice Hammond to Constance Baker Motley, April 12, 1965, Smith Motley Papers, box 8, folder 28; Anonymous to Constance Baker Motley, n.d., Smith Motley Papers, box 8, folder 28.

24. Alice Hammond to Constance Baker Motley, April 12, 1965, Smith Motley Papers, box 8, folder 28; Anonymous to Constance Baker Motley, n.d., Smith Motley Papers, box 8, folder 28.

25. See Clayton Knowles, "Mrs. Motley Wins Manhattan Post," *New York Times*, February 24 1965, 1.

26. See Hoff, *Law, Gender and Injustice*, 230–32, 233; Gallagher, *Black Women and Politics*, 152–53, 173–74, 176–78.

27. George H. Favre, "Manhattan Finds a Spokesman," *Christian Science Monitor*, April 5, 1965, 15; "Constance Baker Motley Thrives Under Pressure," *Philadelphia Tribune*, April 10, 1965, 6; Virginia Pasley, "Profile: Con-

stance Baker Motley," *Newsday*, March 8, 1965, 33; Lillian S. Calhoun, "Confetti," *Chicago Daily Defender*, March 2, 1965, 4; "Manhattan Head," *Chicago Tribune*, February 24, 1965, 28; "Orchid for the Day," *Chicago Daily Defender*, February 25, 1965, 3; "UL Asks Mrs. Motley for Speed," *Chicago Daily Defender*, March 6, 1965, 7.

28. Shirley Chisholm to Constance Baker Motley, March 22, 1965, Smith Motley Papers, box 8, folder 10; Constance Baker Motley to Shirley Chisholm, March 25, 1965, Smith Motley Papers, box 8, folder 10. On Chisholm, see Brownmiller, *Shirley Chisholm*, 75–83.

29. See Dorothy Kenyon to Constance Baker Motley, February 20, 1964, Smith College, Kenyon Papers, box 15, folder 36; Constance Baker Motley to Dorothy Kenyon, February 25, 1964, Kenyon Papers, box 15, folder 36; Constance Baker Motley to Dorothy Kenyon, Kenyon Papers, November 13, 1964, box 15, folder 36. For more on Kenyon, see Kate Weigand and Daniel Horowitz, "Dorothy Kenyon: Feminist Organizing, 1919–1963," *Journal of Women's History* 14, no. 2 (Summer 2002): 126–31.

30. See Dorothy Kenyon to Constance Baker Motley, September 16, 1965, Kenyon Papers, Smith College, box 15, folder 36; Constance Baker Motley to Dorothy Kenyon, October 5, 1965, Kenyon Papers, box 15, folder 36.

31. See Hon. Constance Baker Motley, Acceptance of AAUW Woman of the Year Award, Columbia University Club, October 8, 1965, Smith Motley Papers, box 13, folder 4.

32. See Hon. Constance Baker Motley, Address at the Women's Day of the Abyssinian Baptist Church, March 13, 1966, Smith Motley Papers, box 13, folder 5.

33. Hon. Constance Baker Motley, Address at the Women's Day of the Abyssinian Baptist Church, March 13, 1966, Smith Motley Papers, box 13, folder 5.

34. Constance Baker Motley, Remarks at New York Club of the National Association of Negro Business and Professional Women, n.d., Smith Motley Papers, box 13, folder 5.

35. "Manhattan President," *Evening Times* (Trenton, NJ), February 24, 1965; "Mrs. Motley New Borough Chief," *Afro-American*, March 6, 1965, A1; "NYC Borough President," *Chicago Daily Defender*, February 25, 1965, 6: "UL Asks Mrs. Motley for Speed," *New York Amsterdam News*, March 6, 1965, 7; Gay Pauley, " 'Not Feminist,' Says Boro Prexy," *Chicago Daily Defender*, March 8, 1965, 11.

36. Gallagher, *Black Women and Politics in New York City*, 114–16; 202; Motley Reminiscences, 597.

37. "Mrs. C.B. Motley Is Busy 'Boss,' " *New York Times*, September 12, 1965; Constance Baker Motley, Remarks at YMCA Conference, December 2, 1965, Smith Motley Papers, box 13, folder 4.

38. See "I'm Not a Feminist Says Madame Borough President," *New Journal and Guide* (Norfolk, VA), March 13, 1965, A8; Pasley, "Profile: Constance B. Motley"; Mrs. C.B. Motley Is Busy 'Boss' "; Pauley, " 'Not Feminist,' Says Boro Prexy."

39. See Sara Slack, "Mrs. Motley Marks 2 Big Milestones," *New York Amsterdam News*, September 18, 1965, 29; William Borders, "Mrs. Motley Honored at Yale, Where Her Father Was a Chef," *New York Times*, May 18, 1965, 34; Pasley, "Profile: Constance Baker Motley"; see Donald Drake, "A Child Turned Away," *Newsday*, February 6, 1964, 31; Richard P. Hunt, "Ellison Replaced by Mrs. Motley," *New York Times*, January 24, 1964, 13; Richard P. Hunt, "Mrs. Motley Wins Senate Seat; Wrong Liberal Candidate Listed," *New York Times*, February 5, 1964, 1; "Mrs. Motley Is Sworn In," news clipping no. 234, Columbia Motley Collection; "One Chuckle Missing," news clipping no. 246, Columbia Motley Collection; Clayton Knowles, "Mrs. Motley Wins Manhattan Post," *New York Times*, February 24, 1965, 1.

40. See William Borders, "Mrs. Motley Honored at Yale, Where Her Father Was a Chef," *New York Times*, May 18, 1965, 34; Pasley, "Profile: Constance Baker Motley"; Drake, "A Child Turned Away"; Hunt, "Ellison Replaced by Mrs. Motley"; Hunt, "Mrs. Motley Wins Senate Seat; Wrong Liberal Candidate Listed"; "Mrs. Motley Is Sworn In," news clipping no. 234, Columbia Motley Collection; "One Chuckle Missing," news clipping no. 246, Columbia Motley Collection; Knowles, "Mrs. Motley Wins Manhattan Post." For criticisms of the pantsuit, see Marylin Bender, "The Continuing Story of the Pants Suit: Will It Survive?," *New York Times*, April 10, 1967, 43. "Glamour girl" from Slack, "Mrs. Motley Marks 2 Big Milestones." "Pride in being a woman" from Hon. Ann Claire Williams, "Tribute to Constance Baker Motley," n.d., p. 7 (on file with author).

41. "New BP Looks at Schools, Slums," news clipping, n.d., Columbia Motley Collection.

42. Remarks by Hon. Constance Baker Motley, Women and Work Conference, Smith College, March 10, 1982, p. 22, Smith Motley Papers; "I'm Not a Feminist Says Madame Borough President."

43. "Constance Baker Motley Thrives Under Pressure," *Philadelphia Tribune*, April 10, 1965, 6; George H. Favre, "Manhattan Finds a Spokesman," *Christian Science Monitor*, April 5, 1965, 15; "Mrs. Motley Is Sworn In," news clipping no. 234, Columbia Motley Collection; "One Chuckle Missing," news clipping no. 246, Columbia Motley Collection; Pauley, " 'Not Feminist,' Says Boro Prexy."

18. "FIRST": THE JUDICIAL CONFIRMATION

1. On the history of Lord & Taylor, see Toni Schlesinger, "Dear Lord & Taylor, Retail's Resting Place," *New York Observer*, September 11, 2006, https://

observer.com/2006/09/dear-lord-taylor-retails-resting-place/; Stephanie Amerian, "Dorothy Shaver: Fifth Avenue's First Lady," UCLA Center for the Study of Women, June 1, 2009, https://escholarship.org/uc/item /7w18h2jx. See also Motley, *Equal Justice Under Law*, 213.

2. See "Judge Known as Boat-Rocker in New York Politics," *Globe and Mail*, January 27, 1966, W5.

3. Motley Reminiscences, 685.

4. Motley Reminiscences, 685.

5. Motley, *Equal Justice Under Law*, 213.

6. Marie Smith, "Where Are the Can-Do Women," *Washington Post*, May 30, 1965, F1; Kotz, *Judgment Days*, 43–44, 94.

7. Transcript, Louis Martin Oral History Interview 1, by David G. McComb, May 14, 1969, Lyndon Baines Johnson Oral History Collection, LBJ Presidential Library, p. 8; Transcript, Nicholas deB. Katzenbach Oral History Interview, by Paige E. Mulhollan, Lyndon Baines Johnson Oral History Collection, LBJ Presidential Library, p. 9; Kotz, *Judgment Days*, 43–44, 94.

8. See Navasky, *Kennedy Justice*, 277–78.

9. See Navasky, *Kennedy Justice*, 277-78.

10. See Navasky, *Kennedy Justice*, 278, 279; Motley Reminiscences, 493; "William Harold Cox, Outspoken Federal Judge," *New York Times*, February 27, 1988, 12.

11. See Kotz, *Judgment Days*, 94, 356; on the struggle in the New York Senate, see Motley, *Equal Justice Under Law*, 209–11.

12. Motley, *Equal Justice Under Law*, 213.

13. "Mrs. Motley Is Chosen for a Federal Judgeship Here," *New York Times*, January 26, 1966, 1.

14. Motley, *Equal Justice Under Law*, 215–16.

15. See Annis, *Big Jim Eastland*, 155, 161–62; Marjorie Hunter, "James O. Eastland Is Dead at 81; Leading Senate Foe of Integration," *New York Times*, February 20, 1986; Eagles, *The Price of Defiance*, 74–75.

16. See Annis, *Big Jim Eastland*, 166–67, 170–71, 175–76, 226–34 (discussing the powers associated with Senator Eastland's role and how he deployed them). On Eastland's opposition to Marshall, see Juan Williams, *Thurgood Marshall*, 10, 299–300, 302–3, 336.

17. See 112 *Congressional Record* 21,215 (1966) (statement of Sen. Eastland). On the April hearing, see United States Senate, Report of Proceedings, Subcommittee of the Committee on the Judiciary, Nomination of Constance Baker Motley to the United States District Court, April 4, 1966, Washington, DC.

18. The Supreme Court held that individuals could not be prosecuted for Communist Party membership alone in *Yates v. United States*, 354 U.S.

298, 331–32 (1957), but upheld mandatory registration and the right to penalize suspected subversives in *Communist Party of United States v. Subversive Activities Control Board*, 367 U.S. 1, 81–94 (1961). For a discussion of Supreme Court First Amendment jurisprudence during the Red Scares, see Jay, "The Creation of the First Amendment Right to Free Expression"; Sabin, *In Calmer Times*, 138–42. For an overview of laws, court decisions, and developments related to the Communists, particularly during the two Red Scares, see Haynes, *Red Scare or Red Menace?*, 64–88, 163–89; Storrs, *The Second Red Scare and the Unmaking of the New Deal Left*, 203–4, 286–90; Sabin, *In Calmer Times*, 209–11.

19. See 112 *Congressional Record* 21,215 (1966) (statement of Sen. Eastland); James L. Farmer, Federal Bureau of Investigation File, 100-433744, January. In her memoir, Motley identified an "Estella Segritta." Motley, *Equal Justice Under Law*, 215–16. However, further research indicated that the correct spelling is Sgritta, best known as "Stella." See Stella Sgritta from Stamford in 1940 Census District 1-182.

20. See Woods, *Black Struggle, Red Scare*, 43–44; Annis, *Big Jim Eastland*, 95–115, 155, 182, 210 (discussing Senator Eastland's obsession with alleged Black Communists and with subversive activities by advocates of labor and civil rights). The Senate Internal Security Subcommittee was the analog to the better-known House Un-American Activities Committee. The Senate subcommittee was "charged with investigating the 'extent, nature, and effects' of Communist and subversive activities in the United States." Annis, *Big Jim Eastland*, 100. Senator Eastland drafted the measure that created the subcommittee. Annis, *Big Jim Eastland*, 95.

21. Constance Baker Motley, Statement to Special Agents of the Federal Bureau of Investigation, March 24, 1966.

22. For more discussion of the leftist political context in which Motley came of age, see chapters 2 and 3; Gallagher, *Black Women and Politics in New York City*, 5, 52, 91; Welky, *Marching Across the Color Line*, 7, 12; Haygood, *King of the Cats*, 44–45, 98, 101, 147; McDuffie, *Sojourning for Freedom*, 2–3, 7, 137–46. See also 112 *Congressional Record* 21,215–16 (statement of Sen. Eastland); Motley, *Equal Justice Under Law*, 215–17; "Mrs. Motley Gets Senate Voice OK," *Afro-American*, September 10, 1966, 13.

23. See Gallagher, *Black Women and Politics in New York City*, 5, 52, 91; McDuffie, *Sojourning for Freedom*, 2–3, 7, 137–46. See also 112 *Congressional Record* 21,215–16 (statement of Sen. Eastland); Motley, *Equal Justice Under Law*, 215–17; "Mrs. Motley Gets Senate Voice OK," *Afro-American*, September 10, 1966, 13.

24. Constance Baker Motley File, Federal Bureau of Investigation, Freedom of Information Privacy Office (contents on file with author); Memorandum from W. V. Cleveland to Mr. Gale, March 10, 1966.

25. Memorandum from W. V. Cleveland to Mr. Gale, March 10, 1966; Memo from Special Agent to FBI field office file, NH 161-3994, Bureau File 161-3994, March 30, 1966.

26. See Statement to FBI Special Agents of Constance Baker Motley, March 24, 1966; Motley, *Equal Justice Under Law*, 215–17.

27. See Memorandum from W. V. Cleveland to Mr. Gale, May 11, 1966, in Motley FBI file; see also 112 *Congressional Record* 21,215–16 (statement of Sen. Eastland); Motley, *Equal Justice Under Law*, 215–17; "Mrs. Motley Gets Senate Voice OK," *Afro-American*, September 10, 1966, 13.

28. See Woods, *Black Struggle, Red Scare*, 244–53.

29. Memorandum from N. P. Callahan to J. Edgar Hoover, August 31, 1966, in Motley, FBI file; Summary, Constance Baker Motley Interviews, August 5, 1965, 3–10.

30. 112 *Congressional Record* 21,216 (statement of Sen. Javits).

31. Motley, *Equal Justice Under Law*, 218.

32. See, e.g., Memorandum from Ramsey Clark to President Lyndon B. Johnson (September 14, 1965); Letter from Dave Hitchcock to President Lyndon B. Johnson (September 2, 1966); Letter from Cecile L. Piltz, Attorney at Law, to President Lyndon B. Johnson (September 3, 1966); Letter from Mrs. William A. Harris to President Lyndon B. Johnson (September 27, 1966); Jesse Helms, Editorial, WRAL TV: Viewpoint #1431 (September 6, 1966) (noting that Motley's legal career had then consisted entirely of civil rights litigation); "Mrs. Motley Is Chosen for a Federal Judgeship Here," *New York Times*, January 26, 1966, 1; see also Motley, *Equal Justice Under Law*, 217–18, 218–19, 222.

   The ABA has consistently rated minority and women lawyers lower than white male lawyers. See Sen, "How Judicial Qualifications Ratings May Disadvantage Minority and Female Candidates" (showing that African American and women lawyers are more likely to receive lower ratings, even when controlling for education and experience over the past fifty years); Dylan Matthews, "Has the American Bar Association Kept Our Judges White and Male?," *Washington Post*, February 28, 2013, www.washingtonpost.com/news/wonk/wp/2013/02/28/has-the-american-bar-association-kept-our-judges-white-and-male/?utm_term=.ac6e86e96b90 [http://perma.cc/5R3B-QFBX] (discussing Sen's findings "arguing that the ABA has for the past fifty years been systematically less likely to recommend the judicial confirmations of women or racial minorities"); Adam Serwer, "American Bar Association Under Fire for Underrating Women, Minorities," MSNBC, May 12, 2014, www.msnbc.com/msnbc/american-bar-association-diversity-ratings [http://perma.cc/8Z8J-AG4K] (discussing evidence that shows the ABA "rates women and minority candidates for the federal bench lower than white men").

33. See Letter from Nicholas deB. Katzenbach to President Lyndon B. Johnson (July 14, 1965) (on file with *Columbia Law Review*) (discussing Senator Kennedy's qualified support for Motley).

34. See Juan Williams, *Thurgood Marshall*, 314–15.

35. Transcript of Recording No. WH6507-03-8326, Nicholas Katzenbach and President Lyndon B. Johnson, July 9, 1965, 2:00 p.m., Presidential Recordings Program, Miller Center of Public Affairs, University of Virginia.

36. Nicholas deB. Katzenbach to Lyndon B. Johnson, July 14, 1965; Clifford L. Alexander Jr. to Bill D. Moyers, July 20, 1965, Macy Papers, box 411, CBM folder, LBJ Presidential Library. Motley believed Kennedy had developed second thoughts about that, partly because of Motley's vote against a candidate for state office whom Kennedy opposed. Motley, *Equal Justice Under Law*, 210–12. In reality, much more was at play.

37. Nicholas deB. Katzenbach to Lyndon B. Johnson, July 14, 1965; Clifford L. Alexander Jr. to Bill D. Moyers, July 20, 1965, Macy Papers, box 411, CBM folder, LBJ Presidential Library. Kennedy backed Ed Weinfield. Wilfred Feinberg, also Jewish, was appointed to Marshall's seat in January 1966. Kennedy originally submitted Motley's name for a district court appointment but then developed second thoughts about that, partly because of Motley's vote against a candidate for state office whom Kennedy opposed. Motley, *Equal Justice Under Law*, 210–12.

38. Nicholas deB. Katzenbach to Lyndon B. Johnson, July 14, 1965; Clifford L. Alexander Jr. to Bill D. Moyers, July 20, 1965, Macy Papers, box 411, CBM folder, LBJ Presidential Library. Kennedy backed Ed Weinfield. Wilfred Feinberg, also Jewish, was appointed to Marshall's seat in January 1966.

39. 112 *Congressional Record*, 21,217 (1966).

40. "Re: Appointment of Constance Baker Motley," White House memorandum, n.d., Macy Papers, box 411, CBM folder, LBJ Presidential Library.

41. "Re: Appointment of Constance Baker Motley," White House memorandum, n.d., Macy Papers, box 411, CBM folder, LBJ Presidential Library. Quotes from "Constance Baker Motley," *Hartford Courant*, September 3, 1966, 12, in response to Motley's confirmation vote.

42. "As Constance Motley Becomes a Federal Judge, Lady Lawyer's Cinderella Story Comes to Happy End," *New Journal and Guide* (Norfolk, VA), September 10, 1966; see also Letter from Mabel S. Bouldin, Supreme Basileus, Nat'l Sorority of Phi Delta Kappa, & Helen W. Green, Nat'l Dir. of Pub. Relations, Nat'l Sorority of Phi Delta Kappa, to President Lyn-

don B. Johnson (February 3, 1966); Letter from Judge Anna M. Kross to President Lyndon B. Johnson (January 27, 1966); Letter from LaCretia Lamb, Exec. Dir., Citizens Care Comm., Inc., to President Lyndon B. Johnson (January 27, 1966); Letter from Robert E. Harding, Jr., et al. to President Lyndon B. Johnson (May 10, 1965); Letter from Paul O'Dwyer, Councilman at Large, The Council of the City of N.Y. City Hall, to President Lyndon B. Johnson (April 29, 1965); "Mrs. Motley Is Chosen for a Federal Judgeship Here," *New York Times*, January 26, 1966, 1.

43. See "March Ends in Rock Fight," *Chicago Tribune*, September 5, 1966; "New Lansing Riots Halted by Tear Gas," *Chicago Tribune*, August 9, 1966; "Bar U.S. School Guidelines," *Chicago Tribune*, September 3, 1966; Charles E. Jones, "The Political Repression of the Black Panther Party 1966–1971; "The National Organization for Women's 1966 Statement of Purpose," https://now.org/about/history/statement-of-purpose/ (last accessed February 20, 2019); see also Sugre, *Sweet Land of Liberty*, 356–99.

44. See transcript of Thurgood Marshall interview by T. H. Baker, LBJ Oral History Collection, July 10, 1969, p. 9; Goldman, *Picking Federal Judges*, 180–83; "Mrs. Motley Is Chosen for a Federal Judgeship Here," *New York Times*, 1; Motley, *Equal Justice Under Law*, 214; Memorandum from John B. Clinton to John Macy.

45. Proceedings Held on the Occasion of the Induction of the Honorable Constance Baker Motley as United States District Judge for the Southern District of New York, September 9, 1966, Senator Jacob K. Javits Collection, Stony Brook University, Series 9, Subseries 3, Appointments, 1957–1980, box 5, folder, Judges, 1965–1966; "Civil Rights Attorney Becomes Federal Judge," *Hartford Courant*, September 10, 1966, 43.

46. See "As Constance Motley Becomes a Federal Judge, Lady Lawyer's Cinderella Story Comes to Happy End"; Letter from Mabel S. Bouldin, Supreme Basileus, Nat'l Sorority of Phi Delta Kappa, & Helen W. Green, Nat'l Dir. of Pub. Relations, Nat'l Sorority of Phi Delta Kappa, to President Lyndon B. Johnson (February 3, 1966); Letter from Judge Anna M. Kross to President Lyndon B. Johnson (January 27, 1966); Letter from LaCretia Lamb, Exec. Dir., Citizens Care Comm., Inc., to President Lyndon B. Johnson (January 27, 1966); Letter from Robert E. Harding, Jr., et al. to President Lyndon B. Johnson (May 10, 1965); Letter from Paul O'Dwyer, Councilman at Large, The Council of the City of N.Y. City Hall, to President Lyndon B. Johnson (April 29, 1965).

A few years after Motley's appointment to the district court, the National Women's Political Caucus expressly pointed to "demonstrated commitment to the human issues" as a general requirement for any nominee when it proposed Motley as a nominee for an open seat on the U.S.

Supreme Court. See "Suggest 10 Women for Top Court," *Chicago Tribune*, September 27, 1971.

47. See, e.g., Letter from Mrs. William A. Harris to President Lyndon B. Johnson; Letter from Dave Hitchcock to President Lyndon B. Johnson; Letter from Cecile L. Piltz to President Lyndon B. Johnson.

48. See Cecile L. Piltz to Lyndon B. Johnson, September 3, 1966, Office Files of John Macy, box 411, CBM folder, LBJ Presidential Library; "693 Who Passed the New York Bar Exam," *New York Times*, December 27, 1937, 21; "County Bar Group Lists Committees," *New York Times*, August 8, 1943, 38.

49. James E. Marsh Jr. to Cecile L. Piltz, September 13, 1966, Office Files of John Macy, box 411, CBM folder, LBJ Presidential Library.

19. "A TOUGH OLD BIRD": JUDGE MOTLEY'S COURT

1. "Greatest" from Judge Edward Weinfeld as quoted in "The United States District Court for the Southern District of New York: A Retrospective (1990–2000)," New York County Lawyers' Association Committee on the Federal Courts, December 2002, p. 5, http://web.archive.org/web/20030821105518/www.nycla.org/publications/fedcts.pdf.

2. Motley Reminiscences, 777; author interview with Michael Ratner, September 1, 2018; statements of Kevin Fong and Howard Fischer, Botein, "Judge Motley Memories"; see also Anna Quindlen, "Case History: Judge v. Life," *New York Times*, August 25, 1977. On the court and its stature, see *History of the United States District Court for the Southern District of New York* (New York: Federal Bar Association, 1962).

3. Author interview with Kevin Fong, July 12, 2014; author interview with Dorothy Roberts, July 24, 2014. "Opportunities" from Botein, "Judge Motley Memories."

4. On ongoing efforts to increase law clerk diversity, see Tony Maura, "Law Clerk Diversity: 'It's Complicated,' " *National Law Journal*, September 26, 2019; "Courting Clerkships: The NALP Judicial Clerkship Study," October 2000; author interview with Elizabeth Schneider, July 24, 2014; author interview with Kevin Fong, July 12, 2014; author interview with Leonora Wayland, July 20, 2015.

5. See Anna Quindlen, " 'Ordinary Woman' Makes History," *New York Times*, August 31, 1977, B1; Motley, *Equal Justice Under Law*, 26; author interview with Lan Cao; author interview with Elizabeth Schneider, July 24, 2014; author interview with Kevin Fong, July 12, 2014; author interview with Leonora Wayland, July 20, 2015; author interview with Nell Moskowitz, April 17, 2012; author interview with Hon. Anne Thompson, June 23, 2014; author interview with Richard Blum, July 24, 2014; author interview with Dorothy Roberts, July 24, 2014; Motley Reminiscences, 777.

6. See Howard W. French, "Guiding Wedtech Trial, a Sure Hand," *New York*

Times, n.d.; Lamson, ed., *Few Are Chosen*. On judicial virtues, see, e.g., Solum, "The Virtues and Vices of a Judge," 1735, 1740 (citing intelligence, integrity, and wisdom).

7. See, e.g., Higginbotham, "African-American Women's History and the Metalanguage of Race" (defining respectability politics as the pursuit of belonging and civil rights within the context of embracing of white middle-class notions of proper behavior, particularly for women). "Formidable" from author interview with Hon. Pierre Leval, August 15, 2017. "Scary" from author interview with John Gordon, January 25, 2013. "Bird" from author interview with Lynn Huntley, July 24, 2014.

8. Author interview with Elizabeth Schneider, July 24, 2014; author interview with Kevin Fong, July 12, 2014; author interview with Laura Swain, July 3, 2014; author interview with Lynn Huntley, July 24, 2014; author interview with Nell Moskowitz, April 17, 2012; statement of Simon Procas and Sara Moss, Botein, "Judge Motley Memories." Motley's reference to "harassing" lawyers is found in Motley, *Equal Justice Under Law*, 226, and to anger in ibid., 100. On disrespect to women judges more generally, see Lynn Hecht Schafran, "Not from Central Casting," 953, 958–59.

9. Author interview with Elizabeth Schneider, July 24, 2014; author interview with Kevin Fong, July 12, 2014; author interview with Laura Swain, July 3, 2014; statement of Barbara Botein, Botein, "Judge Motley Memories."

10. See author interview with Lan Cao, July 12, 2014; author interview with Elizabeth Schneider, July 24, 2014; author interview with Dorothy Roberts, July 24, 2014; statement of Linda Calder and the Honorable Lindsey Miller-Lerman, Botein, "Judge Motley Memories."

11. See author interview with Lan Cao, July 12, 2014; author interview with Daniel Steinbock, July 24, 2014; author interview with Elizabeth Schneider, July 24, 2014; author interview with Kevin Fong, July 12, 2014; author interview with Laura Swain, July 3, 2014; Quindlen, "Case History: Judge v. Life."

12. Author interview with Christi Cunningham, July 14, 2014; author interview with Lan Cao, July 12, 2014; author interview with Daniel Steinbock, July 24, 2014; author interview with Kevin Fong, July 12, 2014; author interview with Laura Swain, July 3, 2014; author interview with Richard Blum, July 24, 2014; statement of Bruce Freedman and Scott Optican, Botein, "Judge Motley Memories."

13. Author interview with Laura Swain, July 3, 2014; statement of Sara Moss and Scott Optican, Botein, "Judge Motley Memories"; author interview with Daniel Steinbock, July 24, 2014.

14. Author interview with Lan Cao, July 12, 2014; statement of Susan Davis and Barbara Botein, Botein, "Judge Motley Memories."

15. Author interview with Christi Cunningham, July 14, 2014; author interview with Lan Cao, July 12, 2014; author interview with Daniel Steinbock, July 24, 2014; author interview with Kevin Fong, July 12, 2014; statement of Susan Davis and the Honorable Lindsey Miller-Lerman, Botein, "Judge Motley Memories"; Motley, *Equal Justice Under Law*, 100.

16. Author interview with Leonora Wayland, July 20, 2015; author interview with Isolde Motley, July 15, 2014; Chester Land Trust Application to the Connecticut Freedom Trail, September 12, 2018, p. 5; "Judge Buys Chester Home," *Hartford Courant*, August 19, 1966; Michelle Jacklin, "Baseball Judge Stars on the Bench," *Hartford Courant*, January 7, 1979, H6.

17. Author interview with Christi Cunningham, July 14, 2014; author interview with Dorothy Roberts, July 24, 2014; author interview with Lan Cao, July 12, 2014; author interview with Daniel Steinbock, July 24, 2014; author interview with Kevin Fong, July 12, 2014; author interview with Richard Blum, July 24, 2014; statement of Sara Moss and Bruce Freedman, Botein, "Judge Motley Memories."

20. "THE WEEPING AND THE WAILING":
THE BLACK PANTHER PARTY, THE FBI, AND THE HUGGINS FAMILY

1. Author interview with Constance Royster, June 25, 2014, 16; author interview with Joan and Carolyn Huggins, September 25, 2019, pp. 2–3, 6. See also Motley, *Equal Justice Under Law*, 13. Edward, Motley's uncle (her mother's brother), was John Jr.'s grandfather.

2. "Shooting Victim New Haven Native," *Hartford Courant*, January 21, 1969, 1.

3. Robert Sanford, "Panthers Split on Seale Trial," *St. Louis Post-Dispatch*, March 21, 1971, A2; "Nixon Puts 'Bum' Label on Some College Radicals," *New York Times*, May 2, 1970, 1; Sam Negri, "Slain 'Panther' Active in Rights Drive Here Before Going to L.A.," *New Haven Register*, January 19, 1969, 1; author interview with Joan and Carolyn Huggins, September 25, 2019, p. 3.

4. Author interview with Constance Royster, June 25, 2014, p. 16; author interview with Joan and Carolyn Huggins, September 25, 2019, pp. 2–3, 6. See also Motley, *Equal Justice Under Law*, 13.

5. See Brown-Nagin, *Courage to Dissent*, 255–56; Plummer, *In Search of Power*, 15–17; Joseph, *Stokely*.

6. Gail Sheedy, "Black Against Black: The Agony of Panthermania," *New York*, November 16, 1970.

7. Author interview with Joan and Carolyn Huggins, September 25, 2019, pp. 3–4; Sheedy, "Black Against Black," 47.

8. Author interview with Joan and Carolyn Huggins, September 25, 2019, p. 4. "Five Get Jail Terms in Protest," *Hartford Courant*, November 11,

1967, 1–2; "Welfare Department Demonstrators Plead Innocent," *Hart-ford Courant*, November 19, 1966, 7.

9. Quotes from Ericka found in Freed, *Agony in New Haven*, 62–64; see also Platt and O'Leary, "Two Interviews with Ericka Huggins."

10. Author interview with Constance Royster, June 25, 2014, p. 16; author interview with Joan and Carolyn Huggins, September 25, 2019, p 4. Quotes from Ericka found in Freed, *Agony in New Haven*, 62–64; Platt and O'Leary, "Two Interviews with Ericka Huggins." Quotes from John Sr. found in Sheehy, "Black Against Black."

11. Freed, *Agony in New Haven*, 63; author interview with Joan and Carolyn Huggins, September 25, 2019, p. 4. On the Panthers and context, see Plummer, *In Search of Power*, 208, 219, 231, 235.

12. Author interview with Constance Royster, June 25, 2014, p. 16; author interview with Joan and Carolyn Huggins, September 25, 2019, p. 4;

13. See Bloom and Martin, *Black Against Empire*, 139–40. Author interview with Joan and Carolyn Huggins, September 25, 2019, p. 9.

14. Larry May, "Two Black Men Sought by Police for Slayings in Campbell Hall Friday," *UCLA Daily Bruin*, January 20, 1969, 1; Freed, *Agony in New Haven*, 65; Sam Negri, "Slain 'Panther' Active in Rights Drive Here Before Going to L.A.," *New Haven Register*, January 19, 1969, 1; author interview with Joan and Carolyn Huggins, September 25, 2019, p. 4.

15. Nearly a decade later, a U.S. Senate Select Committee established in 1976 to review the FBI's intelligence activities would concede that the agency's "abusive" COINTELPRO practices had surrounded the Panthers in a "climate of violence," disinformation, and conspiracy theories that led to the slaying of many friends, and foes, of the party, and violated the constitutional rights of numerous Americans. See John Kifner, "F.B.I. Sought Doom of Panther Party," *New York Times*, May 9, 1976, 1.

16. See Spencer, *The Revolution Has Come*, 62, 64–65, 88–89.

17. See Federal Bureau of Investigation, COINTELPRO Black Extremist File, Memorandum from FBI Los Angeles Bureau for FBI Director (September 25, 1968); Memorandum from FBI Los Angeles Bureau for FBI Director (November 29, 1968). The Panthers later sued the FBI over the events described herein, unsuccessfully. See Laura A. Kiernan, "Suit by Black Panthers Against U.S. Is Dismissed," *Washington Post*, January 26, 1980.

18. See Martin Rips, "US Members to Be Arraigned for Panther Shooting Deaths," *UCLA Daily Bruin*, February 19, 1969, 1; Clipping, "Black Militant Power Clash Probed in UCLA Slayings," n.d., Catherine Roraback Collection of Ericka Huggins Papers, John J. Huggins, Jr. file, Yale University, box 4, folder 43; Editorial, "Progress, Not Tension, Must Follow Campus Deaths," *UCLA Daily Bruin*, January 20, 1969, 4; Gail Sheedy,

"Black Against Black: The Agony of Panthermania," *New York*, November 16, 1970, 48; Larry May, "Panther Slaying Suspect Voluntarily Surrenders," *UCLA Daily Bruin*, January 21, 1969, 4; Spencer, *The Revolution Has Come*, 88.

19. See "Shooting Victim New Haven Native," *Hartford Courant*, January 21, 1969, 1; Sam Negri, "Slain 'Panther' Active in Rights Drive Here Before Going to L.A.," *New Haven Register*, January 19, 1969, 1; Paul Indman, "Campus Deaths: A White Response," *UCLA Daily Bruin*, January 24, 1969, 4; Robert Sanford, "Panthers Split on Seale Trial," *St. Louis Post-Dispatch*, March 21, 1971, A2; Sheedy, "Black Against Black," 50. "Couldn't make it" from author interview with Joan and Carolyn Huggins, September 25, 2019, pp. 6, 8.

20. See author interview with Joan and Carolyn Huggins, September 25, 2019, p. 3; Larry May, "Panther Slaying Suspect Voluntarily Surrenders," *UCLA Daily Bruin*, January 21, 1969, 4; Larry May, "Two Black Men Sought by Police for Slayings in Campbell Hall Friday," *UCLA Daily Bruin*, January 20, 1969, 1; Martin Rips, "Seale Denounces Karenga at Funeral for Murder Victim," *UCLA Daily Bruin*, January 27, 1969; Robert Sanford, "Panthers Split on Seale Trial," *St. Louis Post-Dispatch*, March 21, 1971, A2; author interview with Constance Royster, June 25, 2014, p. 17.

21. "Over the top" from author interview with Joel Motley, June 27, 2014, p. 21; Motley, *Equal Justice Under Law*, 27–30, 52–53, 154, 215–17; Motley Reminiscences, 558.

22. Sam Negri, "Slain 'Panther' Active in Rights Drive Here Before Going to L.A.," *New Haven Register*, January 19, 1969, 1; Sheedy, "Black Against Black; Bass and Rae, *Murder in the Model City*, 60, 85; Yohuru Williams, "No Haven."

23. See Bass and Rae, *Murder in the Model City*, 60, 85.

24. See Yohuru Williams, "No Haven"; Leslie Oelsner, "Prosecutor Jabs at Mrs. Huggins," *New York Times*, May 13, 1972, 38.

25. See author interview with Joel Motley, June 27, 2014, p. 21; author interview with Constance Royster, June 25, 2014, p. 16; Freed, *Agony in New Haven*, 36, 80, 83; "Catherine Roraback," Connecticut Women's Hall of Fame, https://connecticuthistory.org/people/catherine-roraback/ (last accessed January 5, 2020).

26. See Bass and Rae, *Murder in the Model City*, 60, 85; Yohuru Williams, "No Haven"; Bloom and Martin, *Black Against Empire*, 247–61; Oelsner, "Prosecutor Jabs at Mrs. Huggins"; author interview with Joan and Carolyn Huggins, September 25, 2019, p. 9; "Paid Notice: Deaths, HUGGINS, ELIZABETH," *New York Times*, June 21, 2004, www.nytimes.com/2004/06/21/classified/paid-notice-deaths-huggins-elizabeth.html.

27. See Freed, *Agony in New Haven*, 36, 80, 83; "Catherine Roraback," Connecticut Women's Hall of Fame, https://connecticuthistory.org/people /catherine-roraback/ (last accessed January 5, 2020).

28. See Bass and Rae, *Murder in the Model City*, 60, 85; Yohuru Williams, "No Haven"; Bloom and Martin, *Black Against Empire*, 247–61; Oelsner, "Prosecutor Jabs at Mrs. Huggins."

29. See Seale v. Manson, 326 F. Supp. 1375 (D. Conn. 1971); Answer at 1–10, Seale and Huggins v. MacDougall, No. 14077, Catherine Roraback Collection of Ericka Huggins Papers, Yale University Library, Jail Pleadings Conditions, box 3, folder 39; "Upheaval in Jails," *New York Times*, October 10, 1970, 12.

21. "PAWNS IN A VERY DANGEROUS GAME":
CRIME, PUNISHMENT, AND PRISONERS' RIGHTS

1. David Daloia and William Randall to Hon. Constance Baker Motley, January 5, 1976, Smith Motley Papers.

2. On the drug laws, see Jeremy W. Peters, "Assembly Votes to End Rockefeller Drug Laws," *New York Times*, March 5, 2009, A25; Deardra Shuler, "Thousands Rally at City Hall to Fight Rockefeller Drug Laws," *New York Amsterdam News*, June 5, 2003, 1; Fortner, *Black Silent Majority*, 173–216. On mass incarceration, see Hinton, *From the War on Poverty to the War on Crime*; Wagner and Rabuy, "Mass Incarceration."

3. See David Daloia and William Randall to Hon. Constance Baker Motley, January 5, 1976, Smith Motley Papers.

4. The landmark case is Cooper v. Pate, 378 U.S. 546 (1964). For an overview of the case and the broader prisoners' rights movement, see Jacobs, "The Prisoners' Rights Movement and Its Impacts, 1960–1980."

5. See Jacobs, "The Prisoners' Rights Movement and Its Impacts, 1960–80"; Freed, *Agony in New Haven*, 186–201; Bloom and Martin, *Black Against Empire*, 374–79; "Upheaval in Jails," *New York Times*, October 10, 1970, 12.

6. See Michael Powell, "Radical's Progress: Another Building," *The Record* (Passaic-Morris, NJ), January 22, 1987; Alexandria Symonds, "Overlooked No More: Martin Sostre, Who Reformed America's Prisons from His Cell," *New York Times*, April 24, 2019; Joseph Shapiro, "How One Inmate Changed the Prison System from the Inside," *Code Switch*, National Public Radio, April 14, 2017 (last accessed January 13, 2020). Quotes from "William Worthy's TV Address on the Martin Sostre Case," *Worker's World* (New York), July 5, 1968.

7. See Powell, "Radical's Progress"; Symonds, "Overlooked No More"; Shapiro, "How One Inmate Changed the Prison System from the Inside."

8. See Cooper v. Pate, 378 U.S. 546 (1964). For background on Sostre and

his prior lawsuits, see Sostre v. Rockefeller, 312 F. Supp. 863 (Motley, J., 1970).

9. See Shapiro, "How One Inmate Changed the Prison System from the Inside."

10. See Devlin, "Sentenced to 41 Years for Selling Books"; Wicker, "The Irony of Martin Sostre."

11. See 309 F. Supp. 611 (1969); see also Sostre v. Rockefeller, 312 F. Supp. 863 at 867–68; Worthy, "Sostre in Solitary."

12. See 309 F. Supp. 611 (1969); see also Sostre v. Rockefeller, 312 F. Supp. 863 at 867–68; Devlin, "Sentenced to 41 Years for Selling Books"; Gelman, "Martin Sostre: Up from Attica."

13. See Martin Sostre, *Letters from Prison* (Martin Sostre Defense Committee, July 1968), 28; Schaich and Hope, "The Prison Letters of Martin Sostre."

14. See Sostre v. Rockefeller, 312 F. Supp. 863 at 865–87; also see Wicker, "Irony of Martin Sostre."

15. See Transcript at 260, Sostre v. Rockefeller, 68 Civ 4058, National Archives; Sostre, *Letters from Prison*, 32; Sostre v. Rockefeller, 312 F. Supp. 863 at 865–87; "A Convict Suing State Charges Cruelty in Solitary Confinement," *New York Times*, October 30, 1969, 51; "Another Round Won in the Long Protracted Struggle to Free Martin Sostre," *Black Panther* 2, issue 18 (August 23, 1969): 7.

16. See Sostre v. Rockefeller, 312 F. Supp. 863 at 865-87; "A Convict Suing State Charges Cruelty in Solitary Confinement," *New York Times*, October 30, 1969, 51; "Martin Sostre v. the Ruling Class," *Black Panther* 3, issue 2 (November 29, 1969): 14; "Victor Rabinowitz, 96, Leftist Lawyer, Dies," *New York Times*, November 20, 2007; Copeland, *The Crime of Martin Sostre*, 175–76.

17. Copeland, *The Crime of Martin Sostre*, 176; "Martin Sostre Launches His Attack on the Ruling Class," *Black Panther* 2, issue 29 (November 15, 1969): 4.

18. See Transcript at 197, 207, 240, 248–49, 253, Sostre v. Rockefeller, 68 Civ 4058, National Archives; Sostre v. Rockefeller, 312 F. Supp. 863 at 865–87.

19. See Transcript at 197, 207, 240, 248–49, 253, Sostre v. Rockefeller, 68 Civ 4058, National Archives; Sostre v. Rockefeller, 312 F. Supp. 863 at 865–87; Copeland, *The Crime of Martin Sostre*, 176; "Martin Sostre v. Nelson Rockefeller," *Black Panther* 3, issue 32 (November 29, 1969): 4.

20. See Sostre v. McGinnis, 442 F.2d at 190; Copeland, *The Crime of Martin Sostre*, 178, 179, 185, 196.

21. See Sostre v. Rockefeller, 312 F. Supp. 863 at 867–68, 871.

22. See Sostre v. Rockefeller, 312 F. Supp. 863 at 868, 870.

23. See Sostre v. Rockefeller, 312 F. Supp. 863 at 871.

24. See Sostre v. Rockefeller, 312 F. Supp. 863 at 868–69, 875.

25. See Sostre v. Rockefeller, 312 F. Supp. 863 at 868–69, 874, 876.

26. See Sostre v. Rockefeller, 312 F. Supp. 863 at 885. Motley's decision expanded the reach of a 1967 decision by the Court of Appeals for the Second Circuit that held that certain prison conditions could violate the Eighth Amendment. Wright v. McMann, 387 F.2d 519 (2d Cir. 1967). Motley rejected one of the allegations made in the Sostre lawsuit. She dismissed claims against Governor Nelson Rockefeller and others for allegedly conspiring to practice racial discrimination in the operation of the prison system. Sostre had noted that the overwhelming majority of prison officials were white, while the overwhelming majority of prisoners were Black—statistics that showed the beginnings of mass incarceration in the United States. See Sostre v. Rockefeller, 312 F. Supp. 863 at 876–77.

27. See Sostre v. Rockefeller, 312 F. Supp. 863 at 885. Sostre did not prevail on his claims against the governor for allegedly maintaining a segregated prison system, where overwhelmingly white wardens and guards governed overwhelmingly Black prisoners.

28. See Sostre v. Rockefeller, 312 F. Supp. 863 at 885. The court of appeals decision is Sostre v. McGinnis, 442 F.2d 178 (en banc) (reversing holding that conditions of prisoner's segregated confinement constituted cruel and unusual punishment, upholding ruling that confinement because of political beliefs and legal activities was unlawful, but holding that inmate could recover from state commissioner of corrections); also see F. B. Taylor Jr., "Does the Bill of Rights Cross Prison Walls?," *Boston Globe*, March 17, 1971, 1.

29. Craig R. Whitney, "U.S. Writ Blamed in Prison Unrest," *New York Times*, June 13, 1970, 33; Craig R. Whitney, "U.S. Judge's Order Fought by State," *New York Times*, August 11, 1970, 30; Tom Wicker, "In the Nation: Due Process for Prisoners," *New York Times*, June 18, 1970, 44; David Gelman, "Martin Sostre: Up from Attica," *Newsday*, Sept. 20, 1971, 4.

30. Tom Wicker, "Irony of Martin Sostre," *New York Times*, December 8, 1974, A18; Wicker, "In the Nation: Due Process for Prisoners"; David Gelman, "Martin Sostre: Up from Attica II," *Newsday*, September 27, 1971, 4; Whitney, "U.S. Judge's Order Fought by State"; "Prisoners Still Have Rights," *Afro-American*, October 17, 1970, 4; William Worthy to Constance Baker Motley, June 22, 1970, Smith Motley Papers; J. Patrick Hazel to Constance Baker Motley, July 1, 1970, Smith Motley Papers; Roberta I. Thomas to Jonathan Shapiro, July 13, 1970, Smith Motley Papers; M. Lawrence Jr., July 6, 1970, Smith Motley Papers.

31. Shapiro, "How One Inmate Changed the Prison System from the Inside."

32. See F. B. Taylor Jr., "Does the Bill of Rights Cross Prison Walls?," *Bos-*

ton *Globe*, March 17, 1971, 1; Michael T. Kaufman, "Rising Protests and Lawsuits Shake Routine in State Prisons," *New York Times*, November 15, 1970, 1.

33. See Taylor, "Does the Bill of Rights Cross Prison Walls?"; Kaufman, "Rising Protests and Lawsuits Shake Routine in State Prisons"; see also Meola v. Fitzpatrick, 322 F. Supp. 878, 886 (D. Mass. 1971) (plaintiff inmate alleged lack of due process in prison transfers and discipline); Urbano v. McCorkle, 346 F. Supp. 51, 54 (D.N.J. 1972) (plaintiff inmate alleged lack of due process in punitive segregation hearing); Soto v. Lord, 693 F. Supp. 8, 20 (S.D.N.Y. 1988) (plaintiff inmate alleged lack of due process in faulty drug test); Rhem v. Malcolm, 377 F. Supp. 995, 999 (S.D.N.Y. 1974) (plaintiff inmates alleged prison conditions violated constitutional rights); Meyers v. Alldredge, 348 F. Supp. 807, 809 (M.D. Pa. 1972) (plaintiff inmates conducted work stoppage, alleged that disciplinary procedures at prison failed to meet due process requirements and constituted cruel and unusual punishment); Souza v. Travisono, 368 F. Supp. 959, 962 (D.R.I. 1973) (plaintiff inmates alleged that warden's eviction of prison legal services program violated right to counsel); Croom v. Manson, 367 F. Supp. 586, 588 (D. Conn. 1973) (plaintiff inmate alleged prison transfer was conducted without due process); Davis v. Lindsay, 321 F. Supp. 1134, 1136 (S.D.N.Y. 1970) (Angela Davis, at the time an inmate, alleged being kept in solitary confinement violated her constitutional rights); Jones v. Wittenberg, 323 F. Supp. 93, 97 (N.D. Ohio 1971) (plaintiff inmates sued alleging prison conditions were unconstitutional; court found conditions "outstandingly" bad); Morales v. Schmidt, 340 F. Supp. 544, 546 (1972) (plaintiff inmate alleged removal of a relative from approved correspondence list violated First Amendment); Shimabuku v. Britton, 357 F. Supp. 825, 826 (D. Kan. 1973) (plaintiff inmates alleged insufficient procedural safeguards in prison disciplinary hearings); Payne v. Whitmore, 325 F. Supp. 1191, 1192 (N.D. Cal. 1971) (plaintiff inmates alleged complete denial of access to books and magazines violated First Amendment); Clutchette v. Procunier, 328 F. Supp. 767, 769 (N.D. Cal. 1971) (plaintiff inmates alleged prison disciplinary hearings violated due process); Brenneman v. Madigan, 343 F. Supp. 128, 130 (N.D. Cal. 1972) (plaintiff inmates alleged confinement solely because of an inability to post bail constituted cruel and unusual punishment); Crafton v. Luttrell, 378 F. Supp. 521, 523 (M.D. Tenn. 1973) (plaintiff inmates alleged absence of due process in disciplinary hearings and in confinement to solitary); Novak v. Beto, 320 F. Supp. 1206, 1207 (S.D. Tex. 1970) (plaintiff inmates alleged prohibition of inmate legal assistance deprived them of their constitutional right to access the courts); Sinclair v. Henderson, 331 F. Supp. 1123, 1125 (E.D. La. 1971) (plaintiff

inmate alleged conditions on death row constituted cruel and unusual punishment).

34. See Sostre, *The New Prisoner*, reprinted in *North Carolina Central Law Journal* 4, no. 2 (Spring 1973): 244, Labadie Collection; Thompson, *Blood in the Water*, 84, 101; author interview with Daniel Steinbock, July 12, 2014.

35. See Jacobs, "The Prisoners' Rights Movement and Its Impacts, 1960–80"; Freed, *Agony in New Haven*, 186–201; Bloom and Martin, *Black Against Empire*, 374–79; "Upheaval in Jails," *New York Times*, October 10, 1970, 12.

36. See Seale v. Manson, 326 F. Supp. 1375 (D. Conn. 1971); Answer at 1–10, Seale and Huggins v. MacDougall, No. 14077, Catherine Roraback Collection of Ericka Huggins Papers, Yale University Library, Jail Pleadings Conditions, box 3, folder 39; "Upheaval in Jails," *New York Times*, October 10, 1970, 12.

37. See Seale v. Manson, 326 F. Supp. 1375 (D. Conn. 1971); Answer at 1–10, Seale and Huggins v. MacDougall, No. 14077, Catherine Roraback Collection of Ericka Huggins Papers, Yale University Library, Jail Pleadings Conditions, box 3, folder 39; "Upheaval in Jails," *New York Times*, October 10, 1970, 12.

38. For the record on appeal, see Sostre v. Rockefeller, 312 F. Supp. 863 (S.D.N.Y. 1970), aff'd in part, rev'd in part, 442 F.2d 178 (1971), cert. denied, 92 S. Ct. 719 (1972). Justice Douglas would have granted certiorari. Pending appellate review, Judge Motley stayed her order to create new disciplinary rules. Sostre v. McGinnis, 442 F.2d at 187.

39. Sostre v. McGinnis, 442 F.2d 178, 183–84, 189, 199, 201–2 (2d Cir. 1971).

40. Sostre v. McGinnis, 442 F.2d 178, 184–85, 191 (2d Cir. 1971). That holding neglected to mention numerous other federal court orders commanding state officials to take corrective action in state and local institutions, or begin to explain why those actions were not relevant to this case.

41. Sostre v. McGinnis, 442 F.2d 178 (2d Cir. 1971). The court of appeals had stayed Motley's order to the prison system to create new disciplinary rules. See Craig R. Whitney, "U.S. Judge's Order Fought by State," *New York Times*, August 11, 1970, 30.

42. David Gelman, "Martin Sostre: Up from Attica II," *New York Times*, September 27, 1971, 4.

43. Numerous psychiatrists and psychologists now attest that solitary confinement can cause a variety of mental health disorders. See, for example, Haney, "Mental Health Issues in Long-Term 'Solitary' and 'Supermax' Confinement." But prison officials still to this day turn to solitary confinement to manage inmates deemed difficult or dangerous.

44. Motley Reminiscences, 15–16.

45. See Botein, "Judge Motley Memories," p. 3.

46. See William Worthy, "Sostre in Solitary," *Boston Globe*, September 8,

1968, A44; William Worthy, "Key Witness Against Sostre Says He Lied," *Afro-American*, April 24, 1971, 1; John L. Hess, "Clemency Given to Sostre and 7," *New York Times*, December 25, 1975, 45; "Unbowed Sostre Leaves N.Y. Prison," *Afro-American*, February 21, 1976, 6.

47. See David Vidal, "A Freed Activist Sees No Change," *New York Times*, February 15, 1976, 28; Joseph Shapiro, "How One Inmate Changed the Prison System from the Inside," *Code Switch*, National Public Radio, April 14, 2017 (last accessed January 13, 2020).

48. See Carmona v. Ward, 436 F. Supp. 1153 (S.D.N.Y. 1977), rev'd, 576 F.2d 1153 (2d Cir. 1978), cert. denied, 439 U.S. 1091 (1979). Justice Marshall would have granted certiorari.

49. 436 F. Supp. at 1156–60.

50. 436 F. Supp. at 1156–60.

51. 576 F.2d 1153, 1157 (2d Cir. 1978); see Arnold Lubasch, "Court Voids 2 Life Terms Imposed Under New York State Drug Laws," *New York Times*, August 6, 1977.

52. 576 F.2d 1153, 1157 (2d Cir. 1978).

53. 439 U.S. 1091 (1979) (Marshall, J.).

54. See Mancuso, "Resentencing After the Fall of the Rockefeller Drug Laws"; Brian G. Gilmore and Reginald Dwayne Betts, "Deconstructing Carmona." On wrongful imprisonment on drug charges, see, for example, Lise Olsen and Anita Hassan, "298 Wrongful Drug Convictions Identified in Ongoing Audit," *Houston Chronicle*, July 16, 2016, 1; "The Women Wrongfully Convicted by Drug War Prosecutors," *Filter*, October 2, 2019; "Record Number of False Convictions Overturned in 2015," *New York Times*, February 3, 2016; Covey, "Police Misconduct and Wrongful Convictions."

55. Hon. Constance Baker Motley, " 'Law and Order' and the Criminal Justice System," Northwestern Univ. School of Law, April 24, 1973, Columbia Motley Collection.

22. A "WOMAN LAWYER" AND A "WOMAN JUDGE": MAKING OPPORTUNITY FOR WOMEN IN LAW

1. Dorothy Kenyon to Constance Baker Motley, January 26, 1966, Smith Motley Papers, box 8, folder 16; Dorothy Kenyon to Constance Baker Motley, October 3, 1966, Smith Motley Papers, box 8, folder 16; Pauli Murray to Constance Baker Motley, January 31, 1966, Smith Motley Papers, box 8, folder 16.

2. See Azaransky, "Jane Crow"; Evans, "The Rebirth of the Women's Movement in the 1960s."

3. See Dorothy Townsend, "Woman's 'Lib' Groups Plan Nationwide Strike," *Los Angeles Times*, August 23, 1970, B1; John H. Fenton, "A Welfare Protest Spurs Boston Riot," *New York Times*, June 3, 1967, 1; "Radcliffe Women

Protest," *Chicago Daily Defender*, December 11, 1968, 6; Brown, "A New Era in American Politics," 1013–14; Grace Lichtenstein, "Feminists Demand 'Liberation' in Ladies' Home Journal Sit-In," *New York Times*, March 19, 1970; "The National Organization for Women's 1966 Statement of Purpose," https://now.org/about/history/statement-of-purpose/ (last accessed May 1, 2019); Combahee River Collective, "A Black Feminist Statement" (1974) (last accessed May 3, 2020), https://www.blackpast .org/african-american-history/combahee-river-collective-statement -1977/

4. See, for example, Bornstein, "A Tribute to Justice Ruth Bader Ginsburg," 1301–3; Randolph, *Florynce "Flo" Kennedy*; see also Griswold v. Connecticut, 381 U.S. 479 (1965) (birth control); Reed v. Reed, 404 U.S. 71 (1971) (estate administration); Frontiero v. Richardson, 411 U.S. 677 (1973) (military benefits); Weinberger v. Wiesenfeld, 420 U.S. 636 (1975) (Social Security benefits).

5. See Lisagor and Lipsius, *A Law Unto Itself*; see also Jonathan Kwitny, "Law Firm Is Stung by Hiring Bias Suit Filed by Woman Lawyer and Heard by a Woman Judge," *Wall Street Journal*, August 8, 1975, 26.

6. See Lisagor and Lipsius, *A Law Unto Itself*; Grant, "Women in the Legal Profession from the 1920s to the 1970s," 2–3. During the 1930s, Sullivan & Cromwell had hired five women; they were never made partners. See Grant, 5.

7. See Biskupic, *Sandra Day O'Connor*, 28; De Hart, *Ruth Bader Ginsburg*, 79. The survey is described in Grant, "Women in the Legal Profession from the 1920s to the 1970s," 11–12.

8. Cynthia Fuchs Epstein, *Women in Law* (2012), 40–41; American Bar Association, "First Year and Total J.D. Enrollment by Gender 1947–2011," www .americanbar.org/content/dam/aba/administrative/legal_education _and_admissions_to_the_bar/statistics/jd_enrollment_1yr_total_gender .authcheckdam.pdf (last accessed June 4, 2019); see also Neumann, "Women in Legal Education" (noting that "the female percentage began to climb" in 1968), available at https://scholarlycommons.law.hofstra .edu/faculty_scholarship/734.

9. Strebeigh, *Equal*, 14, 17–19.

10. Strebeigh, *Equal*, 116, 146, 152–54.

11. U.S. Congress, House, *Discrimination Against Women: Hearings on Section 805 of H.R. 16098 Before the House Committee on Education and Labor, Special Subcommittee on Education*, 91st Cong. 584 (statement of Mrs. Diane Blake and Mrs. Susan D. Ross, Women's Rights Committee of NYU Law), pp. 589, 606, 610; Bowman, "Women in the Legal Profession from the 1920s to the 1970s; transcript of interview with Harriet S. Rabb, Part 4, Gender Discrimination Cases, pp. 6, 8–9.

12. Blank v. Sullivan & Cromwell, 418 F. Supp. 1 (S.D.N.Y. 1975); Laurie John-ston, "2 Law Firms Push Feminism—With All-Women Staffs: Probably a First," *New York Times*, February 17, 1973, 33; Rabb, "Litigating Sex Dis-crimination Cases in the 1970s," 51; See Strebeigh, *Equal*, 152–59, 165.

13. See Lisagor and Lipsius, *A Law Unto Itself*, 220–21; see also Bowman, "Women in the Legal Profession from the 1920s to the 1970s," 12; Strebeigh, *Equal*, 152–59.

14. Blank v. Sullivan and Cromwell, 418 F. Supp. 1 (S.D.N.Y. 1975); Rabb, "Litigating Sex Discrimination Cases in the 1970s," 51; Strebeigh, *Equal*, 152–59, 165.

15. See Lindsy Van Gelder, "Fighting Discrimination: Harriet Rabb Has a Case for Women," *Chicago Tribune*, July 23, 1978, D1; Rabb, "Litigating Sex Discrimination Cases in the 1970s," 51; "Harriet S. Rabb Oral His-tory. Part 1: Family Influence on Career Choice," p. 2; "Part 3: First Case," p. 5; "Part 4: Gender Discrimination Cases in the 1970s." See Strebeigh, *Equal*, 152–59.

16. See Jean M. White, "2500 Women Storm Pentagon over War," *Washington Post*, February 16, 1967, A1; Rabb, "Litigating Sex Discrimination Cases in the 1970s," 50–51; Rabb, interview by J. P. Oglivy, March 6, 2001, Tran-script, National Archive of Legal Clinical Education, Catholic University of America, Washington, DC, pp. 12–13, https://www.law.edu/NACLE /nacle-transcripts.cfm; "Harriet S. Rabb Oral History. Part 1: Family Influence on Career Choice," p. 2; "Part 3: First Case," p. 5; "Part 4: Gen-der Discrimination Cases in the 1970s."

17. See "The Honorable Eleanor Holmes Norton," The HistoryMakers, www .thehistorymakers.org/biography/honorable-eleanor-holmes-norton; "Eleanor Holmes Norton," BlackPast, March 14, 2007. "Zabar's" from Lindsy Van Gelder, "Fighting Discrimination: Harriet Rabb Has a Case for Women," *Chicago Tribune*, July 23, 1978, D1.

18. On the district court's random assignment system, see Macfarlane, "The Danger of Nonrandom Case Assignment"; Arnold H. Lubasch, "'Shop-ping' for Judges Is Curbed," *New York Times*, May 1, 1987, www.nytimes .com/1987/05/01/nyregion/shopping-for-judges-is-curbed.html; Bird, "The Assignment of Cases to Federal District Court Judges."

19. See Glenn Fowler, "Ephraim London, 78, a Lawyer Who Fought Censor-ship, Is Dead," *New York Times*, June 14, 1990; "Bridal Thursday for Pearl Levison," *New York Times*, June 1, 1939, 36.

20. See Affidavit in Support of Request for Disqualification, Blank v. Sullivan & Cromwell, 75 Civ. 189 (Motley, J.) at 13.

21. See Affidavit in Support of Request for Disqualification, Blank v. Sullivan & Cromwell, 75 Civ. 189 (Motley, J.) at 1–2, 5–6, 12–13, 14.

22. 418 F. Supp. at 2, 4. The quote is from Rabb, interview by J. P. Oglivy,

Transcript, National Archive of Legal Clinical Education, Catholic University of America, Washington, DC, p. 9. www.law.edu/_media/imported -media/NACLE/rabb.pdf.

23. 418 F. Supp. at 4. The quote is from Rabb, interview by J. P. Oglivy, p. 9. For empirical data on Motley's rulings in discrimination cases and analysis, see Brown-Nagin, "Identity Matters."

24. 418 F. Supp. at 4.

25. On treatises, see Flamm, *Judicial Disqualification*, 695–96. For laudatory commentary, see Margaret M. Russell, "Beyond 'Sellouts' and 'Race Cards,'" 766, 778–89; Ifill, "Racial Diversity on the Bench."

   828 F.2d at 1543. See also Laird v. Tatum, 409 U.S. 824, 835 (1972) ("proof that a judge's mind was a complete *tabula rasa* would be evidence of lack of qualification, not lack of bias").

26. See Van Gelder, "Fighting Discrimination: Harriet Rabb Has a Case for Women"; Jonathan Kwitny, "Law Firm Is Stung by Hiring-Bias Suit Filed by Woman Lawyer and Heard by Woman Judge," *Wall Street Journal*, August 8, 1975, 26; see also Strebeigh, *Equal*, 187–88.

27. Strebeigh, *Equal*, 195–96.

28. See Blank v. Sullivan & Cromwell, 75 Civ. 189 (1977) at 1–2; Jonathan Kwitney, "New York Law Firm Accepts Conditions in Hiring-Bias Case: Sullivan & Cromwell Settles Female Class-Action Suit Assigned a Woman Judge," *Wall Street Journal*, May 9, 1977.

29. See Arnold Lubasch, "Top Law Firm Bans Sex Discrimination," *New York Times*, May 8, 1977, 1; "Decades-Old Gender Bias Case Marked Turning Point in Big Law," *Bloomberg Law*, May 15, 2017.

30. See Lisagor and Lipsius, *A Law Unto Itself*, 217–20. See, in general, Harrington, *Women Lawyers*, 20–22.

31. See Jonathan Kwitney, "New York Law Firm Accepts Conditions in Hiring-Bias Case: Sullivan & Cromwell Settles Female Class-Action Suit Assigned a Woman Judge," *Wall Street Journal*, May 9, 1977, 21.

32. See Jonathan Kwitney, "New York Law Firm Accepts Conditions in Hiring-Bias Case: Sullivan & Cromwell Settles Female Class-Action Suit Assigned a Woman Judge," *Wall Street Journal*, May 9, 1977, 21; Van Gelder, "Fighting Discrimination: Harriet Rabb Has a Case for Women." On the significance of Title VII in the struggle for race and gender equality, see MacLean, *Freedom Is Not Enough*; Mayeri, *Reasoning from Race*.

33. See Mary L. Clark, "Carter's Groundbreaking Appointment of Women to the Federal Bench"; see also Martin Tolchin, "U.S. Search for Women and Blacks to Serve as Judges Is Going Slowly," *New York Times*, April 22, 1979, www.nytimes.com/1979/04/22/archives/us-search-for-women -and-blacks-to-serve-as-judges-is-going-slowly.html ("When President Carter took office, only one woman and one Black were among the

97 appeals court judges, and there were only 16 Blacks, five women and five Hispanic-Americans out of 399 district court judges."); Remarks by Hon. Constance Baker Motley, Gate City Bar Association, Atlanta, Ga., May 4, 1977, Smith Motley Papers, box 14, folder 2, 12–13.

34. See Clark, "Carter's Groundbreaking Appointment of Women to the Federal Bench"; see also Martin Tolchin, "U.S. Search for Women and Blacks to Serve as Judges Is Going Slowly," *New York Times*, April 22, 1979, www .nytimes.com/1979/04/22/archives/us-search-for-women-and-blacks -to-serve-as-judges-is-going-slowly.html; Marilyn Nejelski to Hon. Arlen Specter, July 25, 1984, National Women's Political Caucus Papers, Schlesinger Library, box 324, folder 18.

35. See, e.g., United States v. Alabama, 828 F.2d 1532, 1541 (11th Cir. 1987) (rejecting a motion to remove a Black judge from a desegregation case because his children might have benefited from his ruling); LeRoy v. City of Houston, 592 F. Supp. 415, 422–24 (S.D. Tex. 1984) (denying a recusal motion made on the grounds that the judge and minority plaintiffs in a vote-dilution case were the same race); Baker v. City of Detroit, 458 F. Supp. 374, 375–77 (E.D. Mich. 1978) (rejecting a recusal motion targeted at Judge Keith in a discrimination case based on his friendship with the Black mayor on grounds that such relationships are common in a small circle of elite Blacks in a predominantly Black city); Pennsylvania v. Local Union 542, Int'l Union of Operating Eng'rs, 388 F. Supp. 155, 157 (E.D. Pa. 1974) (rejecting the recusal of Judge Higginbotham on grounds of judicial bias and prejudice in a case involving a suit by a Black construction worker); MacDraw, Inc. v. CIT Grp. Equip. Fin., Inc., 138 F.3d 33, 35–38 (2d Cir. 1998) (upholding sanctions issued by Judge Denny Chin after counsel called for recusal based, in part, on his race and ethnicity); In re Evans, 801 F.2d 703, 706 (4th Cir. 1986) (disbarring an attorney for sending a judge a letter accusing the judge of "incompetence and/ or religious and racial bias"); Wessmann ex rel. Wessman v. Bos. Sch. Comm., 979 F. Supp. 915, 915–16 (D. Mass. 1997) (rejecting an argument for recusal in a discrimination case based on the judge's background as a civil rights lawyer); Johnson v. State, 430 S.E.2d 821, 822 (Ga. Ct. App. 1993) (affirming the denial of a motion requesting transfer of a rape and kidnapping case from a female judge to a male judge); cf. McCann v. Commc'ns Design Corp., 775 F. Supp. 1506, 1509 (D. Conn. 1991) (rejecting a recusal motion made on grounds that Judge José Cabranes tended to favor defendants over plaintiffs in certain cases as opposed to on grounds of extrajudicial prejudice); see also Robert L. Carter, *A Matter of Law*, 147; Schafran, "Not from Central Casting" (detailing specific examples of and study findings supporting the prevalence of recusal motions based solely on gender).

36. On the litigation over gay marriage and ensuing controversy, see Perry v. Schwarzenegger, 704 F. Supp. 2d 921, 973 (N.D. Cal. 2010) (declaring California's Proposition 8 banning gay marriage unconstitutional because it places "the force of law behind stigmas against gays and lesbians"); John Schwartz, "Conservative Jurist, with Independent Streak," *New York Times*, August 5, 2010, www.nytimes.com/2010/08/06/us /06walker.html (the legal ethics professor observed, "You could say, 'If a gay judge is disqualified, how about a straight judge?' There isn't anybody about whom somebody might say, 'You're not truly impartial in this case.' " On President Trump's criticisms of a Hispanic judge presiding in a case involving "Trump University," see Z. Byron Wolf, "Trump's Attacks on Judge Curiel Are Still Jarring to Read," CNN, February 27, 2018.

23. "FOR A GIRL, YOU KNOW A LOT ABOUT SPORTS": THE NEW YORK YANKEES STRIKE OUT IN JUDGE MOTLEY'S COURTROOM

1. "For a girl" is from a quote by Frank Gifford, a former professional football player and a rising star in broadcast journalism who later became a legendary host of *Monday Night Football*, as recalled by Melissa Ludtke. Author interview with Melissa Ludtke, March 13, 2013, pp. 4, 6, 7–8, 10, 13.

2. See "1976 World Series," Baseball Almanac (last accessed June 19, 2019); "1977 World Series," Baseball Almanac (last accessed June 19, 2019); Stacey Gotsulias, "When Reggie Jackson and Billy Martin Clashed at Fenway," *Sporting News*, June 18, 2017; Bryan Curtis, "Debating America's Pastime(s)," *New York Times*, February 1, 2009; "World Series Television Ratings: TV Ratings for Every World Series in Major League History Since 1968," Baseball Almanac.

3. Author interview with Melissa Ludtke, March 13, 2013, pp. 2, 4, 6. "Wonderful place to grow up" from Melissa Ludtke Interview by Anne Ritchie, Washington Press Club Foundation, February 21, 1993, Washington, DC, p. 3; ibid., p. 6.

4. See Povich, *The Good Girls Revolt*; Jessica Bennett and Jesse Ellison, "Behind 'The Good Girls Revolt': The *Newsweek* Lawsuit that Paved the Way for Women Writers," *Daily Beast*, July 14, 2017; Lindsy Van Gelder, "Fighting Discrimination: Harriet Rabb Has a Case for Women," *Chicago Tribune*, July 23, 1978, D1; Lee Lescaze, "New York Times Agrees to Pay Women $235,000," *Washington Post*, October 7, 1978, A6; "Newsweek Agrees to Speed Promotion of Women," *New York Times*, August 27, 1970, 30; Henry Raymont, "As Newsweek Says, Women Are in Revolt, Even on Newsweek," *New York Times*, March 17, 1970, 30.

5. Author interview with Melissa Ludtke, March 13, 2013, p. 13.

6. Author interview with Melissa Ludtke, March 13, 2013, p. 14.

7. Transcript of Jane Pauley Reporting, ABC News, *Good Morning America*, January 12, 1978, p. 1; see also Ludtke v. Kuhn, 461 F. Supp. 86, 89 (1978); "Former MLB Commissioner Dead at 80," *USA Today*, March 16, 2007.

8. See Larry Eldridge, "Would the Babe Recognize the New Yankee Stadium?," *Christian Science Monitor*, May 18, 1976, 14; Murray Chass, "Yankee Stadium: Modern Comforts and Hairdryers," *New York Times*, March 7, 1976, S1; Francis X. Clines, "About New York: A Look Inside Yankee Stadium," *New York Times*, October 13, 1977, 50; Murray Schumach, "Fans at Yankee Stadium Rewarded by a Title Though Not by a Triumph," *New York Times*, October 2, 1977, S7.

9. See Eldridge, "Would the Babe Recognize the New Yankee Stadium?"; Chass, "Yankee Stadium: Modern Comforts and Hairdryers"; Clines, "About New York: A Look Inside Yankee Stadium"; Schumach, "Fans at Yankee Stadium Rewarded by a Title Though Not by a Triumph." See also Melissa Ludtke to Bowie Kuhn, October 15, 1977, Schlesinger Library, Series 1, Ludtke v. Kuhn, box 1, letters folder, item 4, page 18.

10. Melissa Ludtke to Bowie Kuhn, October 15, 1977, Schlesinger Library, Series 1, Ludtke v. Kuhn, box 1, letters folder, item 4, p. 18.

11. Author interview with Melissa Ludtke, March 13, 2013, 16–17, 18–19; see also 1977 World Series Almanac.

12. Author interview with Melissa Ludtke, March 13, 2013, p. 21.

13. Melissa Ludtke to Bowie Kuhn, October 15, 1977, Schlesinger Library, Series 1, Ludtke v. Kuhn, box 1, letters folder, item 4; author interview with Melissa Ludtke, March 13, 2013, Cambridge, MA, 21.

14. See Red Smith, "The Ultimate Invasion," *Sports of the Times*, January 10, 1978; "Locker Room Sex," *News-Tribune* (Idaho), January 24, 1978; Howard Kleinberg, "Challenges in the Locker Room," *Miami News*, January 25, 1978; Roger Kahn, "Some Modest Proposals," *New York Times*, February 13, 1978; author interview with Melissa Ludtke, March 13, 2013, pp. 24–25.

15. Jane Pauley Interview of Melissa Ludtke, NBC, *Today Show*, Burrelle's T.V. Clips, January 4, 1978, p. 1; author interview with Melissa Ludtke, March 13, 2013, pp. 24–25.

16. Author telephone interview with Frederick A. O. Schwarz, August 14, 2013, pp. 9–10.

17. Author telephone interview with Frederick A. O. Schwarz, August 14, 2013, pp. 9–11.

18. Ludtke v. Kuhn, 461 F. Supp. at 93–98.

19. Ludtke v. Kuhn, 461 F. Supp. at 93 (citing Burton v. Wilmington Parking Auth., 365 U.S. 715 [1961]) (finding that state action may be found

when a private party's actions are entwined with a state agency); id. at 93–95. See, e.g., Jackson v. Statler Found., 496 F.2d 623, 629 (2d Cir. 1974) (discussing the existence of a double "state action" standard—"one, a less onerous test for cases involving racial discrimination, and a more rigorous standard for other claims"). For a leading Supreme Court case narrowly conceiving state action, see Moose Lodge No. 107 v. Irvis, 407 U.S. 163 (1972) (holding that the state liquor board and its practices insufficiently implicated actions of a private club that refused service to a Black guest to make the board's practices "state action" within the meaning of the Equal Protection Clause).

20. Ludtke v. Kuhn, 461 F. Supp. at 86, 93–95.

21. Ludtke v. Kuhn, 461 F. Supp. at 97. The Ginsburg case was Califano v. Goldfarb, 430 U.S. 199, 212 (1977).

22. Ludtke v. Kuhn, 461 F. Supp. at 97 (citing Califano v. Goldfarb, 430 U.S. 199 [1977], as well as Reed v. Reed, 404 U.S. 71, 92 S.Ct. 251, 30 L.Ed.2d 225 [1971]).

23. Ludtke v. Kuhn, 461 F. Supp. at 98 (citing, for example, *Allgeyer v. Louisiana*, 165 U.S. 578, 17 S.Ct. 427, 41 L.Ed. 832 [1897] and Meyer v. Nebraska, 262 U.S. 390, 43 S.Ct. 625, 67 L.Ed. 1042 [1923]). The citation to *Allgeyer* was somewhat odd, because it is associated with Lochner-era jurisprudence in the economic realm long discredited by the Court, at least in part. Motley also cited more recent cases for the same principle.

24. Maury Allen, "Women in the Locker Room? 1,000 Times No!," *New York Daily Metro*, September 29, 1978; Gerald Eskenazi, "Men Have a Right to Keep Fig Leaf," *New York Daily Press*, September 29, 1978, 1.

25. Ludtke v. Kuhn, 461 F. Supp. 86, 88 (S.D.N.Y. 1978).

26. Author telephone interview with Frederick A. O. Schwarz, August 14, 2013, 9–10; Roger Angell, "The Sporting Scene: Sharing the Beat," *New Yorker*, April 9, 1979, 47.

27. See Monell v. Department of Social Services, 357 F. Supp. 1051 (1972); Danna v. New York Telephone Company, 752 F. Supp. 594, 608–9 (S.D.N.Y. 1990).

24. NO "PROTECTING ANGEL": BLACKS, LATINOS, AND ORDINARY PEOPLE IN JUDGE MOTLEY'S COURTROOM

1. Martin, "Gender and Judicial Selection"; "Figures Back Carter on Black Judgeships," *St. Louis Post-Dispatch*, September 7, 1980, 25; Norman Lockman, "Black Federal Judges—a Plus for Carter's Presidency," *Boston Globe*, August 3, 1979, 13.

2. Bella Abzug to Constance Baker Motley, January 25, 1966, Smith Motley Papers, box 8, folder 23; Derrick A. Bell to Constance Baker Motley, January 25, 1966, Smith Motley Papers, box 8, folder 38.

3. Bunche, "A Critical Analysis of the Tactics and Programs of Minority Groups."

4. Author interview with Lynn Huntley, July 24, 2014.

5. Motley Reminiscences, 770; author interview with Justice Sonia Sotomayor, January 19, 2015; author interview with Lynn Huntley, July 24, 2014. "Revolution" from Motley, *Equal Justice Under Law*, 5–6. On her support for affirmative action, see ibid., 229–42. On "common impediment," see ibid., 246.

6. See Blank v. Sullivan & Cromwell, 418 F. Supp. 1, 4 n.1 (S.D.N.Y. 1975). Quotes are from author interview with Hon. Miriam Cedarbaum; author interview with Lan Cao, July 12, 2014; statement of Howard Fischer, Botein, "Judge Motley Memories."

7. See Harold F. Evans Jr., Obituary, *Hartford Courant*, December 5, 2004; "Hartford's Police Priority," December 7, 1979, 28; "Police Complaints Topic of Hearings," *Hartford Courant*, January 5, 1980; Countryman, *Up South*; Brown-Nagin, *Courage to Dissent*; Biondi, *The Black Revolution on Campus*.

8. See Harold F. Evans Jr., Obituary; "Hartford's Police Priority," December 7, 1979, 2; see Dulaney, *Black Police in America*, 19–29. President's Commission on Law Enforcement and Administration of Justice, *Task Force Report: The Police* (1967); Fern Shen, "State Agrees to Double Minority Troopers, Regrade Exams," *Hartford Courant*, February 2, 1984.

9. See Harold F. Evans Jr., Obituary; Gardiner, "Policing Around the Nation"; U.S. Commission on Civil Rights, *Who Is Guarding the Guardians?*, 5–7; Kuykendall and Burns, "The Black Police Officer," 5.

10. See Evans v. Connecticut, 935 F. Supp. at 145, 147, 157 (1996), aff'd 24 Fed. Appx. 35 (2d Cir. 2001). Judge Motley sat by designation in the District of Connecticut.

11. Mark Pazniokas, "Judge Finds State Police in Contempt," *Hartford Courant,* June 25, 1994.

12. Evans v. Connecticut, 935 F. Supp. at 150–51.

13. Evans v. Connecticut, 935 F. Supp. at 153–54, 158, 160.

14. Evans v. Connecticut, 935 F. Supp. at 160.

15. Evans v. Connecticut, 935 F. Supp. at 154; see also Evans v. Connecticut, 24 Fed. Appx. 35 (2d Cir. 2001).

16. Harold F. Evans Jr., Obituary; Mark Pazniokas, "Is It Jail or Home for the Holidays," *Hartford Courant*, December 21, 1999; Evans v. Connecticut, 935 F. Supp. at 158.

17. Harold F. Evans Jr., Obituary.

18. See Brown-Nagin, *Courage to Dissent*, 87; Giddings, *When and Where I Enter*, 101, 147.

19. See Bates Case Summary, Personal Papers of Constance Baker Motley

(on file with author); Constance Baker Motley, "Twenty Years Later: My Personal Recollections of Brown," March 21, 1974, Smith Motley Papers, box 14, folder 2, p. 14.

20. See Du Bois, "Does the Negro Need Separate Schools," 331; Brown-Nagin, *Courage to Dissent*, 103–5; "Bias Against Black Teachers," *Christian Science Monitor*, May 15, 1970, 1; "Ousted Black Teachers," *Chicago Daily Defender*, December 22, 1970, 13. See Smith, "A Comparative Look at African American Teachers After Brown v. Board of Education," 8.

21. Complaint, Gulino v. Board of Education, 96 Civ. 8414 (U.S.D.C. 1996), 1–2, 17.

22. Complaint, Gulino v. Board of Education, 96 Civ. 8414 (U.S.D.C. 1996), 1–2, 7–8.

23. Complaint, Gulino v. Board of Education, 96 Civ. 8414 (U.S.D.C. 1996), 1–2, 7–8.

24. See Kozol, *Savage Inequalities*; James Dao, "Passing of Regents Exams to Be Required for Diploma," *New York Times*, April 24, 1996, 1.

25. 236 F. Supp. 2d 314, 318 (S.D.N.Y. 2002); see also Mark Walsh, "Court Seeks Justice Dept.'s Views in Case over N.Y. Teacher Test," *Education Weekly*, December 5, 2007 (quoting Brief of Respondent New York State Education Department in Support of the Petition at 14, Bd. of Educ. v. Gulino, 554 U.S. 917 [2008] [No. 07-270], 2007 WL 2764264, at *14), www.edweek.org/ew/articles/2007/12/12/15scotus.h27.html (on file with *Columbia Law Review*).

26. Gulino v. Bd. of Educ., 201 F.R.D. 326, 334, 339–42, 334 (S.D.N.Y. 2001).

27. Gulino v. Bd. of Educ., 201 F.R.D. 326, 334, 339–42, 334 (S.D.N.Y. 2001).

28. Gulino v. Bd. of Educ., 201 F.R.D. at 339.

29. Gulino v. N.Y. State Educ. Dep't, 460 F.3d 361, 376 n.15 (2d Cir. 2006).

30. Motley, *Equal Justice Under Law*, 41, 43–44.

31. Motley, *Equal Justice Under Law*, 44–45.

32. Motley, *Equal Justice Under Law*, 33–34, 36.

33. Motley, *Equal Justice Under Law*, 32, 33.

34. Motley, *Equal Justice Under Law*, 78; Gladys Noel Bates, Case Summary, at 2.

35. An Act to Amend the Education Law, #2905, N.Y. Senate, February 12, 1964, Smith Motley Papers, box 10, folder 17; An Act to Amend the Education Law, #3557, N.Y. Senate, February 25, 1964, Smith Motley Papers, box 10, folder 17; Constance B. Motley to Senators, March 3, 1964, Smith Motley Papers, box 10, folder 17; Sonsease Wilson to Hon. Constance Baker Motley, March 23, 1984, Columbia Motley Papers, U.S. District Court files.

36. Remarks by the Hon. Constance Baker Motley, Judicial Luncheon, Phil-

adelphia, Pa., March 24, 1979, Smith Motley Papers, box 14, folder 3, p. 3; Sonsease Wilson to Hon. Constance Baker Motley, March 23, 1984, Motley Papers, U.S. District Court files, on file with author.

37. Gulino v. N.Y. State Educ. Dep't, 460 F.3d at 382-88, 386.

38. See Barnes-Johnson, "Preparing Minority Teachers," 72, 75 (noting that some thought Motley's reputation as a civil rights activist would impact her treatment of the case). On the NAACP LDF's role in the disparate impact cases, see Greenberg, *Crusaders in the Courts*, 418–20, 427. Lydia Chavez, "Study Sees Bias in New York Teacher Exams," *New York Times*, March 11, 1988, www.nytimes.com/1988/03/11/nyregion/study-sees -bias-in-new-york-teacher-exams.html (on file with *Columbia Law Review*).

39. See Duggan v. Local 638, Enter. Ass'n of Steam, Hot Water, Hydraulic Sprinkler, Pneumatic Tube, Ice Mach., Air Conditioning & Gen. Pipe-fitters, 419 F. Supp. 2d 484, 492 (S.D.N.Y. 2005) (holding that union members who brought a race discrimination claim under Title VII failed to demonstrate disparate impact or disparate treatment and citing stringent requirements in Motley's opinion to support its proposition that plaintiffs' statistical analysis did not adequately demonstrate disparate treatment of Black union members); Michael Delikat, Orrick, Herrington & Sutcliffe LLP, "Evidence Issues and Jury Instructions in Employment Cases: Procedure," "Evidence & Jurisdiction in EEOC Lawsuits" 18 (2006) (on file with *Columbia Law Review*) (citing Motley's *Gulino* opinion to support the proposition that there is no consensus among courts as to whether there is "a distinction between 'pattern-or-practice' cases and systemic continuing violations ('policy or practice') cases" for the purposes of Title VII claims); see also Ricci v. DeStefano, 530 F.3d 88, 90 n.1 (2d Cir. 2008) (Parker, J., concurring) (citing *Gulino* in support of the decision to deny en banc rehearing of a decision reject-ing an employment discrimination claim). In *Ricci*, the Second Circuit affirmed the district court's ruling that an employer's use of a test with racially disparate impact did not constitute intentional discrimination against white candidates. See 554 F. Supp. 2d 142, 143 (D. Conn. 2006), aff'd, 530 F.3d 87 (2d Cir. 2008), rev'd, 557 U.S. 557 (2009).

40. On pink-collar work, see Bergmann, "Occupational Segregation, Wages and Profits When Employers Discriminate by Race or Sex"; Charles and Grusky, *Occupational Ghettos*. The "caring" phrase from Baber, "Left Lib-ertarianism," p. 1016, n. 32.

41. See Minetos v. City University of New York, 875 F. Supp. 1046 (1995); author email interview with Ralph B. Pinskey, August 19, 2019. On the history of the college, see Joan M. Williams, *Hunter College*, 9–12. For

a similar case, see Carter v. Cornell University, 976 F. Supp. 224, 226 (S.D.N.Y. 1997).

42. On "intersectional discrimination," see Crenshaw, "Demarginalizing the Intersection of Race and Sex."

43. Minetos, 875 F. Supp. 1049, 1050–52 (1995). Plaintiff brought the age discrimination claim under a different federal statute, the ADEA.

44. Minetos, 875 F. Supp. 1049, 1050–52 (1995).

45. See Leslie Hunter-Gadsen, "The Troubling News About Black Women in the Workplace," *Forbes*, November 6, 2018; see also Harris-Perry, *Sister Citizen*. For discussions of how Dominican Americans are perceived as "Black" in America despite self-identification based on their national origin, see Bailey, "Dominican-American Ethnic/Racial Identities and United States Social Categories," 677, 680, and Oropesa and Jensen, "Dominican Immigrants and Discrimination in a New Destination," 274, 278–79.

46. Minetos, 875 F. Supp. at 1050.

47. Minetos, 925 F. Supp. at 180.

48. Minetos, 925 F. Supp. at 181.

49. Minetos, 925 F. Supp. at 181–82.

50. Minetos, 925 F. Supp. at 180; author email interview with Ralph B. Pinskey, August 19, 2019.

51. Minetos, 925 F. Supp. at 182.

52. Minetos v. City University of New York, 875 F. Supp. 1046 (1995); Harris-Perry, "Sister Citizen"; Leslie Hunter-Gadsen, "The Troubling News about Black Women in the Workplace," *Forbes*, November 6, 2018.

53. Swain v. Alabama, 380 U.S. 202 (1965).

54. See Swain v. Alabama, 380 U.S. 202 (1965); Swain v. State, 156 So.2d 368, 371–72, 374–77 (Ala. Sup. Ct. 1963); Brief for Petitioner, Swain v. Alabama, 1964 WL 81288 at *5–11 (U.S. 1965); Bob Ingrahm, "No Merry Christmas on Death Row," *Montgomery Advertiser*, December 26, 1965, 58; see also Griffin, "Jumping on the Ban Wagon."

55. Batson v. Kentucky, 476 U.S. 79 (1986). Swain was condemned to die but never executed; the state did not execute anyone between 1965 and 1983. "Waldrop Sentenced to Die," *Anniston Star* (Alabama), March 23, 1983, 7. His sentence was commuted to life in prison and in 1977 he won parole. "Pardons and Paroles," *Montgomery Advertiser*, August 21, 1977, 24.

56. Minetos v. City University of New York, 925 F. Supp. 177, 185 (S.D.N.Y. 1996).

57. Author email interview with Ralph B. Pinskey, August 20, 2019.

58. Minetos, 925 F. Supp. at 185–86.

59. Author email interview with Ralph B. Pinskey, August 19, 2019.

60. Botein, "Judge Motley Memories," p. 1.

EPILOGUE: LEGACIES

1. Motley, *Unequal Justice Under Law*, 214, 218–19; Motley, "My Personal Debt to Thurgood Marshall," 23; Cole and Greenaway, "Judge Constance Baker Motley and the Struggle for Equal Justice," 16.

2. The other two women were Judge Shirley Hufstedler of the U.S. Court of Appeals for the Ninth Circuit, and Judge Sarah T. Hughes of the U.S. District Court in Texas. See "Court Prospects Include Three Women," *New York Times*, November 29, 1969, 22; "Black Woman Proposed for Supreme Court," *Pittsburgh Courier*, October 2, 1971, 1; "Suggest 10 Women for Top Court," *Chicago Tribune*, September 28, 1971, A6; "Prospective Court Choices Draw Fire," *Chicago Tribune*, October 17, 1971, 10. On Carter passing Motley over for promotion, see Motley, *Equal Justice Under Law*, 143, 224; author interview with Drew Days, U.S. solicitor general, December 5, 2012; author interview with Margaret McKenna, August 13, 2013; Marie Allen interview with Robert Lipshutz, Counsel to the President, Staff Office Files, Carter Presidential Library, September 29, 1979, pp. 16–17. "We're still waiting" from author interview with Lynn Huntley, July 24, 2014. Carter ended up nominating Amalya Kearse, a Black woman law firm partner and well-known bridge player, to the Second Circuit. See Kearse biography at www.ca2.uscourts.gov/judges/bios/alk.html.

3. See author interview with Hon. Pierre Leval; author interview with Hon. Laura Swain; author interview with Joel Motley III. "Biggest disappointments" from Motley, "My Personal Debt to Thurgood Marshall."

4. See Motley, *Equal Justice Under Law*, 224–25.

5. See author interview with Daniel Steinbock, July 12, 2014.

6. Major League Baseball Properties Inc. v. Sed Non Olet Denarius Ltd., 817 F. Supp. 1103 (S.D.N.Y. 1993), vac'd, 859 F. Supp. 80 (S.D.N.Y. 1994).

7. See Columbia Broadcasting System, Inc., v. Teleprompter Corp., 355 F. Supp. 618, 618–19 (S.D.N.Y. 1972), aff'd, Teleprompter Corp. v. Columbia Broadcasting System, Inc., 415 U.S. 394 (1974).

8. Segal, "Representative Decision Making on the Federal Bench," 144; Massie et al., "The Impact of Gender and Race in the Decisions of Judges on the United States Courts of Appeals," 10–11; Farhang and Wawro, "Institutional Dynamics on the U.S. Court of Appeals," 326; Britt and Steffensmeier, "Judges' Race and Judicial Decision Making," 761–62; Barrow and Walker, "The Diversification of the Federal Bench," 606–7.

9. See Pena v. N.Y. State Div. for Youth, 419 F. Supp. 203, 206 (S.D.N.Y. 1976); Olivieri v. Ward, 613 F. Supp. 616 (S.D.N.Y. 1985); see Arnold H. Lubasch, "Approval Given to Demonstrate at St. Patrick's: Judge Rebuffs the Police on Homosexual Rally," *New York Times*, June 17, 1986.

10. See Williams v. Ward, 671 F. Supp. 225 (S.D.N.Y. 1987), rev'd, 845 F.2d 374 (2d Cir. 1988), cert denied, 109 S.Ct. 818 (1988); Streetwatch v. National

Railroad Passenger Corp., 875 F. Supp. 1055 (1995); see also Arnold H. Lubasch, "U.S. Judge Limits Detention Period After Arrest," *New York Times*, July 7, 1987; Anonymous to Hon. Constance Baker Motley, Smith Motley Papers, box 8, folder 28; Anonymous to Hon. Constance Baker Motley, February 28, 1995, Smith Motley Papers, box 8, folder 28.

11. Oral History Interview of Constance Baker Motley, conducted by Peggy Lamson, ca. 1967, p. 4a, Lamson Papers, Schlesinger Library, Radcliffe Institute, Harvard University.

12. Author interview with Lynn Huntley, July 24, 2014.

13. See author interview with Lan Cao, July 12, 2014; author interview with Elizabeth Schneider, July 24, 2014.

14. See author interview with Lan Cao, July 12, 2014.

15. See Hon. Ann Claire Williams, "Tribute to Constance Baker Motley," n.d., pp. 2, 3 (on file with author); author interview with Hon. Kimba Wood, September 14, 2016; author interview with Hon. William Kuntz, July 24, 2014; author interview with Hon. Anne Thompson, June 23, 2014.

16. See author interview with Hon. Sonia Sotomayor, January 19, 2015.

17. See Sonia Sotomayor, "A Latina Judge's Voice," *New York Times*, May 14, 2009.

18. Washington, *Black Judges on Justice*, 132.

19. Author interview with Hon. Anne Thompson, June 23, 2014.

20. "President Bill Clinton Awards the Presidential Citizens Medals," January 8, 2001; "Presentation of the 88th NAACP Spingarn Medal to the Honorable Constance Baker Motley by Professor Derrick Bell," July 17, 2003, Ann C. Williams Papers, Collection MC 982, "Judge Motley Tributes and Other Events, 2016," Schlesinger Library, Radcliffe Institute, Harvard University; see also Marie Brenner, "Judge Motley's Verdict," *New Yorker*, May 16, 1994, 65.

21. Anna Quindlen, "The Judge Is Black, a Woman—and Sharp," *Dallas Morning News*, September 18, 1977, 8; author interview with Isolde Motley, July 15, 2014.

22. Quotes from Oral History Interview conducted by Peggy Lamson, ca. 1967, Peggy Lamson Papers, Schlesinger Library, Harvard University, and Bill Berry, "Five Strong Black Men Support and Encourage Famous Wives," *Ebony*, April 1978. On gender and earnings, see Tara Siegel Bernard, "When She Earns More: As Roles Shift, Old Ideas on Who Pays the Bills Persist," *New York Times*, July 6, 2018; Clair Cain Miller, "When Wives Earn More Than Husbands, Neither Partner Likes to Admit It," *New York Times*, July 17, 2018.

23. Author interview with Lan Cao, July 12, 2014; see "Constance Baker Motley, 84, Civil Rights Trailblazer, Lawmaker and Judge, Dies," *New York Times*, September 29, 2005.

24. Author interview with Constance Royster, June 25, 2015.

25. Author interview with Constance Royster, June 25, 2015.

26. Ginsburg, "Human Rights Hero"; "Memorial Service for the Honorable Constance Baker Motley," Ceremonial Courtroom, United States District Court, Southern District of New York, December 8, 2005 (transcript on file with author); 109th Congress, Senate Resolution 272 (October 7, 2005); see also Women's Congressional Policy Institute, "Senate Honors Constance Baker Motley"(2005).

27. "Girl in the office" from Brenner, "Judge Motley's Verdict," 65.

28. The quote is a paraphrase of Thurgood Marshall, who upon his resignation from the U.S. Supreme Court said he wanted to be remembered for doing "what he could with what he had." See Keith A. Owens, "Justice Marshall 'Did What He Could with What He Had,' and That Was a Lot," *Sun Sentinel* (South Florida), July 9, 1991.

Sources

MANUSCRIPT COLLECTIONS

Ann C. Williams Papers. Schlesinger Library, Radcliffe Institute, Harvard University, Cambridge.

Catherine Roraback Collection of Ericka Huggins Papers. Yale University Library, New Haven.

Connecticut Conference on Social and Labor Legislation. Social Ethics Pamphlet Collection, Special Collections, Yale Divinity School Library, New Haven.

Constance Baker Motley Papers, 1935–2006. Rare Book and Manuscript Library, Columbia University, New York.

Constance Baker Motley Papers. Sophia Smith Collection of Women's History, Smith College Library, Northampton.

Derrick A. Bell Jr. Papers, 1929–2011. New York University Library, New York.

Dorothy Kenyon Papers. Sophia Smith Collection of Women's History, Smith College Library, Northampton.

Dwight Hall Records. Manuscripts and Archives, Yale University Library, New Haven.

Elizabeth Wade White Papers. New York Public Library, New York.

James Rowland Angell Records. Yale University Library, New Haven.

Lyndon Baines Johnson Oral History Collection. LBJ Presidential Library, University of Texas, Austin.

Martin Luther King Jr. Papers. Stanford University, Palo Alto.

NAACP Legal Defense and Educational Fund. Library of Congress, Washington, DC.

National Archives of St. Kitts and Nevis. Basseterre, St. Kitts.

National Lawyers Guild Records, 1936–1999. Bancroft Library, University of California, Berkeley.

National Women's Political Caucus Papers. Schlesinger Library, Radcliffe Institute, Harvard University, Cambridge.

Office Files of John Macy. LBJ Presidential Library, Austin.

Papers of Melissa Ludtke, 1977–1997. Schlesinger Library, Harvard University, Cambridge.

Papers of Peggy Lamson, ca. 1967. Schlesinger Library, Harvard University, Cambridge.

Presidential Recordings Program. Miller Center of Public Affairs, University of Virginia, Charlottesville.

Robert F. Wagner Documents Collection. LaGuardia Community College, New York.

Senator Jacob K. Javits Collection. Stony Brook University, New York.

White House Central Files. LBJ Presidential Library, Austin.

William Hastie Papers. Harvard Law School Library, Harvard University, Cambridge.

GOVERNMENT DOCUMENTS

Census Records. National Archives, Washington, DC.

Federal Bureau of Investigation, Freedom of Information Privacy Office. *Constance Baker Motley File*. Washington, DC.

Illinois Department of Public Health. *Della Motley, Medical Certificate of Death*. Springfield, December 11, 1955.

National Center for Education Statistics. *120 Years of American Education: A Statistical Portrait*. Edited by Thomas Snyder. Washington, DC, 1993. https://nces.ed.gov/pubs93/93442.pdf.

President's Commission on Law Enforcement and Administration of Justice. *Task Force Report: The Police*. Washington, DC, 1967.

Records of the Selective Service System, 1926–1975. National Archives at St. Louis.

United States Bureau of the Census. *1923 Decatur City Directory*. Washington, DC.

———. *1942 Decatur City Directory*. Washington, DC.

———. *Twelfth Census of the United States Taken in the Year 1900*, vol. 1. Washington, DC.

———. *Fifteenth Census of the United States Taken in the Year 1930, Decatur, Macon, Illinois*. Washington, DC.

———. *Fifteenth Census of the United States Taken in the Year 1930, Joel Motley*. Washington, DC.

———. *Historical Poverty Tables, 1959–2016*. Washington, DC. https://www.census.gov/data/tables/time-series/demo/income-poverty/historical-poverty-people.html.

———. *Historical Statistics of the United States: Colonial Times to 1970*. Washington, DC. http://www.census.gov/library/publications/1975/compendia/hist_stats_colonial-1970.html.

———. *Sixteenth Census of the United States Taken in the Year 1940*, Enumeration Districts 11–129. Washington, DC.

United States Commission on Civil Rights. *Who Is Guarding the Guardians?: A Report on Police Practices*. 1981.

United States Congress. House. Committee on Education and Labor, Special Subcommittee on Education. *Discrimination Against Women: Hearings on Section 805 of H.R. 16098 before the House Committee on Education and Labor, Special Subcommittee on Education*. 91st Congress, 2nd session, 1970.

———. Committee on Internal Security. *Hearings, Reports and Prints of the House Committee on Internal Security*. Washington, DC: Government Printing Office, 1973.

———. Statement of Terri A. Sewell, "Honoring Bishop Calvin Woods." 113th Congress., 1st session. *Congressional Record*, E277. www.govinfo.gov/content/pkg/CREC-2014-02-28/pdf/CREC-2014-02-28-extensions.pdf.

United States Congress. Senate. "Recognizing and honoring the life and achievements of Constance Baker Motley, a judge for the United States District Court, Southern District of New York." 109th Congress, October 7, 2005.

———. "Statement of Senator Eastland." Hearings on the Nomination of Constance Baker Motley to the U.S. District Court. 89th Congress, 2nd session. *Congressional Record*. August 30, 1966.

World War I Selective Service System Draft Registration Cards, 1917–1918. National Archives and Records Administration, Washington, DC.

World War II Draft Cards (Fourth Registration) for the State of Connecticut. National Archives and Records Administration, Washington, DC.

INTERVIEWS

Andrew M. Manis Oral History Interviews. Birmingham Public Library, Birmingham.

Blum, Richard. Interview by the author, July 24, 2014.

Cao, Lan. Interview by the author, July 12, 2014.

Cedarbaum, the Honorable Miriam. Interview by the author, June 18, 2014.

Coleman, William T. Interview by the author, January 13, 2011.

Cunningham, Christi. Interview by the author, email, July 14, 2014.

Days, Drew. Interview by the author, 5 Dec. 2012.

Fong, Kevin. Interview by the author, July 12, 2014.

Gordon, John. Interview by the author, January 25, 2014.

Greenberg, Jack. Columbia Oral History Project, 1994.

Height, Dorothy Irene. Black Women Oral History Project, 1976–1981, Schlesinger Library.

Huggins, Joan and Carolyn. Interview by the author, September 25, 2019.

Huntley, Lynn. Interview by the author, July 24, 2014.

Jones, Clarence. Interview by the author, October 3, 2017.

Kuntz, the Honorable William. Interview by the author, July 24, 2014.

Lassiter, Mai Huggins. Interview by the author, November 22, 2019.

Leval, the Honorable Pierre. Interview by the author, August 15, 2017.

Lipshutz, Robert. By Marie Allen. Carter Presidential Library, September 29, 1979.

Ludtke, Melissa. By Jane Pauley. NBC, *Today*, January 4, 1978.

——. By Anne Ritchie. Washington Press Club Foundation, February 21, 1993.

——. Interview by the author, March 13, 2013.

Marshall, Thurgood. By T. H. Baker. LBJ Oral History Collection, July 10, 1969.

——. Columbia Oral History Project, 1994.

McKenna, Margaret. Interview by the author, August 13, 2013.

Meltzer, Michael. Interview by the author, May 9, 2013.

Moskowitz, Nell. Interview by the author, April 17, 2012.

Motley, Constance Baker. Oral History Archive, National Visionary Leadership Project. www.visionaryproject.org/motleyconstancebaker/.

——. Columbia Oral History Project, 1994.

"The Reminiscences of Judge Constance Baker Motley." By Kitty Gellhorn. Oral History Research Office, Columbia University (1978).

——. Interview with Constance Baker Motley, conducted by Blackside, Inc. on November 2, 1985, for *Eyes on the Prize: America's Civil Rights Years (1954–1965)*. Washington University Libraries, Film and Media Archive, Henry Hampton Collection.

Motley, Isolde. Interview by the author, July 15, 2014.

Motley, Joel, III. Interview by the author, June 27, 2015.

——. Interview by the author, email, December 11, 2016, and September 2, 2020.

Norton, Eleanor Holmes. The History Makers Oral History Collections, August 25, 2018. www.thehistorymakers.org/biography/honorable-eleanor-holmes-norton.

Pinskey, Ralph B. Interview by the author, email, August 19, 2019.

Rabb, Harriet. Interview by J. P. Ogilvy, March 6, 2001. Transcript, National Archive of Legal Clinical Education, Catholic University of America, Washington, DC. www.law.edu/NACLE/nacle-transcripts.cfm.

——. "Harriet S. Rabb Oral History. Part 1: Family Influence on Career Choice." Harriet S. Rabb Oral History, Rockefeller University, 2017. https://digitalcommons.rockefeller.edu/harriet-rabb/2/.

——. "Harriet S. Rabb Oral History. Part 3: First Case." Harriet S. Rabb Oral History, Rockefeller University, 2017. https://digitalcommons.rockefeller.edu/harriet-rabb/5/.

——. "Harriet S. Rabb Oral History. Part 4: Gender Discrimination Cases in the 1970s." Harriet S. Rabb Oral History, Rockefeller University, 2017. https://digitalcommons.rockefeller.edu/harriet-rabb/4/.

Ratner, Michael. Interview by the author, September 1, 2018.

Roberts, Dorothy. Interview by the author, July 14, 2014.

Royster, Constance. Interview by the author, June 24–25, 2014.

——. Interview by the author, email, December 8–9, 2016.

——. Interview by the author, email, December 22, 2017.

Schneider, Elizabeth. Interview by the author, July 24, 2014.

Schwarz, Frederick A. O. Interview by the author, telephone, August 14, 2013.

Sotomayor, the Honorable Sonia. Interview by the author, January 19, 2015.

Steinbock, Daniel. Interview by the author, July 12, 2014.

Swain, the Honorable Laura. Interview by the author, July 3, 2014.

Thompson, the Honorable Anne. Interview by the author, June 23, 2014, and January 19, 2015.

Tushnet, Mark. Interview by the author, March 30, 2016.

Wayland, Leonora. Interview by the author, July 20, 2015.

Williams, Joan, and Shirley. Interview by author, November 1, 2012.

Wood, the Honorable Kimba. Interview by the author, September 14, 2016.

Woods, Reverend Abraham L. Mervyn H. Sterne Library, University of Alabama, October 28, 1975.

Woods, Reverend Calvin Wallace. History Makers, September 7, 2007. www.thehistorymakers.org/biography/reverend-calvin-wallace-woods-sr.

NEWSPAPERS AND PERIODICALS

Afro-American (Baltimore)
American Heritage
Anniston Star (Alabama)
Atlanta Constitution
Atlanta Daily World
Atlanta Journal-Constitution
Birmingham Mirror (Alabama)
The Black Panther
Bloomberg Law
Boston Globe
Bridgeport Telegram (Connecticut)

Business Insider
Call and Post (Cleveland)
Chicago Daily Defender
Chicago Defender
Chicago Tribune
Christian Science Monitor
Clarion-Ledger (Jackson, MS)
The Columbian (Vancouver, Canada)
Commentary magazine
The Crisis (NAACP)
The Daily Beast

Daily Worker

Daily World (New York)

Dallas Morning News

Decatur Daily Review (Illinois)

The Democrat (Nevis)

Ebony

Education Weekly

Forbes

Globe and Mail (Canada)

Harper's Magazine

Hartford Courant (Connecticut)

Houston Chronicle

Jackson Free Press (Mississippi)

Jet

Life

Los Angeles Times

Macon Telegraph (Georgia)

Miami Herald

Miami News

Montgomery Advertiser (Alabama)

National Geographic

National Law Journal

National Public Radio (NPR)

Nevis Recorder (St. Kitts and Nevis)

New Haven Register (Connecticut)

New Journal and Guide (Virginia)

Newsday (New York)

News-Tribune (Idaho)

New York magazine

New York Amsterdam News

New York Daily Metro

New York Daily Press

New Yorker

New York Herald Tribune

New York Journal-American

New York Post

New York Times

New York World-Telegraph

Oneonta Star (New York)

Philadelphia Tribune

Pittsburgh Courier

Plain Dealer (Cleveland)

The Record (New Jersey)

Saturday Evening Post

Southern School News

Sporting News

St. Kitts-Nevis Daily Bulletin
    (St. Kitts and Nevis)

St. Louis Post-Dispatch

Sun Sentinel (South Florida)

Time

Times-Picayune (New Orleans)

Trial magazine

UCLA Daily Bruin (California)

USA Today

Wall Street Journal

The Washington Lawyer

Washington Post

Worcester Telegram & Gazette
    (Massachusetts)

Worker's World (New York)

INTERNET SOURCES

Amerian, Stephanie. "Dorothy Sayer: Fifth Avenue's First Lady." UCLA Center for the Study of Women, June 1, 2009. https://escholarship.org/uc/item/7w18h2jx.

"Approved Application for Membership, The Connecticut Society of the Sons of the American Revolution, Sept. 30, 1914." U.S., Sons of the American Revolution Membership Applications, 1889–1970, Ancestry.com. www.ancestry.com/search/collections/2204/.

Bagall, Whitney S. "A Brief History of Women at Columbia Law School, Pt. 2."

http://web.archive.org/web/20030920070540/http://www.law.columbia.edu/law_school/communications/reports/Fall2002/brief2.

Bryant, Joseph D. "Longtime Birmingham Civil Rights Figure Honored with Marker at Kelly Ingram Park." Al.com, September 14, 2014. www.al.com/news/birmingham/2014/09/longtime_birmingham_civil_righ.html.

"First Year and Total J.D. Enrollment by Gender 1947–2011." American Bar Association, accessed June 4, 2019. www.americanbar.org/content/dam/aba/administrative/legal_education_and_admissions_to_the_bar/statistics/jd_enrollment_1yr_total_gender.authcheckdam.pdf.

Gardiner, Christine. "Policing Around the Nation: Education, Philosophy, and Practice." California State Fullerton, Center for Public Policy, September 2017. www.policefoundation.org/wp-content/uploads/2017/10/PF-Report-Policing-Around-the-Nation_10-2017_Final.pdf.

"The National Organization for Women's 1966 Statement of Purpose." National Organization for Women. https://now.org/about/history/statement-of-purpose/.

Patten, Eileen. "Racial, Gender Wage Gaps Persist in U.S. Despite Some Progress." Pew Research Center, July 1, 2016. www.pewresearch.org/fact-tank/2016/07/01/racial-gender-wage-gaps-persist-in-u-s-despite-some-progress/.

"Sam Cooke and the Song That 'Almost Scared Him.'" *All Things Considered*, National Public Radio, February 1, 2014. www.npr.org/2014/02/01/268995033/sam-cooke-and-the-song-that-almost-scared-him.

"Senate Honors Constance Baker Motley." Women's Congressional Policy Institute. www.wcpinst.org/source/senate-honors-constance-baker-motley/.

Serwer, Adam. "American Bar Association Under Fire for Underrating Women, Minorities." MSNBC, May 12, 2014. www.msnbc.com/msnbc/american-bar-association-diversity-ratings.

Shapiro, Joseph. "How One Inmate Changed the Prison System from the Inside." *Code Switch*, National Public Radio, April 14, 2017. www.npr.org/sections/codeswitch/2017/04/14/507297469/how-one-inmate-changed-the-prison-system-from-the-inside.

"The United States District Court for the Southern District of New York: A Retrospective (1990–2000)." New York County Lawyers' Association Committee on the Federal Courts, December 2002. www.nycla.org/siteFiles/Publications/Publications74_0.pdf.

Wagner, Peter, and Bernadette Rabuy. "Mass Incarceration: The Whole Pie." Prison Policy Initiative, March 14, 2017. www.prisonpolicy.org/reports/pie2017.html.

Wolf, Z. Byron. "Trump's Attacks on Judge Curiel Are Still Jarring to Read."

CNN, February 27, 2018. www.cnn.com/2018/02/27/politics/judge-curiel
-trump-border-wall.

UNPUBLISHED MATERIAL

Botein, Barbara. "Judge Motley Memories: Law Clerk Compilation." On file
with author.

Calder, Linda, and the Honorable Lindsey Miller-Lerman. "Judge Motley
Memories: Law Clerk Compilation." On file with author.

Dargan, Catherine J. "Don't Let Nobody Turn You Around." Third-year paper,
Harvard Law School, April 1994. On file with author.

Davis, Susan, and the Honorable Lindsey Miller-Lerman. "Judge Motley
Memories: Law Clerk Compilation." On file with author.

Fischer, Howard. "Judge Motley Memories: Law Clerk Compilation." On file
with author.

Fong, Kevin. "Judge Motley Memories: Law Clerk Compilation." On file with
author.

Freedman, Bruce, and Sara Moss. "Judge Motley Memories: Law Clerk Compilation." On file with author.

King, Martin Luther, Jr. "Martin Luther King, Jr., Address to the Association
of the Bar of the City of New York." April 21, 1965.

Massie, Tajuana, et al. "The Impact of Gender and Race in the Decisions of
Judges on the United States Courts of Appeals." April 25–28, 2002. Unpub-
lished manuscript. On file with the *Columbia Law Review*.

Moss, Sara, and Scott Optican. "Judge Motley Memories: Law Clerk Compilation." On file with author.

Pauley, Jane. "Transcript of Jane Pauley Reporting." *Good Morning America*,
ABC News, January 12, 1978.

"Transcript, Open Mind Roundtable." NBC News, October 15, 1961.

Williams, the Honorable Ann Claire. "Tribute to Constance Baker Motley."
On file with author.

BOOKS AND JOURNAL ARTICLES

Abramowitz, Mildred W. "Eleanor Roosevelt and the National Youth Administration, 1935–1943: An Extension of the Presidency." *Presidential Studies
Quarterly* 14, no. 4 (1984): 569–80.

Agersborg, H. P. K., and W. D. Hatfield. "The Biology of a Sewage Treatment
Plant." *Sewage Works Journal* 1, no. 4 (1929): 411–24.

Anderson, James D. *The Education of Blacks in the South, 1860–1935*. Chapel
Hill: University of North Carolina Press, 1988.

Anderson, Jervis. *A. Philip Randolph: A Biographical Portrait*. Berkeley: University of California Press, 1986.

Anderson, Sarah A. " 'The Place to Go': The 135th Street Branch Library and the Harlem Renaissance." *Library Quarterly* 73, no. 4 (2003): 383–421.

Annis, J. Lee, Jr. *Big Jim Eastland: The Godfather of Mississippi*. Oxford: University Press of Mississippi, 2016.

Arsenault, Raymond. *Freedom Riders: 1961 and the Struggle for Racial Justice*. Oxford: Oxford University Press, 2011.

Ashmore, Susan Youngblood. *Carry It On: The War on Poverty and the Civil Rights Movement in Alabama, 1964–1972*. Athens: University of Georgia Press, 2008.

Aspinall, Algernon E. *The British West Indies*. London: Pitman & Sons, 1912.

Azaransky, Sarah. "Jane Crow: Pauli Murray's Intersections and Antidiscrimination Law." *Journal of Feminist Studies in Religion* 29, no. 1 (2013): 155–60.

Baber, H. E. "Left Libertarianism: What's In It for Me." *San Diego Law Review* 43 (2006): 995–1016.

Bailey, Benjamin. "Dominican-American Ethnic/Racial Identities and United States Social Categories." *International Migration Review* 35, no. 3 (2001): 677–708.

Baldwin, James. *The Price of the Ticket: Collected Nonfiction*. New York: St. Martin's, 1985.

Ball, Howard. *A Defiant Life: Thurgood Marshall and the Persistence of Racism in America*. New York: Broadway Books, 1998.

Banks, Fred L. "The United States Court of Appeals for the Fifth Circuit: A Personal Perspective." *Mississippi College Law Review* 16, no. 2 (1996): 275–88.

Banks, Taunya L. "Justice Thurgood Marshall, the Race Man, and Gender Equality in the Courts." *Virginia Journal of Social Policy and Law* 18, no. 1 (2010): 16–43.

Barnes-Johnson, Joy M. "Preparing Minority Teachers: Law and Out of Order." *Journal of Negro Education* 77, no. 1 (2008): 72–81.

Barrie, J. M. *Peter and Wendy,* New York: Charles Scribner's Sons, 1911.

Barrow, Deborah J., and Thomas G. Walker. "The Diversification of the Federal Bench: Policy and Process Ramifications." *Journal of Politics* 47, no. 2 (1985): 596–617.

Bass, Paul, and Douglas W. Rae. *Murder in the Model City*. Vol. 1. New York: Basic Books, 2006.

Berg, Allison. "Trauma and Testimony in Black Women's Civil Rights Memoirs: The Montgomery Bus Boycott and the Women Who Started It, Warriors Don't Cry, and From the Mississippi Delta." *Journal of Women's History*, 21 no. 3 (2009): 84–107.

Berger, Lawrence M., and Jane Waldfogel. "Maternity Leave and the Employment of New Mothers in the United States." *Journal of Population Economics* 17, no. 2 (2004): 331–49.

Bergmann, Barbara R. "Occupational Segregation, Wages and Profits When Employers Discriminate by Race or Sex." *Eastern Economic Journal* 103, no. 2 (1974): 103–10.

Biondi, Martha. *The Black Revolution on Campus*. Berkeley: University of California Press, 2012.

Bird, Susan Willett. "The Assignment of Cases to Federal District Court Judges." *Stanford Law Review* 27 (1975): 475–87.

Biskupic, Joan. *Sandra Day O'Connor: How the First Woman on the Supreme Court Became Its Most Influential Justice*. New York: Harper, 2005.

Black, Barbara Aronstein. "Something to Remember, Something to Celebrate: Women at Columbia Law School." *Columbia Law Review* 6, no. 102 (2002): 1451–68.

Bloom, Joshua, and Waldo E. Martin. *Black Against Empire: The History and Politics of the Black Panther Party*. Berkeley: University of California Press, 2016.

Bogle, Donald. *Toms, Coons, Mulattoes, Mammies and Bucks: An Interpretative History of Blacks in American Films*. New York: Bloomsburg Academic, 2016.

Bornstein, Stephanie. "A Tribute to Justice Ruth Bader Ginsburg: The Law of Gender Stereotyping and the Work-Family Conflicts of Men." *Hastings Law Journal* 63 (2012): 1297–1395.

Branch, Taylor. *Pillar of Fire: America in the King Years, 1963–65*. New York: Touchstone, 1998.

Branham, Robert James. " 'I Was Gone on Debating': Malcolm X's Prison Debates and Public Confrontations." *Argumentation and Advocacy* (1995): 117–37.

Britt, Chester L., and Darrell Steffensmeier. "Judges' Race and Judicial Decision Making: Do Black Judges Sentence Differently?" *Social Science Quarterly* 82, no. 4 (2001): 749–64.

Brown, Tammy L. "A New Era in American Politics: Shirley Chisholm and the Discourse of Identity." *Callaloo, A Journal of African Diaspora Arts and Letters* 31, no. 4 (2008): 1013–25.

Brownmiller, Susan. *Shirley Chisholm: A Biography*. Garden City, NY: Doubleday, 1970.

Brown-Nagin, Tomiko. "The Transformation of a Social Movement into Law?: The SCLC and NAACP's Campaigns for Civil Rights Reconsidered in Light of the Educational Activism of Septima P. Clark." *Women's History Review* 8, no. 1 (1999): 81–137.

———. *Courage to Dissent: Atlanta and the Long History of the Civil Rights Movement*. New York: Oxford University Press, 2011.

———. "Identity Matters: The Case of Constance Baker Motley." *Columbia Law Review* 117, no. 7 (2017): 1707–12.

———. "The Civil Rights Canon: Above and Below." *Yale Law Journal* 123, no. 8 (2018): 2698–739.

Bunche, Ralph J. "A Critical Analysis of the Tactics and Programs of Minority Groups." *Journal of Negro Education* 4 (1935): 308–20.

Burhop, Ray. *Okahumpka Florida: The History of a Florida Cracker Community*. CreateSpace Independent Publishing Platform, 2013.

Caplan, Colin M. *Legendary Locals of New Haven*. Charleston, SC: Arcadia, 2013.

Cardozier, V. R. *Colleges and Universities in World War II*. Westport, CT: Praeger, 1993.

Caro, Robert A. *The Passage of Power: The Years of Lyndon Johnson*. New York: Knopf, 2012.

Carter, Dan T. *Scottsboro: A Tragedy of the American South*. Baton Rouge: Louisiana State University Press, 1994.

Carter, Judge Robert L. *A Matter of Law: A Memoir of Struggle in the Cause of Civil Rights*. New York: New Press, 2005.

Casper, Gerhard, and Philip B. Kurland, eds. *Brown v. Board of Education (1954 & 1955)*. In *Landmark Briefs and Arguments of the Supreme Court of the United States: Constitutional Law*, vols. 49 and 49A. Washington, DC: University Publications of America, 1975.

Cha-Jua, Sundiata Keita. "A Warlike Demonstration: Legalism, Armed Resistance and Black Political Mobilization in Decatur, Illinois, 1894–1898." *Journal of Negro History* 83, no. 1 (1998): 57–72.

Charles, Maria, and David B. Grusky. *Occupational Ghettos: The Worldwide Segregation of Women and Men*. Stanford, CA: Stanford University Press, 2004.

Charron, Katherine Mellen. *Freedom's Teacher: The Life of Septima Clark*. Chapel Hill: University of North Carolina Press, 2009.

Chernow, Ron. *Alexander Hamilton*. New York: Penguin, 2004.

Chicoine, Stephen. "One Glorious Season: How Baseball Helped to Integrate Decatur, Illinois." *Journal of the Illinois State History Society* 96, no. 1 (2003): 80–97.

Churchill, Ward, and Jim Vander Wall. *Agents of Repression: The FBI's Secret Wars Against the Black Panther Party and the American Indian Movement*. Boston: South End Press, 1988.

Clark, E. Culpepper. *The Schoolhouse Door: Segregation's Last Stand at the University of Alabama*. New York: Oxford University Press, 1993.

Clark, Kenneth B. *Dark Ghetto: Dilemmas of Social Power*. New York: Harper & Row, 1965.

Clark, Mary L. "Carter's Groundbreaking Appointment of Women to the Federal Bench: His Other Human Rights Record." *American University Journal of Gender, Social Policy, and the Law* 11, no. 3 (2002): 1131–64.

Clark, Robert F. *The War on Poverty: History, Selected Programs and Ongoing Impact*. Lanham, MD: University Press of America, 2002.

Clarke, John Henrik. *Malcolm X: The Man and His Times*. New York: Macmillan, 1969.

Clinton, Catherine. *The Plantation Mistress: Woman's World in the Old South*. New York: Pantheon, 1982.

Cohen, Rodney T. *Fisk University*. Charleston, SC: Arcadia Publishing, 2001.

Cole, Jeffrey, and Joseph A. Greenaway. "Judge Constance Baker Motley and the Struggle for Equal Justice." *Litigation* 29 (2002–3): 6–16.

Colvin, Claudette. *Twice Toward Justice*. New York: Square Fish, 2010.

Combahee River Collective. "A Black Feminist Statement." *Women's Studies Quarterly* 42, no. 3/4 (2014): 271–80.

Copeland, Vincent. *The Crime of Martin Sostre*. New York: McGraw-Hill, 1970.

Cott, Nancy F. *Public Vows: A History of Marriage and the Nation*. Cambridge, MA: Harvard University Press, 2000.

Countryman, Matthew J. *Up South: Civil Rights and Black Power in Philadelphia*. Philadelphia: University of Pennsylvania Press, 2006.

Covey, Russel. "Police Misconduct and Wrongful Convictions." *Washington University Law Review* 90, no. 4 (2013): 1133–89.

Crenshaw, Kimberlé. "Demarginalizing the Intersection of Race and Sex: A Black Feminist Critique of Antidiscrimination Doctrine, Feminist Theory and Antiracist Politics." *University of Chicago Legal Forum* 139 (1989): 139–67.

Cushman, Clare. *Supreme Court Decisions and Women's Rights*. Washington, DC: CQ Press, 2001.

D'Amato, Paul. "The Communist Party and Black Liberation in the 1930s." *International Socialist Review* (1997). www.isreview.org/issues01/cp_blacks_1930s.shtml.

Daniels, Maurice. *Saving the Soul of Georgia: Donald L. Hollowell and the Struggle for Civil Rights*. Athens: University of Georgia Press, 2013.

Davis, Michael D., and Hunter R. Clark. *Thurgood Marshall: Warrior at the Bar, Rebel on the Bench*. New York: Carol Publishing, 1994.

De Hart, Jane Sherron. *Ruth Bader Ginsburg: A Life*. New York: Knopf, 2018.

Dierenfield, Bruce J. *The Civil Rights Movement*. Revised edition. New York: Routledge, 2013.

Dinner, Deborah. "The Universal Childcare Debate: Rights Mobilization, Social Policy, and the Dynamics of Feminist Activism, 1966–1974." *Law and History Review* 28, no. 3 (2010): 577–628.

Dittmer, John. *Local People: The Struggle for Civil Rights in Mississippi*. Urbana: University of Illinois Press, 1994.

Doyle, William. *An American Insurrection: James Meredith and the Battle of Oxford, Mississippi, 1962*. New York: Anchor Books, 2003.

Dubin, Lawrence A. "Virgil Hawkins: A One-Man Civil Rights Movement." *Florida Law Review* 51 (1999): 913–56.

Du Bois, W. E. B. "Does the Negro Need Separate Schools?" *Journal of Negro Education* 4, no. 3 (1934): 328–35.

———. *Darkwater: Voices from Within the Veil*. New York: Washington Square Press, 2004. Originally published by Harcourt, Brace & Howe, 1920.

Dulaney, W. Marvin. *Black Police in America*. Bloomington: Indiana University Press, 1996.

Dunn, Richard S. *Sugar and Slaves: The Rise of the Planter Class in the British West Indies*. Chapel Hill: University of North Carolina Press, 2000.

Dyde, Brian. *Out of the Crowded Vagueness: A History of the Islands of St. Kitts, Nevis and Anguilla*. Oxford, UK: Macmillan, 2005.

Eagles, Charles W. *The Price of Defiance: James Meredith and the Integration of Ole Miss*. Chapel Hill: University of North Carolina Press, 2009.

Eagly, Alice H., and Blair T. Johnson. "Gender and Leadership Style: A Meta-Analysis." *Psychological Bulletin* 108, no. 2 (1990): 233–56.

Emanuel, Anne. *Elbert Parr Tuttle: Chief Jurist of the Civil Rights Revolution*. Athens: University of Georgia Press, 2014.

Epstein, Cynthia Fuchs. *Women in Law*. New Orleans: Quid Pro Books, 2012.

Eskew, Glenn T. *But for Birmingham: The Local and National Movements in the Civil Rights Struggle*. Chapel Hill: University of North Carolina Press, 1997.

Evans, Sara. *Personal Politics: The Roots of Women's Liberation in the Civil Rights Movement and the New Left* (New York: Vintage, 1980).

———. "The Rebirth of the Women's Movement in the 1960s." In *Woman and Power in American History*, edited by Kathryn Kish Sklar and Thomas Dublin, 239–47. Upper Saddle River, NJ: Prentice Hall, 2009.

Fairclough, Adam. *To Redeem the Soul of America: The Southern Christian Leadership Conference and Martin Luther King, Jr.* Athens: University of Georgia Press, 1987.

Farhang, Sean, and Gregory Wawro. "Institutional Dynamics on the U.S. Court of Appeals: Minority Representation Under Panel Decision Making." *Journal of Law, Economics & Organization* 20 (2004): 299–330.

Flamm, Richard. *Judicial Disqualification: Recusal and Disqualification of Judges*. 2nd. ed. Berkeley, CA: Banks & Jordan Law Publishing, 2007.

Fleishman, Joel L. *The Foundation: A Great American Secret: How Private Wealth Is Changing the World*. New York: PublicAffairs, 2009.

Ford, Gary L., Jr. *Constance Baker Motley: One Woman's Fight for Civil Rights and Equal Justice Under Law*. Tuscaloosa: University of Alabama Press, 2017.

Forest, Kay B., et al. "Cohort Differences in the Transition to Motherhood: The Variable Effects of Education and Employment Before Marriage." *Sociological Quarterly* 36, no. 2 (1995): 567–85.

Fortner, Michael Javin. *Black Silent Majority: The Rockefeller Drug Laws and the Politics of Punishment*. Cambridge, MA: Harvard University Press, 2015.

Frazier, E. Franklin. *The Negro Family in the United States*. Chicago: University of Chicago Press, 1939.

———. *Black Bourgeoisie*. New York: Free Press, 1997. Originally published 1957.

Freed, Donald. *Agony in New Haven: The Trial of Bobby Seale, Ericka Huggins, and the Black Panther Party*. New York: Simon & Shuster, 1973.

Friedan, Betty. *The Feminine Mystique*. New York: W. W. Norton, 1963.

Frucht, Richard. "Emigration, Remittances and Social Change: Aspects of the Social Field of Nevis, West Indies." *Anthropologica* 10, no. 2 (1968): 193–208.

Frusciano, Thomas J., and Marilyn H. Pettit. *New York University and the City*. New Brunswick, NJ: Rutgers University Press, 1997.

Fuld, Stanley H. "Professor Milton Handler." *Columbia Law Review* 73, no. 3 (1973): 407–9.

Gallagher, Henry T. *James Meredith and the Ole Miss Riot: A Soldier's Story*. Jackson: University Press of Mississippi, 2012.

Gallagher, Julie A. *Black Women and Politics in New York City*. Urbana: University of Illinois Press, 2012.

Garrow, David. *Bearing the Cross: Martin Luther King, Jr., and the Southern Christian Leadership Conference*. New York: Vintage, 1988. Originally published 1986.

Giddings, Paula J. *When and Where I Enter: The Impact of Black Women on Race and Sex in America*. New York: HarperCollins, 1984.

———. *Ida: A Sword Among Lions: Ida B. Wells and the Campaign Against Lynching*. New York: HarperCollins, 2008.

Gilbert, Lynn, and Gaylen Moore. "Constance Baker Motley." In *Particular Passions: Talks with Women Who Have Shaped Our Times*. New York: Potter, 1981.

Gilmore, Brian G., and Reginald Dwayne Betts. "Deconstructing Carmona: The U.S. War on Drugs and Black Men." *Valparaiso Law Review* 47, no. 3 (2013): 89–129.

Gilmore, Glenda Elizabeth. *Defying Dixie: The Radical Roots of Civil Rights, 1919–1950*. New York: W. W. Norton, 2008.

Gilpin, Patrick J. "Charles S. Johnson and the Race Relations Institutes at Fisk University." *Phylon* 41, no. 3 (1980): 300–311.

Ginsburg, Ruth Bader. "Human Rights Hero: Tribute to Constance Baker Motley." *Human Rights* (2005). www.americanbar.org/groups/crsj /publications/human_rights_magazine_home/human_rights_vol32_2005 /fall2005/hr_Fall05_bakermotley/.

Goebel, Julius. *A History of the School of Law, Columbia University*. New York: Columbia University Press, 1955.

Goldman, Sheldon. *Picking Federal Judges: Lower Court Selection from Roosevelt Through Reagan*. New Haven, CT: Yale University Press, 1999.

Goodman, James. *Stories of Scottsboro*. New York: Vintage, 1995.

Goucher, Candice, Charles LeGuin, and Linda Walton. "Commerce and Change: The Creation of a Global Economy and the Expansion of Europe." In *In the Balance: Themes in Global History*, 491–508. Boston: McGraw-Hill, 1998.

Grant, Cynthia Bowman. "Women in the Legal Profession from the 1920s to the 1970s: What Can We Learn from Their Experience About Law and Social Change." *Maine Law Review* 61, no. 2 (2009): 1–25.

Green, Victor H. *The Negro Motorist Green-Book*. New York: Victor H. Green & Co., 1940.

Greenberg, Jack. *Crusaders in the Courts: How a Dedicated Band of Lawyers Fought for the Civil Rights Revolution*. New York: Basic Books, 1994.

Griffin, Patricia J. "Jumping on the Ban Wagon: Minetos v. City University of New York and the Future of the Peremptory Challenge." *Minnesota Law Review* 81, no. 5 (1997): 1237–70.

Griffler, Keith P. *Front Line of Freedom: African Americans and the Forging of the Underground Railroad in the Ohio Valley*. Louisville: University Press of Kentucky, 2004.

Grob, Gerald N. *Mental Illness and American Society, 1875–1940*. Princeton, NJ: Princeton University Press, 1983.

———. *The Mad Among Us: A History of the Care of America's Mentally Ill*. New York: Free Press, 1994.

Grunebaum, Henry. *Mentally Ill Mothers and Their Children*. Chicago: University of Chicago Press, 1982.

Guillory, Dan. *Decatur, Illinois*. Charleston, SC: Arcadia Publishing, 2004.

Hamilton, Charles V. *Adam Clayton Powell Jr: The Political Biography of an American Dilemma*. New York: Atheneum, 1991.

Haney, Craig. "Mental Health Issues in Long-Term 'Solitary' and 'Supermax' Confinement." *Crime and Delinquency* 49, no. 1 (2003): 124–56.

Harrington, Mona. *Women Lawyers: Rewriting the Rules*. New York: Plume, 1995.

Harris, Abram L., and Sterling D. Spero. *The Black Worker*. New York: Atheneum, 1969.

Harris-Perry, Melissa. *Sister Citizen: Shame, Stereotype, and Black Women in America*. New Haven, CT: Yale University Press, 2011.

Haygood, Will. *King of the Cats: The Life and Times of Adam Clayton Powell*. New York: Amistad, 2006.

Haynes, John. *Red Scare or Red Menace?: American Communism and Anti-Communism in the Cold War Era*. Chicago: Ivan R. Dee, 1996.

Height, Dorothy I. "The Adult Education Program of the YWCA Among Negroes." *Journal of Negro Education* 14, no. 3 (1945): 322–30.

Hickey, Neil, and Ed Edwin. *Adam Clayton Powell and the Politics of Race*. New York: Fleet Publishing, 1965.

Higginbotham, Evelyn Brooks. "African-American Women's History and the Metalanguage of Race." *Signs* 17 (1992): 251–74.

——. *Righteous Discontent: The Women's Movement in the Black Baptist Church, 1880–1920*. Cambridge, MA: Harvard University Press, 1993.

Hinton, Elizabeth. *From the War on Poverty to the War on Crime: The Making of Mass Incarceration*. Cambridge, MA: Harvard University Press, 2017.

Hoff, Joan. *Law, Gender, and Injustice: A Legal History of U.S. Women*. New York: New York University Press, 1991.

Hollars, B. J. *Opening the Doors: The Desegregation of the University of Alabama and the Fight for Civil Rights in Tuscaloosa*. Tuscaloosa: University of Alabama Press, 2013.

Honey, Maureen. *Creating Rosie the Riveter: Class, Gender and Propaganda During World War II*. Amherst: University of Massachusetts Press, 1984.

Hope, John. "The Negro College, Student Protest and the Future." *Journal of Negro Education* 30, no. 4 (1961): 368–76.

Horne, Gerald. *Black Liberation/Red Scare: Ben Davis and the Communist Party*. Newark: University of Delaware Press, 1994.

Hubbard, Vincent K. *Swords, Ships and Sugar: A History of Nevis to 1900*. Corvallis, OR: Premiere Editions International, 2002.

Hughes, C. Alvin. " 'We Demand Our Rights': The Southern Negro Youth Congress." *Phylon* 48, no. 1 (1987): 38–50.

Hunter-Gault, Charlayne. *In My Place*. New York: Vintage, 1992.

Ifill, Sherrilyn A. "Racial Diversity on the Bench: Beyond Role Models and Public Confidence." *Washington & Lee Law Review* 57, no. 2 (2000): 405–95.

Institute for Research in Biography. *Who's Who in Commerce and Industry*. Chicago: Marquis, 1936.

Jackson, Thomas F. *From Civil Rights to Human Rights: Martin Luther King, Jr., and the Struggle for Economic Justice*. Philadelphia: University of Pennsylvania Press, 2007.

Jacobs, James B. "The Prisoners' Rights Movement and Its Impacts, 1960–1980." *Crime and Justice* 2 (1980): 429–70.

Jay, Stewart. "The Creation of the First Amendment Right to Free Expression: From the Eighteenth Century to the Mid-Twentieth Century." *William Mitchell Law Review* 34 (2008): 773–1020.

Jonas, Gilbert. *Freedom's Sword: The NAACP and the Struggle Against Racism in America, 1909–1969*. New York: Routledge, 2005.

Jones, Charles E. "The Political Repression of the Black Panther Party 1966–

1971: The Case of the Oakland Bay Area." *Journal of Black Studies* 18, no. 4 (1988): 415–34.

Jones, Clarence B., and Stuart Connelly. *Behind the Dream: The Making of the Speech That Transformed a Nation*. New York: St. Martin's Press, 2012.

Jones, Jacqueline. *Labor of Love, Labor of Sorrow: Black Women, Work, and the Family, from Slavery to the Present*. New York: Basic Books, 2010.

Joseph, Peniel E. *Dark Days, Bright Nights: From Black Power to Barack Obama*. New York: BasicCivitas, 2010.

———. *Stokely: A Life*. New York: Basic Books, 2014.

———. *The Sword and the Shield: The Revolutionary Lives of Malcolm X and Martin Luther King Jr.* New York: Basic Books, 2020.

Kandel, I. L. *The Impact of War upon American Education*. Chapel Hill: University of North Carolina Press, 1948.

King, Gilbert. *Devil in the Grove: Thurgood Marshall, the Groveland Boys, and the Dawn of a New America*. New York: Harper, 2013.

King, Martin Luther, Jr. *Why We Can't Wait*. Toronto: New American Library, 1964.

Klein, Maury. *History of the Louisville and Nashville Railroad*. New York: Macmillan, 1972.

Kluger, Richard. *Simple Justice: The History of Brown v. Board of Education and Black America's Struggle for Equality*. New York: Knopf, 1975.

Knauer, Christine. *Let Us Fight as Free Men: Black Soldiers and Civil Rights*. Philadelphia: University of Pennsylvania Press, 2014.

Kotz, Nick. *Judgment Days: Lyndon Baines Johnson, Martin Luther King, Jr., and the Laws That Changed America*. Boston: Houghton Mifflin, 2005.

Kozol, Jonathan. *Savage Inequalities: Children in America's Schools*. New York: Crown, 1991.

Kunzel, Regina G. "White Neurosis, Black Pathology: Constructing Out-of-Wedlock Pregnancy in the Wartime and Postwar United States." In *Not June Cleaver*, edited by Joanne Meyerowitz, 304–34. Philadelphia: Temple University Press, 1994.

Kuykendall, Jack, and David E. Burns. "The Black Police Officer: An Historical Perspective." *Journal of Contemporary Criminal Justice* 1, no. 4 (1980): 4–12.

Lamson, Peggy. *Few Are Chosen: American Women in Political Life Today*. Boston: Houghton Mifflin, 1968.

Landon, Michael de L. "The Origins of the University of Mississippi Law Journal." *Mississippi Law Journal* (2003): i–viii.

———. *The University of Mississippi School of Law*. Jackson: University Press of Mississippi, 2006.

Landry, Bart. *Black Working Wives: Pioneers of the American Family Revolution*. Berkeley: University of California Press, 2002.

Lanker, Brian. "Constance Baker Motley Interview." In *I Dream a World: Portraits of Black Women Who Changed America*. New York: Stewart, Tabori & Chang, 1989.

Lassonde, Stephen. *Learning to Forget: Schooling and Family Life in New Haven's Working Class, 1870–1940*. New Haven, CT: Yale University Press, 2005.

Lavergne, Gary M. *Before Brown: Heman Marion Sweatt, Thurgood Marshall, and the Long Road to Justice*. Austin: University of Texas Press, 2010.

Lawson, Steven F. *Black Ballots: Voting Rights in the South, 1944–1969*. New York: Columbia University Press, 1976.

——. *Running for Freedom: Civil Rights and Black Politics in America Since 1941*. 4th ed. New York: Wiley Blackwell, 2015.

Lee, Chana Kai. *For Freedom's Sake: The Life of Fannie Lou Hamer*. Urbana: University of Illinois Press, 2000.

Lee, Helen Shores, and Barbara S. Shores. *The Gentle Giant of Dynamite Hill: The Untold Story of Arthur Shores and His Family's Fight for Civil Rights*. Grand Rapids, MI: Zondervan, 2012.

Levin, Ellen. *Freedom's Children: Young Civil Rights Activists Tell Their Own Stories*. New York: Puffin, 2000. Originally published 1993.

Lewis, David L. *When Harlem Was in Vogue*. New York: Oxford University Press, 1981.

——. *W. E. B. Du Bois, 1868–1919: Biography of a Race*. New York: Henry Holt, 1993.

Lighter, David L. *Asylum, Prison, and Poorhouse: The Writings and Reform Work of Dorothea Dix in Illinois*. Carbondale: Southern Illinois University Press, 1999.

Lisagor, Nancy, and Frank Lipsius. *A Law Unto Itself: The Untold Story of the Law Firm Sullivan & Cromwell*. New York: William Morrow, 1988.

Macfarlane, Katherine A. "The Danger of Nonrandom Case Assignment: How the Southern District of New York's 'Related Cases' Rule Has Shaped the Evolution of Stop-and-Frisk Law." *Michigan Journal of Race & Law* 199 (2014). https://digitalcommons.law.lsu.edu/cgi/viewcontent.cgi?article=1115&context=faculty_scholarship.

Mack, Kenneth W. *Representing the Race: The Creation of the Civil Rights Lawyer*. Cambridge, MA: Harvard University Press, 2014.

MacLean, Nancy. *Freedom Is Not Enough: The Opening of the American Workplace*. Cambridge, MA: Harvard University Press, 2006.

Malcolm X. "Open Mind Roundtable." In *Malcolm X: Collected Speeches, Debates and Interviews (1960–1965)*. Edited by Sandeep S. Atwal. N.p., n.d.

Mancuso, Peter A. "Resentencing After the Fall of the Rockefeller Drug Laws." *Albany Law Review* 173 (2009): 1535–82.

Manis, Andrew M. *A Fire You Can't Put Out: The Civil Rights Life of Birmingham's Reverend Fred Shuttlesworth*. Tuscaloosa: University of Alabama Press, 2010.

Marable, Manning. *Malcolm X: A Life of Reinvention*. New York: Viking, 2011.

Martin, Elaine. "Gender and Judicial Selection: A Comparison of the Reagan and Carter Administrations." *Judicature* 71, no. 3 (1987): 136–42.

Martin, Gordon A., Jr. *Count Them One by One: Black Mississippians Fighting for the Right to Vote*. Jackson: University Press of Mississippi, 2010.

Mason, Gilbert R., and James Patterson Smith. *Beaches, Blood, and Ballots: A Black Doctor's Civil Rights Struggle*. Jackson: University Press of Mississippi, 2000.

May, Gary. *Bending Toward Justice: The Voting Rights Act and the Transformation of American Democracy*. New York: Basic Books, 2013.

Mayeri, Serena. *Reasoning from Race: Feminism, Law, and the Civil Rights Revolution*. Cambridge, MA: Harvard University Press, 2011.

McDuffie, Erik S. *Sojourning for Freedom: Black Women, American Communism and the Making of Black Left Feminism*. Durham, NC: Duke University Press, 2011.

McGee, Meredith Coleman. *James Meredith: Warrior and the America That Created Him*. Praeger; 1st Printing edition, 2013.

McGuire, Danielle L. *At the Dark End of the Street: Black Women, Rape and Resistance: A New History of the Civil Rights Movement from Rosa Parks to the Rise of Black Power*. New York: Knopf, 2011.

McLeod, Jacqueline A. *Daughter of the Empire State: The Life of Judge Jane Bolin*. Urbana: University of Illinois Press, 2011.

McMillen, Neil R. *Dark Journey: Black Mississippians in the Age of Jim Crow*. Chicago: University of Illinois Press, 1990.

McWhorter, Diane. *Carry Me Home: Birmingham, Alabama; The Climactic Battle of the Civil Rights Revolution*. New York: Simon & Schuster, 2001.

Mehr, Joseph. *An Illustrated History of Illinois Public Mental Health Services, 1847 to 2000*. Victoria, BC: Trafford, 2002.

Meier, August, and Elliot Rudwick. "Attorneys Black and White: A Case Study of Race Relations within the NAACP." *Journal of American History* 62, no. 4 (1976): 913–46.

Meredith, James. *Three Years in Mississippi*. Bloomington: Indiana University Press, 1966.

Meyerowitz, Joanne. "Beyond the Feminine Mystique: A Reassessment of Postwar Mass Culture, 1946–1958." *Journal of American History* 79, no. 4 (1993): 1455–82.

Mjagkij, Nina. *Light in the Darkness: African Americans and the YMCA, 1852–1946*. Louisville: University Press of Kentucky, 1994.

Model, Suzanne. *West Indian Immigrants: A Black Success Story*. New York: Russell Sage Foundation Press, 2008.

Morris, Aldon D. *The Origins of the Civil Rights Movement*. New York: Free Press, 1984.

Motley, Constance Baker. "My Personal Debt to Thurgood Marshall." *Yale Law Journal* 101, no. 1 (1991): 19–24.

———. "Standing on His Shoulders." *Howard Law Journal* 35, no. 1 (1991): 23–36.

———. "Thurgood Marshall." *New York University Law Review* 68 (1993): 208–11.

———. *Equal Justice Under Law: An Autobiography*. New York: Farrar, Straus & Giroux, 1998.

———. "Reflections." *Columbia Law Review* 102, no. 6 (2002): 1449–50.

Muhammad, Khalil Gibran. *The Condemnation of Blackness: Race, Crime and the Making of Modern Urban America*. Cambridge, MA: Harvard University Press, 2011.

Murray, Hugh T., Jr. "The NAACP versus the Communist Party: The Scottsboro Rape Case, 1931–32." *Phylon* 28, no. 3 (1967): 276–87.

Navasky, Victor S. *Kennedy Justice*. New York: Atheneum, 1971.

Neumann, Richard K., Jr. "Women in Legal Education: What the Statistics Show." *Journal of Legal Education* 50 (2000): 313–57.

O'Brien, M. J. *We Shall Not Be Moved: The Jackson Woolworth's Sit-in and the Movement It Inspired*. Oxford: University Press of Mississippi, 2014.

Okin, Susan Moller. *Justice, Gender, and the Family*. New York: Basic Books, 1989.

Olwig, Karen Fog. *Global Culture, Island Identity: Continuity and Change in the Afro-Caribbean Community of Nevis*. New York: Routledge, 1993.

Oropesa, R. S., and Leif Jensen. "Dominican Immigrants and Discrimination in a New Destination: The Case of Reading, Pennsylvania." *City & Community* 9 (2010): 274–98.

Painter, Nell Irvin. *Sojourner Truth: A Life, a Symbol*. New York: W. W. Norton, 1996.

Palmer, Phyllis. *Domesticity and Dirt: Housewives and Domestic Servants in the United States, 1920–1945*. Philadelphia: Temple University Press, 2010.

Platt, Tony, and Cecilia O'Leary. "Two Interviews with Ericka Huggins." *Social Justice* 40, no. 1/2 (2014): 54–71.

Plummer, Brenda Gayle. *In Search of Power: African Americans in the Era of Decolonization, 1956–1974*. Cambridge: Cambridge University Press, 2013.

Povich, Lynn. *The Good Girls Revolt: How the Women of Newsweek Sued Their Bosses and Changed the Workplace*. New York: PublicAffairs, 2012.

Pratt, Robert A. *We Shall Not Be Moved: The Desegregation of the University of Georgia*. Athens: University of Georgia Press, 2005.

Rabb, Harriet S. "Litigating Sex Discrimination Cases in the 1970s." *Columbia Journal of Gender and Law* 25, no. 1 (2013): 50–53.

Rabinowitz, Victor, and Tim Ledwith. *A History of the National Lawyers Guild: 1937–1987*. New York: National Lawyers Guild Foundation, 1987.

Randolph, Sherie M. *Florynce "Flo" Kennedy: The Life of a Black Feminist Radical*. Chapel Hill: University of North Carolina Press, 2015.

Ransby, Barbara. *Ella Baker and the Black Freedom Movement*. Chapel Hill: University of North Carolina Press, 2003.

"Report of the Dean." Columbia Law School. New York: Columbia University Press, 1943.

Riccio, Anthony V. *The Italian American Experience in New Haven*. Albany: State University of New York Press, 2006.

Richards, Glen. "The Pursuit of 'Higher Wages' and 'Perfect Personal Freedom': St. Kitts-Nevis, 1836–1956." In *From Chattel Slaves to Wage Slaves: The Dynamics of Labour Bargaining in the Americas*, edited by Mary Turner. Bloomington: Indiana University Press, 1995.

Richardson, Bonham C. *Caribbean Migrants: Environment and Human Survival on St. Kitts and Nevis*. Knoxville: University of Tennessee Press, 1983.

Richardson, Joe M. "Fisk University: The First Critical Years." *Tennessee Historical Quarterly* 29, no. 1 (1970): 29–41.

———. *A History of Fisk University, 1865–1946*. Tuscaloosa: University of Alabama Press, 2002.

Robbins, Alexandra. *The Secrets of the Tomb: Skull and Bones, the Ivy League, and the Hidden Paths of Power*. Boston: Back Bay Books, 2002.

Robinson, Jo Ann. *Montgomery Bus Boycott and the Women Who Started It*. Nashville: University of Tennessee Press, 1987.

Rochelle, Belinda. *Witnesses to Freedom: Young People Who Fought for Civil Rights*. New York: Puffin, 1997.

Rosenberg, Rosalind. *Jane Crow: The Life of Pauli Murray*. New York: Oxford University Press, 2017.

Russell, Margaret M. "Beyond 'Sellouts' and 'Race Cards': Black Attorneys and the Straitjacket of Legal Practice." *Michigan Law Review* 95 (1997): 766–94.

Rustin, Bayard. "From Protest to Politics: The Future of the Civil Rights Community." *Commentary*, February 1, 1965.

Ryan, Yvonne. *Roy Wilkins: The Quiet Revolutionary and the NAACP*. Louisville: University Press of Kentucky, 2014.

Sabin, Arthur J. *In Calmer Times: The Supreme Court and Red Monday*. Philadelphia: University of Pennsylvania Press, 1999.

Salkin, Patricia E., ed. "Constance Baker Motley." In *Pioneering Women Lawyers: From Kate Stoneman to the Present*. Chicago: American Bar Association, 2008.

Samuel, Lawrence R. *New York City 1964: A Cultural History*. Jefferson, NC: McFarland, 2014.

Sansing, David G. *The University of Mississippi: A Sesquicentennial History*. Jackson: University Press of Mississippi, 1999.

Schafran, Lynn Hecht. "Not from Central Casting: The Amazing Rise of Women in the American Judiciary." *University of Toledo Law Review* 36, no. 4 (2005): 953–76.

Schaich, Warren L., and Diane S. Hope. "The Prison Letters of Martin Sostre." *Journal of Black Studies* 7, no. 3 (1977): 281–300.

Schmidt, Taylor T. "White Pervert: Tracing Integration's Queer Desires in African American Novels of the 1950s." *Women's Studies Quarterly* 35, no. 1/2 (2007): 149–71.

Segal, Jennifer A. "Representative Decision Making on the Federal Bench: Clinton's District Court Appointees." *Political Research Quarterly* 53, no. 1 (2000): 137–50.

Sen, Maya. "How Judicial Qualifications Ratings May Disadvantage Minority and Female Candidates." *Journal of Law and Courts* 2 (2014): 33–65.

Slauter, Eric. "From 'Equality Before the Law' to 'Separate but Equal.'" In *Rhetorical Processes and Legal Judgments*, edited by Austin Sarat, 12–30. New York: Cambridge University Press, 2016.

Sletcher, Michael. *New Haven: From Puritanism to the Age of Terrorism*. Charleston, SC: Arcadia Publishing, 2004.

Smead, Howard. *Blood Justice: The Lynching of Mack Charles Parker*. Oxford: Oxford University Press, 1988.

Smith, J. Clay, Jr. *Emancipation: The Making of the Black Lawyer, 1844–1944*. Philadelphia: University of Pennsylvania Press, 1993.

Smith, Tamara. "A Comparative Look at African American Teachers After Brown v. Board of Education." Pro Quest Dissertation Publishing, 2014.

Solinger, Rickie. *Wake Up Little Susie: Single Pregnancy and Race Before Roe v. Wade*. New York: Routledge, 2000.

Solum, Lawrence B. "The Virtues and Vices of a Judge: An Aristotelian Guide to Judicial Selection." *Southern California Law Review* 61 (1988): 1735–56.

Sostre, Martin. *The New Prisoner*. New York: Martin Sostre Book Store, 1973.

Sowell, Thomas. *Civil Rights: Rhetoric or Reality?* New York: William Morrow, 1984.

Spear, Allan H. *Black Chicago: The Making of a Negro Ghetto*. Chicago: University of Chicago Press, 1967.

Spencer, Robyn C. *The Revolution Has Come: Black Power, Gender, and the Black Panther Party in Oakland*. Durham, NC: Duke University Press, 2016.

Spock, Benjamin. *Dr. Spock's Baby and Child Care*. New York: Duell, Sloan & Pearce, 1946.

Stern, Seth, and Stephen Wermiel. *Justice Brennan: Liberal Champion*. Boston: Houghton Mifflin Harcourt, 2010.

St. John's Law Review. "Rent Strike Legislation—New York's Solution to Landlord-Tenant Conflicts." Vol. 40, no. 2 (1966): 253–65.

St. John's Law Review. "The No-Knock and Stop-and-Frisk Provisions of the New York Criminal Code." Vol. 38, no. 2. (1964): 392–405.

Stoltzfus, Emilie. *Citizen, Mother, Worker: Debating Public Responsibility for Child Care After the Second World War*. Chapel Hill: University of North Carolina Press, 2003.

Storrs, Landon R. Y. *The Second Red Scare and the Unmaking of the New Deal Left*. Princeton, NJ: Princeton University Press, 2013.

Strebeigh, Fred. *Equal: Women Reshape American Law*. New York: W. W. Norton, 2009.

Sugre, Thomas. *Sweet Land of Liberty: The Forgotten Struggle for Civil Rights in the North*. New York: Random House, 2008.

Sullivan, Patricia. *Lift Every Voice: The NAACP and the Making of the Civil Rights Movement*. New York: New Press, 2009.

Sutton, Anthony C. *America's Secret Establishment: An Introduction to Skull and Bones*. Chicago: Trine Day, 2004.

Taylor, Betty W. "A History of Race and Gender at the University of Florida Levin College of Law, 1909–2001." *Florida Law Review* 84 (2002): 496–520.

Theoharis, Jeanne. *The Rebellious Life of Mrs. Rosa Parks*. Boston: Beacon, 2013.

Thompson, Heather Ann. *Blood in the Water: The Attica Prison Uprising of 1971 and Its Legacy*. New York: Pantheon, 2016.

Tirella, Joseph. *Tomorrow-Land: The 1964–65 World's Fair and the Transformation of America*. Guilford, CT: Lyons Press, 2014.

Toossi, Mitra. "A Century of Change: The U.S. Labor Force, 1950–2050," *Monthly Labor Review* (May 2002).

Trillin, Calvin. *An Education in Georgia: Charlayne Hunter, Hamilton Holmes, and the Integration of the University of Georgia*. Athens: University of Georgia Press, 2000.

Turner, Wallace B. "Abolitionism in Kentucky." *Register of the Kentucky Historical Society* 69, no. 4 (1971): 319–38.

Tushnet, Mark V. *The NAACP's Legal Strategy Against Segregated Education, 1925–1950*. Chapel Hill: University of North Carolina Press, 1987.

———. *Making Civil Rights Law: Thurgood Marshall and the Supreme Court, 1936–61*. New York: Oxford University Press, 1994.

Tye, Larry. *Bobby Kennedy: The Making of a Liberal Icon*. New York: Random House, 2016.

Vandenberg-Daves, Jodi. "Teaching Motherhood in History." *Women's Studies Quarterly* 30, no. 3/4 (2002): 234–55.

Wallace, William N. *Yale's Ironmen: A Story of Football and Lives in the Years of the Depression*. iUniverse, 2005.

Walsh, Judi, et al. "Attachment and Coping Strategies in Middle Childhood Children Whose Mothers Have a Mental Problem." *British Journal of Social Work* 39, no. 1 (2009): 81–98.

Walter, John C. *The Harlem Fox: J. Raymond Jones and Tammany, 1920–1970*. Albany: State University of New York Press, 1989.

Warner, Robert A. *New Haven Negroes: A Social History*. New York: Arno Press, 1969.

Washington, Linn. *Black Judges on Justice: Perspectives from the Bench*. New York: W. W. Norton, 1994.

Waters, Mary C. *Black Identities: West Indian Immigrant Dreams and American Realities*. Cambridge, MA: Harvard University Press, 1999.

Weigand, Kate, and Daniel Horowitz. "Dorothy Kenyon: Feminist Organizing, 1919–1963," *Journal of Women's History* 14, no. 2 (Summer 2002).

Weisenfeld, Judith. "The Harlem YWCA and the Secular City, 1904–1945." *Journal of Women's History* 6, no. 3 (1994): 62–78.

Welky, David. *Marching Across the Color Line: A. Philip Randolph and Civil Rights in the World War II Era*. New York: Oxford University Press, 2014.

Weller, John L. *The New Haven Railroad: Its Rise and Fall*. New York: Hastings House, 1969.

Wexler, Laura. *Fire in the Canebrake: The Last Mass Lynching in America*. New York: Scribner, 2003.

White, Deborah Gray. *Too Heavy a Load: Black Women in Defense of Themselves, 1894–1994*. New York: W. W. Norton, 1999.

Wiesen Cook, Blanche. *Eleanor Roosevelt: The Defining Years, 1933–1938*. New York: Penguin, 2000.

Williams, Eric. *Capitalism and Slavery*. 1st ed. Chapel Hill: University of North Carolina Press, 1994.

Williams, Joan M. *Hunter College*. Charleston, SC: Arcadia Press, 2000.

Williams, Juan. *Thurgood Marshall: American Revolutionary*. New York: Three Rivers, 1998.

Williams, Michael Vinson. *Medgar Evers: Mississippi Martyr*. Fayetteville: University of Arkansas Press, 2011.

Williams, Yohuru. "No Haven: From Civil Rights to Black Power in New Haven, Connecticut." *The Black Scholar* 31, no. 3/4 (2001): 54–66.

Wolcott, Victoria W. *Remaking Respectability: African American Women in Interwar Detroit*. Chapel Hill: University of North Carolina Press, 2001.

Woods, Jeff. *Black Struggle, Red Scare: Segregation and Anti-Communism in the South, 1948–1968*. Baton Rouge: Louisiana State University Press, 2004.

Young, Andrew. *An Easy Burden: The Civil Rights Movement and the Transformation of America*. Waco, TX: Baylor University Press, 1996.

Zelden, Charles L. *Thurgood Marshall: Race, Rights, and the Struggle for a More Perfect Union*. New York: Routledge, 2013.

Index

Page numbers in *italics* refer to illustrations.

Tomiko Brown-Nagin is dean of the Radcliffe Institute for Advanced Study at Harvard University, the Daniel P.S. Paul Professor of Constitutional Law at Harvard Law School, and a professor of history on Harvard University's Faculty of Arts and Sciences. She is a member of the American Academy of Arts and Sciences, of the American Law Institute, and of the American Philosophical Society, and a fellow of the American Bar Foundation. Her previous book, *Courage to Dissent*, won the Bancroft Prize in 2011. She frequently appears as a commentator about law and history in media. She lives in Boston with her family.

A NOTE ON THE TYPE

The text of this book was set in Filosofia, a typeface designed by Zuzana Licko in 1996 as a revival of the typefaces of Giambattista Bodoni (1740–1813). Basing her design on the letterpress practice of altering the cut of the letters to match the size for which they were to be used, Licko designed Filosofia Regular as a rugged face with reduced contrast to withstand the reduction to text sizes, and Filosofia Grand as a more delicate and refined version for use in larger display sizes.

Typeset by North Market Street Graphics,
Lancaster, Pennsylvania

Printed and bound by Berryville Graphics,
Berryville, Virginia

Designed by Betty Lew